BRADFORD'S
POCKET
CROSSWORD
SOLVER'S
LISTS

D0893035

Collins

HarperCollins Publishers
Westerhill Road
Bishopbriggs
Glasgow
G64 2QT
Great Britain

First Edition 2010

Reprint 10 9 8 7 6 5 4 3 2

© HarperCollins Publishers 2004
Some of the lists in this book have
been adapted from material in
*Collins Bradford's Crossword Solver's
Dictionary*, © Anne R. Bradford, 2003

ISBN 978-0-00-733364-6

Collins® is a registered trademark
of HarperCollins Publishers Limited

www.collinslanguage.com

A catalogue record for this book is
available from the British Library

Technical Production Coordination
by Thomas Callan

Typeset by Wordcraft, Glasgow

Printed in Great Britain by Clays Ltd,
St Ives plc

Note
Entered words that we have reason
to believe constitute trademarks
have been designated as such.
However, neither the presence nor
absence of such designation should
be regarded as affecting the legal
status of any trademark.

CONSULTANT EDITOR
Anne R. Bradford

EDITOR
Christopher Riches

FOR THE PUBLISHER
Lucy Cooper
Kerry Ferguson
Elaine Higgleton

Preface

Since the *Bradford's Crossword Solver's Dictionary* was first published in 1986, it has proved to be an invaluable aid for countless cruciverbalists. Compiled as a daily task since 1957 by Anne R. Bradford, a true crossword lover and an active member of the Crossword Club who still solves around 20 crosswords a week, the book has gone from strength to strength over a number of editions, offering the user over 200,000 crossword solutions as well as advice on solving cryptic clues. The latest edition has proved to be the most successful and popular yet.

Many crosswords are solved on the move and so in 2008, *Bradford's Pocket Crossword Solver's Dictionary*, which gives over 120,000 solutions in a portable format, was added to the range. Now *Bradford's Pocket Crossword Lists* provides the essential companion, with hundreds of word lists covering a wide range of subjects, to help with solving tricky crossword clues. Reflecting its pocket size, the maximum length of possible solutions is restricted to 15 letters.

This brand-new addition to the Bradford's crossword series has been compiled from the Collins thesaurus database, with additional material and advice from Anne Bradford, and gives useful word lists on hundreds of subjects, from **Artists**, **Birds**, and **Collectors** to **Winds**, **Worms**, and **Zoology**. Where the entry consists of a straight list of vocabulary on a given subject – for example at **Fish** – the lists are arranged by number of letters and then alphabetically, so that you can spot the word you need to complete your grid quickly. Where an entry includes additional useful information – for example, at **Capitals**, where both the capital and its country are shown – the list is arranged in columns to allow you to find the relevant material which you need to solve your clue. The book therefore provides both vocabulary lists and encyclopedic information – both of which are invaluable for crossword solving.

Solving crossword clues

Crossword puzzles tend to be basically 'quick' or 'cryptic'. A 'quick' crossword usually relies on a one or two-word clue which is a simple definition of the answer required. As has been stated, many words have different meanings, so that the clue 'ball' could equally well lead to the answer 'sphere', 'orb' or 'dance'. The way to solve 'quick' crosswords is to press on until probable answers begin to interlink, which is a good sign that you are on the right track.

'Cryptic' crosswords are another matter. Here the clue usually consists of a basic definition, given at either the beginning or end of the clue, together with one or more definitions of parts of the answer. Here are some examples taken from alltime favourites recorded over the years:

1. *'Tradesman who bursts into tears'* (**Stationer**)

   Tradesman is a definition of stationer. Bursts is cleverly used as an indication of an anagram, which into tears is of stationer.

2. *'Sunday school tune'* (**Strain**)

   Here Sunday is used to define its abbreviation S, school is a synonym for train, and put together they give strain, which is a synonym of tune.

3. *'Result for everyone when head gets at bottom'* (**Ache**) (used as a 'down' clue)

   This is what is known as an '& lit' clue, meaning that the setter has hit on a happy composition which could literally be true. Everyone here is a synonym for each, move the head (first letter) of the word to the bottom, and the answer is revealed, the whole clue being the definition of the answer in this case.

4. *'Tin out East'* (**Sen**)

   In this example, tin, implying 'money', requires its chemical symbol Sn to go out(side) East, or its abbreviation, E, the whole clue being a definition of a currency (sen) used in the East.

5. *'Information given to communist in return for sex'* (**Gender**)

   Information can be defined as gen; communist is almost always red, in return indicates 'reversed', leading to gen-der, a synonym for sex.

6. *'Row about no enclosure of this with sardines'* (**Tin-opener**)

   Row is a synonym for tier, about indicates 'surrounding', no enclosure can be no pen, leading to ti-no pen-er, and another '& lit' clue.

7. 'Cake-sandwiches-meat, at Uncle Sam's party' (Clambake)

   Meat here is lamb, sandwiches is used as a verb, so we have C-lamb-ake, which is a kind of party in America. Uncle Sam or US is often used to indicate America.

8. 'Initially passionate meeting of boy and girl could result in it' (Pregnancy)

   Initially is usually a sign of a first letter, in this case 'p' for passionate + Reg (a boy) and Nancy (a girl), and another clever '& lit'.

With 'cryptic' clues the solver needs to try to analyse the parts to see what he or she is looking for – which word or words can be the straight definition, and which refer to the parts or hint at anagrams or other subterfuges. Whilst it would be unrealistic to claim total infallibility, practice has shown that in most crosswords some 90% of the answers are to be found in this work.

Anne R. Bradford

How to use the book

This book gives useful vocabulary lists and information on hundreds of subjects which are likely to come up as part of crossword clues. The lists are arranged alphabetically by subject, so finding the one you want is as quick and easy as looking up a dictionary. A full table of the lists, in the order they appear, is also given at the front of the book.

Where the entry consists of a straightforward list of words relevant to a given subject, such as **Pigs**, **Pasta**, or **Birds**, the words are arranged by length, with all three-letter words grouped together in alphabetical order, then all four-letter words, then all five-letter words, and so on, up to fifteen-letter words. Longer words are not shown, so, for example, under **American Football Teams**, teams such as Arizona Cardinals or Tampa Bay Buccaneers do not appear because of their word length.

Where an entry includes additional useful information – for example at **US States** (in the **States** listing), where not only the name of each state is shown, but also its **abbreviation**, **zip code**, **nickname**, and **capital** – the list is arranged in columns to allow you to find the relevant information you need to solve your clue. The book thus provides both vocabulary and encyclopaedic information, set out in whichever way will be most helpful to the user.

Lists such as **Artists** and **Composers**, which consist of people's names, are arranged by length of the surname, or whichever part of the name the person is best known by, and then alphabetically within each length group. First names and other more 'optional' elements, such as nicknames and initials, are shown after the main part of the name, in italics. You can therefore find the person you are looking for straight away, and then choose the part of their name which is relevant to your crossword solution.

Cross-references are also included wherever appropriate at the ends of entries, so that if you happen to be looking up, for example, the entry for **Animals**, you can see straight away that there are also related lists at **Amphibians**, **Birds**, **Insects**, and so on, which may provide further useful information to help you solve your clue. The cross-references are introduced by the line 'See also:' and each is preceded by the symbol ➤ with the cross-referenced list's title shown in bold type.

About the Author

Anne Bradford's love of words began to make itself evident even in her schooldays, when, as Head Girl of her school, she instituted a novel punishment – instead of making rulebreakers write lines, she had them write out pages from a dictionary, on the grounds that this was a more useful exercise. Little did she know this was soon to be her own daily routine!

In time, crosswords became a magnificent obsession for Anne. All lovers of crosswords can understand the irresistible lure of solving them, but Anne's interest went much deeper than most people's, and when she stopped work in 1957 to have her first child, she found herself starting to note down answers to particularly tricky clues as an aid to memory, in case she should come across them again in another puzzle. It was from this simple beginning that this crossword dictionary evolved.

Over the space of 25 years, Anne continued to build on her collection of solutions, analysing every crossword clue as she solved it and adding it to her steadily growing bank of entries. This unique body of material eventually reached such proportions that she had the idea of offering it to her fellow crossword-solvers as a reference book, and since then, the book has gone from strength to strength, providing valuable help to countless cruciverbalists over a number of editions.

Anne Bradford continues to devote time each day to solving crosswords, averaging some 20 a week – both quick and cryptic – and still avidly collects new solutions for her *Crossword Solver's Dictionary* at a rate of around 150 a week, compiling each solution by hand (without the use of a computer!) This latest edition therefore includes much new material, gleaned by a true crossword lover who not only solves crosswords but, as an active member of the Crossword Club, can offer the user an insight into the mind of a cunning crossword compiler.

The Crossword Club

If you are interested in crosswords, you might like to consider joining the Crossword Club. Membership is open to all who enjoy tackling challenging crosswords and who appreciate the finer points of clue-writing and grid construction. The Club's magazine, Crossword, contains two prize puzzles each month. A sample issue and full details are available on request.

The Crossword Club
Coombe Farm
Awbridge
Romsey, Hants.
SO51 0HN
UK

email: bh@thecrosswordclub.co.uk
website address: www.crosswordclub.demon.co.uk

CONTENTS

A

Abbreviations

CLASSIFIED ADVERTISEMENTS

Abbreviation	Meaning
AMC *or* amc	All mod cons
Deps	Deposit
Exc *or* excl	Excluding
F/f	Furnished flat
GCH	Gas central heating
Inc *or* incl	Including
Pcm	Per calendar month
Pw	Per week

LONELY HEARTS COLUMN ABBREVIATIONS

Abbreviation	Meaning
GSOH	Good sense of humour
GWM	Gay white male
LTR	Long term relationship
NS *or* N/S	Non-smoker
SOH	Sense of humour
SWF	Single white female
VGSOH	Very good sense of humour
WLTM	Would like to meet
WSOH	Weird *or* wicked sense of humour

Acids

SPECIFIC ACIDS

2 letters:
PH
3 letters:
DNA
HCL
RNA
4 letters:
Dopa
Uric
5 letters:
Auric
Boric
Caro's
L-dopa

Malic
Mucic
Oleic
Orcin
Trona
6 letters:
Acetic
Adipic
Bromic
Capric
Cholic
Citric
Cyanic
Erucic

Formic
Gallic
Lactic
Lauric
Leucin
Lipoic
Maleic
Niacin
Nitric
Oxalic
Pectic
Phenol
Picric
Quinic

Sialic
Sorbic
Tannic
Tiglic
Valine
7 letters:
Abietic
Alginic
Benzoic
Butyric
Caproic
Cerotic
Chloric
Chromic
Creatin
Ellagic
Ferulic
Folacin
Fumaric
Fusidic
Guanine
Malonic
Meconic
Muramic
Nitrous
Orcinol
Prussic
Pteroic
Pyruvic
Racemic
Sebacic
Selenic
Silicic
Stannic
Stearic
Suberic
Terebic
Titanic
Valeric
Xanthic
Xylonic
8 letters:
Abscisic
Ascorbic
Aspartic
Butanoic
Caprylic
Carbamic
Carbolic
Carbonic
Chlorous
Cinnamic
Creatine
Cresylic
Crotonic
Cyclamic

Decanoic
Ethanoic
Fulminic
Glutamic
Glyceric
Glycolic
Guanylic
Hexanoic
Hippuric
Itaconic
Linoleic
Lysergic
Manganic
Muriatic
Myristic
Nonanoic
Palmitic
Phthalic
Rhodanic
Succinic
Tantalic
Tartaric
Telluric
Tungstic
Tyrosine
Valproic
9 letters:
Aqua-regia
Citydylic
Dichromic
Hydrazoic
Hydriodic
Isocyanic
Linolenic
Methanoic
Nalidixic
Nicotinic
Panthenic
Pentanoic
Propanoic
Propenoic
Pyroboric
Saccharic
Salicylic
Sassolite
Selenious
Sulphonic
Sulphuric
10 letters:
Aquafortis
Asparagine
Barbituric
Citrulline
Dithionous
Dodecanoic
Glucoronic

Glutaminic
Hyaluronic
Methionine
Pelargonic
Perchloric
Phosphoric
Proprionic
Pyrogallic
Ricinoleic
Sulphurous
Thiocyanic
Tryptophan
11 letters:
Arachidonic
Decanedioic
Ethanedioic
Ferricyanic
Ferrocyanic
Gibberellic
Hydnocarpic
Hydrobromic
Methacrylic
Octanedioic
Pantothenic
Permanganic
Phosphorous
Ribonucleic
Sarcolactic
Taurocholic
12 letters:
Aminobenzoic
Chloroacetic
Hydrochloric
Hydrofluoric
Hypochlorous
Indoleacetic
Persulphuric
Phenylalanin
Polyadenalic
Prostacyclin
Pyroligneous
Spiraeic acid
Terephthalic
13 letters:
Galactosamine
Glacial acetic
Heptadecanoic
Indolebutyric
Phenylalanine
Platinocyanic
Prostaglandin
Pyrosulphuric
Thiosulphuric
14 letters:
Hypophosphoric
Metaphosphoric

Polyphosphoric
Pyrophosphoric

15 letters:
Hypophosphorous

Orthophosphoric
Trichloroacetic

TYPES OF ACID

4 letters:
Acyl
Pyro
5 letters:
Amide
Amino
Fatty
Folic
Iodic

Lewis
Osmic
7 letters:
Dibasic
Mineral
Nucleic
Peracid
8 letters:
Periodic

9 letters:
Polybasic
10 letters:
Carboxylic
12 letters:
Dicarboxylic
14 letters:
Polycarboxylic

AMINO ACIDS

6 letters:
Lysine
Serine
7 letters:
Alanine
Cystine
Glycine

Leucine
Proline
8 letters:
Arginine
9 letters:
Ethionine
Glutamine

Histidine
Ornithine
Threonine
10 letters:
Citrulline
Isoleucine

Agriculturalists

4 letters:
Coke, *Thomas William*
Tull, *Jethro*
5 letters:
Lawes, *Sir John Bennet*
Young, *Arthur*
6 letters:
Carver, *George Washington*

7 letters:
Borlaug, *Norman Ernest*
Burbank, *Luther*
8 letters:
Bakewell, *Robert*
9 letters:
McCormick, *Cyrus Hall*
12 letters :
Boussingault, *Jean-Baptiste Joseph*

Aircraft

TYPES OF AIRCRAFT

3 letters:
Jet
MIG
SST
4 letters:
Moth
STOL
VTOL
Wing
5 letters:
Avion

Blimp
Camel
Comet
Drone
Gotha
Jumbo
Rigid
Stuka
Taube
6 letters:
Auster

Bomber
Canard
Chaser
Fokker
Galaxy
Glider
Hunter
Mirage
Ramjet
Tanker
Tri-jet

7 letters:
Airship
Aviette
Balloon
Biplane
Chopper
Fighter
Harrier
Heinkel
Jump jet
Parasol
Penguin
Propjet
Sopwith
Trident

8 letters:
Aerodyne
Aerostat
Airliner
Autogiro
Autogyro
Brabazon
Concorde
Gyrodyne
Jetliner
Jet plane
Jumbo jet
Mosquito
Oerlikon
Scramjet
Seaplane

Skiplane
Spitfire
Triplane
Turbofan
Turbojet
Viscount
Warplane
Zeppelin

9 letters:
Amphibian
Autoflare
Coleopter
Cyclogiro
Delta-wing
Dirigible
Doodlebug
Fixed-wing
Freighter
Hurricane
Lancaster
Liberator
Microlite
Monoplane
Orthopter
Rotaplane
Sailplane
Semi-rigid
Swept-wing
Swing-wing
Taxiplane
Turboprop

10 letters:
Dive bomber
Flying boat
Flying wing
Hang-glider
Helicopter
Microlight
Multiplane
Tankbuster

11 letters:
Intercepter
Interceptor
Lifting body
Ornithopter
Turboramjet

12 letters:
Night fighter
Sopwith Camel
Stealth plane
Stratotanker
Troop carrier

13 letters:
Convertaplane
Convertiplane
Convertoplane
Fighter-bomber
Hot-air balloon
Light aircraft
Messerschmitt
Stealth bomber
Stratocruiser

AIRCRAFT PARTS

3 letters:
Fin
Pod
Tab

4 letters:
Body
Cowl
Flap
Hold
Horn
Keel
Nose
Slat
Tail
Wing

5 letters:
Cabin
Pylon
Rotor
Waist

6 letters:
Basket

Canopy
Elevon
Engine
Galley
Pusher
Ramjet
Rudder
Turret

7 letters:
Aileron
Airlock
Athodyd
Blister
Bomb bay
Capsule
Chassis
Cockpit
Cowling
Fairing
Gondola
Jet pipe
Nacelle

Spinner
Spoiler
Trim tab
Winglet
Wing tip

8 letters:
Aerofoil
Airframe
Air scoop
Airscrew
Anti-icer
Arrester
Black box
Bulkhead
Drop tank
Elevator
Fuel tank
Fuselage
Heat sink
Joystick
Longeron
Pulsejet

Tailskid
9 letters:
Air-intake
Altimeter
Astrodome
Autopilot
Bombsight
Clamshell
Dashboard
Empennage
Engine pod
Jet engine
Main plane
Nose wheel
Pitot tube
Propeller

Tailplane
Tail wheel
10 letters:
Astrohatch
Cantilever
Flight deck
Hydroplane
Launch shoe
Stabilizer
11 letters:
Afterburner
Horn balance
Landing gear
Slinger ring
12 letters:
Control stick

Ejection seat
Inclinometer
Landing light
Ramjet engine
Trailing edge
13 letters:
Aerostructure
All-flying tail
Control column
Launching shoe
Undercarriage
14 letters:
Flight recorder
15 letters:
Instrument panel

Airline flight codes

Code	Airline
AA	American Airlines
AC	Air Canada
AF	Air France
AH	Air Algerie
AI	Air India
AJ	Air Belgium
AM	Aeromexico
AQ	Aloha Airlines (Hawaii)
AR	Aerolineas Argentinas
AY	Finnair
AZ	Alitalia
BA	British Airways
BD	British Midland
BY	Britannia Airways
CA	Air China
CO	Continental Airlines
CP	Canadian Airlines International
CT	Air Sofia
CU	Cubana
CY	Cyprus Airways
DA	Air Georgia
DI	Deutsche BA
DL	Delta Airlines
DX	Danish Air Transport
EI	Aer Lingus
EK	Emirates
FE	Royal Khmer Airlines
FI	Icelandair
FR	Ryanair
GF	Gulf Air
GH	Ghana Airways
GM	Air Slovakia
HA	Hawaiian Airlines
IB	Iberia
IC	Indian Airlines
IL	Istanbul Airways

Code	Airline
IR	Iran Air
JA	Air Bosnia
JE	Manx Airlines
JG	Air Greece
JL	Japan Airlines
JM	Air Jamaica
JU	JAT (Yugoslavia)
KL	KLM
KQ	Kenya Airways
KU	Kuwait Airways
LG	Luxair
LH	Lufthansa
LV	Albanian Airlines
LY	El Al
MA	Malev (Hungary)
MS	Egyptair
NG	Lauda Air (Austria)
NH	All Nippon Airlines
NV	Northwest Territorial Airways (Canada)
NW	Northwest Airlines (USA)
NY	Air Iceland
NZ	Air New Zealand
OA	Olympic Airlines (Greece)
OG	Go
OK	Czech Airlines
OS	Austrian Airlines
OU	Croatia Airlines
OV	Estonian Air
PC	Fiji Air
PK	Pakistan International Airlines
PS	Ukraine International Airlines
QF	Qantas
QR	Qatar Airways
QS	Tatra Air (Slovakia)
QU	Uganda Airlines
QZ	Zambia Airways
RG	Varig (Brazil)
RM	Air Moldova
RO	Tarom (Romania)
RR	Royal Air Force
SA	South African Airways
SK	SAS (Scandinavian Airlines, Sweden)
SN	Sabena Belgian World Airlines
SQ	Singapore Airlines
SR	Swissair
SU	Aeroflot (Russia)
TE	Lithuanian Airlines
TK	Turkish Airlines
TP	TAP Air Portugal
TT	Air Lithuania
TW	TWA (USA)
UA	United Airlines (USA)
UK	KLM UK
UL	Sri Lankan Airlines
UM	Air Zimbabwe
US	USAir

Code	Airline
VS	Virgin Atlantic Airways
WN	Southwest Airlines (USA)
WT	Nigeria Airways
WX	Cityjet (Ireland)
ZB	Monarch Airlines (UK)

Airports

3 letters:
JFK
Lod
4 letters:
Dyce
Faro
Lydd
Orly
Sfax
Wick
5 letters:
Logan
Luton
McCoy
O'Hare
6 letters:
Dulles
Gander
Gerona
Lympne
7 letters:
Ataturk
Dalaman
Entebbe
Gatwick
Kennedy
Kerkyra
Lincoln

Shannon
8 letters:
Beauvais
Ciampino
G Marconi
Heathrow
Idlewild
Keflavik
McCarran
Mohamed V
Schiphol
Stansted
9 letters:
Ben Gurion
Charleroi
Fiumicino
Jose Marti
Marco Polo
Peninsula
Prestwick
Queen Alia
Turnhouse
10 letters:
Hellenikon
King Khaled
Louis Botha
Reina Sofia
Will Rogers

11 letters:
Ninoy Aquino
12 letters:
Benito Juarez
Indira Gandhi
Jomo Kenyatta
Norman Manley
Papola Casale
Queen Beatrix
Santos Dumont
Simon Bolivar
13 letters:
Chiang Kai Shek
Grantley Adams
King Abdul Aziz
14 letters:
Galileo Galilei
Lester B Pearson
Luis Munoz Marin
15 letters:
Charles De Gaulle
General Mitchell
Leonardo da Vinci
Murtala
 Muhammed
Sir Seretse Khama

Alcohols

4 letters:
Diol
5 letters:
Cetyl
Ethal
Ethyl
Meths
Nerol
6 letters:
Cresol
Lauryl
Mescal
Phytol
Propyl

Sterol
7 letters:
Borneol
Choline
Ethanol
Mannite
Xylitol
8 letters:
Acrolein
Aldehyde
Catechol
Farnesol
Fusel-oil
Geraniol

Glycerin
Inositol
Linalool
Mannitol
Methanol
Sorbitol
9 letters:
Glycerine
Isopropyl
Mercaptan
11 letters:
Cholesterol
Citronellol
Sphingosine

Algae

3 letters:
Red
4 letters:
Kelp
5 letters:
Brown
Dulse
Fucus
Green
Jelly
Laver
Wrack
6 letters:
Desmid
Diatom
Fucoid
Lichen
Nostoc
Volvox
7 letters:
Euglena
Isokont

Oarweed
Seaweed
Valonia
8 letters:
Anabaena
Carageen
Conferva
Gulfweed
Plankton
Pleuston
Rockweed
Sargasso
Sea wrack
Ulothrix
9 letters:
Carrageen
Chlorella
Irish moss
Prokaryon
Sargassum
Sea tangle
Spirogyra

Star-jelly
Stonewort
10 letters:
Carragheen
Sea lettuce
11 letters:
Blanketweed
Iceland moss
Protococcus
12 letters:
Bladderwrack
Heterocontae
Reindeer moss
Ulotrichales
Zooxanthella
13 letters:
Blackfish weed
Phytoplankton
14 letters:
Dinoflagellate

Alkalis

5 letters:
Borax
6 letters:
Betane
Emetin
Harmin
Potash
7 letters:
Brucine
Codeine
Emetine
Harmine
Narceen
Quinine
Tropine
8 letters:
Harmalin

Hyoscine
Lobeline
Narceine
Nicotine
Piperine
Thebaine
Veratrin
9 letters:
Bebeerine
Berberine
Capsaicin
Ephedrine
Gelsemine
Guanidine
Harmaline
Reserpine
Rhoeadine

Sparteine
Veratrine
Yohimbine
10 letters:
Colchicine
Papaverine
11 letters:
Apomorphine
Gelseminine
Scopolamine
Theobromine
Vinblastine
Vincristine
12 letters:
Theophylline

Alloys

5 letters:
Brass
Invar®
Monel
Potin
Steel
Terne

6 letters:
Albata
Alnico®
Billon
Bronze
Cermet
Chrome

Latten
Magnox
Marmem
Occamy
Oreide
Ormolu
Oroide

Pewter
Tambac
Tombac
Tombak
7 letters:
Amalgam
Babbitt
Chromel
Nimonic
Nitinol
Paktong
Platina
Shakudo
Similor
Spelter
Tutenag
8 letters:
Electron
Electrum
Gunmetal
Kamacite
Manganin®
Nichrome®
Orichalc

Stellite®
Zircaloy
Zircoloy
9 letters:
Bell metal
Duralumin®
Magnalium
Permalloy
Pinchbeck
Platinoid
Shibuichi
Type metal
White gold
Zircalloy
10 letters:
Bell bronze
Constantan
Misch metal
Nicrosilal
Osmiridium
Soft solder
11 letters:
Babbit metal
Cupronickel

Ferronickel
Monell metal
12 letters:
Ferrosilicon
Nickel silver
Nimonic alloy
13 letters:
Brazing solder
Ferrochromium
Magnolia metal
Platiniridium
Speculum metal
14 letters:
Britannia metal
Ferromanganese
Phosphor bronze
Sterling silver
15 letters:
Ferromolybdenum

Alphabets

RELATED VOCABULARY

3 letters:
ITA
4 letters:
Kana
Ogam
5 letters:
Cufic
Kanji
Kufic
Latin
Ogham
Roman
6 letters:
Brahmi
Glagol
Hangul

Nagari
Pinyin
Romaji
7 letters:
Braille
Futhark
Futhorc
Futhork
Glossic
Grantha
Linear A
Linear B
Pangram
8 letters:
Cyrillic
Hiragana

Katakana
Logogram
Phonetic
9 letters:
Logograph
Syllabary
10 letters:
Devanagari
Estrangelo
Glagolitic
Lexigraphy
11 letters:
Estranghelo

ARABIC ALPHABET

Alif	Khā	Shīn	Ghain	Nūn
Bā	Dāl	S̤ād	Fā	Hā
Tā	Dhāl	Dād	Qāf	Wāw
Thā	Rā	T̤ā	Kāf	Yā
Jīm	Zā	Z̤ā	Lām	
Hā	Sīn	ʿAin	Mīm	

GREEK ALPHABET

Alpha	Eta	Mu	Pi	Theta
Beta	Gamma	Nu	Psi	Upsilon
Chi	Iota	Omega	Rho	Xi
Delta	Kappa	Omicron	Sigma	Zeta
Epsilon	Lambda	Phi	Tau	

HEBREW ALPHABET

Aleph	He	Lamedh	Tsade	Vav
Ayin	Heth	Mem	Samekh	Waw
Ain	Cheth	Nun	Shin	Yod
Beth	Kaph	Pe	Sin	Yodh
Daleth	Koph	Resh	Tav	Zayin
Daled	Qoph	Sadhe	Taw	
Gimel	Lamed	Sade	Teth	

COMMUNICATIONS CODE WORDS FOR THE ALPHABET

Alpha	Golf	Mike	Sierra	Yankee
Bravo	Hotel	November	Tango	Zulu
Charlie	India	Oscar	Uniform	
Delta	Juliet	Papa	Victor	
Echo	Kilo	Quebec	Whiskey	
Foxtrot	Lima	Romeo	X-Ray	

American football teams

11 letters:
New York Jets
St Louis Rams
12 letters:
Buffalo Bills
Chicago Bears
Detroit Lions
13 letters:
Dallas Cowboys
Denver Broncos
Houston Texans

Miami Dolphins
New York Giants
14 letters:
Atlanta Falcons
Oakland Raiders
15 letters:
Baltimore Ravens
Cleveland Browns
Green Bay Packers
Seattle Seahawks
Tennessee Titans

Amphibians

3 letters:
Eft
Olm
4 letters:
Frog
Hyla
Newt
Pipa
Rana

Toad
5 letters:
Anura
Guana
Siren
Snake
6 letters:
Desman
Hassar

7 letters:
Axolotl
Crapaud
Proteus
Tadpole
Urodela
Urodele
8 letters:
Bullfrog

Caecilia
Cane toad
Congo eel
Mud puppy
Tree frog
Urodelan
9 letters:
Ambystoma

Caecilian
Hairy frog
Salientia
10 letters:
Amblystoma
Batrachian
Hellbender
Natterjack

Salamander
11 letters:
Goliath frog
Midwife toad
Surinam toad

Ancient cities

2 letters:
Ur
3 letters:
Bam
4 letters:
Coba
Rome
Susa
Troy
Tula
Tyre
Uruk
5 letters:
Aksum
Argos
Bosra
Copán
Hatra
Huari
Kabah
Khiva
Labna
Mitla
Moche
Nemea
Petra
Sayil
Shloh
Tegea
Tikal
Tultm
Uxmal

6 letters:
Athens
Byblos
Delphi
Jabneh
Jamnia
Megara
Napata
Nippur
Sardis
Sikyon
Sparta
Thebes
Ugarit
Xlapak
7 letters:
Antioch
Babylon
Bukhara
Cahokia
Corinth
Eleusis
El Tajin
Ephesos
Ephesus
Mayapan
Miletus
Mycenae
Mykenae
Nineveh
Olympia
Pompeii

Samaria
Sybaris
8 letters:
Carthage
Cihuatán
Damascus
Palenque
Pergamon
Pergamum
Sigiriya
Tashkent
Thysdrus
9 letters:
Byzantium
Perepolis
Samarkand
Sukhothai
10 letters:
Alexandria
Carchemish
Heliopolis
Hierapolis
11 letters:
Chichén Itzá
Machu Picchu
Polonnaruwa
12 letters:
Anuradhapura
13 letters:
Halicarnassus
14 letters:
Constantinople

Angels

5 letters:
Ariel
Uriel
6 letters:
Abdiel
Arioch
Azrael
Belial
Rimmon

Uzziel
7 letters:
Asmadai
Gabriel
Israfel
Lucifer
Michael
Raphael
Zadkiel

Zephiel
8 letters:
Apollyon
Ithuriel
9 letters:
Beelzebub
10 letters:
Adramelech

ANGELIC ORDERS

6 letters:	**8 letters:**	Archangels
Angels	Cherubim	Princedoms
Powers	Seraphim	**11 letters:**
7 letters:	**9 letters:**	Dominations
Thrones	Dominions	**14 letters:**
Virtues	**10 letters:**	Principalities

Animals

RELATED WORDS

Animal	**Related adjective**
Ant	Formic
Ass	Asinine
Bear	Ursine
Bee	Apian
Bird	Avian *or* ornithic
Bull	Taurine
Cat	Feline
Crab	Cancroid
Crow	Corvine
Deer	Cervine
Dog	Canine
Dove	Columbine
Eagle	Aquiline
Elephant	Elephantine
Falcon	Falconine
Fish	Piscine *or* ichthyoid
Fowl	Gallinaceous
Fox	Vulpine
Goat	Caprine *or* hircine
Goose	Anserine *or* anserous
Gull	Larine
Hare	Leporine
Hawk	Accipitrine
Horse	Equine
Lion	Leonine
Lynx	Lyncean
Mite *or* tick	Acaroid
Monkey	Simian
Ox	Bovine
Parrot	Psittacine
Peacock	Pavonine
Pig	Porcine
Puffin	Alcidine
Seal	Phocine
Sheep	Ovine
Snake	Serpentine, anguine, ophidian, *or* colubrine
Swallow	Hirundine
Wasp	Vespine
Wolf	Lupine

COLLECTIVE ANIMALS

Animal	**Collective noun**
Antelopes	Herd
Apes	Shrewdness
Asses	Pace *or* herd
Badgers	Cete
Bears	Sloth
Bees	Swarm *or* grist
Birds	Flock, congregation, flight, *or* volery
Bitterns	Sedge *or* siege
Boars	Sounder
Bucks	Brace *or* lease
Buffaloes	Herd
Capercailzies	Tok
Cats	Clowder
Cattle	Drove *or* herd
Choughs	Chattering
Colts	Rag
Coots	Covert
Cranes	Herd, sedge, *or* siege
Crows	Murder
Cubs	Litter
Curlews	Herd
Curs	Cowardice
Deer	Herd
Dolphins	School
Doves	Flight *or* dule
Ducks	Paddling *or* team
Dunlins	Flight
Elk	Gang
Fish	Shoal, draught, haul, run, *or* catch
Flies	Swarm *or* grist
Foxes	Skulk
Geese	Gaggle *or* skein
Giraffes	Herd
Gnats	Swarm *or* cloud
Goats	Herd *or* tribe
Goldfinches	Charm
Grouse	Brood, covey, *or* pack
Gulls	Colony
Hares	Down *or* husk
Hawks	Cast
Hens	Brood
Herons	Sedge *or* siege
Herrings	Shoal *or* glean
Hounds	Pack, mute, *or* cry
Insects	Swarm
Kangaroos	Troop
Kittens	Kindle
Lapwings	Desert
Larks	Exaltation
Leopards	Leap
Lions	Pride *or* troop
Mallards	Sord *or* sute
Mares	Stud
Martens	Richesse

Animal	**Collective noun**
Moles	Labour
Monkeys	Troop
Mules	Barren
Nightingales	Watch
Owls	Parliament
Oxen	Yoke, drove, team, *or* herd
Partridges	Covey
Peacocks	Muster
Pheasants	Nye *or* nide
Pigeons	Flock *or* flight
Pigs	Litter
Plovers	Stand *or* wing
Pochards	Flight, rush, bunch, *or* knob
Ponies	Herd
Porpoises	School *or* gam
Poultry	Run
Pups	Litter
Quails	Bevy
Rabbits	Nest
Racehorses	Field *or* string
Ravens	Unkindness
Roes	Bevy
Rooks	Building *or* clamour
Ruffs	Hill
Seals	Herd *or* pod
Sheep	Flock
Sheldrakes	Dopping
Snipe	Walk *or* wisp
Sparrows	Host
Starlings	Murmuration
Swallows	Flight
Swans	Herd *or* bevy
Swifts	Flock
Swine	Herd, sounder, *or* dryft
Teal	Bunch, knob, *or* spring
Whales	School, gam, *or* run
Whelps	Litter
Whiting	Pod
Wigeon	Bunch, company, knob, *or* flight
Wildfowl	Plump, sord, *or* sute
Wolves	Pack, rout, *or* herd
Woodcocks	Fall

HABITATIONS

Animal	**Habitation**
Ant	Ant hill *or* formicary
Badger	Set *or* sett
Beaver	Lodge
Bee	Hive *or* apiary
Bird	Nest
Eagle	Aerie *or* eyrie
Fish	Redd
Fox	Earth
Otter	Holt

Animal	Habitation
Pig	Sty
Puffin	Puffinry
Rabbit	Warren
Rook	Rookery
Seal	Sealery
Squirrel	Drey *or* dray
Termite	Termitarium
Wasp	Vespiary *or* bike

ANIMALS / MALE / FEMALE

Animal	Male	Female
Ass	Jack	Jenny
Bird	Cock	Hen
Cat	Tom	Queen
Deer	Hart *or* stag	Doe *or* hind
Dog	—	Bitch
Donkey	Jack	Jenny
Duck	Drake	—
Elephant	Bull	Cow
Falcon	Tercel *or* tiercel	—
Ferret	Hob	Gill *or* jill
Fowl	Cock	Hen
Fox	Dog	Vixen
Goat	Billy *or* buck	Nanny
Goose	Gander	—
Hare	Buck	Doe
Horse	Stallion	Mare
Kangaroo	Buck *or* old man	—
Leopard	—	Leopardess
Lion	—	Lioness
Lobster	Cock	Hen
Ox	Bull	Cow
Peafowl	Peacock	Peahen
Pig	Boar	Sow
Rabbit	Buck	Doe
Reindeer	Buck	—
Ruff	Ruff	Reeve
Sheep	Ram *or* tup	Ewe
Swan	Cob	Pen
Tiger	—	Tigress
Weasel	Whittret	—
Whale	Bull	Cow
Wolf	—	Bitch
Wren	—	Jenny

YOUNG ANIMALS

Animal	Young
Bear	Cub
Bird	Chick, fledgling, fledgeling, *or* nestling
Butterfly	Caterpillar, chrysalis, *or* chrysalid
Cat	Kitten
Cod	Codling

Animal	Young
Deer	Fawn
Dog	Pup *or* puppy
Duck	Duckling
Eagle	Eaglet
Eel	Elver *or* grig
Elephant	Calf
Falcon	Eyas
Ferret	Kit
Fish	Fry *or* fingerling
Fox	Kit *or* cub
Frog	Tadpole
Goat	Kid *or* yeanling
Goose	Gosling
Hare	Leveret
Herring	Alevin, brit, *or* sparling
Horse	Foal, colt, *or* filly
Kangaroo	Joey
Lion	Cub
Moth	Caterpillar
Owl	Owlet
Ox	Calf
Pig	Piglet
Pigeon	Squab
Salmon	Alevin, grilse, parr, *or* smolt
Seal	Pup
Sheep	Lamb *or* yeanling
Sprat	Brit
Swan	Cygnet
Tiger	Cub
Toad	Tadpole
Whale	Calf
Wolf	Cub *or* whelp

See also:
> ➤ **Amphibians ➤ Anteaters ➤ Antelopes ➤ Birds**
> ➤ **Dinosaurs ➤ Fish ➤ Insects ➤ Invertebrates**
> ➤ **Mammals, extinct ➤ Parasites ➤ Reptiles**

Anniversaries

Year	Traditional	Modern
1st	Paper	Clocks
2nd	Cotton	China
3rd	Leather	Crystal *or* glass
4th	Linen *or* silk	Electrical appliances
5th	Wood	Silverware
6th	Iron	Wood
7th	Wool *or* copper	Desk sets
8th	Bronze	Linen *or* lace
9th	Pottery *or* china	Leather
10th	Tin *or* aluminium	Diamond jewellery
11th	Steel	Fashion jewellery *or* accessories
12th	Silk	Pearls *or* coloured gems
13th	Lace	Textile *or* furs

Year	Traditional	Modern
14th	Ivory	Gold jewellery
15th	Crystal	Watches
20th	China	Platinum
25th	Silver	Sterling silver
30th	Pearl	Diamond
35th	Coral *or* jade	Jade
40th	Ruby	Ruby
45th	Sapphire	Sapphire
50th	Gold	Gold
55th	Emerald	Emerald
60th	Diamond	Diamond

Anteaters and other edentates

2 letters:
Ai
5 letters:
Sloth
6 letters:
Numbat
7 letters:
Echidna

Tamandu
8 letters:
Aardvark
Anteater
Pangolin
Tamandua
9 letters:
Armadillo

13 letters:
Scaly anteater
Spiny anteater
14 letters:
Banded anteater
Lesser anteater

Antelopes

3 letters:
Elk
Gnu
Kob
4 letters:
Kudu
Oryx
Puku
Suni
Thar
Topi
5 letters:
Addax
Bongo
Bubal
Eland
Goral
Kaama
Nagor
Nyala
Oribi
Sable
Saiga
Sasin
Serow
Takin
6 letters:
Dikdik

Duiker
Duyker
Dzeren
Impala
Inyala
Koodoo
Lechwe
Nilgai
Nilgau
Ourebi
Pallah
Pygarg
Reebok
Rhebok
7 letters:
Blaubok
Blesbok
Bloubok
Bubalis
Chamois
Chikara
Gazelle
Gemsbok
Gerenuk
Grysbok
Kongoni
Madoqua
Nylghau

Sassaby
Stembok
8 letters:
Bluebuck
Bontebok
Bushbuck
Hartbees
Pale-buck
Reedbuck
Steenbok
Stemback
Tsessebe
9 letters:
Blackbuck
Prongbuck
Pronghorn
Sitatunga
Situtunga
Steinbock
Tragelaph
Waterbuck
10 letters:
Hartebeest
Wildebeest
12 letters:
Klipspringer

Antibiotics

7 letters:
Opsonin
8 letters:
Colistin
Neomycin
Nystatin
9 letters:
Kanamycin
Mitomycin
Oxacillin
Polymixin
Rifamycin
10 letters:
Bacitracin

Gentamicin
Gramicidin
Lincomycin
Rifampicin
Terramycin®
Tyrocidine
11 letters:
Actinomycin
Cloxacillin
Doxorubicin
Doxycycline
Interleukin
Methicillin
Tyrothricin

12 letters:
Erythromycin
Griseofulvin
Streptomycin
Tetracycline
13 letters:
Cephalosporin
Spectinomycin
14 letters:
Streptothricin
15 letters:
Oxytetracycline

Ants, bees and wasps

3 letters:
Ant
Bee
4 letters:
Wasp
5 letters:
Emmet
Minga
7 letters:
Army ant
Blue ant
Bull ant
Bull Joe
Hive bee
Termite
Wood ant
8 letters:
Gall wasp
Honey ant
Honeybee

Horntail
Kootchar
Mason bee
Sand wasp
Slave ant
White ant
Wood wasp
9 letters:
Amazon ant
Bumblebee
Cuckoo bee
Driver ant
Humblebee
Killer bee
Mason wasp
Mining bee
Mud dauber
Native bee
Sirex wasp
Velvet ant

10 letters:
Bulldog ant
Digger wasp
Flower wasp
Pharaoh ant
11 letters:
Honeypot ant
Sugarbag fly
12 letters:
Carpenter bee
Cicada hunter
Ichneumon fly
Legionary ant
Policeman fly
Ruby-tail wasp
Yellow jacket
13 letters:
Ichneumon wasp
Leafcutter ant
Leafcutter bee

Apocalypse, Four Horsemen of

Colour	Represents
White	Christ
Red	War
Black	Famine
Pale	Death

Apostles

4 letters:
John
Jude
5 letters:
James (the Great)
James (the Less)

Peter
Simon
6 letters:
Andrew
Philip
Thomas

7 letters:
Matthew
8 letters:
Matthias
11 letters:
Bartholomew

Apples

3 letters:
Cox
4 letters:
Crab
Fuji
John
Lobo
Love
Pome
Snow
5 letters:
Pyrus
Sugar
Thorn
6 letters:
Balsam
Biffin
Codlin
Elstar
Empire
Idared
Mammee
Medlar
Pippin
Pomace
Pomroy
Rennet
Russet
Sunset
7 letters:
Baldwin

Bramley
Codling
Costard
Custard
Pomeroy
Ribston
Ruddock
Spartan
Sturmer
Winesap
8 letters:
Braeburn
Greening
Jonagold
Jonathan
Jonathon
Pearmain
Pink Lady
Reinette
Ribstone
Sweeting
9 letters:
Alligator
Charlotte
Crab apple
Discovery
Grenadier
Nonpareil
Quarenden
Quarender
Redstreak

Royal Gala
Worcester
10 letters:
Quarantine
Red Ellison
Sops-in-wine
11 letters:
Charles Ross
Granny Smith
James Grieve
Leather-coat
Quarrington
12 letters:
Greensleeves
Laxton Superb
Prince Albert
Red Delicious
13 letters:
Lord Lambourne
Seek-no-further
14 letters:
Blenheim Orange
Egremont Russet
Rosemary Russet
15 letters:
Golden Delicious

Archaeology

ARCHAEOLOGICAL PERIODS

6 letters:
Ice age
La Tène
Minoan
7 letters:
Azilian
Iron Age

8 letters:
Asturian
Helladic
9 letters:
Acheulean
Acheulian
Bronze Age

Levallois
Mycenaean
Neolithic
Solutrean
10 letters:
Eneolithic
Gravettian

Mesolithic
Mousterian
11 letters:
Aurignacian
Magdalenian
New Stone Age
Old Stone Age

12 letters:
Chalcolithic
Levalloisian
Palaeolithic
13 letters:
Neo-Babylonian
Old Babylonian

15 letters:
Châtelperronian

ARCHAEOLOGICAL TERMS

4 letters:
Celt
Cist
Core
Kist
5 letters:
Baulk
Blade
Burin
Cairn
Flake
Flint
Henge
Mound
Pylon
Stela
Stele
6 letters:
Arcade
Barrow
Bogman
Cirque

Dolmen
Eolith
Larnax
Vallum
7 letters:
Callais
Caveman
Hogback
Ley line
Neolith
Obelisk
Patella
Retouch
Sondage
Tumulus
8 letters:
Bifacial
Cartouch
Cromlech
Graffito
Hillfort
Megalith

Palmette
Palstave
Tribrach
9 letters:
Acropolis
Alignment
Bracteate
Cartouche
Earthwork
Hut circle
Microlith
10 letters:
Souterrain
11 letters:
Clovis point
Cross-dating
Stone circle
12 letters:
Robber trench
Stratigraphy
15 letters:
Archeomagnetism

Archbishops of Canterbury

3 letters:
Oda
4 letters:
Lang, *Cosmo*
Laud, *William*
Pole, *Reginald*
Rich, *Edmund*
Tait, *Archibald*
Wake, *William*
5 letters:
Abbot, *George*
Carey, *George*
Deane, *Henry*
Islip, *Simon*
Juxon, *William*
Kempe, *John*
Moore, *John*
6 letters:
Anselm
Becket, *Thomas à*

Benson, *Edward*
Coggan, *Donald*
Fisher, *Geoffrey*
Howley, *William*
Hutton, *Matthew*
Justus
Lyfing
Mepham, *Simon*
Morton, *John*
Offord, *John*
Parker, *Matthew*
Potter, *John*
Ramsey, *Arthur*
Robert *of Jumieges*
Runcie, *Robert*
Secker, *Thomas*
Sumner, *John*
Sutton, *Charles*
Temple, *Frederick*
Temple, *William*

Walden, *Roger*
Walter, *Hubert*
Warham, *William*
7 letters:
Aelfric
Arundel, *Thomas*
Baldwin
Cranmer, *Thomas*
Dunstan
Eadsige
Grindal, *Edmund*
Herring, *Thomas*
Langham, *Simon*
Langton, *Stephen*
Le Grant, *Richard*
Longley, *Charles*
Nothelm
Peckham, *John*
Richard *of Dover*
Sheldon, *Gilbert*

Sigeric, *Serio*
Stigand
Sudbury, *Simon*
Tatwine
Tenison, *Thomas*
William *of Corbeil*
Wulfred
8 letters:
Aelfheah
Aelfsige
Bancroft, *Richard*
Boniface *of Savoy*
Ceolnoth
Chichele, *Henry*
Davidson, *Randall*
D'Escures, *Ralph*
Honorius
Lanfranc

Mellitus
Plegmund
Reynolds, *Walter*
Sancroft, *William*
Stafford, *John*
Theobald *of Bec*
Theodore
Whitgift, *John*
Williams
Wulfhelm
9 letters:
Aethelgar
Aethelred
Augustine
Bregowine
Courtenay, *William*
Deusdedit
Feologeld

Kilwardby, *Robert*
Stratford, *John*
Tillotson, *John*
10 letters:
Aethelhelm
Aethelnoth
Beorhthelm
Bourgchier, *Thomas*
Cornwallis, *Frederick*
Cuthbeorht
Jaenbeorht
Laurentius
Whittlesey, *William*
Winchelsey, *Robert*
11 letters:
Aethelheard
Beorhtweald
Bradwardine, *Thomas*

Architecture

ARCHITECTURAL STYLES

5 letters:
Doric
Ionic
Roman
Saxon
Tudor
6 letters:
Empire
Gothic
Norman
Rococo
Tuscan
7 letters:
Art Deco
Baroque
Bauhaus
Moderne
Moorish
Morisco
Mudéjar
Regency
Saracen
8 letters:
Colonial

Georgian
Jacobean
9 letters:
Brutalist
Byzantine
Classical
Composite
Decorated
Edwardian
Mannerist
Modernist
Palladian
Queen-Anne
Victorian
10 letters:
Art Nouveau
Corinthian
Federation
Louis Seize
Romanesque
Transition
11 letters:
Elizabethan
Louis Quinze

Louis Treize
Renaissance
12 letters:
Early English
Greek Revival
New brutalist
Transitional
13 letters:
Functionalism
Gothic Revival
Louis Quatorze
Neoclassicist
Perpendicular
Postmodernist
14 letters:
Churrigueresco
Early Christian
15 letters:
Churrigueresque

ARCHITECTURAL TERMS

3 letters:
Hip
4 letters:
Drum
Naos

Rise
5 letters:
Giant
Order
Shaft

Shell
Stria
6 letters:
Filler
Florid

Fluted
Hipped
Invert
Lierne
Lintel
Listed
Loggia
Member
Module
Return
Rhythm
Soffit
Spring
Storey
String
Summer

7 letters:
Abuttal
Astylar
Bolster
Bracket
Castled
Engaged
Galilee
Profile
Rampant
Respond
Stilted
Subbase
Surbase

8 letters:
Abutment
Colossal
Cradling

Diastyle
Diminish
Dipteral
Foliated
Galleria
King post
Lanceted
Moresque
Postiche
Prostyle
Shafting
Stringer
Tail beam
Trabeate
Tympanic

9 letters:
Composite
Crenelate
Discharge
Elevation
Eurhythmy
Floor plan
Floreated
Floriated
Foliation
Hexastyle
Hypostyle
Imbricate
Pulvinate
Queen post
Rendering
Rusticate
Springing
Stylobate

Tailpiece
Trabeated

10 letters:
Cloistered
Crenellate
Flamboyant
Ground plan
Imbricated
Joggle post
Polychromy
Pulvinated
Sexpartite
Summer tree

11 letters:
Castellated
Cinquecento
Denticulate
Fenestrated
High-pitched
Orientation

12 letters:
String course

13 letters:
Architectonic
Architectural
Springing line
Supercolumnar

14 letters:
Architectonics
Springing point

15 letters:
Underpitch vault

ARCHITECTURAL FEATURES

3 letters:
Bow
Cap
Die
Ell
Fan
Rib
Web

4 letters:
Anta
Apse
Arch
Balk
Band
Base
Bead
Beak
Case

Cove
Cusp
Cyma
Dado
Drip
Foil
Jube
Naos
Neck
Ogee
Pace
Pier
Quad
Reed
Sill
Stoa
Term
Tore

Xyst

5 letters:
Aisle
Ancon
Apsis
Arris
Atlas
Attic
Cella
Cheek
Choir
Coign
Conch
Congé
Crown
Doors
Facet
Facia

Gable
Garth
Glyph
Groin
Gutta
Hance
Helix
Label
Newel
Niche
Ogive
Oriel
Ovolo
Patio
Porch
Pylon
Quirk
Quoin
Ridge
Shaft
Spire
Splay
Stela
Stele
Stria
Table
Talon
Tenia
Thumb
Torus
Truss
Vault
Verge

6 letters:
Abacus
Ancone
Arcade
Atrium
Baguet
Belfry
Bezant
Billet
Binder
Breast
Broach
Byzant
Canopy
Casing
Cellar
Coffer
Coigne
Column
Concha
Corbel
Cordon
Corona
Coving

Crenel
Cullis
Cupola
Dentil
Ectype
Exedra
Facade
Facial
Fascia
Fillet
Finial
Flèche
Frieze
Garret
Gazebo
Gradin
Griffe
Grotto
Haunch
Hipped
Impost
Lacuna
Leaded
Listel
Loggia
Louvre
Metope
Mutule
Offset
Perron
Piazza
Pillar
Plinth
Podium
Portal
Reglet
Relief
Return
Reveal
Rosace
Scotia
Screen
Soffit
Squint
Summer
Taenia
Trophy
Turret
Tympan
Volute

7 letters:
Acroter
Annulet
Antefix
Apteral
Balcony
Bezzant

Bracket
Caisson
Calotte
Capital
Cavetto
Ceiling
Channel
Chaplet
Chevron
Corbeil
Cornice
Crochet
Crocket
Cushion
Echinus
Entasis
Fantail
Fascial
Festoon
Fluting
Footing
Frustum
Gadroon
Gallery
Gambrel
Godroon
Hip roof
Landing
Lantern
Lucarne
Mansard
Meander
Minaret
Mullion
Narthex
Necking
Obelisk
Parapet
Pendant
Perpend
Portico
Postern
Reeding
Respond
Rosette
Rotunda
Roundel
Squinch
Steeple
Strigil
Tambour
Telamon
Tracery
Trefoil
Tribune
Trumeau
Veranda

8 letters:
Acanthus
Accolade
Apophyge
Arcature
Astragal
Atlantes
Baguette
Baluster
Banderol
Bannerol
Basement
Buttress
Caryatid
Casement
Chapiter
Cloister
Crenelle
Cresting
Crossing
Crow step
Curb roof
Cymatium
Dancette
Dogtooth
Extrados
Fanlight
Fenestra
Gable end
Gargoyle
Gorgerin
Headwork
Imperial
Intrados
Keystone
Moulding
Ogee arch
Pedestal
Pediment
Pinnacle
Platform
Predella
Semidome
Shafting
Skew arch
Skylight
Spandrel
Spandril
Springer
Tellamon
Terminal
Terminus
Transept
Traverse

Triglyph
Tympanum
Verandah
Vignette
9 letters:
Anthemion
Archivolt
Arcuation
Baldachin
Banderole
Bay window
Bilection
Bolection
Bow window
Cartouche
Choir loft
Colonnade
Corbeille
Decastyle
Dripstone
Embrasure
Footstall
Gatehouse
Headstone
Helicline
Hood mould
Hypophyge
Medallion
Modillion
Onion dome
Penthouse
Peristyle
Poppyhead
Roman arch
Strap work
Stylobate
Triforium
10 letters:
Ambulatory
Arc-boutant
Architrave
Ballflower
Belt course
Cantilever
Cinquefoil
Clerestory
Corbel step
Corbie-step
Egg and dart
Fan tracery
Fenestella
Gothic arch
Hagioscope
Lancet arch

Norman arch
Propylaeum
Quadrangle
Quatrefoil
Rose window
Saddleback
Saddle roof
Sash window
Scrollwork
Stereobate
Wagon vault
Water table
11 letters:
Amphistylar
Barge couple
Barge course
Barrel vault
Bed moulding
Bottom house
Brattishing
Columbarium
Corbie gable
Curtail step
Curtain wall
Cuspidation
Entablature
Gable window
Half landing
Oeil-de-boeuf
Oriel window
Tunnel vault
12 letters:
Articulation
Columniation
Egg and anchor
Egg and tongue
Frontispiece
Lancet window
Palm vaulting
Porte-cochere
Quarter round
String course
13 letters:
Amphiprostyle
Compass window
French windows
Machicolation
14 letters:
Catherine wheel
Flying buttress
Straining piece
15 letters:
Underpitch vault

ARCHITECTS

3 letters:
Oud, *Jacobus Johann Pieter*
Pei, *I(eoh) M(ing)*
4 letters:
Adam, *James*
Adam, *Robert*
Adam, *William*
Kahn, *Louis I(sadore)*
Kent, *William*
Loos, *Adolf*
Nash, *John*
Shaw, *Richard Norman*
Webb, *Aston*
Webb, *Philip*
Wood, *John*
Wren, *Christopher*
5 letters:
Aalto, *Alvar*
Baker, *Herbert*
Barry, *Charles*
Bryce, *David*
Dance, *George*
Doshi, *Balkrishna Vithaldas*
Dudok, *Willem Marinus*
Engel, *Johann Carl Ludwig*
Gaudí, *Antonio*
Gibbs, *James*
Gilly, *Friedrich*
Horta, *Victor*
Jones, *Inigo*
Levau, *Louis*
Moore, *Charles Willard*
Nervi, *Pier Luigi*
Pugin, *Augustus (Welby Northmore)*
Scott, *George Gilbert*
Scott, *Giles Gilbert*
Soane, *John*
Tange, *Kenzo*
Terry, *(John) Quinlan*
Utzon, *Jorn*
Wyatt, *James*
6 letters:
Boulle, *Etienne-Louis*
Breuer, *Marcel Lajos*
Burton, *Decimus*
Casson, *Hugh (Maxwell)*
Coates, *Wells Wintemute*
Foster, *Norman*
Fuller, *(Richard) Buckminster*
Geddes, *Patrick*
Giotto *(di Bondone)*
Howard, *Ebenezer*
Lasdun, *Denys*
Ledoux, *Claude Nicolas*

Lescot, *Pierre*
Nissen, *Godber*
Paxton, *Joseph*
Perret, *Auguste*
Pisano, *Andrea*
Pisano, *Nicola*
Pollio, *Marcus Vitruvius*
Repton, *Humphrey*
Rogers, *Richard*
Romano, *Giulio*
Scopas
Serlio, *Sebastiano*
Smirke, *Robert*
Spence, *Basil (Unwin)*
Street, *George Edmund*
Stuart, *James*
Vasari, *Giorgio*
Voysey, *Charles (Francis Annesley)*
Wagner, *Otto*
Wright, *Frank Lloyd*
7 letters:
Alberti, *Leon Battista*
Asplund, *Erik Gunnar*
Behrens, *Peter*
Berlage, *Hendrick Petrus*
Bernini, *Gian Lorenzo*
Burnham, *David Hudson*
Candela, *Felix*
Columbo, *David*
Da Vinci, *Leonardo*
De l'Orme, *Philibert*
Gabriel, *Ange-Jacques*
Garnier, *Tony (Antoine)*
Gibberd, *Frederick*
Gilbert, *Cass*
Gropius, *Walter*
Guarini, *Guarino*
Holland, *Henry*
Ictinus
Imhotep
Johnson, *Philip Cortelyou*
Lethaby, *William Richard*
Lorimer, *Robert Stodart*
Lutyens, *Edwin*
Maderna, *Carlo*
Maderno, *Carlo*
Mansart, *François*
Mansart, *Jules Hardouin*
Neumann, *Johann Balthasar*
Orcagna *(Andrea di Cionne)*
Peruzzi, *Baldassare Tommaso*
Poelzig, *Hans*
Raphael
Renwick, *James*
Thomson, *Alexander (Greek)*

Venturi, *Robert*
Vignola, *Giacomo*
8 letters:
Bramante, *Donato*
Chambers, *William*
Daedalus
De Brosse, *Salomon*
Di Cambio, *Arnolfo*
Erickson, *Arthur Charles*
Hamilton, *Thomas*
Hoffmann, *Josef*
Jacobsen, *Arne*
Niemeyer, *Oscar*
Palladio, *Andrea*
Piranesi, *Giambattista*
Playfair, *William Henry*
Rietveld, *Gerrit Thomas*
Saarinen, *Eero*
Schinkel, *Karl Friederich*
Smythson, *Robert*
Sottsass, *Ettore Jr*
Soufflot, *Jacques Germain*
Stirling, *James*
Sullivan, *Louis (Henri)*
Vanbrugh, *John*
Yamasaki, *Minoru*
9 letters:
Anthemias *of Tralles*
Bartholdi, *Frédéric August*
Borromini, *Francesco*
Cockerell, *Charles Robert*
Da Cortona, *Pietro*
Da Cortona, *Pietro Berrettini*
Da Vignola, *Giacomo Barozzi*
Di Giorgio, *Francesco*

Haussmann, *Georges Eugene*
Hawksmoor, *Nicholas*
Labrouste, *(Pierre Francois) Henri*
Mackmurdo, *Arthur Heygate*
Macquarie, *Lachlan*
Sansovino, *Jacopo*
Van Campen, *Jacob*
Vitruvius
Von Erlach, *Johann Bernhard Fischer*
10 letters:
Chermayeff, *Serge*
Mackintosh, *Charles Rennie*
Mendelsohn, *Eric*
Michelozzo
Sanmicheli, *Michele*
Trophonius
Van der Rohe, *Ludwig Mies*
Van de Velde, *Henry*
Waterhouse, *Alfred*
11 letters:
Abercrombie, *(Leslie) Patrick*
Butterfield, *William*
Callicrates
Churriguera, *Don Jose*
De Cuvillies, *Francois*
Le Corbusier
Van Doesburg, *Theo*
12 letters:
Brunelleschi, *Filippo*
Michelangelo
Viollet-le-Duc, *Eugène Emmanuel*
14 letters:
Von Hildebrandt, *Johann Lukas*

Armour

4 letters:	Vizor	Tasset
Cush	**6 letters:**	Thorax
Jack	Beaver	Tonlet
Mail	Byrnie	Tuille
Tace	Camail	Voider
Umbo	Corium	**7 letters:**
5 letters:	Couter	Ailette
Armet	Crinet	Basinet
Bevor	Cuisse	Besagew
Cuish	Curiet	Brasset
Culet	Gorget	Buckler
Curat	Greave	Casspir
Fauld	Gusset	Corslet
Jupon	Helmet	Cuirass
Nasal	Jamber	Hauberk
Petta	Poleyn	Jambart
Tasse	Secret	Jambeau
Visor	Taslet	Lamboys

Panoply
Placcat
Placket
Poitrel
Roundel
Sabaton
Ventail
8 letters:
Barbette
Bascinet
Chaffron
Chamfron
Chanfron
Chausses

Corselet
Gauntlet
Jazerant
Pauldron
Pavloron
Plastron
Pouldron
Solleret
Spaudler
Vambrace
9 letters:
Chamfrain
Garniture
Habergeon

Jesserant
Lance rest
Nosepiece
Sword belt
Vantbrass
10 letters:
Brigandine
Cataphract
Coat-of-mail
11 letters:
Breastplate
Genouillère
Mentonnière

Art

ART STYLES AND MOVEMENTS

2 letters:
Op
3 letters:
Pop
4 letters:
Clip
Dada
Deco
Fine
Kano
5 letters:
Cobra
Dedal
Nabis
Tatum
Virtu
6 letters:
Bonsai
Brücke
Cubism
Daedal
Gothic
Kitsch
Rococo
Trouvé
Ukiyo-e
7 letters:
Art Deco
Baroque
Bauhaus
Dadaism
Daedale
De Stijl
Fauvism
Flemish
Kinetic
Minimal

Montage
New Wave
Norwich
Nouveau
Optical
Orphism
Plastic
Realism
Relievo
Sienese
Tachism
Trivium
8 letters:
Abstract
Futurism
Mandorla
Nazarene
Tachisme
Trecento
9 letters:
Mannerism
Modernism
Primitive
Still-life
Symbolism
Tenebrism
Toreutics
Vorticism
10 letters:
Arte Povera
Art Nouveau
Bloomsbury
Classicism
Commercial
Conceptual
Decorative
Jugendstil

Naturalism
Postmodern
Quadratura
Quadrivium
Romanesque
Surrealism
Synthetism
11 letters:
Chiaroscuro
Divisionism
Performance
Perigordian
Pointillism
Psychedelic
Romanticism
Suprematism
Synchronism
Trompe l'oeil
12 letters:
Clair-obscure
Clare-obscure
Neoclassical
13 letters:
Expressionism
Impressionism
Impressionist
Neoclassicism
Neoplasticism
Postmodernism
Pre-Raphaelite
14 letters:
Abstractionism
Barbizon School
Constructivism
Der Blaue Reiter

ART EQUIPMENT

3 letters:
Ink
5 letters:
Brush
Chalk
Easel
Glaze
Paint
6 letters:
Canvas
Crayon
Ground
Pastel

Pencil
7 letters:
Acrylic
Palette
Spatula
Varnish
8 letters:
Airbrush
Charcoal
Fixative
Oil paint
Paintbox
Spray gun

9 letters:
Lay figure
10 letters:
Linseed oil
Paintbrush
Sketchbook
11 letters:
Watercolour
12 letters:
Drawing paper
Palette knife

Arthurian legend

CHARACTERS IN ARTHURIAN LEGEND

4 letters:
Bors
5 letters:
Nimue
6 letters:
Arthur
Elaine
Gawain
Merlin
Modred

7 letters:
Caradoc
Galahad
Gawayne
Igraine
Launfal
Tristan
Viviane
8 letters:
Bedivere

Lancelot
Parsifal
Perceval
Tristram
11 letters:
Morgan Le Fay
14 letters:
Gareth of Orkney
Launcelot du Lac
Uther Pendragon

PLACES IN ARTHURIAN LEGEND

6 letters:
Avalon
7 letters:
Astolat
Camelot

8 letters:
Tintagel
9 letters:
Lyonnesse

11 letters:
Glastonbury

Artists

3 letters:
Arp, *Hans*
Arp, *Jean*
Cox, *David*
Dou, *Gerrit*
Fry, *Roger*
Nay, *Ernst Wilhelm*
Ray, *Man*
Xia *Gui*
4 letters:
Bell, *Vanessa*
Boyd, *Arthur*
Caro, *Anthony*

Cuyp, *Aelbert*
Dadd, *Richard*
Dalí, *Salvador*
Doré, *Gustave*
Dufy, *Raoul*
Etty, *William*
Gabo, *Naum*
Gill, *Eric*
Goya (y Lucientes), *Francisco José de*
Gris, *Juan*
Gros, *Antoine Jean*
Hals, *Frans*

Hsia *Kuei*
Hunt, *William Holman*
John, *Augustus*
John, *Gwen*
Klee, *Paul*
Kuyp, *Aelbert*
Lely, *Peter*
Marc, *Franz*
Miró, *Joan*
Nash, *Paul*
Opie, *John*
Phiz *(Hablot Knigh Browne)*
Reni, *Guido*
Rosa, *Salvator*
West, *Benjamin*
Zorn, *Anders*
5 letters:
Aiken, *John MacDonald*
Appel, *Karel*
Bacon, *Francis*
Bakst, *Leon Nikolayevich*
Beuys, *Joseph*
Blake, *Peter*
Blake, *William*
Bosch, *Hieronymus*
Brown, *Ford Madox*
Burra, *Edward*
Corot, *Jean Baptiste Camille*
Crane, *Walter*
Crome, *John*
Danby, *Francis*
David, *Jacques Louis*
Degas, *Hilaire Germain Edgar*
Denis, *Maurice*
Dulac, *Pierre Charles*
Dürer, *Albrecht*
Ensor, *James*
Ernst, *Max*
Freud, *Lucian*
Gorky, *Arshile*
Grant, *Duncan*
Greco, *El*
Grosz, *George*
Hirst, *Damien*
Hoare, *William*
Homer, *Winslow*
Hooch, *Pieter de*
Johns, *Jasper*
Kitaj, *Ron B(rooks)*
Klimt, *Gustav*
Kline, *Franz*
Leech, *John*
Léger, *Fernand*
Lewis, *Wyndham*
Lippi, *Filippino*
Lotto, *Lorenzo*

Lowry, *L(awrence) S(tephen)*
Manet, *Edouard*
Monet, *Claude Oscar*
Moore, *Henry*
Morse, *Samuel Finley Breese*
Moses, *Grandma*
Munch, *Edvard*
Myron
Nolan, *Sidney*
Nolde, *Emil*
Orpen, *Sir William*
Oudry, *Jean Baptiste*
Pilon, *Germain*
Piper, *John*
Puget, *Pierre*
Redon, *Odilon*
Riley, *Bridget*
Rodin, *Auguste*
Runge, *Philipp Otto*
Seago, *Edward*
Shahn, *Ben*
Sloan, *John*
Smith, *David*
Steen, *Jan*
Steer, *Philip Wilson*
Stoss, *Veit*
Tatum, *Mary*
Watts, *George Frederick*
Zumbo, *Gaetano Giulio*
6 letters:
Albers, *Josef*
Andrei, *Rublev*
Andrei, *Rublyov*
Benton, *Thomas Hart*
Boudin, *Eugène*
Braque, *Georges*
Buffet, *Bernard*
Butler, *Reg*
Calder, *Alexander*
Callot, *Jacques*
Campin, *Robert*
Canova, *Antonio*
Clouet, *François*
Clouet, *Jean*
Copley, *John*
Coypel, *Antoine*
De Goya, *Francisco*
Derain, *André*
De Wint, *Peter*
Dobell, *William*
D'Orsay, *Count Alfred Guillaum Gabriel*
Eakins, *Thomas*
Fuseli, *Henry*
Gérard, *François*
Giotto *(di Bondone)*

Greuze, *Jean Baptiste*
Guardi, *Francesco*
Haydon, *Benjamin Robert*
Hopper, *Edward*
Houdon, *Jean Antoine*
Ingres, *Jean Auguste Dominique*
Knight, *Laura*
Lebrun, *Charles*
Le Nain, *Antoine*
Le Nain, *Louis*
Le Nain, *Mathieu*
Mabuse, *Jan*
Martin, *John*
Massys, *Quentin*
Millet, *Jean François*
Moreau, *Gustave*
Morris, *William*
Newman, *Barnett*
O'Keefe, *Georgia*
Orozco, *José Clemente*
Palmer, *Samuel*
Pisano, *Andrea*
Pisano, *Giovanni*
Pisano, *Nicola*
Potter, *Paulus*
Ramsay, *Allan*
Renoir, *Pierre Auguste*
Ribera, *Jusepe de*
Rivera, *Diego*
Romano, *Giulio*
Romney, *George*
Rothko, *Mark*
Rubens, *Peter Paul*
Scopas
Sendak, *Maurice*
Sesshu, *Toyo*
Seurat, *Georges*
Signac, *Paul*
Sisley, *Alfred*
Sluter, *Claus*
Stubbs, *George*
Tanguy, *Yves*
Tatlin, *Vladimir*
Tissot, *James Jacques Joseph*
Titian
Turner, *J(oseph) M(allord) W(illiam)*
Vasari, *Giorgio*
Villon, *Jacques*
Warhol, *Andy*
Wilson, *Richard*
Wright, *Joseph*
Zeuxis
7 letters:
Alberti, *Leon Battista*
Allston, *Washington*
Apelles

Audubon, *John James*
Balthus *(Balthasar Klossowski de Rola)*
Bellini, *Giovanni*
Bernini, *Gian Lorenzo*
Bomberg, *David*
Bonheur, *Rosa*
Bonnard, *Pierre*
Borglum, *Gutzon*
Boucher, *Francois*
Brassaï, *Gyula*
Bruegel, *Jan*
Bruegel, *Pieter*
Cassatt, *Mary*
Cellini, *Benvenuto*
Cézanne, *Paul*
Chagall, *Marc*
Chardin, *Jean-Baptiste Siméon*
Cimabue, *Giovanni*
Collier, *John*
Courbet, *Gustave*
Cranach, *Lucas*
Daumier, *Honoré*
Da Vinci, *Leonardo*
De Hooch, *Pieter*
De Hoogh, *Pieter*
Delvaux, *Paul*
Duchamp, *Marcel*
Epstein, *Jacob*
Flaxman, *John*
Fouquet, *Jean*
Gauguin, *Paul*
Gibbons, *Grinling*
Hobbema, *Meindert*
Hockney, *David*
Hofmann, *Hans*
Hogarth, *William*
Hokusai, *Katsushika*
Holbein, *Hans*
Hoppner, *John*
Kneller, *Godfrey*
Kossoff, *Leon*
Lindsay, *Norman Alfred William*
Lorrain, *Claude*
Maillol, *Aristide*
Martini, *Simone*
Matisse, *Henri*
Memlinc, *Hans*
Memling, *Hans*
Millais, *John Everett*
Morisot, *Berthe*
Morland, *George*
Murillo, *Bartolomé Esteban*
Nattier, *Jean Marc*
Orcagna, *Andrea di Cionne*
Pasmore, *Victor*
Patinir, *Joachim*

Peruzzi, *Baldassare*
Pevsner, *Antoine*
Phidias
Picabia, *Francis*
Picasso, *Pablo*
Pigalle, *Jean Baptiste*
Pissaro, *Camille*
Pollock, *Jackson*
Poussin, *Nicolas*
Proesch, *Gilbert*
Prud'hon, *Pierre Paul*
Rackham, *Arthur*
Raeburn, *Henry*
Raphael
Rouault, *Geroges*
Sargent, *John Singer*
Schiele, *Egon*
Sickert, *Walter Richard*
Soutine, *Chaim*
Spencer, *Stanley*
Teniers, *David*
Tiepolo, *Giambattista*
Uccello, *Paolo*
Utamaro, *Kitigawa*
Utrillo, *Maurice*
Van Dyck, *Anthony*
Van Eyck, *Jan*
Van Gogh, *Vincent*
Van Rijn, *Rembrandt Harmensz*
Vecchio, *Palma*
Vermeer, *Jan*
Watteau, *Jean Antoine*
Zeuxian
Zoffany, *Johann*
8 letters:
Angelico, *Fra*
Annigoni, *Pietro*
Auerbach, *Frank*
Beckmann, *Max*
Boccioni, *Umberto*
Bramante, *Donato*
Brancusi, *Constantin*
Breughel, *Jan*
Breughel, *Pieter*
Bronzino, *Agnolo*
Brueghel, *Jan*
Brueghel, *Pieter*
Carracci, *Agostino*
Carracci, *Annibale*
Carracci, *Ludovico*
Chadwick, *Lynn*
Daubigny, *Charles François*
De La Tour, *Georges*
Delaunay, *Robert*
De Ribera, *José*
Di Cosimo, *Piero*
Di Duccio, *Agostino*

Drysdale, *George Russell*
Dubuffet, *Jean*
Eastlake, *Sir Charles Lock*
Ghiberti, *Lorenzo*
González, *Julio*
Hamilton, *Richard*
Jongkind, *Johan Barthold*
Jordaens, *Jacob*
Kirchner, *Ernst Ludwig*
Landseer, *Edwin*
Lawrence, *Thomas*
Leighton, *Frederic*
Leonardo
Lipchitz, *Jacques*
Lysippus
Magritte, *René*
Malevich, *Kasimir Severinovich*
Mantegna, *Andrea*
Masaccio *(Thomasso Giovanni di Simone Guidi)*
Mondrian, *Piet*
Munnings, *Alfred*
Nevinson, *Christopher Richard Wynne*
Paolozzi, *Eduardo*
Passmore, *George*
Patenier, *Joachim*
Perugino, *Pietro*
Piranesi, *Giambattista*
Pissarro, *Camille*
Pontormo, *Jacopo Carucci*
Reynolds, *Joshua*
Rossetti, *Dante Gabriel*
Rousseau, *Henri Julien*
Rousseau, *Théodore*
Ter Borch, *Gerard*
Topolski, *Feliks*
Van Goyen, *Jan*
Vasarely, *Victor*
Veronese, *Paolo*
Whistler, *James Abbott McNeill*
Zurbarán, *Francisco*
9 letters:
Altdorfer, *Albrecht*
Bartholdi, *Frédéric August*
Beardsley, *Aubrey Vincent*
Bonington, *Richard Parkes*
Canaletto *(Giovanni Antonio Canal)*
Carpaccio, *Vittore*
Cavallini, *Pietro*
Constable, *John*
Correggio, *Antonio Allegri da*
Da Cortona, *Pietro*
Da Messina, *Antonello*
De Chirico, *Giorgio*
De Kooning, *Willem*

Delacroix, *Eugène*
Delaroche, *Paul*
Donatello *(Donato di Betto Bardi)*
Feininger, *Lyonel*
Fragonard, *Jean Honoré*
Friedrich, *Caspar David*
Géricault, *Théodore*
Giorgione, *Giorgio Barbarelli*
Grünewald, *Isaak*
Hiroshige, *Ando*
Kandinsky, *Wassily*
Kauffmann, *Angelica*
Kokoschka, *Oscar*
Kuniyoshi, *Utagawa*
Lehmbruck, *Wilhelm*
Mestrovic, *Ivan*
Nicholson, *Ben*
Nollekens, *Joseph*
Oldenburg, *Claes*
Pisanello
Rembrandt *(Rembrandt Harmensz van Rijn)*
Rodchenko, *Alexander Mikhailovich*
Roubiliac, *Louis-François*
Roubillac, *Louis-François*
Siqueiros, *David Alfaro*
Thornhill, *James*
Velázquez, *Diego Rodríguez de Silva y*
10 letters:
Alma-Tadema, *Lawrence*
Archipenko, *Aleksandr Porfiryevich*
Arcimboldo, *Giuseppe*
Bonnington, *Richard Parkes*
Botticelli, *Sandro*
Buonarroti, *Michelangelo*
Burne-Jones, *Edward*
Da Corregio, *Antonio Allegri*
Da Fabriano, *Gentile*
De Vlaminck, *Maurice*
Giacometti, *Alberto*
Guillaumin, *Armand*
Mackintosh, *Charles Rennie*
Michelozzo, *Michelozzi*
Modigliani, *Amedeo*
Moholy-Nagy, *László*
Polyclitus
Polygnotus
Praxiteles

Rowlandson, *Thomas*
Schongauer, *Martin*
Schwitters, *Kurt*
Signorelli, *Luca*
Sutherland, *Graham*
Tintoretto, *Jacopo*
Van der Goes, *Hugo*
Van de Velde, *Adriaen*
Van de Velde, *Willem*
11 letters:
Bartolommeo, *Fra*
Callimachus
De Chavannes, *Pierre Puvis*
Del Barbiere, *Domenico*
Della Robbia, *Andrea*
Della Robbia, *Luca*
Domenichino *(Domenico Zampien)*
Ghirlandaio, *Domenico*
Giambologna *(Jean de Boulogne)*
Terbrugghen, *Hendrik*
Thorvaldsen, *Bertel*
Van Ruisdael, *Jacob*
Van Ruysdael, *Salomen*
Vigée-Lebrun, *Élisabeth*
12 letters:
Da Caravaggio, *Michelangelo Merisi*
De Champaigne, *Philippe*
Della Quercia, *Jacopa*
Fantin-Latour, *Henri*
Gainsborough, *Thomas*
Lichtenstein, *Roy*
Michelangelo *(Michelagniolo di Lodovico Buonarriti)*
Parmigianino *(Girolano Francesco Maria Mazzola)*
Pinturicchio *(Bernardino di Betto)*
Rauschenberg, *Robert*
Van der Weyden, *Rogier*
Winterhalter, *Franz Xaver*
13 letters:
Del Pollaiuolo, *Antonio*
Del Pollaiuolo, *Piero*
Del Verrocchio, *Andrea*
Di Buoninsegna, *Duccio*
Messerschmidt, *Franz Xavier*
14 letters:
Da Castelfranco, *Giorgione*
Della Francesca, *Piero*
Gaudier-Brzeska, *Henri*

Asteroids

4 letters:
Eros
Juno
5 letters:
Ceres

6 letters:
Hermes
Pallas

8 letters:
Hesperia
Phaethon

Astronomers

4 letters:
Hale, *Alan*
Oort, *Jan*
5 letters:
Brahe, *Tycho*
Encke, *Johann Franz*
Hoyle, *Sir Fred(erick)*
Jeans, *Sir James Hopwood*
Meton
Reber, *Grote*
Roche, *Edouard*
6 letters:
Bessel, *Friedrich Wilhelm*
Halley, *Edmund*
Hewish, *Antony*
Hubble, *Edwin*
Kepler, *Johannes*
Lovell, *Sir (Alfred Charles)
  Bernard*
7 letters:
Bradley, *James*
Cassini, *Giovanni*
Celsius, *Anders*
Eudoxus
Galileo, *Galilei*

Huggins, *Sir William*
Khayyam, *Omar*
Laplace, *Pierre Simon de*
Lockyer, *Sir Joseph Norman*
Ptolemy *(Claudius Ptolemaeus)*
8 letters:
Almagest
Callipic
Herschel, *Caroline*
Herschel, *Sir William*
9 letters:
Eddington, *Sir Arthur*
Flamsteed, *John*
Leverrier, *Urbain Jean Joseph*
Sosigenes
10 letters:
Copernicus, *Nicolas*
Hipparchus
Tycho Brahe
11 letters:
Aristarchus
12 letters:
Eratosthenes
13 letters:
Schwarzschild, *Karl*

Athletic events

5 letters:
Relay
6 letters:
Discus
Hammer
7 letters:
Hurdles
Javelin
Shot put

Walking
8 letters:
High jump
Long jump
Marathon
9 letters:
Decathlon
Pole vault
Triathlon

10 letters:
Heptathlon
Pentathlon
Triple jump
12 letters:
Half marathon
Orienteering
Steeplechase

Atmosphere, layers of

10 letters:
Ionosphere
Mesosphere
Ozone layer

11 letters:
Ozonosphere
Troposphere

12 letters:
Stratosphere
Thermosphere

B

Bacteria

4 letters:
MRSA
5 letters:
Cocci
Staph
Strep
6 letters:
Aerobe

Vibrio
7 letters:
Bacilli
Lysogen
8 letters:
Listeria
Pathogen
Spirilla

10 letters:
Salmonella
11 letters:
Pasteurella
13 letters:
Streptococcus

Bags

3 letters:
Bum
Cod
Ice
Net
Sea
Tea
4 letters:
Body
Caba
Cool
Dime
Grip
Poke
Port
Sack
Tote
5 letters:
Amaut
Amowt
Bulse
Cabas
Dilli
Dilly
Ditty
Doggy
Jelly
Jiffy®
Nunny
Pikau

Pouch
Purse
Scrip
Water
6 letters:
Bergen
Carpet
Clutch
Duffel
Kitbag
Oxford
Sachet
Saddle
Sponge
Tucker
Valise
Vanity
Wallet
7 letters:
Alforja
Carrier
Daypack
Dorothy
Handbag
Holdall
Satchel
Shopper
Sporran
Weekend
Workbag

8 letters:
Backpack
Carryall
Crumenal
Knapsack
Pochette
Reticule
Ridicule
Rucksack
Shoulder
Sleeping
Suitcase
Survival
9 letters:
Briefcase
Carpetbag
Gladstone
Haversack
Overnight
Saddlebag
Vanity box
10 letters:
Diplomatic
Portmantle
Portmantua
Sabretache
Vanity case
11 letters:
Portmanteau

Ballets

5 letters:
Manon
Rodeo
6 letters:
Bolero
Carmen
Façade
Ondine
Onegin
Parade
7 letters:
Giselle
Masques

Orpheus
8 letters:
Coppélia
Firebird
Les Noces
Serenade
Swan Lake
9 letters:
Les Biches
Spartacus
10 letters:
Cinderella
La Bayadère

Nutcracker
Petroushka
11 letters:
Billy the Kid
12 letters:
Les Sylphides
Rite of Spring
Scheherazade
14 letters:
Romeo and Juliet
Sleeping Beauty

Ballet steps and terms

3 letters:
Pas
4 letters:
Jeté
Plié
5 letters:
Adage
Battu
Brisé
Coupé
Decor
Passé
Tombé
6 letters:
Adagio
Aplomb
Ballon
Chassé
Croisé
Dégagé
Ecarté
En l'air
Failli
Ouvert
Pointe
Relevé
7 letters:
Allegro
Allongé
Balancé
Ciseaux
Déboulé
Échappé
Emboîté
Soutenu
Turn-out
8 letters:
Absolute
Abstract

Assemblé
Attitude
Ballonné
Ballotté
Batterie
Cabriole
Demi-plié
En dedans
En dehors
En pointe
Figurant
Glissade
Pas coupé
Romantic
Sickling
Sur place
Temps lié
Toe-dance
9 letters:
Arabesque
Ballerina
Battement
Classical
Cou-de-pied
Détournée
Dévelopée
Elevation
Entrechat
Pas de chat
Pas de deux
Pirouette
Raccourci
Temps levé
Variation
10 letters:
Changement
Demi-pointe
En couronne
Foudroyant

Grand écart
Grande plié
Pas ciseaux
Pas de brisé
Pas échappé
Soubresaut
Tour en l'air
11 letters:
Ballet blanc
Contretemps
Pas ballotté
Pas de bourée
Pas de chassé
Ports de bras
Rond de jambe
Terre à terre
12 letters:
Ballet de cour
Croisé devant
Enchaînement
Gargouillade
13 letters:
Ballet d'action
En tire-bouchon
Pas de sissonne
Temps de cuisse
Temps de flèche
14 letters:
Benesh notation
Croisé derrière
Entrée de ballet
Premier danseur
Prima ballerina
Temps de poisson
Temps dévelopée
15 letters:
Cecchetti method

Ball games

4 letters:
Golf
5 letters:
Fives
6 letters:
Boules
Hockey
Soccer
Squash
Tennis
7 letters:
Bowling
Croquet
Hurling
Netball

Pinball
Pyramid
Snooker
8 letters:
Baseball
Football
Goalball
Handball
Korfball
Lacrosse
Pushball
Rounders
Subbuteo®
9 letters:
Badminton

Bagatelle
Billiards
Crazy golf
Paintball
Punchball
10 letters:
Volleyball
11 letters:
Bumble-puppy
12 letters:
Bar billiards
15 letters:
Australian Rules
Pocket billiards

Baseball teams

11 letters:
Chicago Cubs
New York Mets
12 letters:
Boston Red Sox
Texas Rangers
Tampa Bay Rays
13 letters:
Anaheim Angels
Atlanta Braves
Detroit Tigers
Houston Astros

14 letters:
Cincinnati Reds
Florida Marlins
Minnesota Twins
New York Yankees
San Diego Padres
15 letters:
Chicago White Sox
Colorado Rockies
Seattle Mariners
Toronto Blue Jays

Bats

5 letters:
Fruit
6 letters:
Kalong
7 letters:
Noctule
Vampire

8 letters:
Serotine
9 letters:
Flying fox
Horseshoe
10 letters:
Hammerhead

11 letters:
Barbastelle
Pipistrelle
12 letters:
False vampire
13 letters:
Insectivorous

Battles

Battle	Year
Aboukir Bay *or* Abukir Bay	1798
Actium	31 BC
Agincourt	1415
Alamo	1836
Arnhem	1944
Atlantic	1939–45
Austerlitz	1805
Balaklava *or* Balaclava	1854

Battle	Year
Bannockburn	1314
Barnet	1471
Bautzen	1813
Belleau Wood	1918
Blenheim	1704
Borodino	1812
Bosworth Field	1485
Boyne	1690
Britain	1940
Bulge	1944−45
Bull Run	1861;1862
Bunker Hill	1775
Cannae	216 BC
Crécy	1346
Culloden	1746
Dien Bien Phu	1954
Edgehill	1642
El Alamein	1942
Falkirk	1298; 1746
Flodden	1513
Gettysburg	1863
Guadalcanal	1942−3
Hastings	1066
Hohenlinden	1800
Imphal	1944
Inkerman	1854
Issus	333 BC
Jemappes	1792
Jena	1806
Killiecrankie	1689
Kursk	1943
Ladysmith	1899−1900
Le Cateau	1914
Leipzig	1813
Lepanto	1571
Leyte Gulf	1944
Little Bighorn	1876
Lützen	1632
Manassas	1861; 1862
Mantinea or Mantineia	418 BC; 362 BC
Marathon	490 BC
Marengo	1800
Marston Moor	1644
Missionary Ridge	1863
Naseby	1645
Navarino	425 BC
Omdurman	1898
Passchendaele	1917
Philippi	42 BC
Plains of Abraham	1759
Plassey	1757
Plataea	479 BC
Poltava	1709
Prestonpans	1745
Pydna	168 BC
Quatre Bras	1815

Battle	Year
Ramillies	1706
Roncesvalles	778
Sadowa *or* Sadová	1866
Saint-Mihiel	1918
Salamis	480 BC
Sedgemoor	1685
Sempach	1386
Shiloh	1862
Shipka Pass	1877–78
Somme	1916; 1918
Stalingrad	1941–42
Stamford Bridge	1066
Stirling Bridge	1297
Tannenberg	1410; 1914
Tewkesbury	1471
Thermopylae	480 BC
Tobruk	1941; 1942
Trafalgar	1805
Trenton	1776
Verdun	1916
Vitoria	1813
Wagram	1809
Waterloo	1815
Ypres	1914; 1915; 1917; 1918
Zama	202 BC

Bays

2 letters:
MA
3 letters:
Ise
4 letters:
Pigs
Vigo
Wick
5 letters:
Algoa
Bonny
Byron
Casco
Dvina
False
Fleet
Fundy
Glace
Green
Hawke
Herne
Horse
James
Korea
Milne
Omura
Osaka
Shark

Sligo
Suvla
Table
Tampa
Tokyo
Urado
6 letters:
Abukir
Ariake
Baffin
Bantry
Bengal
Biscay
Botany
Broken
Callao
Colwyn
Daphne
Dublin
Galway
Golden
Hawke's
Hudson
Jervis
Lobito
Manila
Mobile
Newark

Tasman
Toyama
Tralee
Ungava
Vyborg
Walvis
7 letters:
Aboukir
Cape Cod
Delagoa
Delogoa
Dundalk
Florida
Jiazhou
Montego
Moreton
New York
Pegasus
Poverty
Setúbal
Swansea
Thunder
Walfish
Whitley
8 letters:
Biscayne
Buzzards
Cardigan

Delaware
Georgian
Hangzhou
Quiberon
San Pedro
Santiago
9 letters:
Bay of Acre
Bay of Pigs
Bombetoka
Discovery
Encounter
Famagusta
Frobisher
Guanabara
Inhambane
Kuskokwim

Magdalena
Morecambe
St Austell
10 letters:
Bay of Cádiz
Bay of Fundy
Bay of Vlorë
Caernarvon
Carmarthen
Chesapeake
Cienfuegos
Guantánamo
Lützow-Holm
11 letters:
Bay of Bengal
Bay of Biscay
Bay of Gdansk

Bay of Naples
Bay of Plenty
Port Phillip
12 letters:
Bay of Kaválla
Narragansett
San Francisco
13 letters:
Bay of Campeche
Bay of St Michel
Corpus Christi
Massachusetts
Passamaquoddy
14 letters:
Bay of Gibraltar

Beans and other pulses

3 letters:
Red
4 letters:
Dhal
Gram
Lima
Mung
Navy
Soya
5 letters:
Black
Bobby
Broad
Field
Green
Pinto
6 letters:
Adsuki

Adzuki
Butter
French
Kidney
Lentil
Runner
String
7 letters:
Haricot
Snow pea
8 letters:
Borlotti
Chick pea
Garbanzo
Split pea
9 letters:
Black-eyed
Cannelini

Flageolet
Mangetout
Petit pois
Pigeon pea
Puy lentil
Red kidney
Red lentil
11 letters:
Green lentil
12 letters:
Black-eyed pea
Marrowfat pea
Sugar snap pea

Beds

3 letters:
Air
Box
Cot
Day
Mat
4 letters:
Bunk
Camp
Cott
Crib
Kang
Lilo®

Loft
Sofa
Twin
5 letters:
Berth
Couch
Divan
Field
Futon
Water
6 letters:
Cradle
Double

Litter
Murphy
Pallet
Put-u-up
Single
Sleigh
7 letters:
Amenity
Charpoy
Feather
Folding
Hammock
Trestle

Truckle
Trundle
8 letters:
Apple-pie
Bassinet
Captain's
Carrycot
Foldaway
Hospital

King-size
Mattress
Platform
9 letters:
Couchette
King-sized
Paillasse
Palliasse
Queen-size

Shake down
Stretcher
10 letters:
Four-poster
Queen-sized
11 letters:
Procrustean

Beetles

3 letters:
Bee
Dor
May
Oil
4 letters:
Bark
Cane
Dorr
Dung
Flea
Gold
Huhu
June
King
Leaf
Mall
Maul
Pill
Rose
Rove
Stag
5 letters:
Bacon
Black
Click
Clock
Jewel
Roach
Snout
Tiger
Water
6 letters:
Batler
Carpet
Chafer
Diving
Dor-fly
Elater
Gregor
Ground
Hammer
Larder

Mallet
May bug
Museum
Potato
Scarab
Sexton
Sledge
Spider
Weevil
7 letters:
Asiatic
Blister
Burying
Cabinet
Cadelle
Carrion
Elytron
Elytrum
Firefly
Goldbug
Goliath
Hop-flea
Hornbug
June bug
Ladybug
Leather
Skelter
Soldier
Vedalia
8 letters:
Ambrosia
Bum-clock
Cardinal
Colorado
Curculio
Darkling
Glow-worm
Hercules
Japanese
Ladybird
Longhorn
Māori bug
Scarabee

Skipjack
Snapping
Tortoise
Wireworm
9 letters:
Buprestus
Cantharis
Carpet bug
Christmas
Cockroach
Furniture
Goldsmith
Kekerengu
Longicorn
Pea weevil
Pinchbuck
Scavenger
Timberman
Tumble-bug
Whirligig
Woodborer
10 letters:
Bean weevil
Boll weevil
Bombardier
Churchyard
Cockchafer
Deathwatch
Dumbledore
Long-horned
Rhinoceros
Rose chafer
Spanish fly
Turnip-flea
11 letters:
Bloody-nosed
Typographer
12 letters:
Buzzard-clock
Sledge-hammer

Bible

BOOKS OF THE BIBLE: OLD TESTAMENT

3 letters:
Job
4 letters:
Amos
Ezra
Joel
Ruth
5 letters:
Hosea
Jonah
Kings
Micah
Nahum
6 letters:
Daniel
Esther

Exodus
Haggai
Isaiah
Joshua
Judges
Psalms
Samuel
7 letters:
Ezekiel
Genesis
Malachi
Numbers
Obadiah
8 letters:
Habakkuk
Jeremiah

Nehemiah
Proverbs
9 letters:
Leviticus
Zechariah
Zephaniah
10 letters:
Chronicles
11 letters:
Deuteronomy
12 letters:
Ecclesiastes
Lamentations
13 letters:
Song of Solomon

BOOKS OF THE BIBLE: NEW TESTAMENT

4 letters:
Acts
John
Jude
Luke
Mark
5 letters:
James
Peter
Titus

6 letters:
Romans
7 letters:
Hebrews
Matthew
Timothy
8 letters:
Philemon
9 letters:
Ephesians

Galatians
10 letters:
Colossians
Revelation
11 letters:
Corinthians
Philippians
13 letters:
Thessalonians

BOOKS OF THE BIBLE: APOCRYPHA

5 letters:
Tobit
6 letters:
Baruch
Esdras
Judith
Wisdom

8 letters:
Manasseh
9 letters:
Maccabees
14 letters:
Ecclesiasticus
Song of the Three

CHARACTERS IN THE BIBLE

3 letters:
Dan
Eve
Gad
Ham
Job
Lot
4 letters:
Abel

Adam
Ahab
Amos
Boaz
Cain
Cush
Enos
Esau
Ezra

Jael
Jehu
Joab
Joel
John
Jude
Kush
Leah
Levi

Luke
Mark
Mary
Noah
Paul
Ruth
Saul
Seth
Shem
5 letters:
Aaron
Ammon
Asher
David
Dinah
Dives
Elias
Enoch
Hagar
Herod
Hiram
Hosea
Isaac
Jacob
James
Jesse
Jonah
Jonas
Jubal
Judah
Laban
Magus
Micah
Moses
Nahum
Naomi
Peter
Sarah
Simon
Tobit
Uriah
6 letters:
Andrew
Balaam
Baruch
Belial
Caspar
Daniel
Dorcas
Elijah
Elisha
Esther
Gideon
Gilead
Haggai
Hannah
Isaiah

Jephte
Jethro
Joseph
Joshua
Josiah
Judith
Martha
Midian
Miriam
Naboth
Nathan
Nimrod
Philip
Rachel
Reuben
Salome
Samson
Samuel
Simeon
Thomas
Zilpah
7 letters:
Abigail
Abraham
Absalom
Ananias
Deborah
Delilah
Ephraim
Ezekiel
Gabriel
Goliath
Ishmael
Japheth
Jezebel
Lazarus
Malachi
Matthew
Meshach
Obadiah
Rebecca
Solomon
Susanna
Thadeus
Zachary
Zebedee
Zebulun
8 letters:
Abednego
Barabbas
Benjamin
Caiaphas
Habakkuk
Hezekiah
Issachar
Jephthah
Jeremiah

Jeroboam
Jonathan
Lot's wife
Manasseh
Matthias
Melchior
Mordecai
Naphtali
Nehemiah
Potiphar
Shadrach
Thaddeus
Zedekiah
9 letters:
Ahasuerus
Balthazar
Bathsheba
Beelzebub
Boanerges
Nabonidus
Nathanael
Nicodemus
Tubal-cain
Zachariah
Zacharias
Zechariah
Zephaniah
10 letters:
Achitophel
Ahithophel
Belshazzar
Holofernes
Methuselah
Virgin Mary
11 letters:
Bartholomew
Gog and Magog
Jehoshaphat
Jesus Christ
Melchizedek
Prodigal Son
12 letters:
Melchisedech
Queen of Sheba
13 letters:
Good Samaritan
Judas Iscariot
Mary Magdalene
14 letters:
John the Baptist
Nebuchadnezzar
Nebuchadrezzar
Tetragrammaton
Whore of Babylon

PLACE NAMES IN THE BIBLE

2 letters:
On
4 letters:
Aram
Cana
Eden
Gath
Gaza
Moab
5 letters:
Babel
Horeb
Judah
Judea
Ophir
Sodom
6 letters:
Ararat
Bashan

Canaan
Goshen
Judaea
Shiloh
Shinar
Tadmor
Tophet
7 letters:
Antioch
Calvary
Galilee
Gehenna
Jericho
Samaria
Shittim
Topheth
8 letters:
Aceldama
Bethesda

Golgotha
Gomorrah
Gomorrha
Nazareth
9 letters:
Arimathea
Bethlehem
Capernaum
Jerusalem
Land of Nod
10 letters:
Arimathaea
Gethsemane
Wilderness
12 letters:
Garden of Eden
Rabbath Ammon

TYPES OF BIBLE

2 letters:
AV
NT
OT
RV
3 letters:
NEB
NIV
RSV
4 letters:
NRSV
Whig
5 letters:
Douai
Douay
Itala
6 letters:
Family
Geneva
Gideon

Gospel
Italic
Missal
Tanach
Targum
Wyclif
Zurich
7 letters:
Bamberg
Cranmer
Hexapla
Mazarin
Midrash
Peshito
Psalter
Tyndale
Vulgate
8 letters:
Cromwell
Mazarine

Peshitta
Peshitto
Polyglot
Wycliffe
9 letters:
Apocrypha
Coverdale
Jerusalem
King James
Taverners
10 letters:
Pentateuch
Septuagint
12 letters:
Antilegomena
14 letters:
Revised Version

Bicycles

BICYCLE PARTS

4 letters:
Bell
5 letters:
Pedal
Wheel

6 letters:
Saddle
7 letters:
Pannier
Rat-trap

8 letters:
Crossbar
Mudguard
9 letters:
Kickstand

Saddlebag
10 letters:
Handlebars
Mileometer

Stabilizer
11 letters:
Bicycle pump

12 letters:
Bicycle chain

TYPES OF BICYCLE

3 letters:
BMX
6 letters:
Tandem
7 letters:
Bicycle
Chopper

8 letters:
Roadster
9 letters:
Autocycle
10 letters:
Boneshaker
Fairy cycle

Velocipede
12 letters:
Exercise bike
Mountain bike
13 letters:
Penny-farthing

Biochemists

3 letters:
Dam, *Henrik Carl Peter*
4 letters:
Cori, *Carl Ferdinand*
Cori, *Gerti*
Funk, *Casimir*
Katz, *Bernard*
5 letters:
Bloch, *Konrad Emil*
Boyer, *Herbert*
Cohen, *Stanley*
Doisy, *Edward Adelbert*
Krebs, *Hans Adolf*
Monod, *Jaques Lucien*
Moore, *Stanford*
Ochoa, *Severo*
Stein, *William H(oward)*
Synge, *Richard*
6 letters:
Beadle, *George Wells*
De Duve, *Christian*
Domagk, *Gerhard*
Florey, *Howard Walter*
Holley, *Robert W(illiam)*
Martin, *Archer*
Mullis, *Kary Banks*
Oparin, *Alexandr*
Perutz, *Max Ferdinand*

Porter, *Rodney Robert*
Sanger, *Frederick*
Sumner, *James B(atcheller)*
7 letters:
Buchner, *Eduard*
Edelman, *Gerald M(aurice)*
Fleming, *Alexander*
Gilbert, *Walter*
Hopkins, *Frederick Gowland*
Kendrew, *John C(owdery)*
Khorana, *Har Gobind*
Macleod, *John James Richard*
Rodbell, *Martin*
Stanley, *Wendell Meredith*
Waksman, *Selman Abraham*
Warburg, *Otto Heinrich*
8 letters:
Anfinsen, *Christian Boehmer*
Chargaff, *Erwin*
Kornberg, *Arthur*
Meyerhof, *Otto Fritz*
Northrop, *John H(oward)*
9 letters:
Bergstrom, *Sune K(arl)*
Butenandt, *Adolf Friedrich Johann*
Nirenberg, *Marshall W(arren)*
10 letters:
Samuelsson, *Bengt*

Biology

BRANCHES OF BIOLOGY

6 letters:
Botany
7 letters:
Ecology

Zoology
8 letters:
Biometry
Cytology

Genetics
Taxonomy
9 letters:
Histology

10 letters:
Biophysics
Biostatics
Morphology
Organology
Somatology
Teratology
11 letters:
Aerobiology
Agrobiology
Biodynamics

Cryobiology
12 letters:
Astrobiology
Bacteriology
Biochemistry
Biogeography
Cytogenetics
Microbiology
Oceanography
Organography
Parasitology

Photobiology
Radiobiology
Sociobiology
Stoichiology
13 letters:
Actinobiology
Chronobiology
Palaeontology
Photodynamics

BIOLOGY TERMS

3 letters:
DNA
Egg
RNA
4 letters:
Bone
Cell
Gene
Ovum
Root
Seed
Skin
Soil
5 letters:
Blood
Class
Clone
Fruit
Genus
Gland
Gonad
Order
Organ
Sperm
Spore
Virus
6 letters:
Albino
Allele
Dorsal
Embryo
Enzyme
Family
Flower
Foetus
Fossil
Fungus
Gamete
Growth
Hybrid
Muscle
Phylum

Pollen
Sexual
Zygote
7 letters:
Aerobic
Asexual
Biomass
Diploid
Haploid
Hormone
Kingdom
Meiosis
Mitosis
Nucleus
Osmosis
Progeny
Protein
Puberty
Species
Ventral
Vitamin
8 letters:
Anterior
Bacteria
Division
Dominant
Heredity
Mutation
Parasite
Pathogen
Pectoral
Predator
Ribosome
Skeleton
9 letters:
Anaerobic
Cytoplasm
Diffusion
Digestion
Ecosystem
Epidermis
Evolution

Excretion
Food chain
Gestation
Life cycle
Ovulation
Pollution
Posterior
Pregnancy
Recessive
Symbiosis
10 letters:
Chromosome
Conception
Copulation
Krebs cycle
Metabolism
Protoplasm
Vertebrate
Viviparous
11 letters:
Allelomorph
Blood vessel
Circulation
Codominance
Cold-blooded
Environment
Germination
Inheritance
Nucleic acid
Pollination
Propagation
Respiration
Warm-blooded
X-chromosome
Y-chromosome
12 letters:
Assimilation
Fermentation
Invertebrate
Menstruation
Reproduction
Spermatozoon

13 letters:
Agglutination
Binary fission
Fertilization

Hermaphrodite
Metamorphosis
Nitrogen cycle
Translocation

Transpiration
14 letters:
Photosynthesis
Poikilothermic

BIOLOGISTS

3 letters:
May, *Robert McCredie*
Orr, *John Boyd*
4 letters:
Berg, *Paul*
Koch, *Robert*
5 letters:
Crick, *Francis Harry Compton*
Krebs, *Hans Adolf*
6 letters:
Beadle, *George Well*
Carrel, *Alexis*
Carson, *Rachel*
Claude, *Albert*
Darwin, *Charles (Robert)*
Harvey, *William*
Huxley, *Andrew Fielding*
Huxley, *Julian*
Huxley, *Thomas Henry*
Mendel, *Gregor Johann*

Morgan, *Thomas Hunt*
Watson, *James Dewey*
7 letters:
Fleming, *Alexander*
Haeckel, *Ernst Heinrich*
Pasteur, *Louis*
8 letters:
Delbrück, *Max*
Dulbecco, *Renato*
Franklin, *Rosalind*
Linnaeus
Von Linné, *Carl*
9 letters:
Baltimore, *David*
Von Haller, *Albrecht*
10 letters:
Denisovich, *Trofim*
Dobzhansky, *Theodosius*
14 letters:
Van Leeuwenhoek, *Anton*

See also:
➤ **Bacteria** ➤ **Enzymes** ➤ **Hormones** ➤ **Membranes** ➤ **Proteins**
➤ **Sugars**

Birds

2 letters:	Ruc	Hawk	Pavo
Ka	Tit	Hern	Pawn
3 letters:	Tui	Huma	Pern
Ani	**4 letters:**	Ibis	Piet
Auk	Barb	Iynx	Pink
Boo	Chat	Jynx	Pown
Cob	Cirl	Kagu	Pyot
Emu	Cobb	Kaka	Rail
Fum	Coly	Kite	Rhea
Jay	Coot	Kiwi	Roch
Kae	Crax	Knot	Rook
Kea	Crow	Koel	Ruff
Maw	Dove	Kora	Runt
Mew	Emeu	Lark	Ruru
Nun	Erne	Loon	Rype
Oil	Eyas	Lory	Shag
Owl	Fung	Lyre	Smee
Pea	Gled	Mina	Sora
Pie	Guan	Monk	Swan
Ree	Guga	Myna	Taha
Roc	Gull	Otis	Tara

Teal
Tern
Tody
Tuli
Weka
Whio
Whip
Wren
Xema
Yale
Yite

5 letters:
Agami
Ardea
Ariel
Bennu
Booby
Bosun
Capon
Chook
Colin
Colly
Cooee
Crake
Crane
Diver
Egret
Finch
Fleet
Galah
Galar
Glede
Goose
Goura
Grebe
Heron
Hobby
Homer
Isaac
Junco
Kight
Liver
Lowan
Macaw
Madge
Manch
Mavis
Merle
Micky
Mimus
Mohua
Monal
Mulga
Murre
Mynah
Nandu
Nelly

Noddy
Ousel
Ouzel
Ox-eye
Peggy
Pekan
Pewit
Picus
Piper
Pipit
Pitta
Poaka
Poker
Potoo
Prion
Quail
Quest
Quist
Raven
Reeve
Rifle
Robin
Rotch
Ryper
Saker
Scape
Scart
Scaup
Scops
Scray
Scrub
Serin
Shama
Sitta
Skart
Snipe
Solan
Soree
Spink
Sprug
Squab
Stare
Stilt
Stint
Stork
Sugar
Swift
Sylph
Terek
Tewit
Topaz
Twite
Umber
Umbre
Urubu
Veery
Vireo

Wader
Whaup
Widow
Wonga
Yaffa

6 letters:
Amazon
Aquila
Avocet
Avoset
Bantam
Barbet
Bishop
Bittor
Bittur
Bonxie
Boubou
Brolga
Bulbul
Canary
Chough
Chukar
Condor
Conure
Corbie
Coucal
Cuckoo
Culver
Curlew
Cushat
Darter
Dikkop
Dipper
Drongo
Duiker
Dunlin
Duyker
Elanet
Evejar
Falcon
Fulmar
Gambet
Gander
Gannet
Garuda
Gentle
Gentoo
Gillar
Go-away
Godwit
Gooney
Goslet
Grakle
Grouse
Hagden
Hagdon
Haglet

Hermit
Hoopoe
Houdan
Jabiru
Jaçana
Jaegar
Jaeger
Kakapo
Karoro
Kereru
Kokako
Kotare
Kotuku
Lahore
Lanner
Leipoa
Linnet
Lintie
Locust
Loriot
Lourie
Lungie
Magpie
Martin
Menura
Merlin
Merops
Missel
Mistle
Monaul
Mopoke
Mossie
Motmot
Musket
Nandoo
Oriole
Osprey
Parrot
Parson
Pavone
Peahen
Peewee
Peewit
Pernis
Petrel
Phoebe
Pigeon
Pipipi
Plover
Pouter
Progne
Puffin
Pukeko
Pullet
Queest
Quelea
Quoist

Redcap
Reeler
Roller
Scamel
Scarth
Scaury
Scraye
Sea-cob
Sea-mew
Seapie
Shrike
Simara
Simorg
Simurg
Siskin
Skarth
Smeath
Soland
Sorage
Strich
Sultan
Sylvia
Tailor
Takahe
Tarcel
Tassel
Tauhou
Tewhit
Thrush
Tom-tit
Toucan
Towhee
Trogon
Turaco
Turbit
Tyrant
Tystie
Verdin
Wading
Walker
Waxeye
Weaver
Whidah
Whydah
Willet
Woosel
Yaffle
Ynambu
Yucker
Zoozoo
7 letters:
Amokura
Anhinga
Antbird
Apostle
Apteryx
Axebird

Babbler
Bécasse
Bittern
Bittour
Blighty
Bluecap
Blue-eye
Blue jay
Bluetit
Boobook
Bullbat
Bunting
Buphaga
Bushtit
Bustard
Buzzard
Cacique
Cariama
Catbird
Chewink
Chicken
Coal tit
Coletit
Colibri
Corella
Cotinga
Courlan
Courser
Cowbird
Creeper
Crombec
Cropper
Cumulet
Diamond
Dinorus
Dottrel
Dovekie
Dunnock
Emu-wren
Fantail
Fern-owl
Fig-bird
Finfoot
Flicker
Frigate
Gobbler
Goburra
Gorcrow
Goshawk
Grackle
Grallae
Hacklet
Hadedah
Hagbolt
Hagdown
Halcyon
Hemipod

Hoatzin
Humming
Ice-bird
Jacamar
Jackdaw
Jacobin
Kahawai
Kamichi
Kestrel
Killdee
Kinglet
Lapwing
Leghorn
Limpkin
Manakin
Marabou
Maribou
Martlet
Mesites
Minivet
Mudlark
Ortolan
Oscires
Ostrich
Pandion
Peacock
Peafowl
Pelican
Penguin
Phoenix
Pickmaw
Piculet
Pinnock
Pintado
Pintail
Pochard
Pockard
Poe-bird
Poy-bird
Quetzal
Rainbow
Rasores
Redpoll
Redwing
Regulus
Rooster
Rosella
Rotchie
Ruddock
Sakeret
Sawbill
Scooper
Scourie
Sea-mell
Seriema
Simurgh
Sirgang

Sitella
Skimmer
Skylark
Snow-cap
Soldier
Spadger
Sparrow
Squacco
Staniel
Stinker
Sturnus
Sunbird
Swallow
Tanager
Tarrock
Tattler
Teacher
Teuchat
Tiercel
Tinamou
Titanis
Titlark
Titling
Tokahea
Totanus
Touraco
Tumbler
Tweeter
Vulture
Vulturn
Wagtail
Warbler
Waxbill
Waxwing
Whooper
Widgeon
Wimbrel
Witwall
Wood hen
Woosell
Wren-tit
Wrybill
Wryneck
Yang-win
8 letters:
Aasvogel
Accentor
Adjutant
Aigrette
Alcatras
Altrices
Amadavat
Aquiline
Arapunga
Avadavat
Barnacle
Bee-eater

Bellbird
Blackcap
Bluebird
Blue duck
Blue-wing
Boatbill
Boattail
Bobolink
Bobwhite
Buln-buln
Bush wren
Capuchin
Caracara
Cardinal
Cargoose
Cheewink
Chirn-owl
Cockatoo
Coquette
Curassow
Dabchick
Didapper
Dip-chick
Dobchick
Dotterel
Estridge
Fauvette
Fernbird
Firebird
Fish-hawk
Flamingo
Gambetta
Gang-gang
Garefowl
Garganey
Great tit
Greenlet
Grosbeak
Guacharo
Hackbolt
Hangbird
Hangnest
Hawfinch
Hazelhen
Hemipode
Hernshaw
Hill myna
Hoactzin
Hornbill
Kakariki
Killdeer
Kingbird
Kiskadee
Koromako
Landrail
Lanneret
Laverock

Longspur
Lorikeet
Lovebird
Lyrebird
Magotpie
Makomako
Māori hen
Marsh tit
Megapode
Mire-drum
Miromiro
Morepork
Murrelet
Nightjar
Nuthatch
Ovenbird
Oxpecker
Paradise
Parakeet
Peetweet
Percolin
Petchary
Pheasant
Philomel
Pihoihoi
Podargus
Poorwill
Puffbird
Quarrian
Quarrion
Rainbird
Rallidae
Redshank
Redstart
Reedbird
Reedling
Reed-wren
Ricebird
Rifleman
Ringdove
Ringtail
Riroriro
Rock dove
Sandpeep
Scolopar
Screamer
Shake-bag
Shoebill
Silktail
Skua-gull
Snowbird
Stanniel
Starling
Struthio
Surfbird
Swiftlet
Tantalus

Tapacolo
Tapaculo
Teru-tero
Thrasher
Thresher
Throstle
Tick-bird
Titmouse
Tom-noddy
Toucanet
Tragopan
Trembler
Troopial
Troupial
Umbrella
Umbrette
Water-hen
Weka rail
Wheatear
Whimbrel
Whinchat
Whitecap
White-eye
Woodchat
Woodcock
Wood ibis
Woodlark
Woodwale
Yoldring
9 letters:
Accipiter
Aepyornis
Albatross
Aylesbury
Baldicoot
Baltimore
Beccaccia
Beccafico
Bergander
Blackbird
Blackcock
Blackhead
Blackpoll
Bowerbird
Brambling
Broadbill
Brown duck
Brown kiwi
Bullfinch
Campanero
Cassowary
Chaffinch
Chatterer
Chickadee
Coachwhip
Cockateel
Cockatiel

Cormorant
Corncrake
Crocodile
Crossbill
Currawong
Cushie-doo
Dowitcher
Estreldid
Fieldfare
Fig-pecker
Firecrest
Fledgling
Francolin
Friarbird
Frogmouth
Gallinule
Gerfalcon
Gier-eagle
Goldcrest
Goldfinch
Goosander
Grassquit
Green leek
Grenadier
Guillemot
Happy Jack
Helldiver
Heronshaw
Icteridae
Impundulu
Jacksnipe
Kittiwake
Lintwhite
Mallemuck
Merganser
Mistletoe
Mollymawk
Mousebird
Nighthawk
Nutjobber
Olive-back
Ossifraga
Ossifrage
Pardalote
Parrakeet
Partridge
Peaseweep
Peregrine
Phalarope
Pictarnie
Pied goose
Policeman
Porphyrio
Ptarmigan
Razorbill
Redbreast
Red grouse

Riflebird
Ring ouzel
Rosy finch
Salangane
Sandpiper
Sapsucker
Scansores
Sea-turtle
Secretary
Seedeater
Sheldrake
Shoveller
Silvereye
Skunk-bird
Snakebird
Solitaire
Spoonbill
Standgale
Stock dove
Stonechat
Storm-cock
Swart-back
Swordbill
Talegalla
Thickhead
Thick-knee
Thornbill
Trochilus
Trumpeter
Turnstone
Volucrine
Water rail
Willow tit
Wind-hover
Xanthoura
10 letters:
Aberdevine
Banded rail
Bearded tit
Bell magpie
Bishopbird
Black robin
Bluebreast
Blue grouse
Bluethroat
Brain-fever
Bubbly-jock
Budgerigar
Bush canary
Bush shrike
Butter-bump
Cape pigeon
Chiffchaff
Crested tit
Demoiselle
Dickcissel
Didunculus

Dollarbird
Ember-goose
Eyas-musket
Flycatcher
Fringillid
Goatsucker
Gobemouche
Grassfinch
Greenfinch
Greenshank
Guinea fowl
Hen harrier
Honeyeater
Honey guide
Hooded crow
Jungle fowl
Kingfisher
Kookaburra
Magpie lark
Marsh-robin
Meadowlark
Night heron
Noisy miner
Nutcracker
Pettichaps
Pettychaps
Piwakawaka
Pratincole
Quaker-bird
Racket-tail
Rafter-bird
Regent-bird
Rhampastos
Rhinoceros
Roadrunner
Rockhopper
Rock pigeon
Saddleback
Saddlebill
Sage grouse
Sanderling
Sandgrouse
Sand martin
Scandaroon
Shearwater
Sheathbill
Sicklebill
Silverbill
Snowy egret
Song thrush
Spatchcock
Stone-snipe
Sun bittern
Tailorbird
Tanagridae
Tree-runner
Tropicbird

Turtledove
Water crake
Water ouzel
Wattlebird
Weaverbird
Whisky-jack
Whisky-john
White heron
Wild turkey
Wonga-wonga
Woodpecker
Wood pigeon
Yaffingale
Yellowlegs
Yellowtail
Yellowyite
Zebra finch
11 letters:
Black cuckoo
Black grouse
Bokmakierie
Bristlebird
Butcherbird
Button quail
Cape sparrow
Carrion crow
Coppersmith
Corn bunting
Gnatcatcher
Grallatores
Green plover
Grey warbler
Happy family
Honeysucker
House martin
Hummingbird
Java sparrow
King penguin
Leatherhead
Lily-trotter
Magpie goose
Meadow pipit
Mockingbird
Moss-bluiter
Moss-cheeper
Nightingale
Pied wagtail
Plain turkey
Plantcutter
Pyrrhuloxia
Reed bunting
Reed warbler
Scissortail
Snow bunting
Song sparrow
Stone curlew
Storm petrel

Stymphalian
Tawny pippit
Thunderbird
Titipounamu
Tree creeper
Tree sparrow
Wall creeper
Water thrush
Whitethroat
Wonga pigeon
Woodcreeper
Woodswallow
Wood warbler
Yellow-ammer
Zebra parrot

12 letters:
Bronze-pigeon
Brown creeper
Bustard quail
Capercaillie
Capercailzie
Chimney swift
Cliff swallow
Collared dove
Cuckoo-shrike
Drongo-cuckoo
Drongo-shrike
Flower-pecker
Golden oriole
Hedge sparrow
Homing pigeon
Honey creeper
House sparrow
Marsh harrier
Missel thrush
Mistle thrush
Mosquito hawk
Mountain duck
Mourning dove
Murray magpie
Painted finch

Pallid cuckoo
Paradise duck
Peppershrike
Piping shrike
Plains turkey
Putangitangi
Ring-dotterel
Ringed plover
Ruffed grouse
Sage-thrasher
Sedge warbler
Serpent-eater
Spotted crake
Standard-wing
Stonechatter
Stormy petrel
Throstle-cock
Whippoorwill
Willow grouse
Willy wagtail
Yellowhammer
Yellow-yowley

13 letters:
Bushman's clock
Chaparral cock
Cock-of-the-rock
Crow blackbird
Gouldian finch
Long-tailed tit
Major Mitchell
Numidian crane
Oyster-catcher
Pipiwharauroa
Plantain-eater
Settler's clock
Swamp pheasant
Topknot pigeon
Whistling duck
White cockatoo
Whooping crane
Willow warbler

14 letters:
Banded dotterel
Bird of paradise
Chimney swallow
Cockatoo-parrot
Emperor penguin
Manx shearwater
Noisy friarbird
Ortolan bunting
Pheasant coucal
Pie-billed grebe
Ringneck parrot
Robin redbreast
Satin bowerbird
Scarlet tanager
Superb blue wren
Superb lyrebird
Tawny frogmouth
Woodchat shrike

15 letters:
American ostrich
Australian crane
Baltimore oriole
Blackbacked gull
Blue-wattled crow
Boat-billed heron
Cape Barren goose
Chipping sparrow
Chuck-will's-
  widow
Demoiselle crane
Green woodpecker
Laughing jackass
Native companion
Purple gallinule
Rainbow lorikeet
Red-backed shrike
Regent bowerbird
Shining starling

EXTINCT BIRDS

3 letters:
Moa
4 letters:
Dodo
Huia
6 letters:
Piopio

8 letters:
Great auk
Notornis
9 letters:
Solitaire
11 letters:
Archaeornis

Ichthyornis
13 letters:
Archaeopteryx
15 letters:
Passenger pigeon

See also:
➤ **Ducks** ➤ **Fowl** ➤ **Hawks** ➤ **Prey, birds of** ➤ **Sea birds**

Birthstones

Month	Stone
January	Garnet
February	Amethyst
March	Aquamarine, Bloodstone
April	Diamond
May	Emerald
June	Pearl, Alexandrite, Moonstone
July	Ruby
August	Peridot, Sardonyx
September	Sapphire
October	Opal, Tourmaline
November	Topaz
December	Turquoise, Zircon

Biscuits

3 letters:
Nut
Sea
Tea
4 letters:
Farl
Kiss
Rusk
Soda
Tack
5 letters:
Marie
Matzo
Pilot
Ship's
Wafer
Water
6 letters:
Cookie
Empire
Oliver
Parkin
Perkin
7 letters:
Bannock

Bourbon
Cracker
Fairing
Oatcake
Osborne
Pig's ear
Pretzel
Ratafia
Rich tea
Tararua
8 letters:
Captain's
Charcoal
Cracknel
Flapjack
Hardtack
Macaroon
Mattress
Poppadom
Poppadum
Zwieback
9 letters:
Abernethy
Dandyfunk
Digestive

Garibaldi
Ginger nut
Jaffa cake®
Lebkuchen
Petit four
Shortcake
Sweetmeal
10 letters:
Bath Oliver
Brandy snap
Butterbake
Crispbread
Dunderfunk
Florentine
Ginger snap
Love letter
Shortbread
12 letters:
Caramel wafer
Cream cracker
Langue de chat
13 letters:
Graham cracker
14 letters:
Gingerbread man

Black and white shades

3 letters:
Ash
Jet
4 letters:
Grey
Iron
5 letters:
Black
Cream

Ebony
Ivory
Pearl
Putty
Raven
Sable
Slate
Stone
White

6 letters:
Pewter
Silver
8 letters:
Charcoal
Eggshell
Gunmetal
Off-white
Platinum

9 letters:
Steel grey

10 letters:
Pitch-black

11 letters:
Oyster white

Blemishes

3 letters:
Zit
4 letters:
Boil
Mole
Scab
Scar
Spot
Wart
5 letters:
Stain

6 letters:
Callus
Naevus
Pimple
7 letters:
Freckle
Pustule
Verruca
8 letters:
Pockmark

9 letters:
Birthmark
Blackhead
Carbuncle
Whitehead
12 letters:
Dicoloration
14 letters:
Strawberry mark

Blood cells

9 letters:
Haemocyte
Leucocyte
Macrocyte
Microcyte
Phagocyte

Polymorph
10 letters:
Lymphocyte
11 letters:
Erythrocyte
Poikilocyte

12 letters:
Reticulocyte

Blue, shades of

3 letters:
Sky
4 letters:
Aqua
Bice
Cyan
Navy
Nile
Saxe
Teal
5 letters:
Azure
Clear
Perse
Royal
Saxon
Slate
Steel
6 letters:
Berlin
Cantab
Cobalt

Indigo
Oxford
Petrol
Pewter
Powder
Saxony
Welkin
7 letters:
Celeste
Duck-egg
Gentian
Nattier
Peacock
Watchet
8 letters:
Bleuâtre
Caesious
Cerulean
Eggshell
Electric
Lavender
Mazarine

Midnight
Prussian
Sapphire
Stafford
Wedgwood®
9 letters:
Cambridge
Germander
Robin's egg
Turquoise
10 letters:
Aquamarine
Copenhagen
Cornflower
Heliotrope
Periwinkle
11 letters:
Clair de lune
Lapis lazuli
Ultramarine

Board games

2 letters:
Go

3 letters:
I-go

4 letters:
Ludo

5 letters:
Chess
Halma

6 letters:
Cluedo®

7 letters:
Reversi

8 letters:
Chequers
Draughts
Monopoly®
Scrabble®

9 letters:
Acey-deucy
Bagatelle
Parcheesi®
Solitaire

10 letters:
Backgammon
Kriegspiel
Speed chess

11 letters:
Fox and geese

14 letters:
Lightning chess
Nine men's morris
Shove-halfpenny

15 letters:
Chinese chequers

Boats and ships

1 letter:
Q

2 letters:
MY
PT
VJ

3 letters:
Ark
Cat
Cog
Cot
Dow
Gig
Hoy
MTB
Red
Tub
Tug

4 letters:
Argo
Bark
Brig
Buss
Cock
Dhow
Dory
Duck
Grab
Junk
Koff
Maxi
Nina
Pink
Pont
Pram
Prau
Proa
Punt
Raft

Ro-ro
Saic
Scow
Snow
Tall
Tern
Trow
Yawl
Zulu

5 letters:
Aviso
Barge
Broke
Camel
Canal
Canoe
Coble
Coper
Crare
Dandy
Dingy
Drake
E-boat
Ferry
Funny
Jolly
Kayak
Ketch
Laker
Liner
Moses
Oiler
Pinky
Pinto
Prore
Púcán
Razee
Sabot
Scoot

Screw
Scull
Shell
Skiff
Sloop
Swamp
Tramp
U-boat
Umiak
Whiff
Xebec
Yacht
Zabra
Zebec

6 letters:
Argosy
Banker
Barque
Bateau
Bawley
Beagle
Bethel
Bireme
Boatel
Borley
Bounty
Caïque
Carack
Carvel
Castle
Coaler
Cobble
Cooper
Crayer
Cutter
Decker
Dingey
Dinghy
Dogger

Droger
Dromon
Drover
Dugout
Flotel
Frigot
Galiot
Galley
Gay-you
Hooker
Jigger
Launch
Lorcha
Lugger
Masula
Narrow
Nuggar
Oomiak
Packet
Pedalo
Pequod
Pinkie
Pirate
Pitpan
Pulwar
Puteli
Randan
Rowing
Sampan
Sandal
Schuit
Schuyt
Sealer
Settee
Slaver
Tanker
Tartan
Tender
Tonner

Torpid
Trader
Whaler
Wherry
Zebeck
7 letters:
Airboat
Belfast
Bidarka
Bumboat
Capital
Caravel
Carrack
Carract
Carrect
Catboat
Clipper
Coaster
Collier
Coracle
Counter
Crabber
Cruiser
Currach
Curragh
Dredger
Drifter
Drogher
Dromond
Factory
Felucca
Fishing
Floatel
Flyboat
Foyboat
Frigate
Gabbard
Gabbart
Galleas
Galleon
Galliot
Galloon
Geordie
Gondola
Gunboat
Jet-boat
Jetfoil
Liberty
Lymphad
Man o' war
Masoola
Mistico
Monitor
Mudscow
Oomiack
Patamar
Pelican

Pinnace
Piragua
Pirogue
Polacca
Polacre
Pontoon
Revenge
Rowboat
Sailing
Scooter
Shallop
Sharpie
Steamer
Stew-can
Tartane
Titanic
Torpedo
Towboat
Trawler
Trireme
Tugboat
Vedette
Victory
Vidette
Warship
8 letters:
Acapulco
Bilander
Billyboy
Cabotage
Cockboat
Corocore
Corocoro
Corvette
Dahabieh
Faldboat
Faltboat
Fireboat
Flatboat
Foldboat
Galleass
Galliass
Gallivat
Hoveller
Ice yacht
Indiaman
Ironclad
Keelboat
Lifeboat
Longboat
Longship
Mackinaw
Man-of-war
Mary Rose
Masoolah
Merchant
Monohull

Outboard
Pinafore
Sailboat
Savannah
Schooner
Shanghai
Showboat
Skipjack
Surfboat
Trimaran
9 letters:
Auxiliary
Bucentaur
Catamaran
Cutty Sark
Dahabeeah
Dahabiyah
Dahabiyeh
Destroyer
Dromedary
First-rate
Freighter
Frigatoon
Houseboat
Hydrofoil
Klondiker
Klondyker
Lapstrake
Lapstreak
Leviathan
Lightship
Mayflower
Minelayer
Monoxylon
Motorboat
Multihull
Outrigger
Oysterman
Peter-boat
Powerboat
Shear-hulk
Sheer-hulk
Speedboat
Steamboat
Steamship
Submarine
Troopship
Vaporetto
Whale-back
Whaleboat
10 letters:
Bathyscape
Bathyscaph
Battleship
Bermuda rig
Brigantine
Cockleboat

Golden Hind
Hydroplane
Icebreaker
Knockabout
Minehunter
Motor yacht
Paddleboat
Quadrireme
Santa Maria
Trekschuit
Triaconter
Windjammer
11 letters:
Barquantine
Barquentine
Bathyscaphe
Bellerophon
Berthon-boat
Bulk carrier
Cockleshell
Dreadnaught
Dreadnought
Merchantman
Minesweeper
Penteconter
Quinquereme
Sidewheeler
Skidbladnir
Submersible
Supertanker
Threedecker
Three-master
Weathership
12 letters:
Cabin cruiser
Fore-and-after
Great Eastern
Landing craft
Marie Celeste
Motor torpedo
Square-rigger
Stern-wheeler
13 letters:
Battlecruiser
Paddle steamer
Revenue cutter
Ship of the line
14 letters:
Ocean
 greyhound
Vaucluse
 junior
15 letters:
Aircraft carrier
Destroyer
 escort

Bombs

4 letters:	**7 letters:**	**10 letters:**
Atom	Cluster	Incendiary
Nail	Grenade	**11 letters:**
5 letters:	Neutron	Blockbuster
A-bomb	Nuclear	Depth charge
Mills	Plastic	Hand grenade
6 letters:	**8 letters:**	Stun grenade
Fusion	Bouncing	**15 letters:**
Petrol	Hydrogen	Molotov cocktail

Bones

Bone	**Nontechnical names**
Astragalus	Anklebone
Calcaneus	Heel bone
Carpal	Wrist
Carpus	Wrist
Centrum	—
Clavicle	Collarbone
Coccyx	—
Costa	Rib
Cranium	Brainpan
Cuboid	—
Ethmoid	—
Femur	Thighbone
Fibula	—
Frontal bone	—
Hallux	—
Humerus	Funny
Hyoid	—
Ilium	—
Incus	Anvil
Innominate bone	Hipbone
Ischium	—
Malar	Cheek
Malleus	Hammer
Mandible	Lower jawbone
Mastoid	—
Maxilla	Upper jawbone
Metacarpal	—
Metatarsal	—
Metatarsus	—
Nasal	Nose
Occipital bone	—
Parietal bone	—
Patella	Kneecap
Pelvis	—
Phalanx	—
Pubis	—
Radius	—
Rib	—
Sacrum	—
Scapula	Shoulder blade
Skull	—

Bone	Nontechnical names
Sphenoid	—
Spinal column *or* spine	Backbone
Stapes	Stirrup
Sternum	Breastbone
Talus	Anklebone
Tarsal	—
Tarsus	—
Temporal bone	—
Tibia	Shinbone
Trapezium	—
Ulna	—
Vertebra	—
Vertebral column	Backbone
Zygomatic bone	Cheekbone

Books

TYPES OF BOOK

3 letters:
Log
4 letters:
A to Z
Hymn
Road
Song
5 letters:
Album
Atlas
Bible
Comic
Diary
Novel
Score
6 letters:
Annual
Gradus
Jotter
Ledger
Manual
Missal
Phrase
Prayer
Primer
Reader
7 letters:
Almanac
Anatomy
Bibelot
Cookery
Grammar
Journal

Lexicon
Logbook
Novella
Ordinal
Peerage
Psalter
Service
Speller
Statute
Who's who
8 letters:
Armorial
Baedeker
Bestiary
Breviary
Brochure
Casebook
Copybook
Exercise
Grimoire
Handbook
Notebook
Register
Textbook
Wordbook
Workbook
Yearbook
9 letters:
Anthology
Biography
Catalogue
Catechism
Companion

Directory
Formulary
Gazetteer
Guidebook
Monograph
Novelette
Reference
Scrapbook
Storybook
Thesaurus
Vade mecum
10 letters:
Compendium
Dictionary
Lectionary
Miscellany
Prospectus
Sketchbook
11 letters:
Coffee-table
Commonplace
Concordance
12 letters:
Confessional
Dispensatory
Encyclopedia
Graphic novel
13 letters:
Autobiography
Encyclopaedia
Pharmacopoeia

PARTS OF A BOOK

4 letters:
Back
Leaf
Page
Tail
5 letters:
Blurb
Cover
Folio
Index
Plate
Proem
Recto
Spine
Verso
6 letters:
Errata
Gutter
Margin
Rubric
7 letters:
Binding

Chapter
Flyleaf
Preface
Prelims
Wrapper
8 letters:
Addendum
Appendix
Contents
Endpaper
Epigraph
Epilogue
Fore-edge
Foreword
Glossary
Prologue
Slipcase
9 letters:
Afterword
Half-title
Interleaf
Title page

10 letters:
Back matter
Corrigenda
Dedication
Dust jacket
Postscript
11 letters:
Front matter
Running head
12 letters:
Bibliography
Frontispiece
Illustration
Introduction
Prolegomenon
15 letters:
Acknowledgments

Botany

BRANCHES OF BOTANY

8 letters:
Algology
Bryology
Mycology
9 letters:
Carpology
10 letters:
Dendrology
Floristics

11 letters:
Agrostology
Astrobotany
Ethnobotany
Phytography
Pteridology
12 letters:
Archeobotany
Palaeobotany

Phytogenesis
13 letters:
Archaeobotany
14 letters:
Phytogeography
Phytopathology

BOTANY TERMS

3 letters:
Key
Nut
Sap
4 letters:
Axil
Axis
Bulb
Corm
Leaf
Pith
Root
Seed
Stem

5 letters:
Auxin
Berry
Calyx
Fruit
Hilum
Ovary
Ovule
Sepal
Shoot
Spore
Stoma
Style
Testa

Tuber
Xylem
6 letters:
Anther
Carpel
Corona
Cortex
Flower
Lamina
Legume
Phloem
Pistil
Pollen
Raceme

Runner
Spadix
Stamen
Stigma
Stolon
7 letters:
Cambium
Corolla
Cuticle
Plumule
Radicle
Rhizome
Root cap
Rosette
Seed pod
Tropism
8 letters:
Filament
Lenticel
Meristem
Root hair
Seedcase

9 letters:
Cotyledon
Epidermis
Foliation
Guard cell
Gynaecium
Mesophyll
Micropyle
Operculum
10 letters:
Abscission
Androecium
Geotropism
Integument
Receptacle
Root nodule
Seed vessel
Sporangium
11 letters:
Androgynous
Archegonium
Chlorophyll

Chloroplast
Dicotyledon
Germination
Pollination
Seed capsule
12 letters:
Hydrotropism
Phototropism
13 letters:
Inflorescence
Monocotyledon
Translocation
Transpiration
14 letters:
Nastic movement
Photosynthesis
Vascular bundle
15 letters:
Self-pollination
Spongy mesophyll
Wind pollination

BOTANISTS

3 letters:
Ray, *John*
5 letters:
Banks, *Joseph*
Brown, *Robert*
6 letters:
Carver, *George Washington*
Darwin, *Charles (Robert)*
Hooker, *Joseph Dalton*
Hooker, *William Jackson*
Mendel, *Gregor Johann*

7 letters:
Bellamy, *David (James)*
De Vries, *Hugo*
Eichler, *August Wilhelm*
8 letters:
Linnaeus
Von Linné, *Carl*
10 letters:
De Candolle, *Auguste Pyrame*
Tradescant, *John*

See also:
➤ **Algae** ➤ **Ferns** ➤ **Fungi** ➤ **Grasses** ➤ **Lilies**
➤ **Mosses** ➤ **Palms** ➤ **Plants** ➤ **Sea-weeds** ➤ **Shrubs** ➤ **Trees**

Bottles

5 letters:
Flask
Gourd
Phial
Water
6 letters:
Carboy
Caster
Flacon
Flagon
Lagena

Nansen
Stubby
Woulfe
7 letters:
Ampulla
Feeding
8 letters:
Decanter
Demijohn
Half-jack
Hot-water

Screw top
9 letters:
Miniature
10 letters:
Pycnometer
Soda siphon
11 letters:
Marie-Jeanne
Vinaigrette

Boxes

4 letters:
Case
Coin
Deed
Nest
Poor
Wine
5 letters:
Bulla
Chest
Ditty
Glory
Glove
Grass
Music
Trunk
6 letters:
Ballot

Carton
Casket
Coffer
Coffin
Hatbox
Haybox
Pounce
Saggar
Vanity
Window
7 letters:
Bandbox
Caisson
Cracket
Honesty
Keister
Pillbox
Pouncet

Saltbox
Sandbox
Soapbox
8 letters:
Dispatch
Matchbox
Paintbox
Solander
9 letters:
Cartouche
Papeterie
Strongbox
Tinderbox
10 letters:
Desiccator
11 letters:
Packing case

Boxing weights

Weight	Amateur	Professional
Light flyweight	48 kg	49 kg
Flyweight	51 kg	51 kg
Bantamweight	54 kg	53.5 kg
Featherweight	57 kg	57 kg
Junior lightweight	—	59 kg
Lightweight	60 kg	61 kg
Light welterweight	63.5 kg	63.5 kg
Welterweight	67 kg	66.6 kg
Light middleweight	71 kg	70 kg
Middleweight	75 kg	72.5 kg
Light heavyweight	81 kg	79 kg
Cruiserweight	—	88.5 kg
Heavyweight	91 kg	+88.5 kg
Superheavyweight	+91 kg	—

Brain, parts of

6 letters:
Vermis
8 letters:
Amygdala
Cerebrum
Meninges
Midbrain
Thalamus
9 letters:
Brainstem
10 letters:
Afterbrain
Broca's area

Cerebellum
Grey matter
Pineal body
11 letters:
Frontal lobe
Hippocampus
Pons Varolli
White matter
12 letters:
Diencephalon
Hypothalamus
Infundibulum
Limbic system

Optic chiasma
Parietal lobe
Temporal lobe
13 letters:
Central sulcus
Choroid plexus
Mamillary body
Occipital lobe
Wernicke's area
14 letters:
Cerebral cortex
Corpus callosum
Myelencephalon

Pituitary gland
Substantia alba
Third ventricle

15 letters:
Fourth ventricle

Breads

3 letters:
Bap
Bun
Cob
Nan
Pan
Rye
4 letters:
Corn
Loaf
Naan
Puri
Roll
Roti
Soda
5 letters:
Bagel
Black
Brown
Matza
Matzo
Pitta
Plain
Plait
White
6 letters:
Beigel
Coburg

Damper
French
Gluten
Hallah
Indian
Matzah
Matzoh
Muffin
7 letters:
Bloomer
Brioche
Buttery
Challah
Chapati
Granary®
Long tin
Paratha
Stollen
Wheaten
8 letters:
Baguette
Barm cake
Chapatti
Ciabatta
Corn pone
Focaccia
Poppadom
Poppadum

Quartern
Split tin
Tortilla
9 letters:
Barmbrack
Batch loaf
Croissant
Farmhouse
Fruit loaf
Schnecken
Sourdough
Square tin
Wholemeal
10 letters:
Billy-bread
Bridge roll
Johnny cake
Unleavened
Whole-wheat
11 letters:
Cottage loaf
French stick
12 letters:
Griddlebread
Half-quartern
Pumpernickel

Bridges

BRIDGES

4 letters:
Skye
Tyne
5 letters:
Tower
6 letters:
Humber
London
Rialto
Severn

7 letters:
Rainbow
8 letters:
Brooklyn
Waterloo
9 letters:
Forth Road
Halfpenny
10 letters:
Golden Gate

Millennium
Oakland Bay
11 letters:
Westminster
12 letters:
Forth Railway
13 letters:
Bridge of Sighs
Sydney Harbour

TYPES OF BRIDGE

4 letters:
Deck
Snow
Turn
5 letters:
Pivot
Swing
Truss
6 letters:
Bailey

7 letters:
Balance
Bascule
Clapper
Flyover
Pontoon
Viaduct
8 letters:
Aqueduct
9 letters:
Box-girder

10 letters:
Cantilever
Drawbridge
Footbridge
Suspension
11 letters:
Cable-stayed
12 letters:
Counterpoise

Brown, shades of

3 letters:
Bay
Dun
Tan
4 letters:
Buff
Drab
Ecru
Fawn
Fusc
Rust
Sand
Sore
Teak
5 letters:
Abram
Amber
Beige
Camel
Cocoa
Cream
Hazel
Henna
Khaki
Liver
Mocha
Mousy
Sable
Sepia

Soare
Taupe
Tawny
Tenné
Umber
6 letters:
Almond
Auburn
Bisque
Bistre
Bronze
Burnet
Coffee
Copper
Fallow
Ginger
Nutmeg
Rufous
Russet
Sienna
Sorrel
Walnut
7 letters:
Biscuit
Brindle
Caramel
Caromel
Filemot
Fulvous

Fuscous
Neutral
Oatmeal
Oxblood
Vandyke
8 letters:
Brunette
Chestnut
Cinnabar
Cinnamon
Mahogany
Mushroom
Nutbrown
Philamot
9 letters:
Butternut
Chocolate
Seal brown
10 letters:
Burnt umber
Café au lait
Coromandel
Terracotta
Testaceous
11 letters:
Burnt sienna
13 letters:
Tortoiseshell

Buddhism

3 letters:
Zen
4 letters:
Jodo
Soto

5 letters:
Foism
Geluk
Kagyü
Sakya

6 letters:
Rinjai
Tendai
7 letters:
Lamaism

Nyingma
8 letters:
Hinayana
Mahayana

Nichiren
9 letters:
Theravada
Vajrayana

10 letters:
Soka Gakkai

Bugs

4 letters:
Lace
5 letters:
Māori
Mealy
Stink
Water
6 letters:
Bedbug
Chinch
Cicada

Cicala
Damsel
Debris
Shield
7 letters:
Kissing
Spittle
9 letters:
Harlequin
10 letters:
Froghopper

Leaf-hopper
Pond-skater
11 letters:
Water skater
12 letters:
Water boatman
Water strider
13 letters:
Spittle insect
Water scorpion

Buildings and monuments

5 letters:
Kaaba
6 letters:
Big Ben
Louvre
Masada
7 letters:
Beehive
Knossos
Kremlin
Lateran
Vatican
8 letters:
Alhambra
Barbican
Cenotaph
Monument

Pentagon
Taj Mahal
9 letters:
Charminar
Hermitage
10 letters:
Versailles
White House
11 letters:
Eiffel Tower
Scone Palace
12 letters:
Althorp House
Mansion House
13 letters:
Arc de Triomphe
Crystal Palace

Elysées Palace
Forbidden City
Holyroodhouse
Lambeth Palace
Longleat House
Nelson's Column
Tower of London
14 letters:
Admiralty House
Blenheim Palace
15 letters:
Angel of the North
Edinburgh Castle

Butterflies and moths

2 letters:
Io
3 letters:
Bag
Bee
Fox
Nun
Owl
Wax
4 letters:
Arch
Bell
Blue

Goat
Hawk
Leaf
Luna
Meal
Puss
Wave
5 letters:
Argus
Atlas
Brown
Comma
Eggar

Egger
Flour
Ghost
Gipsy
Grass
Gypsy
Heath
House
Owlet
Snout
Swift
Thorn
Tiger

Tinea
Umber
White
Y-moth
6 letters:
Antler
Apollo
Bogong
Bugong
Burnet
Carpet
Codlin
Copper

Dagger
Ermine
Herald
Kitten
Lackey
Lappet
Lichen
Magpie
Morpho
Muslin
Noctua
Pieris
Psyche
Sphinx
Thecla
Turnip
Veneer
Winter
Yellow

7 letters:
Abraxas
Bagworm
Buff-tip
Cabbage
Clothes
Codling
Drinker
Emperor
Festoon
Hook-tip
Kallima
Leopard
Lobster
Monarch
Noctuid
Old lady
Peacock
Pug-moth
Ringlet
Silver-Y
Skipper
Stamper
Sulphur
Thistle

Tortrix
Tussock
Unicorn
Vanessa
Zygaena

8 letters:
Bobowler
Bombycid
Cardinal
Cecropia
Cinnabar
Dart-moth
Geometer
Goldtail
Grayling
Hesperid
Oak-egger
Peppered
Saturnia
Silkworm
Sphingid
Tapestry
Tineidae
Vapourer
Wainscot

9 letters:
Arctiidae
Brimstone
Brown-tail
Carpenter
Clearwing
Cleopatra
Geometrid
Honeycomb
Notodonta
Orange-tip
Pyralidae
Saturniid
Scavenger
Underwing
Wall brown

10 letters:
Common blue
Death's-head

Fritillary
Gate-keeper
Hairstreak
Large white
Leafroller
Polyphemus
Privet hawk
Red admiral
Silverspot
Small white
Yellowtail

11 letters:
Diamondback
Hummingbird
Large copper
Meadow brown
Painted lady
Swallowtail

12 letters:
Cabbage white
Cactoblastis
Kentish glory
Lymantriidae
Marbled white
Red underwing
Sallow-kitten
Speckled wood
White admiral

13 letters:
Clouded yellow
Mother-of-pearl
Mother Shipton
Mourning cloak
Processionary
Purple emperor

14 letters:
Two-tailed pasha

15 letters:
Yellow underwing

Cakes and pastries

3 letters:
Bun
Nut
Oil
Pan
Set

4 letters:
Baba
Farl
Kueh
Pone
Puff
Puri
Rock
Roti
Rout
Rusk
Slab
Soul
Tart

5 letters:
Angel
Babka
Cream
Donut
Fairy
Farle
Fudge
Genoa
Lardy
Latke
Layer
Poori
Pound
Rosti
Scone
Sushi
Tansy
Tipsy
Torte
Wafer

6 letters:
Almond
Carrot
Cherry
Coburg

Cotton
Dainty
Dundee
Eccles
Eclair
Gateau
Girdle
Hockey
Johnny
Jumbal
Jumble
Kuchen
Marble
Muffin
Parkin
Simnel
Sponge
Tablet
Waffle
Wonder
Yumyum

7 letters:
Baklava
Banbury
Bannock
Brioche
Brownie
Carcake
Chapati
Chupati
Coconut
Cruller
Crumpet
Cupcake
Fritter
Galette
Jannock
Jumbles
Kruller
Linseed
Madeira
Oatmeal
Pancake
Paratha
Pavlova
Pikelet

Pomfret
Ratafia
Rum baba
Savarin
Stollen
Teacake
Vetkoek
Wedding

8 letters:
Agnus dei
Birthday
Black bun
Chapatti
Chillada
Chupatty
Doughnut
Dumpling
Flapjack
Macaroon
Meringue
Mince pie
Napoleon
Pandowdy
Sandwich
Seedcake
Teabread
Tortilla
Turnover

9 letters:
Angel food
Barmbrack
Buckwheat
Chocolate
Christmas
Chupattie
Clapbread
Cream puff
Croquette
Drop scone
Fruitcake
Kuglehopf
Lamington
Madeleine
Panettone
Petit four
Puftaloon

Queencake
Sally Lunn
Swiss roll
10 letters:
Battenberg
Battenburg
Coffee kiss
Devil's food
Frangipane
Frangipani
Koeksister
Ladyfinger

Pontefract
Puftaloona
Religieuse
Upside-down
11 letters:
Gingerbread
Hot cross bun
Linzer torte
Profiterole
Sachertorte
12 letters:
Bakewell tart

Danish pastry
French pastry
Maid of honour
Millefeuille
Singing hinny
Sponge finger
13 letters:
Genoese sponge
14 letters:
Selkirk bannock
Victoria sponge

Cameras

CAMERA PARTS

6 letters:
Tripod
7 letters:
Hot shoe
Shutter
8 letters:
Flash gun
Lens hood

Sprocket
Zoom lens
9 letters:
Amplifier
Macro lens
10 letters:
Autowinder
Viewfinder

12 letters:
Synchroflash
13 letters:
Accessory shoe

TYPES OF CAMERA

3 letters:
Box
4 letters:
Cine
6 letters:
Candid
Reflex
Webcam
7 letters:
Brownie

Compact
Digital
Pinhole
Process
8 letters:
Polaroid
9 letters:
Automatic
Camcorder
Miniature

Steadicam
10 letters:
Programmed
12 letters:
Subminiature

Canals

3 letters:
Suo
4 letters:
Erie
Göta
Kiel
Suez
5 letters:
Grand
6 letters:
Moscow
Panama

Twente
7 letters:
Corinth
Welland
8 letters:
Berezina
9 letters:
Champlain
10 letters:
Caledonian
Grand Union
Mittelland

Rhine-Herne
11 letters:
Bridgewater
Canal du Midi
Dortmund-Ems
Houston Ship
12 letters:
Canal do Norte
14 letters:
Manchester Ship

Capes

3 letters:	Sandy	Good Hope
Cod	Verde	Hatteras
Hoe	Wrath	Palatine
May	**6 letters:**	**9 letters:**
Ras	Helles	Canaveral
4 letters:	Lizard	Dungeness
Fear	Reinga	Guardafui
Hogh	Sontag	Lindesnes
Horn	Ushant	Southwest
Naze	**7 letters:**	St Vincent
Race	Agulhas	Trafalgar
Roca	Comorin	**10 letters:**
Scaw	Delgado	Finisterre
Skaw	Leeuwin	**11 letters:**
5 letters:	Matapan	Fairweather
Byron	Runaway	
Canso	Western	
North	**8 letters:**	
Parry	Farewell	
Sable	Flattery	

Capitals

Capital	**Country, region, state, etc**
Abidjan	Côte d'Ivoire (formerly)
Abu Dhabi	United Arab Emirates
Abuja	Nigeria
Accra	Ghana
Acra	Hunger
Addis Ababa	Ethiopia
Adelaide	South Australia
Agana	Guam
Albany	New York (state capital)
Algiers	Algeria
Amman	Jordan
Amsterdam	Netherlands
Andorra la Vella	Andorra
Ankara	Turkey
Annapolis	Maryland
Antananarivo	Madagascar
Antioch	Ancient Syria
Apia	Samoa
Ashkhabad	Turkmenistan
Asmara	Eritrea
Astana	Kazakhstan
Asunción	Paraguay
Athens	Greece
Atlanta	Georgia
Austin	Texas
Baghdad	Iraq
Baku	Azerbaijan
Bamako	Mali
Bandar Seri Begawan	Brunei
Bangalore	Karnataka

Capital	Country, region, state, etc
Bangkok	Thailand
Bangui	Central African Republic
Banjul	Gambia
Barnaul	Altai
Basseterre	St Kitts and Nevis
Bastia	Corsica
Baton Rouge	Louisiana
Beijing *or* Peking	People's Republic of China
Beirut *or* Beyrouth	Lebanon
Belfast	Northern Ireland
Belgrade	Serbia
Belmopan	Belize
Berlin	Germany
Berne	Switzerland
Bishkek	Kyrgyzstan
Bissau	Guinea-Bissau
Bloemfontein	Judicial capital of South Africa
Bogotá	Colombia
Bonn	Federal Republic of Germany (formerly)
Brasília	Brazil
Bratislava	Slovakia
Brazzaville	Congo (Republic of)
Bridgetown	Barbados
Brisbane	Queensland
Brno	Moravia
Bruges	West Flanders
Brussels	Belgium
Bucharest	Romania
Budapest	Hungary
Buenos Aires	Argentina
Bujumbura	Burundi
Caen	Basse-Normandie
Cagliari	Sardinia
Cairo	Egypt
Calcutta	West Bengal
Cali	Valley of the Cauca, Colombia
Canberra	Australia
Cape Town	Legislative capital of South Africa
Caracas	Venezuela
Cardiff	Wales
Cartagena	Bolivar
Castries	St Lucia
Cayenne	French Guiana
Charleston	West Virginia
Colombo	Sri Lanka
Conakry *or* Konakry	Guinea
Copenhagen	Denmark
Cordoba	Cordoba
Dakar	Senegal
Damascus	Syria
Darwin	Northern Territory, Australia
Delhi	India
Dhaka *or* Dacca	Bangladesh

Capital	Country, region, state, etc
Dili	East Timor
Djibouti *or* Jibouti	Djibouti *or* Jibouti
Dodoma	Tanzania
Doha	Qatar
Douglas	Isle of Man
Dublin	Republic of Ireland
Dushanbe	Tajikistan
Edinburgh	Scotland
Enugu	Enugu State, Nigeria
Faro	The Algarve
Fongafale	Tuvalu
Fort-de-France	Martinique
Freetown	Sierra Leone
Funafuti	Tuvalu
Funchal	Madeira
Gaborone	Botswana
Georgetown	Guyana
Guatemala City	Guatemala
Hanoi	Vietnam
Harare	Zimbabwe
Havana	Cuba
Helsinki	Finland
Heraklion *or* Eraklion	Crete
Hobart	Tasmania
Honiara	Solomon Islands
Honolulu	Hawaii
Ibadan	Oyo State, Nigeria
Ipoh	Perak
Islamabad	Pakistan
Istanbul *or* Constantinople	Turkey (formerly)
Jakarta *or* Djakarta	Indonesia
Jerusalem	Israel
Jos	Plateau (central Nigeria)
Kabul	Afghanistan
Kampala	Uganda
Karachi	Sind
Katmandu *or* Kathmandu	Nepal
Khartoum *or* Khartum	Sudan
Kiel	Schleswig-Holstein
Kiev	Ukraine
Kigali	Rwanda
Kingston	Jamaica
Kingstown	St Vincent and the Grenadines
Kinshasa	Congo (Democratic Republic of)
Kirkwall	Orkney Islands
Kishinev	Moldova
Kobe	Honshu
Koror	Palau
Kuala Lumpur	Malaysia
Kuwait	Kuwait
Lagos	Nigeria (formerly)
La Paz	Administrative capital of Bolivia
Lassa *or* Lhasa	Tibet
Leningrad, St Petersburg, *or* Petrograd	Russia (formerly)
Libreville	Gabon

Capital	**Country, region, state, etc**
Lilongwe	Malawi
Lima	Peru
Lisbon	Portugal
Little Rock	Arkansas
Ljubljana	Slovenia
Lomé	Togo
London	United Kingdom
Luanda	Angola
Lusaka	Zambia
Luxembourg	Luxembourg
Madrid	Spain
Majuro	Marshall Islands
Malabo	Equatorial Guinea
Malé	Maldives
Managua	Nicaragua
Manama	Bahrain
Manila	Philippines
Maputo	Mozambique
Maseru	Lesotho
Mathura	Braj Bhoomi
Mbabane	Swaziland
Memphis	Egypt, Old Kingdom
Mexico City	Mexico
Minsk	Belarus
Mogadishu	Somalia
Monaco-Ville	Monaco
Monrovia	Liberia
Montevideo	Uruguay
Moroni	Comoros
Moscow	Russia
Muscat	Oman
Nairobi	Kenya
Nashville	Tennessee
Nassau	Bahamas
Naypyidaw	Myanmar (Burma)
Ndjamena	Chad
Niamey	Niger
Nicosia	Cyprus
Nineveh	Ancient Assyrian empire
Nouakchott	Mauritania
Nuku'alofa	Tonga
Nuuk	Greenland
Olympia	Washington state
Oslo	Norway
Ottawa	Canada
Ouagadougou	Burkina-Faso
Palermo	Sicily
Palikir	Micronesia
Panama City	Panama
Pandemonium *or* Pandaemonium	Hell
Paramaribo	Suriname
Paris	France
Persepolis	Ancient Persia
Phnom Penh	Cambodia
Pishpek	Kirghizia
Podgorica	Montenegro

Capital	Country, region, state, etc
Port-au-Prince	Haiti
Port Louis	Mauritius
Port Moresby	Papua New Guinea
Port of Spain	Trinidad and Tobago
Porto Novo	Benin
Port Vila	Vanuatu
Prague	Czech Republic
Praia	Cape Verde
Pretoria	Administrative capital of South Africa
Pristina	Kosovo
Providence	Rhode Island
Pyongyang	North Korea
Quito	Ecuador
Rabat	Morocco
Reykjavik	Iceland
Riga	Latvia
Rio	Rio de Janeiro
Rio Branco	Acre
Riyadh	Saudi Arabia
Rome	Italy
Roseau	Dominica
Samarkand	Mongol Empire (14th century)
San'a'	Yemen
San José	Costa Rica
San Juan	Puerto Rico
San Marino	San Marino
San Salvador	El Salvador
Santiago	Chile
Santo Domingo	Dominican Republic
São Tomé	São Tomé and Principe
Sarajevo	Bosnia and Herzegovina
Sendai	Tohoku
Seoul	South Korea
Singapore	Singapore
Skopje	Macedonia
Sofia	Bulgaria
Sokoto	Sokoto
St George's	Grenada
St John's	Antigua and Barbuda
Stockholm	Sweden
Stuttgart	Baden-Württemberg
Sucre	Legislative and judicial capital of Bolivia
Susa	Ancient Persia (Achaemenid dynasty)
Suva	Fiji
Taipei	Taiwan
Tallinn	Estonia
Tarawa	Kiribati
Tashkent	Uzbekistan
Tbilisi	Georgia
Tegucigalpa	Honduras
Tehran *or* Teheran	Iran
Tel Aviv	Israel
Thebes	Ancient Egypt (18th dynasty)

Capital	Country, region, state, etc
Thimphu *or* Thimbu	Bhutan
Tirana	Albania
Tokyo	Japan
Topeka	Kansas
Trebizond	Trebizond
Tripoli	Libya
Tunis	Tunisia
Ufa	Bashkiria
Ulan Bator	Mongolia
Vaduz	Liechtenstein
Valladolid	Castilla-Léon
Valletta	Malta
Vatican City	Vatican City
Victoria	Seychelles
Vienna	Austria
Vientiane	Laos
Vilnius	Lithuania
Warsaw	Poland
Washington DC	United States of America
Wellington	New Zealand
Windhoek	Namibia
Winnipeg	Manitoba
Xanthus	Ancient Lycia
Xian	Shaanxi
Yamoussoukro	Côte d'Ivoire
Yangon (Rangoon)	Myanmar (Burma) (formerly)
Yaoundé *or* Yaunde	Cameroon
Yaren	Nauru
Yerevan	Armenia
Zagreb	Croatia

Caps

3 letters:
Mob
Taj
Tam
4 letters:
Blue
Caul
Coif
Cope
Cowl
Flat
Kepi
5 letters:
Beret
Chaco
Chape
Cloth
Kippa
Mutch
Pagri
Quoif
Shako

Toque
Tuque
Turk's
6 letters:
Abacot
Amorce
Barret
Berret
Biggin
Blakey
Calpac
Chapka
Cornet
Czapka
Dunce's
Forage
Gandhi
Granny
Jockey
Juliet
Kalpak
Kipput

Kiss-me
Morion
Pileus
Pinner
Square
Toorie
7 letters:
Bathing
Bellhop
Bendigo
Biretta
Bycoket
Calotte
Calpack
Chapeau
Chechia
Fatigue
Grannie
Kippoth
Liberty
Monteer
Montero

Morrion
Newsboy
8 letters:
Balmoral
Baseball
Capeline
Chaperon
Garrison
Havelock
Monmouth
Phrygian
Puggaree

Schapska
Skullcap
Stocking
Thinking
Trencher
Yarmulka
Yarmulke
Zuchetto
9 letters:
Balaclava
Glengarry
Trenchard

10 letters:
Cockernony
Kilmarnock
11 letters:
Bonnet-rouge
Deerstalker
Kiss-me-quick
Mortar-board
Tam-o'-shanter
12 letters:
Cheese-cutter
Davy Crockett

Cards

CARD GAMES

3 letters:
Loo
Nap
4 letters:
Faro
Skat
Snap
Solo
5 letters:
Cinch
Monte
Ombre
Poker
Rummy
Stops
Whist
6 letters:
Boston
Bridge
Casino
Chemmy
Écarté

Euchre
Hearts
Piquet
Quinze
Switch
7 letters:
Bezique
Canasta
Cooncan
Old maid
Pinocle
Pontoon
Seven up
8 letters:
Baccarat
Canfield
Conquian
Cribbage
Gin rummy
Napoleon
Patience
Penuchle

Penuckle
Pinochle
Slapjack
9 letters:
Blackjack
Solo whist
Spoilfive
Stud poker
10 letters:
Strip poker
11 letters:
Five hundred
Rouge et noir
12 letters:
Rubber bridge
13 letters:
Auction bridge
Happy families
14 letters:
Contract bridge
15 letters:
Duplicate bridge

BRIDGE TERMS

4 letters:
East
Ruff
Slam
West
5 letters:
Dummy
North
South
Trick

Trump
6 letters:
Double
Rubber
7 letters:
Finesse
No-trump
8 letters:
Contract
Redouble

9 letters:
Grand slam
Singleton
Small slam
10 letters:
Little slam
Vulnerable
Yarborough

POKER TERMS

3 letters:
See
Shy
4 letters:
Ante
Pair
5 letters:
Flush

Raise
8 letters:
Showdown
Stand pat
Straddle
Straight
9 letters:
Full house

10 letters:
Royal flush
13 letters:
Straight flush

OTHER CARD TERMS

3 letters:
Ace
Cut
4 letters:
Deal
Deck
Hand
Jack
King

Suit
Trey
Wild
5 letters:
Clubs
Deuce
Joker
Knave
Queen

6 letters:
Hearts
Revoke
Spades
8 letters:
Diamonds
Face card
9 letters:
Court card

Carnivores

3 letters:
Cat
Dog
Fox
4 letters:
Bear
Coon
Eyra
Lion
Lynx
Mink
Puma
Wolf
5 letters:
Civet
Dhole
Dingo
Genet
Hyena
Otter
Ounce
Panda
Potto
Rasse
Ratel
Sable
Skunk
Stoat
Tayra
Tiger

Zibet
6 letters:
Badger
Bobcat
Chetah
Corsac
Cougar
Coyote
Ermine
Fennec
Ferret
Grison
Hyaena
Jackal
Jaguar
Kit fox
Margay
Marten
Nanook
Ocelot
Racoon
Red fox
Serval
Teledu
Weasel
7 letters:
Caracal
Cheetah
Genette
Glutton

Grey fox
Grizzly
Leopard
Linsang
Meerkat
Panther
Polecat
Raccoon
Rooikat
Sun bear
Zorilla
Zorille
8 letters:
Aardwolf
Carcajou
Grey wolf
Kinkajou
Kolinsky
Mongoose
Sea otter
Swift fox
Tiger cat
Warrigal
Zibeline
9 letters:
Arctic fox
Binturong
Black bear
Brown bear
Cacomixle

Catamount
Hog badger
Honey bear
Ichneumon
Native dog
Palm civet
Polar bear
Silver fox
Sloth bear
Wolverine
10 letters:
Cacomistle
Desert lynx

Giant panda
Jaguarondi
Jaguarundi
Kodiak bear
Otter shrew
Pine marten
Prairie dog
Raccoon dog
Strandwolf
Timber wolf
11 letters:
Grizzly bear
Prairie wolf

Snow leopard
Stone marten
Sweet marten
12 letters:
Catamountain
Cat-o'-mountain
Cinnamon bear
Mountain lion
Spotted hyena
13 letters:
Hognosed skunk
Laughing hyena

See also:
➤ **Cats** ➤ **Dogs**

Carpets and rugs

5 letters:
Kilim
6 letters:
Durrie
Kirman
Numdah
Wilton
7 letters:
Ingrain

8 letters:
Aubusson
Chenille
9 letters:
Axminster
Broadloom
Flat-woven
10 letters:
Bukhara rug

Persian rug
12 letters:
Turkey carpet
13 letters:
Kidderminster
Persian carpet
14 letters:
Brussels carpet

Carriages and carts

3 letters:
Cab
Car
Fly
Gig
Rig
4 letters:
Bier
Cart
Chay
Coch
Drag
Ekka
Pung
Rath
Shay
Sled
Trap
Wain
5 letters:
Bandy
Brake
Buggy
Coach

Coupé
Ratha
Sulky
Tonga
Wagon
6 letters:
Berlin
Britka
Calash
Chaise
Charet
Dennet
Do-si-do
Drosky
Fiacre
Gharry
Go-cart
Hansom
Herdic
Landau
Limber
Pochay
Random
Remise

Sledge
Spider
Surrey
Tandem
Troika
Whisky
7 letters:
Berline
Britska
Britzka
Calèche
Cariole
Caroche
Chariot
Chassis
Dogcart
Dos-a-dos
Droshky
Growler
Norimon
Phaeton
Tilbury
Vetture
Vis-à-vis

Voiture
Whiskey
8 letters:
Barouche
Brougham
Cape cart
Carriage
Carriole
Carryall
Clarence
Curricle
Equipage
Pochaise
Quadriga
Rickshaw
Rockaway
Sociable

Stanhope
Tarantas
Victoria
9 letters:
Britschka
Buckboard
Cabriolet
Gladstone
Horseless
Jaunty car
Landaulet
Tarantass
Wagonette
Whirligig
10 letters:
Four-in-hand
Post chaise

Stagecoach
Tim-whiskey
11 letters:
Hurly-hacket
Jaunting car
12 letters:
Covered wagon
13 letters:
Désobligeante
Spider phaeton
14 letters:
Conestoga wagon
15 letters:
Prairie schooner

Cars

TYPES OF CAR

2 letters:
BL
GT
MG
RR
VW
3 letters:
Cab
Elf
4 letters:
Audi
Biza
Drag
Fiat
Ford
Kart
Lada
Limo
Merc
Mini
Opel
Tank
5 letters:
Astra
Buick
Coupé
Panda
Prowl
Racer

Rolls
Sedan
Skoda
Squad
Stock
Turbo
6 letters:
Beetle
Bubble
Bumper
Dodgem®
Estate
Hearse
Hot-rod
Lancia
Morris
Patrol
Ragtop
Roller
Sports
Tourer
7 letters:
Bugatti
Company
Cortina
Daimler
Formula
Hardtop
Hillman

Lagonda
Sunbeam
Veteran
Vintage
8 letters:
Cadillac
Dragster
Drophead
Fastback
Mercedes
Roadster
9 letters:
Cabriolet
Hatchback
Landaulet
Landrover
Limousine
Notchback
Two-seater
10 letters:
Subcompact
11 letters:
Convertible
Stretch-limo
12 letters:
Station wagon
Three-wheeler

CAR PARTS

3 letters:
Fan
Top
4 letters:
Axle
Body
Boot
Bulb
Coil
Cowl
Door
Fuse
Gear
Hood
Horn
Jack
Lock
Plug
Roof
Seat
Sump
Tank
Trim
Tyre
Wing
5 letters:
Brake
Choke
Crank
Light
Pedal
Valve
Wheel
6 letters:
Air bag
Big end
Bonnet
Bumper
Clutch
Engine
Fascia
Fender
Gasket
Grille
Heater
Hubcap
Piston
Points
Towbar
Window
7 letters:
Ammeter
Ashtray

Battery
Bearing
Chassis
Exhaust
Fan belt
Fog lamp
Fuse box
Gearbox
Hard top
Mud flap
Oil pump
Soft top
Springs
Starter
Sunroof
Wing nut
8 letters:
Brake pad
Camshaft
Cylinder
Demister
Dipstick
Flywheel
Foglight
Headrest
Ignition
Manifold
Odometer
Radiator
Seat belt
Silencer
Sprocket
Tailgate
Tailpipe
Wheel nut
9 letters:
Crankcase
Dashboard
Fuel gauge
Gear lever
Gearshift
Generator
Handbrake
Headlight
Indicator
Little end
Milometer
Oil filter
Petrol cap
Radius arm
Rear light
Sidelight
Taillight

Wheel trim
10 letters:
Alternator
Brake light
Bucket seat
Crankshaft
Disc brakes
Door handle
Driveshaft
Mileometer
Petrol tank
Safety belt
Spare wheel
Suspension
Torsion bar
Wheel brace
Windscreen
Wing mirror
11 letters:
Accelerator
Anti-roll bar
Carburettor
Distributor
Hazard light
Luggage rack
Numberplate
Parcel shelf
Petrol gauge
Speedometer
12 letters:
Cylinder head
Parking light
Sunshine roof
Transmission
13 letters:
Connecting rod
Passenger seat
Shock absorber
Steering wheel
14 letters:
Automatic choke
Childproof lock
Convertible top
Distributor cap
Radiator grille
Rear-view mirror
Reversing light
Steering column
Universal joint
15 letters:
Windscreen wiper

INTERNATIONAL CAR REGISTRATION LETTERS

Letter(s)	Country	Letter(s)	Country
A	Austria	GUY	Guyana
ADN	Yemen	H	Hungary
AFG	Afghanistan	HK	Hong Kong
AL	Albania	HKJ	Jordan
AND	Andorra	HR	Croatia
AUS	Australia	I	Italy
B	Belgium	IL	Israel
BD	Bangladesh	IND	India
BDS	Barbados	IR	Iran
BG	Bulgaria	IRL	Republic of
BH	Belize		Ireland
BR	Brazil	IRQ	Iraq
BRN	Bahrain	IS	Iceland
BRU	Brunei	J	Japan
BS	Bahamas	JA	Jamaica
BUR	Myanmar	K	Cambodia
C	Cuba	KWT	Kuwait
CDN	Canada	L	Luxembourg
CH	Switzerland	LAO	Laos
CI	Côte d'Ivoire	LAR	Libya
CL	Sri Lanka	LB	Liberia
CO	Colombia	LS	Lesotho
CR	Costa Rica	LT	Lithuania
CY	Cyprus	LV	Latvia
CZ	Czech Republic	M	Malta
D	Germany	MA	Morocco
DK	Denmark	MAL	Malaysia
DOM	Dominican	MC	Monaco
	Republic	MEX	Mexico
DY	Benin	MS	Mauritius
DZ	Algeria	MW	Malawi
E	Spain	N	Norway
EAK	Kenya	NA	Netherlands
EAT	Tanzania		Antilles
EAU	Uganda	NIC	Nicaragua
EC	Ecuador	NL	Netherlands
ES	El Salvador	NZ	New Zealand
ET	Egypt	OMAN	Oman
ETH	Ethiopia	P	Portugal
EW	Estonia	PA	Panama
F	France	PE	Peru
FIN	Finland	PK	Pakistan
FJI	Fiji	PL	Poland
FL	Liechtenstein	PNG	Papua New
FR	Faeroe Islands		Guinea
GB	United Kingdom	PY	Paraguay
GBA	Alderney	RA	Argentina
GBG	Guernsey	RB	Botswana
GBJ	Jersey	RC	Taiwan
GBM	Isle of Man	RCA	Central African
GBZ	Gibraltar		Republic
GCA	Guatemala	RCB	Congo Republic
GH	Ghana	RCH	Chile
GR	Greece	RH	Haiti

Letter(s)	Country	Letter(s)	Country
RI	Indonesia	TN	Tunisia
RIM	Mauritania	TR	Turkey
RL	Lebanon	TT	Trindad and
RM	Madagascar		Tobago
RMM	Mali	USA	United States of
RO	Romania		America
ROK	South Korea	V	Vatican City
ROU	Uruguay	VN	Vietnam
RP	Philippines	WAG	Gambia
RSM	San Marino	WAL	Sierra Leone
RU	Burundi	WAN	Nigeria
RUS	Russian Federation	WD	Dominica
RWA	Rwanda	WG	Grenada
S	Sweden	WL	St Lucia
SD	Swaziland	WS	Western Samoa
SGP	Singapore	WV	St Vincent and
SK	Slovakia		the Grenadines
SME	Surinam	YU	Yugoslavia
SN	Senegal	YV	Venezuela
SWA	Namibia	Z	Zambia
SY	Seychelles	ZA	South Africa
SYR	Syria	ZRE	Zaire
T	Thailand	ZW	Zimbabwe
TG	Togo		

Cartoon characters

3 letters:
Doc
Ren
Tom
4 letters:
Dino
Kyle
Stan
5 letters:
Bambi
Bluto
Dopey
Dumbo
Goofy
Happy
Itchy
Jerry
Kenny
Pluto
Snowy
6 letters:
Bam-Bam
Boo-Boo
Grumpy
Krusty
Popeye
Shaggy
Sleepy

Sneezy
Stimpy
Tigger
Tintin
Top Cat
7 letters:
Bashful
Cartman
Muttley
Pebbles
Swee' Pea
8 letters:
Olive Oyl
Scratchy
Yogi Bear
9 letters:
Betty Boop
Daffy Duck
Elmer Fudd
Scooby-Doo
Sylvester
Tweety-Pie
10 letters:
Donald Duck
Roadrunner
11 letters:
Bart Simpson
Betty Rubble

Lisa Simpson
Mickey Mouse
Minnie Mouse
Ned Flanders
Sideshow Bob
Wile E Coyote
Yosemite Sam
12 letters:
Barney Rubble
Homer Simpson
Marge Simpson
13 letters:
Dick Dastardly
Maggie Simpson
Officer Dibble
The Hooded Claw
Winnie the Pooh
14 letters:
Foghorn Leghorn
Fred Flintstone
Speedy Gonzalez
15 letters:
Penelope Pitstop
Wilma Flintstone

Cases

3 letters:
Box
Pod
4 letters:
Aril
Beer
Bere
Etui
Flan
Grip
Hull
Husk
Port
5 letters:
Ascus
Blimp
Burse
Calyx
Chase
Crate
Crust
Etwee
Frame
Ocrea
Theca
Trunk
Volva
6 letters:
Basket

Chitin
Cocoon
Locket
Lorica
Manche
Ochrea
Penner
Quiver
Sheath
Telium
Valise
Walise
Wallet
7 letters:
Cabinet
Capsule
Compact
Elytron
Hanaper
Hold-all
Humidor
Keister
Nacelle
Sheathe
Six-pack
Sporran
Wardian
8 letters:
Bundwall

Canister
Cartouch
Cellaret
Dispatch
Flapjack
Indusium
Nutshell
Scabbard
Tantalus
Tea-chest
Vasculum
9 letters:
Cartouche
Cartridge
Chrysalis
Croustade
Housewife
Papeterie
10 letters:
Canterbury
Phylactery
Sabretache
12 letters:
Plummer-block

Castles

3 letters:
Man
4 letters:
Cheb
Drum
More
Rait
Trim
5 letters:
Aydon
Blois
Cabra
Cahir
Conwy
Corfe
Dinan
Hever
Leeds
Spain
Torún
Vaduz

6 letters:
Brodie
Dublin
Durham
Farney
Forfar
Glamis
Kilkea
Ludlow
Raglan
Rithes
Stuart
7 letters:
Alnwick
Amboise
Arundel
Ashford
Barnard
Beeston
Belvoir
Blarney

Braemar
Canossa
Chillon
Colditz
Crathes
Culzean
Despair
Harlech
Lincoln
Otranto
Schloss
Skipton
St Mawes
Warwick
Windsor
8 letters:
Balmoral
Balvenie
Bamburgh
Bastille
Berkeley

Bunraity
Carbonek
Darnaway
Doubting
Egremont
Elephant
Elsinore
Kilkenny
Killaghy
Leamaneh
Malahide
Malperdy
Monmouth
Pembroke
Portlick
Rackrent
Richmond
Stirling
Stokesay
Taymouth
Tintagel
Urquhart

Wartburg
9 letters:
Beaumaris
Dangerous
Dunnottar
Dunsinane
Edinburgh
Esterháza
Inverness
Kilravock
Lancaster
Leicester
Pendennis
Restormel
Sherborne
Trausnitz
Vincennes
10 letters:
Caernarfon
Caerphilly
Carmarthen
Heidelberg

Kenilworth
Launceston
Pontefract
11 letters:
Aberystwyth
Carisbrooke
Eilean Donan
Gormenghast
Scarborough
12 letters:
Berkhamstead
Caerlaverock
Château-Raoul
Dunstaffnage
Fotheringhay
Herstmonceux
Rock of Cashel
13 letters:
Ballindalloch
Carrickfergus
14 letters:
Ashby de la Zouch

Cats

BREEDS OF CAT

3 letters:
Rex
4 letters:
Manx
5 letters:
Tabby
6 letters:
Angora
Havana

7 letters:
Burmese
Persian
Ragdoll
Siamese
Turkish
9 letters:
Himalayan
Maine Coon

10 letters:
Abyssinian
11 letters:
Colourpoint
Russian blue
13 letters:
Bengal leopard
Tortoiseshell

FAMOUS CATS

3 letters:
Tom
4 letters:
Bast
Jinx
5 letters:
Bucky
Felix
Fritz
Hodge
Salem
6 letters:
Arthur
Bastet
Ginger

Huckle
Muessa
Selima
Top Cat
7 letters:
Bagpuss
Lucifer
Slipper
8 letters:
Garfield
Lady Jane
Scratchy
Snowball
9 letters:
Mehitabel

Mistigris
Thomasina
Tobermory
10 letters:
Grizabella
Heathcliff
11 letters:
Bombalurina
Cat in the Hat
Cheshire Cat
Mungojerrie
Puss-in-Boots
Snagglepuss
13 letters:
Fat Freddy's Cat

Cattle and other artiodactyls

2 letters:
Ox
Zo
3 letters:
Cow
Dzo
Elk
Gnu
Goa
Kob
Pig
Yak
Zho
4 letters:
Axis
Boar
Bull
Deer
Gaur
Goat
Ibex
Kudu
Oont
Oryx
Pudu
Sika
Stag
Tahr
Thar
Zebu
5 letters:
Addax
Argal
Ariel
Bison
Bongo
Bubal
Camel
Eland
Gayal
Goral
Izard
Jacob
Llama
Moose
Nagor
Nyala
Okapi
Oribi
Saiga
Serow

Sheep
Takin
6 letters:
Alpaca
Aoudad
Argali
Bharal
Chital
Dik-dik
Duiker
Duyker
Impala
Koodoo
Nilgai
Reebok
Rhebok
Sambar
Sambur
Vicuña
Wapiti
7 letters:
Alpacca
Blaubok
Blesbok
Brocket
Bubalis
Buffalo
Bushpig
Carabao
Caracul
Caribou
Chamois
Gazelle
Gemsbok
Gerenuk
Giraffe
Grysbok
Guanaco
Jumbuck
Karakul
Kongoni
Kouprey
Markhor
Mouflon
Muntjac
Muntjak
Nilghau
Nylghau
Peccary
Red deer
Roe deer

Sassaby
Wart hog
Water ox
8 letters:
Antelope
Babirusa
Boer goat
Bontebok
Boschbok
Bushbuck
Markhoor
Moufflon
Mule deer
Musk deer
Reedbuck
Reindeer
Steenbok
Wild boar
9 letters:
Blacktail
Dromedary
Hartbeest
Marshbuck
Mouse deer
Pronghorn
Razorback
Springbok
Waterbuck
10 letters:
Camelopard
Chevrotain
Hartebeest
Jacob sheep
Wildebeest
11 letters:
Barking deer
Cape buffalo
Kashmir goat
12 letters:
Hippopotamus
Klipspringer
Mountain goat
Water buffalo
13 letters:
Bactrian camel
Sable antelope
14 letters:
Père David's deer
15 letters:
White-tailed deer

See also:
➤ **Cows** ➤ **Pigs** ➤ **Sheep**

Cattle, breeds of

4 letters:
Aver
Gyal
Neat
Nout
Nowt
Soum
Sowm
Stot

5 letters:
Devon
Heard
Kerry
Kraal
Kyloe
Luing
Owsen
Store

6 letters:
Ankole
Catalo
Dexter
Durham
Jersey
Rother

Sussex

7 letters:
Brahman
Cattalo
Kouprey
Lairage
Lincoln
Red Poll

8 letters:
Alderney
Ayrshire
Charbray
Friesian
Galloway
Gelbvieh
Guernsey
Hereford
Highland
Holstein
Limousin
Longhorn
Normandy

9 letters:
Charolais
Friesland

Illawarra
Red Polled
Shorthorn
Simmental
Teeswater

10 letters:
Africander
Brown Swiss
Piemontese
Simmenthal
Welsh black

11 letters:
Chillingham

12 letters:
Norwegian Red

13 letters:
Aberdeen Angus
Texas Longhorn

14 letters:
Belted Galloway
Santa Gertrudis

Chairs

3 letters:
Pew
Tub

4 letters:
Bath
Camp
Cane
Club
Deck
Easy
Form
Pouf
Wing

5 letters:
Bench
Sedan
Stool
Súgán
Swing

6 letters:
Barrel
Basket
Bosun's
Carver
Corner
Curule

Dining
Estate
Garden
Jampan
Morris
Pouffe
Rocker
Settle
Swivel
Throne

7 letters:
Beanbag
Berbice
Bergère
Dos-à-dos
Folding
Guérite
Hassock
Jampani
Lounger
Ottoman
Rocking
Windsor

8 letters:
Armchair
Bar stool

Bentwood
Birthing
Campaign
Captain's
Cathedra
Electric
Fauteuil
Jampanee
Recliner
Straight
Wainscot

9 letters:
Banquette
Butterfly
Director's
Highchair
Opsitbank
Reclining

10 letters:
Bucket seat
Fiddle-back
Ladder-back
Music stool
Piano stool
Wheelchair
Window seat

11 letters:
Gestatorial
12 letters:
Milking stool

13 letters:
Shooting stick
Windsor rocker

14 letters:
Platform rocker

Champagne bottles

Bottle	Capacity
Magnum	2 bottles
Jeroboam	2 magnums
Rehoboam	3 magnums
Methuselah	4 magnums
Salmanazar	6 magnums
Balthazar	8 magnums
Nebuchadnezzar	10 magnums

Channels

3 letters:
Fox
5 letters:
North
6 letters:
Queen's
7 letters:
Bristol

English
Yucatán
8 letters:
Spithead
9 letters:
St George's
10 letters:
Mozambique

11 letters:
Solway Firth
12 letters:
Saint George's
14 letters:
Molucca Passage

Cheeses

3 letters:
Ewe
Fet
Oka
Pot
4 letters:
Blue
Brie
Curd
Edam
Feta
Goat
Hard
Skyr
Tofu
Yarg
5 letters:
Caboc
Cream
Derby
Esrom
Fynbo
Goats'
Gouda
Islay

Kenno
Quark
Samsø
6 letters:
Cantal
Chèvre
Damson
Dunlop
Ermite
Junket
Orkney
Romano
Tilsit
7 letters:
Boursin
Chaumes
Cheddar
Chessel
Cottage
Crowdie
Fontina
Gjetost
Gruyère
Havarti
Kebbock

Kebbuck
Limburg
Munster
Mycella
Ricotta
Sapsago
Stilton®
8 letters:
American
Bel Paese
Blue vein
Cheshire
Emmental
Halloumi
Huntsman
Muenster
Parmesan
Pecorino
Raclette
Taleggio
Tornegus
Vacherin
Vignotte
9 letters:
Amsterdam

Appenzell
Blue Vinny
Camembert
Emmenthal
Ilchester
Jarlsberg®
Killarney
Leicester
Limburger
Lymeswold®
Mousetrap
Port-Salut
Provolone
Reblochon
Roquefort
Sage Derby
Saint Agur
10 letters:
Blue Vinney

Bonchester
Caerphilly
Cambazolla
Canestrato
Danish blue
Dolcelatte
Emmentaler
Gloucester
Gorgonzola
Lanark Blue
Lancashire
Mascarpone
Mozzarella
Neufchâtel
Red Windsor
Stracchino
11 letters:
Blue Stilton
Coulommiers

Dunsyre Blue
Emmenthaler
Ribblesdale
Wensleydale
12 letters:
Bavarian blue
Bleu de Bresse
Caciocavallo
Fromage frais
Monterey jack
Red Leicester
13 letters:
Bleu d'Auvergne
14 letters:
Blue Shropshire

Chemical elements

Chemical element	Symbol	Atomic number
Actinium	Ac	89
Aluminium *or* aluminum	Al	13
Americium	Am	95
Antimony	Sb	51
Argon	Ar	18
Arsenic	As	33
Astatine	At	85
Barium	Ba	56
Berkelium	Bk	97
Beryllium	Be	4
Bismuth	Bi	83
Bohrium	Bh	107
Boron	B	5
Bromine	Br	35
Cadmium	Cd	48
Caesium *or* cesium	Cs	55
Calcium	Ca	20
Californium	Cf	98
Carbon	C	6
Cerium	Ce	58
Chlorine	Cl	17
Chromium	Cr	24
Cobalt	Co	27
Copper	Cu	29
Curium	Cm	96
Darmstadtium	Ds	110
Dubnium	Db	105
Dysprosium	Dy	66
Einsteinium	Es	99
Erbium	Er	68
Europium	Eu	63
Fermium	Fm	100
Fluorine	F	9

Chemical element	Symbol	Atomic number
Francium	Fr	87
Gadolinium	Gd	64
Gallium	Ga	31
Germanium	Ge	32
Gold	Au	79
Hafnium	Hf	72
Hassium	Hs	108
Helium	He	2
Holmium	Ho	67
Hydrogen	H	1
Indium	In	49
Iodine	I	53
Iridium	Ir	77
Iron	Fe	26
Krypton	Kr	36
Lanthanum	La	57
Lawrencium	Lr	103
Lead	Pb	82
Lithium	Li	3
Lutetium *or* lutecium	Lu	71
Magnesium	Mg	12
Manganese	Mn	25
Meitnerium	Mt	109
Mendelevium	Md	101
Mercury	Hg	80
Molybdenum	Mo	42
Neodymium	Nd	60
Neon	Ne	10
Neptunium	Np	93
Nickel	Ni	28
Niobium	Nb	41
Nitrogen	N	7
Nobelium	No	102
Osmium	Os	76
Oxygen	O	8
Palladium	Pd	46
Phosphorus	P	15
Platinum	Pt	78
Plutonium	Pu	94
Polonium	Po	84
Potassium	K	19
Praseodymium	Pr	59
Promethium	Pm	61
Protactinium	Pa	91
Radium	Ra	88
Radon	Rn	86
Rhenium	Re	75
Rhodium	Rh	45
Roentgenium	Rg	111
Rubidium	Rb	37
Ruthenium	Ru	44
Rutherfordium	Rf	104
Samarium	Sm	62
Scandium	Sc	21
Seaborgium	Sg	106
Selenium	Se	34

Chemical element	Symbol	Atomic number
Silicon	Si	14
Silver	Ag	47
Sodium	Na	11
Strontium	Sr	38
Sulphur *or* sulfur	S	16
Tantalum	Ta	73
Technetium	Tc	43
Tellurium	Te	52
Terbium	Tb	65
Thallium	Tl	81
Thorium	Th	90
Thulium	Tm	69
Tin	Sn	50
Titanium	Ti	22
Tungsten *or* wolfram	W	74
Uranium	U	92
Vanadium	V	23
Xenon	Xe	54
Ytterbium	Yb	70
Yttrium	Y	39
Zinc	Zn	30
Zirconium	Zr	40

Chemistry

BRANCHES OF CHEMISTRY

7 letters:
Nuclear
Organic
Zymurgy
8 letters:
Chemurgy
Kinetics
Physical
9 letters:
Inorganic
10 letters:
Analytical

12 letters:
Biochemistry
Geochemistry
Zoochemistry
13 letters:
Cytochemistry
Stoichiometry
14 letters:
Astrochemistry
Histochemistry
Neurochemistry
Petrochemistry

Phonochemistry
Photochemistry
Phytochemistry
Radiochemistry
15 letters:
Immunochemistry
Stereochemistry
Thermochemistry

CHEMISTRY TERMS

2 letters:
pH
3 letters:
Fat
Gas
Ion
Oil
Ore
4 letters:
Acid
Atom

Base
Bond
Foam
Fuel
Mole
Salt
Soap
5 letters:
Alloy
Anion
Anode

Chain
Ester
Ether
Inert
Metal
Solid
Sugar
6 letters:
Alkali
Alkane
Cation

Dilute
Fusion
Isomer
Liquid
Proton
7 letters:
Alcohol
Cathode
Crystal
Element
Fission
Formula
Halogen
Isotope
Mineral
Mixture
Monomer
Neutral
Neutron
Nucleus
Organic
Plastic
Polymer
Reagent
Soluble
Solvent
Valency
8 letters:
Analysis
Catalyst
Compound
Electron

Emulsion
Equation
Inert gas
Molarity
Molecule
Noble gas
Nonmetal
Reaction
Solution
9 letters:
Allotrope
Amino acid
Corrosion
Diffusion
Electrode
Fatty acid
Inorganic
Insoluble
Ionic bond
Metalloid
Oxidation
Reduction
Saturated
Synthesis
10 letters:
Atomic mass
Combustion
Hydrolysis
Ionization
Lanthanide
Litmus test
Suspension

11 letters:
Alkali metal
Evaporation
Hydrocarbon
Precipitate
Sublimation
Unsaturated
12 letters:
Atomic number
Boiling point
Carbohydrate
Concentrated
Condensation
Covalent bond
Distillation
Electrolysis
Fermentation
Melting point
13 letters:
Chain reaction
Periodic table
Radioactivity
Redox reaction
14 letters:
Brownian motion
Chromatography
Electrovalency
Saponification
15 letters:
Crystallization
Transition metal

CHEMISTS

4 letters:
Auer, *Karl*
Caro, *Heinrich*
Davy, *Humphrey*
Hall, *Charles Martin*
Hill, *Archibald Vivian*
Kipp, *Petrus Jacobus*
Mond, *Ludwig*
Swan, *Joseph Wilson*
Todd, *Alexander Robert*
Urey, *Harold Clayton*
5 letters:
Abney, *William*
Adams, *Roger*
Aston, *Francis William*
Baumé, *Antoine*
Black, *James (Whyte)*
Black, *Joseph*
Bosch, *Carl*
Boyle, *Robert*
Brown, *Herbert Charles*

Curie, *Marie*
Curie, *Pierre*
Dakin, *Henry*
Debye, *Peter Joseph Wilhelm*
Dewar, *James*
Dumas, *Jean-Baptiste André*
Eigen, *Manfred*
Ernst, *Richard Robert*
Haber, *Fritz*
Henry, *William*
Hooke, *Robert*
Libby, *Willard Frank*
Nobel, *Alfred Bernhard*
Prout, *William*
Soddy, *Frederick*
6 letters:
Barton, *Derek*
Brandt, *Georg*
Bunsen, *Robert Wilhelm*
Calvin, *Melvin*
Carver, *Geroge Washington*

Dalton, *John*
Draper, *John William*
Kekulé, *August*
Liebig, *Justus*
Morley, *Edward Williams*
Müller, *Paul Hermann*
Mullis, *Kary Banks*
Nernst, *Walther Hermann*
Perutz, *Max Ferdinand*
Porter, *George*
Proust, *Joseph Louis*
Ramsay, *William*
Schiff, *Hugo*
Solvay, *Ernest*
Tizard, *Henry*
Werner, *Alfred*
Wöhler, *Friedrich*
Woulfe, *Peter*
7 letters:
Abelson, *Philip*
Andrews, *Thomas*
Bergius, *Friedrich (Karl Rudolph)*
Buchner, *Eduard*
Castner, *Hamilton Young*
Crookes, *William*
Faraday, *Michael*
Fischer, *Emil Hermann*
Fischer, *Ernst Otto*
Fischer, *Hans*
Gadolin, *Johan*
Gomberg, *Moses*
Guthrie, *Samuel*
Hodgkin, *Dorothy Crowfoot*
Leblanc, *Nicolas*
Macadam, *John*
Ostwald, *Wilhelm*
Pasteur, *Louis*
Pauling, *Linus Carl*
Piccard, *Jean Félix*
Scheele, *Karl Wilhelm*

Seaborg, *Glenn Theodore*
Von Babo, *Lambert*
Warburg, *Otto Heinrich*
Ziegler, *Carl*
8 letters:
Beckmann, *Ernst Otto*
Grignard, *Victor*
Langmuir, *Irving*
Mulliken, *Robert Sanderson*
Newlands, *John Alexander*
Sabatier, *Paul*
Silliman, *Benjamin*
Smithson, *James*
Sorensen, *Soren Peter Lauritz*
Van't Hoff, *Jacobus Hendricus*
Woodward, *R(obert) B(urns)*
9 letters:
Arrhenius, *Svante August*
Butenandt, *Adolf Frederick Johann*
Cavendish, *Henry*
Cornforth, *John Warcup*
Gay-Lussac, *Joseph Louis*
Lavoisier, *Antoine Laurent*
Pelletier, *Pierre Joseph*
Priestley, *Joseph*
Prigogine, *Ilya*
Von Baeyer, *Johann Friedrich*
    Wilhelm Adolf
Von Hevesy, *George*
Zsigmondy, *Richard Adolf*
10 letters:
Chardonnet, *(Louis Marie)*
    Hilaire Bernigaud
Erlenmeyer, *Emil*
Mendeleyev, *Dmitri Ivanovich*
Van Helmont, *Jean Baptiste*
13 letters:
Von Stradonitz, *(Friedrich)*
    August Kekulé

See also:
➤ Acids ➤ Alcohols ➤ Alkalis ➤ Alloys
➤ Chemical elements ➤ Compounds ➤ Crystals
➤ Hydrocarbons ➤ Minerals ➤ Molecules ➤ Ores
➤ Salts ➤ Silicas and Silicates
➤ Subatomic particles ➤ Sugars

Chinaware

4 letters:	**5 letters:**	Seric
Goss	Delft	Spode®
Ming	Derby	Wally
Waly	Hizen	**6 letters:**
Ware	Imari	Kaolin

Minton
7 letters:
Crackle
Dresden
Limoges
Meissen

8 letters:
Coalport
Eggshell
Etrurian
Wedgwood®

9 letters:
Cameoware
Porcelain
10 letters:
Rockingham
Willowware

Cities

4 letters:	Kazan	Cracow
Baku	Kyoto	Dallas
Bari	Lagos	Dayton
Bonn	La Paz	Denver
Brno	Leeds	Dublin
Cork	Lyons	Dundee
Gifu	Malmo	Durban
Giza	Mecca	El Paso
Graz	Miami	Frunze
Homs	Milan	Fukoka
Hull	Mosul	Fushun
Ipoh	Omaha	Fuzhou
Kano	Osaka	Gdansk
Kiel	Padua	Geneva
Kiev	Paris	Harbin
Kobe	Patna	Havana
Lima	Perth	Ibadan
Lodz	Poona	Indore
Nice	Quito	Jaipur
Omsk	Rabat	Kanpur
Oran	Sakai	Kansas
Oslo	Seoul	Khulna
Riga	Sofia	Kumasi
Rome	Surat	Lahore
5 letters:	Tampa	Lisbon
Accra	Tokyo	London
Adana	Tomsk	Luanda
Amman	Tunis	Lübeck
Basle	Turin	Lusaka
Basra	**6 letters:**	Madras
Belem	Aachen	Madrid
Berne	Abadan	Magpur
Bursa	Aleppo	Málaga
Cairo	Ankara	Malang
Chiba	Asmara	Manila
Dacca	Athens	Mexico
Davao	Austin	Moscow
Delhi	Baroda	Multan
Essen	Beirut	Mumbai
Genoa	Berlin	Munich
Gorky	Bilbao	Mysore
Haifa	Bochum	Nantes
Halle	Bogota	Naples
Hanoi	Bombay	Newark
Izmir	Boston	Odessa
Kabul	Bremen	Oporto

Ottawa
Oxford
Panama
Peking
Penang
Poznan
Prague
Puebla
Quebec
St Paul
Santos
Shiraz
Suzhou
Sydney
Tabriz
Taipei
Talinn
Toledo
Venice
Verona
Vienna
Warsaw
Zagreb
Zürich

7 letters:
Abidjan
Algiers
Antwerp
Atlanta
Baghdad
Bangkok
Barnaul
Belfast
Bologna
Brescia
Bristol
Buffalo
Caracas
Cardiff
Chengdu
Chennai
Chicago
Cologne
Colombo
Córdoba
Corunna
Detroit
Donetsk
Dresden
Firenze
Foochow
Glasgow
Gwalior
Hamburg
Hanover
Houston

Irkutsk
Isfahan
Jakarta
Kalinin
Karachi
Kharkov
Kolkata
Kowloon
Kwangju
La Plata
Leipzig
Lucknow
Managua
Memphis
Messina
Mombasa
Nairobi
Nanjing
New York
Oakland
Palermo
Phoenix
Rangoon
Rosario
St Louis
San Jose
San Juan
Santa Fe
Sapporo
Saratov
Seattle
Seville
Stettin
Taranto
Tbilisi
Teheran
Tel Aviv
Toronto
Trieste
Tripoli
Utrecht

8 letters:
Aberdeen
Adelaide
Amritsar
Auckland
Augsburg
Belgrade
Bordeaux
Bradford
Brasilia
Brisbane
Brussels
Budapest
Bulawayo
Cagliari

Calcutta
Campinas
Canberra
Capetown
Columbus
Coventry
Curitiba
Damascus
Dortmund
Duisborg
Edmonton
Florence
Gorlovka
Hague, The
Haiphong
Hamilton
Hangchou
Helsinki
Honolulu
Istanbul
Katmandu
Katowice
Khartoum
Kingston
Kinshasa
Kumamoto
Kweiyang
Mandalay
Mannheim
Montreal
Murmansk
Nagasaki
Oklahoma
Peshawar
Plymouth
Portland
Port Said
Pretoria
Pyongang
Richmond
Salonika
Salt Lake
San Diego
Santiago
Sao Paulo
Sarajevo
Shanghai
Sholapur
Srinagar
Tashkent
Tientsin
Toulouse
Winnipeg
Yokohama

9 letters:
Ahmedabad

Allahabad
Amagasaki
Amsterdam
Archangel
Asahikawa
Astrakhan
Baltimore
Bangalore
Barcelona
Brunswick
Bucharest
Cambridge
Cartagena
Chengchou
Chihuahua
Cleveland
Des Moines
Edinburgh
Fort Worth
Frankfurt
Guatemala
Guayaquil
Hamamatsu
Hiroshima
Hyderabad
Jerusalem
Karlsruhe
Krasnodar
Krivoi Rog
Kuibyshev
Kwangchou
Las Palmas
Leicester
Leningrad
Liverpool
Magdeburg
Maracaibo
Marrakesh
Melbourne
Milwaukee
Nuremberg

Reykjavik
Rotterdam
Salisbury
Samarkand
Saragossa
Sheffield
Singapore
Stockholm
Stuttgart
Vancouver
Volgograd
Wuppertal
10 letters:
Addis Ababa
Alexandria
Baton Rouge
Birmingham
Bratislava
Canterbury
Casablanca
Chittagong
Cincinnati
Coimbatore
Copenhagen
Düsseldorf
Gothenburg
Jamshedpur
Los Angeles
Louisville
Manchester
Marseilles
Monte Video
New Orleans
Nottingham
Pittsburgh
Portsmouth
Rawalpindi
Sacramento
San Antonio
Strasbourg
Sunderland

Sverdlovsk
Tananarive
Valparaiso
Washington
Wellington
11 letters:
Baranquilla
Braunshweig
Buenos Aires
Chelyabinsk
Dar-es-Salaam
Guadalajara
Kuala Lumpur
Mar del Plata
Novosibirsk
Pondicherry
Rostov-on-Don
San Salvador
Southampton
Vladivostok
12 letters:
Barquisimeto
Bloemfontein
Indianapolis
Jacksonville
Johannesburg
Magnitogorsk
Philadelphia
Port-au-Prince
Rio de Janeiro
San Francisco
Santo Domingo
Stoke-on-Trent
13 letters:
Gelsenkirchen
Karl-Marx-Stadt
Port Elizabeth
Shihkiachwang
Wolverhampton
14 letters:
Dnepropetrovsk

Clothing

ARTICLES OF CLOTHING

3 letters:
Aba
Alb
Tie
4 letters:
Abba
Body
Bubu
Coat
Gown

Haik
Hose
Izar
Kilt
Muff
Rami
Robe
Sari
Sash
Shoe

Slop
Sock
Toga
Vest
Wrap
5 letters:
Abaya
Ao dai
Apron
Burka

Burqa
Cardy
Chaps
Cimar
Cotta
Dress
Ephod
Fanon
Frock
Gilet
Glove
Ihram
Jupon
Kanga
Kanzu
Levis
Pilch
Plaid
Ramée
Ramie
Ruana
Saree
Shawl
Shift
Shirt
Smock
Stola
Stole
Tanga
Thong
Tunic
6 letters:
Barrow
Basque
Bikini
Blouse
Bodice
Bolero
Boubou
Braces
Caftan
Cardie
Chador
Chimer
Cilice
Coatee
Cossie
Dirndl
Dolman
Exomis
Garter
Halter
Jacket
Jerkin
Jersey
Jibbah
Jubbah

Jumper
Kaftan
Kameez
Kaross
Khanga
Kimono
Kittel
Mantle
Mitten
Peplos
Rochet
Sarong
Serape
Shorts
Skivvy
Tabard
Tallit
Tights
Trunks
T-shirt
Zephyr
7 letters:
Baldric
Blouson
Bourkha
Burnous
Bustier
Busuuti
Catsuit
Chapeau
Chuddah
Chuddar
Chudder
Costume
Dashiki
Djibbah
Doublet
Exomion
Hauberk
Leotard
Maillot
Manteau
Necktie
Nightie
Overall
Pajamas
Paletot
Pallium
Partlet
Pelisse
Pyjamas
Rompers
Shalwar
Singlet
Soutane
Sporran
Surcoat

Sweater
Tank top
Tunicle
Unitard
Wrapper
Yashmac
Yashmak
8 letters:
Bathrobe
Bodysuit
Cardigan
Chasuble
Chausses
Codpiece
Dalmatic
Galluses
Gambeson
Himation
Jump suit
Negligée
Overcoat
Pashmina
Peignoir
Pelerine
Pullover
Scapular
Surplice
Swimsuit
Tee shirt
9 letters:
Cover-slut
Dungarees
Housecoat
Loincloth
Mandilion
Mandylion
Nightgown
Overskirt
Pantihose
Pantyhose
Sanbenito
Waistcoat
10 letters:
Chaparajos
Chaparejos
Cote-hardie
Cummerbund
Jeistiecor
Kummerbund
Nightdress
Nightshirt
Oversleeve
Salopettes
Suspenders
11 letters:
Bathing suit
Bib and brace

Breechcloth
Dreadnought
12 letters:
Body stocking

Dressing gown
Undergarment
14 letters:
Bathing costume

Swimming trunks
15 letters:
Swimming
  costume

TYPES OF CLOTHING

4 letters:
Hose
5 letters:
Mufti
Slops
6 letters:
Armour
Civies
Livery
Samfoo
7 letters:
Civvies
Hosiery
Uniform
Weepers
8 letters:
Black tie
Fatigues
Froufrou

Knitwear
Lingerie
Neckwear
Skivvies
Swimwear
White tie
9 letters:
Beachwear
Clericals
Coveralls
Long-coats
Millinery
Nightwear
Sackcloth
Separates
Underwear
10 letters:
Canonicals
Fancy dress

Sportswear
11 letters:
Baby clothes
Coordinates
Long clothes
Underthings
Widow's weeds
12 letters:
Evening dress
Morning dress
Nightclothes
Overgarments
13 letters:
Academic dress
Highland dress
Undergarments

See also:
➤ **Caps** ➤ **Coats and Cloaks** ➤ **Dresses** ➤ **Hats** ➤ **Hoods**
➤ **Jackets** ➤ **Scarves** ➤ **Shirts** ➤ **Shoes and Boots** ➤ **Skirts**
➤ **Sweaters** ➤ **Ties and Cravats** ➤ **Trousers and Shorts**
➤ **Underwear**

Clouds

3 letters:
Fog
4 letters:
Haze
Mist
5 letters:
Storm
6 letters:
Cirrus
Nimbus
7 letters:

Cumulus
Strat(o)us
8 letters:
Water-dog
Woolpack
9 letters:
Goat's hair
Mare's tail
11 letters:
Altocumulus
Altostratus

False cirrus
Thunderhead
12 letters:
Cirrocumulus
Cirrostratus
Cumulonimbus
Nimbostratus
13 letters:
Fractocumulus
Fractostratus
Stratocumulus

Clubs

3 letters:
RAC
4 letters:
Bath

Golf
5 letters:
Disco
Slate

Youth
6 letters:
Brook's
Cotton

Drones
Guards
Jockey
Kitcat
Monday
Reform
Rotary
Savage
Savile
White's
7 letters:
Adelphi
Almack's
Boodles
Carlton
Cavalry
Country

Garrick
Hampden
Jacobin
Kiwanis
Leander
Variety
8 letters:
Atheneum
Hell-fire
Rotarian
9 letters:
Athenaeum
Beefsteak
10 letters:
Crockford's
Devonshire
Landsdowne

Oddfellows
Travellers
11 letters:
Army and Navy
Caterpillar
Discotheque
12 letters:
Conservative
13 letters:
Junior Carlton
Thatched House
14 letters:
Constitutional
United Services
15 letters:
National Liberal

Clubs and bats

3 letters:
Bat
4 letters:
Cosh
Kiri
Mace
Maul
Mell
Mere
Meri
Patu
Polt
5 letters:
Basto
Lathi

Waddy
6 letters:
Alpeen
Cudgel
Kierie
Priest
7 letters:
Bourdon
8 letters:
Bludgeon
Shillala
Trunnion
9 letters:
Blackjack
Knobstick

Truncheon
10 letters:
Knobkerrie
Nightstick
Nulla-nulla
Shillelagh
12 letters:
Quarterstaff
13 letters:
Life preserver

Coats and cloaks

3 letters:
Aba
Box
Car
Fur
Mac
Top
4 letters:
Abba
Capa
Cape
Cope
Hair
Hood
Jack
Jump
Mack

Polo
Rail
Sack
Seal
Tail
Tent
Toga
Warm
Wool
5 letters:
Abaya
Acton
Amice
Dress
Frock
Grego
Jelab

Jemmy
Jupon
Lammy
Loden
Manta
Palla
Parka
Pilch
Sagum
Tails
6 letters:
Abolla
Achkan
Afghan
Anarak
Anorak
Capote

Chimer
Coatee
Covert
Dolman
Domino
Duffel
Duster
Fleece
Fun fur
Jacket
Jerkin
Joseph
Kaross
Lammie
Mantle
Parkee
Peplum
Poncho
Raglan
Riding
Tippet
Trench
Tuxedo
Ulster
Vestry
Visite

7 letters:
Admiral
Burnous
Cassock
Chimere
Chlamys
Chuddah
Chuddar
Crombie®
Cutaway
Galabea
Galabia
Hacking
Jellaba
Manteel
Mantlet
Matinee
Morning
Mozetta
Paenula
Paletot

Pallium
Peacoat
Pelisse
Posteen
Rocklay
Rokelay
Sarafan
Slicker
Snorkel
Spencer
Surcoat
Surtout
Swagger
Topcoat
Zamarra
Zamarro

8 letters:
Barathea
Bathrobe
Benjamin
Burberry®
Burnoose
Burnouse
Capuchin
Cardinal
Chasuble
Djellaba
Galabieh
Gambeson
Hall-robe
Haqueton
Himation
Jellabah
Jodhpuri
Mackinaw
Mantelet
Mantilla
Overcoat
Peignoir
Poshteen
Raincoat
Revestry
Scapular
Sherwani
Taglioni
Tailcoat
Vestiary

9 letters:
Balmacaan
Caracalla
Chlamydes
Coat dress
Djellabah
Gabardine
Gaberdine
Gallabeah
Greatcoat
Hacqueton
Housecoat
Inverness
Macintosh
Newmarket
Opera hood
Pea jacket
Petersham
Redingote
Sheepskin
Sou'wester
Undercoat

10 letters:
Fearnaught
Fearnought
Gallabiyah
Gallabiyeh
Mackintosh
Opera cloak
Roquelaure
Ulsterette
Waterproof
Windjammer
Wrap-rascal

11 letters:
Dreadnaught
Dreadnought
Swallowtail

12 letters:
Chesterfield
Dressing gown
Mousquetaire
Paludamentum
Prince Albert

13 letters:
Swallow-tailed

Coins

1 letter:	Rd	Cob	Flu
D	Xu	Dam	Hao
2 letters:	**3 letters:**	Ecu	Jun
As	Ban	Fen	Kip
DM	Bar	Fil	Lat
Kr	Bob	Fin	Lei

Lek
Leu
Lev
Lew
Mil
Mna
Moy
Ore
Pul
Pya
Red
Sen
Sol
Som
Sou
Won
Yen
Zuz

4 letters:
Anna
Baht
Bani
Birr
Buck
Cedi
Cent
Chon
Dibs
Dime
Doit
Dong
Dram
Duro
Euro
Fiat
Fils
Inti
Jack
Jane
Jiao
Kina
Kobo
Kuna
Kyat
Lari
Lion
Lira
Loti
Maik
Mark
Merk
Mina
Obol
Para
Paul
Peag
Peni

Peso
Pice
Pula
Puli
Punt
Rand
Real
Reis
Rial
Riel
Rock
Ryal
Sene
Slog
Spur
Tael
Taka
Tala
Toea
Vatu
Yuan
Zack

5 letters:
Agora
Angel
Asper
Aurar
Baiza
Bekah
Belga
Bodle
Broad
Brown
Butat
Butut
Chiao
Colon
Conto
Crore
Crown
Daric
Dibbs
Dinar
Dobra
Ducat
Eagle
Eyrir
Franc
Fugio
Gerah
Groat
Grosz
Haler
Krona
Krone
Kroon
Kurus

Laari
Laree
Leone
Liard
Litas
Livre
Louis
Lyart
Maile
Manat
Maneh
Mohur
Mongo
Mopus
Naira
Nakfa
Ngwee
Noble
Obang
Oscar
Paisa
Paolo
Pence
Pengo
Penie
Penni
Penny
Plack
Pound
Razoo
Rider
Royal
Ruble
Rupee
Sceat
Scudo
Scute
Semis
Sente
Shand
Soldo
Souon
Sucre
Sycee
Tenge
Thebe
Tical
Ticky
Tolar
Toman
Tyiyn
Zaire
Zimbi
Zloty

6 letters:
Aureus
Balboa

Bawbee
Bender
Bezant
Boddle
Byzant
Canary
Centas
Copeck
Couter
Dalasi
Danace
Deaner
Décime
Denier
Derham
Dirham
Dirhem
Dodkin
Dollar
Double
Drachm
Ekuele
Escudo
Filler
Florin
Forint
Gilder
Gourde
Guinea
Gulden
Halala
Heller
Hryvna
Jitney
Kobang
Koruna
Kroner
Kroona
Kwacha
Kwanza
Lepton
Likuta
Loonie
Makuta
Mancus
Markka
Mawpus
Pa'anga
Pagoda
Pataca
Pennia
Peseta
Pesewa
Qintar
Rappen
Rouble
Rupiah

Santum
Satang
Sceatt
Seniti
Sequin
Shekel
Sickle
Siglos
Stater
Stiver
Stotin
Talent
Tanner
Tester
Teston
Thaler
Tickey
Toonie
Tugrik
Turner
Vellon
Wakiki

7 letters:
Afghani
Austral
Bolivar
Cardecu
Carolus
Centavo
Chetrum
Cordoba
Crusado
Drachma
Ekpwele
Guarani
Guilder
Hryvnya
Jacobus
Joannes
Kreuzer
Lemoira
Metical
Millime
Milreis
Moidore

Ostmark
Ouguiya
Patrick
Piastre
Piefort
Pistole
Pollard
Quarter
Quetzal
Ringgit
Ruddock
Rufiyaa
Sextans
Solidus
Spanker
Tambala
Testoon
Testril
Thrimsa
Thrymsa
Tughrik
Unicorn
Xerafin

8 letters:
Brockage
Cardecue
Cruzeiro
Denarius
Doubloon
Ducatoon
Emalengi
Farthing
Groschen
Johannes
Kreutzer
Llangeni
Louis d'or
Maravedi
Millieme
Napoleon
Ngultrum
Picayune
Pistolet
Planchet
Portague

Portigue
Quadrans
Rigmarie
Semuncia
Sesterce
Shilling
Skilling
Solidare
Stotinka
Xeraphin
Zecchino

9 letters:
Boliviano
Britannia
Centesimo
Dandiprat
Dandyprat
Didrachma
Dupondius
Luckpenny
Pistareen
Rennminbi
Rix-dollar
Rose noble
Schilling
Sovereign
Spur-royal
Yellowboy
Zwanziger

10 letters:
Broadpiece
Chervonets
Krugerrand
Portcullis
Reichsmark

11 letters:
Deutschmark
Sword-dollar
Tetradrachm

12 letters:
Antoninianus

13 letters:
Rennminbi yuan

Collective nouns

Noun	Collective noun
Actors	Company
Aldermen	Bench, guzzle
Bakers	Tabernacle
Bishops	Bench
Critics	Shrivel
Directors	Board
Eggs	Clutch

Noun	Collective noun
Flowers	Bouquet
Inventions	Budget
Judges	Bench
People	Audience, crowd, congregation, horde, mob
Poems	Garland
Policemen	Posse
Prisoners	Gang
Remedies	Rabble
Rumours	Nest
Sailors	Crew
Ships	Fleet
Stories	Anthology
Thieves	Gang
Workmen	Gang

See also:
➤ **Animals**

Collectors and enthusiasts

Collector/Enthusiast	Object
Ailurophile	Cats
Arctophile	Teddy bears
Audiophile	High-fidelity sound reproduction
Automobilist	Cars
Bibliophile	Books
Brolliologist	Umbrellas
Campanologist	Bell-ringing
Cartophilist	Cigarette cards
Cruciverbalist	Crosswords
Deltiologist	Picture postcards
Discophile	Gramophone records
Fusilatelist	Phonecards
Herbalist	Herbs
Lepidopterist	Moths and butterflies
Medallist	Medals
Numismatist	Coins
Oenophile	Wine
Paranumismatist	Coin-like objects
Philatelist	Stamps
Phillumenist	Matchbox labels
Phraseologist	Phrases
Scripophile	Share certificates
Vexillologist	Flags
Zoophile	Animals

Colleges

3 letters:	Eton	Taft
New	Fife	York
4 letters:	Iona	**5 letters:**
City	Reed	Bates
Dana	Snow	Chase

Clare
Green
Jesus
Keble
King's
Oriel
Peace
Ripon
Salem
Smith
Union
Wells
6 letters:
Bethel
Boston
Darwin
Durham
Exeter
Geneva
Girton
Gordon
Hebrew
Ithaca
Merton
Queen's
Selwyn
Thomas
Vassar
Wadham
7 letters:
Amherst
Aquinas
Balliol
Barnard
Bedford
Bermuda
Bowdoin
Chatham
Christ's
Concord
Cornell
Cypress
Douglas
Downing
Emerson

Erskine
Kellogg
Linacre
Lincoln
Newnham
St Anne's
St Cross
St Hugh's
St John's
St Paul's
Trinity
Wolfson
8 letters:
All Souls
Bryn Mawr
Carleton
Columbia
Emmanuel
Findhorn
Hamilton
Hastings
Hertford
Homerton
Illinois
Imperial
Lewisham
Longwood
Magdalen
Meredith
Monmouth
National
Nuffield
Pembroke
Robinson
St Hilda's
St Peter's
9 letters:
Brasenose
Churchill
Clare Hall
Claremont
Gateshead
Guildford
Hampshire
Haverford

Kalamazoo
Lafayette
Magdalene
Manhattan
Mansfield
Newcastle
St Antony's
St Edmund's
Templeton
Wellesley
Worcester
10 letters:
Chesapeake
Goldsmith's
Greyfriars
Heidelberg
Hughes Hall
Huntingdon
Middlebury
Paul Smith's
Peterhouse
Somerville
St Stephen's
University
Washington
11 letters:
Blackfriars
Campion Hall
Fitzwilliam
King Alfred's
Regent's Park
Springfield
Trinity Hall
12 letters:
Christ Church
Sidney Sussex
St Benet's Hall
St Catharine's
St Catherine's
St Edmund Hall
Wycliffe Hall
13 letters:
Corpus Christi
Lucy Cavendish
Murray Edwards

See also:
➤ **Education terms** ➤ **Ivy League universities** ➤ **Oxbridge colleges** ➤ **Schools**

Colours

3 letters:
Jet
Red
Tan
4 letters:
Anil
Blue
Ecru
Fawn
Gold
Grey
Iris
Jade
Navy
Onyx
Opal
Pink
Plum
Puce
Rose
Ruby
Rust
Sand
Sage
5 letters:
Amber
Beige
Black
Brown
Cocoa
Coral
Cream
Ebony
Green
Hazel
Henna
Ivory
Khaki

Lemon
Lilac
Mauve
Ochre
Olive
Peach
Pearl
Sepia
Slate
Taupe
Topaz
Umber
White
6 letters:
Auburn
Blonde
Bottle
Bronze
Canary
Cerise
Cherry
Claret
Cobalt
Copper
Indigo
Maroon
Orange
Purple
Russet
Salmon
Silver
Violet
Walnut
Yellow
7 letters:
Apricot
Avocado
Biscuit

Caramel
Crimson
Emerald
Fuchsia
Gentian
Magenta
Mustard
Saffron
Scarlet
8 letters:
Burgundy
Charcoal
Chestnut
Cinnamon
Eau de nil
Lavender
Magnolia
Mahogany
Sapphire
Viridian
9 letters:
Aubergine
Chocolate
Pistachio
Tangerine
Turquoise
Vermilion
10 letters:
Aquamarine
Chartreuse
Cobalt blue
Terracotta
11 letters:
Burnt sienna
Lemon yellow
Ultramarine

Comets

4 letters:
Wild
West
8 letters:
Borrelly
Hale-Bopp

Kohoutek
McNaught
9 letters:
Hyakutake
Ikeya-Seki
Oort cloud

11 letters:
Swift-Tuttle
12 letters:
Halley's Comet
13 letters:
Shoemaker-Levy

Commonwealth members

4 letters:
Fiji
5 letters:
Ghana
India
Kenya
Malta
Nauru
Samoa
Tonga
6 letters:
Belize
Brunei
Canada
Cyprus
Guyana
Malawi
Rwanda
Tuvalu
Uganda
Zambia
7 letters:
Grenada

Jamaica
Lesotho
Namibia
Nigeria
St Lucia
Vanuatu
8 letters:
Barbados
Botswana
Cameroon
Dominica
Kiribati
Malaysia
Maldives
Pakistan
Sri Lanka
Tanzania
Zimbabwe
9 letters:
Australia
Mauritius
Singapore
Swaziland

The Gambia
10 letters:
Bangladesh
Mozambique
New Zealand
Seychelles
The Bahamas
11 letters:
Sierra Leone
South Africa
13 letters:
United Kingdom
14 letters:
Papua New Guinea
Solomon Islands
15 letters:
St Kitts and Nevis

Communications

2 letters:
IT
PA
3 letters:
BCD
Cue
Dah
Dit
Dot
DVD
FAQ
Fax
FTP
IAP
ICT
ISP
LAN
Net
Out
TMT
URL
WAN
WAP
Web
XML
4 letters:
Alfa
Byte

CCTA
Code
Dash
Data
E-CRM
E-FIT
HTML
Java
Link
Mail
Mast
Over
Page
SGML
Site
Spam
WiFi
Worm
5 letters:
Bleep
Carry
Comms
Crier
Datum
DOVAP
Email
Flame
GMDSS

Inbox
Media
Modem
Pager
Radar
Radio
Stamp
Telex
Virus
6 letters:
Aerial
Browse
Cipher
Codify
Convey
Decode
Direct
Encode
Letter
Mayday
Medium
Nettie
Newbie
Outbox
Return
Server
Trojan
Usenet

7 letters:
Bleeper
Browser
Courier
Decrypt
DEW line
Digital
Dossier
En clair
Encrypt
Entropy
Evernet
E-wallet
Lurking
Message
Meta tag
Nethead
Netizen
Network
Tapping
Webcast
Web page
Website
8 letters:
Anti-site
Blocking
Boob tube
Chatroom
Codeword
Computer
Coverage
Data bank
Database
Decipher
Diaphone
Dispatch
Disperse
E-address
Envelope
E-payment
Ethernet
Firewall

Internet
Intranet
Listen in
Minidish
New media
Postmark
Register
Registry
Semaphor
Wireless
9 letters:
Aldis lamp
Bandwidth
Bluetooth
Broadband
Cybercafé
Digital TV
Direction
Directory
E-commerce
Facsimile
Frequency
Hypertext
Mass media
Morse code
Paperless
Royal Mail
Satellite
Snail mail
Telephone
Time-stamp
10 letters:
Beam aerial
Come across
Correspond
Dead letter
Degenerate
Fax machine
JavaScript
Media event
Memorandum
Multimedia

Netiquette
Silicon Fen
Ticker tape
Ultrafiche
Undirected
11 letters:
Address book
Chain letter
Communicate
Cryptograph
Dactylology
Mailing list
Mobile phone
Safe surfing
Silicon Glen
12 letters:
Cause célèbre
Conversation
Cryptography
Email address
Registration
Silicon Alley
Silver surfer
13 letters:
Bandspreading
Communication
Communicative
Correspondent
Cryptanalysis
Dead letter box
Dispatch rider
Online banking
Rural delivery
Satellite dish
Silicon Valley
14 letters:
Conversational
Correspondence
Electronic mail
Registered post

Composers

CLASSICAL COMPOSERS

3 letters:
Bax, *Arnold*
4 letters:
Adam, *Adolphe*
Arne, *Thomas*
Bach, *Carl Philipp Emanuel*
Bach, *Johann Christian*
Bach, *Johann Christoph Friedrich*
Bach, *Johann Sebastian*

Bach, *Wilhelm Friedemann*
Berg, *Alban*
Blow, *John*
Bull, *John*
Byrd, *William*
Cage, *John*
Dima, *Gheorghe*
Ives, *Charles*
Lalo, *Édouard*

Nono, *Luigi*
Orff, *Carl*
Pärt, *Arvo*
Peri, *Jacopo*
Raff, *Joachim*
Ward, *David*
Weir, *Judith*
Wolf, *Hugo*
5 letters:
Adams, *John*
Alwyn, *William*
Auber, *Daniel François Espirit*
Auric, *Georges*
Balfe, *Michael William*
Berio, *Luciano*
Biber, *Heinrich*
Bizet, *Georges*
Bliss, *Arthur*
Bloch, *Ernest*
Boito, *Arrigo*
Boyce, *William*
Brian, *Havergal*
Bruch, *Max*
Crumb, *George*
D'Indy, *Vincent*
Dukas, *Paul*
Dupré, *Marcel*
Dutch, *Jan Pieterszoon Sweelinck*
Elgar, *Edward*
Fauré, *Gabriel*
Field, *John*
Finzi, *Gerald*
Glass, *Philip*
Gluck, *Christoph Willibald*
Grieg, *Edvard*
Harty, *Sir (Herbert) Hamilton*
Haydn, *Franz Joseph*
Haydn, *Michael*
Henze, *Hans Werner*
Holst, *Gustav*
Ibert, *Jacques*
Jones, *Daniel*
Lawes, *Henry*
Lawes, *William*
Lehár, *Franz*
Liszt, *Franz*
Lloyd, *George*
Locke, *Matthew*
Loewe, *Karl*
Lully, *Jean Baptiste*
Nyman, *Michael*
Ogdon, *John*
Parry, *Hubert*
Prout, *Ebenezer*
Ravel, *Maurice*
Reger, *Max*
Reich, *Steve*

Rieti, *Vittorio*
Rossi, *Luigi*
Satie, *Erik*
Smyth, *Ethel*
Sousa, *John Philip*
Suppe, *Franz von*
Tosti, *Francesco Paolo*
Verdi, *Giuseppi*
Watts, *Isaac*
6 letters:
Alfven, *Hugo*
Arnold, *Malcolm*
Azione
Barber, *Samuel*
Bartók, *Béla*
Boulez, *Pierre*
Brahms, *Johannes*
Bridge, *Frank*
Burney, *Charles*
Busoni, *Ferruccioni*
Carter, *Eliot*
Carver, *Robert*
Casals, *Pablo*
Chopin, *Frédéric*
Clarke, *Jeremiah*
Coates, *Eric*
Czerny, *Karl*
Davies, *Peter Maxwell*
Delius, *Frederick*
Doráti, *Antal*
Duparc, *Henri*
Dvořák, *Antonín*
Enesco, *Georges*
Farmer, *John*
Flotow, *Friedrich Freiherr von*
Franck, *César*
German, *Sir Edward*
Glière, *Reinhold*
Glinka, *Mikhail Ivanovich*
Gounod, *Charles François*
Gurney, *Ivor*
Halévy, *Fromental*
Handel, *George Frederick*
Harris, *Roy*
Hummel, *Johann Nepomuk*
Joplin, *Scott*
Kodály, *Zoltán*
Lassus, *Orlandus*
Ligeti, *György*
Mahler, *Gustav*
Martin, *Frank*
Mingus, *Charles*
Morley, *Thomas*
Mozart, *Leopold*
Mozart, *Wolfgang Amadeus*
Ogolon
Rameau, *Jean Philippe*

Rubbra, *Edmund*
Schütz, *Heinrich*
Straus, *Oscar*
Tallis, *Thomas*
Thomas, *Ambroise*
Varèse, *Edgar*
Varèse, *Edgard*
Wagner, *Richard*
Walton, *William*
Webern, *Anton*
7 letters:
Albéniz, *Isaac*
Allegri, *Gregorio*
Antheil, *George*
Bantock, *Granville*
Bellini, *Vincenzo*
Bennett, *Richard Rodney*
Berlioz, *Hector*
Berners, *Gerald*
Borodin, *Aleksandr Porfirevich*
Britten, *Benjamin*
Brubeck, *Dave (David Warren)*
Copland, *Aaron*
Corelli, *Arcangelo*
Debussy, *Claude*
De Falla, *Manuel*
Delibes, *Léo*
De Lisle, *Claude Joseph Rouget*
Des Prés, *Josquin*
Di Lasso, *Orlando*
Dowland, *John*
Duruflé, *Maurice*
Gibbons, *Orlando*
Górecki, *Henryk*
Ireland, *John*
Janáček, *Leoš*
Joachim, *Joseph*
Knussen, *Oliver*
Krommer, *Franz*
Kubelik, *Raphael*
Lambert, *Constant*
Lutyens, *Elisabeth*
Martinů, *Bohuslav*
Menotti, *Gian Carlo*
Milhaud, *Darius*
Nicolai, *Carl Otto Ehrenfried*
Nielsen, *Carl*
Poulenc, *Francis*
Puccini, *Giacomo*
Purcell, *Henry*
Purnell, *Alton*
Quilter, *Roger*
Rodrigo, *Joaquín*
Romberg, *Sigmund*
Rossini, *Gioacchino Antonio*
Roussel, *Albert*

Salieri, *Antonio*
Schuman, *William*
Simpson, *Robert*
Smetana, *Bedřich*
Stainer, *John*
Strauss, *Johann*
Strauss, *Richard*
Tartini, *Giuseppe*
Tavener, *John*
Thomson, *Virgil*
Tippett, *Michael*
Vivaldi, *Antonio*
Warlock, *Peter*
Weelkes, *Thomas*
Wellesz, *Egon*
Xenakis, *Yannis*
8 letters:
Alaleona, *Domenico*
Albinoni, *Tomaso*
Benjamin, *Arthur*
Berkeley, *Lennox*
Bonporti, *Francesco Antonio*
Bruckner, *Anton*
Chabrier, *Emmanuel*
Chausson, *Ernest*
Cimarosa, *Domenico*
Couperin, *François*
De Lassus, *Roland*
Gabrieli, *Andrea*
Gabrieli, *Giovanni*
Gershwin, *George*
Gesualdo, *Carlo*
Glazunov, *Aleksandr Konstantinovich*
Goossens, *Eugene*
Grainger, *Percy*
Granados, *Enrique*
Holliger, *Heinz*
Honegger, *Arthur*
Korngold, *Erich*
Kreutzer, *Conradin*
Maconchy, *Elizabeth*
Marcello, *Benedetto*
Marenzio, *Luca*
Martland, *Steve*
Mascagni, *Pietro*
Massenet, *Jules Émile Frédéric*
Messager, *André*
Messiaen, *Olivier*
Musgrave, *Thea*
Ockeghem, *Johannes*
Paganini, *Niccolò*
Panufnik, *Andrzej*
Respighi, *Ottorino*
Schnabel, *Artur*
Schubert, *Franz*
Schumann, *Clara*

Schumann, *Robert*
Scriabin, *Aleksandr Nikolayvich*
Sessions, *Roger*
Sibelius, *Jean*
Stanford, *Charles*
Taverner, *John*
Telemann, *Georg Philipp*
Von Weber, *Carl Maria*
9 letters:
Balakirev, *Mily Alexeyevich*
Bernstein, *Leonard*
Bocherini, *Luigi*
Boulanger, *Nadia*
Broughton, *Bruce*
Buxtehude, *Dietrich*
Carpenter, *John Alden*
Chaminade, *Cecile*
Cherubini, *Luigi*
De Machaut, *Guillaume*
Donizetti, *Gaetano*
Dunstable, *John*
Dutilleux, *Henri*
Ginastera, *Alberto*
Hildegard *of Bingen*
Hindemith, *Paul*
Klemperer, *Otto*
MacMillan, *James*
Meyerbeer, *Giacomo*
Offenbach, *Jacques*
Pachelbel, *Johann*
Pergolesi, *Giovanni Battista*
Prokofiev, *Sergei Sergeyevich*
Scarlatti, *Alessandro*
Scarlatti, *Domenico*
Schnittke, *Alfred*
Takemitsu, *Toru*
Tortelier, *Paul*
Von Flotow, *Friedrich*
Whitehead, *Gillian*
Zemlinsky, *Alexander*
10 letters:
Birtwistle, *Harrison*
Canteloube, *Joseph*
De Victoria, *Tomás Luis*
Monteverdi, *Claudio*
Mussorgsky, *Modest Petrovich*
Paderewski, *Ignace Jan*

Palestrina, *Giovanni Pierluigi da*
Penderecki, *Krzystof*
Ponchielli, *Amilcare*
Praetorius, *Michael*
Rawsthorne, *Alan*
Rubinstein, *Anton Grigorevich*
Saint-Saëns, *Camille*
Schoenberg, *Arnold*
Sculthorpe, *Peter*
Stravinsky, *Igor Fyodorovich*
Villa-Lobos, *Heitor*
Williamson, *Malcolm*
11 letters:
Butterworth, *George*
Charpentier, *Gustave*
Charpentier, *Marc-Antoine*
Frescobaldi, *Girolamo*
Fürtwangler, *Wilhelm*
Humperdinck, *Englebert*
Leoncavallo, *Ruggiero*
Lutosławski, *Witold*
Mendelssohn, *Fanny*
Mendelssohn, *Felix*
Rachmaninov, *Sergei Vassilievich*
Stockhausen, *Karlheinz*
Szymanowski, *Karol*
Tchaikovsky, *Pyotr Ilyich*
Theodorakis, *Mikis*
Von Dohnányi, *Ernst*
Wolf-Ferrari, *Ermanno*
12 letters:
Dallapiccola, *Luigi*
Khachaturian, *Aram Ilich*
Rostropovich, *Mstislav Leopoldovich*
Shostakovich, *Dmitri Dmitriyevich*
Van Beethoven, *Ludwig*
14 letters:
Jaques-Dalcroze, *Émile*
Rimsky-Korsakov, *Nikolai Andreyevich*
15 letters:
Coleridge-Taylor, *Samuel*
Vaughan Williams, *Ralph*

POPULAR COMPOSERS, SONGWRITERS, AND LYRICISTS

4 letters:
Baez, *Joan*
Bart, *Lionel*
Brel, *Jacques*
Cahn, *Sammy*
Duke, *Vernon*

Hart, *Lorenz*
John, *Elton*
Kern, *Jerome (David)*
King, *Carole*
Mann, *Barry*
Monk, *Thelonious (Sphere)*

Rice, *Tim*
Webb, *Jimmy*
Weil, *Cynthia*
5 letters:
Arlen, *Harold*
Barry, *John*
Bowie, *David*
Brown, *Nacio Herb*
Cohan, *George*
Cohen, *Leonard*
Dixon, *Willie*
Dylan, *Bob*
Handy, *W(illiam) C(hristopher)*
Jarre, *Maurice*
Jobim, *Antonio Carlos*
Loewe, *Frederick*
Pomus, *Doc*
Shore, *Howard*
Simon, *Paul*
Styne, *Jule*
Waits, *Tom*
Weill, *Kurt*
6 letters:
Berlin, *Irving*
Coward, *Noel*
Dozier, *Lamont*
Foster, *Stephen*
Goffin, *Gerry*
Herman, *Jerry*
Jagger, *Mick*
Lehrer, *Tom*
Lennon, *John*
Lerner, *Alan Jay*
Lieber, *Jerry*
McColl, *Ewan*
McColl, *Kirsty*
McHugh, *Jimmy*
Nelson, *Willie*
Porter, *Cole*
Strong, *Barrett*
Warren, *Harry*
Wilson, *Brian*
7 letters:
Gilbert, *W(illiam) S(chwenck)*

Guthrie, *Woody*
Holland, *Brian*
Holland, *Eddie*
Johnson, *Robert*
Loesser, *Frank*
Mancini, *Henry*
Manilow, *Barry*
Novello, *Ivor*
Rodgers, *Richard*
Romberg, *Sigmund*
Stoller, *Mike*
Youmans, *Vincent*
8 letters:
Gershwin, *George*
Hamlisch, *Marvin*
Mitchell, *Joni*
Morrison, *Van*
Richards, *Keith*
Robinson, *William 'Smokey'*
Sondheim, *Stephen*
Sullivan, *Arthur*
Williams, *Hank*
Williams, *John*
9 letters:
Bacharach, *Burt*
Bernstein, *Leonard*
Ellington, *Duke*
Goldsmith, *Jerry*
Ledbetter, *Huddie 'Leadbelly'*
McCartney, *Paul*
Strayhorn, *Billy*
Toussaint, *Allen*
Van Heusen, *Johnny*
Whitfield, *Norman*
10 letters:
Carmichael, *Hoagy*
Goldenthal, *Elliot*
Livingston, *Jay*
11 letters:
Hammerstein, *Oscar*
Lloyd-Webber, *Andrew*
13 letters:
Kristofferson, *Kris*

Compounds

3 letters:	Urea	Diene
Azo	**5 letters:**	Dimer
4 letters:	Allyl	Diode
Alum	Amide	Erbia
EDTA	Amino	Ester
Enol	Azide	Furan
Haem	Azine	Halon
Heme	Azole	Imide
TEPP	Diazo	Imine

Lipid
Olein
Oxide
Oxime
Potin
Pyran
Sarin
Tabun
Thiol
Trona
Vinyl
6 letters:
Acetal
Alkane
Alkene
Arsine
Baryta
Borane
Calque
Cetane
Chrome
Cresol
Epimer
Fluate
Glycol
Halide
Haloid
Hexene
Isatin
Isomer
Ketone
Lithia
Niello
Phenol
Pinene
Potash
Purine
Pyrone
Retene
Silane
Speiss
Tartar
Tetryl
Thymol
Triene
Trimer
Uranyl
7 letters:
Acetone
Acridin
Aglycon
Ammonia
Benzene
Betaine
Bromide
Caliche
Calomel

Camphor
Carbide
Chelate
Choline
Cinerin
Creatin
Cumarin
Cyanide
Diamine
Diazine
Diazole
Dioxide
Dvandva
Epoxide
Erinite
Ethanol
Eugenol
Fenuron
Flavone
Hormone
Hydrate
Hydride
Indican
Indoxyl
Lactate
Menthol
Metamer
Monomer
Nitrite
Oxazine
Peptone
Polymer
Protein
Quassia
Quinoid
Quinone
Realgar
Skatole
Steroid
Sulfide
Syncarp
Taurine
Terpene
Toluene
Tritide
Uridine
Wolfram
8 letters:
Acridine
Aglycone
Aldehyde
Alizarin
Arginine
Butyrate
Catenane
Chloride
Chromene

Coenzyme
Coumarin
Creatine
Cyanogen
Datolite
Dieldrin
Dopamine
Farnesol
Fluoride
Glycogen
Hydroxyl
Indoform
Isologue
Ketoxime
Lecithin
Massicot
Melamine
Monoxide
Pentosan
Peroxide
Piperine
Ptomaine
Pyrazole
Rock-alum
Rotenone
Selenate
Silicide
Siloxane
Sodamide
Stilbene
Sulphide
Sulphone
Tautomer
Tetroxid
Thiazide
Thiazine
Thiazole
Thiotepa
Thiourea
Titanate
Triazine
Triazole
Trilling
Tyramine
Urethane
Xanthate
Xanthine
Zirconia
9 letters:
Aflatoxin
Alicyclic
Aliphatic
Anhydride
Biguanide
Carbazole
Carnitine
Cellulose

Cementite
Cortisone
Deuteride
Dipeptide
Disulfram
Endorshin
Ferrocene
Flavanone
Glycoside
Guanosine
Haematein
Histamine
Hydrazide
Hydroxide
Imidazole
Impsonite
Ionophore
Monoamine
Pentoxide
Phenoxide
Pheromone
Phosphide
Piperonal
Polyamine
Porphyrin
Qinghaosu
Quercetus
Quinoline

Serotonin
Tetroxide
Veratrine
10 letters:
Amphoteric
Argyrodite
Dimethoate
Disulphide
Enkephalin
Isocyanate
Lumisterol
Mercaptide
Nucleoside
Phenocaine
Picrotoxin
Piperazine
Piperidine
Propionate
Putrescine
Tatpurusha
Thimerosal
Tocopherol
11 letters:
Acetanilide
Amphetamine
Coprosterol
Dimercaprol
Electrolyte

Fluorescein
Ghitathione
Hydrocarbon
Neostigmine
Sesquioxide
12 letters:
Carbohydrate
Formaldehyde
Haematoxylin
Hydroquinone
Permanganate
Polyurethane
Triglyceride
Trimethadine
13 letters:
Catecholamine
Cycloheximide
Isoproterenol
Metronidazole
Nortriptyline
Trinucleotide
14 letters:
Oxyhaemoglobin
Polycarboxylic
Polyunsaturate
Trohalomethane

Computers

COMPUTER PARTS

3 letters:
ALU
CPU
MTU
VDU
4 letters:
Case
Chip
DIMM
Disk
DRAM
Port
SIMM
5 letters:
Modem
Mouse
SDRAM
6 letters:
DDR-RAM
Memory
Screen
Webcam
7 letters:
Console

Counter
Encoder
Monitor
Printer
Scanner
Speaker
USB port
8 letters:
Disk unit
Emulator
Joystick
Keyboard
LCD panel
9 letters:
Cartridge
Digitizer
Disk drive
DVD reader
DVD writer
Hard drive
Interface
Processor
Sound card
Trackball

10 letters:
CD-rewriter
CD-Rom drive
Control key
Daisywheel
Floppy disk
Transistor
11 letters:
Line printer
Motherboard
Multiplexor
Optical disk
12 letters:
Coaxial cable
Graphics card
Laser printer
13 letters:
Digital camera
14 letters:
Flatbed scanner
Microprocessor
Optical scanner

COMPUTER TERMS

2 letters:
AI
I/O
IT
PC
3 letters:
Bit
Bpi
Bug
Bus
CAD
CAE
CAI
CAL
CAM
CAT
CBT
CIM
COL
COM
DAC
DMA
DOS®
Dpi
DTP
FAT
FTP
Gif
ICL
IDE
Job
LAN
OCR
OEM
PDA
Pdf
RAM
ROM
Run
SAM
USB
WAN
WAP
XML
4 letters:
ADSL
Area
Bomb
Boot
Byte
Cast
CISC
Code
Data
Dump

Echo
Edit
Exit
File
Flag
Gate
Giga-
GIGO
Host
HTML
Icon
IKBS
ISDN
Jpeg
Kilo-
Load
Loop
Mega-
Menu
Midi
Mpeg
Node
Open
PROM
RISC
SCSI
SGML
Sort
UNIX®
WIMP
Word
Worm
5 letters:
Array
ASCII
Brain
CD-Rom
Clock
Crash
Cyber
Cycle
Datel®
Digit
Earom
E-mail
Eniac
EPROM
ERNIE
Field
Flops
Fuzzy
Input
JANET
Key in
Log in

Macro
Micro
Patch
Pixel
Queue
Rerun
Reset
Sense
Stack
Store
Tally
Tower
Virus
Voxel
Warez
6 letters:
Access
Analog
Applet
Backup
Buffer
Bundle
Busbar
CADCAM
CADMAT
Caster
Cookie
Cursor
Device
Driver
Duplex
Earcon
EBCDIC
Editor
EEPROM
Figure
Hacker
Holmes
Hot key
Infect
Kludge
Laptop
Legacy
Linker
Log out
Module
Online
OR gate
Output
Packet
Parser
Prompt
Read in
Reboot
Record

Scroll
Server
Sprite
String
SWITCH
Syntax
System
TAURUS
Toggle
Uptime
Window
Wizard
7 letters:
ActiveX
Address
AND gate
Capture
Chipset
Clip art
Command
Corrupt
Counter
Databus
Default
Desktop
Digital
Freenet
Gateway
Install
Keyword
Lapheld
Manager
Netbook
Network
NOR gate
NOT gate
Numlock
Offline
Package
Palette
Palmtop
Pointer
Power up
Process
Program
Read out
Routine
Run time
Time out
Utility
Vaccine
WYSIWIG
Wysiwyg
8 letters:
Analogue

Assemble
Autosave
Backbone
Beta-test
Black box
Calculus
Checksum
Chiphead
Compiler
Constant
Data bank
Database
Digitize
Document
Download
Downsize
Down time
Emulator
Estimate
Extranet
Fail-safe
Filename
Firewall
FireWire
Firmware
Freeware
Function
Gigabyte
Graphics
Hard card
Hard copy
Hardware
Idle time
Internet
Intranet
Kilobyte
Language
Liveware
Location
Megabyte
Morphing
NAND gate
Optimize
Overflow
Password
Platform
Portable
Printout
Protocol
Pushdown
Realtime
Reckoner
Skinning
Software
TALISMAN
Terabyte
Terminal

Topology
Tristate
Variable
Wild card
9 letters:
Algorithm
Alpha-test
Assembler
Authoring
Bandwidth
Bluetooth
Bootstrap
Broadband
Bus master
Calculate
Character
Co-routine
Cybercafé
Cyberpunk
Debugging
Directory
Dithering
Dot matrix
Ecommerce
Flowchart
Groupware
Handshake
Hard-wired
Hypertext
Interface
Interrupt
Logic bomb
Mainframe
Multi-user
Parameter
Power down
Procedure
Processor
Retrieval
Shareware
Smart card
Statement
Tetrabyte
Trackball
Underflow
User group
10 letters:
3D graphics
Access time
Address bus
Compatible
Core memory
Cyberspace
Encryption
Fileserver
Hypermedia
Initialize

Integrator
Linked list
Main memory
Menu-driven
Patch board
Programmer
README file
Robustness
Scratchpad
Stand-alone
Subroutine
Throughput
Transcribe
Translator
Transputer
Voice input
Webcasting
11 letters:
Antialising
Base address
Binary digit
Bits per inch
Cache memory
Clickstream
Computerate
Computerize
Concordance
Cut and paste
Cybernetics
Data capture
Dots per inch
File manager
Function key
Help screens
Input device
Input/output
Instruction
Interactive
Interpreter
Machine code
Mail bombing
Multiaccess
NAND circuit
Parity check
Screensaver
Spreadsheet
Superserver
Systems disk
Time sharing
Trackerball
Work station
12 letters:
Architecture
Backing store
Digital fount
Disassembler
Dumb terminal

Error message
Expert system
Global search
Housekeeping
Logic circuit
Minicomputer
Mobile device
Remote access
Reserved word
Search engine
Shell program
Telesoftware
World Wide Web
13 letters:
Audio response
Bulletin board
Configuration
Data structure
Decision table
Escape routine
Expansion slot
Memory mapping
Microcomputer
Multi-threaded
Neurocomputer
Object program
Query language

Queuing theory
Source program
Storage device
Supercomputer
Turnkey system
Virtual memory
Voice response
Word processor
14 letters:
Binary notation
Communications
Condition codes
Cross assembler
Data processing
Data protection
Digital imaging
Digital mapping
Document reader
Electronic mail
Hybrid computer
Magnetic bubble
Microprocessor
Neural computer
Number-cruncher
Plug compatible
Read only memory
Source document

Teleprocessing
Text processing
User-defined key
Virtual address
Virtual reality
Virtual storage
Volatile memory
Web development
15 letters:
Absolute address
Archival storage
Automatic repeat
Batch processing
Command language
Computer science
Control commands
Digital computer
Fifth-generation
Machine learning
Machine readable
Operating system
Packet-switching
Palmtop computer
Storage capacity
Store and forward
Systems analysis

COMPUTER SCIENTISTS

4 letters:
Cray, *Seymour*
5 letters:
Aiken, *Howard*
Gates, *Bill*
6 letters:
Eckert, *John Presper*
Turing, *Alan Mathison*
7 letters:
Babbage, *Charles*

Mauchly, *John W.*
8 letters:
Lovelace, *Ada (Countess of)*
Sinclair, *Clive*
9 letters:
Hollerith, *Herman*
10 letters:
Berners-Lee, *Tim*
Von Neumann, *John*

See also:
➤ **Programming languages**

Confectionery

3 letters:
Gem
Gum
4 letters:
Jube
Kiss
Mint

Rock
5 letters:
Candy
Dolly
Fudge
Halva
Lolly

Taffy
6 letters:
Bonbon
Button
Cachou
Comfit
Confit

Dainty
Dragée
Halvah
Humbug
Jujube
Nougat
Sorbet
Sundae
Tablet
Toffee
7 letters:
Brittle
Caramel
Fondant
Gumdrop
Halavah
Lozenge
Panocha
Praline
Sherbet
Truffle
8 letters:
Acid drop

All-sorts
Bull's eye
Licorice
Lollipop
Marzipan
Noisette
Pastille
Peardrop
Scroggin
Stickjaw
9 letters:
Blackball
Chocolate
Fruit drop
Jelly baby
Jelly bean
Lemon drop
Liquorice
Marchpane
10 letters:
Brandyball
Candyfloss
Chewing gum

Coconut ice
Gob-stopper
Nanaimo bar
Peppermint
Pick and mix
Soft-centre
11 letters:
Barley sugar
Boiled sweet
Marshmallow
Toffee apple
12 letters:
Burnt-almonds
Butterscotch
13 letters:
Fruit pastille
14 letters:
Turkish delight

Containers for liquids

3 letters:
Can
Jar
Jug
Keg
Tin
4 letters:
Cask
Tube
5 letters:
Flask
Gourd
Tinny
6 letters:
Barrel

Bottle
Carafe
Carton
Coldie
Firkin
Flagon
Magnum
Stubby
7 letters:
Amphora
Ampulla
Pitcher
Polypin
8 letters:
Decanter

Hogshead
Jeroboam
Rehoboam
Screw-top
Tantalus
9 letters:
Balthazar
Miniature
10 letters:
Half-bottle
Methuselah
Salmanazar
14 letters:
Nebuchadnezzar

Continents

4 letters:
Asia
6 letters:
Africa
Europe

9 letters:
Australia
10 letters:
Antarctica

12 letters:
North America
South America

Cookery

CUISINES AND COOKING STYLES

4 letters:
Ital
Thai
5 letters:
Balti
Greek
Halal
Tapas
Vegan
6 letters:
French
Indian
Kosher
Tex-Mex
7 letters:
Chinese

Italian
Mexican
Seafood
Sichuan
Turkish
8 letters:
Fast food
Japanese
Szechuan
9 letters:
Cantonese
Caribbean
Malaysian
Provençal
10 letters:
Cordon bleu

Indonesian
Vegetarian
11 letters:
Californian
Home cooking
12 letters:
Haute cuisine
13 letters:
Gutbürgerlich
International
Mediterranean
14 letters:
Cuisine minceur
15 letters:
Nouvelle cuisine

Counties

ENGLISH COUNTIES

4 letters:
Kent
5 letters:
Devon
Essex
6 letters:
Dorset
Durham
Surrey
7 letters:
Bristol
Cumbria
Norfolk
Rutland
Suffolk
8 letters:
Cheshire
Cornwall
Somerset
9 letters:
Berkshire

Hampshire
Wiltshire
10 letters:
Cumberland (former)
Derbyshire
East Sussex
Lancashire
Merseyside
Shropshire
West Sussex
11 letters:
Isle of Wight
Oxfordshire
Tyne and Wear
Westmorland
(former)
12 letters:
Bedfordshire
Lincolnshire
Warwickshire
West Midlands

13 letters:
Greater London
Herefordshire
Hertfordshire
Staffordshire
West Yorkshire
14 letters:
Cambridgeshire
Leicestershire
Northumberland
North Yorkshire
South Yorkshire
Worcestershire
15 letters:
Buckinghamshire
Gloucestershire
Nottinghamshire

SCOTTISH COUNTIES

4 letters:
Fife
5 letters:
Angus
Moray
6 letters:
Orkney
7 letters:
Falkirk
8 letters:
Highland
Shetland

Stirling
10 letters:
Dundee City
Eilean Siar
Inverclyde
Midlothian
11 letters:
East Lothian
Glasgow City
West Lothian
12 letters:
Aberdeen City

East Ayrshire
Renfrewshire
Western Isles
13 letters:
Aberdeenshire
Argyll and Bute
North Ayrshire
South Ayrshire
15 letters:
City of Edinburgh
Perth and Kinross
Scottish Borders

FORMER SCOTTISH COUNTIES

4 letters:
Bute
5 letters:
Banff
Nairn
6 letters:
Argyll
Dundee
7 letters:
Glasgow
Kinross
8 letters:
Aberdeen
Ayrshire
Roxburgh

9 letters:
Caithness
Edinburgh
10 letters:
Banffshire
Kincardine
Nairnshire
Perthshire
Sutherland
11 letters:
Lanarkshire
12 letters:
Berwickshire
Kinross-shire
Peeblesshire

Renfrewshire
Selkirkshire
Wigtownshire
13 letters:
Dumfriesshire
Roxburghshire
Stirlingshire
14 letters:
Dunbartonshire
Inverness-shire
15 letters:
Kincardineshire
Ross and Cromarty

WELSH COUNTIES (POST-1998)

5 letters:
Conwy
Powys
7 letters:
Cardiff
Gwynedd
Newport
Swansea
Torfaen
Wrexham

8 letters:
Anglesey
Bridgend
10 letters:
Caerphilly
Ceredigion
Flintshire
12 letters:
Blaenau Gwent
Denbighshire

13 letters:
Merthyr Tydfil
Monmouthshire
Pembrokeshire
15 letters:
Carmarthenshire
Neath Port Talbot
Vale of Glamorgan

FORMER WELSH COUNTIES

5 letters:
Clwyd
Dyfed
Gwent
Powys

7 letters:
Gwynedd
12 letters:
Mid Glamorgan

13 letters:
West Glamorgan
14 letters:
South Glamorgan

TRADITIONAL NORTHERN IRISH COUNTIES

4 letters:
Down
6 letters:
Antrim

Armagh
Tyrone
9 letters:
Fermanagh

11 letters:
Londonderry

REPUBLIC OF IRELAND COUNTIES

4 letters:
Cork
Mayo
5 letters:
Cavan
Clare
Kerry
Laois
Louth
Meath
Sligo

6 letters:
Carlow
Dublin
Galway
Offaly
7 letters:
Donegal
Kildare
Leitrim
Wexford
Wicklow

8 letters:
Kilkenny
Limerick
Longford
Monaghan
9 letters:
Roscommon
Tipperary
Waterford
Westmeath

Countries

4 letters:
Chad
Cuba
Fiji
Iran
Iraq
Laos
Mali
Oman
Peru
Togo
5 letters:
Belau
Benin
Chile
Congo
Egypt
Gabon
Ghana
Haiti
India
Italy
Japan
Kenya
Libya
Malta
Nauru
Nepal
Niger
Qatar
Samoa
Spain

Sudan
Syria
Tonga
Wales
Yemen
6 letters:
Angola
Belize
Bhutan
Brazil
Brunei
Canada
Cyprus
France
Gambia
Greece
Guinea
Guyana
Israel
Jordan
Kuwait
Latvia
Malawi
Mexico
Monaco
Norway
Panama
Poland
Russia
Rwanda
Serbia
Sweden

Taiwan
Turkey
Tuvalu
Uganda
Zambia
7 letters:
Albania
Algeria
Andorra
Armenia
Austria
Bahamas
Bahrain
Belarus
Belgium
Bolivia
Burundi
Comoros
Croatia
Denmark
Ecuador
England
Eritrea
Estonia
Finland
Georgia
Germany
Grenada
Hungary
Iceland
Jamaica
Lebanon

Lesotho
Liberia
Moldova
Morocco
Myanmar
Namibia
Nigeria
Romania
Senegal
Somalia
St Lucia
Surinam
Tunisia
Ukraine
Uruguay
Vanuatu
Vietnam
8 letters:
Barbados
Botswana
Bulgaria
Cambodia
Cameroon
Colombia
Djibouti
Dominica
Ethiopia
Honduras
Kiribati
Malaysia
Mongolia
Pakistan
Paraguay
Portugal
Scotland

Slovakia
Slovenia
Sri Lanka
Tanzania
Thailand
Zimbabwe
9 letters:
Argentina
Australia
Cape Verde
Costa Rica
East Timor
Greenland
Guatemala
Indonesia
Kirghizia
Lithuania
Macedonia
Mauritius
Nicaragua
San Marino
Singapore
Swaziland
Venezuela
10 letters:
Azerbaijan
Bangladesh
El Salvador
Kazakhstan
Luxembourg
Madagascar
Mauritania
Micronesia
Montenegro
Mozambique

New Zealand
North Korea
Puerto Rico
Seychelles
South Korea
Tajikistan
Uzbekistan
Yugoslavia
11 letters:
Afghanistan
Burkina-Faso
Côte d'Ivoire
Netherlands
Philippines
Saudi Arabia
Sierra Leone
South Africa
Switzerland
Vatican City
12 letters:
Guinea-Bissau
Turkmenistan
13 letters:
American Samoa
Czech Republic
Liechtenstein
United Kingdom
14 letters:
Papua New Guinea
Solomon Islands
15 letters:
Marshall Islands
Northern Ireland
St Kitts and Nevis

See also:
➤ **Commonwealth members** ➤ **Dependencies**
➤ **European Union** ➤ **Republics**

Cows

2 letters:
Zo
3 letters:
Dun
Zho
4 letters:
Zebu
5 letters:
Colly
Kyloe
Milch
Mooly

Muley
Stirk
6 letters:
Crummy
Dexter
Heifer
Jersey
Mulley
Rother
7 letters:
Kouprey
Redpoll

8 letters:
Alderney
Galloway
Guernsey
Hereford
9 letters:
Charolais
Red Sindhi
Simmental
Teeswater
11 letters:
Rother-beast

See also:
➤ **Cattle**

Crafts

5 letters:
Batik
6 letters:
Sewing
7 letters:
Crochet
Macramé
Pottery
Weaving
8 letters:
Basketry
Ceramics

Knitting
Knotwork
Quilling
Quilting
Spinning
Tapestry
9 letters:
Decoupage
Patchwork
10 letters:
Crewelwork
Embroidery

Raffia work
Sugarcraft
Wickerwork
11 letters:
Calligraphy
Cloisonnage
Dressmaking
Needlepoint
12 letters:
Basket-making
15 letters:
Flower arranging

Cricket terms

2 letters:
In
3 letters:
Bat
Bye
Cut
Out
Pad
Run
Six
4 letters:
Bail
Ball
Bowl
Duck
Edge
Four
Hook
Over
Pull
Seam
Slip
Spin
Wide
5 letters:
Ashes
Catch
Drive
Extra
Glide
Gully
Mid on
Pitch
Stump
Sweep

Swing
Umpie
6 letters:
Appeal
Bowled
Bowler
Bumper
Caught
Covers
Crease
Glance
Googly
Leg bye
Long on
Maiden
Mid off
No ball
On side
Opener
Run out
Single
Umpire
Wicket
Yorker
7 letters:
Batsman
Bouncer
Century
Declare
Fielder
Fine leg
Innings
Leg side
Leg slip
Long leg

Long off
Off side
Stumped
8 letters:
Boundary
Chinaman
Follow on
Full toss
Leg break
Off break
Short leg
Third man
9 letters:
Fieldsman
Hit wicket
Mid wicket
Square leg
Test match
10 letters:
Cover point
Extra cover
Fast bowler
Maiden over
Silly mid on
Twelfth man
11 letters:
Silly mid off
12 letters:
Wicketkeeper
13 letters:
Nightwatchman
14 letters:
Opening batsman
15 letters:
Leg before wicket

Crime writers

3 letters:
Poe, *Edgar Allan*
4 letters:
Vine, *Barbara*
5 letters:
Block, *Lawrence*
Doyle, *Arthur Conan*
James, *P(hyllis) D(orothy)*
6 letters:
Rankin, *Ian*
Sayers, *Dorothy L(eigh)*
7 letters:
Bateman, *Colin*
Grisham, *John*
Hiaasen, *Carl*
Rendell, *Ruth*

Simenon, *Georges (Joseph Christian)*
Wallace, *Edgar (Richard Horatio)*
8 letters:
Chandler, *Raymond*
Christie, *Dame Agatha (Mary Clarissa)*
Connelly, *Michael*
Connolly, *John*
Cornwell, *Patricia*
9 letters:
Brookmyre, *Christopher*
Highsmith, *Patricia*
10 letters:
Wiesenthal, *Simon*

Crosses

3 letters:
Red
Tau
4 letters:
Ankh
Crux
Iona
Iron
Rood
Tree
5 letters:
Fiery
Greek
Latin
Papal
Pommé
Rouen
6 letters:
Ansate
Barbée
Botone
Celtic
Chiasm
Fitché
Fleury
Fylfot
Geneva
George

Graded (Calvary)
Moline
Pattée
Potent
Raguly
Trefly
7 letters:
Botonne
Calvary
Chiasma
Eleanor
Maltese
Patonce
Potence
Rarulée
Saltier
Saltire
8 letters:
Cercelée
Crosslet
Crucifix
Globical
Holy rood
Lorraine
Military
Millvine
Pectoral
Quadrate

Southern
St Peter's
Svastika
Swastika
Victoria
9 letters:
Encolpion
Jerusalem
St Andrew's
St George's
10 letters:
Canterbury
Clover-leaf
Crux ansata
St Anthony's
11 letters:
Constantine
Patriarchal
12 letters:
Pattée formée
13 letters:
Cross crosslet
14 letters:
Archiepiscopal
15 letters:
Russian Orthodox

Crustaceans

4 letters:
Crab
Craw
5 letters:
Koura
Krill

Prawn
6 letters:
Cyprid

Cypris
Isopod
Marron
Scampi
Scampo
Shrimp
Slater
7 letters:
Camaron
Copepod
Cyclops
Decapod
Foot-jaw
Gribble
Lobster
Macrura
Squilla
8 letters:
Amphipod
Barnacle
Cirriped
Cirripid
Crawfish
Crayfish

Cumacean
Decapoda
King crab
Land crab
Nauplius
Pagurian
Sand flea
Scorpion
9 letters:
Beach flea
Cirripede
Euphausia
Fishlouse
King prawn
Langouste
Ostracoda
Phyllopod
Schizopod
Sea spider
Water flea
Woodlouse
10 letters:
Brachyuran
Cladoceran

Hermit crab
Oyster crab
Robber crab
Sand hopper
Sand shrimp
Spider crab
Stomatopod
11 letters:
Langoustine
Rock lobster
12 letters:
Branchiopoda
Entomostraca
Spiny lobster
13 letters:
Goose barnacle
Horseshoe crab
Malacostracan
Norway lobster
Opossum shrimp
Rhizocephalan
Soft-shell crab
14 letters:
Dublin Bay prawn

Crystals

4 letters:
Lead
Rock
Spar
5 letters:
Beryl
Druse
Glass
Macle
Nicol
Prism
Purin
6 letters:
Liquid
Purine

Quartz
7 letters:
Baccara
Cumarin
Epitaxy
8 letters:
Baccarat
Coumarin
Dendrite
Jarosite
Melamine
Pinacoid
Pinakoid
Sorbitol
Trichite

Trilling
9 letters:
Hemitrope
Love-arrow
Rubicelle
Snowflake
Xenocryst
10 letters:
Phenocryst
Rhinestone
Watch-glass
12 letters:
Enantiomorph
15 letters:
Allotriomorphic

Cupboards and cabinets

4 letters:
Safe
5 letters:
Ambry
Chest
Press
Shelf
Stand

6 letters:
Buffet
Bureau
Closet
Dooket
Drawer
Larder
Locker

Lowboy
Pantry
7 letters:
Armoire
Cabinet
Commode
Console
Dresser

Étagère
Highboy
Tallboy
Vitrine
Whatnot
8 letters:
Bookcase
Cellaret
Credenza
Wardrobe

9 letters:
Garderobe
Sideboard
10 letters:
Canterbury
Chiffonier
11 letters:
Chiffonnier
12 letters:
Chest-on-chest

Clothes-press
Welsh dresser
13 letters:
Court cupboard
Credence table
Filing cabinet
Medicine chest
14 letters:
Chest of drawers
Coolgardie safe

Cups and other drinking vessels

3 letters:
Cup
Mug
Nut
Pot
Tig
Tot
Tyg
4 letters:
Dish
Horn
5 letters:
Calix
Cruse
Cylix
Glass
Hanap
Kylix
Tazza

6 letters:
Beaker
Copita
Cotyle
Fingan
Finjan
Goblet
Loving
Noggin
Porrón
Quaich
Rhyton
Tassie
7 letters:
Canteen
Chalice
Cyathus
Scyphus
Stirrup

Tankard
Tea-dish
Tumbler
8 letters:
Pannikin
Schooner
Tantalus
Tastevin
9 letters:
Cantharus
Demitasse
Moustache
10 letters:
Monstrance
11 letters:
Water bottle
14 letters:
Champagne flute

Currencies

Country	Currency
Afghanistan	Afghani
Albania	Lek
Algeria	Algerian dinar
Andorra	Euro
Angola	Kwanza
Antigua and Barbuda	East Caribbean dollar
Argentina	Peso
Armenia	Dram
Australia	Australian dollar
Austria	Euro
Azerbaijan	Manat
Bahamas	Bahamian dollar
Bahrain	Dinar
Bangladesh	Taka
Barbados	Barbados dollar
Belarus	Rouble
Belgium	Euro
Belize	Belize dollar
Benin	CFA franc

Country	Currency
Bhutan	Ngultrum
Bolivia	Boliviano
Bosnia-Herzegovina	Convertible marka
Botswana	Pula
Brazil	Real
Brunei	Brunei dollar
Bulgaria	Lev
Burkina-Faso	CFA franc
Burundi	Burundi franc
Cambodia	Riel
Cameroon	CFA franc
Canada	Canadian dollar
Cape Verde	Escudo
Central African Republic	CFA franc
Chad	CFA franc
Chile	Peso
China	Yuan
Colombia	Peso
Comoros	Comorian franc
Congo (Democratic Republic of)	Congolese franc
Congo (Republic of)	CFA franc
Costa Rica	Cólon
Côte d'Ivoire	CFA franc
Croatia	Kuna
Cuba	Peso
Cyprus	Euro
Czech Republic	Koruna
Denmark	Krone
Djibouti	Djibouti franc
Dominica	East Caribbean dollar
Dominican Republic	Peso
East Timor	US dollar
Ecuador	US dollar
Egypt	Pound
El Salvador	Cólon
Equatorial Guinea	CFA franc
Eritrea	Nakfa
Estonia	Kroon
Ethiopia	Birr
Fiji	Fiji dollar
Finland	Euro
France	Euro
French Guiana	French franc
Gabon	CFA franc
Gambia	Dalasi
Germany	Euro
Ghana	Cedi
Greece	Euro
Greenland	Danish krone
Grenada	East Caribbean dollar
Guatemala	Quetzal
Guinea	Guinea franc
Guinea-Bissau	CFA franc
Guyana	Guyana dollar
Haiti	Gourde
Honduras	Lempira

Country	Currency
Hungary	Forint
Iceland	Krona
India	Rupee
Indonesia	Rupiah
Iran	Rial
Iraq	Dinar
Ireland (Republic of)	Euro
Israel	Shekel
Italy	Euro
Jamaica	Jamaican dollar
Japan	Yen
Jordan	Dinar
Kazakhstan	Tenge
Kenya	Shilling
Kirghizia	Som
Kiribati	Australian dollar
Kosovo	Dinar; euro
Kuwait	Dinar
Kyrgyzstan	Som
Laos	Kip
Latvia	Lat
Lebanon	Pound
Lesotho	Loti
Liberia	Liberian dollar
Libya	Dinar
Liechtenstein	Swiss franc
Lithuania	Litas
Luxembourg	Euro
Macedonia	Denar
Madagascar	Malagasy franc
Malawi	Kwacha
Malaysia	Ringgit
Maldives (Republic of)	Rufiyaa
Mali	CFA franc
Malta	Euro
Marshall Islands	U.S. dollar
Mauritania	Ouguiya
Mauritius	Rupee
Mexico	Peso
Micronesia	U.S. dollar
Moldova	Leu
Monaco	French franc
Mongolia	Tugrik
Montenegro	Euro
Montserrat	East Caribbean dollar
Morocco	Dirham
Mozambique	Metical
Myanmar	Kyat
Namibia	Namibian dollar
Nauru	Australian dollar
Nepal	Rupee
Netherlands	Euro
New Zealand	New Zealand dollar
Nicaragua	Córdoba
Niger	CFA franc
Nigeria	Naira

Country	Currency
North Korea	Won
Norway	Krone
Oman	Rial
Pakistan	Rupee
Palau	U.S. dollar
Panama	Balboa
Papua New Guinea	Kina
Paraguay	Guarani
Peru	New sol
Philippines	Philippine peso
Poland	Zloty
Portugal	Euro
Qatar	Riyal
Romania	Leu
Russia	Rouble
Rwanda	Rwanda franc
St Kitts and Nevis	East Caribbean dollar
St Lucia	East Caribbean dollar
St Vincent and the Grenadines	East Caribbean dollar
Samoa	Tala
San Marino	Euro
São Tomé and Principe	Dobra
Saudi Arabia	Riyal
Senegal	CFA franc
Seychelles	Rupee
Sierra Leone	Leone
Singapore	Singapore dollar
Slovakia	Euro
Slovenia	Euro
Solomon Islands	Solomon Islands dollar
Somalia	Shilling
South Africa	Rand
South Korea	Won
Spain	Euro
Sri Lanka	Rupee
Sudan	Dinar
Surinam	Guilder
Swaziland	Lilangeni
Sweden	Krona
Switzerland	Swiss franc
Syria	Pound
Taiwan	Taiwan dollar
Tajikistan	Somoni
Tanzania	Shilling
Thailand	Baht
Togo	CFA franc
Tonga	Pa'anga
Trinidad and Tobago	Trinidad and Tobago dollar
Tunisia	Dinar
Turkey	Turkish lira
Turkmenistan	Manat
Tuvalu	Australian dollar
Uganda	Shilling
Ukraine	Hryvna
United Arab Emirates	Dirham
United Kingdom	Pound sterling

Country	Currency
United States of America	U.S. dollar
Uruguay	Peso
Uzbekistan	Sum
Vanuatu	Vatu
Vatican City	Euro
Venezuela	Bolívar
Vietnam	Dong
Yemen	Riyal
Yugoslavia (Serbia)	Dinar
Zambia	Kwacha
Zimbabwe	Zimbabwe dollar

Cutting tools

3 letters:
Axe
Bit
Saw
4 letters:
Adze
Sawn
5 letters:
Dicer

Lance
Mower
6 letters:
Carver
Chisel
Grater
Jigsaw
Padsaw
Ripsaw

Scythe
Shaver
Shears
Sickle
7 letters:
Chopper
Cleaver
Coulter
Handsaw

Scissor
8 letters:
Engraver
9 letters:
Secateurs
11 letters:
Ploughshare

D

Dams

4 letters:
Guri
Hume
Pati
5 letters:
Aswan
Nurek
Rogun
6 letters:
Hoover

Inguri
Itaipu
Kariba
Vaiont
7 letters:
Benmore
8 letters:
Chapetón
9 letters:
Aswan High

10 letters:
Glen Canyon
11 letters:
Grand Coulee
Three Gorges
13 letters:
Grande Dixence
Vishvesvaraya

Dance

DANCES

3 letters:
Fan
Gig
Hay
Hey
Ice
Jig
Lap
Pas
Poi
Sun
Tap
Toe
War

4 letters:
Alma
Ball
Barn
Bump
Clog
Dump
Fado
Folk
Foot
Frug
Giga
Go-go
Haka
Hora
Hula
Jive
Jota
Juba
Juke
Kolo
Lion
Mosh
Nach
Pogo
Polo
Reel
Shag
Slam
Spin
Stag
Step
Taxi
Trip

5 letters:
Belly
Bogle
Brawl
Break

Caper
Carol
Ceroc®
Conga
Disco
Dolin
Fling
Furry
Galop
Ghost
Gigue
Gopak
Horah
Limbo
Loure
Mambo
Mooch
Natch
Paspy
Pavan
Paven
Pavin
Polka
Raver
Round
Rumba
Salsa
Samba
Shake
Skank
Snake
Stomp
Strut
Sword
Tango
Twist
Valse
Vogue
Volta
Waltz
Whirl

6 letters:
Almain
Apache
Ballet
Bolero
Boogie
Boston
Branle
Canary
Cancan
Cha-cha
Do-si-do

Fading
Floral
German
Gigolo
Hustle
Jump-up
Kathak
Lavolt
Maenad
Maxixe
Minuet
Morris
Nautch
Oberek
Pavane
Petipa
Redowa
Shimmy
Spring
Square
Trophe
Valeta
Veleta
Zapata

7 letters:
Baladin
Ballant
Beguine
Bourrée
Bransle
Brantle
Calypso
Cantico
Capuera
Carioca
Coranto
Cossack
Country
Courant
Csardas
Czardas
Farruca
Forlana
Foxtrot
Furlana
Gavotte
Halling
Hetaera
Hetaira
Hoedown
Lambada
Lancers
Ländler

Lavolta
Macaber
Macabre
Mazurka
Moresco
Morisco
Morrice
Moshing
Musette
Old-time
One-step
Pericon
Planxty
Polacca
Pyrrhic
Ridotto
Romaika
Roundel
Roundle
Sardana
Sashaya
Saunter
Shuffle
St Vitus
Tanagra
Tordion
Trenise
Two-step
Ziganka

8 letters:
Baladine
Ballroom
Bayadère
Boogaloo
Bunny hug
Cachucha
Cakewalk
Canticoy
Capoeira
Chaconne
Corybant
Coryphee
Cotillon
Courante
Egg-dance
Excuse-me
Fandango
Flamenco
Flip-flop
Galliard
Habanera
Hay-de-guy
Haymaker

Heythrop
Hoolican
Hornpipe
Hula-hula
Irish jig
Joncanoe
Junkanoo
Kantikoy
Kazachok
Kazatzka
Lindy hop
Macarena
Marinera
Matachin
Medicine
Merengue
Murciana
Orchesis
Pierette
Rigadoon
Rigadon
Robotics
Ronggeng
Saraband
Snowball
Soft-shoe
Trippant
Trucking
Vogueing
9 letters:
Allemande

Ballabile
Bergamask
Bergomask
Bossa nova
Breakdown
Butterfly
Caballero
Cha-cha-cha
Cotillion
Ecossaise
Eightsome
Farandole
Formation
Gallopade
Hoolachan
Jitterbug
Kathakali
Malagueña
Pas de deux
Paso doble
Passepied
Paul Jones
Polonaise
Poussette
Quadrille
Quickstep
Ring-shout
Roundelay
Siciliano
Sink-a-pace
Tambourin

Tripudium
Variation
Zapateado
10 letters:
Antimasque
Carmagnole
Charleston
Cinque-pace
Corroboree
Gay Gordons
Hay-de-guise
Hay-de-guyes
Hey-de-guise
Hokey cokey
Nautch-girl
Passamezzo
Petronella
Saltarello
Seguidilla
Sicilienne
Sinke-a-pace
Strathspey
Tarantella
Trenchmore
Tripudiate
Turkey trot
Tyrolienne
11 letters:
Antistrophe
Black bottom
Body popping

Buck and wing
Contradance
Contredanse
Cracovienne
Lambeth walk
Palais glide
Passacaglia
Pastourelle
Schottische
Shimmy-shake
Terpsichore
Varsovienne
12 letters:
Bharat Natyam
Labanotation
Passemeasure
Passy-measure
Robot dancing
Saltatorious
Virginia reel
13 letters:
Eightsome reel
Highland fling
14 letters:
Jack-in-the-
green
Strip the
willow

GENERAL DANCE STEPS AND TERMS

3 letters:
Pas
Set
4 letters:
Time
5 letters:
Glide
Score
Steps
6 letters:
Chassé
Dosido
In step

Phrase
Rhythm
7 letters:
Pas seul
Routine
Shuffle
8 letters:
Keep step
Sequence
Slip step
9 letters:
Out of step
Promenade

10 letters:
Grand chain
Pigeonwing
11 letters:
Comprimario
Pas de basque
Progressive
12 letters:
Choreography

See also:
➤ **Ballets** ➤ **Ballet steps and terms**

Dependencies

4 letters:
Guam
Niue
5 letters:
Aruba
Macau (S.A.R.)
Undof
6 letters:
Jersey
7 letters:
Bermuda
Mayotte
Reunion
Tokelau
8 letters:
Anguilla
Guernsey
Hong Kong (S.A.R.)
Jan Mayen
Svalbard
9 letters:
Aksai Chin
Gibraltar
Greenland

Isle of Man
Wake Atoll
10 letters:
Antarctica
Guadeloupe
Martinique
Montserrat
Puerto Rico
11 letters:
Baker Island
Cook Islands
Kingman Reef
Saint Helena
12 letters:
Bouvet Island
Cocos Islands
Europa Island
Faroe Islands
French Guiana
Jarvis Island
New Caledonia
Palmyra Atoll
13 letters:
American Samoa

Bassas da India
Cayman Islands
Howland Island
Islas Malvinas
Johnston Atoll
Midway Islands
Navassa Island
Norfolk Island
Virgin Islands
14 letters:
Keeling Islands
Paracel Islands
Spratly Islands
Tromelin Island
15 letters:
Christmas Island
Coral Sea Islands
Falkland Islands
French Polynesia
Glorioso Islands
Pitcairn Islands
Wallis and Futuna

Deserts

4 letters:
Gobi
Thar
6 letters:
Gibson
Libyan
Mohave
Mojave
Nubian
Sahara

7 letters:
Arabian
Atacama
Kara Kum
8 letters:
Kalahari
Kyzyl Kum
9 letters:
Dasht-e-Lut
Dasht-i-Lut

10 letters:
Great Sandy
Rub'al Khali
11 letters:
Death Valley
13 letters:
Great Victoria
15 letters:
Taklimakan Shama

Detectives (Fictional)

7 letters:
Maigret
Taggart
8 letters:
Ironside
Sam Spade
9 letters:
Dick Tracy
Donald Lam
Joe Friday
Lew Archer
Nancy Drew
Nero Wolfe

10 letters:
Jane Marple
Mike Hammer
Paul Temple
Perry Mason
11 letters:
Charlie Chan
Ellery Queen
Father Brown
Jim Bergerac
Jim Rockford
Lord Peter Wimsey
Travis McGee

12 letters:
Sergeant Cuff
Simon Templar
13 letters:
Albert Campion
C Auguste Dupin
Hercule Poirot
Jonathan Creek
Kinky Friedman
Philip Marlowe
14 letters:
Brother Cadfael
Charlie Resnick

Inspector Morse
Inspector Rebus
Sherlock Holmes

15 letters:
Eddie Shoestring
Inspector Bucket

Lieutenant Kojak

Diarists

3 letters:
Nin, *Anaïs*
4 letters:
Gide, *André (Paul Guillaume)*
5 letters:
Frank, *Anne*
Pepys, *Samuel*
6 letters:
Burney, *Fanny*
Evelyn, *John*
7 letters:
Kilvert, *Francis*
8 letters:
Fielding, *Helen (Bridget Jones)*

Townsend, *Sue (Adrian Mole)*
9 letters:
Delafield, *E M*
Grossmith, *George and Weedon
  (Charles Pooter)*
10 letters:
Wordsworth, *Dorothy*
11 letters:
Rivers-Moore, *Marion*
12 letters:
Bashkirtseff, *Marie*

Dinosaurs

8 letters:
Allosaur
Mosasaur
Stegodon
Theropod
9 letters:
Apatosaur
Hadrosaur
Iguanodon
Oviraptor
Pterosaur
Stegodont
Stegosaur
Trachodon
10 letters:
Allosaurus
Ankylosaur
Brontosaur
Ceratosaur
Dimetrodon

Diplodocus
Dromiosaur
Elasmosaur
Iguanodont
Megalosaur
Mosasaurus
Plesiosaur
Pteranodon
Titanosaur
11 letters:
Apatosaurus
Atlantosaur
Brachiosaur
Dolichosaur
Hadrosaurus
Ichthyosaur
Pterodactyl
Stegosaurus
Triceratops
Tyrannosaur

12 letters:
Ankylosaurus
Brontosaurus
Ceratosaurus
Dromiosaurus
Elasmosaurus
Megalosaurus
Plesiosaurus
Titanosaurus
Velociraptor
13 letters:
Atlantosaurus
Brachiosaurus
Compsognathus
Dolichosaurus
Ichthyosaurus
Protoceratops
Tyrannosaurus

Directors, Film

3 letters:
Lee, *Ang*
Lee, *Spike*
Ray, *Satyajit*
Woo, *John*
4 letters:
Coen, *Ethan*
Coen, *Joel*

Ford, *John*
Hall, *Peter*
Hill, *George Roy*
Lang, *Fritz*
Lean, *David*
Penn, *Arthur*
Reed, *Carol*
Roeg, *Nicholas*

Tati, *Jacques*
Weir, *Peter*
Wise, *Robert*
5 letters:
Allen, *Woody*
Brook, *Peter*
Capra, *Frank*
Carné, *Marcel*
Clair, *René*
Dante, *Joe*
Demme, *Johnathan*
Gance, *Abel*
Hawks, *Howard*
Ivory, *James*
Kaige, *Chen*
Kazan, *Elia*
Leigh, *Mike*
Leone, *Sergio*
Loach, *Ken*
Lucas, *George*
Lumet, *Sidney*
Lynch, *David*
Malle, *Louis*
Pabst, *G(eorge) W(ilhelm)*
Reitz, *Edgar*
Roach, *Hal*
Scott, *Ridley*
Stone, *Oliver*
Vadim, *Roger*
Wajda, *Andrei*
Yimou, *Zhang*
6 letters:
Altman, *Robert*
Badham, *John*
Beatty, *Warren*
Besson, *Luc*
Brooks, *Mel*
Buñuel, *Luis*
Burton, *Tim*
Corman, *Roger*
Cuarón, *Alfonso*
Curtiz, *Michael*
De Sica, *Vittoria*
Donner, *Richard*
Forbes, *Bryan*
Forman, *Milös*
Frears, *Stephen*
Godard, *Jean-Luc*
Guitry, *Sacha*
Haneke, *Michael*
Herzog, *Werner*
Huston, *John*
Jarman, *Derek*
Jordan, *Neil*
Kasdan, *Lawrence*
Keaton, *Buster*
Landis, *John*

Lester, *Richard*
Méliès, *Georges*
Mendes, *Sam*
Miller, *George*
Miller, *Jonathon Wolfe*
Ophüls, *Max*
Pagnol, *Marcel*
Parker, *Alan*
Powell, *Michael*
Reiner, *Carl*
Reiner, *Rob*
Renoir, *Jean*
Rohmer, *Eric*
Romero, *George*
Siegel, *Don*
Welles, *Orson*
Wilder, *Billy*
Winner, *Michael*
7 letters:
Aldrich, *Robert*
Asquith, *Anthony*
Bergman, *Ingmar*
Boorman, *John*
Bresson, *Robert*
Cameron, *James*
Campion, *Jane*
Chabrol, *Claude*
Cocteau, *Jean*
Coppola, *Francis Ford*
De Mille, *Cecil B(lount)*
De Palma, *Brian*
Edwards, *Blake*
Fellini, *Federico*
Fleming, *Victor*
Forsyth, *Bill*
Gilliam, *Terry*
Jackson, *Peter*
Kaufman, *Philip*
Kubrick, *Stanley*
McBride, *Jim*
Nichols, *Mike*
Olivier, *Laurence*
Pollack, *Sydney*
Puttnam, *David*
Redford, *Robert*
Resnais, *Alain*
Ritchie, *Guy*
Robbins, *Tim*
Russell, *Ken*
Sturges, *Preston*
Van Sant, *Gus*
Wenders, *Wim*
8 letters:
Anderson, *Lindsay*
Anderson, *Wes*
Columbus, *Christopher*
Eastwood, *Clint*

Friedkin, *William*
Grierson, *John*
Griffith, *D(avid) W(ark)*
Kurosawa, *Akira*
Levinson, *Barry*
Merchant, *Ismail*
Minnelli, *Vincente*
Pasolini, *Pier Paolo*
Polanski, *Roman*
Pudovkin, *Vsevolod*
Scorsese, *Martin*
Truffaut, *François*
Visconti, *Luchino*
Von Trier, *Lars*
Zemeckis, *Robert*
9 letters:
Almódovar, *Pedro*
Antonioni, *Michelangelo*
Armstrong, *Gillian*
Carpenter, *John*
Dovzhenko, *Aleksandr Petrovitch*
Greenaway, *Peter*
Hitchcock, *Alfred*
Minghella, *Anthony*
Mizoguchi, *Kenji*
Peckinpah, *Sam*
Preminger, *Otto*

Spielberg, *Steven*
Stevenson, *Robert*
Tarantino, *Quentin*
Tarkovsky, *Andrei*
Tavernier, *Bertrand*
Zinnemann, *Fred*
10 letters:
Bertolucci, *Bernardo*
Cronenberg, *David*
Eisenstein, *Sergei Mikhailovich*
Fassbinder, *Rainer Werner*
Kieslowski, *Krzysztof*
Mankiewicz, *Joseph*
Rossellini, *Roberto*
Soderbergh, *Steven*
Zeffirelli, *Franco*
11 letters:
Bogdanovich, *Peter*
Mackendrick, *Alexander*
Pressburger, *Emeric*
Riefenstahl, *Leni*
Schlesinger, *John*
Von Stroheim, *Erich*
12 letters:
Attenborough, *Richard*
Von Sternberg, *Joseph*

Disciples

4 letters:
John
Jude
5 letters:
James (*the Great*)
James (*the Less*)

Judas
Peter
Simon
6 letters:
Andrew
Philip

Thomas
7 letters:
Matthew
11 letters:
Bartholomew

Diseases

2 letters:
CD
ME
MS
TB
VD
3 letters:
ALD
BSE
CFS
Flu
Gid
Haw
Pip
Pox
Rot

TSE
Wog
4 letters:
Acne
Ague
AIDS
Boba
Bots
Bunt
Clap
Cold
Conk
Gout
Kuru
Loco
Lues

Lyme
Roup
Scab
Yaws
5 letters:
Bang's
Brand
Braxy
Ebola
Edema
Ergot
Favus
Gapes
Lupus
Lurgi
Lurgy

Mesel
Mumps
Ngana
Palsy
Pinta
Polio
Pott's
Sprue
Surra
Tinea
Weil's
6 letters:
Anbury
Angina
Asthma
Blight
Blotch
Cancer
Canker
Caries
Chagas'
Chorea
Cowpox
Crohn's
Cruels
Dartre
Dengue
Dropsy
Eczema
Farcin
Goitre
Grapes
Graves'
Heaves
Herpes
Income
Iritis
Johne's
Lampas
Mad cow
Meazel
Mildew
Morbus
Nagana
Oedema
Otitis
Paget's
Q fever
Quinsy
Rabies
Sapego
Scurvy
Spavin
Still's
Sweeny
Thrush
Typhus

Ulitis
Urosis
Warble
Zoster
7 letters:
Anthrax
Apraxia
Ascites
Bright's
British
Bulimia
Caisson
Cholera
Coeliac
Colitis
Crewels
Dourine
Earache
Founder
Glue ear
Hansen's
Hard pad
Hydatid
Icterus
Lampers
Leprosy
Lockjaw
Lumbago
Maidism
Malaria
Marburg
Measles
Megrims
Mooneye
Moor-ill
Murrain
Myiasis
Pébrine
Pinkeye
Porrigo
Prurigo
Purples
Purpura
Quittor
Ratbite
Rickets
Roaring
Rosette
Rubella
Scabies
Scrapie
Sequela
Serpigo
Sitfast
Sycosis
Tetanus
Tetters

Typhoid
Uraemia
Uveitis
Variola
Wilson's
8 letters:
Addison's
Alastrim
Anorexia
Aortitis
Beriberi
Blackleg
Bornholm
Bull nose
Bursitis
Carditis
Clubroot
Coxalgia
Cushing's
Cynanche
Cystitis
Diabetes
Dutch elm
Economo's
Epilepsy
Ergotism
Fishskin
Fowl pest
Glanders
Glaucoma
Grand mal
Gummosis
Hidrosis
Hodgkin's
Hookworm
Impetigo
Jaundice
Kala-azar
Loose-cut
Lumpy jaw
Lymphoma
Mastitis
Menière's
Minamata
Myopathy
Myxedema
Osteitis
Pellagra
Petit mal
Phthisis
Phytosis
Pleurisy
Progeria
Pullorum
Rachitis
Raynaud's
Red water

Rhinitis
Ringbone
Ringworm
Rose-rash
Sciatica
Scrofula
Seedy toe
Shingles
Smallpox
Staggers
Suppeago
Swayback
Swinepox
Syphilis
Tay-Sachs
Toe crack
Trachoma
Trembles
Venereal
Vincent's
Vulvitis
Windgall
Zoonosis

9 letters:
Acariasis
Arthritis
Bilharzia
Brown lung
Calenture
Chancroid
Chin cough
Chloracne
Chlorosis
Christmas
Cirrhosis
Dhobi itch
Diarrhoea
Diathesis
Distemper
Dysentery
Emphysema
Enteritis
Exanthema
Gastritis
Glossitis
Gonorrhea
Hepatitis
Idiopathy
Influenza
Ixodiasis
Kawasaki's
Laminitis
Lathyrism
Leucaemia
Leukaemia
Loose smut
Malanders

Milk fever
Myxoedema
Nephritis
Nephrosis
Newcastle
Pellagrin
Pemphigus
Phlebitis
Pneumonia
Porphyria
Psoriasis
Pyorrhoea
Retinitis
Sand crack
Sapraemia
Scratches
Siderosis
Silicosis
Sinusitis
Splenitis
Strangles
Sunstroke
Synovitis
Tarantism
Tick fever
Trichosis
Tularemia
Urticaria
Vaginitis
Vagotonia
Varicosis
Varioloid
Whistling

10 letters:
Absinthism
Acromegaly
Alcoholism
Alzheimer's
Amoebiasis
Asbestosis
Ascariasis
Autoimmune
Babesiosis
Bagassosis
Bell's palsy
Black Death
Broken wind
Bronchitis
Byssinosis
Cellulitis
Chickenpox
Common cold
Dandy-fever
Dermatitis
Diphtheria
Ebola virus
Erysipelas

Fibrositis
Filariasis
Framboesia
Gingivitis
Gonorrhoea
Heartwater
Hemophilia
Hepatitis A
Hepatitis B
Hog cholera
Ichthyosis
Impaludism
Laryngitis
Lassa fever
Leuchaemia
Limber-neck
Lou Gehrig's
Louping ill
Mallanders
Mallenders
Meningitis
Moniliasis
Muscardine
Narcolepsy
Neuropathy
Ornithosis
Parkinson's
Pityriasis
Rinderpest
Salmonella
Scarlatina
Scleriasis
Seborrhoea
Shell shock
Springhalt
Stomatitis
Stringhalt
Swamp fever
Swine fever
Texas fever
Tularaemia
Urethritis
Valvulitis

11 letters:
Anthracosis
Brittle-bone
Brucellosis
Cardiopathy
Consumption
Dead fingers
Farmer's lung
Green monkey
Haemophilia
Hebephrenia
Huntington's
Hypothermia
Jungle fever

Kwashiorkor
Listeriosis
Myxomatosis
Parasitosis
Pharyngitis
Psittacosis
Rickettsial
Salpingitis
Scleroderma
Scrub typhus
Septicaemia
Spina bifida
Spondylitis
Thoroughpin
Tonsillitis
Trench fever
Trench mouth
Trichinosis
Utriculitis
Yellow fever
12 letters:
Aeroneurosis
Anaplasmosis
Appendicitis
Athlete's foot
Avitaminosis
Bilharziasis
Bilharziosis
Black measles
Bush sickness
Constipation
Cor pulmonale
Encephalitis
Endocarditis
Enterobiasis
Fascioliasis
Finger and toe
Foot-and-mouth
Furunculosis
Gallsickness
Herpes zoster
Hoof-and-mouth
Legionnaire's
Milk sickness
Molybdenosis
Motor neurone

Osteomalacia
Osteoporosis
Pericarditis
Quarter crack
Ratbite fever
Sarcomatosis
Scarlet fever
Schizothymia
Sclerodermia
Shaking palsy
Sheep measles
Splenomegaly
Spotted fever
Thalassaemia
Tuberculosis
Typhoid fever
Uncinariasis
13 letters:
Actinomycosis
Blind staggers
Bronchiolitis
Bubonic plague
Elephantiasis
Enterocolitis
Genital herpes
German measles
Greensickness
Herpes simplex
Labyrinthitis
Leichmaniasis
Leishmaniasis
Leishmaniosis
Leptospirosis
Lupus vulgaris
Moon blindness
Non-A hepatitis
Non-B hepatitis
Osteomyelitis
Poliomyelitis
Polycythaemia
Reye's syndrome
Salmonellosis
Schizophrenia
Serum sickness
Syringomyelia
Toxoplasmosis

Tsutsugamushi
Undulant fever
Whooping cough
14 letters:
Bulimia nervosa
Cardiomyopathy
Coal miner's lung
Conjunctivitis
Cystic fibrosis
Diverticulitis
Encephalopathy
Glandular fever
Histoplasmosis
Hypothyroidism
Kaposi's sarcoma
Leucodystrophy
Onchocerciasis
Osteoarthritis
Pneumoconiosis
Relapsing fever
Rheumatic fever
Senile dementia
Spirochaetosis
Sporotrichosis
Swine vesicular
Trichomoniasis
Trichophytosis
Variola porcina
Vincent's angina
Vulvovaginitis
15 letters:
Agranulocytosis
Ancylostomiasis
Ankylostomiasis
Anorexia nervosa
Atherosclerosis
Blackwater fever
Burkitt lymphoma
Double pneumonia
Equine distemper
Gastroenteritis
Pleuropneumonia
Schistosomiasis
Strongyloidosis
Sydenham's chorea
Trypanosomiasis

Dishes

3 letters:
Fry
Pan
Pie
Poi
4 letters:
Dent

Flan
Fool
Hash
Lanx
Mess
Olla
Paté

Puri
Soba
Soss
Soup
Stew
Taco
Tofu

Udon
5 letters:
Balti
Belle
Bhaji
Bitok
Brawn
Brose
Broth
Champ
Chips
Crêpe
Curry
Cutie
Daube
Dolma
Fry-up
Gomer
Grits
Kasha
Kebab
Kibbe
Knish
Kofta
Korma
Laksa
Maror
Paten
Patin
Patty
Pilaf
Pilao
Pilau
Pilaw
Pilow
Pizza
Poori
Quorn®
Raita
Ramen
Roast
Rojak
Salad
Salmi
Sango
Satay
Sushi
Tamal
Thali
Tikka
Toast
6 letters:
Apollo
Bharta
Blintz
Bredie
Bridie

Burgoo
Canapé
Coddle
Cook-up
Croute
Cuscus
Entrée
Faggot
Fondue
Haggis
Hotpot
Houmus
Hummus
Humous
Kimchi
Kishke
Laggen
Laggin
Luggie
Mousse
Muesli
Nachos
Omelet
Paella
Pakora
Panada
Patera
Patine
Pilaff
Pirogi
Pot pie
Quiche
Ragout
Salmis
Samosa
Sanger
Sarmie
Scampi
Scouse
Sowans
Sowens
Subgum
Tagine
Tamale
Tsamba
Wonton
7 letters:
Biriani
Bobotie
Bouchée
Burrito
Calzone
Ceviche
Chafing
Charger
Cocotte
Comport

Compote
Crowdie
Crubeen
Crumble
Custard
Cuvette
Dariole
Dhansak
Dopiaza
Egg roll
Epergne
Fajitas
Falafel
Fel-a-fel
Flasket
Foo yong
Foo Yung
Friture
Goulash
Grav lax
Lasagne
Mousaka
Navarin
Padella
Polenta
Pottage
Poutine
Ramekin
Rarebit
Ravioli
Risotto
Rissole
Roulade
Sashimi
Scallop
Seviche
Skirlie
Sosatie
Soufflé
Stir-fry
Stottie
Stovies
Tartlet
Tempura
Terrine
Timbale
Tostada
8 letters:
Brandade
Caponata
Chop suey
Chow mein
Consommé
Coolamon
Coq au vin
Coquille
Couscous

Crostini
Dolmades
Entremes
Escargot
Feijoada
Fish cake
Gado-gado
Halloumi
Kedgeree
Keftedes
Kickshaw
Kouskous
Kreplach
Kromesky
Matelote
Mazarine
Meat loaf
Mirepoix
Moussaka
Omelette
Pandowdy
Pannikin
Pastrami
Pirozhki
Porridge
Pot-au-feu
Pot roast
Quenelle
Raclette
Ramequin
Salpicon
Sandwich
Shashlik
Sillabub
Souvlaki
Steak pie
Sukiyaki
Syllabub
Teriyaki
Tomalley
Tortilla
Tsatsiki
Tzatziki
Yakimono
Yakitori

9 letters:
Carbonara
Casserole
Cassoulet
Compotier
Croquette
Curry puff
Egg-fo-yang
Enchilada
Entremets
Forcemeat
Fricassee

Galantine
Game chips
Gravad lax
Guacamole
Hamburger
Howtowdie
Irish stew
Jambalaya
Lobscouse
Madrilène
Manicotti
Matelotte
Mutton pie
Osso bucco
Pastitsio
Pepper pot
Reistafel
Rijstafel
Schnitzel
Scotch egg
Scotch pie
Shashlick
Souvlakia
Succotash
Surf 'n' turf
Tyropitta
Vol-au-vent

10 letters:
Avgolemono
Baked beans
Blanquette
Bombay duck
Bruschetta
Cacciatore
Cottage pie
Coulibiaca
Couscousou
Doner kebab
Egg-foo-yung
Fish finger
Fish supper
Hotchpotch
Jugged hare
Koulibiaca
Laver bread
Minestrone
Mixed grill
Nasi goreng
Parmigiana
Provencale
Quesadilla
Red pudding
Rijsttafel
Salmagundi
Salmagundy
Sauerkraut
Scaloppine

Scaloppini
Shish kebab
Smørrebrød
Spatchcock
Spitchcock
Spring roll
Stroganoff
Vegeburger

11 letters:
Buck-rarebit
Caesar salad
Chicken Kiev
Clam chowder
Cock-a-leekie
Corn chowder
Cullen skink
Frankfurter
French toast
Fritto misto
Gefilte fish
Hominy grits
Olla podrida
Palm-oil chop
Ratatouille
Saltimbocca
Sauerbraten
Sausage roll
Scotch broth
Smorgasbord
Spanakopita
Spanish rice
Spanokopita
Suet pudding
Vichyssoise
Welsh rabbit

12 letters:
Cheeseburger
Club sandwich
Cockie-leekie
Cornish pasty
Eggs Benedict
Fish and chips
Forfar bridie
Gefüllte fish
Mulligatawny
Open sandwich
Pease pudding
Prawn cracker
Shepherd's pie
Steak tartare
Taramasalata
Veggieburger
Waldorf salad
Welsh rarebit
White pudding

13 letters:
Prairie oyster

Rumbledethump
Salade niçoise
Scrambled eggs
Toad-in-the-hole
14 letters:
Beef bourguinon

Beef stroganoff
Chilli con carne
Lobster Newburg
Macaroni cheese
Mock turtle soup
Quiche lorraine

Rumbledethumps
15 letters:
Bubble and squeak
Ploughman's lunch

Divination

METHODS OF DIVINATION

4 letters:
Dice
5 letters:
Runes
Tarot
6 letters:
I Ching

7 letters:
Dowsing
Scrying
9 letters:
Astrology
Palmistry
Sortilege

Tea leaves
10 letters:
Numerology
12 letters:
Clairvoyance
13 letters:
Crystal gazing

MEANS OF DIVINATION

Name	Object used
Ailuromancy	Cats
Alphitomancy	Wheat *or* barley cakes
Arachnomancy	Spiders
Astragalomancy	Dice
Bibliomancy	Passages from books
Cartomancy	Cards
Catoptromancy	Mirror
Ceromancy	Melted wax
Chiromancy	Hands
Cleidomancy	Suspended key
Crithomancy	Freshly baked bread
Cromniomancy	Onions
Crystallomancy	Crystal ball
Dactylomancy	Suspended ring
Geomancy	Earth, sand, *or* dust
Hippomancy	Horses
Hydromancy	Water
Lampadomancy	Oil lamps
Lithomancy	Precious stones
Lychnomancy	Flames of wax candles
Molybdomancy	Molten lead
Necromancy	The dead
Oneiromancy	Dreams
Ornithomancy	Birds
Pegomancy	Sacred pool
Pyromancy	Fire *or* flames
Radiesthesia	Pendulum
Rhabdomancy	Rod *or* wand
Sciomancy	Ghosts
Tasseography	Tea leaves
Theomancy	God
Tyromancy	Cheese

Dogs

3 letters:
Cur
Lab
Pom
Pug

4 letters:
Barb
Bush
Chow
Dane
Kuri
Peke
Puli
Stag
Tosa

5 letters:
Akita
Alans
Apsos
Boxer
Brach
Cairn
Coach
Corgi
Husky
Spitz
Spoor

6 letters:
Afghan
Bandog
Barbet
Beagle
Blanch
Borzoi
Briard
Chenet
Cocker
Collie
Eskimo
Goorie
Kelpie
Messan
Pariah
Poodle
Pye-dog
Saluki
Scotch
Setter
Shough
Sleuth
Talbot
Teckel
Vizsla
Westie
Yorkie

7 letters:
Basenji
Boerbul
Bouvier
Brachet
Bulldog
Courser
Griffon
Harrier
Lurcher
Maltese
Maremma
Mastiff
Mongrel
Pointer
Prairie
Raccoon
Samoyed
Sapling
Scottie
Shar-Pei
Sheltie
Shih-tzu
Showghe
Spaniel
Terrier
Volpino
Whippet

8 letters:
Aardwolf
Aberdeen
Airedale
Alsatian
Blenheim
Bratchet
Carriage
Chow-chow
Doberman
Elkhound
Foxhound
Huntaway
Keeshond
Komondor
Labrador
Landseer
Malamute
Malemute
Papillon
Pekinese
Pembroke
Pinscher
Samoyede
Scottish
Sealyham
Springer

Warragal
Warrigal

9 letters:
Buckhound
Chihuahua
Coonhound
Dachshund
Dalmatian
Deerhound
Gazehound
Great Dane
Greyhound
Kerry blue
Lhasa apso
Pekingese
Red setter
Retriever
St Bernard
Schnauzer
Staghound
Wolfhound

10 letters:
Bedlington
Bloodhound
Blue cattle
Blue heeler
Bruxellois
Fox terrier
Otterhound
Pomeranian
Rottweiler
Schipperke
Tripehound
Weimaraner
Welsh corgi

11 letters:
Afghan hound
Basset hound
Bichon Frise
Bull mastiff
Bull terrier
Irish setter
Jack Russell
Rough collie
Skye terrier
Sydney silky

12 letters:
Belvoir hound
Border collie
Cairn terrier
Field spaniel
Gordon setter
Irish terrier
Japanese tosa
Newfoundland

Saint Bernard
Water spaniel
Welsh terrier
West Highland
13 letters:
Affenpinscher
Alpine spaniel
Bearded collie
Border terrier
Boston terrier
Cocker spaniel
Dandie Dinmont
English setter

French bulldog
Scotch terrier
Sussex spaniel
14 letters:
Clumber spaniel
Egyptian basset
German shepherd
Irish wolfhound
Norfolk terrier
Norwich terrier
Pit bull terrier
15 letters:
Aberdeen terrier

Airedale terrier
Alaskan malamute
Blenheim spaniel
Blue Gascon hound
Cuban bloodhound
Golden retriever
Highland terrier
Japanese spaniel
Lakeland terrier
Mexican hairless
Sealyham terrier
Springer spaniel

Drama

2 letters:
No
3 letters:
Noh
5 letters:
Farce
6 letters:
Comedy
Kabuki
Sitcom
Sketch
7 letters:
Tragedy

8 letters:
Jacobean
9 letters:
Kathakali
Melodrama
Soap opera
10 letters:
Shadow play
11 letters:
Kitchen sink
Mystery play
Passion play
Tragicomedy

12 letters:
Costume drama
Costume piece
Grand Guignol
Morality play
13 letters:
Street theatre
14 letters:
Revenge tragedy
15 letters:
Comedy of manners
Situation comedy

Dramatists

2 letters:
Fo, *Dario*
3 letters:
Fry, *Christopher Harris*
Gay, *John*
Kyd, *Thomas*
4 letters:
Amos, *Robert*
Bond, *Edward*
Ford, *John*
Gray, *Oriel*
Hare, *David*
Inge, *William Motter*
Lyly, *John*
Shaw, *George Bernard*
5 letters:
Albee, *Edward (Franklin)*
Behan, *Brendan*
Eliot, *T(homas) S(tearns)*
Esson, *Louis*
Friel, *Brian*
Genet, *Jean*
Gogol, *Nikolai Vasilievich*

Havel, *Václav*
Hayes, *Alfred*
Ibsen, *Henrik*
Lorca, *Federico García*
Mamet, *David*
Odets, *Clifford*
Orton, *Joe*
Otway, *Thomas*
Synge, *(Edmund) J(ohn) M(illington)*
Udall, *Nicholas*
Wilde, *Oscar (Fingal O'Flahertie Wills)*
Yeats, *W(illiam) B(utler)*
6 letters:
Adamov, *Arthur*
Beynon, *Richard*
Brecht, *Bertolt (Eugen Friedrich)*
Bridie, *James (Osborne Henry Mavor)*
Brieux, *Eugene*
Coward, *Noël (Pierce)*
Dekker, *Thomas*

De Vega, *Lope*
Dryden, *John*
Goethe, *Johann Wolfgang von*
Greene, *Robert*
Hebbel, *(Christian) Friedrich*
Hewett, *Dorthy*
Howard, *Sidney*
Jonson, *Ben(jamin)*
Kaiser, *George*
Lawler, *Ray*
Miller, *Arthur*
Oakley, *Barry*
O'Casey, *Sean*
O'Neill, *Eugene (Gladstone)*
Pinero, *Arthur Wing*
Pinter, *Harold*
Porter, *Hal*
Racine, *Jean (Baptiste)*
Sartre, *Jean-Paul*
Seneca, *Lucius Annaeus*
Wilder, *Thornton*
7 letters:
Anouilh, *Jean*
Beckett, *Samuel (Barclay)*
Chapman, *George*
Chekhov, *Anton Pavlovich*
Gilbert, *W(illiam) S(chwenk)*
Goldoni, *Carlo*
Heywood, *Thomas*
Hibberd, *Jack*
Ionesco, *Eugène*
Kushner, *Tony*
Marlowe, *Christopher*
Marston, *John*
Molière
Osborne, *John*
Patrick, *John*
Plautus, *Titus Maccius*
Pushkin, *Aleksander Sergeyevich*
Romeril, *John*
Rostand, *Edmond*
Russell, *Willy*
Seymour, *Alan*
Shaffer, *Peter*
Shepard, *Sam*
Soyinka, *Wole*
Terence
Webster, *John*

8 letters:
Beaumont, *Francis*
Congreve, *William*
Fletcher, *John*
Lochhead, *Liz*
Menander
Rattigan, *Terence (Mervyn)*
Schiller, *Johann Christoph Friedrich von*
Shadwell, *Thomas*
Sheridan, *Richard Brinsley*
Sherwood, *Robert*
Stoppard, *Tom*
Vanbrugh, *Sir John*
Wedekind, *Frank*
Williams, *Tennessee*
Wycherly, *William*
9 letters:
Aeschylus
Ayckbourn, *Alan*
Bleasdale, *Alan*
Corneille, *Pierre*
De la Barca, *Pedro Calderón*
Euripides
Giraudoux, *(Hippolyte) Jean*
Goldsmith, *Oliver*
Hauptmann, *Gerhart Johann Robert*
Massinger, *Philip*
Middleton, *Thomas*
Sackville, *Thomas*
Sophocles
10 letters:
Drinkwater, *John*
Galsworthy, *John*
Pirandello, *Luigi*
Strindberg, *August*
Williamson, *David Keith*
11 letters:
Maeterlinck, *Count Maurice*
Shakespeare, *William*
12 letters:
Aristophanes
Beaumarchais, *Pierre Augustin Caron de*
14 letters:
De Beaumarchais, *Pierre Augustin Caron*

Dresses

4 letters:	**5 letters:**	Tunic
Coat	Burka	**6 letters:**
Midi	Pinny	Caftan
Sack	Saree	Chiton
Sari	Shift	Dirndl

Jumper
Kaftan
Kimono
Mantua
Muu-muu
Nighty
Sheath
7 letters:
Busuuti
Chemise
Gymslip
Nightie
Sweater
Tea gown

Wedding
8 letters:
Ballgown
Cocktail
Negligée
Peignoir
Pinafore
Sundress
9 letters:
Cheongsam
Maxidress
Minidress
Nightgown
Nightrobe

Overdress
10 letters:
Microdress
Nightdress
Nightshirt
Shirtdress
Shirtwaist
11 letters:
Riding habit
12 letters:
Shirtwaister
13 letters:
Button-through
Mother Hubbard

Drinks

2 letters:
It
3 letters:
Ale
Ava
Cha
Cup
Dão
Dop
Gin
Ice
IPA
Keg
Kir
Mum
Nog
Pop
Rum
Rye
Tea
Vin
4 letters:
Arak
Asti
Beef
Bock
Brut
Bull
Bush
Cava
Coke®
Cola
Corn
Dram
Flip
Gavi
Grog
Herb
Hock

Java
Kava
Kola
Korn
Kvas
Malt
Marc
Maté
Mead
Mild
Milk
Mint
Nipa
Nogg
Ouzo
Palm
Pils
Port
Purl
Raki
Rosé
Rosy
Sack
Saké
Saki
Sekt
Soda
Soma
Sour
Sura
Tent
Tutu
Yill
5 letters:
Anise
Anjou
Assam
Bingo
Black

Blend
Bohea
Bombo
Brown
Bumbo
China
Cider
Cocoa
Congo
Crème
Crush
Cyder
Decaf
Fitou
Float
Fruit
Glogg
Grain
Grass
Green
Guest
Haoma
Heavy
Hogan
Hooch
Hyson
Irish
Juice
Julep
Kefir
Kirsh
Kvass
Lager
Latte
Ledum
Lemon
Light
Lirac
Mâcon

Mauby
Meath
Medoc
Meths
Mirin
Mobby
Mocha
Mosel
Mulse
Nappy
Negus
Noyau
Pekoe
Pepsi®
Perry
Pinot
Plain
Polly
Pombe
Punch
Quass
Rakee
Rhine
Rioja
Roero
Rueda
Rully
Rummy
Salop
Senna
Shake
Shrub
Sixty
Sling
Soave
Stout
Straw
Syrah
Tavel

Tizer®
Toddy
Tokay
Tonic
Twist
Yerba
Vimto®
Vodka
Water
Wheat
White
Xeres
6 letters:
Arrack
Atomic
Bandol
Barley
Barolo
Barsac
Beaune
Bishop
Bovril®
Brandy
Burton
Busera
Cahors
Canary
Carema
Cassis
Caudle
Cauker
Ceylon
Chaser
Claret
Coffee
Cognac
Congou
Cooler
Cooper
Crusta
Doctor
Eggnog
Eighty
Enzian
Export
Frappé
Gaelic
Gibson
Gimlet
Ginger
Glayva®
Grappa
Graves
Gueuze
Herbal
Indian
Kaffir

Kahlua
Kenyan
Kephir
Kirsch
Kölsch
Koumis
Kumiss
Kümmel
Lambic
Lisbon
Málaga
Malibu®
Meathe
Merlot
Mescal
Midori
Mocker
Mojito
Muscat
Nectar
Nobbie
Oolong
Oulong
Orgasm
Orgeat
Pastis
Pernod®
Poitín
Porter
Posset
Poteen
Pulque
Quincy
Redeye
Ribena®
Rickey
Samshu
Saumur
Scotch
Shandy
Sherry
Shiraz
Squash
Stingo
Strega
Taffia
Tisane
Tokaji
Waragi
Whisky
Yaqona
Zombie
Zythum
7 letters:
Absinth
Akvavit
Alcopop

Alicant
Amarone
Amoroso
Aquavit
Arabica
Auslese
Bacardi®
Banyuls
Bastard
Bellini
Bitters
Blended
Bourbon
Bucelas
Campari®
Catawba
Chablis
Chanoyu
Chianti
Chinese
Cinzano®
Cobbler
Collins
Cordial
Cowslip
Curaçao
Curaçoa
Daquiri
Dark rum
Draught
Eggflip
Eiswein
Essence
Fendant
Fleurie
Fustian
Gaillac
Guarana
Gunfire
Herb tea
Hokonui
Instant
Italian
Jasmine
Koumiss
Koumyss
Lapsang
Limeade
Liqueur
Madeira
Malmsey
Margaux
Marsala
Martini®
Mineral
Moselle
Negroni

Oenomel
Oloroso
Orvieto
Pale ale
Palinka
Parrina
Perrier®
Persico
Pilsner
Pink gin
Pomerol
Pommard
Ratafee
Ratafia
Real ale
Red-root
Retsina
Rhenish
Robusta
Rooibos
Russian
Sambuca
Sangria
Sazerac
Schnaps
Scrumpy
Seltzer
Seventy
Shebean
Shebeen
Sherbet
Sherris
Shnapps
Shooter
Sidecar
Slammer
Sloe gin
Special
Stengah
Stinger
Swizzle
Tequila
Tio Pepe®
Turkish
Twankay
Vouvray
8 letters:
Absinthe
Advocaat
Aleberry
Amaretto
Ambrosia
Anisette
Apéritif
Armagnac
Bairrada
Bergerac

Bordeaux
Brouilly
Brown ale
Bucellas
Bullshot
Burgundy
Cabernet
Café noir
Calvados
Camomile
Champers
Charneco
Ciderkin
Coca-Cola®
Cocktail
Cold duck
Condrieu
Daiquiri
Dog's nose
Drambuie®
Dubonnet®
Earl Grey
Eau de vie
Espresso
Espumoso
Essencia
Faugères
Frascati
Fruit tea
Galliano®
Geropiga
Gigondas
Gin sling
Gluhwein
Highball
Hollands
Home brew
Hydromel
Iron brew
Jerepigo
Jurançon
Kabinett
Labrador
Lemonade
Lemon tea
Light ale
Lucozade®
Mahogany
Malvasia
Malvesie
Montilla
Muscadel
Muscadet
Muscatel
Palm wine
Paraguay
Pauillac

Persicot
Pilsener
Pink lady
Pinotage
Pradikat
Prunelle
Red biddy
Resinata
Resinate
Rice beer
Rice wine
Riesling
Root beer
Sambucca
Sancerre
Sangaree
Sauterne
Schnapps
Sillabub
Skokiaan
Smoothie
Snowball
Souchong
Sour mash
Spätlese
Spremuta
Spritzer
Spumante
Switchel
Syllabub
Tequilla
Tia Maria®
Trappist
Verdelho
Vermouth
White rum
Witblitz

9 letters:
Alexander
Americano
Applejack
Aqua vitae
Ayahuasco
Bacharach
Badminton
Bardolino
Bourgogne
Bourgueil
Brazilian
Buck's fizz
Chamomile
Champagne
Chocolate
Christmas
Claret cup
Cointreau®
Colombian

Corbières
Côte Rôtie
Cream soda
Cuba libre
Falernian
Firewater
Framboise
Fumé Blanc
Gattinara
Gingerade
Ginger ale
Gladstone
Grenadine
Gunpowder
Hard cider
Hermitage
Hippocras
Hoccamore
Lambrusco
Lambswool
Languedoc
Macchiato
Malvoisie
Manhattan
Margarita
Meersault
Metheglin
Meursault
Milk punch
Milk shake
Milk stout
Minervois
Mint julep
Mirabelle
Muscadine
Nor'wester
Orangeade
Pinot noir
Rauchbier
Rusty Nail
Sauternes
Sauvignon
Slivovitz
Snakebite
Soda water
St Emilion
Sundowner
Tarragona
Triple sec
Van der Hum
Weissbier
Whisky mac
White lady
Zinfandel

10 letters:
Apple juice
Barbaresco

Barley wine
Beaujolais
Bloody Mary
Bull's Blood
Buttermilk
Café au lait
Cappuccino
Chambertin
Chardonnay
Chartreuse®
Constantia
Costa Rican
Darjeeling
Dry martini
Elderberry
Frangelico
Fruit juice
Genevrette
Ginger beer
Ginger wine
Hochheimer
Hogan-mogen
Lolly water
Malt liquor
Manzanilla
Maraschino
Mochaccino
Montrachet
Moscow Mule
Mulled wine
Peter-see-me
Piesporter
Piña colada
Pousse-café
Rosé d'Anjou
Russian tea
Saint-Véran
Shandygaff
Single malt
Spruce beer
Sweet stout
Tom Collins
Valdepeñas
Vatted malt
Verdicchio
Vichy water
Vinho Verde
Weizenbier

11 letters:
Aguardiente
Amontillado
Apple brandy
Barley water
Benedictine
Bitter lemon
Black and tan
Black velvet

Boiler-maker
Continental
Crusted port
Egri Bikaver
Frappuccino
French roast
Half-and-half
Irish coffee
Kirshwasser
Lemon squash
Lime cordial
Monbazillac
Niersteiner
Orange juice
Orange pekoe
Pinot Grigio
Pouilly-Fumé
Post-and-rail
Rosso Cònero
Rüdesheimer
Saint-Julien
Screwdriver
Scuppernong
Skinny latte
Soapolallie
Steinberger
Tomato juice
Yerba de Maté
Whiskey sour

12 letters:
Asti Spumante
Barbera d'Albi
Barbera d'Asti
Bière de Garde
Black Russian
Blue mountain
Cherry brandy

Christmas ale
Colheita Port
Côtes du Rhône
Crème de cacao
Gaelic coffee
Grand Marnier®
Hot chocolate
Humpty-dumpty
Ice-cream soda
India Pale Ale
Irish whiskey
Johannisberg
Kirschwasser
Liqueur Tokay
Marcobrunner
Mineral water
Moscato d'Asti
Old-fashioned
Perrier water®
Saint-Émilion
Saint-Estèphe
Sarsaparilla
Seltzer water
Tome-and-Jerry
Valpolicella
Vin ordinaire
Vosne-Romanée

13 letters:
Amendoa Amarga
Blanc de blancs
Crème de menthe
Decaffeinated
Eau des creoles
Entre-Deux-Mers
Liebfraumilch
Liqueur Muscat
Long Island Tea

Mâcon-Villages
Peach schnapps
Pessac-Léognan
Planter's punch
Pouilly-Fousse
Pouilly-Fuissé
Prairie oyster
Sixty shilling

14 letters:
Crémant d'Alsace
Crémant de Loire
Eighty shilling
Elderberry wine
French vermouth
Gewürztraminer
Herbal infusion
Johannisberger
John Barleycorn
Quarts de Chaume
Singapore sling
Tokay-Pinot Gris
Veuve Jacquolot

15 letters:
Alcohol-free beer
Applejack brandy
Brandy Alexander
Cask-conditioned
Crozes-Hermitage
Grange Hermitage
Grapefruit juice
Italian vermouth
Lachryma Christi
Lapsang Souchong
Salice Salentino
Seventy shilling
Southern Comfort®

Drugs and drug terms

1 letter:	Ice	Alum	Hash
E	INH	Bang	Head
Q	Jag	Blow	Hemp
2 letters:	Kif	Bong	High
Do	LSD	Bust	Hype
LD	Man	Bute	Junk
OD	MLD	Buzz	Kick
3 letters:	PCP®	Coke	Line
Ana	Pop	Dopa	Mass
Cop	Pot	Dope	Nail
DET	STP	Dose	Narc
DMT	Tab	Drop	Oral
Eve	Tea	Gear	Sida
Fix	**4 letters:**	Gone	Soft
Hit	Acid	Goof	Soma
Hop	Adam	Hard	Toke

Toot
Trip
Unit
User
Wine
Wrap
5 letters:
Aloes
Aloin
Benny
Bhang
Candy
Crack
Crank
Dagga
Ganja
Grass
Habit
Hocus
Hop up
Intal®
Joint
L-dopa
Lit up
Local
Mummy
NSAID
Opium
Poppy
Quina
Roach
Route
Rutin
Salep
Salop
Salts
Score
Smack
Smoke
Snort
Speed
Stash
Stuff
Sugar
Sulfa
Taxol
Tonic
Upper
Vomit
Wafer
6 letters:
Amulet
Amytal®
Ativan®
Bombed
Bromal
Bummer

Burned
Charas
Cocain
Cook up
Curare
Curari
Dealer
Dosage
Downer
Dragée
Dry out
Elixir
Emetic
Get off
Heroin
Hooked
Inulin
Ipecac
Jack up
Joypop
Junkie
Kaolin
Liquor
Loaded
Make it
Mescla
Monkey
Mummia
Nod out
Normal
Number
Opiate
Peyote
Pituri
Popper
Prozac®
Pusher
Reefer
Remedy
Saloop
Skin up
Spaced
Spirit
Spliff
Squill
Step on
Stoned
Sulpha
Turn on
Valium®
Viagra®
Wasted
Weight
Zonked
7 letters:
Anodyne
Araroba

Argyrol®
Aspirin
Atabrin
Atebrin®
Atropin
Blocker
Botanic
Calomel
Cardiac
Cascara
Charlie
Chillum
Churrus
Cocaine
Codeine
Crank up
Damiana
Dapsone
Ecbolic
Ecstasy
Errhine
Ethical
Eucaine
Exhaust
Extract
Guarana
Hashish
Hemagog
Hemlock
Henbane
Hepatic
Hophead
Hyped up
Hypnone
Insulin
Jellies
Kaoline
Librium®
Linctus
Metopon
Miltown®
Mixture
Mogadon®
Morphia
Nervine
Patulin
Pep pill
Pessary
Placebo
Pothead
Quinine
Reactor
Rhatany
Salicin
Seconal®
Shoot up
Skin-pop

Smashed
Steroid
Styptic
Suramin
Swacked
Synergy
Tetanic
Topical
Trional
Turpeth
Vehicle
Veronal®
Vinegar
Wrecked
8 letters:
Acidhead
Adjuvant
Antabuse®
Antidote
Aromatic
Atabrine®
Ataraxic
Atropine
Autacoid
Bacterin
Banthine
Barbital
Benadryl®
Bioassay
Blockade
Caffeine
Cannabis
Cinchona
Cohobate
Comedown
Cortisol
Curarine
Designer
Diazepam
Diuretic
Emulsion
Endermic
Ephedrin
Excitant
External
Fentanyl
Freebase
Goofball
Hyoscine
Hypnotic
Inhalant
Ketamine
Krameria
Laetrile
Laudanum
Laxative
Lenitive

Mainline
Mersalyl
Mescalin
Methadon
Miticide
Moonrock
Morphine
Naloxone
Narcotic
Nembutal®
Neomycin
Nepenthe
Nicotine
Nystatin
Opium den
Overdose
Oxytocic
Pectoral
Positive
Psilocin
Pulmonic
Reaction
Relaxant
Retrovir®
Rifampin
Roborant
Salicine
Santonin
Scammony
Scopolia
Sedative
Serevent®
Snowball
Spansule
Specific
Switch on
Terebene
Tetronal
Thiazide
Tincture
Tolerant
Valerian
Vesicant
Viricide
Wormseed
Zerumbet
9 letters:
Acyclovir
Addiction
Addictive
Analeptic
Analgesic
Angel dust
Anovulant
Antrycide
Arsenical
Ataractic

Attenuant
Augmentin
Azedarach
Barbitone
Berberine
Biguanide
Botanical
Bring down
Busulphan
Calmative
Captopril
Carbachol
Cathartic
Cisplatin
Clozapine
Corticoid
Cortisone
Crackhead
Cyclizine
Cytotoxin
Decoction
Demulcent
Digitalis
Dramamine®
Electuary
Ephedrine
Excipient
Expellant
Expellent
Febrifuge
Foscarnet
Frusemide
Galenical
Glycoside
Goa powder
Hemagogue
Ibuprofen
Inotropic
Iprindole
Isoniazid
Jaborandi
Lorazepam
Magistral
Marihuana
Marijuana
Menstruum
Mepacrine
Merbromin
Mercurial
Mescaline
Methadone
Mydriasis
Novocaine®
Nux vomica
Officinal
Oleoresin
Paludrine®

Paregoric
Pethidine
Phenytoin
Practolol
Purgative
Quercetin
Quercitin
Quinidine
Quinquina
Reserpine
Resolvent
Revulsive
Safflower
Scopoline
Senna leaf
Senna pods
Sensitise
Sensitize
Signature
Smackhead
Soporific
Spaced out
Speedball
Stimulant
Strung out
Sudorific
Synergism
Synergist
Tamoxifen
Temazepam
Teniacide
Teniafuge
Totaquine
Tricyclic
Trinitrum
Verapamil
Vermifuge
Vulnerary
Wych hazel
Yohimbine
10 letters:
Abirritant
Absorption
Acetanilid
Agrypnotic
Alterative
Amantadine
Ampicillin
Anesthetic
Antagonist
Antibiotic
Antiemetic
Antimonial
Antipyrine
Anxiolytic
Astringent
Atracurium

Bacitracin
Belladonna
Benzedrine®
Benzocaine
Biological
Bufotenine
Chalybeate
Cholagogue
Cimetedine
Cimetidine
Cinchonine
Clofibrate
Clomiphene
Cold turkey
Colestipol
Confection
Connection
Convulsant
Dependency
Depressant
Disulfiram
Ergotamine
Ethambutol
Euphoriant
Formestane
Get through
Haemagogue
Helminthic
Hemostatic
Hypodermic
Imipramine
Indapamide
Isoniazide
Ivermectin
Lethal dose
Long-acting
Medication
Mefloquine
Meperidine
Methyldopa
Mickey Finn
Nalbuphine
Nifedipine
Nitrazepam
Painkiller
Palliative
Papaverine
Parenteral
Penicillin
Pentaquine
Phenacaine
Phenacetin
Phenformin
Potash alum
Potentiate
Prednisone
Preventive

Primaquine
Probenecid
Psilocybin
Quinacrine
Rifampicin
Salbutamol
Selegiline
Side effect
Space cadet
Speedfreak
Spermicide
Stramonium
Sucralfate
Taeniacide
Taeniafuge
Terramycin®
Thiouracil
Unofficial
Vesicatory
Witch hazel
Withdrawal
Ziduvidine
11 letters:
Acetanilide
Acriflavine
Adiaphorous
Allopurinol
Aminobutene
Amphetamine
Amyl nitrite
Anaesthetic
Antifebrile
Antimycotic
Antipyretic
Antitussive
Aphrodisiac
Apomorphine
Barbiturate
Beta-blocker
Bitter aloes
Bupivacaine
Cantharides
Carbimazole
Carminative
Chloroquine
Chrysarobin
Cinnarizine
Clenbuterol
Clindamycin
Contrayerva
Deserpidine
Diamorphine
Diaphoretic
Distalgesic
Embrocation
Emmenagogue
Expectorant

Fluconazole
Gemfibrozil
Haemostatic
Haloperidol
Hyoscyamine
Ipecacuanha
Ipratropium
Isoxsuprine
Laughing gas
Magic bullet
Masticatory
Meprobamate
Neuroleptic
Nikethamide
Paracetamol
Paraldehyde
Pentamidine
Pentazocine
Pravastatin
Propranolol
Proprietary
Psychedelic
Psychodelic
Purple heart
Restorative
Sanguinaria
Scopolamine
Sensitivity
Short-acting
Succedaneum
Suppository
Suppurative
Thalidomide
Theobromine
Tolbutamide
Tous-les-mois
Trituration
Tropomyosin
Tumefacient
Vasodilator
Vinblastine
Vincristine
12 letters:
ACE inhibitor
Alexipharmic
Alpha-blocker
Anthelmintic
Antimalarial
Antiperiodic
Arsphenamine
Azathioprine
Chlorambucil
Control group
Cyclopropane
Cyclosporin-A
Decongestant
False saffron

Fluidextract
Fluphenazine
Glue-sniffing
Gonadotropin
Guanethidine
Hallucinogen
Idiosyncrasy
Incompatible
Indomethacin
Intoxicating
Mecamylamine
Methaqualone
Methotrexate
Mifepristone
Nitrous oxide
Perphenazine
Physotigmine
Prednisolone
Prescription
Promethazine
Prophylactic
Psychoactive
Radio mimetic
Recreational
Solvent abuse
Sorbefacient
Spermatocide
Streptomycin
Stupefacient
Tetracycline
Tranquilizer
Trimethoprim
Venepuncture
Venipuncture
13 letters:
Abortifacient
Amitriptyline
Anaphrodisiac
Anthelminthic
Antihistamine
Antispasmodic
Carbamazepine
Contraceptive
Co-trimoxazole
Depressomotor
Knockout drops
Magic mushroom
Materia medica
Mind-expanding
Penicillamine
Phencyclidine
Phenothiazine
Pyrimethamine
Sulphadiazine
Sympatholytic
Tachyphylaxis
Thiabendazole

Tranquilliser
Tranquillizer
Triamcinolone
Vasoinhibitor
Vinca alkaloid
14 letters:
Anticonvulsant
Antidepressant
Antimetabolite
Antiphlogistic
Bendrofluozide
Benzodiazepine
Bronchodilator
Butyrhophenone
Cascara sagrada
Chlorothiazide
Chlorpromazine
Chlorpropamide
Chlorthalidone

Contraindicate
Dimenhydrinate
Flucloxacillin
Hydrocortisone
Hypersensitive
Mean lethal dose
Mercaptopurine
Norethisterone
Over-the-counter
Pentobarbitone
Phenacyclidine
Phenobarbitone
Phenylbutazone
Rochelle powder
Seidlitz powder
Sulfamethazine
Sulphadimidine
Sulphanilamide
Sulphathiozole

Sulphisoxazole
15 letters:
Acetophenetidin
Alkylating agent
Anticholinergic
Bioavailability
Chloramphenicol
Dinitrogen oxide
Local anesthetic
Methamphetamine
Phenolphthalein
Psychotomimetic
Seidlitz powders
Shooting gallery
Sodium Pentothal®
Sympathomimetic
Vasoconstrictor

Ducks

4 letters:
Blue
Musk
Smee
Smew
Sord
Surf
Teal
Wood
5 letters:
Eider
Ruddy
Scaup
6 letters:
Garrot
Hareld
Herald
Runner
Scoter
Smeath
Smeeth

Tufted
Wigeon
7 letters:
Flapper
Gadwall
Mallard
Muscovy
Pintail
Pochard
Spatula
Widgeon
8 letters:
Bald-pate
Garganey
Mandarin
Oldsquaw
Paradise
Shelduck
Shoveler
9 letters:
Aylesbury

Bargander
Bergander
Golden-eye
Goosander
Greenhead
Harlequin
Sheldduck
Shoveller
Sprigtail
Whistling
10 letters:
Bufflehead
Canvasback
Long-tailed
Shieldrake
Surfscoter
11 letters:
Ferruginous
12 letters:
Velvet scoter

Dwarfs

3 letters:
Doc
5 letters:
Dopey

Happy
6 letters:
Grumpy
Sleepy

Sneezy
7 letters:
Bashful

Dyes

3 letters:
Azo
Vat
4 letters:
Anil
Chay
Choy
Ikat
Kohl
Wald
Weld
Woad
Wold
5 letters:
Batik
Chaya
Chica
Congo
Eosin
Grain
Henna
Shaya
Sumac
Woald
6 letters:
Archil
Battik
Cobalt
Corkir
Crotal
Direct
Flavin
Fustic
Fustoc
Gambir
Indigo
Kamala
Kermes

Korkir
Madder
Orcein
Orchel
Orchil
Raddle
Sumach
Tannin
Tie-dye
7 letters:
Alkanet
Camwood
Crocein
Crottle
Cudbear
Engrain
Flavine
Fuchsin
Gambier
Indican
Indoxyl
Indulin
Magenta
Mauvein
Para-red
Puccoon
Sunfast
Valonia
8 letters:
Catechin
Cinnabar
Fuchsine
Indamine
Induline
Mauveine
Nigrosin
Orchella
Purpurin

Pyronine
Safranin
Stone-rag
Stone-raw
Turnsole
Xanthium
Xylidine
9 letters:
Cochineal
Envermeil
Indirubin
Myrobalan
Nigrosine
Phthalein
Primuline
Quinoline
Rhodamine
Rosanilin
Safranine
10 letters:
Anthracene
Azobenzine
Carthamine
Quercitron
Resorcinol
Rosaniline
Tartrazine
Tropaeolin
11 letters:
Incarnadine
13 letters:
Anthraquinone
Canthaxanthin
14 letters:
Dinitrobenzene
15 letters:
Phenolphthalein

See also:
➤ **Pigments**

Ear, parts of

5 letters:
Ancus
Incus
Pinna
6 letters:
Meatus
Stapes
Tragus
7 letters:
Cochlea

Eardrum
Ear lobe
Malleus
Saccule
Utricle
8 letters:
Tympanum
10 letters:
Oval window

11 letters:
Round window
12 letters:
Organ of Corti
13 letters:
Auditory canal
Auditory nerve
14 letters:
Eustachian tube

Earth's crust

4 letters:
Sial
Sima
7 letters:
Oceanic

8 letters:
Basement
11 letters:
Continental
Lithosphere
Lower mantle
Upper mantle

13 letters:
Asthenosphere
14 letters:
Transition zone

Eating habits

Food	**Name of habit**
Fellow humans	Anthropophagic *or* anthropophagous
Bees	Apivorous
Other members of the same species	Cannibalistic
Meat	Carnivorous
Fruit	Carpophagous, frugivorous, *or* fruitarian
Dead and rotting flesh	Carrion
Dung	Coprophagous
Earth	Geophagous
Plants	Herbivorous
Wood	Hylophagous
Insects	Insectivorous
Mud	Limivorous
Large pieces of food	Macrophagous
Only one food	Monophagous
Fungi	Mycetophagous
Ants	Myrmecophagous
Nectar	Nectarivorous
Nuts	Nucivorous

Food

	Name of habit
Meat and plants	Omnivorous
Raw food	Omophagic *or* omophagous
Fish	Piscivorous
Gods	Theophagous
No animal products	Vegan
No flesh	Vegetarian
Animals	Zoophagous

Ecclesiastical terms

1 letter:
R
S
V
X
Y

2 letters:
BV
CE
DG
DV
HC
MS
PB
PP
RR
Sr
SS
St
VG
VW
Xn
XP
Xt

3 letters:
Abp
Alb
BVM
Cup
Dip
Fra
God
IDN
IHS
Lay
LDS
Mgr
Nun
Par
Pie
Pit
Pix
Pye
Pyx
Rev

See
Sta
STD
Ste
Sun
Use
Ven
Vow
WCC
Zen

4 letters:
Abbé
Alms
Ambo
Amen
Apse
Bans
Bapt
Beat
Bell
Cell
Chap
C of E
Cope
Cowl
Crib
Cure
Dame
Dean
Dove
Ebor
Eccl
Fall
Fold
Font
Hadg
Hajj
Halo
Holy
Host
Hymn
Idol
Kirk
Laic
Lent

Mass
Monk
None
Pall
Revd
Rite
Rood
Rule
Sain
Seal
Sext
Sign
Sion
Slip
Suff
Text
Veil
V Rev
Wake
Whit
Xmas
Xnty
YMCA
Yule
YWCA
Zion

5 letters:
Abbey
Abbot
Agape
Allah
Altar
Ambry
Amice
Amish
Angel
Banns
Bedel
Bible
Bless
Canon
Carol
Catho
Cense
Chant

Choir	Paten	Eparch
Clerk	Patin	Exarch
Close	Pietà	Exodus
Cloth	Piety	Father
Credo	Plate	Ferial
Creed	Prior	Friary
Cross	Psalm	Fundie
Cruet	Pyxis	Gloria
Crypt	Rabbi	Gnosis
Curse	Saint	God man
Deify	Satan	Godson
Deism	Stall	Gospel
Deist	Stole	Gradin
Deity	Stoop	Hallow
Demon	Stoup	Harrow
Denom	Suffr	Heaven
Devil	Synod	Hebrew
Dirge	Teind	Heresy
Dogma	Tithe	Homily
Dowry	Title	Housel
Druid	Trump	Hymnal
Elder	Vigil	Impose
Elect	Wafer	Intone
Epiph	**6 letters:**	Israel
Exeat	Abbacy	Jesuit
Faith	Abbess	Jewish
Flock	Advent	Judaic
Friar	Almuce	Lavabo
Frock	Anoint	Lector
Glebe	Anthem	Legend
Glory	Archbp	Lenten
Godly	Assume	Lesson
Grace	Aumbry	Litany
Hindu	Austin	Living
Hours	Beadle	Marian
House	Bishop	Martyr
Islam	Cantor	Matins
Jesus	Censer	Maundy
Jewry	Chapel	Mormon
Karma	Cherub	Mosaic
Koran	Chrism	Moslem
Laity	Christ	Mosque
Laver	Church	Mother
Maker	Clergy	Muslim
Manna	Cleric	Novice
Manse	Coming	Nuncio
Matin	Common	Oblate
Miter	Crèche	Octave
Mitre	Curacy	Office
Mt Rev	Curate	Old man
Myrrh	Curtal	Ordain
Nones	Deacon	Orders
Offer	Devout	Papacy
Order	Divine	Papism
Padre	Dossal	Papist
Pagan	Dragon	Parish
Papal	Easter	Parson

Pastor
Patron
Paynim
Person
Postil
Prayer
Preach
Priest
Priory
Proper
Pulpit
Purify
Purple
Quaker
Redeem
Revert
Ritual
Rosary
Rt Revd
Rubric
Sacral
Sacred
Schism
Season
Secret
Sermon
Server
Sexton
Shiite
Shinto
Shrine
Shroud
Simony
Sinful
Sinner
Sister
Solemn
Stigma
Sufism
Sunday
Suttee
Talmud
Tantra
Taoism
Te Deum
Temple
Theism
Tippet
Tongue
Venite
Verger
Vesper
Vestal
Vestry
Virgin
Votary
Warden

7 letters:
Aaronic
Acolyte
Agrapha
Ampulla
Anagoge
Apostle
Article
Ascetic
Asperse
Atheism
Atheist
Bahaism
Bambino
Baptism
Baptist
Baptize
Benison
Blessed
Brother
Canonry
Cantuar
Cassock
Cenacle
Chalice
Chancel
Chantry
Chapter
Chrisom
Classis
Cluniac
Collate
Collect
College
Commune
Confess
Confirm
Conform
Convent
Council
Counsel
Crosier
Crozier
Deanery
Decanal
Defrock
Deified
Devotee
Diocese
Dissent
Dominie
Element
Epistle
Eremite
Errancy
Evangel
Evil One

Expiate
Frontal
Genesis
Gentile
Glorify
Gnostic
Godhead
Godhood
Halidom
Hassock
Heathen
Holy day
Holy Joe
Hosanna
Idolize
Immerse
Incense
Infulae
Inspire
Introit
Jainism
Jehovah
Judaism
Kenosis
Kerygma
Kirkman
Labarum
Lady Day
Laicize
Liturgy
Low Mass
Lustral
Madonna
Maniple
Martyry
Mattins
Maurist
Messiah
Minster
Miracle
Mission
Monkery
Monkish
Mortify
Mourner
Movable
Mystery
Notitia
Nunhood
Nunnery
Old Nick
Oratory
Ordinal
Our Lady
Parlour
Paschal
Pauline

Peccant
Penance
Pietism
Pilgrim
Pontiff
Prebend
Prelacy
Prelate
Present
Primacy
Primate
Profane
Prophet
Proverb
Provide
Puritan
Ramadan
Recluse
Rectory
Regular
Reredos
Respond
Retable
Revival
Sabbath
Sacring
Sanctum
Sanctus
Saviour
Secular
Sedilia
Service
Species
Sponsor
Spousal
Station
Stylite
Tantric
Titulus
Tribune
Trinity
Unction
Unfrock
Vatican
Vespers
Whitsun
Worship
Xmas Day
Yule log
Zionism
8 letters:
Abbatial
Ablution
Advowson
Affusion
Agnus Dei
Alleluia

Altar boy
Anathema
Anglican
Antiphon
Beadsman
Bedesman
Benefice
Brownist
Buddhism
Buddhist
Canonist
Canonize
Canon law
Canticle
Cathedra
Catholic
Celibacy
Cellarer
Cenobite
Chancery
Chapelry
Chaplain
Charisma
Chasuble
Cherubim
Choirboy
Christen
Ciborium
Clerical
Cloister
Coenacle
Colloquy
Creation
Crucifix
Deaconry
Dedicate
Devotion
Diaconal
Dies Irae
Diocesan
Diriment
Disciple
Disfrock
Docetism
Doxology
Druidess
Druidism
Ecce Homo
Ecclesia
Emmanuel
Empyrean
Epiphany
Epistler
Evensong
Expiable
Faithful
Footpace

Fraction
Frontlet
Galilean
Gallican
Godchild
God's acre
Godsquad
Guardian
Hail Mary
Hallowed
Heavenly
Hierarch
Hieratic
High Mass
Holiness
Holy City
Holy Land
Holy rood
Holy Week
Hymn book
Immanent
Immanuel
Jacobite
Jubilate
Lavatory
Libellee
Lord's Day
Lustrate
Lutheran
Man of God
Maronite
Marriage
Menology
Ministry
Miserere
Mohammed
Monachal
Monastic
Monition
Monkhood
Nativity
Oblation
Offering
Ordinand
Ordinary
Orthodox
Paradise
Parament
Parclose
Pastoral
Pelagian
Penitent
Pericope
Piacular
Postlude
Priestly
Prophesy

Province
Psalmody
Redeemer
Registry
Response
Reverend
Rigorism
Rogation
Sacristy
Sanctify
Sanctity
Sarum use
Scapular
Sentence
Separate
Silenced
Simoniac
Sinecure
Son of God
Suffrage
Superior
Tantrism
Tertiary
Thurible
Thurifer
Tithable
Traditor
Transept
Unchurch
Unhallow
Veronica
Versicle
Vesperal
Vestment
Viaticum
Vicarage
Vicarial

9 letters:
Adoration
Alleluiah
Allelujah
Ambrosian
Antiphony
Apostolic
Archangel
Aspersion
Augustine
Avoidance
Baptistry
Beelzebub
Bishopric
Blasphemy
Born-again
Calvinism
Calvinist
Candlemas
Canonical

Cantorial
Capitular
Catechism
Catechize
Cathedral
Celebrant
Celestial
Christian
Christmas
Churchman
City of God
Claustral
Clergyman
Clericals
Cloistral
Coadjutor
Coenobite
Collation
Collative
Collegium
Comforter
Commendam
Communion
Conciliar
Confessor
Confirmed
Dalai Lama
Damnation
Deaconess
Dei gratia
Diaconate
Dimissory
Directory
Discalced
Dissenter
Dog collar
Dominical
Easter Day
Ecumenism
Epiclesis
Episcopal
Establish
Eucharist
Exarchate
Expectant
Expiation
Expiatory
Formalism
Formulary
Godfather
Godmother
Godparent
Gospeller
Graveyard
Hagiarchy
Halloween
Hallowmas

Hermitage
Hierarchy
High altar
Holocaust
Holy Ghost
Holy Grail
Holy water
Homiletic
Immersion
Impeccant
Incensory
Incumbent
Institute
Interdict
Jerusalem
Last rites
Lay sister
Libellant
Liturgics
Liturgist
Love feast
Low Sunday
Martinmas
Martyrdom
Mercy seat
Methodism
Methodist
Millenary
Miscreant
Missioner
Monastery
Mortal sin
Novitiate
Obedience
Offertory
Officiant
Officiate
Our Father
Out sister
Paraclete
Parochial
Parsonage
Pastorate
Patriarch
Patrimony
Patristic
Patrology
Patroness
Pentecost
Perdition
Pluralism
Plurality
Pluralize
Polyptych
Precentor
Preceptor
Predicant

Prelatism
Presbyter
Proselyte
Provision
Quakerism
Recession
Reconcile
Reconvert
Reformism
Religieux
Religious
Reliquary
Remission
Ritualism
Ritualize
Rubrician
Rural dean
Sacrament
Sacrarium
Sacrifice
Sacrilege
Sacristan
Saint's day
Salvation
Sanctuary
Scientist
Seneschal
Shintoism
Solemnize
Spiritual
Succentor
Succursal
Suffragan
Surrogate
Sutteeism
Synagogue
Testament
Tradition
Translate
Venerable
Venial sin
Vestryman
Vicariate
Yom Kippur
10 letters:
Act of faith
Allhallows
Altar cloth
Amen corner
Antinomian
Antiphonal
Apostolate
Archbishop
Archdeacon
Archpriest
Asceticism
Ascription

Assumption
Athanasian
Bar mitzvah
Benedicite
Benedictus
Canonicals
Canonicate
Canonicity
Canto fermo
Catechumen
Ceremonial
Chancellor
Childermas
Churchgoer
Circumcise
Cloistered
Conference
Confessant
Confession
Confirmand
Conformist
Conformity
Connection
Consecrate
Consistory
Conventual
Dedication
Deo gratias
Deo volente
Devotional
Discipline
Ecumenical
Enthusiasm
Enthusiast
Episcopacy
Episcopate
Evangelism
Evangelist
Evangelize
Fellowship
Fenestella
Free Church
Gnosticize
Good Friday
Gospel oath
Hagiolatry
Halleluiah
Hallelujah
Hierocracy
High Church
High Priest
Holy Family
Holy orders
Holy Spirit
Homiletics
Horologium
House group

House of God
Idolatrize
Impanation
Impeccable
Insufflate
Intinction
Invitatory
Invocation
Irreligion
Lammastide
Last Supper
Lay brother
Lectionary
Limitarian
Liturgical
Lord's table
Magnificat
Metropolis
Millennium
Miscreance
Misericord
Missionary
Mother's Day
Ordination
Palm Sunday
Pancake Day
Pilgrimage
Pontifical
Prayer book
Preachment
Prebendary
Presbytery
Priesthood
Profession
Protestant
Providence
Provincial
Puritanism
Religieuse
Requiescat
Reredorter
Responsory
Retrochoir
Reunionist
Revelation
Revivalism
Revivalist
Sacerdotal
Sacrosanct
Sanctified
Sanctitude
Scriptures
Secularize
Sexagesima
Shrovetide
Sisterhood
Solifidian

Subreption
Subsellium
Superaltar
Tabernacle
Twelfth Day
Unhallowed
Unhouseled
Versicular
Vigil light
Virgin Mary
Visitation
Whit Monday
Whit Sunday
11 letters:
All Souls' Day
Antependium
Antiphonary
Archdiocese
Aspersorium
Augustinian
Benediction
Beneficiary
Blasphemous
Book of hours
Brotherhood
Calefactory
Cardinalate
Catholicism
Celtic cross
Christening
Christingle
Churchwoman
Clericalism
Cockleshell
Coessential
Commandment
Communicant
Communicate
Contemplate
Conventicle
Convocation
Crucifixion
Evangelical
Externalism
Gloria Patri
Glossolalia
Goddaughter
Hare Krishna
House church
Immanentism
Impropriate
Incarnation
Incorporeal
Independent
Institution
Irreligious
Jesus Christ

Judgment Day
Lord of Hosts
Lord's Prayer
Lord's Supper
Martyrology
Millenarian
Monasticism
Monseigneur
Mother of God
Oecumenical
Parish clerk
Parishioner
Paschal Lamb
Passiontide
Passion Week
Patron saint
Pelagianism
Pentecostal
Preparation
Priestcraft
Prodigal Son
Proselytize
Protomartyr
Purificator
Rastafarian
Recessional
Ritualistic
Sabbatarian
Sacramental
Sanctus bell
Scriptorium
Stabat Mater
Sursum corda
Temporality
Thaumaturge
Twelfthtide
Whitsuntide
Year of grace
Zen Buddhism
12 letters:
Advent Sunday
All Saints' Day
Anathematize
Annunciation
Apostolic See
Archdeaconry
Ascension Day
Ash Wednesday
Body of Christ
Chapel of ease
Chapterhouse
Christmas Day
Christmas Eve
Churchwarden
Circuit rider
Concelebrate
Confessional

Confirmation
Confucianism
Congregation
Deconsecrate
Disestablish
Dispensation
Ecclesiastic
Ecclesiology
Eleanor Cross
Episcopalian
Episcopalism
Good Shepherd
Heteroousian
Holy Saturday
Holy Thursday
Immersionism
Independency
Intercession
Judgement Day
Kyrie eleison
Last Judgment
Messeigneurs
Metropolitan
Ministration
Most Reverend
New Testament
Non-Christian
Obedientiary
Old Testament
Palingenesis
Patriarchate
Presbyterian
Presentation
Presentative
Procathedral
Processional
Providential
Quadragesima
Real presence
Residentiary
Rogation Days
Satisfaction
Satisfactory
Septuagesima
Spirituality
Spiritualize
Spy Wednesday
Subapostolic
Subscription
Sunday school
Superhumeral
Thanksgiving
Traducianism
Twelfth Night
Very Reverend
Vicar general
Well dressing

Winding sheet
13 letters:
Allhallowtide
Apostles' Creed
Archbishopric
Archidiaconal
Ascensiontide
Autocephalous
Baptism of fire
Burnt offering
Canonical hour
Contemplation
Contemplative
Corpus Christi
Credence table
Day of Judgment
Divine service
Ecclesiolatry
Excommunicate
Gift of tongues
Glorification
Holy Communion
Incardination
Last Judgement
Mater dolorosa
Metrical psalm
Mortification

Nonpractising
Passion Sunday
Premillennial
Protestantism
Quadragesimal
Quinquagesima
Right Reverend
Roman Catholic
Sacerdotalism
Salvation Army
Sanctuary lamp
Shrove Tuesday
Spoiled priest
Trinity Sunday
Unconsecrated
14 letters:
Archidiaconate
Archiepiscopal
Article of faith
Day of Judgement
Ecclesiastical
Exclaustration
Extracanonical
Fundamentalism
Gregorian chant
Indifferentism
Intercommunion

Maundy Thursday
Millenarianism
Orthodox Church
Parish register
Peculiar people
Pontifical Mass
Rastafarianism
Recording Angel
Reverend Mother
Sacramentalism
Sacramentarian
Territorialism
15 letters:
Act of contrition
Archiepiscopate
Athanasian Creed
Church of England
Dominical letter
Ecclesiasticism
Excommunication
Father confessor
General Assembly
Jehovah's Witness
Mothering Sunday
Presbyterianism
Ten Commandments

Economics

ECONOMICS TERMS

2 letters:
HP
3 letters:
Bid
GDP
GNP
NIC
Pay
PEP
RPI
RRP
Tax
UBR
VAT
4 letters:
Bank
Boom
Cash
Cost
Debt
Duty
Hire
Loan
Loss

MCAs
Mint
PAYE
PSBR
Rent
Shop
Wage
5 letters:
Asset
Audit
Lease
Money
Price
Sales
Scale
Share
Slump
Stock
Trade
Trust
Yield
6 letters:
Barter
Budget

Buy-out
Cartel
Credit
Demand
Equity
Export
Import
Income
Labour
Lender
Market
Merger
Patent
Picket
Profit
Retail
Salary
Saving
Sector
Supply
Tariff
Wealth
7 letters:
Autarky

Balance
Boycott
Capital
Dumping
Duopoly
Embargo
Finance
Freight
Funding
Hedging
Holding
Invoice
Lockout
Payment
Payroll
Pension
Premium
Revenue
Subsidy
Surplus
Synergy
Trustee
Utility
8 letters:
Base rate
Capacity
Consumer
Currency
Discount
Dividend
Earnings
Employee
Employer
Exchange
Freeport
Hoarding
Hot money
Interest
Junk bond
Monopoly
Mortgage
Offshore
Overtime
Producer
Recovery
Supplier
Takeover
Taxation
Tax haven
Training
9 letters:
Commodity
Deflation
Franchise
Free rider
Free trade
Gilt-edged

Income tax
Inflation
Insurance
Liability
Liquidity
Means test
Mediation
Middleman
Net profit
Oligopoly
Overheads
Piecework
Portfolio
Rationing
Recession
Recycling
Reflation
Sanctions
Trademark
Unit trust
10 letters:
Agronomics
Automation
Bankruptcy
Bear market
Bull market
Capitalism
Closed shop
Commission
Depression
Divestment
Employment
Fiscal drag
Fiscal year
Fixed costs
Forfaiting
Game theory
Green money
Insolvency
Investment
Joint-stock
Monetarism
Pawnbroker
Production
Redundancy
Share issue
Tax evasion
Trade union
Wholesaler
11 letters:
Arbitration
Capital good
Central bank
Cliometrics
Competition
Consumption
Cooperative

Corporation
Devaluation
Durable good
Expenditure
Fixed assets
Foreclosure
Gross profit
Index-linked
Indirect tax
Intangibles
Legal tender
Liquid asset
Liquidation
Money supply
Overheating
Overmanning
Pension fund
Poverty trap
Premium bond
Public works
Pump priming
Revaluation
Savings bank
Self service
Shareholder
Share market
Shop steward
Social costs
Speculation
Stagflation
Stockbroker
Stock market
Stop-go cycle
Transaction
Underwriter
12 letters:
Balance sheet
Black economy
Bridging loan
Buyer's market
Clearing bank
Common market
Consumer good
Cost of living
Customs union
Depreciation
Deregulation
Discount rate
Disinflation
Dutch disease
Earned income
Econometrics
Entrepreneur
Exchange rate
Fiscal policy
Five-Year Plan
Gold standard

Hard currency
Hire purchase
Human capital
Interest rate
Joint venture
Labour market
Laisser faire
Laissez faire
Mercantilism
Merchant bank
Mixed economy
Moonlighting
National debt
Pay-as-you-earn
Productivity
Profit margin
Rent controls
Risk analysis
Soft currency
Stock control
Tax avoidance
Terms of trade
Trade barrier
Unemployment
Welfare state
13 letters:
Budget deficit
Business cycle
Credit squeeze
Discount house
Financial year
Free trade area
Free trade zone
Futures market
Income support
Invisible hand
Listed company

Market failure
Multinational
Primary sector
Privatization
Profitability
Profit sharing
Protectionism
Public finance
Public utility
Ratchet effect
Seller's market
Sequestration
Service sector
Stock exchange
Unit of account
Value-added tax
Variable costs
Wage restraint
14 letters:
Balanced budget
Balance of trade
Barriers to exit
Command economy
Commercial bank
Corporation tax
Credit controls
Current account
Deposit account
Disequilibrium
Economic growth
Economic policy
Fringe benefits
Full employment
Gains from trade
Government bond
Hyperinflation
Infrastructure

Inheritance tax
Macroeconomics
Mass production
Microeconomics
Monetary policy
National income
Nondurable good
Planned economy
Public interest
Quality control
Regional policy
Self-employment
Simple interest
Specialization
Tangible assets
Unearned income
Venture capital
Working capital
15 letters:
Barriers to entry
Building society
Diversification
Economic history
Fixed investment
Foreign exchange
Friendly society
Marginal revenue
Marginal utility
Nationalization
National product
Per capita income
Private property
Purchasing power
Rationalization
Self-sufficiency
Share price index

ECONOMICS SCHOOLS AND THEORIES

7 letters:
Chicago
Marxism
8 letters:
Austrian
9 letters:
Classical

10 letters:
Monetarism
11 letters:
Physiocrats
Reaganomics
Rogernomics
Thatcherism

12 letters:
Keynesianism
Mercantilism
Neoclassical
13 letters:
NeoKeynesians

ECONOMISTS

4 letters:
Hume, *David*
Marx, *Karl*
Mill, *James*
Mill, *John Stuart*

Ward, *Dame Barbara (Mary)*
Webb, *Sidney*
West, *Arthur Lewis*
5 letters:
Passy, *Frédéric*

Smith, *Adam*
Weber, *Max*
6 letters:
Angell, *Norman*
Bright, *John*
Cobden, *Richard*
Delors, *Jacques*
Frisch, *Ragnar*
George, *Henry*
Jevons, *William Stanley*
Keynes, *John Maynard*
Laffer, *Arthur*
Monnet, *Jean*
Pareto, *Vilfredo*
Turgot, *Anne Robert Jacques*
Veblen, *Thorstein*
7 letters:
Bagehot, *Walter*
Cournot, *Augustin*
D' Oresme, *Nicole*
Douglas, *C(lifford) H(ugh)*
Kuznets, *Simon*
Leacock, *Stephen Butler*

Malthus, *Thomas Robert*
Quesnay, *François*
Ricardo, *David*
Toynbee, *Arnold*
Wootton, *Barbara (Frances)*
8 letters:
Beccaria, *Cesare Bonesana*
Friedman, *Milton*
Mansholt, *Sicco Leendert*
Marshall, *Alfred*
Phillips, *A(lban) W(illiam) H(ousego)*
Von Hayek, *Friedrich August*
9 letters:
Beveridge, *William Henry*
Galbraith, *J(ohn) K(enneth)*
Tinbergen, *Jan*
10 letters:
De Sismondi, *Jean Charles Léonard Simonde*
Papandreou, *Andreas (George)*
Schumacher, *Ernst Friedrich*
Schumpeter, *Joseph*

Education terms

2 letters:	Term	Bedder
UE	Test	Binary
3 letters:	Year	Bursar
COP	**5 letters:**	Campus
Don	Class	Credit
Dux	Dunce	Degree
GCE	Entry	Docent
GPS	Essay	Fellow
Jig	Expel	Ferule
LMS	Flunk	Greats
ONC	Gaudy	Higher
PTA	Grade	Honors
SCE	Grant	Hookey
Set	Hooky	Incept
Wag	House	Infant
4 letters:	Lines	Junior
Co-ed	Lycée	Master
CPVE	Mitch	Matric
Crib	Mocks	O grade
Dean	Pandy	O level
Exam	Resit	Pedant
Fail	Shell	Porter
GCSE	Sizar	Reader
Gown	Stage	Recess
Hall	Tutee	Rector
Hood	Tutor	Regent
Mich	Union	Remove
Pass	**6 letters:**	Report
Pipe	A level	Second
SATS	Alumna	Senate

Senior
Stream
Thesis
Truant
Warden
7 letters:
Adviser
Advisor
Alumnus
Banding
Battels
Boarder
Bursary
Crammer
Deanery
Dominie
Donnish
Dropout
Educate
Faculty
Federal
Fresher
Honours
Janitor
Lecture
Marking
Midterm
Prefect
Prelims
Primers
Proctor
Provost
Seminar
Session
Subject
Teach-in
Tuition
8 letters:
A bursary
Academic
Accredit
Aegrotat
B bursary
Comedown
Commoner
Delegacy
Dunce cap
Emeritus
Exercise
External
Freshman
Graduand
Graduate
Headship
Homework
Internal
Key stage

Lecturer
Manciple
Mistress
Parietal
Redbrick
Remedial
Semester
Send down
Sorority
Transfer
Tutorial
Wrangler
9 letters:
Assistant
Associate
Bubs grade
Bursarial
Catalogue
Catchment
Classmate
Classroom
Collegial
Collegian
Detention
Education
Extension
Gymnasium
Moderator
Muck-up day
Principal
Professor
Reception
Registrar
Rusticate
Schoolman
Sixth form
Sophomore
Speech day
Sports day
Statement
Trimester
10 letters:
Assignment
Attainment
Bursarship
Chancellor
Collegiate
Coursework
Curricular
Curriculum
Department
Easter term
Eleven-plus
Exhibition
Extramural
Fellowship
Graded post

Graduation
Grant-in-aid
Headmaster
High school
Hilary term
Imposition
Instructor
Intramural
Invigilate
Prepositor
Prospectus
Readership
Recreation
Sabbatical
Scholastic
Schoolmarm
Supervisor
Transcript
University
Unstreamed
11 letters:
Coeducation
Convocation
Educational
Examination
Housefather
Housemaster
Housemother
In residence
Invigilator
Lower school
Matriculate
Trinity term
Upper school
12 letters:
Accumulation
Chapterhouse
Commencement
Congregation
Core subjects
Dissertation
Exhibitioner
Headmistress
Open learning
Postgraduate
Privatdocent
Public school
Schoolleaver
Schoolmaster
Self-educated
Subprincipal
13 letters:
Advanced level
Baccalaureate
Boarding house
Cuisenaire rod®
Full professor

Lowerclassman
Matriculation
Mature student
Ordinary grade
Ordinary level
Private school
Professoriate
Schoolteacher
Standard Grade
Summa cum laude
Undergraduate

14 letters:
Common Entrance
Family grouping
Headmastership
Liaison officer
Michaelmas term
Sandwich course
Schoolmistress
Student teacher
Tutorial system
Vice chancellor

15 letters:
Advisory teacher
Cross-curricular
Extracurricular
Grant-maintained
Hall of residence
Interscholastic
Refresher course
Regius professor
Tertiary bursary

Electronics terms

3 letters:
Bar
Bus
CCD
Eye
Key
LCD
LED
Pad
4 letters:
Bell
Bulb
Card
Chip
Coil
Cord
Dial
Disc
Duct
Flex
Fuse
Gate
Gobo
Jack
Lead
Lobe
Loop
Mike
Neon
Plug
Port
Slug
Tube
Wire
5 letters:
Array
Balun
Cable
Choke
Clock
Coder
Diode

Donor
Drain
Latch
Maser
Mixer
Motor
Plate
Shunt
Spool
Tuner
Valve
Wafer
Wiper
6 letters:
Aerial
Bridge
Buffer
Busbar
Button
Buzzer
Bypass
Carbon
Driver
Feeder
Heater
Mosaic
Needle
Outlet
Phasor
Pick-up
Radome
Scaler
Screen
Sensor
Sheath
Sleeve
Slicer
Socket
Stator
Stylus
Switch
Triode

Woofer
7 letters:
Acetate
Adaptor
Antenna
Battery
Bimorph
Booster
Breaker
Bushing
Capstan
Charger
Chassis
Chopper
Clipper
Console
Counter
Coupler
Crystal
Display
Divider
Element
Emitter
Exciter
Excitor
Fuse box
Gyrator
Harness
Igniter
Krytron
Limiter
Mag tape
Monitor
Negator
Pentode
Reactor
Scanner
Speaker
Tetrode
Tone arm
Trimmer
Tweeter

8 letters:
Acceptor
Black box
Detector
Diffuser
Digitron
Envelope
Expander
Filament
Heat sink
Ignitron
Inverter
Live wire
Magic eye
Neon lamp
Orthicon
Radiator
Receiver
Recorder
Repeater
Resistor
Rheostat
Sleeving
Slip ring
Solenoid
Varactor
Varistor
Vibrator

9 letters:
Amplifier
Autometer
Autotimer
Bolometer
Call alarm
Capacitor
Cartridge
Choke coil
Component
Condenser
Conductor
Contactor
Delay line
Drift tube
Dummy load
Dynamotor
Equalizer
Flame lamp
Fluxmeter
Hygristor
Image tube
Kinescope
Labyrinth
Leyden jar
Light bulb
Magnetron
Metal tape
Microchip

Nixie tube
Optophone
Phono plug
Phototube
Pilot lamp
Plugboard
Plumbicon
Power pack
Rectifier
Reflector
Resnatron
Resonator
Sequencer
Spark coil
Tesla coil
Thyratron
Thyristor
Turntable
Voltmeter
Wattmeter

10 letters:
Acorn valve
Alternator
Banana plug
Breadboard
Camera tube
Chrome tape
Commutator
Comparator
Compressor
Controller
Coulometer
Esaki diode
Goniometer
Harmonizer
Hydrophone
LCD display
LED display
Microphone
Mimic panel
Moving coil
Multimeter
NOT circuit
Oscillator
Patch board
Photodiode
P-n junction
Push button
Radio valve
Reproducer
Rhumbatron
Screen grid
Servomotor
Shadow mask
Sodium lamp
Solar panel
Stabilizer

Suppressor
Switchgear
Thermistor
Time switch
Transducer
Transistor
Trip switch
Vacuum tube
Variometer
Voltameter
Wander plug
Welding rod
Zener diode

11 letters:
Anticathode
Autochanger
Cat's whisker
Cold cathode
Electric eye
Faraday cage
Interrupter
Junction box
Knife switch
Loading coil
Loudspeaker
Microswitch
Motherboard
NAND circuit
Open circuit
Picture tube
Ring circuit
Silicon chip
Space heater
Storage tube
Strobe tuner
Switchboard
Tickler coil
Transformer
Tunnel diode
Voltammeter

12 letters:
Bow collector
Circuit board
Coaxial cable
Electrometer
Electron tube
Friction tape
Magnetic tape
Microcircuit
Oscillograph
Oscilloscope
Preamplifier
Squirrel cage
Standard cell
Toggle switch

13 letters:
Crystal pick-up

Discharge tube
Discriminator
Electric motor
Image orthicon
Induction coil
Low-pass filter
Mercury switch
Multivibrator
Potentiometer
Quartz crystal
Record-changer
Rhombic aerial
Ripple control
Semiconductor
Tumbler switch
14 letters:
Band-pass filter
Circuit breaker
Heating element
High-pass filter
Image converter

Induction motor
Long-wire aerial
Magnetic pick-up
Magnetic stripe
Mesh connection
Motor generator
Noise generator
Peltier element
Power amplifier
Printed circuit
Schmitt trigger
Servomechanism
Star connection
Television tube
Trickle charger
Turbogenerator
Universal motor
Voltage divider
15 letters:
Alloyed junction
Autotransformer

Bleeder resistor
Bridge rectifier
Cavity resonator
Class-A amplifier
Class-B amplifier
Class-C amplifier
Crystal detector
Drift transistor
Electric circuit
Local oscillator
Majority carrier
Minority carrier
Phototransistor
Shuttle armature
Signal generator
Thermionic valve

Embroidery stitches

3 letters:
Fly
4 letters:
Back
Barb
Coil
Fern
Post
Rice
Stem
5 letters:
Briar
Catch
Chain
Coral
Cross
Daisy
Greek
Satin
Split
6 letters:
Basque
Beaded
Berlin
Cast on
Cretan
Crewel
Damask
Eyelet
Ladder
Scroll

7 letters:
Berwick
Blanket
Bullion
Chevron
Chinese
Convent
Feather
Kloster
Outline
Plaited
Running
Russian
Sampler
Sham Hem
8 letters:
Pekinese
Scottish
Wheatear
9 letters:
Arrowhead
Crow's-foot
Lazy Daisy
Open Chain
Quilt Knot
10 letters:
Buttonhole
Casalguidi
French Knot
German Knot
Portuguese

Roman Chain
Whipped Fly
11 letters:
Caterpillar
Double Cross
Herringbone
Montenegrin
Renaissance
Ribbed Wheel
Threaded Fly
Whipped Back
Whipped Stem
Zigzag Chain
12 letters:
Ghiordes Knot
Russian Cross
Twisted Chain
Whipped Chain
13 letters:
Buttonhole Bar
Closed Feather
Porto Rico rose
14 letters:
Crossed corners
Feathered Chain
Whipped Running
15 letters:
Buttonhole Wheel
Threaded Running

Emperors

TITLES OF EMPERORS

3 letters:
Imp
Rex
4 letters:
Inca
King
Tsar
5 letters:
Kesar

Mpret
Negus
Rosco
Ruler
Shang
Tenno
6 letters:
Kaiser
Keasar

Mikado
Purple
Sultan
9 letters:
Sovereign

FAMOUS EMPERORS

3 letters:
Leo
4 letters:
John
Ming
Nero
Otho
Otto
Pu-yi
Wu Di
5 letters:
Akbar
Asoka
Babur
Gaius
Henry
Jimmu
Kesar
Meiji
Negus
Nerva
Pedro
Rosco
Shang
Tenno
Titus
6 letters:
Caesar
George
Joseph
Kaiser
Keaser
Trajan

Valens
Yong Lo
7 letters:
Akihito
Charles
Francis
Gratian
Hadrian
Leopold
Lothair
Menelik
Severus
William
8 letters:
Agramant
Augustan
Augustus
Caligula
Claudius
Commodus
Hirohito
Matthias
Napoleon
Octavian
Qian Long
Theodore
Tiberius
Valerian
Xuan Zong
9 letters:
Agramante
Atahualpa
Aurangzeb

Bonaparte
Caracalla
Diomitian
Ferdinand
Frederick
Heraclius
Justinian
Montezuma
Shah Jahan
Vespasian
Vitellius
10 letters:
Barbarossa
Dessalines
Diocletian
Franz Josef
Kublai Khan
Maximilian
Theodosius
Theophilus
Wenceslaus
11 letters:
Charlemagne
Constantine
Genghis Khan
Valentinian
13 letters:
Akbar the Great
Antoninus Pius
Haile Selassie
Peter the Great

Engineering, types of

5 letters:
Civil
Naval
6 letters:
Mining
7 letters:
Genetic
Nuclear
Process
Traffic
8 letters:
Chemical
Military
Sanitary
9 letters:
Aerospace

10 letters:
Automotive
Electrical
Ergonomics
Hydraulics
Mechanical
Production
Structural
11 letters:
Electronics
Geotechnics
12 letters:
Aerodynamics
Aeronautical
Agricultural
Astronautics

Cosmonautics
Mechatronics
13 letters:
Computer-aided
Environmental
Fluid dynamics
14 letters:
Bioengineering

Entertainment

TYPES OF ENTERTAINMENT

3 letters:
Gig
4 letters:
Agon
Ball
Fair
Fête
Film
Gala
Play
Rave
Show
5 letters:
Dance
Farce
Feast
Gaudy
Levee
Magic
Opera
Party
Revue
Rodeo
6 letters:
Ballet
Circus
Comedy
Kermis
Masque
Review
Soiree
7 letters:
Airshow

Banquet
Busking
Cabaret
Ceilidh
Charade
Concert
Ice show
Karaoke
Kirmess
Musical
Reading
Recital
Ridotto
Tragedy
Variety
Waltzer
8 letters:
All-dayer
Après-ski
Aquashow
Carnival
Cotillon
Juggling
Operetta
Road show
Sideshow
Singsong
Zarzuela
9 letters:
Conjuring
Cotillion
Fireworks
Floor show

Light show
Melodrama
Music hall
Pantomime
Raree show
Reception
Slide show
Video game
10 letters:
Acrobatics
Aerobatics
All-nighter
Antimasque
Escapology
Exhibition
Masked ball
Puppet show
Recitation
Shadow play
Striptease
Vaudeville
Whist drive
11 letters:
Bear-baiting
Fashion show
Funambulism
Galanty show
Garden party
Slot machine
Wall of death
12 letters:
Bullfighting
Cockfighting

Minstrel show
Pyrotechnics
Son et lumière

13 letters:
Burlesque show
Street theatre

Ventriloquism
14 letters:
Warehouse party

TYPES OF ENTERTAINER

4 letters:
Diva
Fool
5 letters:
Actor
Clown
Mimic
6 letters:
Artist
Busker
Dancer
Guiser
Jester
Mummer
Singer
7 letters:
Acrobat
Actress
Artiste
Auguste
Juggler
Trouper
Tumbler
8 letters:
Comedian
Conjurer

Funnyman
Gracioso
Jongleur
Magician
Minstrel
Musician
Show girl
Stripper
9 letters:
Fire eater
Harlequin
Lion tamer
Performer
Puppeteer
Raconteur
Strongman
Tragedian
10 letters:
Chorus girl
Comedienne
Go-go dancer
Prima donna
Ringmaster
Unicyclist
11 letters:
Equilibrist

Funambulist
Illusionist
Merry-andrew
Stripteaser
Tragedienne
12 letters:
Circus artist
Escapologist
Exotic dancer
Impersonator
Organ-grinder
Snake charmer
Vaudevillian
13 letters:
Bareback rider
Contortionist
Impressionist
Trapeze artist
Ventriloquist
14 letters:
Prima ballerina
Sword swallower
15 letters:
Strolling player
Tightrope walker

PLACES OF ENTERTAINMENT

3 letters:
Zoo
4 letters:
Hall
Lido
5 letters:
Arena
Disco
6 letters:
Big top
Cinema
Circus
Museum
7 letters:
Funfair
Gallery

Marquee
Niterie
Stadium
Theatre
8 letters:
Ballroom
Carnival
Coliseum
Waxworks
9 letters:
Bandstand
Bingo hall
Colosseum
Dance hall
Music hall
Nightclub

Nightspot
10 letters:
Auditorium
Fairground
Opera house
Social club
Vaudeville
11 letters:
Concert hall
12 letters:
Amphitheatre
13 letters:
Leisure centre
15 letters:
Amusement arcade

Enzymes

3 letters:
ACE
5 letters:
Lyase
Lysin
Renin
6 letters:
Cytase
Kinase
Ligase
Lipase
Mutase
Papain
Pepsin
Rennin
Urease
Zymase
7 letters:
Amylase
Apyrase
Casease
Cyclase
Enolase
Erepsin
Guanase
Hydrase
Inulase
Lactase
Maltase
Oxidase
Pectase
Pepsine
Plasmin
Ptyalin
Trypsin

8 letters:
Aldolase
Arginase
Bromelin
Catalase
Diastase
Elastase
Esterase
Lysozyme
Nuclease
Permease
Protease
Steapsin
Thrombin
9 letters:
Amylopsin
Autolysin
Bromelain
Cathepsin
Cellulase
Deaminase
Hydrolase
Invertase
Isomerase
Oxygenase
Reductase
Sulfatase
Trehalase
Urokinase
10 letters:
Allosteric
Kallikrein
Luciferase
Peroxidase
Polymerase

Proteinase
Saccharase
Subtilisin
Sulphatase
Tyrosinase
11 letters:
Carboxylase
Chymopapain
Collagenase
Dipeptidase
Histaminase
Phosphatase
Restriction
Transferase
12 letters:
Asparaginase
Carbohydrase
Chymotrypsin
Enterokinase
Fibrinolysin
Flavoprotein
Ribonuclease
Transaminase
13 letters:
Decarboxylase
Oxdoreductase
Streptokinase
Transcriptase
14 letters:
Cholinesterase
Pectinesterase
Streptodornase
Thromboplastin

Equestrianism

EQUESTRIAN EVENTS AND SPORTS

4 letters:
Hunt
Oaks
Polo
5 letters:
Ascot
Derby
Joust
Plate
7 letters:
Classic
Jump-off
Meeting
8 letters:
Dressage

Eventing
Gymkhana
Races, the
9 letters:
Badminton
Cavalcade
Puissance
10 letters:
Picnic race
Saint Leger
Sweepstake
11 letters:
Buckjumping
Horse racing
Race meeting

Showjumping
Sweepstakes
12 letters:
Claiming race
Point-to-point
Steeplechase
13 letters:
Grand National
Harness racing
Kentucky Derby
Nursery stakes
Three-day event

CLASSIC ENGLISH HORSE RACES

Race	Course	Distance
One Thousand Guineas (fillies)	Newmarket	One mile
Two Thousand Guineas (colts)	Newmarket	One mile
Derby (colts)	Epsom	One and a half miles
The Oaks (fillies)	Epsom	One and a half miles
St Leger (colts and fillies)	Doncaster	One and three quarter miles

HORSE RACING TERMS

3 letters:
Nap
4 letters:
Away
Card
Colt
Draw
Flat
Gate
Head
Neck
Pole
Post
Turf
Wire
5 letters:
Break
Chase
Fence
Filly
Going
Handy
Pacer
Place
Plate
Sweat
Track
6 letters:
Boring
Chaser
Come in
Course
Faller
Finish
Flight
Hurdle
Impost
Jockey
Length
Maiden
Novice

Plater
Scurry
Stakes
Stayer
7 letters:
Also-ran
Classic
Each way
Furlong
Meeting
Paddock
Roughie
Scratch
Starter
Steward
Stretch
Sweat up
Trainer
Weigh in
8 letters:
Dead heat
Distance
Handicap
Hurdling
Milepost
Race card
Straight
Ticktack
Unplaced
Walkover
Yearling
9 letters:
Allowance
Break away
Dope sheet
Objection
Pacemaker
Short head
10 letters:
Apprentice
Flat jockey

Flat racing
Green horse
Jockey Club
Jump jockey
Pacesetter
Silver ring
11 letters:
Accumulator
Daily double
Handicapper
Harness race
Home stretch
Photo finish
Selling race
Winning post
12 letters:
Auction plate
Claiming race
Home straight
National Hunt
Point-to-point
Starting gate
Starting post
Steeplechase
Straightaway
Trotting race
13 letters:
Blanket finish
Starting price
Unseated rider
14 letters:
Across-the-board
Starting stalls
15 letters:
Ante post betting
Stewards' inquiry

TYPES OF JUMP

4 letters:
Gate
Wall
6 letters:
Planks
8 letters:
Hog's back

9 letters:
Water jump
10 letters:
Double oxer
Triple bars
11 letters:
Narrow stile

12 letters:
Post and rails
13 letters:
Brush and rails
Parallel poles

European Union

Year joined	Member Country
1958	Belgium
1958	France
1958	Germany
1958	Italy
1958	Luxembourg
1958	The Netherlands
Year joined	**Member Country**
1973	Denmark
1973	Republic of Ireland
1973	United Kingdom
1981	Greece
1986	Portugal
1986	Spain
1995	Finland
1995	Sweden
1995	Austria
2004	Cyprus
2004	Czech Republic
2004	Estonia
2004	Hungary
2004	Latvia
2004	Lithuania
2004	Malta
2004	Poland
2004	Slovakia
2004	Slovenia
2007	Bulgaria
2007	Romania

Explosives

2 letters:
HE
3 letters:
Cap
SAM
TNT
4 letters:
Mine
5 letters:
Agene
Jelly

Petar
6 letters:
Amatol
Dualin
Petard
Semtex®
Tetryl
Tonite
Trotyl
7 letters:
Ammonal

Cordite
Dunnite
Grenade
Warhead
8 letters:
Cheddite
Fireball
Firedamp
Firework
Landmine
Melinite

Roburite
Xyloidin
9 letters:
Gelignite
Guncotton
Gunpowder

Xyloidine
10 letters:
Aquafortis
Euchlorine
11 letters:
Firecracker

12 letters:
Thunderflash
14 letters:
Nitroglycerine
15 letters:
Trinitrobenzene

Eye

PARTS OF THE EYE

3 letters:
Rod
4 letters:
Cone
Iris
Lens
5 letters:
Fovea
Pupil
6 letters:
Cornea

Retina
Sclera
7 letters:
Choroid
Eyeball
8 letters:
Chorioid
9 letters:
Blind spot
10 letters:
Optic nerve

11 letters:
Ciliary body
Conjunctiva
12 letters:
Ocular muscle
Vitreous body
13 letters:
Aqueous humour
14 letters:
Retinal vessels
Vitreous humour

AFFLICTIONS OF THE EYE

6 letters:
Iritis
Miosis
Myosis
Nebula
Xeroma
7 letters:
Leucoma
Scotoma
Thylose
Tylosis
Wall-eye
8 letters:
Cataract
Coloboma
Diplopia
Glaucoma

Hemiopia
Synechia
Thylosis
Trachoma
9 letters:
Amblyopia
Ametropia
Ceratitis
Entropion
Keratitis
Lippitude
Micropsia
Nystagmus
Retinitis
Scotomata
10 letters:
Asthenopia

Nyctalopia
Presbyopia
Stigmatism
Strabismus
Teichopsia
Tritanopia
11 letters:
Aniseikonia
Astigmatism
Hemeralopia
Hemianopsia
12 letters:
Exophthalmus
13 letters:
Anisomatropia
Hypermetropia
Xerophthalmia

Fabrics

3 letters:
Abb
Fur
Net
Rep
Say
Web

4 letters:
Aida
Baft
Ciré
Cord
Doek
Drab
Duck
Felt
Fent
Gair
Haik
Harn
Huck
Hyke
Ikat
Jean
Kelt
Knit
Lace
Lamé
Lawn
Leno
Line
Mull
Nude
Puke
Rund
Shag
Silk
Slop
Sulu
Tick
Wool

5 letters:
Atlas
Baize
Batik

Beige
Binca
Budge
Chino
Crape
Crash
Crepe
Denim
Dobby
Drill
Duroy
Fanon
Foulé
Frisé
Gauze
Gunny
Haick
Honan
Jaspe
Kanga
Kente
Khadi
Khaki
Kikoi
Linen
Lisle
Llama
Loden
Lurex®
Lycra®
Moiré
Mongo
Mungo
Ninon
Orlon®
Panne
Perse
Piqué
Plaid
Plush
Poult
Rayon
Satin
Scrim
Serge

Slops
Stuff
Stupe
Surah
Surat
Surge
Tabby
Tamin
Tammy
Terry
Tibet
Toile
Towel
Tulle
Tweed
Tweel
Twill
Union
Voile
Wigan

6 letters:
Aertex®
Alpaca
Angora
Armure
Barège
Battik
Beaver
Bouclé
Broche
Burlap
Burnet
Burrel
Byssus
Caddis
Calico
Camlet
Camlot
Canvas
Chintz
Cilice
Cloqué
Coburg
Cotton
Coutil

Crepon
Cubica
Cyprus
Dacron®
Damask
Devoré
Dimity
Domett
Dossal
Dossel
Dowlas
Dralon®
Duffel
Duffle
Dupion
Durrie
Etamin
Faille
Fannel
Fleece
Frieze
Gloria
Greige
Gurrah
Haique
Harden
Herden
Hodden
Humhum
Hurden
Jersey
Kersey
Khanga
Kincob
Lampas
Madras
Medley
Melton
Merino
Mohair
Mongoe
Moreen
Muslin
Nankin
Oxford
Pongee
Poplin
Rateen
Ratine
Runner
Russel
Russet
Samite
Satara
Sateen
Saxony
Sendal

Shalli
Sherpa
Shoddy
Sindon
Soneri
Stroud
Tamine
Tartan
Thibet
Tricot
Tussah
Tusser
Velour
Velure
Velvet
Vicuna
Wadmal
Wincey
Winsey
7 letters:
Abattre
Acrilan®
Alepine
Baracan
Batiste
Brocade
Bunting
Cabbage
Cambric
Camelot
Challie
Challis
Cheviot
Chiffon
Crombie
Cypress
Delaine
Dhurrie
Doeskin
Dornick
Drabbet
Drapery
Droguet
Drugget
Duvetyn
Etamine
Façonné
Fannell
Fishnet
Flannel
Foulard
Fustian
Galatea
Genappe
Gingham
Gore-Tex®
Grogram

Hessian
Holland
Hopsack
Jaconet
Jamdani
Khaddar
Kitenge
Leather
Lockram
Marabou
Mockado
Nankeen
Oilskin
Organza
Orleans
Ottoman
Paisley
Percale
Rabanna
Raploch
Raschel
Ratteen
Rattine
Sacking
Sagathy
Satinet
Schappe
Silesia
Sinamay
Spandex
Stammel
Suiting
Tabaret
Tabinet
Taffeta
Ticking
Tiffany
Tussore
Veiling
Velours
Viyella®
Wadmaal
Webbing
Woolsey
Worsted
Zanella
8 letters:
Algerine
American
Armozeen
Armozine
Arresine
Bagheera
Barathea
Barracan
Bayadere
Bird's-eye

Bobbinet
Brocatel
Buckskin
Cameline
Cashmere
Casimere
Celanese
Chambray
Chamelot
Chenille
Ciclaton
Corduroy
Corporal
Coteline
Coutille
Cretonne
Diamanté
Drabette
Duchesse
Dungaree
Duvetine
Duvetyne
Eolienne
Gambroon
Gossamer
Homespun
Jacquard
Jeanette
Lambskin
Lava-lava
Lustring
Mackinaw
Mantling
Marcella
Marocain
Mazarine
Moleskin
Moquette
Nainsook
Organdie
Osnaburg
Paduasoy
Pashmina
Prunella
Prunelle
Prunello
Rodevore
Sarcenet
Sarsenet
Shabrack
Shalloon
Shantung
Sheeting
Shirting
Sicilian
Spun silk
Swanskin

Tabbinet
Tarlatan
Terylene®
Toilinet
Whipcord
Wild silk
Zibeline

9 letters:
Balzarine
Bengaline
Bombasine
Bombazine
Calamanco
Cassimere
Cerecloth
Charmeuse®
Ciclatoun
Corporale
Cottonade
Crepoline
Crimplene®
Crinoline
Evenweave
Farandine
Filoselle
Folk weave
Gaberdine
Georgette
Grenadine
Grosgrain
Haircloth
Horsehair
Huckaback
Indiennes
Levantine
Mandylion
Marseille
Matelassé
Messaline
Nun's cloth
Organzine
Paramatta
Penistone
Percaline
Persienne
Petersham
Piña cloth
Polyester
Ravenduck
Sailcloth
Satinette
Sharkskin
Silkaline
Stockinet
Swan's-down
Tarpaulin
Towelling

Tricotine
Velveteen
Wire gauze
Worcester
Zibelline

10 letters:
Balbriggan
Broadcloth
Brocatelle
Candlewick
Farrandine
Fearnaught
Fearnought
Ferrandine
Florentine
India print
Kerseymere
Lutestring
Marseilles
Monk's cloth
Mousseline
Needlecord
Parramatta
Peau de soie
Polycotton
Ravensduck
Seersucker
Shabracque
Sicilienne
Tattersall
Toilinette
Tuftaffeta
Winceyette

11 letters:
Abercrombie
Cheesecloth
Cloth of gold
Covert cloth
Dotted Swiss
Drap-de-berry
Dreadnought
Hammercloth
Harris Tweed®
Interfacing
Kendal green
Marquisette
Poult-de-soie
Sempiternum
Stockinette
Stretch knit
Swiss muslin

12 letters:
Brilliantine
Cavalry twill
Crepe de chine
Donegal tweed
Leather-cloth

Slipper satin
13 letters:
Cotton flannel

Gros de Londres
Jacquard weave
Linsey-woolsey

14 letters:
Paisley pattern

See also:
➤ **Materials** ➤ **Silks**

Fates

6 letters:
Clotho

7 letters:
Atropos

8 letters:
Lachesis

Fencing terms

4 letters:
Mask
Volt
5 letters:
Carte
Feint
Guard
Parry
Piste
Prime
Reach

Sabre
Sixte
Terce
Touch
6 letters:
Bracer
Octave
Parade
Quarte
Quinte
Tierce

Touché
7 letters:
Seconde
Septime
9 letters:
Backsword
Repechage
11 letters:
Singlestick

Ferns

3 letters:
Oak
4 letters:
Hard
Lady
Male
Tara
Tree
5 letters:
Beech
Cycad
Filmy
Grape
Marsh
Ponga
Punga
Royal
Sword
6 letters:
Azolla
Meadow
Nardoo
Pteris
Shield
Silver
7 letters:
Bladder

Bracken
Buckler
Cyathea
Elkhorn
Filices
Isoetes
Osmunda
Parsley
Polypod
Walking
Wall rue
Woodsia
8 letters:
Adiantum
Aspidium
Barometz
Bungwall
Ceterach
Cinnamon
Fishbone
Marsilea
Marsilia
Moonwort
Mosquito
Mulewort
Pillwort
Rachilla

Schizaea
Staghorn
9 letters:
Asparagus
Asplenium
Bird's nest
Cryptogam
Dicksonia
Filicales
Rock brake
10 letters:
Maidenhair
Pepperwort
Spleenwort
Venus's-hair
11 letters:
Hart's-tongue
Nephrolepis
12 letters:
Adder's-tongue
Ophioglossum
13 letters:
Scolopendrium

Festivals

3 letters:
Mod
Tet
4 letters:
Feis
Gaff
Holi
Mela
Noel
Obon
Puja
Utas
Yule
5 letters:
Doseh
Druid
Hosay
Litha
Mabon
Miraj
Pasch
Pesah
Pooja
Purim
Seder
Vesak
Wesak
6 letters:
Adonia
Ashura
Bairam
Dewali
Divali
Diwali
Easter
Eostra
Fringe
Hosein
Imbolc
Lammas
Ostara
Pardon

Pesach
Pongal
Poojah
Shrove
Yomtov
7 letters:
Al Hijra
Baisaki
Beltane
Gregory
Harvest
Holy-ale
Kermess
Kermiss
Kirmess
Lady-day
Lemural
Lemuria
Matsuri
Palilia
Potlach
Samhain
Vinalia
8 letters:
Al Hijrah
Baisakhi
Bayreuth
Biennale
Cerealia
Chanukah
Dassehra
Dionysia
Encaenia
Epiphany
Hanukkah
Hock-tide
Id-al-fitr
Panegyry
Passover
Shabuath
Shavuath
Yuletide

9 letters:
Aldeburgh
Candlemas
Chanukkah
Church-ale
Crouchmas
Hallowmas
Navaratra
Navaratri
Pentecost
Thargelia
Up-Helly-Aa
10 letters:
Ambarvalia
Childermas
Eisteddfod
Lughnasadh
Lupercalia
Merry-night
Michaelmas
Quirinalia
Saturnalia
Semi-double
Shrovetide
Terminalia
Visitation
11 letters:
Anthesteria
12 letters:
All Saints' Day
Circumcision
Lailat-ul-Qadr
Lesser Bairam
Panathenaean
Rosh Hashanah
Simchat Torah
Thesmophoria
13 letters:
Corpus Christi
Laylat-al-Miraj

Fibres

3 letters:
Tow
4 letters:
Bass
Bast
Coir
Flax
Hemp
Herl

Jute
Noil
Pita
Pons
Pulu
Rami
Rhea
5 letters:
Abaca

Buaze
Bwazi
Istle
Ixtle
Kapok
Kenaf
Noils
Nylon
Orlon®

Ramee
Viver
Watap
6 letters:
Aramid
Arghan
Cotton
Cuscus
Dralon®
Kevlar®
Kittul
Strick
7 letters:
Acrilan®

Acrylic
Cantala
Filasse
Funicle
Gore-Tex®
Monofil
Pontine
Tampico
Whisker
8 letters:
Elastane
Henequen
Henequin
Monomode

Peduncle
Piassaba
Piassava
Sunn-hemp
Toquilla
9 letters:
Courtelle®
11 letters:
Monkey-grass

Figures of speech

5 letters:
Irony
6 letters:
Aporia
Climax
Simile
Tmesis
Zeugma
7 letters:
Analogy
Kenning
Litotes
Meiosis
Sarcasm
8 letters:
Allusion
Anaphora
Chiasmus
Emphasis
Metaphor
Metonymy
Oxymoron

Pleonasm
9 letters:
Apophasis
Hendiadys
Hypallage
Hyperbole
Inversion
Prolepsis
Syllepsis
10 letters:
Anastrophe
Antithesis
Apostrophe
Epanaphora
Gemination
Hyperbaton
Paralipsis
Repetition
Spoonerism
Synecdoche
11 letters:
Anacoluthia

Anadiplosis
Antiphrasis
Antonomasia
Aposiopesis
Catachresis
Exclamation
Malapropism
Paraleipsis
Parenthesis
Periphrasis
Prosopopeia
12 letters:
Alliteration
Epanorthosis
Onomatopoeia
Polysyndeton
Prosopopoeia
14 letters:
Circumlocution
15 letters:
Personification

Film and television

1 letter:
A
U
2 letters:
AA
PG
3 letters:
BFI
CGI
Cut
Dub
Pan
SFX

Zap
4 letters:
BBFC
Boom
Edit
Emmy
Grip
HDTV
IMAX
Sync
TiVo
5 letters:
Anime

BAFTA
Cameo
Frame
Oscar
Short
Weepy
6 letters:
Action
Biopic
B movie
Co-star
Editor
Gaffer

Razzie
Repeat
Romcom
X-rated
7 letters:
Animate
Backlot
Betacam
Cable TV
Credits
Fleapit
Footage
Key grip
Prequel
Ratings
Trailer
Western
Zapping
8 letters:
Actioner
Art house
Britpack
Game show
Long shot
Stuntman
Subtitle
Talk show
Typecast
9 letters:
Animation

Big screen
Bollywood
Celluloid
Cinematic
Digital TV
Docu-drama
Flashback
Footprint
Hollywood
LCD screen
Reality TV
Road movie
Satellite
Set-top box
Stop-frame
10 letters:
Access card
Adult movie
Blue screen
Body double
Chick flick
Flat screen
Home cinema
Neorealism
Screen test
Slow motion
Snuff movie
Soundtrack
Stop-motion
Storyboard

Video nasty
Widescreen
11 letters:
Channel-surf
Chapter stop
Cinemascope
Cliffhanger
Freeze-frame
Reality show
Satellite TV
Small screen
Synthespian
12 letters:
Animatronics
Cinematheque
Plasma screen
Screenwriter
Slasher movie
Sneak preview
13 letters:
Interactive TV
Motion capture
Remote control
Satellite dish
14 letters:
Channel-surfing
Postproduction
Shooting script
Special effects

Fireworks

3 letters:
SIB
4 letters:
Cake
Mine
Pioy
5 letters:
Gerbe
Peeoy
Pioye
Squib
Wheel
6 letters:
Banger

Fizgig
Maroon
Petard
Rocket
7 letters:
Cracker
Serpent
8 letters:
Fountain
Pinwheel
Sparkler
9 letters:
Girandole
Skyrocket

Whizzbang
10 letters:
Cherry bomb
11 letters:
Bengal light
Roman candle
Tourbillion
14 letters:
Catherine wheel

Fish

2 letters:
Ai
Id
3 letters:
Aua

Ayu
Bar
Bib
But
Cat

Cod
Cow
Dab
Dib
Dog

Eel
Gar
Ged
Hag
Ice
Ide
Koi
Lax
Lob
Par
Pod
Ray
Rig
Sar
Tai
Top

4 letters:
Bass
Blay
Bley
Brim
Brit
Butt
Carp
Cero
Chad
Char
Chub
Chum
Coho
Cray
Cusk
Dace
Dare
Dart
Dory
Fugu
Gade
Goby
Gump
Hake
Harl
Hoki
Huso
Huss
Jack
Kelt
Keta
Lant
Leaf
Ling
Luce
Lump
Maid
Maze
Moki
Mort

Opah
Orfe
Parr
Peal
Peel
Pike
Pogy
Pope
Pout
Raun
Rawn
Rigg
Rudd
Ruff
Scad
Scar
Scat
Scup
Seer
Seir
Shad
Sild
Slip
Snig
Sole
Star
Tope
Trot
Tuna
Tusk
Woof

5 letters:
Ablet
Ahuru
Allis
Angel
Apode
Barra
Basse
Betta
Bleak
Bream
Brill
Bully
Capon
Charr
Cisco
Clown
Cobia
Cohoe
Coley
Cuddy
Danio
Dorad
Doras
Doree
Dorse

Elops
Elver
Fluke
Gadus
Gibel
Grunt
Guppy
Jewie
Jurel
Koaea
Laker
Lance
Loach
Lythe
Maise
Maize
Manta
Masus
Mease
Molly
Moray
Murre
Murry
Nerka
Padle
Perai
Perca
Perch
Pilot
Piper
Pirai
Platy
Pogge
Porae
Porgy
Powan
Prawn
Roach
Roker
Ruffe
Saith
Sargo
Saury
Scrod
Sewen
Sewin
Shark
Sheat
Skate
Slope
Smelt
Snoek
Snook
Solen
Speck
Sprat
Sprod

Tench
Tetra
Toado
Togue
Torsk
Trout
Tunny
Umber
Wahoo
Whiff
Wirra
Witch
Yabby
Zebra
6 letters:
Alevin
Allice
Anabas
Angler
Araara
Archer
Ballan
Barbel
Belone
Beluga
Bigeye
Blenny
Bonito
Bounce
Bowfin
Braise
Braize
Bumalo
Burbot
Callop
Caplin
Caranx
Caribe
Cheven
Clupea
Cockle
Comber
Conger
Conner
Cottus
Cudden
Cuddie
Cuddin
Cunner
Cuttle
Darter
Dentex
Diodon
Dipnoi
Discus
Doctor
Dorado

Dun-cow
Finnac
Finnan
Flying
Fogash
Fumado
Gadoid
Garvie
Gilgie
Goramy
Grilse
Groper
Gulper
Gunnel
Gurami
Gurnet
Haddie
Hapuka
Hapuku
Hassar
Inanga
Jerker
Jilgie
Kelpie
Kipper
Kokopu
Labrus
Lancet
Launce
Lizard
Louvar
Lunker
Mad Tom
Mahsir
Maomao
Marari
Marlin
Meagre
Medaka
Medusa
Megrim
Milter
Minnow
Morgay
Mudcat
Mullet
Murena
Nerite
Nigger
Oyster
Paddle
Paidle
Pakoko
Parore
Parrot
Patiki
Pholas

Pillie
Piraña
Piraya
Plaice
Podley
Pollan
Porgie
Puffer
Rawaru
Red cod
Redfin
Remora
Robalo
Roughy
Runner
Saithe
Salmon
Samlet
Samson
Sander
Sardel
Sargus
Sauger
Saurel
Scampi
Sea-bat
Sea-owl
Seeder
Serran
Shanny
Sheath
Shiner
Skelly
Sparid
Sucker
Tailor
Tarpon
Tautog
Toitoi
Tomcod
Trygon
Turbot
Twaite
Ulicon
Ulikon
Vendis
Weever
Wirrah
Wrasse
Yabbie
Zander
Zingel
7 letters:
Alewife
Anchovy
Anemone
Asterid

Azurine
Batfish
Beardie
Bellows
Bergylt
Bloater
Bluecap
Blue cod
Boxfish
Brassie
Buffalo
Bummalo
Cabezon
Capelin
Catfish
Cavalla
Cavally
Ceviche
Cichlid
Codfish
Copepod
Cowfish
Crappie
Croaker
Crucian
Crusian
Cutlass
Dogfish
Eelfare
Eelpout
Escolar
Findram
Finnack
Finnock
Flattie
Garfish
Garpike
Garvock
Geelbek
Gemfish
Goldeye
Gourami
Grouper
Growler
Grunion
Gudgeon
Gurnard
Gwiniad
Gwyniad
Haddock
Hagdown
Hagfish
Halibut
Herling
Herring
Hirling
Hogfish

Homelyn
Houting
Ichthys
Inconnu
Javelin
Jewfish
Kahawai
Keeling
Koi carp
Kokanee
Lampern
Lamprey
Lampuki
Lantern
Lingcod
Lobster
Lyomeri
Mahseer
Medacca
Merling
Mojarra
Mooneye
Morwong
Mudfish
Muraena
Oarfish
Old-wife
Oolakan
Opaleye
Osseter
Oulakan
Oulicon
Panchax
Pandora
Pegasus
Pigfish
Pinfish
Piranha
Pollack
Pollock
Pomfret
Pompano
Ragfish
Rasbora
Ratfish
Rat-tail
Redfish
Rock cod
Rorqual
Sand dab
Sand eel
Sardine
Sawfish
Scalare
Scallop
Sculpin
Sea bass

Sea-cock
Sea-dace
Sea-moth
Sea-pike
Sea-star
Sea-wife
Sillock
Skegger
Skipper
Sleeper
Snapper
Sockeye
Sparoid
Speldin
Sterlet
Sunfish
Surgeon
Teleost
Tiddler
Tilapia
Titling
Torgoch
Torpedo
Ulichon
Vendace
Walleye
Warehou
Whipray
Whiting
Wide-gab
8 letters:
Albacore
Anableps
Arapaima
Asteroid
Atherine
Ballahoo
Bay trout
Billfish
Black cod
Blind eel
Bloodfin
Blowfish
Blueback
Bluefish
Bluegill
Blue moki
Blue nose
Boarfish
Bonefish
Brisling
Bullhead
Bullhorn
Cabezone
Cabrilla
Cardinal
Cavefish

Characid
Characin
Chimaera
Climbing
Coalfish
Corkwing
Cucumber
Cyprinid
Dealfish
Devil ray
Dragonet
Drumfish
Eagle-ray
Escallop
Eulachon
Fallfish
Fighting
Filefish
Flatfish
Flathead
Flounder
Four-eyed
Four-eyes
Frogfish
Ganoidei
Gillaroo
Gilthead
Goatfish
Gobiidae
Goldfish
Graining
Grayling
Hackbolt
Hairtail
Halfbeak
Hard-head
Holostei
Hornbeak
Hornpout
Jackfish
John Dory
Kabeljou
Kelpfish
Killfish
Kingfish
Kingklip
Kukukuma
Lionfish
Luderick
Lumpfish
Lungfish
Mackerel
Mahi-mahi
Mangrove
Manta ray
Mata Hari
Menhaden

Milkfish
Monkfish
Moonfish
Mulloway
Nannygai
Nennigai
Nine-eyes
Oulachon
Paradise
Patutuki
Pickerel
Pilchard
Pipefish
Pirarucu
Redbelly
Red bream
Rock bass
Rock-cook
Rockfish
Rockling
Roncador
Rosefish
Saibling
Sailfish
Saltfish
Sardelle
Scabbard
Sciaenid
Scorpion
Scuppaug
Sea bream
Sea-devil
Sea horse
Sea-lemon
Sea perch
Sea raven
Sea robin
Sea snail
Sea trout
Sergeant
Serranus
Skipjack
Smear-dab
Snake-eel
Sparling
Stenlock
Stingray
Stonecat
Sturgeon
Tarakihi
Tarwhine
Teraglin
Terakihi
Tilefish
Toadfish
Trevalla
Trevally

Tropical
Tubenose
Tullibee
Weakfish
Whitling
Wobegong
Wolffish
Wollamai
Wollomai

9 letters:
Alfonsino
Amberjack
Anabantid
Anchoveta
Angelfish
Argentine
Barracuda
Black bass
Blackfish
Blindfish
Bony bream
Bull trout
Butterfly
Cascadura
Ceratodus
Chaetodon
Chavender
Clingfish
Clupeidae
Coregonus
Coryphene
Devilfish
Gaspereau
Glassfish
Globefish
Goldfinny
Goldsinny
Golomynka
Goosefish
Greenbone
Greenling
Grenadier
Haberdine
Hornyhead
Hottentot
Houndfish
Ichthyoid
Jacksmelt
Jewelfish
Kabeljouw
Killifish
Labyrinth
Lamper eel
Latimeria
Lemon sole
Menominee
Mudhopper

Neon tetra
Pikeperch
Placoderm
Porbeagle
Porcupine
Quillback
Red mullet
Red salmon
Roussette
Sand lance
Scaldfish
Schnapper
Scorpaena
Selachian
Shubunkin
Siluridae
Slickhead
Snailfish
Snakehead
Snipefish
Solenette
Spadefish
Spearfish
Speldring
Stargazer
Steelhead
Steenbras
Stingaree
Stockfish
Stone bass
Stonefish
Surfperch
Surmullet
Swellfish
Swordfish
Swordtail
Thornback
Threadfin
Tittlebat
Tommy ruff
Topminnow
Trachinus
Troutfish
Trunkfish
Whitebait
White-bass
Whitefish
Wobbegong
Wobbygong
Wreckfish
Yellowfin
10 letters:
Archerfish
Barracoota
Barracouta
Barramunda
Barramundi

Bitterling
Black bream
Black perch
Bombay duck
Bottlehead
Brook trout
Brown trout
Butterfish
Candlefish
Cockabully
Coelacanth
Coral trout
Cornetfish
Cyclostome
Damselfish
Demoiselle
Dollarfish
Etheostoma
Fingerling
Flutemouth
Giant perch
Groundling
Guitarfish
Horned pout
King salmon
Lumpsucker
Māori chief
Maskalonge
Maskanonge
Maskinonge
Midshipman
Mirror carp
Mossbunker
Mudskipper
Needlefish
Nurse-hound
Ouananiche
Paddlefish
Pakirikiri
Parrotfish
Pearl perch
Rabbitfish
Red emperor
Red snapper
Ribbonfish
Rock salmon
Rudderfish
Scopelidae
Sea lamprey
Sea-poacher
Sea-surgeon
Serrasalmo
Sheepshead
Shovelnose
Silverfish
Silverside
Springfish

Squeteague
Teleostome
Titarakura
Tommy rough
Tripletail
Yellow jack
Yellowtail
11 letters:
Bluefin tuna
Chondrostei
Dolly Varden
Electric eel
Golden perch
Istiophorus
Lake herring
Lepidosiren
Maskallonge
Moorish idol
Murray perch
Muskellunge
Ostracoderm
Oxyrhynchus
Plagiostome
Pumpkinseed
Salmon trout
Scolopendra
Sea scorpion
Seventy-four
Silver belly
Silversides
Sleeper goby
Smooth hound
Soldierfish
Stickleback
Stone roller
Surgeonfish
Triggerfish
Trumpetfish
Whiting pout
Yellow-belly
12 letters:
Baggie minnow
Ballan-wrasse
Elasmobranch
Father lasher
Heterosomata
Histiophorus
Mangrove Jack
Miller's thumb
Mouthbreeder
Native salmon
Orange roughy
Ox-eye herring
Plectognathi
Rainbow trout
River lamprey
Silver salmon

Skipjack tuna
Squirrelfish
Walleyed pike
Yarra herring
13 letters:
Armed bullhead
Black kingfish
Black rockfish
Brown bullhead
Chinook salmon
Climbing perch

Flying gurnard
Horse mackerel
Leatherjacket
Northern porgy
Quinnat salmon
Sailor's choice
Sergeant Baker
Sergeant major
Speckled trout
14 letters:
Largemouth bass

Orange chromide
School mackerel
Smallmouth bass
15 letters:
Crossopterygian
Freshwater bream
Siamese fighting
Spanish mackerel
Spotted mackerel

See also:
➤ **Seafood** ➤ **Sharks**

Flags

7 letters:
Saltire
8 letters:
Lone Star
Old Glory
Swastika
9 letters:
Betsy Ross
Blue Peter
Maple Leaf
Red Dragon
Red Duster
Rising Sun
Tricolore

Tricolour
Union Jack
10 letters:
Blue Ensign
Bonnie Blue
Jolly Roger
Lonely Star
Single Star
11 letters:
Golden Arrow
White Duster
12 letters:
Federal Cross
Herring Salad

Stars and Bars
13 letters:
Southern Cross
14 letters:
Flag of the South
15 letters:
Cross of St George
Hammer and Sickle
Stainless Banner
Stars and Stripes

Flies

3 letters:
Bee
Bot
Fly
Fox
4 letters:
Bulb
Bush
Cleg
Deer
Dung
Frit
Gnat
Horn
Moth
Pium
Zimb
5 letters:
Alder
Aphid
Aphis

Baker
Black
Brize
Crane
Drake
Drone
Flesh
Fruit
Hover
Musca
Nymph
Onion
Sedge
Snake
Snipe
Zebub
6 letters:
Blowie
Botfly
Breese
Breeze

Caddis
Carrot
Dayfly
Dragon
Gadfly
Mayfly
Medfly
Motuca
Mutuca
Needle
Pomace
Robber
Stable
Thrips
Tipula
Tsetse
Tzetze
Warble
Willow
7 letters:
Antlion

Beetfly
Blowfly
Brommer
Bushfly
Chalcid
Cluster
Diptera
Gallfly
Grannom
Harvest
Hessian
Lantern
Mangold
Sandfly
Spanish
Tabanid
Tachina
Vinegar
Watchet
8 letters:
Assassin
Bedstead
Blackfly
Dutchman

Glossina
Greenfly
Horsefly
Housefly
Lacewing
Mosquito
Ox-warble
Scorpion
Simulium
Stonefly
Whitefly
9 letters:
Bean aphid
Bee killer
Blue-arsed
Damselfly
Dobsonfly
Dragonfly
Greenhead
Homoptera
Ichneumon
Jock Scott
Sciaridae
Screwworm

Syrphidae
10 letters:
Bluebottle
Cecidomyia
Drosophila
Plant louse
Silverhorn
11 letters:
Apple blight
Buffalo gnat
Greenbottle
Plecopteran
12 letters:
Cheesehopper
Green blowfly
Jenny-spinner
Trichopteran
13 letters:
Cheese skipper
Daddy-longlegs
14 letters:
American blight
15 letters:
Welshman's button

Flowers

4 letters:
Aloe
Arum
Cyme
Disa
Flag
Gold
Gool
Gule
Irid
Iris
Lily
Pink
Rose
5 letters:
Agave
Aster
Brook
Bugle
Camas
Daisy
Enemy
Hosta
Lotus
Lupin
Oxlip
Padma
Pansy

Peony
Phlox
Poppy
Stock
Tansy
Toran
Tulip
Umbel
Yulan
6 letters:
Acacia
Adonis
Arabis
Azalea
Betony
Cactus
Camash
Camass
Corymb
Crants
Crocus
Dahlia
Gollan
Henbit
Madder
Maguey
Mallow
Nuphar

Onagra
Orchid
Paeony
Pompom
Pompon
Protea
Safety
Scilla
Sesame
Silene
Smilax
Spadix
Tassel
Torana
Vernal
Violet
Yarrow
Zinnia
7 letters:
Aconite
Alyssum
Anemone
Arbutus
Astilbe
Begonia
Bugloss
Burdock
Campion

Cowslip
Dog rose
Freesia
Fumaria
Gentian
Gilt-cup
Glacier
Godetia
Golland
Gowland
Hemlock
Ipomoea
Jasmine
Jonquil
Kikumon
Lobelia
Melilot
Petunia
Picotee
Primula
Quamash
Ragweed
Rampion
Saffron
Sulphur
Verbena
8 letters:
Abutilon
Acanthus
Amaranth
Argemone
Asphodel
Aubretia
Aubrieta
Bignonia
Bindi-eye
Bluebell
Camellia
Camomile
Carolina
Clematis
Cyclamen
Daffodil
Floscule
Foxglove
Gardenia
Geranium
Gillyvor
Glory-pea
Harebell
Hepatica
Hibiscus
Hyacinth
Kok-sagyz
Larkspur
Lavender

Magnolia
Mandrake
Marigold
Marjoram
Myosotis
Oleander
Oxtongue
Primrose
Samphire
Scabious
Snowdrop
Stapelia
Sweet pea
Trollius
Tuberose
Turnsole
Valerian
Wisteria
Woodbine
9 letters:
Amaryllis
Aubrietia
Bald-money
Belamoure
Buttercup
Calendula
Carnation
Celandine
Chamomile
Clianthus
Columbine
Dandelion
Desert pea
Digitalis
Edelweiss
Eglantine
Gessamine
Gladiolus
Groundsel
Hellebore
Hollyhock
Hydrangea
Jessamine
Melampode
Monkshood
Narcissus
Pimpernel
Pre-vernal
Rudbeckia
Santonica
Saxifrage
Speedwell
Strobilus
Sunflower
Tiger lily
Water lily

10 letters:
Aspidistra
Bellamoure
Busy Lizzie
Cornflower
Coronation
Delphinium
Gypsophila
Heart's-ease
Heliotrope
Immortelle
Marguerite
Nasturtium
Oxeye daisy
Pentstemon
Poinsettia
Snapdragon
Stavesacre
Sweetbrier
Tibouchine
Touch-me-not
Wallflower
Willowherb
11 letters:
Bog asphodel
Bur-marigold
Cotoneaster
Forget-me-not
Gilliflower
Gillyflower
Guelder-rose
London pride
Loose-strife
Meadowsweet
Ragged robin
Wintergreen
Wood anemone
12 letters:
Hortus siccus
Morning-glory
None-so-pretty
Old man's beard
Sweet william
Tradescantia
13 letters:
African violet
Babe-in-a-cradle
Bougainvillea
Chrysanthemum
Grape hyacinth
Passionflower
14 letters:
Black-eyed Susan
Cardinal flower
Cooktown orchid
Love-in-idleness

Football clubs

EUROPEAN FOOTBALL CLUBS

4 letters:
Ajax
Genk
Lyon
Roma
5 letters:
Lazio
Parma
6 letters:
Brugge
Lierse
Monaco
7 letters:
AC Milan
Beveren
Brondby
FC Porto
Hamburg
8 letters:
Besiktas

Juventus
Valencia
9 letters:
AEK Athens
Barcelona
Celta Vigo
Feyenoord
Stuttgart
Villareal
10 letters:
Anderlecht
Dynamo Kiev
Heerenveen
Inter Milan
Olympiacos
Real Madrid
11 letters:
Ferencvaros
Galatasaray
Rapid Vienna

RCD Mallorca
12 letters:
Bayern Munich
Dinamo Zagreb
PSV Eindhoven
Real Sociedad
Sparta Prague
13 letters:
Austria Vienna
Panathenaikos
14 letters:
Paris St Germain
15 letters:
Lokomotiv Moscow
Red Star Belgrade
Steaua Bucharest

UK FOOTBALL CLUBS

Club	Nickname	Ground
Aberdeen	Dons	Pittodrie
Arsenal	Gunners	Emirates Stadium
Aston Villa	Villa	Villa Park
Birmingham City	Blues	St Andrews
Blackburn Rovers	Rovers	Ewood Park
Bolton	Trotters	Reebok Stadium
Bradford	Bantams	Valley Parade
Bristol City	Robins	Ashton Gate
Burnley	Clarets	Turf Moor
Cardiff	Bluebirds	Cardiff City Stadium
Celtic	Celts, Hoops	Parkhead
Charlton	Addicks	The Valley
Chelsea	Pensioners	Stamford Bridge
Coventry City	Sky Blues	Highfield Road
Crewe	Railwaymen	Gresty Road
Crystal Palace	Glaziers	Selhurst Park
Derby County	Rams	Pride Park
Dundee	Dark Blues	Dens Park
Dundee United	Tangerines	Tannadice
Dunfermline Athletic	Pars	East End Park
Everton	Toffee Men	Goodison Park

Club	Nickname	Ground
Fulham	Cottagers	Craven Cottage
Gillingham	Gills	Prestfield Stadium
Hearts	Jambos, Jam Tarts	Tynecastle
Hibernian	Hibs, Hibees	Easter Road
Inverness Caledonian Thistle	Caley, The Jags	Tulloch Caledonian Stadium
Ipswich	Blues	Portman Road
Kilmarnock	The Killies	Rugby Park
Leeds United	United	Elland Road
Leicester City	Filberts	Filbert Street
Leyton Orient	Orient	Brisbane Road
Liverpool	Reds	Anfield
Livingston	Thistle, Wee Jags	Almondvale
Manchester City	City	City of Manchester Stadium
Manchester United	Reds, Red Devils	Old Trafford
Middlesbrough	Boro	Riverside Stadium
Millwall	Lions	The Den
Motherwell	Steelmen, Well	Fir Park
Newcastle	Magpies, Toon	St James Park
Norwich	Canaries	Carrow Road
Nottingham Forest	Forest	City Ground
Partick Thistle	Jags	Firhill
Peterborough	Posh	London Road
Portsmouth	Pompey	Fratton Park
Preston	Lilywhites	Deepdale
Queen of the South	The Doonhamers	Palmerston Park
Queen's Park Rangers	QPR	Loftus Road
Rangers	Gers, The Blues	Ibrox
Reading	Royals, Biscuitmen	Madejski Stadium
Rotherham	Merry Millers	Don Valley Stadium
St Johnstone	The Saints	McDiarmid Park
St Mirren	The Buddies	Love Street
Sheffield United	Blades	Bramall Lane
Sheffield Wednesday	Owls	Hillsborough
Southampton	Saints	St Mary's Stadium
Stenhousemuir	The Warriors	Ochilview Park
Stoke	Potteries	Britannia Stadium
Sunderland	Rokerites	Stadium of Light
Tottenham Hotspur	Spurs	White Hart Lane
Tranmere Rovers	Rovers	Prenton Park
Walsall	Saddlers	Bescot Stadium
Watford	Hornets	Vicarage Road
West Bromwich Albion	Throstles, Raggies	The Hawthorns
West Ham	Hammers	Upton Park
Wigan	Latics	JJB Stadium
Wolverhampton Wanderers	Wolves	Molineux

Fossils

5 letters:
Amber
6 letters:
Eozoon
Olenus
7 letters:
Exuviae
Ichnite
Zoolite
8 letters:
Ammonite
Baculite
Blastoid
Calamite
Conchite
Conodont
Eohippus
Mosasaur
Pliosaur
Ram's horn
Scaphite
Solenite
Volulite
Volutite
Wood-opal
9 letters:
Belemnite

Buccinite
Ceratodus
Chondrite
Cordaites
Encrinite
Goniatite
Ichnolite
Miliolite
Muscalite
Nummulite
Ostracite
Patellite
Phytolite
Serpulite
Stigmaria
Strombite
Tellinite
Trilobite
Turbinate
Turrilite
10 letters:
Blastoidea
Eurypterus
Graptolite
Lingulella
Mosasauros
Orthoceras

Osteolepis
Plesiosaur
Pliohippus
Pterygotus
Sigillaria
Snakestone
11 letters:
Gongiatites
Ichthyolite
Ostracoderm
12 letters:
Pythonomorph
Sinanthropus
Stromatolite
Uintatherium
13 letters:
Titanotherium
Zinganthropus
14 letters:
Conchyliaceous
15 letters:
Ichthyodurolite

Fowl

3 letters:
Cob
Hen
Ree
4 letters:
Cock
Coot
Duck
Gnow
Kora
Nene
Smew
Swan
Teal
5 letters:
Capon
Chock
Chook
Eider
Ember
Goose
Layer

Quail
Reeve
Rumpy
Scaup
Solan
6 letters:
Ancona
Bantam
Boiler
Brahma
Cochin
Eirack
Guinea
Houdan
Jungle
Pullet
Rumkin
Sitter
Sultan
Sussex
Tappit
Turkey

Wigeon
7 letters:
Campine
Chicken
Dorking
Gadwall
Greylag
Hamburg
Leghorn
Mallard
Minorca
Moorhen
Partlet
Pintado
Pintail
Pochard
Poulard
Redhead
Rooster
Sawbill
Sea duck
Sumatra

Whooper
Widgeon
8 letters:
Baldpate
Blue duck
Cockerel
Hamburgh
Langshan
Marsh hen
Megapode
Musk duck
Mute swan
Pheasant
Screamer
Shelduck
Shoveler
Wood duck
9 letters:
Black swan
Blue goose
Eider duck
Faverolle
Goldeneye

Goosander
Merganser
Orpington
Partridge
Pertelote
Ruddy duck
Scaup duck
Snow goose
Welsummer
Wyandotte
10 letters:
Andalusian
Australorp
Bufflehead
Burrow-duck
Canvasback
Chittagong
Mallee fowl
Spatchcock
Spitchcock
11 letters:
Bewick's swan
Brissle-cock

Brush turkey
Canada goose
Magpie goose
Muscovy duck
Scrub turkey
Whooper swan
12 letters:
Greylag goose
Mandarin duck
New Hampshire
Paradise duck
Plymouth Rock
Velvet scoter
13 letters:
Barnacle goose
Buff Orpington
Harlequin duck
Trumpeter swan
Whistling swan
14 letters:
American wigeon
Rhode Island Red

Fruits

3 letters:
Fig
Haw
Hep
Hip
Hop
Jak
4 letters:
Akee
Bael
Bito
Date
Gage
Gean
Jack
Kaki
Kiwi
Lime
Pear
Pepo
Plum
Pome
Sloe
Sorb
Star
Tuna
UGLI®
5 letters:
Anana
Anona

Apple
Assai
Berry
Bread
Choko
Gourd
Grape
Guava
Jaffa
Lemon
Lichi
Lotus
Mango
Melon
Nancy
Naras
Nashi
Nelis
Olive
Papaw
Peach
Prune
Rowan
Whort
6 letters:
Almond
Ananas
Babaco
Banana
Banian

Banyan
Carica
Casaba
Cherry
Chocho
Citron
Citrus
Damson
Durian
Durion
Emblic
Feijoa
Kiwano®
Lichee
Litchi
Longan
Loquat
Lychee
Mammee
Medlar
Narras
Nelies
Orange
Papaya
Pawpaw
Pepino
Pepper
Pomelo
Pruine
Quince

Raisin
Russet
Samara
Sapota
Sharon
Squash
Sweety
Tomato
Wampee
7 letters:
Apricot
Avocado
Bramble
Bullace
Cedrate
Chayote
Crab-nut
Cumquat
Geebung
Genipap
Kumquat
Leechee
Litchee
Manjack
Morello
Naartje
Passion
Pimento
Pinguin
Poperin
Pumpkin
Pupunha
Ruddock
Satsuma
Soursop
Sultana
Sweetie
Tangelo
Winesap
8 letters:
Abricock
Apricock
Bergamot
Bilberry
Blimbing
Boxberry
Calabash
Dewberry
Fraughan
Goosegog
Hagberry
Hastings
Hedgehog
Kalumpit
Mandarin
May apple
Minneola

Mulberry
Physalis
Plantain
Rambutan
Sebesten
Shaddock
Sunberry
Sweetsop
Tamarind
Tayberry
Victoria
9 letters:
Algarroba
Apple-john
Asian pear
Aubergine
Bakeapple
Beach plum
Blaeberry
Blueberry
Cantaloup
Canteloup
Carambola
Chempaduk
Cherimoya
Cranberry
Greengage
Haanepoot
Hackberry
Jackfruit
Japan plum
Love apple
Mirabelle
Muskmelon
Myrobalan
Naseberry
Nectarine
Neesberry
Ogen melon
Ortanique
Persimmon
Pineapple
Plumdamas
Poppering
Raspberry
Rockmelon
Sapodilla
Saskatoon
Shadberry
Snowberry
Sour gourd
Star-apple
Tamarillo
Tangerine
Tomatillo
Victorine
Whimberry

10 letters:
Blackberry
Breadfruit
Calamondin
Canteloupe
Cherimoyer
Clementine
Cloudberry
Elderberry
Galia melon
Gooseberry
Granadilla
Grapefruit
Grenadilla
Jargonelle
Loganberry
Mangosteen
Pick-cheese
Redcurrant
Scaldberry
Sour cherry
Strawberry
Tree tomato
Watermelon
Youngberry
11 letters:
Anchovy pear
Avocado pear
Black cherry
Blood orange
Boysenberry
Chokecherry
Heart cherry
Hesperidium
Huckleberry
Jaffa orange
Marionberry
Navel orange
Pampelmoose
Pampelmouse
Pomegranate
Pompelmoose
Pompelmouse
Prickly pear
Salmonberry
Sweet cherry
Winter melon
12 letters:
Bartlett pear
Bergamot pear
Blackcurrant
Cassaba melon
Concord grape
Custard apple
Serviceberry
Victoria plum
White currant

Whortleberry
Williams pear
13 letters:
Alligator pear
Honeydew melon
Morello cherry
Sapodilla plum
Seville orange

14 letters:
Cape gooseberry
Conference pear
Queensland blue
Worcesterberry
15 letters:
Beurre Hardy pear
Bigarreau cherry

Bon Chretien pear
Cantaloupe melon
Charentais melon

Fungi

3 letters:
Cup
4 letters:
Bunt
Rust
Smut
5 letters:
Black
Ergot
Favus
Honey
Jelly
Morel
Mould
Mucor
Spunk
Yeast
6 letters:
Agaric
Amadou
Dry rot
Elf-cup
Empusa
Ink-cap
Mildew
Miller
Peziza
Torula
Wax cap
Wet rot
7 letters:
Amanita
Blewits
Boletus
Bracket
Candida
Jew's ear
Milk cap
Monilia
Phallus

Pythium
Russula
Tarspot
Truffle
8 letters:
Ambrosia
Bootlace
Clubroot
Death cap
Death-cup
Fuss-ball
Fuzz-ball
Merulius
Mushroom
Noble rot
Puccinia
Puckfist
Puffball
Rhizopus
Rhytisma
Sariodes
Sickener
Tremella
Tuckahoe
Ustilago
9 letters:
Beefsteak
Blackknot
Cramp ball
Earthstar
Eumycetes
Funnel cap
Horsehair
Mucorales
Shaggy cap
Stinkhorn
Toadstool
10 letters:
Gibberella
Liberty cap

Oak-leather
Orange-peel
Rust fungus
Shoestring
Sooty mould
Yellow rust
11 letters:
Anthracnose
Aspergillus
Chantarelle
Chanterelle
Cladosporum
Craterellus
Ithyphallus
Jelly fungus
Penicillium
Phycomycete
Saprolegnia
Sulphur tuft
Velvet shank
12 letters:
Cryptococcus
Discomycetes
Horn of plenty
Hypersarcoma
Trichophyton
Wood hedgehog
13 letters:
Bracket fungus
Magic mushroom
Saccharomyces
Witches' butter
14 letters:
Wood woollyfoot
15 letters:
Bird's-nest fungus
Dermatophytosis
Destroying angel

Furies

6 letters:	**7 letters:**	**9 letters:**
Alecto	Megaera	Tisiphone

Furniture

TYPES OF FURNITURE

6 letters:
Canopy
Litter
Screen
Tester
7 letters:
Bedpost
Epergne
Lectern
Trolley

8 letters:
Bedstead
Hatstand
Vanitory
9 letters:
Coatstand
Footstool
Girandola
Girandole
Hallstand

Headboard
Washstand
10 letters:
Dumbwaiter
Vanity unit
11 letters:
Cheval glass
13 letters:
Longcase clock
Umbrella stand

FURNITURE STYLES

5 letters:
Saxon
Tudor
6 letters:
Empire
Gothic
Norman
Shaker
7 letters:
Art Deco
Bauhaus
Puritan
Regency

8 letters:
Georgian
Jacobean
Medieval
9 letters:
Cape Dutch
Edwardian
Queen Anne
Victorian
10 letters:
Louis Seize
11 letters:
Elizabethan

Louis Quinze
Louis Treize
New Georgian
Restoration
12 letters:
Greek Revival
Second Empire
13 letters:
Louis Quatorze
14 letters:
William and Mary

FURNITURE DESIGNERS

4 letters:
Adam, *Robert*
Heal, *Ambrose*
Kent, *William*
5 letters:
Aalto, *Alvar*
Bevan, *Charles*
Jones, *Inigo*
Jones, *William*
Klint, *Kaara*
Marot, *Daniel*
Phyfe, *Duncan*
Pugin, *Augustus*
Smith, *George*

6 letters:
Breuer, *Marcel Lajos*
Burges, *William*
Morris, *William*
Voysey, *Charles*
8 letters:
Sheraton, *Thomas*
9 letters:
Pergolesi, *Michael Angelo*
10 letters:
Mackintosh, *Charles Rennie*
11 letters:
Chippendale, *Thomas*
Hepplewhite, *George*

Galaxies

4 letters:
Arp's
5 letters:
Bode's
Draco
Dwarf
Giant
Helix
Radio
Virgo
6 letters:
Baade's
Carafe
Carina
Cygnus
Fornax
Maffei
Quasar
Spiral
Zwicky
7 letters:
Barbon's

Cluster
Garland
Pancake
Regular
Seyfert
Spindle
Tadpole
8 letters:
Aquarius
Barnard's
Bear's Paw
Black Eye
Circinus
Holmberg
Lacertid
Milky Way
Papillon
Pinwheel
Reinmuth
Sculptor
Seashell
Sombrero

9 letters:
Andromeda
Blue fuzzy
Capricorn
Cartwheel
Centaurus
Great Wall
Irregular
Whirlpool
10 letters:
Elliptical
Horologium
Local Group
12 letters:
Supercluster
13 letters:
Burbidge Chain
15 letters:
Exclamation Mark

Games

2 letters:
Eo
Go
RU
3 letters:
Cat
Hob
Loo
Maw
Nap
Nim
Pit
Put
Swy
Tag
Tig
War
4 letters:
Base

Brag
Bull
Crap
Dibs
Fa-fi
Faro
Goff
Golf
Grab
I-spy
Keno
Kino
Loto
Ludo
Main
Mora
Polo
Pool
Putt

Ruff
Scat
Skat
Snap
Solo
Taws
Vint
5 letters:
Bingo
Bocce
Bowls
Catch
Chess
Cinch
Craps
Darts
Fives
Goose
Halma

House
Jacks
Keeno
Lotto
Lurch
Merel
Meril
Monte
Morra
Noddy
Novum
Omber
Ombre
Poker
Quino
Rebus
Roque
Rummy
Shogi
Spoof
Tarok
Tarot
Trugo
Two-up
Whisk
Whist
6 letters:
Animal
Basset
Beetle
Boston
Boules
Casino
Chemmy
Clumps
Crambo
Ecarté
Euchre
Fantan
Footer
Gammon
Gobang
Gomoku
Hockey
Hoopla
Hurley
Kitcat
Merell
Pelota
Piquet
Quinze
Quoits
Raffle
Shinny
Shinty
Soccer
Socker

Squash
Tipcat
Uckers
Vigoro
7 letters:
Anagram
Ba'spiel
Bezique
Braemar
Camogie
Canasta
Cassino
Charade
Codille
Conkers
Coon-can
Croquet
Curling
Diabolo
Hangman
Hurling
In-and-In
Jai Alai
Jukskei
Kabaddi
Lottery
Mahjong
Mancala
Marbles
Matador
Muggins
Netball
Old Maid
Pachisi
Pallone
Peekabo
Pharaoh
Pinball
Plafond
Primero
Rackets
Reversi
Ring taw
Seven-up
Snooker
Squails
Statues
Tangram
Vingt-un
War game
8 letters:
Acrostic
All-fours
Baccarat
Bumpball
Canfield
Charades

Chouette
Cottabus
Cribbage
Dominoes
Fivepins
Football
Forfeits
Handball
Klondike
Klondyke
Korfball
Leapfrog
Mah-jongg
Monopoly®
Ninepins
Nintendo®
Octopush
Pachinko
Pall-mall
Pastance
Patience
Peekaboo
Pegboard
Penneech
Penneeck
Penuchle
Petanque
Ping-pong
Pinochle
Pintable
Pope Joan
Reversis
Rolypoly
Roulette
Rounders
Sack race
Scrabble®
Skipping
Skittles
Slapjack
Softball
Sphairee
Subbuteo®
Teetotum
Tray-trip
Tredille
Trictrac
Verquere
Verquire
Wall game
9 letters:
Badminton
Bagatelle
Billiards
Black-cock
Black-jack
Broomball

Crossword
Duplicate
Fillipeen
Hopscotch
Jingo-ring
Lanterloo
Level-coil
Logogriph
Matrimony
Mistigris
Mumchance
Newmarket
Or mineral
Paintball
Parcheesi®
Pelmanism
Punchball
Quadrille
Quidditch®
Simon says
Solitaire
Spoilfive
Stoolball
Tip-and-run
Tredrille
Twenty-one
Vegetable
Vingt-et-un
10 letters:
Angel-beast
Basketball
Bouillotte
Candlepins
Cat's cradle
Deck tennis
Dumb Crambo

See also:
➤ **Board games**

Five-stones
Handy-dandy
Horseshoes
Jackstones
Jackstraws
Knurr-spell
Lansquenet
Paddleball
Phillipina
Phillipine
Philopoena
Spillikins
Tablanette
Tchoukball
Thimblerig
Tricktrack
Troll-madam
Trou-madame
Volley-ball
11 letters:
Barley-brake
Battleships
Bumble-puppy
Catch-the-ten
Hide-and-seek
Racquetball
Rouge et noir
Sancho-pedro
Shovelboard
Speculation
Tick-tack-toe
Tiddlywinks
Troll-my-dame
12 letters:
Bar billiards
Caber tossing

Commonwealth
Consequences
Housey-housey
Jigsaw puzzle
Knur and spell
One-and-thirty
Pitch-and-toss
Shuffleboard
Span-farthing
Troll-my-dames
13 letters:
Blind man's buff
French cricket
Musical chairs
Postman's knock
Prisoner's base
Scavenger hunt
14 letters:
British bulldog
Crown and anchor
Ducks and drakes
Follow-my-leader
Shove-halfpenny
Snip-snap-snorum
Three-card monte
15 letters:
Chinese whispers
Crossword puzzle
King of the castle
Russian roulette
The Minister's Cat
Twenty questions

Gases

1 letter:
H
O
2 letters:
BZ
CN
CS
He
Kr
Ne
RN
VX

3 letters:
Air
CNG
LNG
LPG
Nox
SNG
4 letters:
Coal
Damp
Flue
Mace®

Neon
Tail
Tear
Town
5 letters:
Argon
Calor®
Ether
Marsh
Nerve
Ozone
Radon

Sarin
Soman
Tabun
Water
Xenon
6 letters:
Arsine
Biogas
Bottle
Butane
Butene
Ethane
Ethene
Ethyne
Helium
Ketene
Oilgas
Olefin
Oxygen
Plasma
Sewage
Silane
Thoron
V-agent
7 letters:
Ammonia
Argonon
Blister
Bottled
Coal-oil
Crypton

Fluorin
Krypton
Methane
Mofette
Mustard
Natural
Olefine
Propane
Propene
Stibine
8 letters:
Chlorine
Cyanogen
Diborane
Etherion
Ethylene
Firedamp
Fluorine
Hydrogen
Laughing
Lewisite
Nitrogen
Phosgene
Producer
9 letters:
Acetylene
Afterdamp
Butadiene
Chokedamp
Phosphine
Propylene

Protostar
Solfatara
Synthesis
Whitedamp
10 letters:
Diphosgene
Greenhouse
11 letters:
Methylamine
Nitric oxide
12 letters:
Carbonic-acid
Diazomethane
Electrolytic
Formaldehyde
Nitrous oxide
Oxyacetylene
13 letters:
Carbon dioxide
Methyl bromide
Vinyl chloride
14 letters:
Carbon monoxide
Hydrogen iodide
Methyl chloride
Sulphur dioxide
15 letters:
Hydrogen bromide
Nitrogen dioxide
Nitrogen mustard

Gemstones

2 letters:
ID
3 letters:
Jet
4 letters:
Jade
Onyx
Opal
Ruby
Sard
5 letters:
Agate
Balas
Beryl
Idaho
Pearl
Prase
Topaz
6 letters:
Garnet
Iolite
Jargon

Jasper
Jaspis
Morion
Plasma
Pyrope
Quartz
Sphene
Spinel
Zircon
7 letters:
Cat's-eye
Citrine
Diamond
Emerald
Girasol
Girosol
Helidor
Jacinth
Jadeite
Jargoon
Kunzite
Peridot

Sardine
Smaragd
8 letters:
Adularia
Amethyst
Corundum
Diopside
Fire opal
Girasole
Hawk's-eye
Heliodor
Hyacinth
Melanite
Menilite
Peridote
Sapphire
Sardonyx
Sunstone
Titanite
9 letters:
Almandine
Amazonite

Andradite
Aventurin
Black opal
Cairngorm
Carnelian
Cornelian
Cymophane
Demantoid
Hessonite
Hiddenite
Liver opal
Moonstone
Morganite
Moss agate
Rhodolite
Rubellite
Spodumene
Starstone
Tiger's eye
Turquoise

Uvarovite
10 letters:
Andalusite
Aquamarine
Avanturine
Aventurine
Bloodstone
Chalcedony
Chrysolite
Heliotrope
Indicolite
Indigolite
Odontolite
Rhinestone
Rose quartz
Staurolite
Topazolite
Tourmaline
11 letters:
Alexandrite

Chrysoberyl
Chrysoprase
Lapis lazuli
Smoky quartz
Spessartite
Verd antique
Vesuvianite
12 letters:
Colorado ruby
Dumortierite
Grossularite
Spanish topaz
13 letters:
Bone turquoise
Colorado topaz
Water sapphire
White sapphire
15 letters:
Oriental emerald

Generals

3 letters:
Ike *(Dwight David Eisenhower)*
Lee, *Robert E(dward)*
5 letters:
Booth, *William*
Condé, *Louis de Bourbon, Prince de*
De Wet, *Christian*
Grant, *Ulysses Simpson*
Smuts, *Jan*
Wolfe, *James*
6 letters:
Custer, *George Armstrong*
Franco, *Francisco*
Gordon, *Charles George*
Joshua
Leslie, *David*
Napier, *Lord Robert*
Patton, *George*
Pompey
Raglan, *Fitzroy James Henry Somerset*
Rommel, *Erwin*
Scipio, *Publius Cornelius*
7 letters:
Agrippa, *Marcus Vipsanius*
Allenby, *Viscount Edmund*
Crassus, *Marcus Licinius*
Gamelin, *Maurice Gustave*
Hadrian
Sherman, *William Tecumseh*

Turenne
8 letters:
Agricola, *Gnaeus Julius*
De Gaulle, *Charles (André Joseph Marie)*
Hannibal
Marshall, *George Catlett*
Montcalm, *Louis Joseph de*
Napoleon *(Bonaparte)*
Pershing, *John Joseph*
Shrapnel, *Henry*
Stilwell, *Joseph Warren*
Stratton, *Charles Sherwood*
Tom Thumb *(Charles Sherwood Stratton)*
9 letters:
Agamemnon
Antigonus
Antipater
Boulanger, *George Ernest Jean Marie*
Kitchener, *Earl Herbert*
Lafayette, *Marie Joseph, Marquis de*
Macarthur, *Douglas*
10 letters:
Alcibiades
Cornwallis, *Charles, Marquis*
Eisenhower, *Dwight D(avid) (Ike)*
Holofernes

Geography

BRANCHES OF GEOGRAPHY

5 letters:
Human
7 letters:
Geology
Orology
8 letters:
Pedology
Physical
9 letters:
Chorology
Hydrology

Orography
Political
10 letters:
Demography
Glaciology
Oceanology
Seismology
Topography
11 letters:
Cartography
Chorography

Climatology
Geopolitics
Meteorology
Vulcanology
12 letters:
Biogeography
Oceanography
13 letters:
Geomorphology

GEOGRAPHY TERMS AND FEATURES

3 letters:
Bay
Col
Cwm
Map
Tor
4 letters:
Core
Crag
Dyke
Fell
Glen
Loch
Reef
Rill
Spit
Spur
Tarn
Veld
Wadi
5 letters:
Arête
Atlas
Atoll
Basin
Beach
Cliff
Crust
Delta
Fault
Fjord
Glade
Levée
Ocean
Ridge
Scree

Stack
Veldt
6 letters:
Canyon
Cirque
Coombe
Corrie
Crater
Desert
Ice cap
Isobar
Jungle
Lagoon
Mantle
Sierra
Spring
Steppe
Suburb
Tundra
7 letters:
Climate
Contour
Culvert
Equator
Erosion
Estuary
Glacier
Isobath
Isohyet
Isthmus
Meander
Moraine
New town
Rivulet
Sand bar
Savanna

Subsoil
Topsoil
Tropics
Tsunami
Volcano
Wetland
8 letters:
Crevasse
Eastings
Headland
Isotherm
Latitude
Oriental
Salt flat
Salt lake
Sandbank
Sand dune
Savannah
Snow line
9 letters:
Antipodes
Continent
Coral reef
Dormitory
Epicentre
Green belt
Longitude
Northings
North Pole
Pollution
Relief map
South Pole
Temperate
Waterfall
Watershed
Whirlpool

10 letters:
Atmosphere
Earthquake
Escarpment
Flood plain
Glaciation
Irrigation
Occidental
Ozone layer
Permafrost
Rainforest
Rain shadow
Rift valley
River basin

Third World
Water cycle
Water table
Weathering
11 letters:
Conurbation
Environment
Watercourse
12 letters:
Conservation
Urbanization
13 letters:
Afforestation
Deforestation

Global warming
Grid reference
Hanging valley
Precipitation
14 letters:
Infrastructure
Longshore drift
Ordnance Survey
Plate tectonics
15 letters:
Desertification

GEOGRAPHERS

6 letters:
Kremer, *Gerhard*
Strabo
7 letters:
Hakluyt, *Richard*
Ptolemy

8 letters:
Mercator, *Gerardus*
9 letters:
Mackinder, *Sir
Halford John*
Pausanias

10 letters:
Somerville, *Mary*

See also:
➤ Canals ➤ Capes ➤ Capitals ➤ Channels ➤ Cities ➤ Continents
➤ Countries ➤ Deserts ➤ Earth's crust ➤ Hills ➤ Islands and
island groups ➤ Lakes, lochs and loughs ➤ Peninsulas ➤ Ports
➤ Rivers ➤ Seas and oceans ➤ Sounds ➤ Straits ➤ Towns
➤ Volcanoes ➤ Waterfalls

Geology

GEOLOGICAL ERAS

8 letters:
Cenozoic
Mesozoic

10 letters:
Palaeozoic

11 letters:
Precambrian

GEOLOGICAL PERIODS

7 letters:
Permian
8 letters:
Cambrian
Devonian
Jurassic

Silurian
Tertiary
Triassic
10 letters:
Cretaceous
Ordovician

Quaternary
13 letters:
Carboniferous

EPOCHS OF THE CENOZOIC ERA

6 letters:
Eocene
7 letters:
Miocene

8 letters:
Holocene
Pliocene
9 letters:
Oligocene

10 letters:
Palaeocene
11 letters:
Pleistocene

See also:
➤ **Earth's crust** ➤ **Minerals** ➤ **Rocks** ➤ **Stones**

Giants and giantesses

2 letters:
Og
3 letters:
Gog
4 letters:
Anak
Bran
Otus
Ymir
5 letters:
Argus
Balan
Balor
Cacus
Hymir
Idris
Magog
Mimir
Talos
Talus
Thrym
6 letters:
Coltys
Cottus

Gefion
Krasir
Pallas
Tityus
Triton
Typhon
Urizen
7 letters:
Antaeus
Cyclops
Despair
Gabbara
Geirred
Goliath
Harapha
Skrymir
8 letters:
Ascapart
Bellerus
Briareus
Colbrand
Cormoran
Cyclopes
Ferragus

Hrungnir
Slaygood
9 letters:
Alcyoneus
Archiloro
Colbronde
Enceladus
Ephialtes
Gargantua
Lestrigon
Leviathan
Rounceval
Tregeagle
Tryphoeus
10 letters:
Pantagruel
Patagonian
Polyphemus
11 letters:
Alifanfaron
Blunderbore
Galligantus

Glands

3 letters:
Oil
4 letters:
Silk
5 letters:
Green
Liver
Lymph
Mucus
Ovary
Scent
Sweat
6 letters:
Ink-sac
Pineal

Tarsel
Testis
Thymus
Tonsil
7 letters:
Adenoid
Adrenal
Cowper's
Eccrine
Mammary
Musk-sac
Nectary
Parotid
Parotis
Thyroid

8 letters:
Apocrine
Conarium
Exocrine
Lacrimal
Pancreas
Pope's eye
Prostate
Salivary
Testicle
9 letters:
Digestive
Endocrine
Epiphysis
Holocrine

Lachrymal
Meibomian
Pituitary
Sebaceous
Uropygial
10 letters:
Bartholin's

Hypophysis
Osmeterium
Suprarenal
11 letters:
Colleterial
Paranephros
Parathyroid

Prothoracic
12 letters:
Hypothalamus
13 letters:
Bulbourethral

Glass, types of

3 letters:
Cut
4 letters:
Eden
Jena
Lead
Milk
Opal
Spun
Vita
Wire
5 letters:
Crown
Flint
Float
Paste
Plate
Pyrex®
Silex
Smalt
6 letters:
Bottle

Cullet
Quartz
Smalto
Strass
7 letters:
Baccara
Crookes
Crystal
Favrile
Lalique
Murrine
Opaline
Perlite
Schmelz
Stained
Tektite
Tiffany
Triplex®
Vitrail
8 letters:
Baccarat
Murrhine

Obsidian
Pearlite
Venetian
Volcanic
9 letters:
Fulgurite
Lanthanum
Tachilite
Tachylite
Tachylyte
Waterford
10 letters:
Avanturine
Aventurine
Calcedonio
Latticinio
Millefiori
Mousseline
Pitchstone
12 letters:
Vitro-di-trina

Gods and goddesses

AZTEC

3 letters:
Atl
4 letters:
Tena
5 letters:
Innan
Itzli
Teteo
6 letters:
Atlaua
Paynal
Tlaloc
Xolotl
7 letters:
Amimitl
Ehecatl
Omacatl

Xilonen
8 letters:
Camaxtli
Centeotl
Chantico
Mayahuel
Mixcoatl
Patecatl
Techlotl
Tonatiuh
Tzapotla
Xippilli
9 letters:
Coatlicue
Cochimetl
Ixtlilton
Techalotl

Tzintetol
Tzontemoc
Xipe Totec
Xiuhcoatl
10 letters:
Acolmiztli
Chiconahui
Cihuacoatl
Nanauatzin
Omecihuatl
Xochipilli
11 letters:
Huehueteotl
Itzpapalotl
Ometecuhtli
Tepeyollotl
Tlazolteotl

Uixtociuatl
Xiuhteuctli
12 letters:
Chicomecoatl
Coyolxauhqui
Malinalxochi
Quetzalcoatl
Tecciztecatl
Tezcatlipoca
Tlaltecuhtli

Xochiquetzal
Yacatecuhtli
13 letters:
Acolnahuacatl
Huixtocihuatl
Ilamatecuhtli
Macuilxochitl
14 letters:
Chicomexochtli
Itzlacoliuhque

Mictlantecutli
Tonacatecuhtli
15 letters:
Centzonuitznaua
Chalchiuhtlicue
Chalchiutotolin
Chalmecacihuilt
Huitzilopochtli

CELTIC

3 letters:
Anu
Dôn
Lir
4 letters:
Áine
Badb
Bíle
Bodb
Dana
Danu
Donn
Ériu
Esus
Fand
Llyr
Lugh
Medb
Ogma
5 letters:
Artio

Balor
Banba
Bóand
Dagda
Epona
Mabon
Macha
Midir
Núadu
6 letters:
Bécuma
Brigid
Nemain
Sirona
7 letters:
Belenus
Nechtan
Sequana
Taranis
8 letters:
Ceridwen

Manannán
Morrígan
Nemetona
Rhiannon
Rosmerta
Sucellus
Teutates
9 letters:
Arianhrod
Blodeuedd
Cernunnos
Manawydan
11 letters:
Nantosuelta
Óengus Mac Óc
14 letters:
Lleu Llaw Gyffes
Vagdavercustis

EGYPTIAN

2 letters:
Ra
Re
3 letters:
Set
4 letters:
Isis

Maat
Ptah
5 letters:
Horus
Thoth
6 letters:
Amen-Ra

Anubis
Hathor
Osiris
7 letters:
Serapis

GREEK

God or goddess	**Area or place ruled**
Aeolus	Winds
Aphrodite	Love and beauty
Apollo	Light, youth, and music
Ares	War
Artemis	Hunting and the moon
Asclepius	Healing

God or goddess	**Area or place ruled**
Athene *or* Pallas Athene	Wisdom
Bacchus	Wine
Boreas	North wind
Cronos	Fertility of the earth
Demeter	Agriculture
Dionysus	Wine
Eos	Dawn
Eros	Love
Fates	Destiny
Gaea *or* Gaia	The earth
Graces	Charm and beauty
Hades	Underworld
Hebe	Youth and spring
Hecate	Underworld
Helios	Sun
Hephaestus	Fire and metalworking
Hera	Queen of the gods
Hermes	Messenger of the gods
Horae *or* the Hours	Seasons
Hymen	Marriage
Hyperion	Sun
Hypnos	Sleep
Iris	Rainbow
Momus	Blame and mockery
Morpheus	Sleep and dreams
Nemesis	Vengeance
Nike	Victory
Pan	Woods and shepherds
Poseidon	Sea and earthquakes
Rhea	Fertility
Selene	Moon
Uranus	Sky
Zephyrus	West wind
Zeus	King of the gods

HINDU

4 letters:
Agni
Devi
Kali
Kama
Maya
Rama
Siva

5 letters:
Durga
Indra
Shiva
Ushas
6 letters:
Brahma
Ganesa

Varuna
Vishnu
7 letters:
Hanuman
Krishna
Lakshmi

INCAN

3 letters:
Apo
4 letters:
Inti
5 letters:
Huaca
Supay
6 letters:
Chasca
Ekkeko
Illapa
7 letters:
Paricia
Punchau

Vichama
8 letters:
Catequil
Cocomama
Coniraya
Copacati
Zaramama
9 letters:
Apu Illapu
Cavillaca
Mama Allpa
Mama Cocha
Mama Oello
Mama Pacha

Pariacaca
Urcaguary
Viracocha
10 letters:
Apu Punchau
Mama Quilla
Manco Capac
Pachacamac
11 letters:
Apocatequil
13 letters:
Chasca Coyllur
Ka-Ata-Killa Kon

MAYAN

2 letters:
Ix
3 letters:
Kan
K'in
4 letters:
Acan
Acat
Alom
Chac
Naum
Zotz
5 letters:
Ah Kin
Ah Mun
Ajbit
Balam
Bitol
Cauac
Cizin
Ixtab
Mulac
Tohil
Votan
Yaluk
6 letters:
Ah Peku
Ah Puch
Chamer
Coyopa
Cum Hau

Ghanan
Ixchel
Kianto
Tzakol
7 letters:
Ac Yanto
Ahau-Kin
Ah Ciliz
Ahmakiq
Ah Tabai
Ahulane
Cakulha
Ekchuah
Hunab Ku
Hun Came
Hurakan
Itzamna
Xaman Ek
Yum Caax
8 letters:
Ah Cancum
Ah Cun Can
Ah Cuxtal
Ah Hulneb
Cabaguil
Camaxtli
Camazotz
Caprakan
Colel Cab
Gucumatz
Ixzaluoh

Kukulcan
9 letters:
Ah Chuy Kak
Akhushtal
Chibirias
Hacha'kyum
Kan-xib-yui
Tlacolotl
10 letters:
Ah Chun Caan
Ah Muzencab
Ah Uuc Ticab
Hun Hunahpu
Kinich Ahau
11 letters:
Alaghom Naom
Cit Bolon Tum
Itzananohk'u
Ix Chebel Yax
Kan-u-Uayeyab
Nohochacyum
12 letters:
Backlum Chaam
Buluc Chabtan
Chac Uayab Xoc
13 letters:
Ah Bolom Tzacab
Colop U Uichkin
14 letters:
Ah Uincir Dz'acab

NORSE

3 letters:	**5 letters:**	**6 letters:**
Hel	Aegir	Balder
Tyr	Aesir	Freyja
4 letters:	Bragi	Frigga
Frey	Freya	Ithunn
Hela	Freyr	Njorth
Idun	Frigg	**7 letters:**
Loki	Njord	Heimdal
Odin	Norns	**8 letters:**
Thor	Othin	Heimdall
Tyrr	Vanir	**9 letters:**
		Heimdallr

ROMAN

God or goddess	**Area or place ruled**
Aesculapius	Medicine
Apollo	Light, youth, and music
Aurora	Dawn
Bacchus	Wine
Bellona	War
Bona Dea	Fertility
Ceres	Agriculture
Cupid	Love
Cybele	Nature
Diana	Hunting and the moon
Faunus	Forests
Flora	Flowers
Janus	Doors and beginnings
Juno	Queen of the gods
Jupiter *or* Jove	King of the gods
Lares	Household
Luna	Moon
Mars	War
Mercury	Messenger of the gods
Minerva	Wisdom
Neptune	Sea
Penates	Storeroom
Phoebus	Sun
Pluto	Underworld
Quirinus	War
Saturn	Agriculture and vegetation
Sol	Sun
Somnus	Sleep
Trivia	Crossroads
Venus	Love
Victoria	Victory
Vulcan	Fire and metalworking

Gorgons

6 letters:
Medusa
Stheno

7 letters:
Euryale

Governments

Name	Meaning
Absolutism	By an absolute ruler
Anarchy	Absence of government
Aristocracy	By nobility
Autarchy *or* autocracy	By an unrestricted individual
Bureaucracy	By officials
Communalism	By self-governing communities
Constitutionalism	According to a constitution
Corporatism	By corporate groups
Democracy	By the people
Despotism	By a despot or absolute ruler
Diarchy *or* dyarchy	By two rulers
Dictatorship	By dictator
Ergatocracy	By the workers
Gerontocracy	By old people
Gynaecocracy *or* gynarchy	By women
Hagiocracy *or* hagiarchy	By holy men
Heptarchy	By seven rulers
Hexarchy	By six rulers
Hierocracy *or* hierarchy	By priests
Imperialism	By an emperor or empire
Isocracy	By equals
Meritocracy	By rulers chosen according to ability
Mobocracy	By the mob
Monarchy	By monarch
Monocracy	By one ruler
Nomocracy	By rule of law
Ochlocracy	By mob
Octarchy	By eight rulers
Oligarchy	By the few
Pantisocracy	By all equally
Pentarchy	By five rulers
Plutocracy	By the rich
Pornocracy	By whores
Ptochocracy	By the poor
Quangocracy	By quangos
Slavocracy	By slaveholders
Squirearchy *or* squirarchy	By squires
Stratocracy	By the army
Technocracy	By experts
Tetrarchy	By four rulers
Theocracy *or* thearchy	By a deity
Triarchy	By three rulers
Tyranny	By a tyrant

Graces

6 letters:
Aglaia
Thalia

10 letters:
Euphrosyne

Grammatical cases

6 letters:
Dative
7 letters:
Elative
Oblique
8 letters:
Ablative
Agentive

Ergative
Genitive
Illative
Locative
Vocative
9 letters:
Objective

10 letters:
Accusative
Nominative
Possessive
Subjective
12 letters:
Instrumental

Grand Prix circuits

5 letters:
Monza
6 letters:
Monaco
Sepang
Suzuka
7 letters:
Bahrain

8 letters:
Shanghai
9 letters:
Catalunya
10 letters:
Albert Park
11 letters:
Hungaroring

Nurburgring
Silverstone
12 letters:
Indianapolis
13 letters:
Francorchamps
14 letters:
Hockenheimring
Jose Carlos Pace

Grapes

3 letters:
Fox
5 letters:
Gamay
Pinot
Steen
Syrah
Tokay
Viura
6 letters:
Malbec
Merlot
Muscat
Shiraz
Spanna
7 letters:
Aligoté
Barbera
Catawba
Concord
Furmint
Hamburg

Malmsey
Sercial
8 letters:
Cabernet
Cinsault
Delaware
Dolcetto
Garnacha
Grenache
Hamburgh
Hanepoot
Honeypot
Malvasia
Malvesie
Marsanne
Moscatel
Muscadel
Muscatel
Nebbiolo
Pinotage
Riesling
Ruländer

Sémillon
Silvaner
Sylvaner
Verdelho
Viognier
9 letters:
Colombard
Haanepoot
Lambrusco
Malvoisie
Mourvèdre
Muscadine
Pinot gris
Pinot noir
Sauvignon
Scheurebe
Trebbiano
Ugni blanc
Véronique
Zinfandel
10 letters:
Chardonnay

Hárslevelü
Kékfrankos
Muscadelle
Negroamoro
Pinot blanc
Sangiovese
Sweet-water
Verdicchio
11 letters:
Chenin blanc

Pinot grigio
Scuppernong
Seyval blanc
Tempranillo
12 letters:
Laski rizling
Olasz rizling
13 letters:
Cabernet franc
Montepulciano

Müller-thurgau
Rhine riesling
Spätburgunder
14 letters:
Gewürztraminer
Sauvignon blanc
Tokay-Pinot Gris
Welschriesling
15 letters:
Grüner veltliner

Grasses

3 letters:
Eel
Lop
Oat
Poa
Rye
Saw
Seg
Tef
4 letters:
Alfa
Bent
Cane
Cord
Crab
Culm
Dari
Diss
Doob
Dura
Hair
Kans
Knot
Lyme
Milo
Rami
Reed
Rice
Rips
Rusa
Salt
Snow
Stag
Star
Tape
Teff
Tell
Wire
Worm
5 letters:
Alang

Avena
Bahia
Blady
Canna
Chess
Cogon
Couch
Cutty
Dhura
Doura
Durra
Emmer
Flote
Goose
Grama
Halfa
Heath
Jawar
Jowar
Kunai
Lemon
Maize
Manna
Melic
Oryza
Pamir
Panic
Peach
Plume
Quack
Quick
Ramee
Ramie
Roosa
Sedge
Sisal
Spear
Spelt
Starr
Stipa
Storm

Sword
Wheat
Witch
6 letters:
Bamboo
Barley
Bennet
Bladey
Bromus
Buffel
Canary
Carpet
Clover
Cotton
Cuscus
Darnel
Dhurra
Eddish
Fescue
Fiorin
Jawari
Jowari
Kikuyu
Lalang
Lolium
Lucern
Marram
Marrum
Melick
Millet
Pampas
Phleum
Puszta
Quitch
Redtop
Ribbon
Scurvy
Scutch
Sesame
Toetoe
Toitoi

Twitch
Zoysia
7 letters:
Alfalfa
Bermuda
Bristle
Buffalo
Cannach
Clivers
Esparto
Feather
Foxtail
Heather
Johnson
Locusta
Lucerne
Matweed
Quaking
Sacaton
Sea-reed
Sorghum
Squitch
Timothy
Vetiver
Wallaby

Whangee
Whitlow
Wild oat
Wild rye
Zizania
Zostera
8 letters:
Barnyard
Cat's tail
Cleavers
Dactylis
Dogstail
Eelwrack
Elephant
Flinders
Kangaroo
Khuskhus
Materass
Paspalum
Rye-grass
Scorpion
Spinifex
Teosinte
9 letters:
Bluegrass

Cocksfoot
Corkscrew
Danthonia
Deergrass
Gama-grass
Harestail
Job's tears
Porcupine
Snowgrass
Sour-gourd
Sugar cane
Triticale
10 letters:
Brome-grass
Citronella
Cochlearia
Cortaderia
Miscanthus
Pennisetum
Persicaria
12 letters:
Kentucky blue
Squirrel-tail
Yorkshire fog

Greeks

4 letters:
Ajax
Nike
5 letters:
Homer
Momus
Timon
Zorba
6 letters:
Epirus
Euclid
Nestor
Nostos
Strabo

7 letters:
Orestes
Paestum
Pelopid
Perseus
Theseus
8 letters:
Achilles
Diomedes
Leonidas
Xenophon
9 letters:
Agamemnon
Aristides

Isocrates
Patroclus
Spartacus
Thersites
10 letters:
Archimedes
Pythagoras
11 letters:
Epaminondas

Green, shades of

3 letters:
Pea
Sea
4 letters:
Aqua
Cyan
Jade
Lime
Nile
Pine

Teal
5 letters:
Apple
Olive
6 letters:
Almond
Citron
7 letters:
Avocado
Celadon

Emerald
Lincoln
8 letters:
Eau de nil
9 letters:
Pistachio
Turquoise
10 letters:
Aquamarine
Chartreuse

Guns

2 letters:
HA
3 letters:
BAR
Dag
Gat
Ray
Tea
Uzi®
Zip
4 letters:
Bren
Burp
Colt
Owen
Pump
Riot
Sten
Stun
Tier
5 letters:
Flame
Fusil
Lewis
Luger®
Maxim
Radar
Rifle
Saker
Siege
Spear
Spray
Taser®
Tommy
6 letters:
Ack-ack
Archie
Barker
Bofors
Breech
Falcon
Fowler
Garand
Gingal
Jezail
Jingal
Magnum®
Mauser
Minnie

Minute
Mortar
Musket
Pistol
Pom-pom
Quaker
Roscoe
Squirt
Staple
Swivel
Tupelo
7 letters:
Bazooka
Bulldog
Bundook
Caliver
Carbine
Coehorn
Gatling
Gingall
Hackbut
Long Tom
Machine
Noonday
Pedrero
Pelican
Perrier
Shotgun
8 letters:
Amusette
Armalite®
Arquebus
Biscayan
Browning
Culverin
Deringer
Electron
Elephant
Falconet
Firelock
Howitzer
Oerlikon
Paderero
Paterero
Pederero
Petronel
Pistolet
Repeater
Revolver

Starting
Sterling
Thompson
9 letters:
Archibald
Automatic
Big Bertha
Brown Bess
Carronade
Chassepot
Chokebore
Derringer
Escopette
Flintlock
Forty-five
Harquebus
Matchlock
Morris Meg
Musketoon
Sarbacane
Snaphance
Sterculia
10 letters:
Scatter-gun
Self-cocker
Six-shooter
Smoothbore
Snaphaunce
11 letters:
Blunderbuss
Garand rifle
Kalashnikov
Stern-cannon
Stern-chaser
Thirty eight
12 letters:
Anti-aircraft
Breech-loader
Enfield rifle
Fowlingpiece
Martini-Henry®
Mitrailleuse
Muzzle-loader
Trench mortar
13 letters:
Sub-machine-gun
15 letters:
Winchester rifle

Gymnastic events

4 letters:
Beam
5 letters:
Rings
7 letters:
High bar

10 letters:
Horse vault
11 letters:
Pommel horse
12 letters:
Parallel bars

13 letters:
Horizontal bar
14 letters:
Asymmetric bars
Floor exercises
Side horse vault

Hairstyles

2 letters:
DA
3 letters:
Bob
Bun
4 letters:
Afro
Crop
Perm
Pouf
5 letters:
Plait
Wedge
6 letters:
Marcel
Mullet

7 letters:
Beehive
Bunches
Buzz cut
Chignon
Corn row
Crew cut
Flat top
Mohican
Pageboy
Pigtail
Shingle
8 letters:
Bouffant
Eton crop
Ponytail

Razor-cut
Skinhead
9 letters:
Duck's arse
Pompadour
10 letters:
Dreadlocks
Feather-cut
French roll
Marcel wave
11 letters:
French pleat
13 letters:
Permanent wave

Harpies

5 letters:
Aello

7 letters:
Celaeno

Ocypete

Hats

3 letters:
Cap
Fez
Lum
Mob
Nab
Red
Taj
Tam

Tin
Tit
Top
4 letters:
Coif
Hard
Hood
Kepi
Poke

Silk
Sola
Tile
Topi
Ugly
Veil
5 letters:
Akuba
Ascot

Beany
Beret
Boxer
Busby
Crown
Curch
Derby
Envoy
Gibus
Mitre
Mutch
Opera
Pagri
Paper
Pilos
Salet
Shako
Snood
Solah
Straw
Tammy
Terai
Tiara
Topee
Toque
Tuque
Visor
Vizor

6 letters:
Akubra®
Anadem
Barret
Basher
Beanie
Beaver
Boater
Bonnet
Bowler
Breton
Calash
Calpac
Castor
Cloche
Cocked
Coolie
Cornet
Cowboy
Diadem
Fedora
Gaucho
Heaume
Helmet
Hennin
Kalpak
Lum-hat
Mobcap
Morion

Panama
Pilion
Pinner
Safari
Sailor
Salade
Sallet
Shacko
Shovel
Slouch
Sunhat
Titfer
Toorie
Topper
Tourie
Trilby
Turban
Wimple

7 letters:
Bandana
Bandeau
Basinet
Biretta
Bluecap
Caleche
Calotte
Calpack
Capouch
Capuche
Chaplet
Circlet
Commode
Coronet
Cossack
Crusher
Curchef
Earmuff
Flat cap
Frontal
Hattock
Homburg
Kufiyah
Laurels
Leghorn
Matador
Montero
Petasus
Picture
Pillbox
Pilleus
Plateau
Pork-pie
Profile
Puritan
Skimmer
Songkok
Stetson

Sundown
Tarbush
Tricorn

8 letters:
Babushka
Balmoral
Bandanna
Bascinet
Bearskin
Berretta
Blackcap
Capotain
Cloth cap
Coonskin
Dunce cap
Fool's cap
Frontlet
Havelock
Headband
Kaffiyeh
Keffiyeh
Mountie's
Mushroom
Nightcap
Planter's
Puggaree
Ramilies
Runcible
Skullcap
Snap-brim
Sola-topi
Sombrero
Tarboosh
Tarboush
Trencher
Tricorne
Tyrolean
Watch cap
Yarmulke

9 letters:
Astrakhan
Balaclava
Billycock
Bollinger
Broadbrim
Cartwheel
Cockle-hat
Dunstable
Forage cap
Gandhi cap
Glengarry
Headdress
Juliet cap
Nor'wester
Peaked cap
Ramillies
Shower cap

Sou'wester
Stovepipe
Sugarloaf
Sunbonnet
Tarbouche
Tarpaulin
Ten-gallon
Wide-awake
10 letters:
Balibuntal
Bluebonnet
Chimneypot

Fascinator
Liberty cap
Pith helmet
Poke bonnet
Sola-helmet
11 letters:
Baseball cap
Crash helmet
Deerstalker
Dolly Varden
Kamelaukion
Mortarboard

Phrygian cap
Stocking cap
Tam-o'-shanter
Trencher cap
12 letters:
Cheese cutter
Fore-and-after
Steeple-crown
15 letters:
Balaclava helmet

Hawks

4 letters:
Eyas
Kite
Nyas
Soar
Sore
5 letters:
Eagle
Hobby
Marsh
Soare
6 letters:
Auceps
Elanet
Falcon
Keelie
Lanner
Merlin
Musket

Osprey
Sorage
Tarsal
Tarsel
Tassel
Tercel
7 letters:
Buzzard
Cooper's
Goshawk
Haggard
Harrier
Kestrel
Sparrow
Staniel
Tarsell
Tiersel
8 letters:
Caracara

Lanneret
Ringtail
Tercelet
9 letters:
Gerfalcon
Gier-eagle
Ossifraga
Ossifrage
Peregrine
Sore-eagle
Wind-hover
10 letters:
Hen harrier
11 letters:
Accipitrine
Lammergeier
12 letters:
Marsh harrier

Heart, parts of

5 letters:
Aorta
6 letters:
Atrium
Septum
7 letters:
Auricle

8 letters:
Vena cava
9 letters:
Ventricle
13 letters:
Bicuspid valve
Pulmonary vein

14 letters:
Semilunar valve
Tricuspid valve
15 letters:
Pulmonary artery

Heraldry terms

2 letters:
Or
3 letters:
Bar
Fur
Vol

4 letters:
Bars
Base
Bend
Coue
Fess

File
Fret
Golp
Lion
Lyon
Orle

Pale
Pall
Paly
Pean
Pile
Semé
Urdé
Vair
Vert
Yale
5 letters:
Azure
Baton
Chief
Crest
Cross
Crown
Eagle
Fesse
Field
Flory
Fusil
Giron
Golpe
Gules
Gyron
Label
Party
Rebus
Sable
Scarp
Semée
Torse
Trick
Urdée
6 letters:
Argent
Armory
Bezant
Blazon
Byzant
Canton
Charge
Checky
Coupee
Coward
Dexter
Empale
Erased
Ermine
Falcon
Fecial
Fetial
Fillet
Fleury
Herald

Impale
Lionel
Lodged
Mascle
Moline
Mullet
Naiant
Norroy
Pallet
Parted
Potent
Proper
Sejant
Shield
Verdoy
Voided
Volant
Vorant
Wreath
Wyvern
7 letters:
Annulet
Armiger
Bandeau
Bearing
Bezzant
Bordure
Cadency
Chaplet
Chevron
Compone
Compony
Coronet
Dormant
Endorse
Gardant
Garland
Gironny
Griffon
Gyronny
Issuant
Leopard
Lozenge
Lozengy
Martlet
Nascent
Nombril
Passant
Purpure
Quarter
Rampant
Red Hand
Roundel
Roundle
Salient
Saltire

Sea lion
Sejeant
Statant
Trangle
Trundle
Urinant
8 letters:
Bendwise
Blazonry
Caboched
Cicerone
Couchant
Crescent
Crosslet
Emblazon
Guardant
Hauriant
Heraldic
Mantling
Naissant
Octofoil
Opinicus
Ordinary
Segreant
Sinister
Tressure
Trippant
Umbrated
9 letters:
Abatement
Dimidiate
Displayed
Embattled
Hatchment
Quartered
Quarterly
Regardant
Scutcheon
Supporter
10 letters:
Bloody Hand
Bluemantle
Cinquefoil
Clarenceux
Coat armour
Coat of arms
Cockatrice
Cognisance
Cognizance
Difference
Escutcheon
Fleur-de-lis
Fleur-de-lys
King-of-arms
Lambrequin
Portcullis

Pursuivant
Quartering
11 letters:
Achievement
Canting arms
Clarencieux
Spread eagle

Subordinary
12 letters:
Bend sinister
Inescutcheon
13 letters:
College of arms
Matriculation

Officer of arms
Voided lozenge
14 letters:
Armes parlantes
Counter-passant
Lyon King of Arms
Sun in splendour

Herbs, spices and seasonings

3 letters:
Bay
Oca
Pia
Rue
4 letters:
Dill
Forb
Mace
Mint
Miso
Moly
Sage
Salt
Wort
5 letters:
Anise
Avens
Basil
Chive
Clove
Cress
Cumin
Eruca
Inula
Maror
Medic
Orval
Senna
Shoyu
Tacca
Tansy
Thyme
Typha
Yerba
6 letters:
Bennet
Borage
Capers
Chilli
Cummin
Exacum
Fennel
Ferula
Garlic
Ginger

Hyssop
Lovage
Madder
Nam pla
Nutmeg
Origan
Purpie
Savory
Sesame
Sorrel
Tamari
Wasabi
Willow
Yarrow
7 letters:
Aconite
Aniseed
Arugula
Bayleaf
Canella
Chervil
Cilanto
Coconut
Comfrey
Dittany
Felicia
Gentian
Gunnera
Madwort
Mustard
Oregano
Origane
Paprika
Parsley
Saffron
Salsify
Vervain
8 letters:
Allspice
Angelica
Bergamot
Cardamom
Centaury
Cinnamon
Costmary
Feverfew

Fireweed
Fluellin
Galangal
Knapweed
Mandrake
Marjoram
Origanum
Plantain
Purslane
Rosemary
Soapwort
Soy sauce
Staragen
Szechuan
Szechwan
Tarragon
Turmeric
Valerian
Wormwood
9 letters:
Asafetida
Calendula
Chamomile
Coriander
Echinacea
Eyebright
Fenugreek
Fish sauce
Galingale
Germander
Haworthia
Kalanchoe
Lamb's ears
Laserwort
Poppy seed
Pussytoes
Red pepper
Rhizocarp
Rocambole
Rodgersia
Soya sauce
Spearmint
Star anise
Tormentil
10 letters:
Asafoetida

Cassia bark
Lemon grass
Peppercorn
Pipsissewa
Rest-harrow
Sesame seed
11 letters:
Black pepper
Caraway seed
Coconut milk

Curry powder
Fines herbes
Garam masala
Laserpicium
Sweet cicely
White pepper
12 letters:
Aristolochia
Ornithogalum
Southernwood

13 letters:
Cayenne pepper
Good-King-Henry
Sunflower seed
14 letters:
Kaffir lime leaf
15 letters:
Alligator pepper
Five spice powder

Hercules, labours of

Number	Labour
First	The slaying of the Nemean lion
Second	The slaying of the Lernaean hydra
Third	The capture of the hind of Ceryneia
Fourth	The capture of the wild boar of Erymanthus
Fifth	The cleansing of the Augean stables
Sixth	The shooting of the Stymphalian birds
Seventh	The capture of the Cretan bull
Eighth	The capture of the horses of Diomedes
Ninth	The taking of the girdle of Hippolyte
Tenth	The capture of the cattle of Geryon
Eleventh	The recovery of the golden apples of Hesperides
Twelfth	The taking of Cerberus

Heroes

3 letters:
Cid
4 letters:
Aitu
Ajax
Eric
Finn
Kami
Lion
Tell
5 letters:
Faust
Jason
6 letters:
Amadis
Cyrano
Fingal
Hector
Kaleva
Nestor
Oliver
Onegin
Roland
Rustem
Rustum
Sigurd

7 letters:
Alcides
Beowulf
Couplet
Lothair
Marmion
Paladin
Perseus
Rinaldo
Saladin
Tancred
Theseus
Tristam
Tristan
Ulysses
Volsung
8 letters:
Achilles
Crockett
Heracles
Hercules
Hiawatha
Leonidas
Meleager
Owlglass
Parsifal

Pericles
Roderego
Roderick
Superman
Tristram
9 letters:
Agamemnon
Cuchulain
Garibaldi
Lochinvar
Owleglass
Owspiegle
Siegfried
10 letters:
Cuchullain
Howleglass
Owlspiegle
11 letters:
Bellerophon
Finn MacCool
Tam o'Shanter
Triptolemus
White knight
13 letters:
Vercingetorix

Hills

3 letters:
How
Kip
Kop
Law
Man
Nab
Tel
4 letters:
Bent
Chin
Cone
Kipp
Knot
Loma
Mesa
Pike
Pnyx
Sion
Tara
Tell
Zion
5 letters:
Bluff
Cleve
Gebel
Horst
Jebel

Kopje
Morro
Pingo
Wolds
6 letters:
Arafar
Broken
Calvan
Coteau
Djebel
Mendip
Wrekin
7 letters:
Beverly
Caelian
Capitol
Drumlin
Hammock
Ludgate
Mamelon
Merrick
Nanatak
Silbury
Viminal
8 letters:
Aventine
Cheviots
Chiltern

Golgotha
Highgate
Lavender
Palatine
Pennines
Quirinal
9 letters:
Areopagus
Esquiline
Grampians
Helvellyn
Janiculum
Monadnock
Monticule
Quantocks
10 letters:
Capitoline
Lammermuir
North Downs
Saddleback
Tweedsmuir
11 letters:
Crag-and-tail
Otway Ranges
12 letters:
Golan Heights

Hindu denominations and sects

6 letters:
Saktas

8 letters:
Saivaism

11 letters:
Hare Krishna
Vaishnavism

Historians

4 letters:
Bede, *the Venerable*
Livy
Oman, *Sir Charles William Chadwick*
5 letters:
Acton, *John Emerich Edward Dalberg*
Green, *John Richard*
Pliny *(the Elder)*
Renan, *(Joseph) Ernest*
Wells, *H(erbert) G(eorge)*
6 letters:
Arrian

Bryant, *Sir Arthur (Wynne Morgan)*
Buckle, *Henry Thomas*
Camden, *William*
Froude, *James Anthony*
Gibbon, *Edward*
Gildas
Schama, *Simon*
Taylor, *A(lan) J(ohn) P(ercivale)*
Thiers, *(Louis) Adolphe*
7 letters:
Asellio, *Sempronius*
Carlyle, *Thomas*
Sallust

Starkey, *David*
Tacitus
Toynbee, *Arnold Joseph*
8 letters:
Macaulay, *Thomas Babbington*
Plutarch
Ponsonby, *Lord Arthur*
Strachey, *(Giles) Lytton*
Xenophon
9 letters:
Herodotus

Suetonius
Trevelyan, *G(eorge) M(acaulay)*
10 letters:
Thucydides
11 letters:
Trevor-Roper, *Hugh*
13 letters:
Knickerbocker, *Diedrick*

History

HISTORICAL CHARACTERS

3 letters:
Lee, *Robert E(dward)*
Mao *Zedong*
4 letters:
Cody, *William Frederick*
Cook, *Captain James*
Khan, *Genghis*
King, *Martin Luther*
Polo, *Marco*
5 letters:
Drake, *Francis*
El Cid
James, *Jesse*
Jesus
Lenin, *Vladimir Ilyich*
Oates, *Lawrence Edward Grace*
Scott, *Robert Falcon*
6 letters:
Borgia, *Lucrezia*
Brutus
Buddha
Caesar, *Julius*
Cortés, *Hernando*
Custer, *George Armstrong*
Fawkes, *Guy*
Gandhi, *Mahatma*
Hickok, *James Butler*
Hickok, *Wild Bill*
Hitler, *Adolf*
Luther, *Martin*
Nelson, *Horatio*
Pompey
Stalin, *Joseph*
Stuart, *Charles Edward*
Wright, *Orville and Wilbur*
Zapata, *Emiliano*
7 letters:
À Becket, *Thomas*
Gagarin, *Yuri*

Guevara, *Che*
Lincoln, *Abraham*
Raleigh, *Walter*
Saladin
Trotsky, *Leon*
Wallace, *William*
8 letters:
Augustus
Boadicea
Boudicca
Columbus, *Christopher*
Crockett, *Davy*
Cromwell, *Oliver*
Geronimo
Hannibal
Hiawatha
Mohammed
Muhammad
Pericles
Rasputin, *Grigori Efimovich*
Selassie, *Haile*
Socrates
9 letters:
Bonaparte, *Napoleon*
Churchill, *Winston*
Cleopatra
Garibaldi, *Giuseppe*
Joan of Arc
Montezuma
Mussolini, *Benito*
10 letters:
Antoinette, *Marie*
Crazy Horse
Mark Antony
Washington, *George*
11 letters:
Billy the Kid
Buffalo Bill
Charlemagne

Nightingale, *Florence*
Sitting Bull
12 letters:
Attila the Hun
Captain Oates
Clive of India
De Torquemada, *Tomás*

14 letters:
Alfred the Great
Robert the Bruce
The Black Prince
15 letters:
Hereward the Wake
Ivan the Terrible

HISTORICAL EVENTS

4 letters:
D-day
5 letters:
Alamo
7 letters:
Boer War
Cold War
8 letters:
Civil War
Crusades
Waterloo
9 letters:
Agincourt
Armistice
Great Trek
Hiroshima
Holocaust
Korean War
Long March
Trafalgar
Watergate
10 letters:
Black Death

Crimean War
Depression
Magna Carta
Suez Crisis
Vietnam War
11 letters:
Diet of Worms
Gordon Riots
Great Schism
Pearl Harbor
Reformation
Renaissance
Restoration
12 letters:
Bloody Sunday
Crystal Night
Easter Rising
Indian Mutiny
Potato Famine
Risorgimento
13 letters:
General Strike
Gunpowder Plot

Kristallnacht
Reign of Terror
Spanish Armada
14 letters:
Boston Tea Party
Boxer Rebellion
Napoleonic Wars
Norman Conquest
Peasants' Revolt
South Sea Bubble
Thirty Years' War
Wars of the Roses
15 letters:
Hundred Years' War
Munich Agreement
Spanish Civil War
Wall Street Crash

Homes

2 letters:
Ho
3 letters:
Cot
Hut
Inn
Mas
4 letters:
Bush
Casa
Chez
Cote
Crib
Dail
Digs
Drum
Flat
Gite

Hall
Home
Iglu
Keys
Mews
Pent
Rath
Safe
Semi
Slum
Tent
Tied
Town
York
5 letters:
Adobe
Booth
Cabin

Croft
Dacha
Dower
Frame
Hogan
Hotel
House
Hovel
Igloo
Lodge
Lords
Manor
Manse
Motel
Opera
Ranch
Shack
Tepee

Tower
Tudor
Tupek
Tupik
Usher
Villa
Wendy
Whare
6 letters:
Bhavan
Bhawan
Biggin
Bunker
Castle
Chalet
Custom
Des res
Duplex
Flotel
Garret
Grange
Hostel
Insula
Maison
Mobile
Mud hut
Orange
Palace
Prefab
Priory
Shanty
Stuart
Tavern
Wigwam
7 letters:
Althing
Barrack
Bastide
Caboose
Caravan
Chamber
Chapter
Charnel
Château
Commons
Convent
Cottage

Council
Crannog
Customs
Deanery
Embassy
Fashion
Flatlet
Habitat
Halfway
Hanover
Harbour
Knesset
Mansion
Meeting
Osborne
Rectory
Schloss
Starter
Stately
Terrace
Theatre
Trailer
Trinity
Windsor
8 letters:
Boarding
Bungalow
Burghley
Camboose
Clearing
Dwelling
Hacienda
Lagthing
Log cabin
Longleat
Montagne
Rest-home
Somerset
Tenement
Vicarage
9 letters:
Admiralty
Apartment
Bedsitter
Bundestag
But and ben
Clapboard

Consulate
Doss house
Farmhouse
Flophouse
Houseboat
Lancaster
Long house
Mattamore
Odelsting
Parsonage
Penthouse
Roadhouse
Show house
Single-end
Town house
Tree house
10 letters:
Back-to-back
Black house
Brownstone
Chatsworth
Commercial
Guest house
Heartbreak
Maisonette
Odelsthing
Parliament
Pied-à-terre
Studio flat
11 letters:
Cottage flat
Plantagenet
Shooting box
12 letters:
Broadcasting
Chattel house
Lake dwelling
Motor caravan
Weatherboard
13 letters:
Boarding house
14 letters:
Cape Cod cottage
15 letters:
Board-and-shingle
Duplex apartment

Hoods

4 letters:
Coif
Cope
Cowl
5 letters:
Amaut

Amice
Amowt
Pixie
Snood
6 letters:
Almuce

Apache
Biggin
Calash
Mantle
7 letters:
Bashlik

Calèche
Capuche
Jacobin
8 letters:
Calyptra
Capeline

Capuccio
Chaperon
Trot-cozy
9 letters:
Balaclava
Chaperone

Trot-cosey

Hormones

3 letters:
Sex
5 letters:
Auxin
Kinin
6 letters:
Growth
7 letters:
Gastrin
Inhibin
Insulin
Relaxin
Steroid
Thyroid
8 letters:
Androgen
Autacoid
Bursicon
Ecdysone
Estrogen
Florigen
Glucagon
Juvenile
Oestriol
Oestrone
Oxytocin
Secretin
Thymosin
9 letters:
Adrenalin®

Corticoid
Cortisone
Cytokinin
Endocrine
Melatonin
Oestrogen
Prolactin
Secretion
Serotonin
Thyroxine
10 letters:
Adrenaline
Calcitonin
Intermedin
Lactogenic
Lipotropin
Oestradiol
11 letters:
Aldosterone
Angiotensin
Epinephrine
Gibberellin
Luteinizing
Parathyroid
Progestogen
Somatomedin
Thyrotropin
Vasopressin
12 letters:
Androsterone

Antidiuretic
Biosynthesis
Corpus luteum
Gonadotropin
Luteotrophin
Noradrenalin
Pancreozymin
Progesterone
Secretagogue
Somatostatin
Somatotropin
Stilboestrol
Testosterone
Thyrotrophin
13 letters:
Gonadotrophic
Gonadotrophin
Noradrenaline
Prostaglandin
Somatotrophin
14 letters:
Corticosteroid
Corticosterone
Enterogastrone
Erythropoietin
Hydrocortisone
15 letters:
Cholecystokinin
Gibberellic acid

Horses

TYPES/BREEDS OF HORSE

2 letters:
Kt
3 letters:
Ass
Bay
Cob
Don
Dun
Nag
Pad
Pot

Rip
Tit
4 letters:
Arab
Aver
Barb
Colt
Dale
Deli
Fell
Foal

Hack
Jade
Mare
Plug
Pole
Pony
Post
Prad
Roan
Shan
Snow

Stud
Taki
Turk
Weed
Wild
Yale
Yaud
5 letters:
Airer
Arion
Arkle
Batak
Bevis
Bidet
Borer
Caple
Capul
Crock
Favel
Filly
Genet
Huçul
Iomud
Konik
Lokai
Morel
Neddy
Night
Pacer
Pinto
Poler
Punch
Rogue
Screw
Seian
Shire
Spiti
Steed
Tacky
Takhi
Waler
Wheel
White
Zebra
6 letters:
Ambler
Basuto
Bayard
Breton
Bronco
Brumby
Calico
Canuck
Cayuse
Chaser
Cooser
Crollo

Curtal
Cusser
Danish
Exmoor
Favell
Garran
Garron
Gennet
Gidran
Hogget
Hunter
Jennet
Kanuck
Keffel
Lampos
Morgan
Mudder
Nonius
Novice
Pad-nag
Plater
Poster
Quagga
Randem
Remuda
Roarer
Rouncy
Runner
Sabino
Saddle
Shagya
Sorrel
Stayer
String
Summer
Tandem
Tarpan
Tracer
Vanner
Viatka
7 letters:
Beetewk
Bobtail
Burmese
Cavalry
Charger
Clipper
Courser
Cow pony
Criollo
Cuisser
Dappled
Eclipse
Eventer
Finnish
Flemish
Gelding

Hackney
Hobbler
Jutland
Kabarda
Klepper
Liberty
Manipur
Marengo
Marocco
Marwari
Morocco
Mustang
Palfrey
Piebald
Quarter
Rhenish
Saddler
Sheltie
Shirazi
Smudish
Spanker
Starter
Strelet
Suffolk
Sumpter
Swallow
Swinger
Trigger
Trooper
Walking
Wheeler
Yamoote
Zeeland
Zmudzin
8 letters:
Aquiline
Ardennes
Balearic
Bangtail
Bathorse
Boerperd
Camargue
Clay-bank
Cocktail
Dartmoor
Destrier
Eohippus
Fell pony
Friesian
Galloway
Gulf Arab
Highland
Holstein
Hyperion
Karabair
Karabakh
Karadagh

Kochlani
Limousin
Lusitano
Palomino
Polo pony
Schimmel
Shetland
Skewbald
Sleipnir
Springer
Stalking
Stallion
Stibbler
Turkoman
Warhorse
Warragal
Warragle
Warragul
Warregal
Warrigal
Welsh Cob
Whistler
Yarraman
Yearling
9 letters:
Akhal-Teke
Anglo-Arab
Appaloosa
Black Bess
Brabançon
Caballine
Carthorse
Clavileno
Coldblood
Connemara
Dales pony
Drayhorse
Esthonian
Fjord pony
Gringolet

Groningen
Houyhnhnm
Icelandic
Kladruber
Knabstrup
Miohippus
Mongolian
Oldenburg
Packhorse
Percheron
Pinzgauer
Racehorse
Rosinante
Rozinante
Schleswig
Tarbenian
Timor pony
Trakehner
Warmblood
Welsh pony
Workhorse
10 letters:
Andalusian
Bloodstock
Bucephalus
Buckjumper
Buttermilk
Clydesdale
Copenhagen
Gelderland
Hafflinger
Hanoverian
Kathiawari
Lipizzaner
Lippizaner
Pliohippus
Polish Arab
Przewalski
Show jumper
Stockhorse

Svadilfari
Zemaitukas
11 letters:
Anglo-Norman
High-stepper
Iceland pony
Mecklenburg
Merychippus
Persian Arab
Przewalski's
Running mate
12 letters:
Cleveland Bay
Dartmoor pony
Dutch Draught
Gudbrandsdal
Hambletonian
Highland pony
North Swedish
Orlov Trotter
Shetland pony
Standard Bred
Suffolk Punch
Thoroughbred
13 letters:
Hyracotherium
Kurdistan pony
New Forest pony
Russian saddle
Spanish Jennet
Stalking-horse
14 letters:
American Saddle
Polish Half-bred
Yorkshire Coach
15 letters:
American Quarter
Orlov Rostopchin
Swedish Ardennes

LEGENDARY/FICTIONAL/HISTORICAL HORSES

5 letters:
Boxer
6 letters:
Bayard
Flicka
Silver
7 letters:
Pegasus
Trigger

8 letters:
Champion
Hercules
Mister Ed
Sleipnir
Traveler
9 letters:
Black Bess
El Fideldo

Incitatus
Rosinante
10 letters:
Bucephalus
11 letters:
Black Beauty

HORSE COLOURS

3 letters:
Bay
Dun
4 letters:
Grey
Roan
5 letters:
Black
Cream
Mealy

Pinto
6 letters:
Albino
Dapple
Sorrel
7 letters:
Piebald
8 letters:
Blue roan
Chestnut

Claybank
Palomino
Skewbald
10 letters:
Dapplegrey
Fleabitten
14 letters:
Strawberry roan

HORSE MARKINGS

4 letters:
Snip
Sock
Star
5 letters:
Blaze

6 letters:
Stripe
7 letters:
Coronet
8 letters:
Stocking

9 letters:
White face

HORSE GAITS

4 letters:
Lope
Pace
Rack
Trot
Walk
5 letters:
Amble

6 letters:
Canter
Gallop
Prance
7 letters:
Jog trot
10 letters:
Rising trot

Single-foot
11 letters:
Sitting trot
12 letters:
Extended trot

HORSE PARTS

3 letters:
Bar
Haw
Toe
4 letters:
Back
Dock
Frog
Heel
Hock
Hoof
Mane
Neck
Poll
Sole
Tail
Tusk

Wall
5 letters:
Croup
Ergot
Flank
Loins
Shank
6 letters:
Barrel
Croupe
Gaskin
Haunch
Muzzle
Saddle
Sheath
7 letters:
Brisket

Counter
Forearm
Foreleg
Gambrel
Off-fore
Off-hind
Pastern
Quarter
Shannon
Withers
8 letters:
Buttress
Chestnut
Coupling
Diagonal
Forehand
Forelock

Near-fore
Near-hind
9 letters:
Hamstring
White line
10 letters:
Cannon bone

Chin groove
Coffin bone
Splint bone
11 letters:
Coronet band
Second thigh
Stifle joint

12 letters:
Fetlock joint
Forequarters

Humours of the body

5 letters:
Blood
6 letters:

Phlegm
9 letters:
Black bile

10 letters:
Yellow bile

Huts

4 letters:
Shed
Skeo
Skio
Tilt
5 letters:
Banda
Booth
Bothy
Cabin
Hogan
Humpy
Igloo
Shack
Sheal
Shiel
Wilja

6 letters:
Bothie
Bustee
Chalet
Gunyah
Mia-mia
Nissen
Pondok
Rancho
Shanty
Succah
Sukkah
Tolsel
Tolsey
Tolzey
Wigwam
Wikiup

Wiltja
Wurley
7 letters:
Choltry
Quonset®
Shebang
Wanigan
Wickiup
8 letters:
Rondavel
Shealing
Shieling
Wannigan
9 letters:
Pondokkie
Rancheria

Hydrocarbons

3 letters:
Wax
5 letters:
Alkyl
Arene
Diene
Gutta
Halon
Hexyl
Phene
Xylol
6 letters:
Aldrin
Alkane
Alkene
Alkyne
Butane
Butene

Cetane
Cubane
Decane
Dioxin
Ethane
Hexane
Hexene
Indene
Nonane
Octane
Pinene
Pyrene
Retene
Xylene
7 letters:
Amylene
Benzene
Heptane

Ligroin
Naphtha
Olefine
Pentane
Pentene
Polyene
Propane
Styrene
Terpene
Toluene
8 letters:
Camphane
Camphene
Carotene
Diphenyl
Hexylene
Isoprene
Limonene

Paraffin
Squalene
Stilbene
Triptane
9 letters:
Acetylene
Butadiene
Isobutane

Isooctane
Pentylene
10 letters:
Asphaltite
Mesitylene
11 letters:
Cycloalkane
Cyclohexane

Hatchettite
Naphthalene
12 letters:
Cyclopropane
Phenanthrene
15 letters:
Cyclopentadiene

Inflammations

3 letters:
Sty
4 letters:
Acne
Noma
Stye
5 letters:
Croup
Felon
6 letters:
Ancome
Angina
Bunion
Eczema
Garget
Iritis
Otitis
Quinsy
Thrush
Ulitis
7 letters:
Colitis
Ecthyma
Founder
Ignatis
Onychia
Pinkeye
Prurigo
Sunburn
Sycosis

Tylosis
Whitlow
8 letters:
Adenitis
Aortisis
Bursitis
Carditis
Cystisis
Fibrosis
Hyalitis
Mastitis
Metritis
Mycetoma
Myelitis
Myositis
Neuritis
Orchitis
Osteitis
Ovaritis
Phlegmon
Pleurisy
Pyelitis
Rachitis
Rhinitis
Uvulitis
Windburn
9 letters:
Arteritis
Arthritis
Balanitis

Cheilitis
Enteritis
Gastritis
Glossitis
Keratitis
Laminitis
Nephritis
Parotitis
Phlebitis
Phrenitis
Pneumonia
Proctitis
Pyorrhoea
Retinitis
Scleritis
Sinusitis
Splenitis
Strumitis
Synovitis
Typhlitis
Vaginitis
10 letters:
Asbestosis
Bronchitis
Cellulitis
Cervicitis
Dermatitis
Erysipelas
Fibrositis
Gingivitis

Hepatitis A
Hepatitis B
Intertrigo
Laryngitis
Meningitis
Oophoritis
Ophthalmia
Paronychia
Phlegmasia
Stomatitis
Tendinitis
Thrombosis
Tracheitis
Urethritis
Valvulitis
Vasculitis
11 letters:
Blepharitis
Farmer's lung

Mastoiditis
Myocarditis
Peritonitis
Pharyngitis
Prostatitis
Salpingitis
Shin splints
Spondylitis
Thoroughpin
Thyroiditis
Tonsillitis
12 letters:
Appendicitis
Encephalitis
Endocarditis
Folliculitis
Mesenteritis
Osteoporosis
Pancreatitis

Pericarditis
Polyneuritis
Swimmer's itch
13 letters:
Enterocolitis
Labyrinthitis
Osteomyelitis
Perihepatitis
Perinephritis
Periodontisis
Perityphlitis
Tenosynovitis
14 letters:
Conjunctivitis
Diverticulitis
Osteoarthritis
Vincent's angina
15 letters:
Gastroenteritis

Insects

TYPES OF INSECT

3 letters:
Ant
Bee
Bot
Fly
Lac
Nit
Wax
4 letters:
Crab
Flea
Gnat
Grig
Kutu
Lice
Mite
Moth
Pium
Tick
Wasp
Weta
Zimb
5 letters:
Aphis
Cimex
Emmet
Louse
Midge
Ox-bot
Scale
Stick
Zebub

6 letters:
Acarid
Breeze
Capsid
Chigoe
Cicada
Cicala
Cootie
Day-fly
Earwig
Gadfly
Hopper
Hornet
Locust
Looper
Mantid
Mantis
Mayfly
Psocid
Psylla
Punkie
Redbug
Sawfly
Scarab
Slater
Spider
Tettix
Thrips
Walker
Weevil
7 letters:
Antlion

Buzzard
Chalcid
Chigger
Cornfly
Cricket
Daphnid
Ergates
Firefly
Gallfly
Grayfly
Hive-bee
Humbuzz
Katydid
Ladybug
Odonata
Oestrus
Oniscus
Phasmid
Pill-bug
Pyralis
Sandfly
Spectre
Stylops
Termite
8 letters:
Alderfly
Bollworm
Bookworm
Caseworm
Circutio
Coccidae
Crane-fly

Dipteras
Firebrat
Gall-wasp
Glossina
Horntail
Horsefly
Inchworm
Itchmite
Lacewing
Ladybird
Lygus bug
Mealybug
Metabola
Milliped
Mosquito
Myriapod
Puss-moth
Reduviid
Ruby-tail
Scarabee
Sheep ked
Silkworm
Snowflea
Stinkbug
Stonefly
Waterbug
Wheel bug
Whitefly
Wireworm
Woodworm
9 letters:
Ametabola
Body louse
Booklouse
Caddis-fly
Centipede
Clipshear
Cochineal
Cockroach
Compodeid

Crab louse
Croton bug
Damselfly
Dobsonfly
Dragonfly
Ephemerid
Hemiptera
Homoptera
Mecoptera
Millepede
Millipede
Rearhorse
Sheep tick
Tabanidae
Tiger-moth
Woodlouse
10 letters:
Apterygota
Bark mantis
Bluebottle
Caddis worm
Cankerworm
Casebearer
Chironomid
Clipshears
Cockchafer
Coleoptera
Collembola
Fan-cricket
Fen-cricket
Froghopper
Harvestman
Leaf-cutter
Leafhopper
Mallophaga
Orthoptera
Phylloxera
Plant-louse
Pond-skater
Psocoptera

Rhipiptera
Silverfish
Springtail
Thysanuran
Treehopper
Web spinner
11 letters:
Apple maggot
Bristletail
Cabbageworm
Dermopteran
Grasshopper
Greenbottle
Hymenoptera
Mole cricket
Neuropteran
Tiger-beetle
Trichoptera
12 letters:
Bishop's mitre
Dictyopteran
Heteropteran
Rhipidoptera
Strepsiptera
Sucking louse
Thousand-legs
Thysanoptera
Walking stick
13 letters:
Cotton stainer
Daddy-long-legs
Jenny-longlegs
Leatherjacket
Measuring worm
Praying mantis
Staphylinidae
15 letters:
German cockroach
Tent caterpillar

PARTS OF INSECTS

3 letters:
Jaw
4 letters:
Coxa
5 letters:
Femur
Ileum
Notum
Scape
Snout
Thigh
Tibia

6 letters:
Air sac
Arista
Cercus
Cirrus
Corium
Glossa
Labium
Labrum
Ligula
Proleg
Scutum

Stigma
Tarsus
Tegmen
Thorax
7 letters:
Antenna
Clasper
Clypeus
Elytron
Gonopod
Hamulus
Maxilla

Ocellus
Pedicel
Trachea
8 letters:
Forewing
Mandible
Pronotum
Spiracle
9 letters:
Flagellum
Proboscis

Prothorax
Pulvillus
Scutellum
Spinneret
Underwing
10 letters:
Acetabulum
Epicuticle
Exocuticle
Haustellum
Hemelytron

Mesothorax
Metathorax
Ovipositor
Prosternum
Trochanter
11 letters:
Compound eye
Endocuticle
Ventriculus
14 letters:
Proventriculus

See also:
➤ **Ants, bees and wasps** ➤ **Beetles** ➤ **Bugs** ➤ **Butterflies and moths** ➤ **Flies**

Instruments

3 letters:
Fan
4 letters:
Celt
Clam
Fork
Mike
Prog
Rasp
Rote
Tram
5 letters:
Brake
Fleam
Float
Gadge
Groma
Meter
Miser
Probe
Sonde
Wecht
6 letters:
Bougie
Broach
Etalon
Scythe
Strobe
Trocar
7 letters:
Alidade
Cadrans
Caltrop
Curette
Forceps
Pelican
Pointel
Probang

Scriber
Sextant
Spatula
Strigil
Swazzle
Swingle
Swozzle
Syringe
Trammel
8 letters:
Ablative
Barnacle
Diagraph
Dividers
Ecraseur
Odometer
Otoscope
Oximeter
Quadrant
Scissors
Strickle
Trephine
Waywiser
9 letters:
Alphonsin
Astrolabe
Atmometer
Auxometer
Barometer
Baryscope
Bolometer
Coelostat
Crows-bill
Cymograph
Dermatome
Dip-circle
Dropsonde
Eriometer

Haemostat
Heliostat
Hodometer
Konimeter
Machmeter
Manometer
Marigraph
Megascope
Metronome
Nocturnal
Potometer
Raspatory
Retractor
Rheometer
Tasimeter
Telemeter
Telescope
Tellurian
Tellurion
Tenaculum
Tonometer
Tripmeter
Voltmeter
Wavemeter
10 letters:
Almacantar
Almucantar
Altazimuth
Anemometer
Ceilometer
Clinometer
Colposcope
Cryophorus
Cystoscope
Fibrescope
Hydrometer
Hydroscope
Hygrometer

Hypsometer
Micrometer
Microphone
Pilliwinks
Protractor
Radiosonde
Spirograph
Spirometer
Tachigraph
Tachometer
Tensometer
Theodolite
Tribometer
11 letters:
Auxanometer
Chronograph
Chronometer
Chronoscope

Helicograph
Jacob's staff
Laparoscope
Pinnywinkle
Polarimeter
Rocketsonde
Seismograph
Solarimeter
Stauroscope
Stethoscope
Stroboscope
Synthesizer
Tacheometer
Tensiometer
Thermometer
Voltammeter
12 letters:
Aethrioscope

Bronchoscope
Cephalometer
Keraunograph
Myringoscope
Penetrometer
Pinniewinkle
Respirometer
Scarificator
Sensitometer
Spectroscope
Synchroscope
Turbidimeter
Zenith-sector
13 letters:
Tachistoscope
14 letters:
Interferometer
Ophthalmoscope

Invertebrates

3 letters:
Lug
4 letters:
Clam
Cone
Kina
Pipi
Worm
5 letters:
Ameba
Bardi
Bardy
Coral
Cunje
Gaper
Leech
Polyp
Squid
Ugari
6 letters:
Amoeba
Bardie
Chiton
Cockle
Cuttle
Mussel
Oyster
Quahog
Sea mat
Sea pen
Sponge
Tellin
Teredo
7 letters:
Bivalve

Blubber
Catworm
Crinoid
Daphnia
Decapod
Eelworm
Lobworm
Lugworm
Mollusc
Octopus
Piddock
Ragworm
Rotifer
Scallop
Sea lily
Sea wasp
Sunstar
Trepang
Tubifex
8 letters:
Ammonite
Annelida
Argonaut
Bryozoan
Clamworm
Cunjevoi
Echinoid
Gapeworm
Lancelet
Lungworm
Milleped
Nautilus
Parazoan
Pauropod
Pumpworm

Red coral
Sandworm
Sea mouse
Shipworm
Starfish
Tapeworm
Tube worm
Whipworm
White cat
Zoophyte
9 letters:
Amphioxus
Anthozoan
Arrowworm
Arthropod
Belemnite
Brandling
Centipede
Clabby-doo
Clappy-doo
Comb jelly
Cone shell
Devilfish
Earthworm
Gastropod
Hard-shell
Hydrozoan
Jellyfish
Lamp shell
Millepede
Millipede
Peritrich
Poriferan
Razor clam
Round clam

Roundworm
Sea slater
Sea squirt
Sea urchin
Soft-shell
Trilobite
Tusk shell
Water bear
Wheatworm
White worm
Woodborer
10 letters:
Animalcule
Balmain bug
Bêche-de-mer
Bluebottle
Brachiopod
Ctenophore
Cuttlefish
Echinoderm
Euripterid
Eurypterid
Gasteropod

Graptolite
Guinea worm
Horseleech
Liver fluke
Otter shell
Paddle worm
Protostome
Razor-shell
Scyphozoan
Sea anemone
Seed oyster
Stony coral
Tardigrade
Tooth shell
Venus shell
Vinegar eel
Water louse
11 letters:
Animalculum
Bladder worm
Bluff oyster
Feather star
Globigerina

Sea cucumber
Stomach worm
Vinegar worm
Water slater
12 letters:
Box jellyfish
Chicken louse
Gastropodart
Onychophoran
Trochelminth
Venus's-girdle
13 letters:
Crown-of-thorns
Hard-shell clam
Paper nautilus
Precious coral
Soft-shell clam
Water measurer
14 letters:
Pearly nautilus
15 letters:
Coat-of-mail shell

See also:
➤ **Insects** ➤ **Shellfish** ➤ **Snails, slugs and other gastropods**
➤ **Spiders and other arachnids** ➤ **Worms**

Islands and island groups

2 letters:	Cook	Mona
TT	Cuba	Motu
3 letters:	Dogs	Muck
Aru	Eigg	Mull
Cos	Elba	Niue
Diu	Erin	Oahu
Fyn	Fair	Rhum
Hoy	Fiji	Rona
Kos	Guam	Ross
Man	Heat	Saba
May	Herm	Sark
Rat	Holy	Seil
Rum	Hova	Skye
Sea	Idse	Truk
Yap	Iona	Uist
4 letters:	Java	Ulva
Amoy	Jolo	Unst
Aran	Jura	Wake
Arru	Keos	Yell
Attu	King	**5 letters:**
Bali	Line	Aland
Biak	Long	Apple
Bute	Mahé	Arran
Calf	Malé	Aruba
Cebú	Maui	Banka
Coll	Mazu	Banks

Barra
Batan
Belau
Belle
Bioko
Bohol
Bonin
Caldy
Canna
Capri
Ceram
Cheju
Chios
Clare
Cocos
Coney
Coral
Corfu
Crete
Delos
Disko
Ellis
Faial
Farne
Faroe
Fayal
Foula
Funen
Gigha
Haiti
Handa
Ibiza
Islay
Isola
Jerba
Kauai
Kiska
Kuril
Lanai
Lewis
Leyte
Longa
Luing
Lundy
Luzon
Maewo
Malta
Matsu
Melos
Nauru
Naxos
Nevis
North
Oland
Ormuz
Panay
Páros

Pemba
Qeshm
Qishm
Reil's
Rhode
Samar
Samoa
Samos
Saria
Seram
South
Spice
Sumba
Sunda
Thera
Thule
Timor
Tiree
Tombo
Tonga
Turks
Upolu
Whale
White
Wight
Youth
Zante

6 letters:
Achill
Aegean
Aegina
Amager
Andros
Avalon
Azores
Baffin
Banaba
Bangka
Barrow
Bikini
Borneo
Bounty
Butung
Caicos
Canary
Canvey
Cayman
Ceylon
Chiloé
Cyprus
Devil's
Diomed
Djerba
Easter
Ellice
Euboea
Flores

Fraser
Hainan
Harris
Hawaii
Hobart
Honshu
Hormuz
Icaria
Imbros
Indies
Insula
Ionian
Ischia
Ithaca
Jersey
Kiushu
Kodiak
Kosrae
Kurile
Kyushu
Labuan
Laputa
Lemnos
Lesbos
Leucas
Leukas
Levkás
Lipari
Lizard
Lombok
Madura
Majuro
Marajó
Mercer
Mersea
Midway
Negros
Ogygia
Orkney
Paphos
Patmos
Penang
Pharos
Philae
Pladdy
Ponape
Quemoy
Raasay
Ramsey
Rhodes
Rialto
Rjukyu
Robben
Ryukyu
Safety
St John
Saipan

Saltee
Savaii
Scilly
Scyros
Sicily
Skerry
Skomer
Skyros
Snares
Soemba
Soenda
Staffa
Staten
Stroma
Summer
Tahiti
Taiwan
Thanet
Thásos
Tobago
Tresco
Tubuai
Tuvalu
Unimak
Ushant
Veneti
Virgin
Walney

7 letters:
Aeolian
Aldabra
Amboina
Andaman
Antigua
Austral
Bahamas
Baranof
Barbuda
Bardsey
Basilan
Battery
Bedloe's
Bermuda
Bonaire
British
Cartier
Celebes
Channel
Chatham
Cipango
Corsica
Crannog
Curaçao
Cythera
Diomede
Emerald
Eriskay

Faeroes
Falster
Flannan
Frisian
Fur Seal
Gambier
Gilbert
Gotland
Grenada
Hawaiki
Hayling
Heimaey
Howland
Iceland
Ireland
Iwo Jima
Jamaica
Kerrera
Laaland
La Palma
Leeward
Liberty
Lismore
Lofoten
Lolland
Madeira
Majorca
Masbate
Mayotte
Mindoro
Minorca
Molokai
Moreton
Mykonos
Nicobar
Norfolk
Oceania
Okinawa
Orcades
Orkneys
Palawan
Palmyra
Phoenix
Rathlin
Réunion
Roanoke
Rockall
St Croix
St Kilda
St Kitts
St Lucia
Salamis
San Juan
Sao Tomé
Scalpay
Sheppey
Shikoku

Skikoku
Society
Socotra
Solomon
Stewart
Sumatra
Sumbawa
Surtsey
Tenedos
Tokelau
Tortola
Tortuga
Tuamotu
Tutuila
Vanuatu
Visayan
Volcano
Waihake
Western
Wrangel
Zealand
Zetland

8 letters:
Alcatraz
Alderney
Aleutian
Anglesey
Anguilla
Antilles
Atlantis
Auckland
Balearic
Barbados
Bathurst
Billiton
Blefuscu
Bora Bora
Bornholm
Canaries
Caroline
Catalina
Choiseul
Colonsay
Cyclades
Dominica
Falkland
Farquhar
Flinders
Foulness
Friendly
Gothland
Gottland
Guernsey
Hamilton
Hebrides
Hokkaido
Hong Kong

Jan Mayen
Kangaroo
Kermadec
Krakatau
Krakatoa
Ladrones
Lavongai
Lilliput
Lord Howe
Luggnagg
Mackinac
Mainland
Maldives
Mallorca
Marianas
Marquesa
Marshall
Melville
Mindanao
Miquelon
Moluccas
Mustique
Pelagian
Pitcairn
Portland
Pribilof
Principe
St Helena
St Martin
Sakhalin
Sardinia
Schouten
Shetland
Sjælland
Skokholm
Soembawa
Somerset
Sporades
Sri Lanka
Sulawesi
Sverdrup
Tasmania
Tenerife
Terceira
Thousand
Thursday
Trinidad
Tsushima
Unalaska
Venetian
Victoria
Viti Levu
Windward
Zanzibar
9 letters:
Admiralty
Alexander

Andreanof
Anticosti
Antipodes
Ascension
Barataria
Benbecula
Calf of Man
Chichagof
Christmas
Elephanta
Ellesmere
Falklands
Fortunate
Galápagos
Governors
Greenland
Hainan Tao
Halmahera
Innisfree
Jamestown
Kerguelen
Lampedusa
Lanzarote
Macquarie
Manhattan
Margarita
Marquesas
Mascarene
Mauritius
Melanesia
Nantucket
New Guinea
North Uist
Polynesia
Rangitoto
Rarotonga
Runnymede
St Tudwal's
St Vincent
Sao Miguel
Shetlands
Singapore
Sjaelland
South Uist
Stromboli
Teneriffe
Trobriand
Vancouver
Vanua Levu
Walcheren
10 letters:
Basse-Terre
Bermoothes
Campobello
Cape Breton
Cephalonia
Corregidor

Dodecanese
Formentera
Grand Manan
Grand Terre
Grenadines
Heligoland
Hispaniola
Isle Royale
Kiritimati
Langerhans
Madagascar
Manitoulin
Marinduque
Martinique
Micronesia
Montserrat
New Britain
New Georgia
New Ireland
Pescadores
Poor Knight
Samothrace
Seychelles
Three Kings
West Indies
Whitsunday
11 letters:
Dry Tortugas
Florida Keys
Glubdubdrib
Grand Bahama
Grand Canary
Grande-Terre
Guadalcanal
Lakshadweep
Lindisfarne
Mount Desert
New Siberian
Pantelleria
Philippines
San Salvador
Southampton
South Orkney
Spitsbergen
12 letters:
Bougainville
Cassiterides
Glubbdubdrib
Greater Sunda
Marie Galante
New Caledonia
Newfoundland
Nusa Tenggara
Prince Edward
San Cristóbal
Santa Barbara
South Georgia

Torres Strait
13 letters:
Espíritu Santo
Forneaux Group
Fuerteventura
Juan Fernández
New Providence
Prince of Wales
St Christopher

Santa Catalina
South Shetland
14 letters:
D'Entrecasteaux
Franz Josef Land
Lesser Antilles
Lewis and Harris
Queen Charlotte
Queen Elizabeth

Tristan da Cunha
Turks and Caicos
Vestmannaeyjar
15 letters:
Greater Antilles
Lewis with Harris
Wallis and Futuna

Ivy League universities

4 letters:
Yale
5 letters:
Brown

7 letters:
Cornell
Harvard

8 letters:
Columbia
9 letters:
Princeton

J

Jackets

3 letters:
Bed
Cag
Mao
Pea
Tux
4 letters:
Baju
Boxy
Bush
Coat
Eton
Flak
Life
Mess
Sack
5 letters:
Acton
Bania
Biker
Cymar
Denim
Duvet
Gilet

Grego
Jupon
Nehru
Parka
Pilot
Polka
Shell
Shrug
Simar
Tunic
Wamus
Water
6 letters:
Amauti
Anorak
Báinín
Banian
Banyan
Basque
Battle
Blazer
Bolero
Bomber
Cagoul

Combat
Dinner
Dolman
Donkey
Jerkin
Kagool
Lumber
Monkey
Reefer
Sacque
Safari
Sports
Strait
Tabard
Tuxedo
Wammus
Wampus
Zouave
7 letters:
Amautik
Barbour®
Blouson
Cagoule
Doublet

Fustian
Hacking
Leather
Mae West
Matinée
Norfolk
Reefing
Simarre
Smoking
Spencer
Vareuse
8 letters:
Camisole
Cardigan

Gambeson
Gendarme
Haqueton
Mackinaw
Mandarin
Tailcoat
Toreador
9 letters:
Habergeon
Hacqueton
Newmarket
Pourpoint
Shortgown
Waistcoat

10 letters:
Body warmer
Bumfreezer
Carmagnole
Fearnought
Hug-me-tight
Windjammer
11 letters:
Afghanistan
Windbreaker®
Windcheater
12 letters:
Lumberjacket
Mackinaw coat

Jazz forms

3 letters:
Bop
4 letters:
Free
Scat
Trad
5 letters:
Swing
6 letters:
Modern

7 letters:
Hard bop
Ragtime
8 letters:
Highlife
9 letters:
Afro-Cuban
Dixieland
Gutbucket
West Coast

10 letters:
Mainstream
New Orleans
11 letters:
Barrelhouse
Thirdstream
Traditional
12 letters:
Boogie-woogie
Western swing

Jazz musicians

3 letters:
Bix
4 letters:
Getz, *Stanley 'Stan'*
Pine, *Courtney*
Shaw, *Artie*
5 letters:
Basie, *William*
Davis, *Miles (Dewey)*
Haden, *Charles (Edward)*
Tatum, *Art (Arthur Tatum)*
6 letters:
Bechet, *Leon Bismarcke*
Bechet, *Sidney*
Blakey, *Art(hur)*
Garner, *Erroll*
Gordon, *Dexter*
Mingus, *Charles 'Charlie'*
Oliver, *Joseph*
Waller, *Fats (Thomas Waller)*
7 letters:
Brubeck, *Dave*

Coleman, *Ornette*
Hampton, *Lionel*
Hawkins, *Coleman*
Jarrett, *Keith*
Vaughan, *Sarah (Lois)*
8 letters:
Coltrane, *John (William)*
Marsalis, *Wynton*
Peterson, *Oscar (Emmanuel)*
9 letters:
Carpenter, *John Alden*
Christian, *Charlie*
Dankworth, *John (Philip William)*
Grappelli, *Stéphane*
Lyttelton, *Humphrey*
10 letters:
Count Basie
Fitzgerald, *Ella*
King Oliver

Jazz terms

3 letters:
Gig
4 letters:
Band
Cool
Jazz
Jive
Riff
Skin
5 letters:
Combo
Jazzy
Major
Minor
Sound
Stomp
Swing
Vocal

6 letters:
Hepcat
Jazz up
Number
Vibist
7 letters:
Bassist
Big band
Hipster
Jug band
Sideman
Stomper
8 letters:
Slap bass
Vocalist
9 letters:
Augmented
Jitterbug

Mouldy fig
Ring-shout
Saxophone
10 letters:
Added sixth
Diminished
Jam session
Ninth chord
Vibraphone
13 letters:
Eleventh chord
15 letters:
Thirteenth chord

Jewish denominations and sects

7 letters:
Zionism
8 letters:
Hasidism
9 letters:
Chasidism
Hassidism

10 letters:
Chassidism
13 letters:
Reform Judaism

14 letters:
Liberal Judaism
15 letters:
Orthodox Judaism

Judges

3 letters:
Ito, *Lance A(llan)*
4 letters:
Coke, *Sir Edward*
More, *Sir Thomas*
5 letters:
Draco
Solon
Woolf, *Lord Henry*
6 letters:
Gideon
Holmes, *Oliver Wendell*
Hutton, *Lord (James) Brian
(Edward)*
Irvine, *Lord Alexander*
Mackay, *Lord James*
7 letters:
Deborah
De Burgh, *Hubert*
Denning, *Lord Alfred*

Jephtha
Pickles
Roy Bean
Solomon
8 letters:
Falconer, *Lord Charles*
Hailsham, *Viscount Quintin
McGarel Hogg*
Jeffreys, *Lord George*
Marshall, *Thurgood*
9 letters:
Judge Judy
10 letters:
Elwyn-Jones, *Lord Frederick*
13 letters:
Judge 'Joe' Dredd
Pontius Pilate

K

Kings

2 letters:
ER
Og
3 letters:
Asa
Ine
Lir
Log
Lud
Roi
Zog
4 letters:
Agag
Agis
Ahab
Brut
Ceyx
Cnut
Cole
Edwy
Fahd
Jehu
Lear
Nudd
Numa
Offa
Olaf
Saul
5 letters:
Balak
Brute
Creon
Cyrus
David
Edgar
Edwin
Gyges
Herod
Hiram
Idris
Ixion
James
Lludd
Louis
Midas

Minos
Mpret
Ninus
Penda
Priam
Rufus
Uther
6 letters:
Aegeus
Alfred
Alonso
Amasis
Arthur
Attila
Baliol
Brutus
Canute
Cheops
Clovis
Darius
Duncan
Edmund
Egbert
Farouk
Fergus
Harold
Hyksos
Lucomo
Ludwig
Memnon
Nestor
Oberon
Ogyges
Paphos
Philip
Ramses
Rhesus
Xerxes
7 letters:
Acestes
Baldwin
Balliol
Beowulf
Busiris
Caradoc

Cecrops
Croesus
Elidure
Evander
Kenneth
Macbeth
Malcolm
Oedipus
Ptolemy
Pyrrhus
Rameses
Servius
Solomon
Stephen
Tarquin
Umberto
8 letters:
Cambyses
Cophetua
Endymion
Ethelred
Hezekiah
Jereboam
Jonathan
Leonidas
Menander
Menelaus
Milesius
Odysseus
Rehoboam
Tantalus
Thyestes
Tigranes
Zedekiah
9 letters:
Agamemnon
Ahasuerus
Alexander
Athelstan
Bretwalda
Brian Boru
Conchobar
Cunobelin
Cymbeline
Ethelbert

Florestan
Frederick
Gargantua
Pygmalion
Ras Tafari
Tarquinus
Vortigern
Wenceslas

10 letters:
Belshazzar
Cadwaladar
Caractacus
Ozymandias
Wenceslaus
11 letters:
Charlemagne

Hardicanute
Jehoshaphat
Sennacherib
12 letters:
Wayland Smith
14 letters:
Nebuchadnezzar
Uther Pendragon

Knights

3 letters:
Kay
4 letters:
Bors
5 letters:
Guyon
Pinel
6 letters:
Bliant
Cambel
Gareth
Gawain
Lionel
Melius
Modred
Ritter
7 letters:
Accolon

Artegal
Caradoc
Galahad
Launfal
Orlando
Paladin
Tristan
8 letters:
Alphagus
Banneret
Bedivere
Calidore
Lancelot
Maecenas
Palmerin
Parsifal
Perceval
Percival

Tristram
Vavasour
9 letters:
Aguecheek
Britomart
Caballero
Launcelot
Lochinvar
Lohengrin
Pharamond
Valvassor
10 letters:
Tannhauser
11 letters:
Perceforest

Knitting stitches

3 letters:
Box
Rib
4 letters:
Moss
Seed
Slip
5 letters:
Cable
6 letters:
Garter

7 letters:
Layette
8 letters:
Pavilion
Stocking
9 letters:
Garter rib
10 letters:
Double moss
Double seed
Mistake rib

Moss panels
11 letters:
Diagonal rib
Roman stripe
13 letters:
Fisherman's rib

Knots

3 letters:
Bow
Tie
4 letters:
Bend
Flat

Loop
Love
Mesh
Reef
Slip
Wale

Wall
5 letters:
Hitch
Mouse
Picot
Quipu

Thumb
Water
6 letters:
Clinch
French
Granny
Lover's
Prusik
Shroud
Square
7 letters:
Barrell
Bowknot
Bowline
Cat's paw
Crochet
Diamond
Gordian
Rosette
Running
Sailor's

Windsor
8 letters:
Hangman's
Overhand
Slipknot
Surgeon's
Truelove
9 letters:
Bowstring
Half-hitch
Sheet bend
Swab hitch
Turk's-head
10 letters:
Becket bend
Clove hitch
Fisherman's
Girth hitch
Hawser bend
Monkey fist
Sheepshank

Stevedore's
Truelover's
11 letters:
Carrick bend
Englishman's
Magnus hitch
Timber hitch
12 letters:
Harness hitch
Rolling hitch
Weaver's hitch
13 letters:
Figure of eight
Matthew Walker
Slippery hitch
14 letters:
Blackwall hitch
Englishman's tie
Fisherman's bend
Running bowline

Lakes, lochs and loughs

2 letters:
No
3 letters:
Ard
Awe
Ewe
Tay
Van
Zug
4 letters:
Bala
Biel
Bled
Chad
Como
Earn
Erie
Erne
Eyre
Fyne

Kivu
Mead
Ness
Nyos
Taal
Tana
Thun
Tien
5 letters:
Allen
Atlin
Cowan
Frome
Garda
Gatún
Huron
Ilmen
Léman
Leven
Lochy

Lower
Malar
Meech
Morar
Mungo
Mweru
Myall
Nam Co
Neagh
Nyasa
Onega
Patos
Playa
Poopó
Pskov
Sevan
Sween
Tahoe
Taupo
Tsana

Urmia
Volta
6 letters:
Albert
Annecy
Argyle
Averno
Baikal
Barlee
Bitter
Broads
Cayuga
Corrib
Edward
Geneva
Kariba
Ladoga
Laggan
Linnhe
Lomond
Lugano
Malawi
Miveru
Mobutu
Nakuru
Nam Tso
Nasser
Oneida
Peipus
P'o-yang
Rudolf
Saimaa
Te Anau
Tekapo
Tummel
Vanern
Zürich
7 letters:
Amadeus
Aral Sea
Avernus
Axolotl
Balaton
Belfast
Dead Sea
Iliamna
Katrine
Koko Nor
Kuku Nor
Lucerne
Managua

Nipigon
Ontario
Rannoch
Rotorua
Toronto
Torrens
Turkana
8 letters:
Balkhash
Bodensee
Carnegie
Dongting
Gairdner
Grasmere
Issyk-Kul
Kootenay
Lake Aral
Maggiore
Manitoba
Menindee
Menteith
Michigan
Naumachy
Okanagan
Onondaga
Regillus
Reindeer
Superior
Titicaca
Tonle Sap
Torridon
Veronica
Victoria
Wakatipu
Wanawaka
Winnipeg
9 letters:
Athabasca
Athabaska
Bangweulu
Champlain
Constance
Ennerdale
Everglade
Great Bear
Great Salt
Innisfree
Killarney
Macquarie
Manapouri
Maracaibo

Naumachia
Neuchâtel
Nicaragua
Nipissing
Saint John
Serbonian
Thirlmere
Trasimene
Trasimono
Ullswater
Wairarapa
Wast Water
Winnebago
Ysselmeer
10 letters:
Buttermere
Caspian Sea
Clearwater
Great Lakes
Great Slave
Hawes Water
Ijsselmeer
Miraflores
Mistassini
Okeechobee
Okefenokee
Saint Clair
Serpentine
Tanganyika
Washington
Windermere
11 letters:
Great Bitter
Lesser Slave
Stanley Pool
12 letters:
Derwentwater
Little Bitter
Memphremagog
Sea of Galilee
Waikaremoana
13 letters:
Bassenthwaite
Coniston Water
Crummock Water
Pontchartrain
14 letters:
Disappointment
Ennerdale Water
Lake of the Woods

Languages

AFRICAN LANGUAGES

2 letters:
Ga
Gã
3 letters:
Edo
Ewe
Ibo
Luo
Tiv
Twi
4 letters:
Akan
Beni
Bini
Efik
Fang
Fula
Hutu
Igbo
Krio
Lozi
Luba
Nama
Nuba
Nupe
Pedi
Susu
Zulu
5 letters:
Bemba
Chewa
Duala
Dyula
Fanti
Fulah

Galla
Ganda
Hausa
Kongo
Masai
Moore
Mossi
Nyoro
Pondo
Sango
Shona
Sotho
Swazi
Temne
Tigré
Tonga
Venda
Wolof
Xhosa
6 letters:
Berber
Coptic
Damara
Fulani
Grikwa
Griqua
Herero
Ibibio
Kabyle
Kikuyu
Nyanja
Ovambo
Rwanda
Somali
Tsonga

Tswana
Tuareg
Yoruba
7 letters:
Adamawa
Amharic
Ashanti
Bambara
Barotse
Bashkir
Kirundi
Luganda
Malinke
Maninke
Namaqua
Ndebele
Sesotho
Songhai
Swahili
8 letters:
Chichewa
Fanagalo
Fanakalo
Kingwana
Malagasy
Matabele
Tigrinya
Tshiluba
9 letters:
Afrikaans
Hottentot
13 letters:
Northern Sotho

ASIAN LANGUAGES

3 letters:
Lao
Mon
4 letters:
Ainu
Cham
Moro
Naga
Nuri
Shan
Thai
Urdu

5 letters:
Dinka
Farsi
Gondi
Hindi
Karen
Kazak
Khmer
Malay
Oriya
Tamil
Tatar

Uigur
Uzbek
Yakut
6 letters:
Abkhaz
Adygei
Adyghe
Afghan
Arabic
Bihari
Brahui
Buriat

Buryat
Divehi
Evenki
Hebrew
Kafiri
Kalmyk
Kazakh
Korean
Lahnda
Lepcha
Manchu
Mishmi
Mongol
Nepali
Ostyak
Pashto
Pushto
Pushtu
Sindhi
Telegu
Telugu
Tungus
Uighur
7 letters:
Abkhazi
Aramaic
Balochi
Baluchi
Bengali
Burmese

Chinese
Chukchi
Chuvash
Dzongka
Iranian
Kalmuck
Kannada
Khalkha
Kirghiz
Kurdish
Marathi
Ossetic
Punjabi
Sogdian
Tadzhik
Tagalog
Tibetan
Turkman
Turkmen
8 letters:
Armenian
Assamese
Balinese
Canarese
Chukchee
Filipino
Gujarati
Gujerati
Gurkhali
Japanese

Javanese
Kanarese
Kashmiri
Mahratti
Mandarin
Ossetian
Tadzhiki
Turkoman
9 letters:
Abkhazian
Cantonese
Kabardian
Malayalam
Mongolian
Sinhalese
10 letters:
Circassian
Hindostani
Hindustani
Kara-Kalpak
Kazan Tatar
Malayalaam
Vietnamese
11 letters:
Azerbaijani
Hindoostani
15 letters:
Bahasa Indonesia

AUSTRALASIAN LANGUAGES

4 letters:
Krio
Motu
5 letters:
Dinka
Māori
6 letters:
Aranda
Fijian
Papuan

Samoan
Tongan
7 letters:
Moriori
Nauruan
Pintubi
8 letters:
Gurindji
Hawaiian
Hiri Motu

Tuvaluan
Warlpiri
9 letters:
Kamilaroi
10 letters:
Beach-la-Mar
Police Motu
13 letters:
Neo-Melanesian

EUROPEAN LANGUAGES

4 letters:
Erse
Komi
Lapp
Manx
5 letters:
Czech
Dutch
Greek

Ladin
Vogul
Welsh
6 letters:
Basque
Bokmål
Breton
Cymric
Danish

French
Gaelic
German
Kymric
Ladino
Lallan
Magyar
Polish
Romany

Shelta
Slovak
Udmurt
Votyak
Zyrian
7 letters:
Catalan
Cornish
English
Finnish
Flemish
Frisian
Gagauzi
Italian
Lallans
Latvian
Lettish
Maltese
Mingrel
Mordvin
Nynorsk
Romanes
Romansh

Russian
Samoyed
Slovene
Sorbian
Spanish
Swedish
Turkish
Yiddish
8 letters:
Albanian
Bohemian
Cheremis
Croatian
Estonian
Faeroese
Friulian
Galician
Georgian
Karelian
Landsmål
Lusatian
Romanian
Romansch

9 letters:
Alemannic
Bulgarian
Castilian
Cheremiss
Hungarian
Icelandic
Norwegian
Provençal
Sardinian
Ukrainian
10 letters:
Lithuanian
Macedonian
Mingrelian
Portuguese
Serbo-Croat
12 letters:
Byelorussian
13 letters:
Serbo-Croatian

NORTH AMERICAN LANGUAGES

3 letters:
Fox
Ute
4 letters:
Crow
Erie
Hopi
Zuñi
5 letters:
Aleut
Creek
Haida
Huron
Osage
Piute
Sioux
Taino
6 letters:
Abnaki
Apache
Cayuga
Eskimo
Micmac
Mixtec
Mohave
Mohawk
Mojave
Navaho

Navajo
Nootka
Ojibwa
Oneida
Paiute
Pawnee
Pequot
Seneca
7 letters:
Arapaho
Caddoan
Catawba
Chinook
Choctaw
Mahican
Mohican
Shawnee
Tahltan
Tlingit
8 letters:
Aleutian
Algonkin
Cherokee
Cheyenne
Comanche
Delaware
Iroquois
Kwakiutl

Menomini
Nez Percé
Okanagan
Okanogan
Okinagan
Onondaga
Sahaptan
Sahaptin
Seminole
Shoshone
Shoshoni
9 letters:
Algonquin
Blackfoot
Chickasaw
Inuktitut
Sahaptian
Tuscarora
Winnebago
11 letters:
Assiniboine
Massachuset
Narraganset
12 letters:
Narragansett
13 letters:
Massachusetts

SOUTH AMERICAN LANGUAGES

4 letters:
Tupi
6 letters:
Aymara
Galibi
Kechua

7 letters:
Guarani
Nahuatl
Quechua
Quichua
Zapotec

8 letters:
Chibchan
10 letters:
Araucanian

ANCIENT LANGUAGES

4 letters:
Avar
Ge'ez
Inca
Maya
Norn
Pali
5 letters:
Aztec
Ionic
Koine
Latin
Mayan
Oscan
Punic
Vedic
6 letters:
Gothic
Hebrew
Libyan
Lycian
Lydian
Sabean
Syriac
7 letters:
Avestan
Avestic
Chaldee

Edomite
Elamite
Hittite
Pahlavi
Pehlevi
Pictish
Sabaean
Umbrian
Venetic
Wendish
8 letters:
Akkadian
Assyrian
Egyptian
Ethiopic
Etruscan
Faliscan
Frankish
Illyrian
Messapïc
Old Norse
Phrygian
Sanskrit
Scythian
Sumerian
Thracian
Ugaritic
Volscian

9 letters:
Canaanite
Langue d'oc
Messapian
Sabellian
Tocharian
Tokharian
10 letters:
Anglo-Saxon
Babylonian
Gallo-Roman
Himyaritic
Langue d'oïl
Phoenician
11 letters:
Celtiberian
Langobardic
Old Prussian
Osso-Umbrian
12 letters:
Ancient Greek
Gallo-Romance
13 letters:
Old High German
14 letters:
Thraco-Phrygian

ARTIFICIAL LANGUAGES

3 letters:
Ido
7 letters:
Volapuk
Volapük

9 letters:
Esperanto
11 letters:
Interlingua

LANGUAGE GROUPS

3 letters:
Gur
Kwa
San

5 letters:
Bantu
Carib
Indic

Mande
Mayan
Munda
Nguni

Norse
Ugric
Yuman
6 letters:
Altaic
Baltic
Celtic
Chadic
Cymric
Dardic
Eskimo
Finnic
Italic
Na-Déné
Pahari
Salish
Siouan
Turkic
Uralic
7 letters:
Caddoan
Hamitic
Iranian
Khoisan
Nilotic
Oceanic
Romance
Saharan
Semitic
Sinitic
Sudanic
Voltaic
8 letters:
Albanian

Arawakan
Armenian
Cushitic
Germanic
Hellenic
Mongolic
Mon-Khmer
Penutian
Rhaetian
Salishan
Slavonic
Tungusic
Wakashan
9 letters:
Algonkian
Anatolian
Brythonic
Caucasian
Chari-Nile
Dravidian
Indo-Aryan
Iroquoian
Muskogean
Semi-Bantu
10 letters:
Algonquian
Athabascan
Athabaskan
Athapascan
Athapaskan
Australian
Benue-Congo
Canaanitic
Hindustani

Melanesian
Muskhogean
Niger-Congo
Polynesian
Sanskritic
Shoshonean
Uto-Aztecan
11 letters:
Afro-Asiatic
East Iranian
Indo-Iranian
Indo-Pacific
Kordofanian
Micronesian
Nilo-Saharan
Pama-Nyungan
Sino-Tibetan
Tupi-Guarani
West Iranian
12 letters:
Austronesian
East Germanic
Indo-European
Tibeto-Burman
West Atlantic
West Germanic
West Slavonic
13 letters:
Austro-Asiatic
Hamito-Semitic
North Germanic
Semito-Hamitic

Law sittings

6 letters:
Easter
Hilary

7 letters:
Trinity

10 letters:
Michaelmas

Leather

3 letters:
Kid
Kip
4 letters:
Buff
Calf
Cuir
Hide
Napa
Roan
Yuft

5 letters:
Mocha
Nappa
Suede
6 letters:
Corium
Deacon
Levant
Nubuck®
Oxhide
Patent

Rexine®
Russia
Shammy
7 letters:
Box-calf
Chamois
Cowhide
Dogskin
Hog-skin
Kip-skin
Morocco

Pigskin
Rawhide
Saffian
8 letters:
Buckskin
Cabretta
Capeskin
Cheverel
Cordovan

Cordwain
Deerskin
Marocain
Maroquin
Rough-out
Shagreen
9 letters:
Chevrette
Horsehide

Sharkskin
Sheepskin
10 letters:
Checklaton
Shecklaton
11 letters:
Cuir-bouilli
Whitleather

Lilies

3 letters:
Day
4 letters:
Aloe
Arum
Corn
Lent
Lote
Sego
5 letters:
Calla
Camas
Lotus
Padma
Regal
Tiger
Water
Yucca
6 letters:
Camash
Camass
Canada
Crinum
Easter

Jacob's
Nerine
Nuphar
Smilax
Zephyr
7 letters:
African
Candock
Madonna
Nelumbo
Quamash
8 letters:
Asphodel
Galtonia
Martagon
Nenuphar
Phormium
Plantain
Trillium
Turk's cap
Victoria
9 letters:
Amaryllis
Colchicum

Colocasia
Herb-paris
Kniphofia
10 letters:
Agapanthus
Aspidistra
Belladonna
Fleur de lys
Haemanthus
11 letters:
Convallaria
12 letters:
Annunciation
Hemerocallis
Skunk cabbage
Solomon's seal
14 letters:
Chincherinchee
15 letters:
Star of Bethlehem

Literature

LITERATURE TERMS

2 letters:
SF
4 letters:
Coda
Epic
Myth
Plot
Saga
5 letters:
Beats
Cento
Drama
Essay
Fable

Gloss
Maxim
Motif
Novel
Roman
Story
Theme
Trope
Verse
6 letters:
Bathos
Comedy
Gothic
Legend

Parody
Pathos
Satire
Simile
Sketch
Theory
Thesis
7 letters:
Bombast
Byronic
Chiller
Conceit
Epistle
Epitaph

Erasure
Faction
Fantasy
Homeric
Imagery
Janeite
Joycean
Kenning
Lampoon
Novella
Polemic
Realism
Subplot
Subtext
Tragedy
8 letters:
Allegory
Allusion
Anti-hero
Aphorism
Archaism
Augustan
Causerie
Dialogue
Epilogue
Exegesis
Fabulist
Foreword
Futurism
Horatian
Jacobean
Kailyard
Kiddy lit
Metaphor
Narrator
Oxymoron
Pastiche
Pastoral
Samizdat
Swiftian
Vignette
9 letters:
Amphigory
Antinovel
Anti-roman
Brechtian
Bricolage
Cyberpunk
Decadence
Derridian

Dialectic
Discourse
Gongorism
Hellenism
Invective
Melodrama
Modernism
Narrative
Novelette
Pot-boiler
10 letters:
Amphigouri
Bakhtinian
Belletrist
Ciceronian
Classicism
Denouement
Dickensian
Johnsonian
Journalese
Juvenalian
Kafkaesque
Laurentian
Lawrentian
Mock-heroic
Mythopoeia
Naturalism
Nom de plume
Palindrome
Paraphrase
Picaresque
Plagiarism
Post-theory
Roman à clef
Short story
Spoonerism
Surrealism
11 letters:
Black comedy
Campus novel
Courtly love
Fantastique
Festschrift
Fin de siècle
Foucauldian
Hagiography
Historicism
Littérateur
Metafiction
Narratology

Pornography
Queer theory
Romanticism
Tragicomedy
12 letters:
Alliteration
Bibliography
Bodice-ripper
Hermeneutics
Magic realism
Metalanguage
New criticism
Nouveau roman
Onomatopoeia
Splatterpunk
13 letters:
Angry Young Men
Belles-lettres
Bildungsroman
Carnivalesque
Celtic Revival
Colloquialism
Expressionism
Marxist theory
Postmodernism
Structuralism
Sturm und Drang
14 letters:
Beat Generation
Bowdlerization
Cut-up technique
Deconstruction
Double entendre
Feminist theory
Figure of speech
Locus classicus
Lost Generation
Magical realism
New historicism
Science fiction
15 letters:
Bloomsbury group
Comedy of
  manners
Epistolary novel
Historical novel
Intertextuality
Post-colonialism

See also:
➤ **Diarists** ➤ **Dramatists** ➤ **Musketeers** ➤ **Novelists** ➤ **Poetry**
➤ **Shakespeare** ➤ **Works of literature and music** ➤ **Writers**

Lizards

3 letters:
Eft
Jew
4 letters:
Abas
Gila
Newt
Sand
Tegu
Wall
Worm
5 letters:
Agama
Anole
Draco
Gecko
Guana
Skink
Snake
Tokay
Varan
6 letters:
Anguis
Goanna

Horned
Iguana
Komodo
Leguan
Moloch
Worral
Worrel
7 letters:
Bearded
Frilled
Geckone
Lacerta
Leguaan
Monitor
Perenty
Stellio
Tuatara
Tuatera
Zandoli
8 letters:
Basilisk
Dinosaur
Hatteria
Menopome

Mosasaur
Perentie
Stellion
Sungazer
Teguexin
Whiptail
9 letters:
Blindworm
Chameleon
Galliwasp
Mastigure
10 letters:
Chuckwalla
Glass snake
Hellbender
Kabaragoya
Mosasaurus
11 letters:
Amphisboena
Blue-tongued
Brontosurus
12 letters:
Komodo dragon

Locomotives

7 letters:
Mallard
9 letters:
Blue Peter
Britannia
City Class
Hall Class
King Class

10 letters:
Black Class
The General
11 letters:
Golden Arrow
West Country
12 letters:
General Stamp

Merchant Navy
Schools Class
14 letters:
Flying Scotsman
15 letters:
Coronation Class
Midland
  Compound

London, boroughs of

5 letters:
Brent
6 letters:
Barnet
Bexley
Camden
Ealing
Harrow
Merton
Newham
Sutton
7 letters:
Bromley

Croydon
Enfield
Hackney
Lambeth
8 letters:
Haringey
Havering
Hounslow
Kingston
Lewisham
Richmond
9 letters:
Greenwich

Islington
Redbridge
Southwark
10 letters:
Hillingdon
Wandsworth
11 letters:
Westminster
12 letters:
Tower Hamlets
13 letters:
Waltham Forest

Lovers

Antony and Cleopatra
Bonnie (Parker) and Clyde (Barrow)
Richard Burton and Elizabeth Taylor
Julius Caesar and Cleopatra
Casanova
Cathy and Heathcliffe
Dante and Beatrice
Darby and Joan
Dido and Aeneas
Don Juan
Edward VIII and Wallis Simpson
Eloise and Abelard
Harlequin and Columbine
Hero and Leander
Jane Eyre and Edward Rochester
Lancelot and Guinevere
Lochinvar and Ellen
Napoleon and Josephine
Scarlett O'Hara and Rhett Butler
Orpheus and Eurydice
Paris and Helen of Troy
Pelleas and Melisande
Petrarch and Laura
Porgy and Bess
Pyramus and Thisbe
Robin Hood and Maid Marian
Romeo and Juliet
Rosalind and Orlando
Samson and Delilah
Tosca and Cavaradossi
Tristan and Isolde
Troilus and Cressida
Zeus and Hera

Mammals, extinct

6 letters:
Apeman
Quagga
Tarpan
7 letters:
Aurochs
Mammoth
8 letters:
Creodont
Eohippus
Irish elk

Mastodon
9 letters:
Dinoceras
Dinothere
Megathere
10 letters:
Glyptodont
Uintathere
11 letters:
Nototherium
Titanothere

12 letters:
Chalicothere
13 letters:
Dryopithecine
14 letters:
Baluchitherium
Labyrinthodont
15 letters:
Sabre-toothed cat

For mammals, see:
➤ **Anteaters and other edentates** ➤ **Antelopes** ➤ **Bats**
➤ **Carnivores** ➤ **Cats** ➤ **Cattle, breeds of** ➤ **Cows** ➤ **Dogs**
➤ **Horses** ➤ **Marsupials** ➤ **Monkeys, apes and other primates**
➤ **Pigs** ➤ **Rabbits and hares** ➤ **Rodents** ➤ **Seals** ➤ **Sea mammals**
➤ **Sheep** ➤ **Shrews and other insectivores** ➤ **Whales and dolphins**

Mania

Mania	Object
Ablutomania	Washing
Agoramania	Open spaces
Ailuromania	Cats
Andromania	Men
Anglomania	England
Anthomania	Flowers
Apimania	Bees
Arithmomania	Counting
Automania	Solitude
Autophonomania	Suicide
Balletomania	Ballet
Ballistomania	Bullets
Bibliomania	Books
Chionomania	Snow
Choreomania	Dancing
Chrematomania	Money
Cremnomania	Cliffs
Cynomania	Dogs
Dipsomania	Alcohol
Doramania	Fur
Dromomania	Travelling
Egomania	Your self
Eleuthromania	Freedom
Entheomania	Religion
Entomomania	Insects
Ergasiomania	Work
Eroticomania	Erotica
Erotomania	Sex
Florimania	Plants
Gamomania	Marriage
Graphomania	Writing
Gymnomania	Nakedness
Gynomania	Women
Hamartiomania	Sin
Hedonomania	Pleasure
Heliomania	Sun
Hippomania	Horses
Homicidomania	Murder
Hydromania	Water
Hylomania	Woods
Hypnomania	Sleep
Ichthyomania	Fish
Iconomania	Icons
Kinesomania	Movement
Kleptomania	Stealing
Logomania	Talking
Macromania	Becoming larger
Megalomania	Your own importance
Melomania	Music
Mentulomania	Penises
Micromania	Becoming smaller
Monomania	One thing
Musicomania	Music
Musomania	Mice

Mania	Object
Mythomania	Lies
Necromania	Death
Noctimania	Night
Nudomania	Nudity
Nymphomania	Sex
Ochlomania	Crowds
Oikomania	Home
Oinomania	Wine
Ophidiomania	Reptiles
Orchidomania	Testicles
Ornithomania	Birds
Phagomania	Eating
Pharmacomania	Medicines
Phonomania	Noise
Photomania	Light
Plutomania	Great wealth
Potomania	Drinking
Pyromania	Fire
Scribomania	Writing
Siderodromomania	Railway travel
Sitomania	Food
Sophomania	Your own wisdom
Thalassomania	The sea
Thanatomania	Death
Theatromania	Theatre
Timbromania	Stamps
Trichomania	Hair
Verbomania	Words
Xenomania	Foreigners
Zoomania	Animals

Marsupials

3 letters:
Roo
4 letters:
Dama
Marl
Tait
Tuan
Uroo
5 letters:
Bilby
Damar
Koala
Mardo
Marlu
Pongo
Quoll
Tungo
Yapok
6 letters:
Badger
Bobuck
Boodie

Cuscus
Glider
Jerboa
Kowari
Merrin
Mongan
Numbat
Possum
Quenda
Quokka
Tammar
Toolah
Tungoo
Warabi
Wogoit
Wombat
Woylie
Yapock
7 letters:
Bettong
Biggada
Dalgite

Dalgyte
Dasyure
Dibbler
Dunnart
Kultarr
Mulgara
Munning
Ningaui
Opossum
Potoroo
Wallaby
Wild cat
Wurrung
Yallara
8 letters:
Boongary
Burramys
Dasyurid
Duckbill
Forester
Kangaroo
Karrabul

Macropod
Platypus
Ringtail
Squeaker
Tiger cat
Toolache
Wallaroo
Wintarro
Wuhl-wuhl
9 letters:
Bandicoot
Boodie rat
Didelphia
Koala bear
Larapinta
Native cat
Pademelon
Petaurist
Phalanger
Thylacine
Wambenger
10 letters:
Antechinus
Diprotodon
Honey mouse
Native bear
Noolbenger
Notoryctes
Paddymelon
Phascogale
Red wallaby
Rock possum
Satanellus
11 letters:
Diprotodont
Fairy possum
Flying mouse
Hare-wallaby
Honey possum
Nototherium
Pygmy glider
Pygmy possum
Rat kangaroo
Red kangaroo
Rock wallaby
Sugar glider
Tcharibeena
12 letters:
Agile wallaby

Black wallaby
Fluffy glider
Grey forester
Marsupial cat
Parma wallaby
Pitchi-pitchi
River wallaby
Sandy wallaby
Scrub wallaby
Swamp wallaby
Tree kangaroo
13 letters:
Brush kangaroo
Feather glider
Marsupial mole
Rufous wallaby
Sooty kangaroo
Striped possum
Tasmanian wolf
Ursine dasyure
14 letters:
Banded anteater
Brown bandicoot
Flying squirrel
Forest kangaroo
Gunn's bandicoot
Jerboa kangaroo
Jungle kangaroo
Mallee kangaroo
Marsupial mouse
Mountain possum
Plains kangaroo
Ringtail possum
Squirrel glider
Tasmanian devil
Tasmanian tiger
15 letters:
Barred bandicoot
Bennett's wallaby
Brush-tail possum
Desert bandicoot
Flying phalanger
Golden bandicoot
Naked-nose wombat
Rabbit bandicoot
Whiptail wallaby

Martial arts

MARTIAL ARTS

4 letters:
Judo
Sumo
5 letters:
Iai-do
Kendo
Kyudo
6 letters:
Aikido
Karate
Kung fu
Tukido®
7 letters:
Hapkido
Ju jitsu
Ju-jutsu
8 letters:
Capoeira
Iai-jutsu

Jiu jitsu
Karate-do
Muay Thai
Ninjitsu
Ninjutsu
Wing Chun
9 letters:
Tae kwon-do
Yari-jutsu
10 letters:
Jeet Kune Do
Kick boxing
Naginata-do
Thai boxing
11 letters:
Tai chi chuan
12 letters:
Tai chi qi gong
Tomiki aikido

13 letters:
Goju Kai karate
Goju Ryu karate
Hung Gar kung fu
Sumo wrestling
Wado Ryu karate
14 letters:
Ishin Ryu karate
Sankukai karate
Shito Ryu karate
Shotokai karate
Shotokan karate
Shukokai karate
Wing Tsun kung fu

MARTIAL ARTS TERMS

Term	Meaning
Basho	Sumo turnament
Bo	Staff
Bogu	Kendo armour
Bokuto	Kendo wooden sword
Budo *or* bushido	Warrior's way
Dan	Black belt grade
Do	Kendo breastplate
-do	The way
Dohyo	Sumo ring
Dojo	Practice room or mat
Gi	Suit
Hachimaki *or* tenugui	Kendo headcloth
Hakama	Divided skirt
Ippon	One competition point
Jiu-kumite	Freestyle karate competition
-jutsu	Fighting art
-ka	Student
Kama	Hand sickle
Kata	Sequence of techniques
Katana	Kendo sword
Katsu	Resuscitation techniques
Keikogi	Kendo jacket
Kesho-mawashi	Embroidered sumo apron
Ki, chi, *or* qi	Inner power
Kiai	Yell accompanying movement
Kihon	Repetition of techniques
Kote	Kendo gauntlets
Kyu	Student grade
Makiwara	Practice block

Term	Meaning
Mawashi	Sumo fighting belt
Men	Kendo mask
Nage-waza *or* tachi-waza	Ju jitsu competition
Naginata	Curved-blade spear
Ne-waza	Ju jitsu competition
Ninin-dori	Aikido competition
Ninja	Japanese trained assassin
Nunchaku	Hinged flails
Obi	Coloured belt
Ozeki	Sumo champion
Qi gong	Breath control
Randori kyoghi	Aikido competition
Rikishi	Sumo wrestler
Rokushakubo	Six-foot staff
Ryu	Martial arts school
Sai	Short trident
Samurai	Japanese warrior caste
Sensei	Teacher
Shinai	Kendo bamboo sword
Sifu	Teacher
Suneate	Naginata shin guards
Tanto randori	Aikido competition
Tare	Kendo apron
Te	Hand fighting
Ton-fa *or* tui-fa	Hardwood weapon
Tsuna	Sumo grand champion's belt
Waza-ari	Half competition point
Yari	Spear
Yokozuna	Sumo grand champion
Zanshin	Total awareness

Materials

3 letters:
Say
4 letters:
Lamé
Lawn
Tape
Wool
5 letters:
Crash
Toile
Twill
6 letters:
Canvas
Cermet
Coburg
Dimity
Russel
Soneri
Tusser
7 letters:
Batiste

Cambric
Ceramic
Chiffon
Galatea
Genappe
Hessian
Oilskin
Sagathy
8 letters:
Cretonne
Gossamer
Homespun
Illusion
Jeanette
Marocain
Moquette
Prunella
Toilinet
9 letters:
Calamanco
Cellulose

Charmeuse®
Fibrefill
Gaberdine
Macintosh
Pina-cloth
Polyester
Sackcloth
Stockinet
Swansdown
Tarpaulin
Towelling
Worcester
10 letters:
Fibreglass
Toilinette
Winceyette
11 letters:
Stockinette

Mathematics

BRANCHES OF MATHEMATICS

4 letters:
Pure
6 letters:
Conics
7 letters:
Algebra
Applied
8 letters:
Analysis
Calculus

Geometry
Topology
9 letters:
Set theory
10 letters:
Arithmetic
Game theory
Nomography
Statistics

11 letters:
Group theory
12 letters:
Number theory
Trigonometry
13 letters:
Chaos geometry
14 letters:
Boolean algebra

MATHEMATICAL TERMS

2 letters:
Pi
3 letters:
Arc
Log
Odd
Set
Sum
4 letters:
Area
Axis
Base
Cone
Cube
Cusp
Even
Mean
Mode
Node
Plus
Root
Sine
Surd
Zero
5 letters:
Angle
Chord
Curve
Digit
Graph
Helix
Index
Locus
Minus
Power
Prism
Proof
Ratio
Solid

Torus
Union
Value
X-axis
Y-axis
Z-axis
6 letters:
Binary
Circle
Cosine
Cuboid
Denary
Equals
Factor
Matrix
Median
Number
Oblong
Origin
Radian
Radius
Scalar
Secant
Sector
Sphere
Square
Subset
Vector
Volume
7 letters:
Average
Decagon
Decimal
Ellipse
Formula
Hexagon
Integer
Nonagon
Octagon

Open set
Polygon
Product
Rhombus
Scalene
Tangent
8 letters:
Addition
Algorism
Binomial
Constant
Cosecant
Cube root
Cylinder
Diagonal
Diameter
Division
Equation
Fraction
Function
Heptagon
Infinity
Integral
Operator
Parabola
Parallel
Pentagon
Quadrant
Quotient
Triangle
Variable
9 letters:
Algorithm
Closed set
Cotangent
Factorial
Frequency
Hyperbola
Isosceles

Logarithm
Numerator
Operation
Rectangle
Remainder
Slide rule
Trapezium
10 letters:
Acute angle
Concentric
Co-ordinate
Hemisphere
Hypotenuse
Octahedron
Percentage
Polyhedron
Polynomial
Real number
Reciprocal

Right angle
Semicircle
Square root
11 letters:
Coefficient
Denominator
Equilateral
Exponential
Icosahedron
Obtuse angle
Prime number
Probability
Reflex angle
Subtraction
Tetrahedron
Venn diagram
12 letters:
Common factor
Dodecahedron

Intersection
Universal set
13 letters:
Circumference
Complex number
Mandelbrot set
Natural number
Ordinal number
Parallelogram
Perfect number
Quadrilateral
14 letters:
Cardinal number
Multiplication
Proper fraction
Rational number
Vulgar fraction
15 letters:
Imaginary number

MATHEMATICIANS

3 letters:
Dee, *John*
Lie, *Marius Sophus*
4 letters:
Hero
Kahn, *Herman*
Weyl, *Hermann*
Zeno *(of Elea)*
5 letters:
Aiken, *Howard Hathaway*
Bondi, *Hermann*
Boole, *George*
Comte, *Isidore Auguste*
Euler, *Leonhard*
Gauss, *Karl Friedrich*
Gibbs, *Josiah Willard*
Gödel, *Kurt*
6 letters:
Agnesi, *Maria Gaetana*
Ampère, *André Marie*
Balmer, *Johann Jakob*
Bessel, *Friedrich Wilhelm*
Briggs, *Henry*
Cantor, *Georg*
Cauchy, *Augustin Louis*
Cayley, *Arthur*
Cocker, *Edward*
Darwin, *George Howard*
Euclid
Fermat, *Pierre De*
Gunter, *Edmund*
Halley, *Edmund*
Jacobi, *Karl Gustav Jacob*
Napier, *John*

Newton, *Isaac*
Pappus *of Alexandria*
Pascal, *Blaise*
Peirce, *Charles Sanders*
Penney, *William George*
Taylor, *Brook*
Thales
Turing, *Alan Mathison*
Wiener, *Norbert*
7 letters:
Babbage, *Charles*
D'Oresme, *Nicole*
Eudoxus *of Cnidus*
Fourier, *Jean Baptiste Joseph*
Galileo
Hawking, *Stephen William*
Hilbert, *David*
Khayyám, *Omar*
Laplace, *Pierre Simon*
Leibniz
Pearson, *Karl*
Penrose, *Roger*
Poisson, *Siméon Denis*
Ptolemy
Pytheas
Riemann, *Georg Friedrich Bernhard*
Russell, *Bertrand*
Shannon, *Claude*
8 letters:
Archytas
Clausius, *Rudolf Julius*
Dedekind, *Julius Wilhelm Richard*
De Fermat, *Pierre*

Einstein, *Albert*
Goldbach, *Christian*
Hamilton, *William Rowan*
Lagrange, *Joseph Louis*
Legendre, *Adrien Marie*
Lovelace, *Ada*
Mercator, *Gerardus*
Playfair, *John*
Poincaré, *Jules Henri*
9 letters:
Bernoulli, *Daniel*
Bernoulli, *Jacques*
Bernoulli, *Jean*
Descartes, *René*
Dirichlet, *Peter Gustav Lejeune*
Dunstable, *John*
Fibonacci, *Leonardo*
Minkowski, *Hermann*
Whitehead, *Alfred North*
10 letters:
Apollonius *of Perga*

Archimedes
Diophantos
Kolmogorov, *Andrei Nikolaevich*
Pythagoras
Torricelli, *Evangelista*
Von Neumann, *John*
11 letters:
Anaximander
Lobachevsky, *Nikolai Ivanovich*
Von Leibnitz, *Gottfried Wilhelm*
12 letters:
De Maupertuis, *Pierre Louis
Moreau*
Eratosthenes
13 letters:
Regiomontanus, *Johann Müller*
14 letters:
Le Rond Alembert, *Jean*

Medals

9 letters:
Iron Cross
10 letters:
Bronze Star
Silver Star
11 letters:
George Cross
Purple Heart

13 letters:
Croix de Guerre
Legion of Merit
Royal Red Cross
Victoria Cross
14 letters:
Légion d'Honneur

Medicine

BRANCHES OF MEDICINE

5 letters:
Legal
Space
6 letters:
Sports
7 letters:
Anatomy
Myology
Nuclear
Otology
Surgery
Urology
8 letters:
Aviation
Etiology
Forensic
Internal
Nosology

Oncology
Physical
Posology
Serology
Tocology
Tokology
Virology
9 letters:
Aetiology
Anaplasty
Andrology
Angiology
Audiology
Chiropody
Dentistry
Midwifery
Neurology
Nostology

Nutrition
Optometry
Orthotics
Osteology
Pathology
Radiology
Rhinology
10 letters:
Balneology
Cardiology
Embryology
Exodontics
Geratology
Geriatrics
Gynecology
Hematology
Immunology
Industrial

Nephrology
Obstetrics
Odontology
Orthoptics
Pediatrics
Preventive
Proctology
Psychiatry
Psychology
Toxicology
Trichology
Veterinary
11 letters:
Biomedicine
Dermatology
Diagnostics
Eccrinology
Endodontics
Gerontology
Gynaecology
Haematology
Laryngology

Neonatology
Oral hygiene
Orthodontia
Orthoptics
Osteoplasty
Paediatrics
Physiatrics
Stomatology
Syphilology
Venereology
12 letters:
Anaesthetics
Bacteriology
Epidemiology
Neuroanatomy
Neurosurgery
Orthodontics
Orthopaedics
Periodontics
Pharyngology
Rheumatology
Therapeutics

13 letters:
Dental hygiene
Dental surgery
Endocrinology
Genitourinary
Materia medica
Morbid anatomy
Ophthalmology
Physiotherapy
Speech therapy
14 letters:
Neuropathology
Otolaryngology
Plastic surgery
Psychoanalysis
Symptomatology
15 letters:
Bioastronautics
Encephalography
Immunochemistry
Neurophysiology
Neuropsychiatry

MEDICAL PRACTITIONERS AND SPECIALISTS

2 letters:
GP
3 letters:
Vet
5 letters:
Nurse
6 letters:
Doctor
Extern
Intern
Matron
Physio
7 letters:
Dentist
Externe
Interne
Midwife
Orderly
Surgeon
8 letters:
Houseman
Optician
Resident
9 letters:
Anatomist
Dietitian
Internist
Myologist
Orthotist
Otologist
Paramedic

Registrar
Therapist
Urologist
10 letters:
Consultant
Etiologist
Exodontist
Geriatrist
Nosologist
Oncologist
Orthoptist
Serologist
Virologist
11 letters:
Aetiologist
Andrologist
Audiologist
Chiropodist
Endodontist
Neurologist
Optometrist
Orthopedist
Osteologist
Pathologist
Radiologist
Rhinologist
12 letters:
Anaesthetist
Balneologist
Cardiologist
Embryologist

Geriatrician
Gynecologist
Hematologist
Immunologist
Junior doctor
Nephrologist
Neurosurgeon
Nutritionist
Obstetrician
Odontologist
Orthodontist
Orthopaedist
Pediatrician
Proctologist
Psychiatrist
Psychologist
Radiographer
Toxicologist
Trichologist
Veterinarian
13 letters:
Dental surgeon
Dermatologist
Diagnostician
District nurse
Gerontologist
Gynaecologist
Haematologist
Health visitor
Laryngologist
Neonatologist

Oral hygienist
Paediatrician
Psychoanalyst
Syphilologist
Venereologist
14 letters:
Bacteriologist
Barefoot doctor

Epidemiologist
House physician
Hydrotherapist
Neuroanatomist
Nursing officer
Pharyngologist
Plastic surgeon
Rheumatologist

15 letters:
Dental hygienist
Endocrinologist
Ophthalmologist
Physiotherapist
Speech therapist

MEDICAL AND SURGICAL INSTRUMENTS AND EQUIPMENT

4 letters:
Swab
5 letters:
Clamp
Curet
Drain
Lance
Probe
Sling
Sound
Stupe
6 letters:
Bedpan
Canula
Lancet
Needle
Splint
Stylet
Suture
Trepan
Trocar
7 letters:
Bandage
Cannula
Catling
Curette
Forceps
Packing
Scalpel
Scanner
Syringe
Wet pack
8 letters:
Bistoury
Catheter
Heat lamp
Hemostat
Iron lung
Otoscope
Pulmotor®
Speculum
Trephine

9 letters:
Aspirator
CT scanner
Cymograph
Depressor
Endoscope
Fetoscope
Haemostat
Inhalator
Kymograph
Nebulizer
Pacemaker
Perimeter
Raspatory
Retractor
Rheometer
Skiascope
Stretcher
10 letters:
CAT scanner
Colposcope
Compressor
Cystoscope
Fiberscope
Fibrescope
Gonioscope
Hypodermic
Inspirator
Microscope
Orthoscope
Oxygen mask
Oxygen tent
Respirator
Rhinoscope
Spirograph
Spirometer
Tourniquet
Urinometer
Ventilator
11 letters:
Arthroscope
Cardiograph

Colonoscope
Fluoroscope
Gamma camera
Gastroscope
Laparoscope
Nephroscope
Plaster cast
Pneumograph
Proctoscope
Retinoscope
Stethoscope
Stomach pump
X-ray machine
12 letters:
Bronchoscope
Laryngoscope
Resuscitator
Sphygmograph
Thoracoscope
Urethroscope
13 letters:
Defibrillator
Encephalogram
Esophagoscope
Kidney machine
Pharyngoscope
Pneumatometer
Röntgenoscope
Styptic pencil
14 letters:
Oesophagoscope
Ophthalmoscope
Roentgenoscope
Specimen bottle
15 letters:
Artificial heart
Dialysis machine
Electromyograph

BRANCHES OF ALTERNATIVE MEDICINE

7 letters:
Massage
Shiatsu
8 letters:
Hypnosis
9 letters:
Herbalism
Iridology
Radionics

10 letters:
Homeopathy
Osteopathy
11 letters:
Acupressure
Acupuncture
Biofeedback
Homoeopathy
Kinesiology

Moxibustion
Naturopathy
Reflexology
12 letters:
Aromatherapy
Chiropractic
Hydrotherapy
Hypnotherapy

PEOPLE IN MEDICINE

4 letters:
Bell, *Sir Charles*
Drew, *Charles*
Jung, *Carl*
Koch, *Robert*
Lind, *James*
Mayo, *Charles*
Reed, *Walter*
Ross, *Sir Ronald*
Salk, *Jonas E(dward)*
5 letters:
Broca, *Paul*
Bruce, *Sir David*
Cajal, *Santiago Ramon y*
Crick, *Francis*
Curie, *Marie*
Freud, *Sigmund*
Galen
Henle, *Friedrich*
Kenny, *Elizabeth*
Krebs, *Sir Edwin*
Leach, *Penelope*
Lower, *Richard*
Osler, *Sir William*
Paget, *Sir James*
Remak, *Robert*
Sharp, *Phillip*
Spock, *Benjamin*
Steno, *Nicolaus*
6 letters:
Barton, *Clara*
Bichat, *Marie*
Bishop, *Michael*
Bright, *Richard*
Carrel, *Alexis*
Cavell, *Edith Louisa*
Cooper, *Sir Astley*
Cuvier, *Georges*
Fernel, *Jean*
Finsen, *Niels*
Garrod, *Sir Archibald*

Harvey, *William*
Hunter, *John*
Inglis, *Elsie*
Jenner, *Edward*
Lister, *Joseph*
Manson, *Sir Patrick*
Mesmer, *Franz Anton*
Mullis, *Kary*
Pavlov, *Ivan*
Sanger, *Margaret*
Treves, *Sir Frederick*
Varmus, *Harold*
Watson, *James*
Watson, *John*
Willis, *Thomas*
7 letters:
Addison, *Thomas*
Axelrod, *Julius*
Banting, *Sir Frederick*
Barnard, *Christiaan*
Bethune, *Henry Norman*
Burkitt, *Denis*
Cushing, *Harvey*
Ehrlich, *Paul*
Eijkman, *Christian*
Fleming, *Sir Alexander*
Gilbert, *William*
Hodgkin, *Dorothy*
Hodgkin, *Thomas*
Laennec, *Rene*
Laveran, *Charles*
Linacre, *Thomas*
MacEwen, *Sir William*
McIndoe, *Sir Archibald*
Medawar, *Sir Peter*
Nicolle, *Charles*
Pasteur, *Louis*
Röntgen, *Wilhelm Conrad*
Seacole, *Mary Jane*
Simpson, *Sir James Young*
Warburg, *Otto*

Winston, *Lord Robert*
8 letters:
Anderson, *Elizabeth Garrett*
Avicenna
Beaumont, *William*
Billroth, *Theodor*
Charnley, *Sir John*
Delbruck, *Max*
Duchenne, *Guillaume*
Dulbecco, *Renato*
Geronimo
Jex-Blake, *Sophia*
Leishman, *Sir William*
Magendie, *Francois*
Malpighi, *Marcello*
Morgagni, *Giovanni*
Pattison, *Dorothy*
Stoppard, *Miriam*
Sydenham, *Thomas*
Tournier, *Paul*
Vesalius
9 letters:
Alzheimer, *Alois*

Bartholin, *Erasmus*
Blackwell, *Elizabeth*
Boerhaave, *Hermann*
Dupuytren, *Guillaume*
Dutrochet, *Henri*
Hahnemann, *Samuel*
Mackenzie, *Sir James*
Parkinson, *James*
10 letters:
Fracastoro, *Girolamo*
Greenfield, *Susan*
Langerhans, *Paul*
Paracelsus
Stephenson, *Elsie*
11 letters:
Hippocrates
Livingstone, *David*
Nightingale, *Florence*
Szent-Gyorgi, *Albert*
12 letters:
Erasistratus

Membranes

3 letters:
Haw
4 letters:
Dura
5 letters:
Exine
Mater
6 letters:
Amnion
Cornea
Extine
Intima
Intine
Meninx
Mucosa
Mucous
Pleura
Sclera
Serosa
Serous
Tympan
7 letters:
Chorion
Choroid
Decidua

Hyaloid
Periost
Putamen
8 letters:
Axilemma
Ependyma
Frenulum
Indusium
Patagium
Pericarp
Pia mater
Synovial
Tympanic
Vacuolar
9 letters:
Arachnoid
Dura mater
Endostium
Involucre
Mesentery
Tonoplast
Vitelline
10 letters:
Periosteum
Peritoneum

Sarcolemma
11 letters:
Chromoplast
Conjunctiva
Dissepiment
Endocardium
Endometrium
Mediastinum
Nictitating
Pericardium
Pericranium
Peritonaeum
Third eyelid
Trophoblast
12 letters:
Schneiderian
13 letters:
Choroid plexus
Perichondrium
15 letters:
Chorioallantois

Metals

Metal	Symbol	Metal	Symbol
Actinium	Ac	Molybdenum	Mo
Aluminium	Al	Neodymium	Nd
Americium	Am	Neptunium	Np
Antimony	Sb	Nickel	Ni
Barium	Ba	Niobium	Nb
Berkelium	Bk	Nobelium	No
Beryllium	Be	Osmium	Os
Bismuth	Bi	Palladium	Pd
Cadmium	Cd	Platinum	Pt
Caesium *or* cesium	Cs	Plutonium	Pu
Calcium	Ca	Polonium	Po
Californium	Cf	Potassium	K
Cerium	Ce	Praseodymium	Pr
Chromium	Cr	Promethium	Pm
Cobalt	Co	Protactinium	Pa
Copper	Cu	Radium	Ra
Curium	Cm	Rhenium	Re
Dysprosium	Dy	Rhodium	Rh
Einsteinium	Es	Rubidium	Rb
Erbium	Er	Ruthenium	Ru
Europium	Eu	Samarium	Sm
Fermium	Fm	Scandium	Sc
Francium	Fr	Silver	Ag
Gadolinium	Gd	Sodium	Na
Gallium	Ga	Strontium	Sr
Germanium	Ge	Tantalum	Ta
Gold	Au	Technetium	Tc
Hafnium	Hf	Terbium	Tb
Holmium	Ho	Thallium	Tl
Indium	In	Thorium	Th
Iridium	Ir	Thulium	Tm
Iron	Fe	Tin	Sn
Lanthanum	La	Titanium	Ti
Lawrencium	Lr	Tungsten *or* wolfram	W
Lead	Pb	Uranium	U
Lithium	Li	Vanadium	V
Lutetium	Lu	Ytterbium	Yb
Magnesium	Mg	Yttrium	Y
Manganese	Mn	Zinc	Zn
Mendelevium	Md	Zirconium	Zr
Mercury	Hg		

Meteor showers

6 letters:
Boötes
Cetids
Lyrids
Ursids
Velids
7 letters:
Corvids
Cygnids

Hydrids
Leonids
Librids
Mensids
Normids
Piscids
Puppids
Scutids
Taurids

8 letters:
Aquilids
Arietids
Aurigids
Cancrids
Geminids
Orionids
Pavonids
Pegasids

Perseids
9 letters:
Aquariids
Craterids
Draconids
Eridanids
Herculids
Scorpiids
Virginids
10 letters:
Centaurids

Phoenicids
Sextantids
11 letters:
Andromedids
Quadrantids
Triangulids
12 letters:
Capricornids
Monocerotids
Sagittariids
Ursa Majorids

13 letters:
Canis Minorids
14 letters:
Coma Berenicids

Military ranks

2 letters:
AB
AC
AM
BO
CO
FM
FO
Lt
MO
OS
PO
QM
RA
SM
VA
WO
3 letters:
ACM
Adm
AVM
Cdr
Col
COS
Cpl
CPO
CSM
Gen
LAC
Maj
NCO
Pte
RSM
Sgt
SMO
Tpr
4 letters:
Brig
Capt
Cdre
C-in-C

Corp
Genl
L-Cpl
MRAF
Sub L
5 letters:
Flt Lt
G Capt
Lt-Col
Lt-Gen
Major
Sergt
6 letters:
Col Sgt
Flt Sgt
Lt-Comm
Maj-Gen
Marine
Sqn-Ldr
7 letters:
Admiral
Captain
Colonel
General
Marshal
Private
8 letters:
Corporal
Sergeant
9 letters:
Brigadier
Commander
Commodore
Drum major
Subaltern
10 letters:
Able rating
Able seaman
Air marshal
Air officer
Lieutenant

Midshipman
11 letters:
Aircraftmen
Rear admiral
Vice admiral
12 letters:
Air commodore
Chief of staff
Field marshal
Field officer
Fleet admiral
Group captain
Major general
Petty officer
Pilot officer
13 letters:
Branch officer
Flying officer
Lance corporal
Leading rating
Master aircrew
Quartermaster
Sergeant major
Staff sergeant
Sublieutenant
Wing commander
14 letters:
Air vice-marshal
Colour sergeant
Flight engineer
Flight mechanic
Flight sergeant
Medical officer
Ordinary rating
Ordinary seaman
Squadron leader
Warrant officer
15 letters:
Air chief marshal
Chief technician

Minerals

4 letters:
Gang
Mica
Opal
Sard
Spar
Talc
Trap
Urao
5 letters:
Agate
Balas
Beryl
Borax
Chert
Emery
Flint
Fluor
Mafic
Nitre
Prase
Topaz
Trona
Umber
6 letters:
Acmite
Albite
Augite
Blende
Galena
Gangue
Garnet
Glance
Gypsum
Halite
Hauyne
Illite
Jargon
Jasper
Lithia
Norite
Nosean
Pinite
Pyrite
Quartz
Rutile
Schorl
Silica
Sphene
Spinel
Tincal
Zircon
7 letters:
Alunite
Amalgam

Anatase
Apatite
Axinite
Azurite
Barytes
Bauxite
Biotite
Bornite
Brucite
Calcite
Calomel
Catseye
Cuprite
Cyanite
Diamond
Dysodil
Epidote
Euclase
Eucrite
Fahlore
Felspar
Gahnite
Göthite
Gummite
Hessite
Ice spar
Jadeite
Jargoon
Kainite
Kernite
Kunzite
Kyanite
Leucite
Mellite
Mullite
Nacrite
Olivine
Pennine
Peridot
Pyrites
Realgar
Rosaker
Sylvine
Sylvite
Thorite
Thulite
Tripoli
Turgite
Ulexite
Uralite
Uranite
Uranium
Zeolite
Zincite
Zoisite

Zorgite
8 letters:
Adularia
Allanite
Analcime
Analcite
Andesine
Ankerite
Antimony
Aphanite
Asbestos
Autunite
Blue john
Boehmite
Boracite
Braunite
Brookite
Calamine
Cerusite
Chlorite
Chromite
Cinnabar
Cleveite
Corundum
Crocoite
Cryolite
Datolite
Dendrite
Diallage
Diaspore
Diopside
Dioptase
Disthene
Dolomite
Dysodile
Dysodyle
Epsomite
Erionite
Euxenite
Fayalite
Feldspar
Flinkite
Fluorite
Galenite
Gibbsite
Goethite
Graphite
Gyrolite
Hematite
Hyacinth
Idocrase
Ilmenite
Iodyrite
Jarosite
Lazulite

Lazurite
Lewisite
Limonite
Massicot
Melilite
Metamict
Mimetite
Monazite
Nephrite
Noselite
Orpiment
Petuntse
Petuntze
Prehnite
Pyroxene
Resalgar
Rock-salt
Sanidine
Saponite
Siderite
Smaltite
Smectite
Sodalite
Stannite
Stibnite
Stilbite
Taconite
Tenorite
Titanite
Troilite
Xenotime
Zaratite

9 letters:
Alabaster
Allophane
Amazonite
Amphibole
Anglesite
Anhydrite
Anorthite
Aragonite
Argentite
Atacamite
Blackjack
Blacklead
Carnelian
Carnotite
Celestine
Celestite
Cerussite
Chabazite
Cheralite
Chondrule
Cobaltine
Cobaltite
Coccolite
Columbate

Columbite
Covellite
Elaeolite
Enhydrite
Enstatite
Erythrite
Fibrolite®
Fluorspar
Gehlenite
Germanite
Geyserite
Gmelinite
Goslarite
Haematite
Harmotome
Hercynite
Hiddenite
Kaolinite
Kermesite
Kieserite
Magnesite
Magnetite
Malachite
Manganite
Marcasite
Margarite
Marialite
Microlite
Microlith
Millerite
Mispickel
Mizzonite
Monzonite
Moonstone
Muscovite
Natrolite
Nepheline
Nephelite
Niccolite
Nitratine
Olivenite
Ottrelite
Ozocerite
Ozokerite
Pargasite
Pectolite
Periclase
Pericline
Phenacite
Phenakite
Pleonaste
Polianite
Pollucite
Powellite
Proustite
Rhodonite
Rubellite

Scapolite
Scheelite
Scolecite
Spodumene
Sylvanite
Tantalite
Tremolite
Troostite
Tungstite
Turquoise
Uraninite
Uvarovite
Variscite
Vulpinite
Wavellite
Wernerite
Willemite
Witherite
Wulfenite
Zinkenite

10 letters:
Actinolite
Alabandine
Alabandite
Andalusite
Bastnasite
Calaverite
Carnallite
Chalcocite
Chessylite
Chrysolite
Chrysotile
Colemanite
Cordierite
Crocoisite
Dyscrasite
Forsterite
Gadolinite
Garnierite
Glauconite
Halloysite
Heulandite
Honey-stone
Hornblende
Indicolite
Indigolite
Jamesonite
Laurdalite
Meerschaum
Microcline
Oligoclase
Orthoclase
Perovskite
Phosgenite
Polybasite
Polyhalite
Pyrolusite

Pyroxenite
Pyrrhotine
Pyrrhotite
Redruthite
Riebeckite
Ripidolite
Samarskite
Sapphirine
Serpentine
Smaragdite
Sperrylite
Sphalerite
Staurolite
Tennantite
Thaumasite
Thenardite
Thorianite
Tiemannite
Torbernite
Tourmaline
Triphylite
Vanadinite
Wolframite
Zinckenite
11 letters:
Alexandrite
Amblygonite
Annabergite
Apophyllite

Baddeleyite
Bastnaesite
Cassiterite
Cerargyrite
Chiastolite
Chrysoberyl
Clay mineral
Clinochlore
Crocidolite
Dendrachate
Franklinite
Greenockite
Hypersthene
Josephinite
Labradorite
Lapis lazuli
Molybdenite
Pentlandite
Phosphorite
Piedmontite
Pitchblende
Psilomelane
Pyrargyrite
Sillimanite
Smithsonite
Tetradymite
Vermiculite
Vesuvianite
Ythro-cerite

12 letters:
Arfvedsonite
Arsenopyrite
Babingtonite
Bismuthinite
Chalcanthite
Chalcopyrite
Cristobalite
Dumortierite
Feldspathoid
Fluorapatite
Hemimorphite
Pyromorphite
Pyrophyllite
Senarmontite
Skutterudite
Strontianite
Synadelphite
Tetrahedrite
Wollastonite
13 letters:
Bismuth glance
Clinopyroxene
Cummingtonite
Rhodochrosite
15 letters:
Montmorillonite

Missiles

3 letters:
SAM
SSM
UAM
4 letters:
Ammo
Ball
Bolt
Bomb
Dart
ICBM
MIRV
Scud
Shot
SLBM
SLCM
Styx
Thor
5 letters:
Arrow
Atlas
Bolas
Kiley

Kyley
Kylie
Onion
Shell
Spear
Titan
6 letters:
Bullet
Cruise
Dum-dum
Exocet
Guided
Pellet
Rocket
Tracer
7 letters:
Dingbat
Grenade
Harpoon
Patriot
Polaris
Quarrel
Torpedo

Trident
Warhead
8 letters:
Air-to-air
Buzz bomb
Maverick
Pershing
Poseidon
Snowball
Standoff
9 letters:
Ballistic
Boomerang
Doodlebug
Fléchette
Minuteman
Smart bomb
10 letters:
Blue streak
Flying bomb
Side-winder
11 letters:
Interceptor

12 letters:
Surface to air

13 letters:
Anti-ballistic

Molecules

3 letters:
DNA
5 letters:
Codon
Dimer
Kinin
6 letters:
Chiral
Hapten
Isomer
Ligand
Trimer
7 letters:
Carbene

Monomer
Peptide
Polymer
Uridine
8 letters:
Acceptor
Cavitand
Coenzyme
Cofactor
Replicon
9 letters:
Buckyball
Cobalamin
Fullerene

Long-chain
Metameric
Semantide
10 letters:
Metabolite
11 letters:
Chromophore
Closed chain
Footballene
12 letters:
Enantiomorph
Stereoisomer
14 letters:
Polysaccharide

Monastic orders

6 letters:
Sangha
7 letters:
Cluniac
Saivite
Shaolin
8 letters:
Basilian
Trappist
Vaisnava
9 letters:
Capuchins
Carmelite

Celestine
Dominican
Mathurins
Red Friars
10 letters:
Bendictine
Carthusian
Cistercian
Feuillants
Franciscan
11 letters:
Augustinian
Bridgettine

Camaldolese
Gilbertines
Tironensian
White Canons
12 letters:
Redemptorist
Trinitarians
14 letters:
Knights Templar
Premonstratian

Monkeys, apes and other primates

3 letters:
Pug
Sai
4 letters:
Douc
Leaf
Mico
Mona
Nala
Saki
Tana
Titi
Zati
5 letters:
Cebus
Chimp

Diana
Drill
Green
Indri
Jocko
Lemur
Loris
Magot
Midas
Orang
Sajou
Silen
Toque
6 letters:
Aye-aye
Baboon

Bandar
Bonnet
Bonobo
Chacma
Coaita
Colugo
Galago
Gelada
Gibbon
Grison
Grivet
Guenon
Howler
Indris
Jackey
Langur

Macaco
Malmag
Monkey
Rhesus
Sagoin
Saguin
Sifaka
Simpai
Spider
Tee-tee
Uakari
Vervet
Wou-wou
Wow-wow
7 letters:
Cebidae
Colobus
Gorilla
Guereza
Hanuman
Hoolock
Jacchus
Macaque
Meerkat
Mycetes

Nasalis
Ouakari
Sagouin
Saimiri
Sapajou
Siamang
Silenus
Tamarin
Tarsier
Wistiti
8 letters:
Bushbaby
Capuchin
Durukuli
Entellus
Mandrill
Mangabey
Marmoset
Ouistiti
Squirrel
Talapoin
Wanderoo
9 letters:
Hylobates
Orang-utan

Phalanger
Proboscis
10 letters:
Barbary ape
Chimpanzee
Cynomolgus
Jackanapes
Silverback
11 letters:
Douroucouli
Flying lemur
Green monkey
Orang-outang
Platyrrhine
12 letters:
Bonnet monkey
Howler monkey
Rhesus monkey
Slender loris
Spider monkey
14 letters:
Squirrel monkey
15 letters:
Proboscis monkey

Monks

3 letters:
Dan
Dom
4 letters:
Bede
Lama
5 letters:
Abbot
Arhat
Black
Bonze
Bruno
Friar
Prior
6 letters:
Austin
Bhikhu
Culdee
Jerome
Mendel
Oblate
Sangha
7 letters:
Beghard
Brother

Caedmon
Caloyer
Cluniac
Félibre
Hegumen
Jacobin
Maurist
8 letters:
Acoemeti
Basilian
Cenobite
Jacobite
Olivetan
Pelagian
Rasputin
Salesian
Talapoin
Theatine
Trappist
9 letters:
Celestine
Coenobite
Dominican
Gyrovague
Hesychast

Thelemite
10 letters:
Bernardine
Carthusian
Cistercian
Hildebrand
Norbertine
Savonarola
Thelonious
11 letters:
Abbey-lubber
Augustinian
Benedictine
Bonaventura
Ignorantine
Mekhitarist
Tironensian
12 letters:
Bethlehemite
Mechitharist
13 letters:
Archimandrite
Thomas à Kempis

Monsters

3 letters:
Orc
4 letters:
Eten
Ogre
5 letters:
Ettin
Giant
Harpy
Hydra
Lamia
Snark
Teras
Troll
Yowie
6 letters:
Alecto
Bunyip
Dragon
Erebus
Geryon
Gorgon
Kraken
Medusa
Moloch

Nessie
Scylla
Simorg
Simurg
Sphinx
Typhon
Wyvern
7 letters:
Caliban
Chimera
Cyclops
Grendel
Simurgh
Taniwha
Vampire
Wendego
Wendigo
Werwolf
Ziffius
8 letters:
Asmodeus
Behemoth
Cerberus
Chimaera
Mastodon

Minotaur
Opinicus
Stegodon
Typhoeus
Werewolf
9 letters:
Dinoceras
Fire-drake
Leviathan
Stegosaur
Wasserman
10 letters:
Cockatrice
Hippogriff
Jabberwock
Sarsquatch
11 letters:
Chichevache
Hippocampus
Triceratops
12 letters:
Bandersnatch
Frankenstein

Mosses

3 letters:
Fog
Hag
4 letters:
Club
Hagg
Peat
Rose
5 letters:
Agate
Irish
Marsh
Usnea
6 letters:
Ceylon
Hypnum

Lichen
Litmus
7 letters:
Acrogen
Iceland
Lycopod
Muscoid
Parella
Spanish
8 letters:
Reindeer
Sphagnum
Staghorn
9 letters:
Carrageen
Lecanoram

Wolf's claw
10 letters:
Carragheen
Fontinalis
11 letters:
Polytrichum
Selaginella

Motor sports

7 letters:
Karting
8 letters:
Rallying
Speedway
9 letters:
Autocross

Motocross
10 letters:
Drag racing
Rallycross
Scrambling
11 letters:
Motor racing

13 letters:
Motor rallying
14 letters:
Stock car racing

Mountains

2 letters:
K2
3 letters:
Apo
Ida
Kaf
Ore
4 letters:
Alai
Blue
Bona
Cook
Etna
Fuji
Harz
Hoss
Isto
Jaya
Jura
Meru
Nebo
Oeta
Ossa
Rigi
Rosa
Viso
Zeil
5 letters:
Abora
Adams
Aldan
Altai
Amara
Andes
Aneto
Arber
Athos
Atlas
Badon
Black
Blanc
Coast
Corno
Djaja

Eiger
Ellis
Ghats
Green
Guyot
Hekla
Horeb
Idris
Kamet
Kenya
Leone
Logan
Marcy
Munro
Ozark
Rocky
Rydal
Sinai
Siple
Snowy
Table
Tabor
Tatra
Teide
Tyree
Urals
Welsh
6 letters:
Amhara
Anadyr
Arafat
Ararat
Averno
Balkan
Bogong
Carmel
Cho Oyu
Dragon
Egmont
Elbert
Elberz
Elbrus
Erebus
Gilead

Hermon
Hoggar
Hoosac
Kunlun
Lhotse
Makalu
Mourne
Musala
Negoiu
Ortles
Pamirs
Pelion
Pisgah
Pocono
Robson
Scopus
Sorata
Steele
Tasman
Taunus
Taurus
Vernon
Vosges
Zagros
7 letters:
Aorangi
Aragats
Arcadia
Belukha
Bernina
Brocken
Buffalo
Calvary
Cariboo
Cascade
Chianti
Corbett
Dapsang
Everest
Helicon
Kennedy
Khingan
Kuenlun
Lebanon

Lucania
Manaslu
Markham
Nan Shan
Olympus
Palomar
Perdido
Pilatus
Rainier
Rhodope
Scafell
Selkirk
Skiddaw
Snowdon
Sperrin
Stanley
Sudeten
Toubkal
Travers
Troglav
Whitney
Wicklow
Zard Kuh
8 letters:
Anai Mudi
Ben Nevis
Cambrian
Cevennes
Demavend
Estrella
Grampian
Hymettus
Illimani
Jungfrau
Kinabalu
King Peak
Klínovec
Leibnitz
McKinley
Mitchell
Mulhacén
Pennines
Pyrenees
Rushmore
Skalitsy
Smólikas
St Helen's
Taraniki
Tien Shan
Vesuvius
Victoria
Waun Fach
Wrangell
9 letters:
Aconcagua
Allegheny
Annapurna

Apennines
Argentera
Ben Lomond
Blackburn
Blue Ridge
Cairngorm
Catskills
Caucasian
Connemara
Corcovado
Demavrand
Dolomites
El Capitan
Emi Koussi
Grampians
Guadalupe
Helvellyn
Highlands
Himalayas
Hindu Kush
Inselberg
Jebel Musa
Karakoram
Kings Peak
Kosciusko
Lenin Peak
Longs Peak
Mansfield
Marmolada
Mont Blanc
Nanda Devi
Narodnaya
Parnassus
Pikes Peak
Puy de Dôme
Rock Creek
Sugarloaf
Tirich Mir
Vancouver
Venusberg
Weisshorn
Woodroffe
Zugspitze
10 letters:
Arakan Yoma
Ben Macdhui
Blanca Peak
Cantabrian
Carpathian
Delectable
Dhaulagiri
Erymanthus
Erzgebirge
Gannet Peak
Grand Teton
Great Gable
Harney Peak

Horselberg
Kongur Shan
Laurentian
Masharbrum
Matterhorn
Monte Corno
Montserrat
Pentelikon
Piz Bernina
Pobeda Peak
Puncak Jaya
Puy de Sancy
St Michael's
Tengri Khan
Timpanogos
Waddington
Washington
Wellington
11 letters:
Adirondacks
Alaska Range
Appalachian
Aran Fawddwy
Bartle Frere
Bimberi Peak
Brooks Range
Drakensberg
Fairweather
Gerlachovka
Kilimanjaro
Kolyma Range
Munku-Sardyk
Nanga Parbat
Salmon River
Scafell Pike
Schneekoppe
Sierra Madre
Sir Sandford
12 letters:
Albert Edward
Cascade Range
Citlaltépetl
Godwin Austen
Gran Paradiso
Kanchenjunga
Ruahine Range
Sierra Nevada
Slieve Donard
Tararua Range
Ulugh Muztagh
Victoria Peak
Vinson Massif
Western Ghats
13 letters:
Carmarthen Van
Carrantuohill
Clingman's Dome

Croagh Patrick
Flinders Range
Grossglockner
Humphreys Peak
Kangchenjunga
Massif Central
Mount of Olives
Petermann Peak
San Bernardino
Slide Mountain

Table Mountain
White Mountain
14 letters:
Bohemian Forest
Carnarvon Range
Finsteraarhorn
Hamersley Range
Kaikoura Ranges
Kommunizma
  Peak

Liverpool Range
Musgrove Ranges
Ruwenzori Range
Stirling Ranges
15 letters:
Cerro de Mulhacén
Uncompahgre
  Peak

Murderers

4 letters:
Cain
Gacy, *John*
Gein, *Ed*
Ruby, *Jack*
West, *Fred*
West, *Rosemary*
5 letters:
Booth, *John Wilkes*
Brady, *Ian*
Ellis, *Ruth*
6 letters:
Bonney, *William*
Borden, *Lizzie*
Corday, *Charlotte*
Graham, *Barbara*

Manson, *Charles*
Oswald, *Lee Harvey*
Pearce, *Charlie*
Sirhan, *Sirhan*
7 letters:
Chapman, *Mark*
Crippen, *Hawley*
Gilmore, *Gary*
Hindley, *Myra*
Huntley, *Ian*
Macbeth
Panzram, *Carl*
Shipman, *Harold*
Wuornos, *Aileen*
8 letters:
Chessman, *Caryl*

Christie, *John*
9 letters:
Bible John
Hauptmann, *Bruno*
Sutcliffe, *Peter*
11 letters:
Billy the Kid
13 letters:
Jack the Ripper
14 letters:
Leopold and Loeb
Moors Murderers
15 letters:
Boston Strangler
Yorkshire Ripper

Muscles

3 letters:
Abs
Lat
Pec
4 letters:
Pecs
Quad
5 letters:
Psoas
Teres
Tonus
6 letters:
Biceps
Flexor
Pathos
Rectus
Smooth
Soleus
Tensor
Thenar
7 letters:
Agonist
Ciliary

Deltoid
Dilator
Erecter
Erector
Evertor
Gluteus
Iliacus
Laxator
Levator
Pylorus
Rotator
Sarcous
Scalene
Sthenic
Triceps
8 letters:
Abductor
Adductor
Effector
Elevator
Extensor
Glutaeus
Kreatine

Masseter
Occlusor
Omohyoid
Opponent
Pectoral
Peroneus
Platysma
Pronator
Risorius
Scalenus
Serratus
Splenial
Striated
9 letters:
Arytenoid
Attollens
Cremaster
Depressor
Diaphragm
Digastric
Hamstring
Perforans
Quadratus

Retractor
Sartorius
Sphincter
Supinator
Suspensor
Tenaculum
Trapezius
Voluntary
10 letters:
Antagonist
Buccinator

Compressor
Contractor
Corrugator
Perforatus
Protractor
Quadriceps
Sarcolemma
Suspensory
11 letters:
Accelerator
Accessorius

Constrictor
Lumbricalis
Rhomboideus
13 letters:
Gastrocnemius
14 letters:
Gluteus maximus
Peroneal muscle
15 letters:
Latissimus dorsi

Muses

Name	Muse of
Calliope	Epic poetry
Clio	History
Erato	Love poetry
Euterpe	Lyric poetry and music
Melpomene	Tragedy
Polyhymnia	Singing, mime, and sacred dance
Terpsichore	Dance and choral song
Thalia	Comedy and pastoral poetry
Urania	Astronomy

Mushrooms and other edible fungi

3 letters:
Cep
5 letters:
Enoki
Horse
Hypha
Magic
Morel
6 letters:
Agaric
Blewit
Button
Hyphal
Ink-cap
Meadow
Oyster
Waxcap
7 letters:
Blewits

Parasol
Porcini
Porcino
Truffle
8 letters:
Penny-bun
Puffball
Shiitake
9 letters:
Fly agaric
Gyromitra
10 letters:
Champignon
Lawyer's wig
Liberty cap
Shaggymane
11 letters:
Chanterelle
Velvet shank

12 letters:
Black truffle
Horn of plenty
Scotch bonnet
Shaggy ink cap
White truffle
13 letters:
Straw mushroom
14 letters:
Button mushroom
Meadow mushroom
Oyster mushroom
15 letters:
Wood ear mushroom

Music

CLASSICAL MUSIC GENRES

5 letters:
Early
Salon
6 letters:
Galant
Gothic
Rococo
Serial
7 letters:
Ars nova
Baroque

8 letters:
Romantic
9 letters:
Classical
10 letters:
Ars antiqua
Minimalist
Twelve-tone
11 letters:
Nationalist
Renaissance

12 letters:
Dodecaphonic
Neoclassical
Post-romantic
13 letters:
Expressionist
Impressionist
Music concrète

TYPES OF COMPOSITION

3 letters:
Air
Duo
4 letters:
Aria
Duet
Lied
Mass
Raga
Reel
Song
Trio
5 letters:
Canon
Dirge
Dumka
Elegy
Étude
Fugue
Galop
Gigue
March
Motet
Nonet
Octet
Opera
Polka
Psalm
Suite
Waltz
6 letters:
Anthem
Ballet
Bolero
Chorus
Lament
Medley
Minuet

Pavane
Septet
Sextet
Sonata
7 letters:
Ballade
Bourrée
Cantata
Canzona
Canzone
Chorale
Czardas
Fantasy
Gavotte
Ländler
Mazurka
Partita
Passion
Pibroch
Prelude
Quartet
Quintet
Requiem
Romance
Scherzo
Toccata
8 letters:
Barceuse
Canticle
Cavatina
Chaconne
Concerto
Fantasia
Galliard
Hornpipe
Madrigal
Nocturne
Notturno

Operetta
Oratorio
Overture
Part song
Pastiche
Phantasy
Rhapsody
Ricercar
Rigadoon
Rigadoun
Serenade
Sonatina
Symphony
Tone poem
9 letters:
Allemande
Bagatelle
Barcarole
Capriccio
Ecossaise
Farandole
Impromptu
Interlude
Passepied
Pastorale
Polonaise
Quadrille
Ricercare
Singspiel
Song cycle
10 letters:
Albumblatt
Canzonetta
Concertino
Grand opera
Humoresque
Opera buffa
Opera seria

Strathspey
Trio sonata
11 letters:
Concertante
Contradance
Contredanse

Passacaglia
Schottische
Sinfonietta
12 letters:
Concertstück
Divertimento

13 letters:
Symphonic poem
14 letters:
Concerto grosso
Divertissement

POPULAR MUSIC TYPES

3 letters:
AOR
Bop
Dub
Pop
Rag
Rai
Rap
Ska
4 letters:
Folk
Funk
Go-go
Goth
Jazz
Loco
Punk
Rave
Rock
Romo
Soca
Soul
Trad
Zouk
5 letters:
Bebop
Blues
Cajun
Cu-bop
Disco
Dream
Early
House
Indie
Kwela
Muzak®
Neume
P-funk
Piped
Ragga
Salon
Salsa
Sokah
Swing
6 letters:
Bebung
Doo-wop

Fusion
Gagaku
Garage
Gospel
Gothic
Grunge
Hip-hop
Jungle
Khayal
Marabi
Motown®
New Age
Reggae
Techno
Thrash
Trance
Zydeco
7 letters:
Ambient
Bhangra
Britpop
Calypso
Ceilidh
Chamber
Country
Gangsta
Hardbag
Hardbop
Klezmer
New Wave
Pibroch
Qawwali
Ragtime
Skiffle
Soukous
Trip hop
Ziganka
8 letters:
Acid jazz
Acid rock
Bluebeat
Concrete
Cool jazz
Flamenco
Folk rock
Free jazz
Glam rock

Hardcore
Hard rock
High life
Jazz-funk
Jazz-rock
Karnatak
Lollipop
Mariachi
Mbaqanga
Punk rock
Trad jazz
9 letters:
Acid house
Bluegrass
Bubblegum
Dixieland
Folk music
Hillbilly
Honky-tonk
Rock'n'roll
Spiritual
Surf music
Swingbeat
Technopop
Warehouse
10 letters:
Chopsticks
Death metal
Gangsta rap
Gothic rock
Heavy metal
Hindustani
Industrial
Merseybeat
Modern jazz
New Country
Rockabilly
Rocksteady
Urban blues
World music
11 letters:
Country rock
Harmolodics
Motor rhythm
New romantic
Psychobilly
Raggamuffin

Rock and roll
Stadium rock
Third stream
Thrash metal
12 letters:
Boogie-woogie

Country blues
13 letters:
Detroit techno
14 letters:
Mainstream jazz
New Orleans jazz

Rhythm and blues
15 letters:
Musique concrete
Progressive rock

MUSICAL MODES

Mode	Final note
I Dorian	D
II Hypodorian	A
III Phrygian	E
IV Hypophrygian	B
V Lydian	F
VI Hypolydian	C
VII Mixolydian	G
VIII Hypomixolydian	D
IX Aeolian	A
X Hypoaeolian	E
XI Ionian	C
XII Hypoionian	G

MUSICAL INSTRUMENTS

2 letters:
Ax
Gu
3 letters:
Axe
Gue
Kit
Lur
Oud
Saz
Uke
Zel
4 letters:
Bell
Crwd
Drum
Fife
Gong
Harp
Horn
Kora
Koto
Lure
Lute
Lyre
Moog®
Oboe
Pipa
Pipe
Rate

Reed
Rote
Sang
Tuba
Vina
Viol
Whip
Zeze
5 letters:
Aulos
Banjo
Bongo
Bugle
Cello
Chime
Clave
Cobza
Conga
Corno
Crowd
Crwth
Dobro®
Flute
Guiro
Gusla
Gusle
Gusli
Kazoo
Mbira
Naker

Nebel
Ngoma
Organ
Piano
Quena
Rebec
Regal
Sanko
Sansa
Sarod
Shalm
Shawm
Sitar
Tabla
Tabor
Tibia
Veena
Viola
Zanze
Zinke
6 letters:
Antara
Cither
Citole
Cornet
Cymbal
Euphon
Fiddle
Flugel
Guitar

Kanoon
Maraca
Poogye
Racket
Rebeck
Ribibe
Sancho
Santir
Santur
Shalme
Sittar
Spinet
Syrinx
Tabour
Tam-tam
Timbal
Tom-tom
Trigon
Tymbal
Vielle
Violin
Zither
Zufolo
7 letters:
Alphorn
Althorn
Bagpipe
Bandore
Bandura
Baryton
Bassoon
Bazooka
Bodhrán
Celesta
Celeste
Cembalo
Chikara
Cithara
Cithern
Cittern
Clarion
Clavier
Console
Cornett
Cowbell
Cymbalo
Dichord
Dulcian
Fagotto
Flutina
Gamelan
Gittern
Hautboy
Helicon
High-hat
Kalimba
Kantela

Kantele
Kithara
Klavier
Lyricon
Mandola
Marimba
Musette
Ocarina
Pandora
Pandore
Pandura
Pianola®
Piccolo
Poogyee
Posaune
Rackett
Sackbut
Sambuca
Samisen
Santour
Sarangi
Saxhorn
Saxtuba
Serpent
Sistrum
Tambour
Tambura
Theorbo
Timbrel
Timpani
Trumpet
Tympani
Tympany
Ukelele
Ukulele
Vihuela
Violone
Vocoder
Whistle
Zuffolo
8 letters:
Angklung
Archlute
Autoharp®
Bagpipes
Barytone
Bass drum
Bass viol
Bouzouki
Calliope
Canorous
Carillon
Charango
Cimbalom
Cimbalon
Clarinet
Clarsach

Clavecin
Cornetto
Cornpipe
Cromorna
Cromorne
Crumhorn
Cymbalon
Dulcimer
Gemshorn
Guarneri
Guimbard
Handbell
Hautbois
Hornpipe
Humstrum
Jew's-harp
Keyboard
Key-bugle
Langspel
Lyra viol
Mandolin
Manzello
Martenot
Melodeon
Melodica
Melodion
Mirliton
Ottavino
Panpipes
Phorminx
Polyphon
Psaltery
Recorder
Reco-reco
Reed pipe
Side drum
Slughorn
Spinette
Sticcado
Sticcato
Surbahar
Tamboura
Tamburin
Tenoroon
Theremin®
Triangle
Trombone
Virginal
Vocalion
Zambomba
Zampogna
9 letters:
Accordion
Alpenhorn
Baby grand
Balalaika
Bandoneon

Baryulele
Böhm flute
Bombardon
Castanets
Chalumeau
Cornemuse
Decachord
Euphonium
Flageolet
Flexatone
Gittarone
Gran cassa
Gutbucket
Harmonica
Harmonium
Idiophone
Kent-bugle
Krummhorn
Langspiel
Mandoline
Monochord
Mouth-harp
Nose flute
Octachord
Orpharion
Pantaleon
Pastorale
Polyphone
Reed organ
Saxophone
Seraphine
Slughorne
Snare drum
Sopranino
Stockhorn
Trompette
Washboard
Welsh harp
Wood block
Wurlitzer®
Xylophone
Xylorimba
10 letters:
Basset horn
Bass guitar
Bullroarer

Chitarrone
Clavichord
Concertina
Contrabass
Cor anglais
Didgeridoo
Double bass
Flugelhorn
French horn
Gramophone
Grand piano
Hurdy-gurdy
Kettledrum
Mellophone
Mouth organ
Oboe d'amore
Ophicleide
Orpheoreon
Pantachord
Shakuhachi
Sousaphone
Squeeze-box
Steam organ
Stylophone
Symphonium
Tambourine
Thumb piano
Vibraphone
11 letters:
Aeolian harp
Bach trumpet
Barrel organ
Chordophone
Clairschach
Contrabasso
Drum machine
English horn
Harmoniphon
Harpsichord
Heckelphone
Hunting horn
Nickelodeon
Orchestrina
Orchestrion
Phonofiddle
Player piano

Slide guitar
Square piano
Steel guitar
Straduarius
Synthesizer
Trump-marine
Viola d'amore
Violoncello
12 letters:
Boudoir grand
Chamber organ
Chapman stick®
Chinese block
Clavicembalo
Concert grand
Cottage piano
Glockenspiel
Hammond organ®
Harmoniphone
Metallophone
Oboe da caccia
Penny whistle
Sarrusophone
Stock and horn
Stradivarius
Tromba-marina
Tubular bells
Uillean pipes
Upright piano
Viola da gamba
13 letters:
Contrabassoon
Contrafagotto
Double bassoon
Ondes Martenot
Panharmonicon
Physharmonica
Spanish guitar
14 letters:
Electric guitar
Glass harmonica
Hawaiian guitar
Portative organ
Viola da braccio
15 letters:
Electronic organ

See also:
➤ **Composers** ➤ **Jazz forms** ➤ **Jazz musicians** ➤ **Jazz terms**
➤ **Notes and rests** ➤ **Orchestral instruments** ➤ **Works of literature and music**

Musketeers

5 letters:
Athos
6 letters:

Aramis
7 letters:
Porthos

9 letters:
D'Artagnan

Mythology

CHARACTERS IN CLASSICAL MYTHOLOGY

2 letters:
Io
4 letters:
Ajax
Dido
Echo
Leda
5 letters:
Atlas
Circe
Helen
Ixion
Jason
Medea
Midas
Minos
Muses
Niobe
Orion
Paris
Priam
Remus
Sibyl
6 letters:
Adonis
Aeneas
Castor
Charon
Europa
Hector
Hecuba
Icarus

Medusa
Pollux
Psyche
Semele
Thisbe
7 letters:
Actaeon
Amazons
Arachne
Ariadne
Calypso
Electra
Galatea
Jocasta
Oedipus
Orestes
Orpheus
Pandora
Perseus
Pyramus
Romulus
Silenus
Theseus
Ulysses
8 letters:
Achilles
Antigone
Atalanta
Callisto
Daedalus
Eurydice
Ganymede

Heracles
Hercules
Menelaus
Odysseus
Penelope
Pleiades
Sisyphus
Tantalus
Tiresias
9 letters:
Agamemnon
Andromeda
Argonauts
Cassandra
Narcissus
Pygmalion
10 letters:
Andromache
Cassiopeia
Hippolytus
Hyacinthus
Persephone
Polydeuces
Polyphemus
Prometheus
Proserpina
12 letters:
Clytemnestra
14 letters:
Hermaphroditus

PLACES IN CLASSICAL MYTHOLOGY

4 letters:
Styx
Troy
5 letters:
Hades
Lethe
6 letters:
Erebus
Thebes
7 letters:
Acheron

Colchis
Elysium
Helicon
Olympus
8 letters:
Tartarus
9 letters:
Parnassus
10 letters:
Phlegethon

MYTHOLOGICAL CREATURES

3 letters:
Elf
Fay
Nix
Orc
Roc
4 letters:
Faun
Fury
Peri
5 letters:
Afrit
Dryad
Dwarf
Fairy
Genie
Giant
Harpy
Hydra
Jinni
Kylin
Lamia
Naiad
Nixie
Nymph
Oread
Pixie
Satyr
Siren
Sylph

Troll
6 letters:
Afreet
Bunyip
Djinni
Djinny
Dragon
Geryon
Goblin
Gorgon
Hobbit
Jinnee
Kelpie
Kraken
Merman
Nereid
Scylla
Sphinx
7 letters:
Banshee
Centaur
Chimera
Cyclops
Echidna
Erlking
Gremlin
Grendel
Griffin
Griffon
Gryphon

Mermaid
Oceanid
Phoenix
Tricorn
Unicorn
8 letters:
Basilisk
Behemoth
Cerberus
Chimaera
Minotaur
9 letters:
Charybdis
Hamadryad
Hobgoblin
Impundulu
Leviathan
Tokoloshe
Wood nymph
10 letters:
Cockatrice
Hippogriff
Hippogryph
Leprechaun
Salamander
Water nymph
11 letters:
Androsphinx
Hippocampus

CHARACTERS IN NORSE MYTHOLOGY

3 letters:
Ask
Lif
4 letters:
Atli
5 letters:
Mimir
Regin

6 letters:
Fafnir
Gudrun
Gunnar
Sigurd
7 letters:
Andvari
Sigmund

Wayland
8 letters:
Brynhild
Gutthorn
Hreidmar
10 letters:
Lifthrasir

PLACES IN NORSE MYTHOLOGY

3 letters:
Hel
4 letters:
Hela
6 letters:
Asgard
Utgard

7 letters:
Asgarth
Bifrost
Midgard
8 letters:
Midgarth
Niflheim

Valhalla
9 letters:
Jotunheim
10 letters:
Jotunnheim

See also:
➤ **Ancient cities** ➤ **Arthurian legend** ➤ **Fates** ➤ **Giants and giantesses** ➤ **Gods and Goddesses** ➤ **Gorgons** ➤ **Graces** ➤ **Greeks** ➤ **Harpies** ➤ **Hercules** ➤ **Monsters** ➤ **Muses** ➤ **Rivers of Hell** ➤ **Seven against Thebes** ➤ **Wonders of the ancient world**

Nerves

4 letters:	**7 letters:**	**10 letters:**
Axon	Cranial	Commissure
5 letters:	Excitor	Perikaryon
Cyton	Sciatic	Trigeminal
Nidus	Synapse	**11 letters:**
Optic	**8 letters:**	Octulomotor
Ulnar	Acoustic	Solar plexus
Vagus	Ganglion	**12 letters:**
6 letters:	**9 letters:**	Baroreceptor
Bouton	Depressor	Electrotonus
Facial	Epicritic	**13 letters:**
Myelon	Trochlear	Proprioceptor
Radial		

Nobility

RANKS OF BRITISH NOBILITY (IN ORDER OF PRECEDENCE)

Royal duke	Marquis	Viscountess
Royal duchess	Marchioness	Baron
Duke	Earl	Baroness
Duchess	Countess	Baronet
Marquess	Viscount	

RANKS OF FOREIGN NOBILITY

5 letters:
Boyar
Count
6 letters:
Prince
7 letters:
Grandee
Marquis
Vicomte
8 letters:
Archduke
Burgrave

Countess
Marchesa
Marchese
Margrave
Marquise
Princess
9 letters:
Grand duke
Landgrave
10 letters:
Margravine
Vicomtesse

11 letters:
Archduchess
Landgravine
12 letters:
Grand duchess

Notes and rests

British name	American name
Breve	Double-whole note
Semibreve	Whole note
Minim	Half note
Crotchet	Quarter note
Quaver	Eighth note
Semiquaver	Sixteenth note
Demisemiquaver	Thirty-second note
Hemidemisemiquaver	Sixty-fourth note

Novelists

2 letters:
Mo, *Timothy*
Oë, *Kenzaburo*
3 letters:
Eco, *Umberto*
Lee, *Harper*
Lee, *Laurie*
Nye, *Robert*
Rao, *Raja*
4 letters:
Amis, *Kingsley*
Amis, *Martin (Louis)*
Behn, *Aphra*
Bely, *Andrei*
Böll, *Heinrich*
Boyd, *William*
Buck, *Pearl*
Cela, *Camilo José*
Dunn, *Nell*
Fast, *Howard*
Ford, *Ford Madox*
Ford, *Richard*
Gide, *André (Paul Guillaume)*
Gold, *Herbert*

Gray, *Alasdair*
Hill, *Susan*
Hogg, *James*
Hope (Hawkins), *Sir Anthony*
Hugo, *Victor (Marie)*
Jong, *Erica*
King, *Francis*
King, *Stephen (Edwin)*
Levi, *Primo*
Mann, *Thomas*
Okri, *Ben*
Puzo, *Mario*
Read, *Piers Paul*
Rhys, *Jean*
Roth, *Henry*
Saki
Sand, *George*
Snow, *C(harles) P(ercy)*
Uris, *Leon*
Wain, *John*
West, *Morris*
West, *Rebecca*
Wouk, *Herman*
Zola, *Émile*

5 letters:
Adams, *Douglas*
Adams, *Richard*
Anand, *Mulk Raj*
Banks, *Iain*
Banks, *Lynne Reid*
Barth, *John*
Bates, *H(erbert) E(rnest)*
Bowen, *Elizabeth*
Bragg, *Melvin*
Brink, *André*
Brown, *George Douglas*
Brown, *George Mackay*
Byatt, *A(ntonia) S(usan)*
Camus, *Albert*
Carey, *Peter*
Crane, *Stephen*
Defoe, *Daniel*
Desai, *Anita*
Doyle, *Arthur Conan*
Doyle, *Roddy*
Duffy, *Maureen*
Dumas, *Alexandre*
Eliot, *George*
Elkin, *Stanley*
Ellis, *Alice Thomas*
Elton, *Ben*
Figes, *Eva*
Frame, *Janet Paterson*
Frayn, *Michael*
Gogol, *Nikolai Vasilievich*
Gorky, *Maxim*
Gosse, *Sir Edmund (William)*
Grass, *Günter (Wilhelm)*
Hardy, *Thomas*
Hesse, *Hermann*
Heyer, *Georgette*
Hines, *Barry*
Hoban, *Russell*
Hulme, *Keri*
Innes, *(Ralph) Hammond*
James, *Henry*
James, *P(hyllis) D(orothy)*
Joyce, *James (Augustine Aloysius)*
Kafka, *Franz*
Keane, *Molly*
Kesey, *Ken*
Lewis, *(Harry) Sinclair*
Llosa, *Mario Vargos*
Lodge, *David (John)*
Lowry, *(Clarence) Malcolm*
Lurie, *Alison*
Marsh, *Ngaio*
Moore, *Brian*
Newby, *P(ercy) H(oward)*
Oates, *Joyce Carol*
O'Hara, *John*

Orczy, *Baroness Emmuska*
Ouida
Ozick, *Cynthia*
Paton, *Alan (Stewart)*
Peake, *Mervyn*
Powys, *John Cowper*
Queen, *Ellery*
Rolfe, *Frederick William*
Scott, *Sir Walter*
Selby, *Hubert Jr*
Shute, *Nevil*
Simon, *Claude*
Smith, *Iain Crichton*
Smith, *Zadie*
Spark, *Dame Muriel (Sarah)*
Stead, *C K*
Stein, *Gertrude*
Stone, *Robert*
Stowe, *Harriet Elizabeth Beecher*
Swift, *Graham*
Swift, *Jonathan*
Toole, *John Kennedy*
Tuohy, *Frank*
Twain, *Mark (Samuel L Clemens)*
Tyler, *Anne*
Verne, *Jules*
Vidal, *Gore*
Waugh, *Evelyn (Arthur St John)*
Wells, *H(erbert) G(eorge)*
Welsh, *Irvine*
Welty, *Eudora*
White, *Antonia*
White, *Patrick*
White, *T(erence) H(anbury)*
Wilde, *Oscar (Fingal O'Flahertie
    Wills)*
Wolfe, *Thomas Clayton*
Wolfe, *Tom*
Wolff, *Tobias*
Woolf, *(Adeline) Virginia*
Yerby, *Frank*
6 letters:
Achebe, *Chinua*
Aldiss, *Brian*
Ambler, *Eric*
Archer, *Jeffrey*
Asimov, *Isaac*
Atwood, *Margaret*
Austen, *Jane*
Barker, *Elspeth*
Barker, *Pat*
Barnes, *Julian*
Bawden, *Nina*
Bellow, *Saul*
Berger, *John*
Berger, *Thomas*
Binchy, *Maeve*

Bowles, *Paul*
Braine, *John (Gerard)*
Brontë, *Anne*
Brontë, *Charlotte*
Brontë, *Emily (Jane)*
Brophy, *Brigid*
Buchan, *John*
Bunyan, *John*
Burney, *Fanny*
Butler, *Samuel*
Capote, *Truman*
Carter, *Angela*
Cather, *Willa*
Clarke, *Arthur C(harles)*
Cleary, *Jon*
Condon, *Richard*
Conrad, *Joseph*
Cooper, *James Fenimore*
Cooper, *Jilly*
Cooper, *William*
Davies, *(William) Robertson*
De Sade, *Marquis*
Didion, *Joan*
Farmer, *Philip José*
Fowles, *John (Robert)*
Fraser, *Antonia*
French, *Marilyn*
Fuller, *Roy*
Gaddis, *William*
Garner, *Helen*
Gibbon, *Lewis Grassic*
Godden, *(Margaret) Rumer*
Godwin, *William*
Goethe, *Johann Wolfgang von*
Graham, *Winston*
Graves, *Robert (Ranke)*
Greene, *(Henry) Graham*
Hailey, *Arthur*
Heller, *Joseph*
Hilton, *James*
Holtby, *Winifred*
Horgan, *Paul*
Howard, *Elizabeth Jane*
Hughes, *Thomas*
Hunter, *Evan*
Huxley, *Aldous (Leonard)*
Irving, *John*
Kaplan, *Johanna*
Kelman, *James*
Le Fanu, *(Joseph) Sheridan*
Le Guin, *Ursula*
Lively, *Penelope*
London, *Jack*
Mailer, *Norman (Kingsley)*
Malouf, *David*
Massie, *Allan*
McEwan, *Ian*

Miller, *Henry (Valentine)*
Mosley, *Nicholas*
O'Brien, *Edna*
O'Brien, *Flann*
Orwell, *George*
Passos, *John Roderigo Dos*
Porter, *Harold*
Porter, *Katherine Anne*
Powell, *Anthony*
Proulx, *E Annie*
Proust, *Marcel*
Rankin, *Ian*
Sartre, *Jean-Paul*
Sayers, *Dorothy L(eigh)*
Sharpe, *Tom*
Singer, *Isaac Bashevis*
Spring, *Howard*
Sterne, *Laurence*
Stoker, *Bram*
Storey, *David (Malcolm)*
Styron, *William*
Symons, *Julian*
Trevor, *William*
Updike, *John (Hoyer)*
Upward, *Edward (Falaise)*
Walker, *Alice*
Warner, *Marina*
Warren, *Robert Penn*
Weldon, *Fay*
Wesley, *Mary*
Wilder, *Thornton*
Wilson, *A(ndrew) N(orman)*
Wright, *Richard Nathaniel*
7 letters:
Ackroyd, *Peter*
Alvarez, *Al*
Angelou, *Maya*
Ballard, *J(ames) G(raham)*
Barstow, *Stanley*
Bedford, *Sybille*
Bennett, *(Enoch) Arnold*
Burgess, *Anthony*
Burrows, *Edgar Rice*
Calvino, *Italo*
Canetti, *Elias*
Clavell, *James*
Coetzee, *J(ohn) M(ichael)*
Colette, *(Sidonie-Gabrielle)*
Collins, *Wilkie (William)*
Connell, *Evan*
Cookson, *Catherine*
DeLillo, *Don*
De Vries, *Peter*
Dickens, *Charles (John Huffam)*
Dickens, *Monica*
Dinesen, *Isak*
Drabble, *Margaret*

Durrell, *Gerald (Malcolm)*
Durrell, *Laurence*
Fleming, *Ian*
Forster, *E(dward) M(organ)*
Forsyth, *Frederick*
Francis, *Dick*
Gaskell, *Elizabeth*
Gibbons, *Stella*
Gilliat, *Penelope*
Gissing, *George (Robert)*
Glasgow, *Ellen*
Golding, *Sir William (Gerald)*
Goldman, *William*
Grisham, *John*
Haggard, *Sir H(enry) Rider*
Hartley, *L(eslie) P(oles)*
Hazzard, *Shirley*
Hurston, *Zora Neale*
Kennedy, *Margaret*
Kerouac, *Jack*
Kipling, *(Joseph) Rudyard*
Kundera, *Milan*
Lamming, *George*
Le Carré, *John*
Lehmann, *Rosamond*
Lessing, *Doris*
MacLean, *Alistair*
Mahfouz, *Naguib*
Malamud, *Bernard*
Manning, *Olivia*
Márquez, *Gabriel García*
Marryat, *(Captain) Frederick*
Maugham, *W(illiam) Somerset*
Mauriac, *François*
Mishima, *Yukio*
Mitford, *Nancy*
Murdoch, *Dame (Jean) Iris*
Nabokov, *Vladimir (Vladimirovich)*
Naipaul, *Sir V(idiadhar) S(urajprasad)*
Peacock, *Thomas Love*
Pynchon, *Thomas*
Raphael, *Frederic*
Renault, *Mary*
Rendell, *Ruth*
Richler, *Mordecai*
Robbins, *Harold*
Rushdie, *(Ahmed) Salman*
Saroyan, *William*
Shelley, *Mary (Wollstonecraft)*
Shields, *Carol*
Simenon, *Georges (Joseph Christian)*
Stewart, *J(ohn) I(nnes) M(ackintosh)*
Stewart, *Mary*
Süskind, *Patrick*

Tennant, *Emma*
Theroux, *Paul*
Tolkien, *J(ohn) R(onald) R(euel)*
Tolstoy, *Count Leo (Nikolayevich)*
Tranter, *Nigel*
Tremain, *Rose*
Tutuola, *Amos*
Walpole, *Horace*
Wharton, *Edith (Newbold)*
Wilding, *Michael*

8 letters:
Abrahams, *Peter*
Aldridge, *James*
Apuleius, *Lucius*
Beerbohm, *Max*
Bradbury, *Malcolm*
Bradford, *Barbara Taylor*
Brittain, *Vera*
Brookner, *Anita*
Bulgakov, *Mikhail Afanaseyev*
Cartland, *Barbara*
Chandler, *Raymond*
Christie, *Dame Agatha (Mary Clarissa)*
Correlli, *Maria*
Davidson, *Lionel*
De Balzac, *Honoré*
Deighton, *Len*
De Laclos, *Pierre Choderlos*
De Quincy, *Thomas*
Disraeli, *Benjamin*
Donleavy, *J(ames) P(atrick)*
Faulkner, *William*
Fielding, *Helen*
Fielding, *Henry*
Flaubert, *Gustave*
Forester, *C(ecil) S(cott)*
Freeling, *Nicholas*
Galloway, *Janice*
Gordimer, *Nadine*
Guterson, *David*
Heinlein, *Robert A(nson)*
Ishiguro, *Kazuo*
Jhabvala, *Ruth Prawer*
Keneally, *Thomas*
Kingsley, *Charles*
Lawrence, *D(avid) H(erbert)*
Macauley, *Rose*
MacInnes, *Colin*
Melville, *Herman*
Meredith, *George*
Michener, *James A(lbert)*
Mitchell, *Julian*
Mitchell, *Margaret*
Moorcock, *Michael*
Morrison, *Toni*
Mortimer, *John*

Mortimer, *Penelope*
Oliphant, *Margaret*
Ondaatje, *Michael*
Remarque, *Erich Maria*
Salinger, *J(erome) D(avid)*
Sillitoe, *Alan*
Smollett, *Tobias George*
Stendhal
Trollope, *Anthony*
Trollope, *Joanna*
Turgenev, *Ivan Sergeyevich*
Voltaire
Vonnegut, *Kurt*
Zamyatin, *Evgeny Ivanovich*
9 letters:
Blackmore, *R(ichard) D(oddridge)*
Bleasdale, *Alan*
Bromfield, *Louis*
Burroughs, *William*
Delafield, *E M*
Du Maurier, *Dame Daphne*
Edgeworth, *Maria*
Feinstein, *Elaine*
Gerhardie, *William Alexander*
Goldsmith, *Oliver*
Goncharov, *Ivan Aleksandrovich*
Grossmith, *George*
Grossmith, *Weedon*
Hawthorne, *Nathaniel*
Hemingway, *Ernest (Millar)*
Highsmith, *Patricia*
Isherwood, *Christopher (William Bradshaw)*
Lermontov, *Mikhail Yurievich*
MacDonald, *George*
Mackenzie, *Sir (Edward Montague) Compton*
MacKenzie, *Henry*
Mankowitz, *(Cyril) Wolf*
McCullers, *Carson*
McLaverty, *Bernard*
Mitchison, *Naomi*
Monsarrat, *Nicholas*
O'Flaherty, *Liam*
Pasternak, *Boris Leonidovich*
Pratchett, *Terry*
Priestley, *J(ohn) B(oynton)*
Pritchett, *V(ictor) S(awdon)*
Radcliffe, *Ann*

Schreiner, *Olive*
Sholokhov, *Mikhail Aleksandrovich*
Steinbeck, *John (Ernest)*
Stevenson, *Robert Louis (Balfour)*
Thackeray, *William Makepeace*
Wa Thiong'o, *Ngugi*
Winterson, *Jeanette*
Wodehouse, *Sir P(elham) G(renville)*
Yourcenar, *Marguerite*
10 letters:
Bainbridge, *Beryl*
Ballantyne, *R(obert) M(ichael)*
Benedictus, *David*
Brooke-Rose, *Christina*
Chesterton, *G(ilbert) K(eith)*
De Beauvoir, *Simone*
Dostoevsky, *Fyodor Mikhailovich*
Fairbairns, *Zöe*
Fitzgerald, *F(rancis) Scott (Key)*
Fitzgerald, *Penelope*
Galsworthy, *John*
Markandaya, *Kamala*
McIlvanney, *William*
Richardson, *Dorothy*
Richardson, *Samuel*
Van der Post, *Laurens*
Vansittart, *Peter*
Waterhouse, *Keith*
11 letters:
Auchincloss, *Louis*
De Cervantes, *Miguel*
Di Lampedusa, *Guiseppe Tomasi*
12 letters:
De Maupassant, *(Henri René Albert) Guy*
Kazantazakis, *Nikos*
Solzhenitsyn, *Alexander Isayevich*
13 letters:
Alain-Fournier
Sackville-West, *Vita (Victoria Mary)*
14 letters:
Compton-Burnett, *Ivy*
De Saint-Exupéry, *Antoine*

Nuts

3 letters:
Cob
4 letters:
Cola
Kola
Mast
Pine
Rhus
5 letters:
Acorn
Areca
Arnut
Beech
Betel
Hazel
Lichi
Pecan
6 letters:
Acajou
Almond
Bauple
Brazil
Cashew
Cobnut

Illipe
Lichee
Litchi
Lychee
Marron
Monkey
Peanut
Pignut
Supari
Walnut
7 letters:
Arachis
Babassu
Coquina
Filberd
Filbert
Hickory
Praline
Prawlin
8 letters:
Chestnut
Earthnut
Hazelnut
Quandong

Sapucaia
9 letters:
Amygdalus
Barcelona
Beech-mast
Butternut
Chincapin
Chinkapin
Coco de mer
Groundnut
Macadamia
Mockernut
Pistachio
Sassafras
10 letters:
Chinquapin
Pine kernel
Queensland
12 letters:
Bertholletia
13 letters:
Dwarf chestnut

Officials

2 letters:
MC
SL
3 letters:
Aga
GOC
4 letters:
Agha
Cigs
Dean
Exon
Imam
Prog
Suit
5 letters:
Amban
Chair

Ephor
Imaum
Jurat
Mayor
Mirza
Sewer
Usher
6 letters:
Ataman
Beadle
Bursar
Censor
Consul
Datary
Deacon
Hetman
Keeper

Lictor
Master
Notary
Purser
Sexton
Syndic
Verger
Warden
Yeoman
7 letters:
Agistor
Attaché
Bailiff
Coroner
Darogha
Equerry
Filacer

Filazer
Hayward
Jamadar
Jemadar
Jemidar
Marshal
Mueddin
Pooh-Bah
Proctor
Provost
Sheriff
Speaker
Steward
Tribune
8 letters:
Bimbashi
Black rod
Chairman
Claviger
Cursitor
Decurion
Delegate
Mandarin
Palatine
Tipstaff
Verderer
Whiffler

9 letters:
Apparitor
Catchpole
Catchpoll
Commissar
Constable
Ealdorman
Escheator
Exciseman
Gauleiter
Intendant
Jobsworth
Landdrost
Moderator
Ombudsman
Polemarch
Precentor
President
Principal
Tahsildar
Treasurer
Waldgrave
10 letters:
Ambassador
Bumbailiff
Bureaucrat
Chairwoman

Chancellor
Magistrate
Postmaster
Procurator
Proveditor
Pursuivant
Silentiary
Subchanter
Supercargo
Tidewaiter
Timekeeper
11 letters:
Chairperson
Chamberlain
Functionary
Infirmarian
Shop steward
12 letters:
Commissioner
Jack-in-office
Remembrancer
13 letters:
Quartermaster
14 letters:
Provost-marshal
15 letters:
Plenipotentiary

Oils

3 letters:
Gas
Nim
Nut
4 letters:
Bone
Coal
Corn
Fuel
Musk
Neem
Oleo
Palm
Poon
Soya
Tung
Yolk
5 letters:
Ajwan
Argan
Attar
Benne
Benni
Clove
Colza
Crude

Fixed
Fusel
Heavy
Maize
Olive
Pulza
Rosin
Savin
Shale
Sperm
Spike
Stand
Train
Whale
6 letters:
Ajowan
Banana
Canola
Carapa
Carron
Castor
Croton
Diesel
Drying
Elaeis
Jojoba

Neroli
Peanut
Ramtil
Savine
Semsem
Sesame
Virgin
7 letters:
Butyrin
Cajeput
Cajuput
Camphor
Coconut
Dittany
Gingili
Linalol
Linseed
Lumbang
Menthol
Mineral
Mustard
Myrrhol
Naphtha
Picamar
Retinol
Ricinus

Tea tree
Vitriol
8 letters:
Bergamot
Camphire
Cod-liver
Gingelli
Gingelly
Lavender
Linalool
Macassar
Oiticica
Paraffin
Pristane
Rapeseed
9 letters:
Groundnut
Neat's foot

Parathion
Patchouli
Sassafras
Spikenard
Star-anise
Sunflower
Vegetable
10 letters:
Citronella
Cottonseed
Eucalyptus
Peppermint
Sandalwood
Turpentine
Ylang-ylang
11 letters:
Camphorated
Chaulmoogra

Chinese wood
Wintergreen
12 letters:
Benzaldehyde
13 letters:
Pentyl acetate
Sunflower seed
14 letters:
Glutaraldehyde
15 letters:
Evening primrose

Orange, shades of

4 letters:
Gold
5 letters:
Amber
Ochre
Peach

9 letters:
Grenadine
Tangerine

10 letters:
Terracotta
11 letters:
Burnt sienna

Orchestral instruments

4 letters:
Gong
Harp
Oboe
Tuba
5 letters:
Cello
Flute
Piano
Viola
6 letters:
Violin

7 letters:
Bassoon
Celesta
Piccolo
Timpani
Trumpet
8 letters:
Bass-drum
Clarinet
Trombone
9 letters:
Snare drum

Xylophone
10 letters:
Cor anglais
Double bass
French horn
11 letters:
Violoncello
12 letters:
Tubular bells
13 letters:
Contra-bassoon

Ores

3 letters:
Tin
Wad
4 letters:
Alga
Wadd
6 letters:
Copper
Glance

7 letters:
Bauxite
Bornite
Niobite
Oligist
Peacock
Realgar
8 letters:
Calamine

Cerusite
Crocoite
Galenite
Ilmenite
Limonite
Smaltite
Tenorite
9 letters:
Coffinite

Haematite
Hedyphane
Ironstone
Phacolite
Proustite
Stream-tin
10 letters:
Calaverite
Chalcocite

Horseflesh
Iridosmine
Melaconite
Sphalerite
Stephanite
11 letters:
Pitchblende
Psilomelane
Pyrargyrite

12 letters:
Babingtonite
Chalcopyrite
Pyromorphite
Tetrahedrite
15 letters:
Stilpnosiderite

Organs

3 letters:
Ear
Fin
4 letters:
Gill
5 letters:
Corti
Ctene
Gonad
Liver
Serra
6 letters:
Carpel
Feeler
Fundus
Kidney
Radula
Spleen
Stamen
Syrinx

Thymus
Tongue
Tonsil
Uterus
Viscus
Vitals
7 letters:
Isomere
Medulla
Nectary
Oogonia
Saprobe
Viscera
8 letters:
Hapteron
Pancreas
Placenta
Pulmones
Receptor
Tentacle

Tympanum
9 letters:
Sensillum
Spinneret
10 letters:
Nephridium
Ovipositor
Parapodium
Photophore
Sporangium
Sporophore
11 letters:
Archegonium
12 letters:
Exteroceptor
13 letters:
Chemoreceptor
Photoreceptor

Oxbridge colleges

3 letters:
New
5 letters:
Clare
Green
Jesus
Keble
King's
Oriel
6 letters:
Darwin
Exeter
Girton
Merton
Queen's
Selwyn
Wadham
7 letters:
Balliol
Christ's

Downing
Kellogg
Linacre
Lincoln
Newnham
St Anne's
St Cross
St Hugh's
St John's
Trinity
Wolfson
8 letters:
All Souls
Emmanuel
Homerton
Magdalen
Nuffield
Pembroke
Robinson
St Hilda's

St Peter's
9 letters:
Brasenose
Churchill
Clare Hall
Magdalene
Mansfield
St Antony's
St Edmund's
Templeton
Worcester
10 letters:
Greyfriars
Hughes Hall
Peterhouse
St Stephen's
Somerville
University
11 letters:
Blackfriars

Campion Hall
Fitzwilliam
Regent's Park
Trinity Hall
12 letters:
Christ Church

St Benet's Hall
St Catharine's
St Catherine's
St Edmund Hall
Sidney Sussex
Wycliffe Hall

13 letters:
Corpus Christi
Lucy Cavendish
Murray Edwards

P

Palms

3 letters:
Ita
4 letters:
Atap
Coco
Date
Doum
Nipa
5 letters:
Areca
Assai
Betel
Bussu
Macaw
Nikau
Ratan
Sabal
6 letters:
Buriti
Corozo
Elaeis

Gomuti
Gomuto
Gru-gru
Jupati
Kentia
Macoya
Raffia
Raphia
Rattan
Trooly
7 letters:
Babassu
Calamus
Coquito
Corypha
Euterpe
Jipyapa
Moriche
Palmyra
Paxiuba
Pupunha

Talipat
Talipot
Troelie
Troolie
8 letters:
Carnauba
Date tree
Groo-groo
Jipi-Japa
Macahuba
9 letters:
Burrawang
Carnahuba
10 letters:
Chamaerops
Jippi-Jappa
12 letters:
Chiqui-chiqui
Washingtonia

Papers

3 letters:
Art
Rag
Wax
4 letters:
Bond
Chad
Demy
Exam

File
Laid
Note
Rice
Test
Wove
5 letters:
Bible
Brown

Crepe
Crown
Emery
Flock
Glass
Graph
Green
India
Kraft

Linen
Sheet
Sugar
Touch
Waste
Waxed
White
6 letters:
Ballot
Baryta
Carbon
Filter
Garnet
Litmus
Manila
Retree

Tissue
Toilet
Vellum
7 letters:
Bromide
Manilla
Papyrus
Torchon
Tracing
Whatman®
Writing
8 letters:
Document
Foolscap
Glassine
Turmeric

Wrapping
9 letters:
Cartridge
Chiyogami
Cigarette
Cream-laid
Cream-wove
Hieratica
Onion-skin
Papillote
Parchment
Willesden
10 letters:
Cellophane®
11 letters:
Greaseproof

Parasites

3 letters:
Bot
Ked
Nit
4 letters:
Conk
Flea
Kade
Tick
Tryp
5 letters:
Leech
Louse
Worms
6 letters:
Coccus
Dodder
Isopod
Viscum
7 letters:
Ascarid
Bonamia
Candida
Copepod
Epizoon
Giardia
Hair-eel
Lamprey

Pinworm
Stylops
8 letters:
Entozoon
Epiphyte
Filarium
Hook-worm
Lungworm
Nematode
Puccinia
Sporozoa
Tapeworm
Trichina
9 letters:
Bilharzia
Ectophyte
Endamoeba
Endophyte
Entophyte
Heartworm
Ichneumon
Inquiline
Macdonald
Mistletoe
Orobanche
Rafflesia
Roundworm
Sporozoan

Strongyle
Trematode
10 letters:
Autoecious
Babesiasis
Liverfluke
Monogenean
Plasmodium
Rickettsia
Smut-fungus
Toxoplasma
11 letters:
Bladder-worm
Cryptozoite
Gregarinida
Haematozoon
Schistosoma
Strongyloid
Trypanosoma
12 letters:
Heteroecious
Licktrencher
Mallophagous
Rhipidoptera
Strepsiptera
15 letters:
Cryptosporidium

Parliaments

4 letters:
Dail
Diet
Rump
Sejm
5 letters:
Lords
Thing
6 letters:
Cortes
Majlis
Seanad
7 letters:
Althing
Commons
Knesset

Lagting
Riksdag
Tynwald
8 letters:
Congress
Lagthing
Lok Sabha
Stannary
Stormont
Storting
9 letters:
Barebones
Bundestag
Eduskunta
Folketing
Landsting

Odelsting
Reichstag
Sanhedrin
Stirthing
Storthing
10 letters:
Landsthing
Odelsthing
Rajya Sabha
St Stephens
11 letters:
Volkskammer
Westminster
13 letters:
Seanad Eireann

Pasta

4 letters:
Pipe
Zita
Ziti
5 letters:
Penne
Ruote
6 letters:
Ditali
7 letters:
Bavette
Fusilli
Gnocchi
Lasagne
Lumache
Noodles
Ravioli

Spätzle
8 letters:
Bucatini
Farfalle
Linguine
Macaroni
Rigatoni
Spaetzle
Taglioni
9 letters:
Agnolotti
Fettucine
Fettucini
Spaghetti
10 letters:
Bombolotti
Cannelloni

Cellentani
Conchiglie
Fettuccine
Gnocchetti
Lasagnette
Tortellini
Tortelloni
Vermicelli
11 letters:
Cappelletti
Maultaschen
Orecchiette
Pappardelle
Tagliatelle
Tortiglioni
12 letters:
Paglia e fieno

Peninsulas

4 letters:
Ards
Cape
Eyre
Kola
5 letters:
Gaspé
Gower
Lleyn
Malay
Sinai
Yorke
6 letters:
Alaska

Avalon
Balkan
Bataan
Crimea
Deccan
Iberia
Istria
Palmer
Tasman
Wirral
7 letters:
Arabian
Boothia
Cape Cod

Chukchi
Florida
Iberian
Jutland
Kintyre
Kowloon
Leizhou
8 letters:
Delmarva
East Cape
Labrador
Melville
9 letters:
Antarctic

Cape Verde
Gallipoli
Indo-China
Kamchatka
Kathiawar
The Lizard

10 letters:
Chalcidice
Chersonese
Nova Scotia
11 letters:
Peloponnese

12 letters:
Scandinavian
14 letters:
Baja California

Peoples

AFRICAN PEOPLES

3 letters:
Edo
Ewe
Ibo
Luo
Rif
San
Tiv
Twi
4 letters:
Akan
Boer
Efik
Fang
Fula
Hutu
Igbo
Lozi
Luba
Moor
Munt
Mzee
Nama
Nuba
Nuer
Nupe
Pedi
Riff
Rifi
Susu
Tshi
Xosa
Zulu
5 letters:
Bantu
Bemba
Bintu
Chewa
Dinka
Duala
Dyula
Fanti
Fingo
Fulah
Galla

Ganda
Hausa
Ibibi
Kongo
Lango
Mande
Masai
Mende
Mossi
Muntu
Negro
Nguni
Nilot
Nyoro
Oromo
Pigmy
Pondo
Pygmy
Shluh
Shona
Sotho
Swazi
Temne
Tonga
Tutsi
Venda
Wolof
Xhosa
6 letters:
Basuto
Beento
Berber
Damara
Grikwa
Griqua
Hamite
Herero
Ibibio
Kabyle
Kenyan
Kikuyu
Libyan
Malawi
Malian
Nilote

Nubian
Nyanja
Ovambo
Somali
Tsonga
Tswana
Tuareg
Watusi
Yoruba
7 letters:
Angolan
Ashanti
Baganda
Bambara
Barbary
Barotse
Basotho
Biafran
Bushman
Cairene
Flytaal
Gambian
Ghanian
Gullash
Lesotho
Lowveld
Maghreb
Maghrib
Malinke
Maninke
Mashona
Mosotho
Namaqua
Ndebele
Shilluk
Songhai
Swahili
Voltaic
Watutsi
Yoruban
Zairean
8 letters:
Botswana
Cushitic
Eritrean

Gabonese
Ghanaian
Khoikhoi
Liberian
Mandingo
Matabele
Moroccan
Namibian
Negrillo
Shangaan

Sudanese
Transkei
Tunisian
9 letters:
Congolese
Ethiopian
Gazankulu
Hottentot
Rhodesian
Transvaal

10 letters:
Abyssinian
Mozambican
11 letters:
Rastafarian
Strandloper
12 letters:
Carthaginian

ASIAN PEOPLES

3 letters:
Hui
Hun
Jat
Lao
Mon
4 letters:
Ainu
Arab
Cham
Chin
Dani
Dard
Dyak
Gond
Jain
Kurd
Mede
Moro
Motu
Naga
Nair
Nuri
Shan
Sikh
Sind
Thai
Turk
5 letters:
Dayak
Hindu
Kafir
Karen
Kazak
Khmer
Kisan
Malay
Mogul
Munda
Nayar
Nogay
Oriya
Parsi

Sindh
Tajik
Tamil
Tatar
Uigur
Uzbek
Vedda
Yakut
6 letters:
Beduin
Bihari
Buryat
Cumans
Essene
Evenki
Fulani
Gurkha
Harsha
Igorot
Jewish
Kalmyk
Kazakh
Khalsa
Lepcha
Lycian
Lydian
Mazhbi
Mishmi
Mongol
Parsee
Pashto
Pathan
Pushto
Pushtu
Sabean
Semite
Sherpa
Sindhi
Tadjik
Tartar
Telegu
Tongan
Tungus

Uighur
Veddah
7 letters:
Adivasi
Adivisi
Amorite
Balochi
Baluchi
Bashkir
Bedouin
Bengali
Bisayan
Burmese
Chinese
Chukchi
Chuvash
Cossack
Elamite
Harijan
Hittite
Hurrian
Israeli
Kalmuck
Kassite
Maratha
Maratta
Negrito
Panjabi
Punjabi
Sabaean
Samoyed
Saracen
Sogdian
Tadzhik
Tagalog
Talaing
Turkmen
Visayan
8 letters:
Accadian
Akkadian
Canarese
Chaldean

Chukchee
Ephesian
Gujarati
Gujerati
Igorrote
Kanarese
Kashmiri
Mahratta
Sumerian
Turanian
9 letters:
Amalekite

Bakhtyari
Chaldaean
Dravidian
Kabardian
Sinhalese
Tocharian
Tokharian
10 letters:
Andamanese
Babylonian
Ephraimite
Kara-Kalpak

Kshatriyas
Montagnard
Phoenician
11 letters:
Palestinian

AUSTRALASIAN PEOPLES

5 letters:
Dayak
Māori
6 letters:
Aranda

7 letters:
Tagalog
8 letters:
Gurindji

9 letters:
Aborigine
10 letters:
Melanesian
Polynesian

CENTRAL AND SOUTH AMERICAN INDIAN PEOPLES

2 letters:
Ge
4 letters:
Inca
Maya
Tupi
5 letters:
Aztec
Carib
Chimú

6 letters:
Aymara
Chibca
Kechua
Makuna
Mixtec
Toltec
7 letters:
Guarani
Nahuatl

Quechua
Quichua
Zapotec
8 letters:
Arawakan
10 letters:
Araucanian
Cashinahua

INUIT PEOPLES

5 letters:
Aleut
Inuit
Yupik

6 letters:
Innuit
8 letters:
Aleutian

13 letters:
Caribou Eskimo

EUROPEAN PEOPLES

4 letters:
Celt
Dane
Finn
Gaul
Goth
Jute
Komi
Lapp
Manx

Pict
Pole
Scot
Slav
Sorb
Turk
Wend
5 letters:
Angle
Aryan

Azeri
Croat
Cymry
Czech
Dutch
Frank
Gipsy
Greek
Gypsy
Iceni

Irish
Kymry
Latin
Norse
Saxon
Swede
Swiss
Vlach
Welsh
6 letters:
Basque
Belgae
Breton
Briton
Bulgar
Cimbri
Dorian
Eolian
French
Gaelic
Gascon
German
Goidel
Ingush
Ionian
Magyar
Norman
Ostyak
Sabine
Salain
Slovak
Teuton
Ugrian
Vandal
Viking
Volsci
Votyak
Walach
7 letters:
Achaean
Achaian
Aeolian

Azorean
Brython
Catalan
Chechen
Cornish
English
Fleming
Frisian
Iberian
Latvian
Lombard
Maltese
Mordvin
Russian
Samnite
Samoyed
Serbian
Silures
Slovene
Swabian
Walloon
8 letters:
Albanian
Alemanni
Armenian
Austrian
Bavarian
Cheremis
Corsican
Croatian
Ephesian
Estonian
Etrurian
Etruscan
Faeroese
Galician
Georgian
Hellenic
Illyrian
Karelian
Lusatian
Prussian

Romanian
Scythian
Sephardi
Sicilian
Thracian
Tyrolese
Visigoth
9 letters:
Aragonese
Ashkenazi
Bulgarian
Castilian
Celtiberi
Cheremiss
Esthonian
Icelandic
Langobard
Norwegian
Ostrogoth
Provençal
Sabellian
Sardinian
Ukrainian
10 letters:
Andalusian
Anglo-Saxon
Burgundian
Carinthian
Lithuanian
Macedonian
Portuguese
11 letters:
Anglo-Norman
Azerbaijani
Belorussian
Celtiberian
Montenegrin
12 letters:
Indo-European
Luxembourger
13 letters:
Bosnian Muslim

NATIVE AMERICAN TRIBES

3 letters:
Fox
Ute
4 letters:
Cree
Crow
Dene
Hopi
Hupa
Inca

Iowa
Maya
Moki
Pima
Pomo
Sauk
Tewa
Tico
Tiwa
Tupi

Yuma
Zuni
5 letters:
Aztec
Blood
Caddo
Cajun
Campa
Carib
Creek

Haida
Huron
Kansa
Kiowa
Lipan
Miami
Moqui
Olmec
Omaha
Osage
Ponca
Sioux
Teton
Wappo
Yaqui
Yuchi
Yuman
Yunca
6 letters:
Abnaki
Apache
Aymara
Biloxi
Cayuga
Cocopa
Dakota
Dogrib
Kechua
Kichai
Lakota
Mandan
Micmac
Mistec
Mixtec
Mohave
Mohawk
Mojave
Navaho
Navajo
Nootka
Oglala
Ojibwa
Oneida
Ostiak
Ottawa
Paiute
Papago
Pawnee
Pequot
Pericu
Piegan
Plains
Pueblo
Quakaw
Quapaw
Salish

Santee
Sarcee
Seneca
Siwash
Toltec
Warrau
Yanqui
7 letters:
Abenaki
Arapaho
Araucan
Arikara
Caddoan
Catawba
Chibcha
Chilcal
Chinook
Choctaw
Hidatsa
Kutenai
Mahican
Mapuche
Mohegan
Mohican
Nahuatl
Natchez
Ojibway
Orejone
Palouse
Pontiac
Quechua
Quichua
Senecan
Serrano
Shawnee
Stonies
Tlingit
Tonkawa
Wichita
Wyandot
Yalkama
8 letters:
Aguaruna
Algonkin
Cherokee
Cheyenne
Chippewa
Comanche
Delaware
Flathead
Illinois
Iroquois
Kickapoo
Kootenai
Kootenay
Kwakiutl

Malecite
Menomini
Mikasuki
Mogollon
Muskogee
Nez Percé
Okanagon
Onondaga
Powhatan
Seminole
Shoshone
Shoshoni
Shushwap
9 letters:
Algonkian
Algonquan
Algonquin
Apalachee
Ashochimi
Blackfoot
Chickasaw
Chipewyan
Chippeway
Karankawa
Manhattan
Melungeon
Menominee
Mescalero
Muskogean
Penobscot
Potawatom
Suquamash
Tsimshian
Tuscarora
Wampanoag
Winnebago
Wyandotte
10 letters:
Algonquian
Athabascan
Bella Coola
Leni-Lenapé
Miniconjou
Minnetaree
Montagnais
Montagnard
Muskhogean
Root-digger
Tarahumara
11 letters:
Assiniboine
Kiowa Apache
Massachuset
Minneconjou
Narraganset
Susquehanna

Philosophy

PHILOSOPHICAL SCHOOLS AND DOCTRINES

5 letters:
Deism
6 letters:
Monism
Taoism
Theism
7 letters:
Animism
Atomism
Dualism
Fideism
Marxism
Realism
Thomism
8 letters:
Cynicism
Fatalism
Hedonism
Humanism
Idealism
Nihilism

Stoicism
9 letters:
Platonism
Pluralism
10 letters:
Eleaticism
Empiricism
Kantianism
Nominalism
Positivism
Pragmatism
Pyrrhonism
Scepticism
Utopianism
11 letters:
Determinism
Hegelianism
Materialism
Rationalism
12 letters:
Behaviourism

Cartesianism
Confucianism
Epicureanism
Essentialism
Neo-Platonism
13 letters:
Conceptualism
Immaterialism
Phenomenalism
Scholasticism
Structuralism
14 letters:
Existentialism
Logical atomism
Pythagoreanism
Sensationalism
Utilitarianism
15 letters:
Aristotelianism
Conventionalism
Critical realism

PHILOSOPHERS

3 letters:
Han *Feizi*
Lao *Zi*
Xun *Zi*
Zhu *Xi*
4 letters:
Ayer, *A(lfred) J(ules)*
Cato, *Marcus Porcius*
Hume, *David*
Kant, *Immanuel*
Mach, *Ernst*
Marx, *Karl*
Mill, *James*
Mill, *John Stuart*
More, *Henry*
Mo-Zi
Reid, *Thomas*
Ryle, *Gilbert*
Vico, *Giovanni Battista*
Weil, *Simone*
Wolf, *Friedrich August*

5 letters:
Amiel, *Henri Frédéric*
Bacon, *Francis*
Bacon, *Roger*
Bayle, *Pierre*
Benda, *Julien*
Bruno, *Giordano*
Buber, *Martin*
Burke, *Edmund*
Comte, *Auguste*
Croce, *Benedetto*
Dewey, *John*
Frege, *Gottlob*
Fromm, *Erich*
Godel, *Kurt*
Green, *T(homas) H(ill)*
Hegel, *Georg Wilhelm Friedrich*
Iqbal, *Muhammad*
James, *William*
Locke, *John*
Lully, *Ramón*

Moore, *G(eorge) E(dward)*
Paine, *Thomas*
Paley, *William*
Plato
Rawls, *John*
Renan, *(Joseph) Ernest*
Royce, *Josiah*
Smith, *Adam*
Sorel, *Georges*
Taine, *Hippolyte Adophe*
6 letters:
Adorno, *Theodor Wiesengrund*
Agnesi, *Maria Gaetana*
Arendt, *Hannah*
Austin, *J(ohn) L(angshaw)*
Berlin, *Isaiah*
Carnap, *Rudolf*
Cicero, *Marcus Tallius*
Cousin, *Victor*
Engels, *Friedrich*
Eucken, *Rudolph Christoph*
Fichte, *Johann Gottlieb*
Ficino, *Marsilio*
Gasset, *José Ortega y*
Godwin, *William*
Herder, *Johann Gottfried*
Herzen, *Aleksandr Ivanovich*
Hobbes, *Thomas*
Langer, *Suzanne*
Lukács, *Georg*
Magnus, *Albertus*
Marcel, *Gabriel*
Mengzi
Newton, *Isaac*
Ortega (y Gasset), *José*
Pascal, *Blaise*
Peirce, *Charles Sanders*
Popper, *Karl*
Pyrrho
Sartre, *Jean-Paul*
Scotus, *John Duns*
Seneca, *Lucius Annaeus*
Tagore, *Rabindranath*
Tarski, *Alfred*
Thales
7 letters:
Abelard, *Peter*
Aquinas, *Thomas*
Bentham, *Jeremy*
Bergson, *Henri Louis*
Bradley, *F(rancis) H(erbert)*
Buridan, *Jean*
Derrida, *Jacques*
Diderot, *Denis*
Emerson, *Ralph Waldo*
Erasmus, *Desiderius*
Erigena, *John Scotus*

Fechner, *Gustav Theodor*
Gentile, *Giovanni*
Gorgias
Haeckel, *Ernst Heinrich*
Hah-Levi, *Judah*
Hartley, *David*
Herbart, *Johann Friedrich*
Herbert, *Edward*
Husserl, *Edmund*
Hypatia
Jaspers, *Karl*
Judaeus, *Philo*
Leibniz, *Gottfried Wilhelm*
Malthus, *Thomas Robert*
Marcuse, *Herbert*
Masaryk, *Tomáš Garrigue*
Mencius
Murdoch, *Dame (Jean) Iris*
Proclus
Ricoeur, *Paul*
Russell, *Bertrand*
Sankara
Sankhya
Schlick, *Moritz*
Spencer, *Herbert*
Spinoza, *Baruch*
Steiner, *Rudolf*
Tillich, *Paul Johannes*
Tolstoy, *Count Leo (Nikolayevich)*
8 letters:
Al-Farabi, *Mohammed ibn Tarkhan*
Averroës
Avicenna
Berkeley, *George*
Boethius, *Anicius Manlius Severinus*
Cassirer, *Ernst*
Cudworth, *Ralph*
Davidson, *Donald*
De Suárez, *Francisco*
Diogenes
Eberhard, *Johann August*
Epicurus
Foucault, *Michel*
Gassendi, *Pierre*
Hamilton, *William*
Harrison, *Frederic*
Leopardi, *Giacomo*
Maritain, *Jacques*
Menippus
Plotinus
Plutarch
Poincaré, *Jules Henri*
Porphyry
Ramanuja
Rousseau, *Jean Jacques*

Shankara
Socrates
Spengler, *Oswald*
Strawson, *Peter*
Voltaire, *François-Marie Arouet de*
Von Hayek, *Friedrich August*
Williams, *Bernard*
Xenophon
Zhuangzi
9 letters:
Althusser, *Louis*
Aristotle
Berdyayev, *Nikolai Aleksandrovich*
Bosanquet, *Bernard*
Chuang-tzu
Cleanthes
Confucius
Copleston, *Frederick (Charles)*
De Chardin, *Pierre Teilhard*
Descartes, *René*
De Unamuno, *Miguel*
Epictetus
Euhemerus
Feuerbach, *Ludwig Andreas*
Heidegger, *Martin*
Helvétius, *Claude Adrien*
Hutcheson, *Francis*
Leucippus
Lévy-Bruhl, *Lucien*
Lucretius
Nietzsche, *Friedrich Wilhelm*
Santayana, *George*
Schelling, *Friedrich Wilhelm Joseph Von*
Von Herder, *Johann Gottfried*
Whitehead, *A(lfred) N(orth)*
10 letters:
Anacharsis
Anaxagoras
Anaximenes
Apemanthus
Apollonius
Aristippus
Baumgarten, *Alexander Gottlieb*
Campanella, *Tommaso*
Chrysippus
Chrysostom, *Dio*
Churchland, *Paul*
Cumberland, *Richard*
De Beauvoir, *Simone*
Democritus
Empedocles
Heraclitus

Ibn-Gabirol, *Solomon*
Ibn-Khaldun
Maimonides
Parmenides
Protagoras
Pythagoras
Schweitzer, *Albert*
Swedenborg, *Emanuel*
Xenocrates
Xenophanes
Zeno of Elea
11 letters:
Anaximander
Antisthenes
Bonaventura
De Condillac, *Étienne Bonnot*
Heracleides
Kierkegaard, *Søren Aabye*
Machiavelli, *Niccolò*
Malebranche, *Nicolas*
Montesquieu, *Charles de Secondat (Baron de la Brède et de)*
Reichenbach, *Hans*
Von Leibnitz, *Gottfried Wilhelm*
Von Schlegel, *Friedrich*
12 letters:
Callisthenes
De Fontenelle, *Bernard le Bovier*
De Saint-Simon, *Comte*
Merleau-Ponty, *Maurice*
Schopenhauer, *Arthur*
Theophrastus
Von Pufendorf, *Samuel*
Von Schelling, *Friedrich Wilhelm Joseph*
Wittgenstein, *Ludwig Josef Johann*
Zeno of Citium
13 letters:
De Montesquieu, *Baron de la Brède et*
Van Orman Quine, *Willard*
14 letters:
Della Mirandola, *Giovanni Pico*
Nicholas of Cusa
Rosmini-Serbati, *Antonio*
Schleiermacher, *Friedrich Ernst Daniel*
Shankaracharya
15 letters:
Le Rond d'Alembert, *Jean*
William of Ockham

Phobias

Phobia	Object	Phobia	Object
Acerophobia	Sourness	Ergasiophobia	Work
Achluophobia	Darkness	Genophobia	Sex
Acrophobia	Heights	Geumaphobia	Taste
Aerophobia	Air	Graphophobia	Writing
Agoraphobia	Open spaces	Gymnophobia	Nudity
Aichurophobia	Points	Gynophobia	Women
Ailurophobia	Cats	Hadephobia	Hell
Akousticophobia	Sound	Haematophobia	Blood
Algophobia	Pain	Hamartiophobia	Sin
Amakaphobia	Carriages	Haptophobia	Touch
Amathophobia	Dust	Harpaxophobia	Robbers
Androphobia	Men	Hedonophobia	Pleasure
Anemophobia	Wind	Helminthophobia	Worms
Anginophobia	Narrowness	Hodophobia	Travel
Anthropophobia	Man	Homichlophobia	Fog
Antlophobia	Flood	Homophobia	Homosexuals
Apeirophobia	Infinity	Hormephobia	Shock
Aquaphobia	Water	Hydrephobia	Water
Arachnophobia	Spiders	Hypegiaphobia	Responsibility
Asthenophobia	Weakness	Hypnophobia	Sleep
Astraphobia	Lightning	Ideophobia	Ideas
Atephobia	Ruin	Kakorraphiaphobia	Failure
Aulophobia	Flute	Katagelophobia	Ridicule
Bacilliphobia	Microbes	Kenophobia	Void
Barophobia	Gravity	Kinesophobia	Motion
Basophobia	Walking	Kleptophobia	Stealing
Batrachophobia	Reptiles	Kopophobia	Fatigue
Belonephobia	Needles	Kristallophobia	Ice
Bibliophobia	Books	Laliophobia	Stuttering
Brontophobia	Thunder	Linonophobia	String
Cancerophobia	Cancer	Logophobia	Words
Cheimaphobia	Cold	Lyssophobia	Insanity
Chionophobia	Snow	Maniaphobia	Insanity
Chrematophobia	Money	Mastigophobia	Flogging
Chronophobia	Duration	Mechanophobia	Machinery
Chrystallophobia	Crystals	Metallophobia	Metals
Claustrophobia	Closed spaces	Meteorophobia	Meteors
Cnidophobia	Stings	Misophobia	Contamination
Cometophobia	Comets	Monophobia	One thing
Cromophobia	Colour	Musicophobia	Music
Cyberphobia	Computers	Musophobia	Mice
Cynophobia	Dogs	Necrophobia	Corpses
Demonophobia	Demons	Nelophobia	Glass
Demophobia	Crowds	Neophobia	Newness
Dermatophobia	Skin	Nephophobia	Clouds
Dikephobia	Justice	Nosophobia	Disease
Doraphobia	Fur	Nyctophobia	Night
Eisoptrophobia	Mirrors	Ochlophobia	Crowds
Electrophobia	Electricity	Ochophobia	Vehicles
Enetephobia	Pins	Odontophobia	Teeth
Entomophobia	Insects	Oikophobia	Home
Eosophobia	Dawn	Olfactophobia	Smell
Eremophobia	Solitude	Ommatophobia	Eyes
Ereuthophobia	Blushing	Oneirophobia	Dreams

Phobia	Object	Phobia	Object
Ophidiophobia	Snakes	Spermaphobia	Germs
Ornithophobia	Birds	Spermatophobia	Germs
Ouranophobia	Heaven	Stasiphobia	Standing
Panphobia	Everything	Stygiophobia	Hell
Pantophobia	Everything	Taphephobia	Being buried alive
Parthenophobia	Girls		
Pathophobia	Disease	Technophobia	Technology
Peniaphobia	Poverty	Teratophobia	Giving birth to a monster
Phasmophobia	Ghosts		
Phobophobia	Fears	Thaasophobia	Sitting
Photophobia	Light	Thalassophobia	Sea
Pnigerophobia	Smothering	Thanatophobia	Death
Poinephobia	Punishment	Theophobia	God
Polyphobia	Many things	Thermophobia	Heat
Potophobia	Drink	Tonitrophobia	Thunder
Pteronophobia	Feathers	Toxiphobia	Poison
Pyrophobia	Fire	Tremophobia	Trembling
Russophobia	Russia	Triskaidekaphobia	Thirteen
Rypophobia	Soiling	Xenophobia	Strangers *or* foreigners
Satanophobia	Satan		
Selaphobia	Flesh	Zelophobia	Jealousy
Siderophobia	Stars	Zoophobia	Animals
Sitophobia	Food		

Physics

BRANCHES OF PHYSICS

5 letters:
Solar
6 letters:
Atomic
Optics
Sonics
7 letters:
Applied
Nuclear
Quantum
Statics
8 letters:
Dynamics
Kinetics
Particle
Rheology
9 letters:
Acoustics

Cosmology
Harmonics
Magnetics
Magnetism
Mechanics
10 letters:
Biophysics
Cryogenics
Geophysics
High-energy
Nucleonics
Photometry
Pneumatics
Solid-state
11 letters:
Aerostatics
Electronics
Mesoscopics

Theoretical
Thermometry
Ultrasonics
12 letters:
Aerodynamics
Astrophysics
Macrophysics
Microphysics
Spectroscopy
13 letters:
Thermostatics
14 letters:
Electrostatics
Low-temperature
Magnetostatics
Thermodynamics
15 letters:
Condensed-matter

PHYSICS TERMS

3 letters:
Ohm
4 letters:
Atom
Fuse

Lens
Mass
Muon
Volt
Watt

Wave
X-ray
5 letters:
Anion
Diode

Earth
Farad
Field
Force
Hertz
Joule
Laser
Meson
6 letters:
Ampere
Baryon
Cacion
Charge
Energy
Fusion
Kelvin
Lepton
Matter
Moment
Newton
Pascal
Proton
Vacuum
7 letters:
Calorie
Coulomb
Current
Decibel
Density
Fission
Gravity
Hyperon
Impetus
Inertia
Neutron
Nucleon

Nucleus
Ohm's law
Quantum
Tension
8 letters:
Angstrom
Electron
Friction
Gamma ray
Half-life
Infrared
Momentum
Neutrino
Particle
Red shift
Spectrum
Velocity
9 letters:
Amplifier
Becquerel
Boyle's law
Conductor
Cosmic ray
Cyclotron
Diffusion
Frequency
Generator
Microwave
Radiation
Radio wave
Viscosity
10 letters:
Antimatter
Cathode ray
Charles' law
Convection

Inductance
Reflection
Refraction
Relativity
Resistance
Rutherford
Thermostat
Transistor
Wavelength
11 letters:
Capacitance
Diffraction
Electricity
Tau particle
Transformer
Ultraviolet
12 letters:
Acceleration
Fluorescence
Luminescence
13 letters:
Direct current
Doppler effect
Kinetic energy
Radioactivity
Semiconductor
Superfluidity
14 letters:
Brownian motion
Planck constant
Surface tension
15 letters:
Centre of gravity
Planck's constant
Potential energy

PHYSICISTS

3 letters:
Lee *Tsung-Dao*
Ohm, *Georg Simon*
4 letters:
Abbe, *Ernst*
Bohr, *Aage Niels*
Bohr, *Niels (Henrik David)*
Born, *Max*
Bose, *Jagadis Chandra*
Bose, *Satyendra Nath*
Hahn, *Otto*
Hess, *Victor Francis*
Kerr, *John*
Lamb, *Willis Eugene*
Lawe, *William C*
Mach, *Ernst*
Néel, *Louis*

Rabi, *Isidor Isaac*
Snow, *C(harles) P(ercy)*
Swan, *Joseph Wilson*
Ting, *Samuel Chao Chung*
Wien, *Wilhelm*
Yang, *Chen Ning*
5 letters:
Aston, *Francis William*
Auger, *Pierre*
Basov, *Nikolai*
Bethe, *Hans Albrecht*
Bloch, *Felix*
Bothe, *Walter*
Boyle, *Robert*
Bragg, *Sir William Henry*
Braun, *Karl Ferdinand*
Curie, *Marie*

Curie, *Pierre*
Debye, *Peter Joseph Wilhelm*
Dewar, *James*
Dirac, *Paul Adrien Maurice*
Fabry, *Charles*
Fermi, *Enrico*
Fuchs, *Klaus*
Gauss, *Carl Friedrich*
Gibbs, *Josiah Willard*
Henry, *Joseph*
Hertz, *Gustav*
Hertz, *Heinrich Rudolph*
Hooke, *Robert*
Jeans, *James Hopwood*
Joule, *James Prescott*
Lodge, *Oliver*
Pauli, *Wolfgang*
Popov, *Alexander Stepanovich*
Sègre, *Emilio*
Stark, *Johannes*
Volta, *Alessandro*
Weber, *Wilhelm Eduard*
Young, *Thomas*
6 letters:
Alfren
Alfvén, *Hannes Olaf Gösta*
Ampère, *André Marie*
Barkla, *Charles Glover*
Binnig, *Gerd*
Carnot, *Nicolas Leonard Sadi*
Cooper, *Leon*
Cronin, *James Watson*
Dalton, *John*
Franck, *James*
Frisch, *Otto*
Geiger, *Hans*
Giorgi, *Filippo*
Glaser, *Donald Arthur*
Graham, *Thomas*
Kelvin, *William Thomson*
Landau, *Lev Davidovich*
Newton, *Isaac*
Pascal, *Blaise*
Perrin, *Jean Baptiste*
Picard, *Jean*
Planck, *Max (Karl Ernst Ludwig)*
Powell, *Celic*
Talbot, *William Henry Fox*
Teller, *Edward*
Townes, *Charles Hard*
Walton, *Ernest Thomas Sinton*
Wigner, *Eugene Paul*
Wilson, *Charles Thomson Rees*
Yukawa, *Hideki*
Zwicky, *Fritz*
7 letters:
Alvarez, *Luis Walter*

Babinet, *Jacques*
Bardeen, *John*
Bravais, *Auguste*
Broglie, *Maurice*
Charles, *Jacques*
Compton, *Arthur Holly*
Coulomb, *Charles Augustin De*
Crookes, *William*
Doppler, *C(hristian) J(ohann)*
Faraday, *Michael*
Fechner, *Gustav*
Feynman, *Richard*
Fresnel, *Augustin*
Galilei, *Galileo*
Galileo
Gell-Man, *Murray*
Gilbert, *William*
Goddard, *Robert Hutchings*
Hawking, *Stephen William*
Heitler, *Walter*
Huygens, *Christiaan*
Kapitza, *Piotr Leonidovich*
Langley, *Samuel Pierpont*
Laplace, *Pierre Simon*
Lippman, *Gabriel*
Lorentz, *Hendrik Antoon*
Marconi, *Guglielmo*
Maxwell, *James Clerk*
Meitner, *Lise*
Milikin, *Robert*
Moseley, *Henry Gwyn-Jeffreys*
Oersted, *Hans Christian*
Penrose, *Roger*
Piccard, *Auguste*
Prandtl, *Ludwig*
Purcell, *Edward Mill*
Réaumur, *René Antoine*
  Ferchault De
Richter, *Burton*
Röntgen, *Wilhelm Konrad Von*
Seaborg, *Glenn*
Szilard, *Leo*
Thomson, *Benjamin*
Thomson, *George Paget*
Thomson, *Joseph John*
Tyndall, *John*
Von Laue, *Max Theodor Felix*
Wheeler, *John Archibald*
8 letters:
Anderson, *Carl David*
Anderson, *Elizabeth Garrett*
Anderson, *Philip Warren*
Ångström, *Anders Jonas*
Appleton, *Edward*
Avogadro, *Amedeo*
Blackett, *Patrick Maynard Stuart*
Brattain, *Walter Houser*

Brewster, *David*
Bridgman, *Percy*
Chadwick, *James*
Cherwell, *Frederick Alexander Lindemann*
Clausius, *Rudolf*
Davisson, *Clinton Joseph*
Einstein, *Albert*
Foucault, *Jean Bernard Léon*
Gassendi, *Pierre*
Ipatieff, *Vladimir Nikolaievich*
Lawrence, *Ernest Orlando*
McMillan, *Edwin*
Mullikin, *Robert Sanderson*
Oliphant, *Mark Laurence Elwin*
Poincaré, *Jules Henri*
Rayleigh, *John William Strutt*
Roentgen, *Wilhelm Konrad*
Sakharov, *Andrei*
Shockley, *William Bradfield*
Siegbahn, *Kai*
Van Allen, *James*
Von Mayer, *Julius Robert*
Weinberg, *Steven*
Zworykin, *Vladimir Kosma*
9 letters:
Arrhenius, *Svante August*
Becquerel, *Antoine Henri*
Bernoulli, *Daniel*
Boltzmann, *Ludwig*
Cavendish, *Henry*
Cherenkov, *Pavel Alekseyevich*
Cockcroft, *John Douglas*
De Coulomb, *Charles Augustin*
Eddington, *Arthur Stanley*

Gay-Lussac, *Joseph Louis*
Heaviside, *Oliver*
Josephson, *Brian David*
Kirchhoff, *Gustav*
Lindemann, *Frederick*
Michelson, *Albert*
Von Békésy, *Georg*
Von Eötvös, *Roland*
10 letters:
Archimedes
Barkhausen, *Heinrich Georg*
Fahrenheit, *Gabriel Daniel*
Heisenburg, *Werner Karl*
Richardson, *Owen Willans*
Rutherford, *Ernest*
Torricelli, *Evangelista*
Watson-Watt, *Robert Alexander*
11 letters:
Chamberlain, *Owen*
Joliot-Curie, *Irène*
Oppenheimer, *J(ulius) Robert*
Schrödinger, *Erwin*
Van de Graaff, *R(obert) J(emison)*
Van der Waals, *Johannes Diderik*
Von Guericke, *Otto*
12 letters:
Von Helmholtz, *Hermann Ludwig Ferdinand*
13 letters:
Von Fraunhofer, *Joseph*
14 letters:
Le Rond Alembert, *Jean*
15 letters:
Kamerlingh-Onnes, *Heike*

See also:
➤ **Molecules** ➤ **Subatomic particles**

Pigments

3 letters:	Cobalt	Sinopia
Hem	Flavin	Tapetum
4 letters:	Lutein	Tempera
Haem	Madder	**8 letters:**
Heme	Naevus	Carotene
5 letters:	Pterin	Gossypol
Ochre	Sienna	Iodopsin
Opsin	**7 letters:**	Luteolin
Sepia	Argyria	Orpiment
Smalt	Carmine	Retinene
Umber	Carotin	Verditer
6 letters:	Etiolin	Viridian
Bister	Flavine	**9 letters:**
Bistre	Gamboge	Anthocyan
Chrome	Melanin	Bilirubin

Chromogen
Colcothar
Lamp-black
Lithopone
Liverspot
Nigrosine
Porphyrin
Quercetin
Rhodopsin
Urochrome
10 letters:
Anthoclore
Betacyanin

Biliverdin
Carotenoid
Carotinoid
Hemocyanin
Hemoglobin
Paris-green
Riboflavin
Terre-verte
11 letters:
Anthocyanin
Chlorophyll
Fucoxanthin
Haemocyanin

Haemoglobin
Phytochrome
Xanthophyll
12 letters:
Cappagh-brown
Phycoxanthin
Xanthopterin
13 letters:
Phycoerythrin
Xanthopterine
14 letters:
Phthalocyanine

Pigs

5 letters:
Duroc
Welsh
8 letters:
Cheshire
Landrace
Pietrain

Tamworth
9 letters:
Berkshire
Hampshire
10 letters:
Large Black
Large White

Saddleback
Small White
11 letters:
Middle White
12 letters:
Chester White

Places and their nicknames

Place	Nickname
Aberdeen	The Granite City
Adelaide	The City of Churches
Amsterdam	The Venice of the North
Birmingham	Brum *or* the Venice of the North
Boston	Bean Town
Bruges	The Venice of the North
California	The Golden State
Chicago	The Windy City
Dallas	The Big D
Detroit	The Motor City
Dresden	Florence on the Elbe
Dublin	The Fair City
Dumfries	Queen of the South
Edinburgh	Auld Reekie *or* the Athens of the North
Florida	The Sunshine State
Fraserburgh	The Broch
Fremantle	Freo
Glasgow	The Dear Green Place
Hamburg	The Venice of the North
Indiana	The Hoosier State
Iowa	The Hawkeye State
Ireland	The Emerald Isle
Jamaica	J.A. *or* the Yard
Jerusalem	The Holy City
Kentucky	The Bluegrass State
Kuala Lumpur	K.L.
London	The Big Smoke *or* the Great Wen
Los Angeles	L.A.

Place	**Nickname**
New Jersey	The Garden State
New Orleans	The Crescent City *or* the Big Easy
New South Wales	Ma State
New York (City)	The Big Apple
New York (State)	The Empire State
New Zealand	Pig Island
North Carolina	The Tarheel State
Nottingham	Queen of the Midlands
Oklahoma	The Sooner State
Pennsylvania	The Keystone State
Philadelphia	Philly
Portsmouth	Pompey
Prince Edward Island	Spud Island
Queensland	Bananaland *or* the Deep North *(both derogatory)*
Rome	The Eternal City
San Francisco	Frisco
Southeastern U.S.A.	Dixie, Dixieland, *or* the Deep South
Tasmania	Tassie *or* the Apple Isle
Texas	The Lone Star State
Utah	The Beehive State
Venice	La Serenissima

Planets

4 letters:
Mars
5 letters:
Earth
Pluto (dwarf planet)

6 letters:
Saturn
Uranus

Venus

7 letters:
Jupiter
Mercury
Neptune

Plants

VARIETIES OF PLANT

3 letters:
Dal
Kex
Meu
Pia
Rue
Set
Til
Udo
Urd
Yam
4 letters:
Alga
Aloe
Anil
Deme
Fern
Forb
Herb

Ixia
Kali
Loco
More
Nard
Ombu
Rhus
Sego
Sola
Sunn
Taro
Thea
Vine
Yarr
5 letters:
Ajwan
Anise
Aroid
Benni

Blite
Boree
Buchu
Bucku
Bugle
Calla
Canna
Clary
Clote
Cress
Fouat
Fouet
Gemma
Glaux
Gorse
Guaco
Hosta
Inula
Jalap

Kenaf
Kudzu
Lathe
Lotus
Lurgi
Medic
Morel
Murva
Musci
Orpin
Orris
Oshac
Panax
Sedge
Sedum
Spink
Tetra
Timbo
Urena
6 letters:
Acacia
Acorus
Ajowan
Alisma
Alpine
Arnica
Bablah
Betony
Burnet
Cactus
Cassia
Catnep
Cnicus
Cosmea
Cosmos
Croton
Datura
Derris
Dodder
Exogen
Gnetum
Hyssop
Iberis
Knawel
Madder
Mallow
Medick
Mimosa
Moorva
Nerium
Nettle
Nuphar
Orchis
Orpine
Pachak
Phloem
Protea

Rattle
Reseda
Retama
Rubber
Sesame
Silene
Smilax
Spider
Spurge
Spurry
Squill
Styrax
Teasel
Thrift
Tulipa
Tutsan
Yarrow
7 letters:
Alkanet
All-good
Allseed
Alyssum
Brinjal
Burdock
Caltrop
Cardoon
Carduus
Carline
Cat's ear
Chervil
Dasheen
Dioecia
Dittany
Ephedra
Filaree
Fly-trap
Freesia
Frogbit
Gentian
Gerbera
Haemony
Henbane
Ipomoea
Isoetes
Lantana
Lucerne
Lychnis
Mahonia
Melilot
Mercury
Mullein
Nemesia
Nigella
Nonsuch
Opuntia
Palmiet
Pareira

Petunia
Ragwort
Rhodora
Ruellia
Saffron
Salfern
Salsola
Sampire
Sanicle
Scandix
Setwall
Skirret
Spignel
Spiraea
Spurrey
Stapela
Syringa
Tagetes
Thallus
Triffid
Tritoma
Vanilla
Vervain
Zedoary
8 letters:
Acanthus
Agrimony
Angelica
Arenaria
Asphodel
Bindi-eye
Buckbean
Buplever
Camomile
Canaigre
Centaury
Costmary
Diandria
Dielytra
Dumbcane
Fluellin
Fumitory
Geophyte
Gesneria
Gnetales
Gromwell
Hag-taper
Henequen
Hepatica
Hibiscus
Larkspur
Lavender
Mandrake
Monstera
Oleander
Opopanax
Plumbago

Psilotum
Putchock
Ratsbane
Roly-poly
Samphire
Scammony
Self-heal
Silphium
Sparaxis
Spergula
Stapelia
Staragen
Starwort
Tamarisk
Tritonia
Tuberose
Tuckahoe
Wait-a-bit
9 letters:
Adderwort
Andromeda
Arrowroot
Artemisia
Aubrietia
Bald-money
Brooklime
Broom-rape
Butterbur
Colocasia
Coltsfoot
Cordaites
Coreopsis
Coriander
Dittander
Erythrina
Euphorbia
Eyebright
Fenugreek
Germander

Groundsel
Herb-paris
Horse-tail
Liver-wort
Lousewort
Mare's-tail
Moneywort
Moschatel
Patchouli
Pimpernel
Portulaca
Rocambole
Screwpine
Spearmint
Spearwort
Spikenard
Stone-crop
Sweet-gale
Tomatillo
Tormentil
Wake-robin
Wincopipe
Wolf's bane
10 letters:
Alexanders
Angiosperm
Aspidistra
Astralagus
Dyer's-broom
Earth-smoke
Five-finger
Fraxinella
Fritillary
Goat-sallow
Goats-thorn
Goat-willow
Goldilocks
Icosandria
Maidenhair

Mignonette
Parkleaves
Rest-harrow
Salicornia
Touch-me-not
Tropophyte
Yellowroot
11 letters:
Acidanthera
Bears-breech
Bristle-fern
Callitriche
Convolvulus
Dusty-miller
Hurtleberry
Loosestrife
Meadowsweet
Nancy-pretty
Schizophyte
Sempervivum
Thallophyte
12 letters:
Adam's flannel
Epacridaceae
Midsummermen
Morning glory
Parsley-piert
Pasqueflower
Phytobenthos
Southernwood
Water-soldier
13 letters:
Townhall clock
14 letters:
Chincherinchee
Lords and ladies
Shepherd's purse

PARTS OF PLANTS

3 letters:
Bud
Lip
Pod
4 letters:
Cyme
Head
Leaf
Root
Seed
Spur
Stem
5 letters:
Bract

Calyx
Costa
Fruit
Glume
Joint
Lemma
Ovary
Ovule
Palea
Petal
Sepal
Spike
Stoma
Style

Tepal
Torus
Umbel
Xylem
6 letters:
Anther
Bulbil
Carpel
Catkin
Caulis
Corymb
Floret
Phloem
Pistil

Pollen
Raceme
Rachis
Sheath
Spadix
Spathe
Stamen
Stigma
Tassel
7 letters:
Blossom
Corolla
Foliage
Nectary
Panicle
Pedicel
Root cap
Seed pod
Taproot
8 letters:
Cyathium

Filament
Nucellus
Offshoot
Peduncle
Perianth
Placenta
Root hair
Spikelet
Thalamus
9 letters:
Capitulum
Dichasium
Epidermis
Guard cell
Gynoecium
Internode
Involucel
Involucre
Micropyle
Pollinium
Secundine

10 letters:
Androecium
Anthophore
Carpophore
Commissure
Hypanthium
Receptacle
11 letters:
Clinandrium
Gametophore
Monochasium
Pollen grain
12 letters:
Hibernaculum
13 letters:
Inflorescence
14 letters:
Floral envelope
Vascular bundle

See also:
➤ **Algae** ➤ **Botany** ➤ **Ferns** ➤ **Flowers** ➤ **Fungi**
➤ **Grasses** ➤ **Lilies** ➤ **Mosses** ➤ **Palms** ➤ **Seaweeds** ➤ **Shrubs**
➤ **Trees**

Poetry

POETRY AND PROSODY TERMS

3 letters:
Bob
4 letters:
Foot
Iamb
5 letters:
Arsis
Canto
Envoi
Envoy
Epode
Ictus
Ionic
Metre
Octet
Paeon
Rhyme
Wheel
6 letters:
Adonic
Alcaic
Cesura
Cretic
Dactyl
Dipody

Iambic
Iambus
Octave
Rhythm
Septet
Sestet
Stanza
Tercet
7 letters:
Anapest
Cadence
Cadency
Caesura
Couplet
Distich
Elision
Paeonic
Pyhrric
Quintet
Refrain
Sapphic
Sestina
Sextain
Spondee
Stichic

Strophe
Triplet
Trochee
8 letters:
Amoebean
Anapaest
Bacchius
Choriamb
Dactylic
Dieresis
Eye rhyme
Pindaric
Quatrain
Quintain
Scansion
Spondaic
Trochaic
9 letters:
Amoebaean
Anacrusis
Anapestic
Assonance
Diaeresis
Free verse
Full rhyme

Half-rhyme
Hemistich
Hexameter
Long metre
Macaronic
Octameter
Pararhyme
Rime riche
Terza rima
Tetrapody
Unstopped
Vers libre
10 letters:
Amphibrach
Amphimacer
Anapaestic
Blank verse
Catalectic
Choriambus
Consonance
Consonancy

End-stopped
Heptameter
Heptastich
Hypermeter
Ottava rima
Pentameter
Pentastich
Rhyme royal
Short metre
Tetrabrach
Tetrameter
Tetrastich
11 letters:
Alexandrine
Antistrophe
Common metre
Enjambement
Jabberwocky
Rhyme scheme
12 letters:
Alliteration

Ballad stanza
Leonine rhyme
Onomatopoeia
Perfect rhyme
Sprung rhythm
13 letters:
Closed couplet
Common measure
Feminine rhyme
Heroic couplet
Internal rhyme
Syllabic metre
14 letters:
Accentual metre
Feminine ending
Masculine rhyme
Verse paragraph
15 letters:
Masculine ending

POETRY MOVEMENTS AND GROUPINGS

8 letters:
Imagists
9 letters:
Decadents
Lake Poets
Romantics

10 letters:
Symbolists
11 letters:
Petrarchans
The Movement

12 letters:
Alexandrians
13 letters:
Georgian Poets
14 letters:
Liverpool Poets

POETS

2 letters:
AE
HD
3 letters:
Gay, *John*
Paz, *Octavio*
Poe, *Edgar Allan*
4 letters:
Abse, *Dannie*
Beer, *Patricia*
Blok, *Alexander Alexandrovich*
Cory, *William Johnson*
Dunn, *Douglas*
Dyer, *Sir Edward*
Gray, *Thomas*
Gunn, *Thom*
Hill, *Geoffrey*
Hogg, *James*
Hood, *Thomas*
Hugo, *Victor (Marie)*
Hunt, *(James Henry) Leigh*

Lang, *Andrew*
Muir, *Edwin*
Nash, *(Frederic) Ogden*
Ovid
Owen, *Wilfred*
Pope, *Alexander*
Rich, *Adrienne*
Rowe, *Nicholas*
Rumi, *Jelaluddin*
Tate, *(John Orley) Allen*
Vega, *(Garcilaso de la)*
Webb, *Francis Charles*
5 letters:
Aiken, *Conrad (Potter)*
Arion
Auden, *W(ystan) H(ugh)*
Blair, *Robert*
Blake, *William*
Burns, *Robert*
Byron, *(George Gordon)*
Cadou, *René-Guy*

Carew, *Thomas*
Cinna, *Gaius Helvius*
Clare, *John*
Dante *(Alighieri)*
Donne, *John*
Duffy, *Carol Ann*
Eliot, *T(homas) S(tearns)*
Frost, *Robert (Lee)*
Gower, *John*
Heine, *Heinrich*
Henri, *Adrian*
Hesse, *Hermann*
Homer
Horne, *Richard Henry (√Hengist')*
Hulme, *Thomas Ernest*
Iqbal, *Sir Mohammed*
Keats, *John*
Keyes, *Sidney*
Lewis, *Cecil Day*
Logue, *Christopher*
Lorca, *Federico García*
Lucan *(Marcus Annaeus Lucanus)*
Marot, *Clément*
Meyer, *Conrad Ferdinand*
Moore, *Marianne*
Nashe, *Thomas*
Noyes, *Alfred*
O'Hara, *Frank*
Perse, *Saint-John*
Plath, *Sylvia*
Pound, *Ezra (Loomis)*
Prior, *Matthew*
Raine, *Kathleen*
Rilke, *Rainer Maria*
Sachs, *Hans*
Scott, *Sir Walter*
Smart, *Christopher*
Smith, *Stevie*
Tasso, *Torquato*
Theon
Wyatt, *Thomas*
Yeats, *W(illiam) B(utler)*
Young, *Edward*
6 letters:
Adcock, *(Karen) Fleur*
Arnold, *Matthew*
Austin, *Alfred*
Barham, *Richard Harris*
Barnes, *William*
Belloc, *(Joseph) Hilaire (Pierre)*
Bishop, *Elizabeth*
Brecht, *Bertolt Eugen Friedrich*
Brooke, *Rupert (Chawner)*
Brooks, *Gwendolyn*
Butler, *Samuel*
Carver, *Raymond*
Clough, *Arthur Hugh*

Cowper, *William*
Crabbe, *George*
Dowson, *Ernest Christopher*
Dryden, *John*
Dunbar, *William*
Dutton, *Geoffrey*
Elliot, *Ebenezer*
Éluard, *Paul*
Empson, *William*
Ennius, *Quintus*
George, *Stefan*
Glycon
Goethe, *Johann Wolfgang von*
Graves, *Robert (Ranke)*
Heaney, *Seamus*
Hesiod
Horace
Hughes, *Ted*
Jonson, *Ben(jamin)*
Landor, *Walter Savage*
Larkin, *Philip*
Lawman
Lowell, *Amy*
Lowell, *Robert*
Millay, *Edna St Vincent*
Milton, *John*
Morgan, *Edwin (George)*
Morris, *Sir Lewis*
Motion, *Andrew*
Neruda, *Pablo*
Ossian
Patten, *Brian*
Pindar
Porter, *Peter*
Racine, *Jean (Baptiste)*
Rhymer, *Corn Law*
Riding, *Laura*
Sappho
Seaman, *Sir Owen*
Shanks, *Edward*
Sidney, *Sir Philip*
Tagore, *Sir Rabindranath*
Thomas, *Dylan (Marlais)*
Thomas, *Edward*
Thomas, *R(onald) S(tuart)*
Trench, *Frederick Herbert*
Villon, *François*
Virgil
Waller, *Edmund*
Wright, *Judith*
7 letters:
Addison, *Joseph*
Alcaeus
Angelou, *Maya*
Aretino, *Pietro*
Ariosto, *Ludovico*
Beddoes, *Thomas*

Belleau, *Rémy*
Blunden, *Edmund*
Bridges, *Robert Seymour*
Brodsky, *Joseph*
Caedmon
Campion, *Thomas*
Causley, *Charles*
Chapman, *George*
Chaucer, *Geoffrey*
Collins, *Wilkie (William)*
Corinna
Cynwulf
De Vigny, *Alfred Victor*
Emerson, *Ralph Waldo*
Flaccus, *Horace (Quintus Horatius)*
Flecker, *James Elroy*
Herbert, *George*
Heredia, *José María*
Herrick, *Robert*
Hodgson, *Ralph*
Hopkins, *Gerard Manley*
Housman, *A(lfred) E(dward)*
Johnson, *Samuel*
Juvenal
Khayyam, *Omar*
Kipling, *(Joseph) Rudyard*
Layamon
Leonard, *Tom*
MacCaig, *Norman*
MacLean, *Sorley*
Martial
Marvell, *Andrew*
McGough, *Roger*
Mistral, *Frédéric*
Newbolt, *Sir Henry John*
Orpheus
Pushkin, *Aleksander Sergeyevich*
Rimbaud, *Arthur*
Roethke, *Theodore Huebner*
Ronsard, *Pierre de*
Russell, *George William*
Sassoon, *Siegfried (Louvain)*
Schwarz, *Delmore*
Seifert, *Jaroslav*
Service, *Robert William*
Shelley, *Percy Bysshe*
Sitwell, *Edith*
Skelton, *John*
Southey, *Robert*
Spender, *Stephen*
Spenser, *Edmund*
Statius, *Publius Papinius*
Stevens, *Wallace*
Terence *(Publius Terentius Afer)*
Thomson, *James*
Vaughan, *Henry*

Vaughan, *William*
Walcott, *Derek*
Whitman, *Walt(er)*
8 letters:
Anacreon
Berryman, *John*
Betjeman, *John*
Browning, *Elizabeth Barrett*
Browning, *Robert*
Campbell, *Thomas*
Catullus, *Gaius Valerius*
Clampitt, *Amy*
Cummings, *E(dward) E(stlin)*
Cynewulf
Davenant, *Sir William*
de la Mare, *Walter (John)*
Ginsberg, *Allen*
Hamilton, *William*
Henryson, *Robert*
Jennings, *Elizabeth*
Kavanagh, *Patrick*
Kynewulf
Langland, *William*
Leopardi, *Giacomo*
Lovelace, *Richard*
Macauley, *Thomas*
MacNeice, *Louis*
Mallarmé, *Stéphane*
Menander
Petrarch
Rossetti, *Christina Georgina*
Rossetti, *Dante Gabriel*
Schiller, *(Johann Cristoph) Friedrich von*
Shadwell, *Thomas*
Stephens, *James*
Suckling, *John*
Taliesin
Tennyson, *Lord Alfred*
Thompson, *Francis*
Traherne, *Thomas*
Tyrtaeus
Verlaine, *Paul*
Whittier, *John Greenleaf*
9 letters:
Aeschylus
Akhmatova, *Anna*
Bunthorne, *Reginald*
Coleridge, *Samuel Taylor*
De Camoëns, *Luis Vaz*
Dickinson, *Emily*
Doolittle, *Hilda (H D)*
Euripides
Goldsmith, *Oliver*
Lamartine, *Alphone Marie Loius De*
Lucretius

Marinetti, *Emilio Filippo Tommaso*
Masefield, *John*
Quasimodo, *Salvatore*
Rochester, *(John Wilmot)*
Rosenberg, *Isaac*
Shenstone, *William*
Simonides *(of Ceos)*
Sophocles
Stevenson, *Robert Louis (Balfour)*
Swinburne, *Algernon Charles*
10 letters:
Baudelaire, *Charles Pierre*
Chatterton, *Thomas*
Cumberland, *Richard*
Drinkwater, *John*
Fitzgerald, *Edward*
Fitzgerald, *Robert*
Longfellow, *Henry Wadsworth*
MacDiarmid, *Hugh*

Propertius, *Sextus*
Szymborska, *Wislawa*
Tannhauser
Theocritus
Wordsworth, *William*
11 letters:
Apollinaire, *Guillaume*
Archilochus
Asclepiades
Callimachus
De Lamartine, *Alphonse Marie Louis de Prat*
Maeterlinck, *Count Maurice*
Shakespeare, *William*
12 letters:
Aristophanes
De La Fontaine, *Jean*
15 letters:
Ettrick Shepherd

Poisons

POISONOUS SUBSTANCES AND GASES

4 letters:
Bane
Lead
Tutu
Upas
5 letters:
Aspic
Conin
Ergot
Sarin
Sassy
Soman
Timbo
Urali
6 letters:
Aldrin
Antiar
Arsine
Cicuta
Conine
Curare
Curari
Datura
Dioxin
Emetin
Hebona
Ourali
Ourari
Phenol

Wabain
7 letters:
Aconite
Amanita
Aniline
Arsenic
Atropin
Benzene
Brucine
Cacodyl
Coniine
Cowbane
Cyanide
Emetine
Hebenon
Hemlock
Henbane
Lindane
Neurine
Ouabain
Phallin
Red lead
Safrole
Solpuga
Stibine
Stibium
Surinam
Tanghin
Tropine

Woorali
Woorara
Wourali
8 letters:
Acrolein
Adamsite
Apocynum
Atropine
Barbasco
Botulism
Cyanogen
Cyanuret
Daturine
Death cap
Dumbcane
Foxglove
Gossypol
Laburnum
Lewisite
Lobeline
Locoweed
Methanol
Mezereon
Nerve gas
Oleander
Paraquat
Phosgene
Pokeroot
Pokeweed

Ratsbane
Samnitis
Santonin
Sasswood
Solanine
Thallium
Thebaine
Urushiol
Veratrin
Warfarin
9 letters:
Aflatoxin
Afterdamp
Baneberry
Benzidine
Coyotillo
Digitalin
Echidnine
Fly agaric
Gelsemine
Monkshood
Muscarine
Nux vomica
Poison gas
Poison ivy
Poison oak
Pokeberry
Sassy wood
Saxitoxin
Stonefish
Tanghinin
Toxaphene
Veratrine
Whitedamp
Wolf's-bane

Yohimbine
10 letters:
Aqua-tofana
Belladonna
Cadaverine
Colchicine
Cyanic acid
Death angel
Hydrastine
Liberty cap
Limberneck
Manchineel
Mandragora
Mustard gas
Oxalic acid
Paris green
Phalloidin
Picrotoxin
Stavesacre
Strychnine
Tetrotoxin
Thorn apple
11 letters:
Agent Orange
Black bryony
Calabar-bean
Death camass
Dog's mercury
Gelseminine
Hyoscyamine
Pilocarpine
Poison elder
Prussic acid
Staggerbush
Sugar of lead

Veratridine
12 letters:
Allyl alcohol
Formaldehyde
Lead monoxide
Noogoora burr
Poison sumach
Strophanthus
Tetrodotoxin
Water hemlock
Zinc chloride
13 letters:
Dieffenbachia
Mercuric oxide
Methyl bromide
Poison dogwood
Silver nitrate
Sodium cyanide
14 letters:
Carbon monoxide
Castor-oil plant
Hydrogen iodide
Mountain laurel
15 letters:
Arsenic trioxide
Barium hydroxide
Black nightshade
Destroying angel
Hydrogen cyanide
Indian liquorice
Nitrogen dioxide
Osmium tetroxide
Woody nightshade

TYPES OF POISONING

4 letters:
Lead
6 letters:
Iodism
7 letters:
Bromism
8 letters:
Botulism

Ergotism
Plumbism
Ptomaine
9 letters:
Fluorosis
Saturnism
10 letters:
Digitalism

Salmonella
11 letters:
Hydrargyria
Listeriosis
Phosphorism
12 letters:
Mercurialism
Strychninism

Politicians

4 letters:
Eden, *Sir (Robert) Anthony*
5 letters:
Laski, *Harold Joseph*
6 letters:
Bright, *John*
7 letters:
Parnell, *Charles Stewart*

Trotsky, *Leon*
8 letters:
Disraeli, *Benjamin*
11 letters:
Wilberforce, *William*
12 letters:
Chesterfield, *Philip Dormer Stanhope*

See also:
➤ **Presidents of the U.S.** ➤ **Prime Ministers**

Popes

Pope	Pontificate	Pope	Pontificate
Peter	Until c.64	Innocent I	402–17
Linus	c.64–c.76	Zosimus	417–18
Anacletus	c.76–c.90	Boniface I	418–22
Clement I	c.90–c.99	Celestine I	422–32
Evaristus	c.99–c.105	Sixtus III	432–40
Alexander I	c.105–c.117	Leo I	440–61
Sixtus I	c.117–c.127	Hilarus	461–68
Telesphorus	c.127–c.137	Simplicius	468–83
Hyginus	c.137–c.140	Felix III (II)	483–92
Pius I	c.140–c.154	Gelasius I	492–96
Anicetus	c.154–c.166	Anastasius II	496–98
Soter	c.166–c.175	Symmachus	498–514
Eleutherius	175–89	Hormisdas	514–23
Victor I	189–98	John I	523–26
Zephyrinus	198–217	Felix IV (III)	526–30
Callistus I	217–22	Boniface II	530–32
Urban I	222–30	John II	533–35
Pontian	230–35	Agapetus I	535–36
Anterus	235–36	Silverius	536–37
Fabian	236–50	Vigilius	537–55
Cornelius	251–53	Pelagius I	556–61
Lucius I	253–54	John III	561–74
Stephen I	254–57	Benedict I	575–79
Sixtus II	257–58	Pelagius II	579–90
Dionysius	259–68	Gregory I	590–604
Felix I	269–74	Sabinianus	604–06
Eutychianus	275–83	Boniface III	607
Caius	283–96	Boniface IV	608–15
Marcellinus	296–304	Deusdedit *or* Adeodatus I	615–18
Marcellus I	308–09		
Eusebius	310	Boniface V	619–25
Miltiades	311–14	Honorious I	625–38
Sylvester I	314–35	Severinus	640
Mark	336	John IV	640–42
Julius I	337–52	Theodore I	642–49
Liberius	352–66	Martin I	649–54
Damasus I	366–84	Eugenius I	654–57
Siricius	384–99	Vitalian	657–72
Anastasius I	399–401	Adeotatus II	672–6

Pope	Pontificate	Pope	Pontificate
Donus	676–78	Benedict V	964–66
Agatho	678–81	John XIII	965–72
Leo II	682–83	Benedict VI	973–74
Benedict II	684–85	Benedict VII	974–83
John V	685–86	John XIV	983–84
Cono	686–87	John XV	985–96
Sergius I	687–701	Gregory V	996–99
John VI	701–05	Sylvester II	999–1003
John VII	705–07	John XVII	1003
Sisinnius	708	John XVIII	1004–09
Constantine	708–15	Sergius IV	1009–12
Gregory II	715–31	Benedict VIII	1012–24
Gregory III	731–41	John XIX	1024–32
Zacharias	741–52	Benedict IX (first reign)	1032–44
Stephen II (not consecrated)	752	Sylvester III	1045
Stephen II (III)	752–7	Benedict IX (second reign)	1045
Paul I	757–67	Gregory VI	1045–46
Stephen III (IV)	768–72	Clement II	1046–47
Hadrian I	772–95	Benedict IX (third reign)	1047–48
Leo III	795–816	Damasus II	1048
Stephen IV (V)	816–17	Leo IX	1048–54
Paschal I	817–24	Victor II	1055–57
Eugenius II	824–27	Stephen IX (X)	1057–58
Valentine	827	Nicholas II	1059–61
Gregory IV	827–44	Alexander II	1061–73
Sergius II	844–47	Gregory VII	1073–85
Leo IV	847–55	Victor III	1086–87
Benedict III	855–58	Urban II	1088–99
Nicholas I	858–67	Paschal II	1099–1118
Hadrian II	867–72	Gelasius II	1118–19
John VIII	872–82	Callistus II	1119–24
Marinus I	882–84	Honorious II	1124–30
Hadrian III	884–85	Innocent II	1130–43
Stephen V (VI)	885–91	Celestine II	1143–44
Formosus	891–96	Lucius II	1144–45
Boniface VI	896	Eugenius III	1145–53
Stephen VI (VII)	896–97	Anastasius IV	1153–54
Romanus	897	Hadrian IV	1154–59
Theodore II	897	Alexander III	1159–81
John IX	898–900	Lucius III	1181–85
Benedict IV	900–03	Urban III	1185–87
Leo V	903	Gregory VIII	1187
Sergius III	904–11	Clement III	1187–91
Anastasius III	911–13	Celestine III	1191–98
Lando	913–14	Innocent III	1198–1216
John X	914–28	Honorious III	1216–27
Leo VI	928	Gregory IX	1227–41
Stephen VII (VIII)	928–31	Celestine IV	1241
John XI	931–35	Innocent IV	1243–54
Leo VII	936–39	Alexander IV	1254–61
Stephen IX	939–42	Urban IV	1261–64
Marinus II	942–46	Clement IV	1265–68
Agapetus II	946–55	Gregory X	1271–76
John XII	955–64		
Leo VIII	963–65		

Pope	Pontificate	Pope	Pontificate
Innocent V	1276	Gregory XIII	1572–85
Hadrian V	1276	Sixtus V	1585–90
John XXI	1276–77	Urban VII	1590
Nicholas III	1277–80	Gregory XIV	1590–91
Martin IV	1281–85	Innocent IX	1591
Honorious IV	1285–87	Clement VIII	1592–1605
Nicholas IV	1288–92	Leo XI	1605
Celestine V	1294	Paul V	1605–21
Boniface VIII	1294–1303	Gregory XV	1621–23
Benedict XI	1303–04	Urban VIII	1623–44
Clement V	1305–14	Innocent X	1644–55
John XXII	1316–34	Alexander VII	1655–67
Benedict XII	1334–42	Clement IX	1667–69
Clement VI	1342–52	Clement X	1670–76
Innocent VI	1352–62	Innocent XI	1676–89
Urban V	1362–70	Alexander VIII	1689–91
Gregory XI	1370–78	Innocent XII	1691–1700
Urban VI	1378–89	Clement XI	1700–21
Boniface IX	1389–1404	Innocent XIII	1721–24
Innocent VII	1404–06	Benedict XIII	1724–30
Gregory XII	1406–15	Clement XII	1730–40
Martin V	1417–41	Benedict XIV	1740–58
Eugenius IV	1431–47	Clement XIII	1758–69
Nicholas V	1447–55	Clement XIV	1769–74
Callistus III	1455–58	Pius VI	1775–99
Pius II	1458–64	Pius VII	1800–23
Paul II	1464–71	Leo XII	1823–29
Sixtus IV	1471–84	Pius VIII	1829–30
Innocent VIII	1484–92	Gregory XVI	1831–46
Alexander VI	1492–1503	Pius IX	1846–78
Pius III	1503	Leo XIII	1878–1903
Julius II	1503–13	Pius X	1903–14
Leo X	1513–21	Benedict XV	1914–22
Hadrian VI	1522–23	Pius XI	1922–39
Clement VII	1523–34	Pius XII	1939–58
Paul III	1534–49	John XXIII	1958–63
Julius III	1550–55	Paul VI	1963–78
Marcellus II	1555	John Paul I	1978
Paul IV	1555–59	John Paul II	1978–2005
Pius IV	1559–65	Benedict XVI	2005–
Pius V	1566–72		

Ports

3 letters:	Amoy	Hull
Abo	Apia	Icel
Ayr	Baku	Kiel
Gao	Bari	Kobe
Hué	Cebu	Lima
Rio	Cóbh	Lomé
Rye	Cork	Oban
4 letters:	Deal	Omsk
Acre	Dill	Oran
Aden	Elat	Oslo
Akko	Hilo	Perm

Pula
Puri
Riga
Said
Suez
Suva
Tyre
Vigo
Wick

5 letters:
Accra
Aqaba
Arhus
Arica
Aulis
Barry
Basra
Batum
Beira
Belem
Brest
Cádiz
Cairo
Colón
Dakar
Derry
Dilli
Dover
Dubai
Eilat
Emden
Galle
Genoa
Gijón
Haifa
Izmir
Jaffa
Jedda
Jidda
Kerch
Kochi
Lagos
Larne
Leith
Lulea
Macao
Malmo
Mocha
Newry
Osaka
Ostia
Poole
Pusan
Rabat
Salto
Sidon
Sligo

Split
Surat
Tampa
Tokyo
Tunis
Turku
Visby
Yalta

6 letters:
Aarhus
Abadan
Agadir
Albany
Ancona
Ashdod
Bastia
Batumi
Beirut
Belize
Bergen
Bilbao
Bissau
Bombay
Bootle
Boston
Bremen
Burgas
Calais
Callao
Cannes
Canton
Cochin
Danzig
Darwin
Dieppe
Duluth
Dundee
Durban
Elblag
Galata
Galway
Gdańsk
Gdynia
Harbin
Havana
Hobart
Iloilo
Inchon
Juneau
Kisumu
Kuwait
Lisbon
Lobito
London
Luanda
Lübeck
Madras

Malaga
Manama
Manaus
Manila
Maputo
Mobile
Muscat
Nantes
Naples
Narvik
Nassau
Nelson
Odense
Odessa
Oporto
Ostend
Padang
Quincy
Ragusa
Recife
Rimini
Rostov
Santos
Smyrna
St Malo
Sydney
Tacoma
Tallin
Venice
Whitby
Yangon

7 letters:
Abidjan
Ajaccio
Algiers
Antibes
Antwerp
Augusta
Bangkok
Belfast
Bristol
Buffalo
Cardiff
Catania
Chicago
Cologne
Colombo
Conakry
Corinth
Dunedin
Dunkirk
Ephesus
Esbjerg
Foochow
Funchal
Geelong
Glasgow

Grimsby
Halifax
Hamburg
Harwich
Incheon
Iquique
Iquitos
Karachi
Kinsale
Kowloon
Latakia
Legaspi
Le Havre
Lerwick
Livorno
Lorient
Marsala
Messina
Milazzo
Mombasa
Munster
Newport
New York
Oakland
Okayama
Palermo
Piraeus
Rangoon
Rapallo
Rosario
Rostock
Runcorn
Salerno
San Juan
Seattle
Seville
Stettin
Swansea
Tallinn
Tampico
Tangier
Taranto
Trieste
Tripoli
Ushuaia
Wexford
Wicklow
8 letters:
Aberdeen
Acapulco
Alicante
Arbroath
Auckland
Batangas
Bathurst
Benghazi
Bordeaux

Boulogne
Brindisi
Brisbane
Cagliari
Calcutta
Cape Town
Djibouti
Flushing
Freetown
Geropiga
Göteborg
Greenock
Hamilton
Harfleur
Helsinki
Holyhead
Honolulu
Istanbul
Kanazawa
Kawasaki
Keflavik
Kingston
La Coruña
La Guaira
Limassol
Limerick
Monrovia
Montreal
Murmansk
Nagasaki
Newhaven
Penzance
Pevensey
Plymouth
Portland
Port Said
Ramsgate
Rosslare
Salvador
San Diego
Sandwich
Savannah
Schiedam
Shanghai
Syracuse
Szczecin
Takoradi
Valencia
Veracruz
Weymouth
Yokohama
9 letters:
Amsterdam
Anchorage
Angostura
Annapolis
Archangel

Baltimore
Barcelona
Cartagena
Cherbourg
Dartmouth
Dubrovnik
Dunkerque
Ellesmere
Esperance
Europoort
Famagusta
Fishguard
Fleetwood
Fremantle
Gallipoli
Gateshead
Gravesend
Guayaquil
Immingham
Inhambane
Kaohsiung
Kirkcaldy
Las Palmas
Liverpool
Lowestoft
Marseille
Melbourne
Mogadishu
Morecambe
Newcastle
Phnom Penh
Port Louis
Port Sudan
Reykjavik
Rotterdam
Santander
Schleswig
Sheerness
Singapore
Stavanger
Stockholm
Stornoway
Stranraer
Tarragona
Trondheim
Tynemouth
Vancouver
Volgograd
Walvis Bay
Waterford
Zeebrugge
10 letters:
Alexandria
Birkenhead
Bratislava
Bridgetown
Caernarfon

Cap-Haitien
Casablanca
Charleston
Chittagong
Copenhagen
East London
Folkestone
Fray Bentos
Georgetown
Gothenburg
Hammerfest
Launceston
Los Angeles
Mogadiscio
Montego Bay
Montevideo
New Orleans
Paramaribo
Portsmouth
Port Talbot
Queenstown

Sevastopol
Sunderland
Townsville
Valparaíso
Wellington
11 letters:
Buenos Aires
Dar es Salaam
Grangemouth
Londonderry
Mar del Plata
Port Moresby
Punta Arenas
Scarborough
Southampton
Trincomalee
Vladivostok
12 letters:
Barranquilla
Buenaventura
Dún Laoghaire

Jacksonville
Milford Haven
Port Adelaide
Port au Prince
Rio de Janeiro
San Francisco
San Sebastian
Santo Domingo
South Shields
13 letters:
Ellesmere Port
Great Yarmouth
Ho Chi Minh City
Hook of Holland
Port Elizabeth
Tandjungpriok
14 letters:
Vishakhapatnam
15 letters:
Saint Petersburg

Potatoes

4 letters:
Cara
5 letters:
Wilja
6 letters:
Estima
Romano
7 letters:
Desiree
Marfona
Roseval
8 letters:
Catriona

9 letters:
Charlotte
Kerr's Pink
Maris Bard
10 letters:
Arran Comet
Arran Pilot
King Edward
Maris Piper
11 letters:
Jersey Royal
12 letters:
Arran Victory

Golden Wonder
Pentland Dell
Pink Fir Apple
13 letters:
Pentland Crown
Ulster Sceptre
14 letters:
Pentland Squire
Sharpe's Express
15 letters:
Belle de Fontenay
Pentland Javelin

Pottery

4 letters:
Delf
Ming
Raku
Song
Sung
Ware
5 letters:
China
Delft
Spode
6 letters:
Bisque

Wemyss
7 letters:
Celadon
Ceramic
Etruria
Faience
Satsuma
8 letters:
Flatback
Gombroon
Majolica
Slipware
Wedgwood®

Whieldon
9 letters:
Agatewear
Creamware
Stoneware
10 letters:
Crouch-ware
Hollowware
Spongeware
11 letters:
Granitewear

Presidents of the USA

President	Party	Term of office
1. George Washington	Federalist	1789–97
2. John Adams	Federalist	1797–1801
3. Thomas Jefferson	Democratic Republican	1801–1809
4. James Madison	Democratic Republican	1809–1817
5. James Monroe	Democratic Republican	1817–25
6. John Quincy Adams	Democratic Republican	1825–29
7. Andrew Jackson	Democrat	1829–37
8. Martin Van Buren	Democrat	1837–41
9. William Henry Harrison	Whig	1841
10. John Tyler	Whig	1841–45
11. James K. Polk	Democrat	1845–49
12. Zachary Taylor	Whig	1849–50
13. Millard Fillmore	Whig	1850–53
14. Franklin Pierce	Democrat	1853–57
15. James Buchanan	Democrat	1857–61
16. Abraham Lincoln	Republican	1861–65
17. Andrew Johnson	Republican	1865–69
18. Ulysses S. Grant	Republican	1869–77
19. Rutherford B. Hayes	Republican	1877–81
20. James A. Garfield	Republican	1881
21. Chester A. Arthur	Republican	1881–85
22. Grover Cleveland	Democrat	1885–89
23. Benjamin Harrison	Republican	1889–93
24. Grover Cleveland	Democrat	1893–97
25. William McKinley	Republican	1897–1901
26. Theodore Roosevelt	Republican	1901–1909
27. William Howard Taft	Republican	1909–13
28. Woodrow Wilson	Democrat	1913–21
29. Warren G. Harding	Republican	1921–23
30. Calvin Coolidge	Republican	1923–29
31. Herbert C. Hoover	Republican	1929–33
32. Franklin D. Roosevelt	Democrat	1933–45
33. Harry S. Truman	Democrat	1945–53
34. Dwight D. Eisenhower	Republican	1953–61
35. John F. Kennedy	Democrat	1961–63
36. Lyndon B. Johnson	Democrat	1963–69
37. Richard M. Nixon	Republican	1969–74
38. Gerald R. Ford	Republican	1974–77
39. James E. Carter, Jr	Democrat	1977–81
40. Ronald W. Reagan	Republican	1981–89
41. George H. W. Bush	Republican	1989–93
42. William J. Clinton	Democrat	1993–2001
43. George W. Bush	Republican	2001–2009
44. Barack Obama	Democrat	2009–

Prey, birds of

3 letters:	Hawk	Hobby
Ern	Kite	Saker
Owl	Ruru	**6 letters:**
4 letters:	**5 letters:**	Condor
Erne	Eagle	Falcon
Gled	Glede	Lanner

Merlin
Mopoke
Osprey
7 letters:
Barn owl
Boobook
Buzzard
Goshawk
Harrier
Hawk owl
Hoot owl
Kestrel
Red kite
Vulture
8 letters:
Brown owl
Bush-hawk
Caracara
Duck hawk
Falconet
Karearea

Sea eagle
Snowy owl
Tawny owl
9 letters:
Accipiter
Bald eagle
Eagle-hawk
Fish eagle
Gerfalcon
Gier-eagle
Gyrfalcon
Horned owl
Little owl
Ossifraga
Ossifrage
Wind-hover
10 letters:
Hen harrier
Screech owl
11 letters:
Chicken hawk

Cooper's hawk
Golden eagle
Lammergeier
Lammergeyer
Sparrowhawk
12 letters:
Honey buzzard
Long-eared owl
Marsh harrier
13 letters:
Bateleur eagle
Secretary bird
Turkey buzzard
14 letters:
Bearded vulture
15 letters:
Montagu's harrier
Peregrine falcon

Prime Ministers

BRITISH PRIME MINISTERS

Prime Minister	Party	Term of office
Robert Walpole	Whig	1721–42
Earl of Wilmington	Whig	1742–43
Henry Pelham	Whig	1743–54
Duke of Newcastle	Whig	1754–56
Duke of Devonshire	Whig	1756–57
Duke of Newcastle	Whig	1757–62
Earl of Bute	Tory	1762–63
George Grenville	Whig	1763–65
Marquess of Rockingham	Whig	1765–66
Duke of Grafton	Whig	1766–70
Lord North	Tory	1770–82
Marquess of Rockingham	Whig	1782
Earl of Shelburne	Whig	1782–83
Duke of Portland	Coalition	1783
William Pitt	Tory	1783–1801
Henry Addington	Tory	1801–04
William Pitt	Tory	1804–06
Lord Grenville	Whig	1806–7
Duke of Portland	Tory	1807–09
Spencer Perceval	Tory	1809–12
Earl of Liverpool	Tory	1812–27
George Canning	Tory	1827
Viscount Goderich	Tory	1827–28
Duke of Wellington	Tory	1828–30
Earl Grey	Whig	1830–34
Viscount Melbourne	Whig	1834
Robert Peel	Conservative	1834–35
Viscount Melbourne	Whig	1835–41
Robert Peel	Conservative	1841–46

Prime Minister	Party	Term of office
Lord John Russell	Liberal	1846–52
Earl of Derby	Conservative	1852
Lord Aberdeen	Peelite	1852–55
Viscount Palmerston	Liberal	1855–58
Earl of Derby	Conservative	1858–59
Viscount Palmerston	Liberal	1859–65
Lord John Russell	Liberal	1865–66
Earl of Derby	Conservative	1866–68
Benjamin Disraeli	Conservative	1868
William Gladstone	Liberal	1868–74
Benjamin Disraeli	Conservative	1874–80
William Gladstone	Liberal	1880–85
Marquess of Salisbury	Conservative	1885–86
William Gladstone	Liberal	1886
Marquess of Salisbury	Conservative	1886–92
William Gladstone	Liberal	1892–94
Earl of Rosebery	Liberal	1894–95
Marquess of Salisbury	Conservative	1895–1902
Arthur James Balfour	Conservative	1902–05
Henry Campbell-Bannerman	Liberal	1905–08
Herbert Henry Asquith	Liberal	1908–15
Herbert Henry Asquith	Coalition	1915–16
David Lloyd George	Coalition	1916–22
Andrew Bonar Law	Conservative	1922–23
Stanley Baldwin	Conservative	1923–24
James Ramsay MacDonald	Labour	1924
Stanley Baldwin	Conservative	1924–29
James Ramsay MacDonald	Labour	1929–31
James Ramsay MacDonald	Nationalist	1931–35
Stanley Baldwin	Nationalist	1935–37
Arthur Neville Chamberlain	Nationalist	1937–40
Winston Churchill	Coalition	1940–45
Clement Attlee	Labour	1945–51
Winston Churchill	Conservative	1951–55
Anthony Eden	Conservative	1955–57
Harold Macmillan	Conservative	1957–63
Alec Douglas-Home	Conservative	1963–64
Harold Wilson	Labour	1964–70
Edward Heath	Conservative	1970–74
Harold Wilson	Labour	1974–76
James Callaghan	Labour	1976–79
Margaret Thatcher	Conservative	1979–90
John Major	Conservative	1990–97
Tony Blair	Labour	1997–2007
Gordon Brown	Labour	2007–

AUSTRALIAN PRIME MINISTERS

Prime Minister	Party	Term of office
Edmund Barton	Protectionist	1901–03
Alfred Deakin	Protectionist	1903–04
John Christian Watson	Labor	1904
George Houston Reid	Free Trade	1904–05
Alfred Deakin	Protectionist	1905–08

Prime Minister	Party	Term of office
Andrew Fisher	Labor	1908–09
Alfred Deakin	Fusion	1909–10
Andrew Fisher	Labor	1910–13
Joseph Cook	Liberal	1913–14
Andrew Fisher	Labor	1914–15
William Morris Hughes	National Labor	1915–17
William Morris Hughes	Nationalist	1917–23
Stanley Melbourne Bruce	Nationalist	1923–29
James Henry Scullin	Labor	1929–31
Joseph Aloysius Lyons	United	1931–39
Earle Christmas Page	Country	1939
Robert Gordon Menzies	United	1939–41
Arthur William Fadden	Country	1941
John Joseph Curtin	Labor	1941–45
Joseph Benedict Chifley	Labor	1945–49
Robert Gordon Menzies	Liberal	1949–66
Harold Edward Holt	Liberal	1966–67
John McEwen	Country	1967–68
John Grey Gorton	Liberal	1968–71
William McMahon	Liberal	1971–72
Edward Gough Whitlam	Labor	1972–75
John Malcolm Fraser	Liberal	1975–83
Robert James Lee Hawke	Labor	1983–91
Paul Keating	Labor	1991–96
John Howard	Liberal	1996–2007
Kevin Rudd	Labor	2007–

CANADIAN PRIME MINISTERS

Prime Minister	Party	Term of office
John A. MacDonald	Conservative	1867–73
Alexander Mackenzie	Liberal	1873–78
John A. MacDonald	Conservative	1878–91
John J.C. Abbot	Conservative	1891–92
John S.D. Thompson	Conservative	1892–94
Mackenzie Bowell	Conservative	1894–96
Charles Tupper	Conservative	1896
Wilfrid Laurier	Liberal	1896–1911
Robert Borden	Conservative	1911–20
Arthur Meighen	Conservative	1920–21
William Lyon Mackenzie King	Liberal	1921–26
Arthur Meighen	Conservative	1926
William Lyon Mackenzie King	Liberal	1926–30
Richard Bedford Bennet	Conservative	1930–35
William Lyon Mackenzie King	Liberal	1935–48
Louis St Laurent	Liberal	1948–57
John George Diefenbaker	Conservative	1957–63
Lester Bowles Pearson	Liberal	1963–68
Pierre Elliott Trudeau	Liberal	1968–79
Joseph Clark	Conservative	1979–80
Pierre Elliott Trudeau	Liberal	1980–84
John Turner	Liberal	1984
Brian Mulroney	Conservative	1984–93
Kim Campbell	Conservative	1993
Joseph Jacques Jean Chrétien	Liberal	1993–2003

Prime Minister	Party	Term of office
Paul Martin	Liberal	2003–6
Stephen Joseph Harper	Conservative	2006–

NEW ZEALAND PRIME MINISTERS

Prime Minister	Party	Term of office
Henry Sewell	—	1856
William Fox	—	1856
Edward William Stafford	—	1856–61
William Fox	—	1861–62
Alfred Domett	—	1862–63
Frederick Whitaker	—	1863–64
Frederick Aloysius Weld	—	1864–65
Edward William Stafford	—	1865–69
William Fox	—	1869–72
Edward William Stafford	—	1872
William Fox	—	1873
Julius Vogel	—	1873–75
Daniel Pollen	—	1875–76
Julius Vogel	—	1876
Harry Albert Atkinson	—	1876–77
George Grey	—	1877–79
John Hall	—	1879–82
Frederick Whitaker	—	1882–83
Harry Albert Atkinson	—	1883–84
Robert Stout	—	1884
Harry Albert Atkinson	—	1884
Robert Stout	—	1884–87
Harry Albert Atkinson	—	1887–91
John Ballance	—	1891–93
Richard John Seddon	Liberal	1893–1906
William Hall-Jones	Liberal	1906
Joseph George Ward	Liberal/National	1906–12
Thomas Mackenzie	National	1912
William Ferguson Massey	Reform	1912–25
Francis Henry Dillon Bell	Reform	1925
Joseph Gordon Coates	Reform	1925–28
Joseph George Ward	Liberal/National	1928–30
George William Forbes	United	1930–35
Michael Joseph Savage	Labour	1935–40
Peter Fraser	Labour	1940–49
Sidney George Holland	National	1949–57
Keith Jacka Holyoake	National	1957
Walter Nash	Labour	1957–60
Keith Jacka Holyoake	National	1960–72
John Ross Marshall	National	1972
Norman Eric Kirk	Labour	1972–74
Wallace Edward Rowling	Labour	1974–75
Robert David Muldoon	National	1975–84
David Russell Lange	Labour	1984–89
Geoffrey Palmer	Labour	1989–90
Mike Moore	Labour	1990
Jim Bolger	National	1990–97
Jenny Shipley	National	1997–99
Helen Clark	Labour	1999–2008
John Key	National	2008–

Programming languages

1 letter:
C
3 letters:
Ada
RPG
SQL
4 letters:
Java
LISP
LOGO
Perl

5 letters:
Algol
BASIC
Basic
COBOL
CORAL
FORTH
OCCAM
6 letters:
Pascal
PROLOG

Simula
SNOBOL
7 letters:
FORTRAN
Haskell
9 letters:
Smalltalk
10 letters:
Postscript

Proteins

4 letters:
Zein
5 letters:
Abrin
Actin
Opsin
Prion
Renin
Ricin
6 letters:
Avidin
Capsid
Enzyme
Fibrin
Globin
Gluten
Lectin
Leptin
Myosin
Ossein
7 letters:
Adipsin
Albumen
Albumin
Aleuron
Amyloid
Elastin
Fibroin
Gliadin
Hordein
Keratin

Legumin
Opsonin
Sericin
Spongin
Tubulin
8 letters:
Aleurone
Amandine
Collagen
Cytokine
Ferritin
Gliadine
Globulin
Prolamin
Spectrin
Troponin
Vitellin
9 letters:
Capsomere
Flagellin
Myoglobin
Ovalbumin
Phaseolin
Prolamine
Properdin
Protamine
Repressor
Sclerotin
10 letters:
Actomyosin
Apoprotein

Bradykinin
Calmodulin
Caseinogen
Conchiolin
Dystrophin
Factor VIII
Fibrinogen
Interferon
Lymphokine
Thrombogen
Toxalbumin
11 letters:
Angiotensin
Haploglobin
Interleukin
Lactalbumin
Transferrin
Tropomyosin
12 letters:
Lactoprotein
Serum albumin
13 letters:
Ceruloplasmin
Serum globulin
14 letters:
Immunoglobulin

Provinces of Canada

Province	Abbreviation
Alberta	AB
British Columbia	BC
Manitoba	MB
New Brunswick	NB

Province	Abbreviation
Newfoundland	NF
Northwest Territories	NWT
Nova Scotia	NS
Nunavut	NU
Ontario	ON
Prince Edward Island	PE
Quebec	PQ
Saskatchewan	SK
Yukon Territory	YT

Provinces of South Africa

Province	Capital
Eastern Cape	Bisho
Free State	Bloemfontein
Gauteng	Johannesburg
KwaZulu-Natal	Pietermaritzburg
Limpopo	Pietersburg
Mpumalanga	Nelspruit
North-West	Mafikeng
Northern Cape	Kimberley
Western Cape	Cape Town

Psychology

BRANCHES OF PSYCHOLOGY

5 letters:
Child
6 letters:
Social
8 letters:
Analytic
Clinical
Hedonics

10 letters:
Industrial
11 letters:
Comparative
Educational
12 letters:
Experimental

13 letters:
Developmental
Psychometrics
Psychophysics
14 letters:
Organizational
Parapsychology
15 letters:
Neuropsychology

PSYCHOLOGY TERMS

2 letters:
Id
3 letters:
Ego
4 letters:
Anal
Mind
Self
5 letters:
Angst

Mania
6 letters:
Phobia
Psyche
Stress
Trauma
7 letters:
Anxiety
Complex
Persona

8 letters:
Alter ego
Analysis
Delusion
Dementia
Fixation
Hypnosis
Hysteria
Neurosis
Paranoia

Superego
Syndrome
9 letters:
Death wish
Extrovert
Introvert
Obsession
Psychosis
10 letters:
Compulsion
Depression
Regression

Repression
11 letters:
Inkblot test
Personality
Sublimation
Unconscious
12 letters:
Conditioning
Freudian slip
Group therapy
Hypochondria
Subconscious

13 letters:
Consciousness
Primal therapy
Psychosomatic
Rorschach test
Schizophrenia
14 letters:
Electra complex
Gestalt therapy
Oedipus complex
Psychoanalysis

PSYCHOLOGISTS

4 letters:
Coué, *Émile*
Jung, *Carl Gustav*
5 letters:
Adler, *Alfred*
Freud, *Sigmund*
Fromm, *Erich*
James, *William*
Janet, *Pierre Marie Félix*
Luria, *Alexander Romanovich*
Reich, *Wilhelm*
Wundt, *Wilhelm Max*
6 letters:
Hering, *Ewald*
Horney, *Karen*

Köhler, *Wolfgang*
Müller, *Johannes Peter*
Pavlov, *Ivan Petrovich*
Piaget, *Jean*
Watson, *John*
7 letters:
Eysenck, *Hans Jürgen*
Fechner, *Gustav Theodor*
Skinner, *B(urrhus) F(rederic)*
9 letters:
Thorndike, *Edward Lee*
10 letters:
Ebbinghaus, *Hermann*
11 letters:
Münsterberg, *Hugo*

Purple, shades of

4 letters:
Plum
Puce
Wine
5 letters:
Lilac
Mauve
Pansy
Royal
6 letters:
Claret

Indigo
Tyrian
Violet
7 letters:
Carmine
Gentian
Heather
Magenta
8 letters:
Amethyst
Burgundy

Dubonnet
Lavender
Mulberry
9 letters:
Aubergine
Peach-blow
10 letters:
Heliotrope
Periwinkle
11 letters:
Gentian blue

Queens

3 letters:
Mab
May
4 letters:
Anna
Anne
Bess
Dido
Juno
Leda
Mary
5 letters:
Helen
Maeve
Sheba
6 letters:
Atossa
Balkis
Esther
Hecuba
Isabel

Ishtar
Isolde
7 letters:
Camilla
Candace
Eleanor
Jocasta
Matilda
Omphale
Titania
8 letters:
Adelaide
Alcestis
Boadicea
Boudicca
Brunhild
Caroline
Eleanora
Gertrude
Hermione
Penelope

Phaedram
Victoria
9 letters:
Alexandra
Artemesia
Brunhilde
Cleopatra
Elizabeth
Guinevere
Hippolyta
Nefertiti
Semiramis
10 letters:
Hatshepset
Hatshepsut
Persephone
Proserpina
15 letters:
Marie Antoinette

Rabbits and hares

4 letters:
Cony
Hare
Pika
5 letters:
Coney
6 letters:
Rabbit

10 letters:
Arctic hare
Cottontail
Jack rabbit
11 letters:
Belgian hare
12 letters:
Angora rabbit

Snowshoe hare
14 letters:
Snowshoe rabbit

Red, shades of

3 letters:
Bay
4 letters:
Foxy
Pink
Plum
Puce
Rose
Rosy
Ruby
Rust
Wine
5 letters:
Coral
Flame
Flesh
Gules
Henna
Liver
Peach
Poppy
Sandy
6 letters:
Auburn
Cerise

Cherry
Claret
Copper
Damask
Ginger
Maroon
Russet
Titian
Turkey
7 letters:
Carmine
Carroty
Coppery
Crimson
Fuchsia
Magenta
Old rose
Oxblood
Roseate
Scarlet
Tea rose
Vermeil
8 letters:
Baby pink
Burgundy

Cardinal
Chestnut
Cinnabar
Cyclamen
Dubonnet
Mulberry
9 letters:
Carnation
Grenadine
Peach-blow
Raspberry
Shell pink
Vermilion
10 letters:
Oyster pink
Salmon pink
Strawberry
Terracotta
11 letters:
Burnt sienna

Regions, Administrative

FRENCH REGIONS

6 letters:
Alsace
Centre
7 letters:
Corsica
8 letters:
Auvergne
Brittany
Burgundy
Limousin
Lorraine

Picardie
9 letters:
Aquitaine
10 letters:
Rhône-Alpes
11 letters:
Île-de-France
Pays de Loire
12 letters:
Franche-Comté
Midi-Pyrénées

14 letters:
Basse-Normandie
Haute-Normandie
15 letters:
Nord-Pas-de-Calais
Poitou-Charentes

FRENCH DÉPARTEMENTS

3 letters:
Ain
Lot
Var
4 letters:
Aube
Aude
Cher
Eure

Gard
Gers
Jura
Nord
Oise
Orne
Tarn
5 letters:
Aisne

Corse
Doubs
Drôme
Indre
Isère
Loire
Marne
Meuse
Paris

Rhône
Saône
Somme
Yonne
6 letters:
Allier
Ariège
Cantal
Creuse
Essone
Gayane
Landes
Loiret
Lozère
Manche
Sarthe
Savoie
Vendée
Vienne
Vosges
7 letters:
Ardèche
Aveyron
Bas Rhin
Corrèze
Cote d'Or
Gironde

Hérault
Mayenne
Moselle
Niveres
Réunion
8 letters:
Ardennes
Calvados
Charente
Dordogne
Haut Rhin
Morbihan
Val d'Oise
Vaucluse
Yvelines
9 letters:
Finistère
Puy de Dôme
10 letters:
Deux Sèvres
Eure et Loir
Guadeloupe
Haute Loire
Haute Marne
Loir et Cher
Martinique
Val de Marne

11 letters:
Côtes du Nord
Hautes Alpes
Haute Savoie
Haute Vienne
Pas de Calais
12 letters:
Haute Garonne
Hauts de Seine
Indre et Loire
Lot et Garonne
Maine et Loire
Saône et Loire
Seine et Marne
13 letters:
Ille et Vilaine
Seine Maritime
Tarn et Garonne
14 letters:
Alpes Maritimes
Bouches du Rhône
Hautes Pyrénées
15 letters:
Loire Atlantique
Seine Saint Denis

GERMAN STATES

6 letters:
Berlin
Bremen
Hessen
Saxony
7 letters:

Bavaria
Hamburg
8 letters:
Saarland
9 letters:
Thuringia

11 letters:
Brandenburg
Lower Saxony
12 letters:
Saxony-Anhalt

ITALIAN REGIONS

5 letters:
Lazio
6 letters:
Marche
Molise
Puglia
Sicily
Umbria
Veneto

7 letters:
Abruzzo
Liguria
Tuscany
8 letters:
Calabria
Campania
Lombardy
Piedmont

Sardinia
10 letters:
Basilicata
11 letters:
Valle d'Aosta
13 letters:
Emilia-Romagna

ITALIAN PROVINCES

4 letters:
Asti
Bari
Como
Enna
Lodi
Pisa
Roma
5 letters:
Aosta
Cuneo
Forlì
Lecce
Lecco
Lucca
Nuoro
Parma
Pavia
Prato
Rieti
Siena
Terni
Udine
6 letters:
Ancona
Arezzo
Chieti
Foggia
Genova
Latina
Matera
Milano
Modena
Napoli
Novara
Padova
Pesaro

Ragusa
Rimini
Rovigo
Savona
Teramo
Torino
Trento
Varese
Verona
7 letters:
Belluno
Bergamo
Bologna
Bolzano
Brescia
Caserta
Catania
Cosenza
Cremona
Crotone
Ferrara
Firenze
Gorizia
Imperia
Isernia
L'Aquila
Livorno
Mantova
Messina
Palermo
Perugia
Pescara
Pistoia
Potenza
Ravenna
Salerno
Sassari

Sondrio
Taranto
Trapani
Treviso
Trieste
Venezia
Vicenza
Viterbo
8 letters:
Avellino
Brindisi
Cagliari
Grosseto
La Spezia
Macerata
Oristano
Piacenza
Siracusa
Verbania
Vercelli
9 letters:
Agrigento
Benevento
Catanzaro
Frosinone
Pordenone
10 letters:
Campobasso
11 letters:
Alessandria
12 letters:
Ascoli Piceno
Massa Carrara
Reggio Emilia
Vibo Valentia
13 letters:
Caltanissetta

SPANISH REGIONS

5 letters:
Ceuta
6 letters:
Aragón
Madrid
Murcia
7 letters:
Galicia
La Rioja
Melilla
Navarra

8 letters:
Asturias
9 letters:
Andalucía
Cantabria
Catalonia
11 letters:
Extremadura
12 letters:
Castilla-León

13 letters:
Basque Country
Canary Islands
15 letters:
Balearic Islands

SPANISH PROVINCES

4 letters:
Jaén
León
Lugo
5 letters:
Álava
Ávila
Cádiz
Ceuta
Soria
6 letters:
Burgos
Cuenca
Girona
Huelva
Huesca
Lleida
Madrid
Málaga
Murcia
Orense

Teruel
Toledo
Zamora
7 letters:
Almerìa
Badajoz
Cácares
Cordoba
Granada
La Rioja
Melilla
Navarra
Segovia
Sevilla
Vizcaya
8 letters:
Albacete
Alicante
Asturias
La Coruna
Palencia

Valencia
Zaragoza
9 letters:
Alhucemas
Balearics
Barcelona
Cantabria
Castellón
Guipúzcoa
Las Palmas
Salamanca
Tarragona
10 letters:
Chafarinas
Ciudad Real
Pontevedra
Valladolid
11 letters:
Gualalajara
15 letters:
Vélez de la Gomera

Religion

RELIGIONS

4 letters:
Babi
Druz
Jain
5 letters:
Baha'i
Druse
Druze
Hasid
Islam
Jaina
Jewry
Sunna
6 letters:
Babism
Culdee
Gueber
Guebre
Hadith
Hassid
Jesuit
Loyola
Sabian
Shaker
Shango
Shembe
Shinto
Taoism

Voodoo
Zabian
7 letters:
Animism
Baha'ism
Bogomil
Ismaili
Jainism
Judaism
Lamaism
Macumba
Mahatma
Orphism
Parsism
Piarist
Sikhism
Tsabian
Yezidis
8 letters:
Buddhism
Druidism
Hinduism
Lutheran
Manichee
Mazdaism
Mazdeism
Paganism
Santeria

Satanism
Theatine
9 letters:
Celestine
Coenobite
Hindooism
Jansenism
Mithraism
Mormonism
Pantheist
Shamanism
Shintoism
Utraquist
Voodooism
Zoroaster
10 letters:
Carthusian
Cistercian
Gilbertine
Heliolatry
Hospitaler
Manicheism
Zend-avesta
11 letters:
Camaldolite
Hare Krishna
Hospitaller
Ignorantine

Manichaeism
Mithraicism
Ryobu Shinto
Scientology®
Zoroastrism
12 letters:
Christianity

Confucianism
Zarathustric
13 letters:
Sons of Freedom
Tractarianism
14 letters:
Rastafarianism

Zoroastrianism
15 letters:
Christadelphian
Jehovah's Witness

RELIGIOUS BOOKS

2 letters:
Lu
4 letters:
Veda
5 letters:
Bible
Koran
Li Chi
Quran
Torah
6 letters:
Granth
I Ching
Talmud

7 letters:
Rigveda
Shi Jing
8 letters:
Ayurveda
Ramayana
Samaveda
Shi Ching
Tipitaka
9 letters:
Adi Granth
Apocrypha
Atharveda
Siddhanta

Tripitaka
Yajurveda
11 letters:
Mahabharata
12 letters:
Bhagavad-Gita
Book of Mormon
New Testament
Old Testament
15 letters:
Guru Granth Sahib

RELIGIOUS BUILDINGS

5 letters:
Abbey
Kaaba
Marae
6 letters:
Bethel
Chapel

Church
Mosque
Temple
7 letters:
Convent
8 letters:
Gurdwara

9 letters:
Cathedral
Monastery
Synagogue
10 letters:
Tabernacle

RELIGIOUS CLOTHING

3 letters:
Alb
4 letters:
Coif
Cope
Cowl
5 letters:
Amice
Cotta
Habit
Mitre
6 letters:
Almuce
Chimar
Chimer
Cornet

Guimpe
Peplos
Peplus
Rochet
Tippet
Wimple
7 letters:
Biretta
Calotte
Capuche
Cassock
Chimere
Gremial
Infulae
Maniple
Mozetta

Pallium
Soutane
Tunicle
8 letters:
Berretta
Capouche
Chasuble
Dalmatic
Mozzetta
Scapular
Surplice
9 letters:
Clericals
Dog collar
Shovel hat
Surcingle

Zucchetto
10 letters:
Canonicals

11 letters:
Mantelletta
Pontificals

12 letters:
Superhumeral
14 letters:
Clerical collar

RELIGIOUS FESTIVALS

4 letters:
Holi
Lent
5 letters:
Hirja
Purim
Wesak
6 letters:
Advent
Diwali
Easter
Pesach
7 letters:
Ramadan
Shavuot
Succoth
Sukkoth
Trinity
Whitsun
Yuan Tan
8 letters:
Al Hijrah
Baisakhi
Bodhi Day

Chanukah
Dussehra
Epiphany
Hanukkah
Id-ul-Adha
Id-ul-Fitr
Passover
Rogation
9 letters:
Candlemas
Ching Ming
Christmas
Eid ul-Adha
Eid ul-Fitr
Pentecost
Rama Naumi
Yom Kippur
10 letters:
Good Friday
Michaelmas
Palm Sunday
Sexagesima
11 letters:
Dhammacakka

Hola Mohalla
12 letters:
Ascension Day
Ash Wednesday
Janamashtami
Lailat ul-Qadr
Moon Festival
Quadragesima
Rosh Hashanah
Septuagesima
13 letters:
Corpus Christi
Lailat ul-Barah
Passion Sunday
Quinquagesima
Raksha Bandhan
Shrove Tuesday
14 letters:
Day of Atonement
Mahashivaratri
Maundy Thursday
Winter Festival

See also:
➤ **Angels** ➤ **Apocalypse, Four Horsemen of** ➤ **Apostles**
➤ **Archbishops of Canterbury** ➤ **Bible** ➤ **Buddhism** ➤ **Disciples**
➤ **Ecclesiastical terms** ➤ **Gods and Goddesses** ➤ **Hindu**
denominations and sects ➤ **Jewish denominations and sects**
➤ **Monastic orders** ➤ **Monks** ➤ **Saints**

Reptiles

2 letters:
Go
3 letters:
Asp
Boa
4 letters:
Habu
5 letters:
Adder
Agama
Anole
Cobra
Gecko
Krait
Mamba

Racer
Skink
Snake
Swift
Tokay
Viper
6 letters:
Agamid
Caiman
Cayman
Dugite
Dukite
Elapid
Freshy
Garial

Gavial
Goanna
Iguana
Leguan
Lizard
Moloch
Python
Saltie
Taipan
Turtle
7 letters:
Camoodi
Frillie
Gharial
Monitor

Ngarara
Perenty
Rattler
Tuatara
8 letters:
Anaconda
Bungarra
Cerastes
Hawkbill
Moccasin
Perentie
Pit viper
Rat snake
Ringhals
Sea snake
Slowworm
Terrapin
Tortoise
9 letters:
Alligator
Blindworm
Blue racer
Boomslang
Box turtle
Bull snake
Chameleon
Crocodile
Deaf adder
Galliwasp
Hamadryad
Hawksbill
Hoop snake
Jew lizard
King cobra
King snake
Milk snake
Mud turtle
Puff adder

Rock snake
Sand viper
Sphenodon
Tree snake
Whip snake
10 letters:
Bandy-bandy
Black snake
Blind snake
Blue tongue
Brown snake
Bushmaster
Chuckwalla
Copperhead
Coral snake
Death adder
Fer-de-lance
Glass snake
Grass snake
Horned toad
Kabaragoya
Loggerhead
Massasauga
Rock python
Sand lizard
Sidewinder
Tiger snake
Wall lizard
Water snake
Worm lizard
11 letters:
Amphisbaena
Carpet snake
Constrictor
Cottonmouth
Diamondback
Gaboon viper
Garter snake

Gila monster
Gopher snake
Green turtle
Horned viper
Indigo snake
Leatherback
Mallee snake
Rattlesnake
Smooth snake
Thorn lizard
Thorny devil
12 letters:
Diamond snake
Flying dragon
Flying lizard
Hognose snake
Komodo dragon
Komodo lizard
13 letters:
Bearded dragon
Bearded lizard
Bicycle lizard
Cycling lizard
Diamond python
Frilled lizard
Giant tortoise
Mountain devil
Water moccasin
14 letters:
Boa constrictor
Cobra de capello
Harlequin snake
Leathery turtle
Malayan monitor
Snapping turtle
15 letters:
Hawksbill turtle
Schneider python

See also:
➤ **Dinosaurs** ➤ **Lizards** ➤ **Snakes**

Republics

3 letters:	Togo	Malta
UAR	**5 letters:**	Nauru
4 letters:	Belau	Niger
Chad	Benin	Palau
Cuba	Chile	Sudan
Eire	Czech	Syria
Fiji	Egypt	Yemen
Iran	Gabon	Zaire
Komi	Ghana	**6 letters:**
Laos	Haiti	Angola
Mali	Italy	Bukavu
Peru	Khmer	Gambia

Guinea
Guyana
Ingush
Israel
Kalmyk
Latvia
Malawi
Mexico
Myanma
Panama
Rwanda
Serbia
Turkey
Weimar
Zambia
7 letters:
Albania
Algeria
Andorra
Bashkir
Belarus
Bolivia
Burundi
Chechen
Comoros
Croatia
Ecuador
Estonia
Finland
Hungary
Iceland
Kalmuck
Khakass
Lebanon
Liberia
Moldova
Myanmar
Namibia

Nigeria
Romania
Senegal
Somalia
Surinam
Tunisia
Ukraine
Uruguay
Vanuatu
Vietnam
8 letters:
Botswana
Bulgaria
Cambodia
Cameroon
Chechnya
Colombia
Dagestan
Djibouti
Dominica
Esthonia
Honduras
Karelian
Kiribati
Malagasy
Maldives
Mongolia
Paraguay
Sinn Fein
Slovakia
Slovenia
Sri Lanka
Tanzania
Udmurtia
Zimbabwe
9 letters:
Argentina
Cape Verde

Costa Rica
Dominican
Guatemala
Indonesia
Kazakstan
Lithuania
Macedonia
Mauritius
Nicaragua
San Marino
Venezuela
10 letters:
Azerbaijan
Bangladesh
Belarussia
El Salvador
Kazakhstan
Kyrgyzstan
Madagascar
Mauritania
Montenegro
Mordvinian
Mozambique
Tajikistan
Ubang-Shari
Yugoslavia
11 letters:
Afghanistan
Byelorussia
Philippines
Sierra Leone
Switzerland
12 letters:
Guinea-Bissau
Turkmenistan
13 letters:
Bashkortostan

Resins

3 letters:
Gum
Lac
4 letters:
Arar
Hing
Kino
Urea
5 letters:
Amber
Amino
Copai
Copal
Damar
Elemi

Epoxy
Myrrh
Roset
Rosin
Rosit
Rozet
Rozit
Saran®
6 letters:
Balsam
Charas
Conima
Copalm
Dammar
Dammer

Gambir
Mastic
Storax
Styrax
7 letters:
Acaroid
Benzoin
Caranna
Carauna
Churrus
Copaiba
Copaiva
Galipot
Gambier
Gamboge

Glyptal
Hashish
Jalapin
Ladanum
Polymer
Shellac
Xylenol
8 letters:
Bakelite®
Benjamin
Cannabin
Galbanum
Guaiacum

Hasheesh
Melamine
Olibanum
Opopanax
Phenolic
Propolis
Retinite
Sandarac
Scammony
Takamaka
9 letters:
Asafetida
Courbaril

Polyester
Sagapenum
Sandarach
10 letters:
Asafoetida
11 letters:
Podophyllin
12 letters:
Dragon's blood
Frankincense

Rice and other cereals

4 letters:
Bran
Corn
Oats
Ragi
Sago
5 letters:
Maize
Wheat
6 letters:
Millet

7 letters:
Oatmeal
Tapioca
8 letters:
Couscous
Wild rice
9 letters:
Brown rice
Patna rice
10 letters:
Indian rice

11 letters:
Arborio rice
Basmati rice
Bulgur wheat
13 letters:
Long grain rice
14 letters:
Short grain rice

Rivers

2 letters:
Ob
Po
Si
Xi
3 letters:
Aar
Ain
Aln
Axe
Ayr
Bug
Cam
Dee
Don
Ems
Esk
Exe
Fal
Fly
Han
Hsi
Inn
Lee
Lot

Nar
Ord
Red
San
Tay
Tet
Ure
Usk
Var
Wye
4 letters:
Abus
Abzu
Acis
Adur
Aire
Alma
Alph
Amur
Aran
Aras
Arno
Aube
Aude
Avon

Back
Beni
Bomu
Cher
Dart
Deva
Doon
Dove
Drin
Earn
Ebbw
Ebro
Eden
Eder
Elbe
Erne
Esla
Eure
Gila
Göta
Huon
Idle
Isar
Iser
Isis

Juba
Kama
Kill
Kura
Kwai
Lahn
Lech
Lena
Liao
Lune
Maas
Main
Meta
Milk
Miño
Mole
Nene
Neva
Nile
Nith
Oder
Ohio
Oise
Ouse
Oxus
Prut
Ruhr
Saar
Sava
Save
Soar
Spey
Styx
Swan
Swat
Taff
Tana
Tarn
Tees
Teme
Test
Tyne
Uele
Ural
Vaal
Waal
Wear
Xero
Yalu
Yare
Yate
Yser
Yüan
Yüen

5 letters:
Abana
Acton

Adige
Afton
Agate
Aisne
Aldan
Apure
Argun
Avoca
Benue
Boyne
Cauca
Chari
Clyde
Congo
Cross
Dasht
Desna
Doubs
Douro
Drava
Drave
Duero
Dvina
Eblis
Firth
Fleet
Forth
Gogra
Green
Havel
Indre
Indus
Isère
James
Jumna
Juruá
Kabul
Kasai
Kenga
Kuban
Lethe
Liard
Lippe
Loire
Marne
Meuse
Minho
Mosel
Mulla
Namoi
Negro
Neman
Niger
Ogowe
Onega
Oreti
Peace

Pearl
Pecos
Pelly
Piave
Pison
Plate
Purús
Rance
Rhein
Rhine
Rhône
Rogue
Saône
Seine
Shari
Shiré
Siang
Siret
Skien
Slave
Snake
Snowy
Somme
Spree
Staff
Stour
Swale
Tagus
Tamar
Tapti
Tarim
Teign
Terek
Tiber
Tisza
Tobol
Trent
Tweed
Volga
Volta
Warta
Weser
Xiang
Xingú
Yaqui
Yarra
Yonne
Yssel
Yukon

6 letters:
Albany
Allier
Amazon
Anadyr
Angara
Arzina
Atbara

Barcoo
Barrow
Bío-Bío
Calder
Canton
Chenab
Clutha
Crouch
Cuiaba
Cydnus
Danube
Dawson
Donets
Duddon
Durack
Finlay
Fraser
Gambia
Ganges
Glomma
Granta
Hodder
Hsiang
Hudson
Humber
Iguaçú
IJssel
Irtish
Irwell
Itchen
Japurá
Javari
Javary
Jhelum
Jordan
Kagera
Kaveri
Kennet
Kolyma
Komati
Liffey
Mamoré
Medway
Mekong
Mersey
Mohawk
Molopo
Morava
Moskva
Murray
Neckar
Neisse
Nelson
Nyeman
Ogooué
Orange
Orwell

Ottawa
Pahang
Paraná
Pripet
Rakaia
Ribble
Riffle
Rother
Sabine
Salado
Salado
Sambre
Santee
Severn
Struma
Sutlej
Sutley
Swanee
Tanana
Tarsus
Teviot
Thames
Ticino
Tigris
Tugela
Tyburn
Ubangi
Ussuri
Vardar
Vienne
Vltava
Wabash
Wairau
Wensum
Wharfe
Yarrow
Yellow
7 letters:
Acheron
Alabama
Aruwimi
Bermejo
Caquetá
Cauvery
Chagres
Cocytus
Damodar
Darling
Derwent
Detroit
Dnieper
Dubglas
Durance
Ettrick
Fitzroy
Garonne
Genesee

Gironde
Guaporé
Helmand
Hooghly
Huang He
Hwangho
Iguassú
Irawadi
Kanawha
Krishna
Lachlan
Limpopo
Lualaba
Madeira
Manning
Marañón
Maritsa
Mataura
Meander
Moselle
Narmada
Niagara
Orinoco
Orontes
Paraíba
Pechora
Pharpar
Potomac
Rubicon
Sabrina
Salinas
Salween
Salzach
Sanders
Scheldt
Senegal
Shannon
Songhua
Swannee
Tapajós
Thomson
Ucayali
Uruguay
Vistula
Waikato
Washita
Welland
Yangtse
Yangtze
Yenisei
Yenisey
Zambese
Zambezi
8 letters:
Amu Darya
Anderson
Apurimac

Araguaia
Arkansas
Berezina
Blue Nile
Canadian
Charente
Cherwell
Chindwin
Clarence
Colorado
Columbia
Daintree
Delaware
Demerara
Dneister
Dniester
Dordogne
Flinders
Franklin
Gascoyne
Godavari
Guadiana
Illinois
Kentucky
Klondike
Kootenai
Kootenay
Maeander
Mahanadi
Menderes
Missouri
Mitchell
Okanagan
Okavango
Ouachita
Pactolus
Paraguay
Parnaíba
Putumayo
Rio Negro

Safid Rud
Saguenay
Savannah
Suwannee
Syr Darya
Torridge
Toulouse
Tunguska
Victoria
Volturno
Wanganui
Windrush
Zhu Jiang
9 letters:
Ashburton
Athabaska
Billabong
Churchill
Crocodile
Des Moines
Essequibo
Euphrates
Irrawaddy
Kuskokwim
Mackenzie
Macquarie
Magdalena
Minnesota
Murchison
Parnahiba
Pilcomayo
Porcupine
Qu'Appelle
Rangitata
Richelieu
Rio Branco
Rio Grande
Saint John
Salambria
Santa Cruz

Tennessee
Tocantins
White Nile
Wisconsin
10 letters:
Black Volta
Blackwater
Chao Phraya
Courantyne
Housatonic
Kizil Irmak
Phlegethon
Rangitaiki
Rangitikei
Sacramento
Saint Croix
St Lawrence
White Volta
11 letters:
Assiniboine
Brahmaputra
Connecticut
Cooper Creek
Lesser Slave
Madre de Dios
Mississippi
Monongahela
Shatt-al-Arab
Susquehanna
Yellowstone
12 letters:
Cooper's Creek
Guadalquivir
Murrumbidgee
Saskatchewan
13 letters:
Little Bighorn
Saint Lawrence

Rivers of Hell

4 letters:
Styx (River of Oath)
5 letters:
Lethe (River of Forgetfulness)
7 letters:
Acheron (River of Woe)
Cocytus (River of Lament)
10 letters:
Phlegethon (River of Fire)

Rocks

2 letters:
Aa
3 letters:
Gem
Gib
Jow
Tor
4 letters:
Bell
Clay
Coal
Crag
Gang
Glam
Grit
Jura
Lava
Lias
Noup
Reef
Sill
Sima
Trap
Tufa
Tuff
Zoic
5 letters:
Ayers
Brash
Calpe
Chair
Chalk
Chert
Cliff
Craig
Elvan
Flint
Geode
Glass
Krans
Loess
Magma
Nappe
Scalp
Scree
Shale
Skarn
Slate
Solid
Stone
Trass
Uluru
Wacke
6 letters:
Aplite

Arkose
Banket
Basalt
Dacite
Diapir
Dunite
Flaser
Flysch
Fossil
Gabbro
Gangue
Gibber
Gneiss
Gossan
Gozzan
Gravel
Inlier
Kingle
Marble
Masada
Norite
Oolite
Pelite
Pluton
Pumice
Rognon
Sarsen
Schist
Sinter
Skerry
Sklate
S. Peter
Stonen
Synroc
Tephra
7 letters:
Aquifer
Boulder
Breccia
Clastic
Cuprite
Cyanean
Diamond
Diorite
Eucrite
Fastnet
Felsite
Granite
Greisen
Lignite
Lorelei
Marlite
Minette
Molasse
Moraine

Needles
Nunatak
Olivine
Ophites
Outcrop
Outlier
Peridot
Picrite
Remanie
Rhaetic
Sinking
Spilite
Syenite
Thulite
Tripoli
Wenlock
8 letters:
Adularia
Aegirine
Andesite
Aphanite
Basanite
Brockram
Burstone
Calcrete
Calc-tufa
Calc-tuff
Ciminite
Diabasic
Dolerite
Dolomite
Eclogite
Eklogite
Elvanite
Eutaxite
Fahlband
Felstone
Ganister
Hepatite
Hornfels
Idocrase
Inchcape
Laterite
Lopolith
Mesolite
Mudstone
Mylonite
Obsidian
Peperino
Perknite
Petuntse
Phyllite
Pisolite
Plutonic
Plymouth

Porphyry
Psammite
Psephite
Ragstone
Regolith
Rhyolite
Rocaille
Roe-stone
Saxatile
Saxonite
Scorpion
Sunstone
Taconite
Tarpeian
Tephrite
The Olgas
Tonalite
Trachyte
Trappean
Xenolith
9 letters:
Anticline
Argillite
Batholite
Bentonite
Bluestone
Buhrstone
Claystone
Cockhorse
Colluvium
Cornstone
Dalradian
Eddystone
Edinburgh
Evaporite
Firestone
Flowstone
Gannister
Gibraltar
Goslarite
Granulite
Graywacke
Greensand
Greystone
Greywacke
Hornstone
Impactite
Intrusion
Ironstone
Laccolite
Laccolith

Limestone
Meteorite
Migmatite
Monadnock
Monocline
Monzonite
Mortstone
Mugearite
Natrolite
Neocomian
Nunatakkr
Ophiolite
Ottrelite
Pegmatite
Petrology
Phonolite
Phosphate
Pleonaste
Protogine
Quartzite
Reservoir
Sandstone
Saprolite
Scablands
Schistose
Siltstone
Soapstone
Tachylyte
Theralite
Tinguaite
Toadstone
Travertin
Variolite
Vulcanite
Whinstone
Whunstane
Zechstein
10 letters:
Ailsa Craig
Amygdaloid
Anthracite
Camptonite
Epidiorite
Foundation
Granophyre
Greenstone
Hypabyssal
Ignimbrite
Kersantite
Kimberlite
Lherzolite

Limburgite
Novaculite
Palagonite
Peridotite
Permafrost
Phenocryst
Pitchstone
Pyroxenite
Rupestrian
Schalstein
Serpentine
Sparagmite
Stinkstone
Stonebrash
Stonehenge
Syntagmata
Teschenite
Touchstone
Travertine
Troctolite
11 letters:
Agglomerate
Amphibolite
Annabergite
Anorthosite
Carbonatite
Geanticline
Halleflinta
Lamprophyre
Monchiquite
Napoleonite
Nephelinite
Phillipsite
Pyroclastic
Sedimentary
Symplegades
12 letters:
Babingtonite
Conglomerate
Granodiorite
Grossularite
Hornblendite
Slickenslide
Stromatolite
Syntagmatite
Thunderstone
13 letters:
Hypersthenite
14 letters:
Roche moutonnée

See also:
➤ **Minerals** ➤ **Ores** ➤ **Stones**

Rodents

3 letters:
Mus
Rat
4 letters:
Cavy
Jird
Mara
Paca
Vole
5 letters:
Aguti
Bobac
Bobak
Civet
Coypu
Hutia
Hyrax
Kiore
Mouse
Murid
Ratel
Shrew
Taira
6 letters:
Agouti
Beaver
Boomer
Dassie
Gerbil
Glires
Gopher
Hog-rat
Jerbil
Jerboa
Marmot
Nutria
Ratton
Suslik

Taguan
7 letters:
Acouchi
Acouchy
Cane rat
Chincha
Glutton
Hamster
Lemming
Mole rat
Muskrat
Ondatra
Pack rat
Potoroo
Souslik
8 letters:
Banxring
Biscacha
Bizcacha
Black rat
Brown rat
Capybara
Chipmunk
Cricetus
Dormouse
Gerbille
Hampster
Hedgehog
Māori rat
Musquash
Ochotona
Sciurine
Sewellel
Squirrel
Tucutuco
Tucu-tuco
Viscacha
Vizcacha

Water rat
White rat
9 letters:
Bandicoot
Bangsring
Chickaree
Deer mouse
Delundung
Desert rat
Groundhog
Guinea pig
Jerboa rat
Norway rat
Porcupine
Water vole
Woodchuck
10 letters:
Chinchilla
Dargawarra
Fieldmouse
House mouse
Springhaas
Springhase
11 letters:
Fox squirrel
Kangaroo rat
Pocket mouse
Red squirrel
Spermophile
12 letters:
Grey squirrel
Harvest mouse
Hopping mouse
Jumping mouse
Pocket gopher
14 letters:
Flying squirrel
Ground squirrel

Roman numerals

Numeral	Equivalent	Numeral	Equivalent
A	50	N	90
B	300	O	11
C	100	P	400
D	500	Q	500
E	250	R	80
F	40	S	7 or 70
G	400	T	160
H	200	V	5
I	1	X	10
K	250	Y	150
L	50	Z	2000
M	1000		

Rome, the seven hills of

7 letters:
Caelian
Viminal

8 letters:
Aventine
Palatine
Quirinal

9 letters:
Esquiline
10 letters:
Capitoline

Roofing

3 letters:
Hip
4 letters:
Bell
Dome
5 letters:
Gable
Skirt
6 letters:
French

Hipped
Pop-top
Saddle
Thatch
Thetch
7 letters:
Belfast
Gambrel
Hardtop
Mansard

Shingle
8 letters:
Imperial
Pavilion
9 letters:
Monopitch
10 letters:
Jerkin-head
12 letters:
Porte-cochère

Ropes

3 letters:
Guy
Tow
4 letters:
Balk
Cord
Fall
Jeff
Line
Stay
Vang
5 letters:
Baulk
Brail
Cable
Guide
Lasso
Longe
Lunge
Riata
Sheet
Sugan
Trace
Wanty
Widdy
6 letters:
Cablet
Cordon

Earing
Halser
Halter
Hawser
Inhaul
Marlin
Prusik
Roband
Robbin
Runner
Shroud
String
Tackle
7 letters:
Bobstay
Cringle
Halyard
Lanyard
Marline
Mooring
Outhaul
Painter
Pastern
Rawhide
Stirrup
Swifter
Towline
Triatic

8 letters:
Backstay
Boltrope
Bunt-line
Downhaul
Forestay
Gantline
Halliard
Headfast
Jack-stay
Prolonge
Selvagee
Spun-yarn
9 letters:
Breeching
Foresheet
Mainbrace
Mainsheet
Reef point
Sternfast
Timenoguy
10 letters:
Hawser-laid
Kernmantel
11 letters:
Triatic stay
13 letters:
Futtock-shroud

Rulers

TITLES OF RULERS

3 letters:
Ban
Bey
Dey
Mir
Oba
Raj
Rex
4 letters:
Amir
Cham
Czar
Doge
Duce
Duke
Emir
Imam
Inca
Khan
King
Pope
Raja
Rana
Rani
Shah
Tsar
Vali
Wali
5 letters:
Ameer
Ardri
Calif
Chief
Dewan
Diwan
Imaum
Kalif
Mogul
Mpret
Mudir
Nabob
Nawab
Negus
Nizam
Pacha
Pasha
Queen
Rajah
Ranee
Shaka

Sheik
Sophi
Sophy
Tenno
6 letters:
Atabeg
Atabek
Caesar
Caliph
Chagan
Dergue
Despot
Dynast
Exarch
Führer
Kabaka
Kaiser
Khalif
Manchu
Mikado
Prince
Regent
Sachem
Satrap
Sharif
Sheikh
Sherif
Shogun
Sirdar
Squier
Squire
Sultan
Tycoon
Tyrant
7 letters:
Abbasid
Ardrigh
Bajayet
Bajazet
Catapan
Chogyal
Elector
Emperor
Empress
Gaekwar
Gaikwar
Jamshid
Jamshyd
Khedive
Lesbian

Monarch
Pharaoh
Podesta
Shereef
Souldan
Toparch
Viceroy
8 letters:
Archduke
Autocrat
Burgrave
Caudillo
Dictator
Ethnarch
Heptarch
Hierarch
Hospodar
Maharaja
Maharani
Mameluke
Mistress
Oligarch
Padishah
Sagamore
Sassanid
Suzerain
Tetrarch
9 letters:
Bretwalda
Cosmocrat
Dalai Lama
Maharajah
Maharanee
Ochlocrat
Pendragon
Plutocrat
Potentate
Sovereign
Vicereine
10 letters:
Aristocrat
Great Mogul
Plantocrat
Rajpramukh
Stadholder
Stratocrat
11 letters:
Stadtholder

FAMOUS RULERS

4 letters:
Nero
5 letters:
Herod
Lenin
Louis
6 letters:
Castro
Cheops
Franco
Hitler
Nasser
Stalin
7 letters:
Idi Amin
Saladin
8 letters:
Augustus
Bismarck

Boadicea
Boudicca
Caligula
Cromwell
De Gaulle
Hirohito
Nicholas
Pericles
Victoria
9 letters:
Churchill
Cleopatra
Elizabeth
Mao Zedong
Montezuma
Mussolini
Tamerlane
10 letters:
Caractacus

Kublai Khan
Mao Tse-tung
11 letters:
Charlemagne
Genghis Khan
Prester John
Tamburlaine
Tutankhamen
Tutankhamun
12 letters:
Chandragupta
Julius Caesar
13 letters:
Haile Selassie
Peter the Great
14 letters:
Alfred the Great
15 letters:
Ivan the Terrible

ENGLISH RULERS (IN CHRONOLOGICAL ORDER)

Saxons
Egbert
Ethelwulf
Ethelbald
Ethelbert
Ethel(d)red I
Alfred the Great
Edward the Elder
Athelstan
Edmund (I)
Edred
Edwy
Edgar
Edward the Martyr
Ethel(d)red II (the Unready)
Edmund II (Ironside)
Danes
Canute
Harold I
Hardecanute
Saxons
Edward the Confessor
Harold II
Normans
William (I) the Conqueror
William II Rufus
Henry I
Stephen
Plantagenets
Henry II
Richard I The Lionheart

John
Henry III
Edward I
Edward II
Edward III
Richard II
Lancasters
Henry IV
Henry V
Henry VI
Yorks
Edward IV
Edward V
Richard III
Tudors
Henry VII
Henry VIII
Edward VI
Lady Jane Grey
Mary (I)
Elizabeth (I)
Stuarts
James I (VI of Scotland)
Charles I (Stuart)
Commonwealth Protectors
Oliver Cromwell
Richard Cromwell
Stuarts
Charles II
James II (Interregnum)
William III and Mary II

Anne
Hanovers
George I
George II
George III
George IV
William IV

Victoria
Edward VII (Saxe-Coburg-Gotha)
Windsors
George V
Edward VIII (abdicated)
George VI
Elizabeth II

SCOTTISH RULERS (IN CHRONOLOGICAL ORDER)

Kenneth (I) M(a)cAlpin
Donald
Constantine I
Aedh
Eocha
Donald
Constantine II
Malcolm I
Indulph
Dubh
Cuilean
Kenneth II
Constantine III
Malcolm II
Duncan I
Macbeth
Lulach
Malcolm III
Donald Bane

Duncan II
Donald Bane
Edmund
Edgar
Alexander I
David I
John Baliol
Robert (the) Bruce
David II
Robert II
Robert III
James I
James II
James III
James IV
James V
Mary (Queen of Scots)
James VI

Saints

Saint	**Feast day**
Agatha	5 February
Agnes	31 January
Aidan	31 August
Alban	22 June
Albertus Magnus	15 November
Aloysius (patron saint of youth)	21 June
Ambrose	7 December
Andrew (Scotland)	30 November
Anne	26 July
Anselm	21 April

Saint	Feast day
Anthony *or* Antony	17 January
Anthony *or* Antony of Padua	13 June
Athanasius	2 May
Augustine of Hippo	28 August
Barnabas	11 June
Bartholomew	24 August
Basil	2 January
Bede	25 May
Benedict	11 July
Bernadette of Lourdes	16 April
Bernard of Clairvaux	20 August
Bernard of Menthon	28 May
Bonaventura *or* Bonaventure	15 July
Boniface	5 June
Brendan	16 May
Bridget, Bride *or* Brigid (Ireland)	1 February
Bridget *or* Birgitta (Sweden)	23 July
Catherine of Alexandria	25 November
Catherine of Siena (the Dominican Order)	29 April
Cecilia (music)	22 November
Charles Borromeo	4 November
Christopher (travellers)	25 July
Clare of Assisi	11 August
Clement I	23 November
Clement of Alexandria	5 December
Columba *or* Colmcille	9 June
Crispin (shoemakers)	25 October
Crispinian (shoemakers)	25 October
Cuthbert	20 March
Cyprian	16 September
Cyril	14 February
Cyril of Alexandria	27 June
David (Wales)	1 March
Denis (France)	9 October
Dominic	7 August
Dorothy	6 February
Dunstan	19 May
Edmund	20 November
Edward the Confessor	13 October
Edward the Martyr	18 March
Elizabeth	5 November
Elizabeth of Hungary	17 November
Elmo	2 June
Ethelbert *or* Æthelbert	25 February
Francis of Assisi	4 October
Francis of Sales	24 January
Francis Xavier	3 December
Geneviève (Paris)	3 January
George (England)	23 April
Gertrude	16 November
Gilbert of Sempringham	4 February
Giles (cripples, beggars, and lepers)	1 September
Gregory I (the Great)	3 September
Gregory VII *or* Hildebrand	25 May
Gregory of Nazianzus	2 January
Gregory of Nyssa	9 March

Saint	Feast day
Gregory of Tours	17 November
Hilary of Poitiers	13 January
Hildegard of Bingen	17 September
Helen *or* Helena	18 August
Helier	16 July
Ignatius	17 October
Ignatius of Loyola	31 July
Isidore of Seville	4 April
James	23 October
James the Less	3 May
Jane Frances de Chantal	12 December
Jerome	30 September
Joachim	26 July
Joan of Arc	30 May
John	27 December
John Bosco	31 January
John Chrysostom	13 September
John Ogilvie	10 March
John of Damascus	4 December
John of the Cross	14 December
John the Baptist	24 June
Joseph	19 March
Joseph of Arimathaea	17 March
Joseph of Copertino	18 September
Jude	28 October
Justin	1 June
Kentigern *or* Mungo	14 January
Kevin	3 June
Lawrence	10 August
Lawrence O'Toole	14 November
Leger	2 October
Leo I (the Great)	10 November
Leo II	3 July
Leo III	12 June
Leo IV	17 July
Leonard	6 November
Lucy	13 December
Luke	18 October
Malachy	3 November
Margaret	20 July
Margaret of Scotland	10 June, 16 November (in Scotland)
Maria Goretti	6 July
Mark	25 April
Martha	29 July
Martin de Porres	3 November
Martin of Tours (France)	11 November
Mary	15 August
Mary Magdalene	22 July
Matthew *or* Levi	21 September
Matthias	14 May
Methodius	14 February
Michael	29 September
Neot	31 July
Nicholas (Russia, children, sailors, merchants, and pawnbrokers)	6 December

Saint	Feast day
Nicholas I (the Great)	13 November
Ninian	16 September
Olaf or Olav (Norway)	29 July
Oliver Plunket or Plunkett	1 July
Oswald	28 February
Pachomius	14 May
Patrick (Ireland)	17 March
Paul	29 June
Paulinus	10 October
Paulinus of Nola	22 June
Peter or Simon Peter	29 June
Philip	3 May
Philip Neri	26 May
Pius V	30 April
Pius X	21 August
Polycarp	26 January or 23 February
Rose of Lima	23 August
Sebastian	20 January
Silas	13 July
Simon Zelotes	28 October
Stanislaw or Stanislaus (Poland)	11 April
Stanislaus Kostka	13 November
Stephen	26 or 27 December
Stephen of Hungary	16 or 20 August
Swithin or Swithun	15 July
Teresa or Theresa of Avila	15 October
Thérèse de Lisieux	1 October
Thomas	3 July
Thomas à Becket	29 December
Thomas Aquinas	28 January
Thomas More	22 June
Timothy	26 January
Titus	26 January
Ursula	21 October
Valentine	14 February
Veronica	12 July
Vincent de Paul	27 September
Vitus	15 June
Vladimir	15 July
Wenceslaus or Wenceslas	28 September
Wilfrid	12 October

Salts

2 letters:
AB
4 letters:
Corn
NaCl
Rock
Soap
Urao
5 letters:
Azide

Borax
Urate
6 letters:
Aurate
Borate
Halite
Iodide
Malate
Mucate
Oleate

Osmate
Sebate
Sodium
Uranin
7 letters:
Bromate
Bromide
Caprate
Citrate
Cyanate

Formate
Glauber
Ioduret
Lactate
Lithate
Muriate
Nitrate
Nitrite
Osmiate
Oxalate
Picrate
Sulfite
Tannate
8 letters:
Alginate
Caproate
Cerusite
Chlorate
Chlorite
Chromate
Datolite
Malonate
Plumbite
Pyruvate
Resinate
Rochelle

Selenate
Stannate
Stearate
Suberate
Sulphate
Sulphite
Tartrate
Titanate
Vanadate
Xanthate
9 letters:
Aluminate
Aspartite
Caprylate
Carbamate
Carbonate
Cyclamate
Glutamate
Magnesium
Manganate
Palmitate
Periodate
Phosphate
Phthalate
Potassium
Succinate

Tellurate
Tungstate
10 letters:
Andalusite
Bichromate
Dithionate
Isocyanide
Pandermite
Propionate
Sulphonate
11 letters:
Bicarbonate
Carboxylate
Microcosmic
Monohydrate
Perchlorate
Sal ammoniac
Sal volatile
Thiocyanate
12 letters:
Ferricyanide
Thiosulphate
13 letters:
Hydrochloride

Satellites

EARTH
4 letters:
Moon

5 letters:
Astra (artificial)

Tiros (artificial)

JUPITER

2 letters:
Io
4 letters:
Leda
Teba
5 letters:
Carme
Elara
Karme
Metis

Thebe
6 letters:
Ananke
Europa
Metida
Pacife
Sinope
7 letters:
Amaltea
Gimalia

Himalia
Lisitea
8 letters:
Adrastea
Amalthea
Callisto
Galilean
Ganymede
Lysithia
Pasiphaë

SATURN

3 letters:
Pan
4 letters:
Rhea
5 letters:
Atlas
Dione
Janus
Mimas

Titan
6 letters:
Helene
Phoebe
Tethys
7 letters:
Calypso
Iapetus
Pandora

Telesto
8 letters:
Hyperion
9 letters:
Enceladus
10 letters:
Epimetheus
Prometheus

URANUS

4 letters:
Puck
5 letters:
Ariel
6 letters:
Bianca
Juliet
Oberon

Portia
7 letters:
Belinda
Caliban
Miranda
Ophelia
Sycorax
Titania

Umbriel
8 letters:
Cordelia
Cressida
Rosalind
9 letters:
Desdemona

NEPTUNE

5 letters:
Naian
6 letters:
Nereid

Triton
7 letters:
Despina
Galatea

Larissa
Proteus
8 letters:
Thalassa

MARS

6 letters:
Deimos
Phobos

PLUTO

6 letters:
Charon

Sauces

2 letters:
HP®
3 letters:
Soy
4 letters:
Fish
Hard
Mint
Mole

Soja
Soya
Wine
5 letters:
Apple
Bread
Brown
Caper
Cream

Curry
Fudge
Garum
Gravy
Melba
Pesto
Salsa
Satay
Shoyu

White
6 letters:
Cheese
Chilli
Coulis
Creole
Fondue
Fu yong
Fu yung
Hoisin
Mornay
Nam pia
Orange
Oxymal
Oyster
Panada
Pistou
Relish
Sambal
Tamari
Tartar
Tomato
7 letters:
A la king
Alfredo
Custard
Ketchup
Newburg
Nuoc mam
Parsley
Passata

Rouille
Sabayon
Soubise
Suprême
Tabasco®
Tartare
Velouté
8 letters:
Barbecue
Béchamel
Chasseur
Chow-chow
Fenberry
Marinara
Matelote
Meunière
Mirepoix
Piri-piri
Ravigote
Red pesto
Salpicon
Verjuice
9 letters:
Allemanse
Béarnaise
Black bean
Bolognese
Carbonara
Chocolate
Cranberry
Enchilada

Espagnole
Rémoulade
Worcester
10 letters:
Bolognaise
Bordelaise
Chaudfroid
Cumberland
Mayonnaise
Mousseline
Piccalilli
Salad cream
Salsa verde
Stroganoff
11 letters:
Hollandaise
Horseradish
Vinaigrette
12 letters:
Brandy butter
Sweet-and-sour
13 letters:
Bourguignonne
Salad dressing
14 letters:
French dressing
Worcestershire
15 letters:
Russian dressing

Sausages

3 letters:
Sav
4 letters:
Lola
5 letters:
Black
Blood
Devon
Kiska
Kiske
Liver
Lorne
Lyons
Metts
Sujuk
Wurst
6 letters:
Banger
Garlic
Haggis
Hot dog
Kishka

Kishke
Lolita
Mirkas
Polony
Salami
Summer
Tuscan
Vienna
Wiener
Wienie
7 letters:
Abruzzo
Bologna
Cheerio
Chorizo
Frizzes
Kolbasa
Merguez
Saveloy
Soujouk
Yershig
Zampone

8 letters:
Cervelat
Chaurice
Chourico
Drisheen
Kielbasa
Lap chong
Lap chung
Linguica
Linguisa
Lop chong
Morcilla
Peperoni
Rohwurst
Teewurst
Toulouse
9 letters:
Andouille
Blutwurst
Bockwurst
Boerewors
Bratwurst

Chipolata
Cotechino
Knoblauch
Landjager
Lap cheong
Longanisa
Longaniza
Loukanika
Mettwurst
Pepperoni
Red boudin
Saucisson
Sulzwurst
10 letters:
Bauerwurst
Boerewurst
Bruehwurst
Cumberland

Knackwurst
Knockwurst
Landjaeger
Liverwurst
Mettwaurst
Mortadella
Potato korv
Weisswurst
11 letters:
Bauernwurst
Boudin blanc
Boudin rouge
Frankfurter
Genoa salami
Grutzewurst
Knublewurst
Kochwuerste
Pinkelwurst

Weisswurste
White boudin
Wienerwurst
Zungenwurst
12 letters:
Andouillette
Bierschinken
Black pudding
Fleischwurst
White pudding
13 letters:
Schinkenwurst
14 letters:
Braunschweiger
Lebanon bologna
Medisterpoelse
15 letters:
Katenrauchwurst

Scarves

4 letters:
Doek
Haik
Hyke
5 letters:
Curch
Fichu
Haick
Pagri
Stole
6 letters:
Cravat
Haique

Madras
Rebozo
Tippet
7 letters:
Belcher
Dupatta
Muffler
Orarium
Tallith
8 letters:
Babushka
Cataract
Mantilla

Neckatee
Palatine
Trot-cosy
Trot-cozy
Vexillum
9 letters:
Comforter
Muffettee
10 letters:
Lambrequin
11 letters:
Nightingale

Schools

NAMES OF SCHOOLS

3 letters:
RAM
4 letters:
Dada
Eton
RADA
5 letters:
Perse
Slade
Stowe
6 letters:
Fettes
Harrow
Oundle
Repton

7 letters:
Bauhaus
Flemish
Lancing
Loretto
Roedean
Rossall
8 letters:
Barbizon
Benenden
Downside
Mannheim
9 letters:
Chartreux
Frankfurt

Tonbridge
10 letters:
Ampleforth
Manchester
Stonyhurst
Wellington
Winchester
11 letters:
Giggleswick
Gordonstoun
Marlborough
12 letters:
Charterhouse

TYPES OF SCHOOL

3 letters:
CAT
CTC
GPS
LSE
Uni
4 letters:
Co-ed
Poly
Prep
Tech
5 letters:
Kindy
Lycée
6 letters:
Hostel
Kindie
7 letters:
Academe
Academy
College
Convent
Crammer
Nursery
Varsity
Yeshiva
8 letters:
Seminary
9 letters:
Alma mater
Day school
Gymnasien
Gymnasium
Institute
Ivy League
Madrassah
Palaestra

10 letters:
Chautauqua
Dame school
High school
Pensionnat
Prep school
University
11 letters:
Charm school
Choir school
Drama school
First school
Grade school
Hedge-school
List D school
Lower school
Mixed school
Night school
Open College
Polytechnic
Reformatory
State school
Trade school
Upper school
12 letters:
Church school
Conservatory
Infant school
Junior school
Kindergarten
Magnet school
Middle school
Multiversity
Normal school
Progymnasium
Public school
Ragged school

Reform school
Summer school
Sunday school
13 letters:
Community home
Comprehensive
Conservatoire
Convent school
Council school
Grammar school
Junior college
Nursery school
Primary school
Private school
Sabbath school
Special school
14 letters:
Approved school
Bluecoat school
Boarding school
Hospital school
National School
Open University
Schola cantorum
Separate school
Village college
15 letters:
Civic university
Community school
Composite school
Finishing school
Parochial school
Secondary school
Single-sex school
Tertiary college

See also:
➤ **Colleges** ➤ **Education terms** ➤ **Ivy League universities**
➤ **Oxbridge colleges**

Sea birds

3 letters:
Auk
Cob
Ern
Mew
4 letters:
Cobb
Coot
Erne

Gull
Shag
Skua
Tara
Titi
5 letters:
Booby
Kawau
Prion

6 letters:
Auklet
Fulmar
Gannet
Korora
Petrel
Scoter
Sea-cob
Sea-mew

Seapie
Takapu
7 letters:
Oldwife
Sea duck
Seagull
Taranui
8 letters:
Black cap
Blue shag
Fish hawk
Murrelet
Old squaw
Skua-gull
Surf duck
9 letters:
Albatross

Black shag
Cormorant
Guillemot
Ivory gull
Kittiwake
Razorbill
10 letters:
Gooney bird
Mutton bird
Sea swallow
Shearwater
Surf scoter
11 letters:
Blue penguin
Caspian tern
Frigate bird
Herring gull

Kahawai bird
Storm petrel
12 letters:
Fairy penguin
Glaucous gull
Man-of-war bird
Stormy petrel
Velvet scoter
13 letters:
Little penguin
Oystercatcher
Wilson's petrel
14 letters:
Black guillemot
Razor-billed auk
15 letters:
Black-backed gull

Seafood

3 letters:
Cod
Dab
Eel
4 letters:
Bass
Carp
Clam
Crab
Hake
Huss
Ling
Pike
Pipi
Pout
Shad
Sild
Sole
Tuna
5 letters:
Bream
Brill
Koura
Perch
Prawn
Roach
Shark
Skate
Snoek
Snook
Sprat
Squid
Trout
Tunny
Wahoo
Whelk

Witch
Yabby
6 letters:
Bonito
Callop
Cockle
Dorado
Kipper
Marron
Megrim
Mullet
Mussel
Oyster
Pillie
Plaice
Saithe
Salmon
Shrimp
Turbot
Winkle
Yabbie
Zander
7 letters:
Abalone
Anchovy
Bloater
Blue cod
Catfish
Codling
Crawbob
Craybob
Craydab
Dogfish
Gemfish
Haddock
Halibut

Herring
Jewfish
Kahawai
Lobster
Morwong
Mud crab
Octopus
Pollack
Pomfret
Queenie
Redfish
Sardine
Scallop
Scollop
Snapper
Sockeye
Whiting
8 letters:
Clawchie
Coalfish
Crawfish
Crayfish
Flounder
Grayling
John Dory
Kingfish
Lumpfish
Mackerel
Monkfish
Mulloway
Nannygai
Pilchard
Rockfish
Sand crab
Tarakihi
Teraglin

Terakihi
Tilefish
Trevally
Wolffish
9 letters:
Blackfish
Blue manna
Clabby-doo
Clappy-doo
Dover sole
King prawn
Lemon sole
Red salmon

Swordfish
Whitebait
10 letters:
Balmain bug
Barramundi
Butterfish
Parrotfish
Red snapper
Tiger prawn
11 letters:
Banana prawn
Blue swimmer
Langoustine

School prawn
Sea cucumber
Yellow belly
12 letters:
Queen scallop
Rainbow trout
Skipjack tuna
13 letters:
Moreton Bay bug
Norway lobster
14 letters:
Dublin Bay prawn

Seals

4 letters:
Harp
Monk
5 letters:
Eared
Great
Otary
Phoca
Silky
6 letters:
Hooded
Hudson

Ringed
Sealch
Sealgh
Selkie
Silkie
7 letters:
Earless
Harbour
Sea-bear
Weddell
8 letters:
Elephant

Seecatch
Zalophus
9 letters:
Crab-eater
Greenland
Pintadera
10 letters:
Pinnipedia
Seecatchie
11 letters:
Bladdernose

Sea mammals

4 letters:
Seal
6 letters:
Dugong
Sea cow
Walrus
7 letters:
Manatee

Sea lion
8 letters:
Harp seal
Sea horse
9 letters:
Eared seal
10 letters:
Hooded seal

11 letters:
Earless seal
12 letters:
Elephant seal

Seas and oceans

3 letters:
Ler
Med
Red
4 letters:
Aral
Azov
Dead
Java
Kara
Ross
Sulu

5 letters:
Banda
Black
Ceram
China
Coral
Hadal
Irish
Japan
North
South
Timor

White
6 letters:
Abssal
Aegean
Arctic
Baltic
Bering
Biscay
Celtic
Euxine
Flores
Indian

Inland
Ionian
Laptev
Scotia
Tasman
Tethys
Yellow
7 letters:
Andaman
Arabian
Arafura
Barents
Caspian
Celebes
Channel
Chukchi
Euripus
Galilee
Icarian
Lincoln
Marmara
Marmora
Okhotsk

Pacific
Pelagic
Polynya
Solomon
Weddell
8 letters:
Adriatic
Amundsen
Atlantic
Beaufort
Bismarck
Bosporus
Hwang Hai
Labrador
Ligurian
Sargasso
Southern
Tiberias
9 letters:
Antarctic
Bosphorus
Caribbean
East China

Greenland
Hudson Bay
Melanesia
Norwegian
Polynesia
Skagerrak
Thalassic
10 letters:
Philippine
South China
Tyrrhenian
11 letters:
Herring-pond
Spanish main
12 letters:
East Siberian
Nordenskjöld
13 letters:
Mediterranean
14 letters:
Bellingshausen

Seasons

Season	**Related adjective**
Spring	Vernal
Summer	Aestival *or* estival
Autumn	Autumnal
Winter	Hibernal *or* hiemal

Seats

3 letters:
Box
Pew
Pit
4 letters:
Banc
Love
Sofa
Sunk
5 letters:
Bench
Chair
Couch
Dicky
Divan
Perch
Sedes
Siege
Squab
Stool

6 letters:
Bucket
Canapé
Dickey
Houdah
Howdah
Humpty
Pouffe
Rumble
Saddle
Settee
Settle
Sunkie
Throne
7 letters:
Ejector
Ottoman
Palfrey
Pillion
Tonneau

8 letters:
Sedilium
Woolsack
9 letters:
Banquette
Bleachers
Davenport
Deckchair
Faldstool
Palanquin
10 letters:
Faldistory
Knifeboard
Strapontin
Subsellium
Sunlounger
Synthronus
12 letters:
Chaise longue
Rumble-tumble

Seaweeds

3 letters:
Ore
4 letters:
Agar
Alga
Kelp
Kilp
Nori
Tang
Ulva
Ware
5 letters:
Algae
Arame
Dulse
Fucus
Kombu
Laver
Varec
Vraic
Wrack
6 letters:
Desmid

Diatom
Sea-mat
Varech
Wakame
Wakane
7 letters:
Oarweed
Redware
Sea-lace
Sea-moss
Seaware
8 letters:
Chondrus
Conferva
Gulfweed
Porphyra
Rockweed
Sargasso
Sea-wrack
9 letters:
Carrageen
Coralline
Cystocarp

Laminaria
Nullipore
Seabottle
Sea-tangle
10 letters:
Badderlock
Carragheen
Ceylon moss
Sea-lettuce
Sea-whistle
11 letters:
Bladderwort
Sea-furbelow
12 letters:
Bladderwrack
Enteromorpha
Heterocontae
Peacock's tail

Seven against Thebes

6 letters:
Tydeus
8 letters:
Adrasyus
Capaneus

9 letters:
Polynices
10 letters:
Amphiaraüs
Hippomedon

13 letters:
Parthenopaeus

Seven deadly sins

4 letters:
Envy
Lust
5 letters:
Anger
Pride

Sloth
7 letters:
Avarice
8 letters:
Gluttony

12 letters:
Covetousness

Shakespeare

CHARACTERS IN SHAKESPEARE

Character	**Play**
Sir Andrew Aguecheek	Twelfth Night
Antonio	The Merchant of Venice
Antony	Antony and Cleopatra, Julius Caesar
Ariel	The Tempest
Aufidius	Coriolanus
Autolycus	The Winter's Tale

Character	Play
Banquo	Macbeth
Bassanio	The Merchant of Venice
Beatrice	Much Ado About Nothing
Sir Toby Belch	Twelfth Night
Benedick	Much Ado About Nothing
Bolingbroke	Richard II
Bottom	A Midsummer Night's Dream
Brutus	Julius Caesar
Caliban	The Tempest
Casca	Julius Caesar
Cassio	Othello
Cassius	Julius Caesar
Claudio	Much Ado About Nothing, Measure for Measure
Claudius	Hamlet
Cleopatra	Antony and Cleopatra
Cordelia	King Lear
Coriolanus	Coriolanus
Cressida	Troilus and Cressida
Demetrius	A Midsummer Night's Dream
Desdemona	Othello
Dogberry	Much Ado About Nothing
Edmund	King Lear
Enobarbus	Antony and Cleopatra
Falstaff	Henry IV Parts I and II, The Merry Wives of Windsor
Ferdinand	The Tempest
Feste	Twelfth Night
Fluellen	Henry V
Fool	King Lear
Gertrude	Hamlet
Gloucester	King Lear
Goneril	King Lear
Guildenstern	Hamlet
Hamlet	Hamlet
Helena	All's Well that Ends Well, A Midsummer Night's Dream
Hermia	A Midsummer Night's Dream
Hero	Much Ado About Nothing
Hotspur	Henry IV Part I
Iago	Othello
Jaques	As You Like It
John of Gaunt	Richard II
Juliet	Romeo and Juliet
Julius Caesar	Julius Caesar
Katharina _or_ Kate	The Taming of the Shrew
Kent	King Lear
Laertes	Hamlet
Lear	King Lear
Lysander	A Midsummer Night's Dream
Macbeth	Macbeth
Lady Macbeth	Macbeth
Macduff	Macbeth
Malcolm	Macbeth
Malvolio	Twelfth Night
Mercutio	Romeo and Juliet

Character	**Play**
Miranda	The Tempest
Oberon	A Midsummer Night's Dream
Octavius	Antony and Cleopatra
Olivia	Twelfth Night
Ophelia	Hamlet
Orlando	As You Like It
Orsino	Twelfth Night
Othello	Othello
Pandarus	Troilus and Cressida
Perdita	The Winter's Tale
Petruchio	The Taming of the Shrew
Pistol	Henry IV Part II, Henry V, The Merry Wives of Windsor
Polonius	Hamlet
Portia	The Merchant of Venice
Prospero	The Tempest
Puck	A Midsummer Night's Dream
Mistress Quickly	The Merry Wives of Windsor
Regan	King Lear
Romeo	Romeo and Juliet
Rosalind	As You Like It
Rosencrantz	Hamlet
Sebastian	The Tempest, Twelfth Night
Shylock	The Merchant of Venice
Thersites	Troilus and Cressida
Timon	Timon of Athens
Titania	A Midsummer Night's Dream
Touchstone	As You Like It
Troilus	Troilus and Cressida
Tybalt	Romeo and Juliet
Viola	Twelfth Night

PLAYS OF SHAKESPEARE

6 letters:
Hamlet
Henry V
7 letters:
Macbeth
Othello
8 letters:
King John
King Lear
9 letters:
Cymbeline
Henry VIII
Richard II
10 letters:
Coriolanus
Richard III
The Tempest

11 letters:
As You Like It
12 letters:
Henry IV Part I
Henry VI Part I
Julius Caesar
Twelfth Night
13 letters:
Henry IV Part II
Henry VI Part II
Timon of Athens
14 letters:
Henry VI Part III
Romeo and Juliet
The Winter's Tale
15 letters:
Titus Andronicus

POEMS OF SHAKESPEARE

7 letters:
Sonnets

14 letters:
Venus and Adonis

Sharks

3 letters:
Cow
Dog
4 letters:
Blue
Huss
Mako
Noah
Rigg
Tope
5 letters:
Angel
Gummy
Nurse
Tiger
Whale
6 letters:
Beagle
Carpet
School
Sea-ape

Whaler
7 letters:
Basking
Dogfish
Requiem
Reremai
Soupfin
Zygaena
8 letters:
Mackerel
Monkfish
Penny-dog
Rhinodon
Sailfish
Thrasher
Thresher
9 letters:
Angelfish
Grey nurse
Houndfish
Lemonfish

Porbeagle
Rhineodon
Seven-gill
Six-gilled
Wobbegong
10 letters:
Blue whaler
Bonnethead
Cestracion
Demoiselle
Hammerhead
Nursehound
Shovelhead
11 letters:
Blue pointer
Plagiostomi
Smoothhound
12 letters:
Bronze whaler

Sheep

4 letters:
Down
Kent
Lonk
Mule
Soay
Udad
5 letters:
Ammon
Ancon
Jacob
Lleyn
Texel
Urial
6 letters:
Aoudad
Argali
Bharal
Bident
Burhel
Burrel
Exmoor
Masham

Merino
Muflon
Musmon
Oorial
Orkney
Oxford
7 letters:
Ancones
Bighorn
Boreray
Burrell
Caracul
Cheviot
Colbred
Dinmont
Karakul
Lincoln
Loghtan
Loghtyn
Mouflon
Musimon
Ryeland
St Kilda

Suffolk
8 letters:
Cheviots
Cotswold
Dartmoor
Drysdale
Herdwick
Loaghtan
Moufflon
Mountain
Polwarth
Portland
Shetland
9 letters:
Blackface
Blue-faced
Broadtail
Cambridge
Coopworth
Dalesbred
Fat-tailed
Hampshire
Hebridian

Kerry Hill
Leicester
Llanwenog
Marco Polo
Perendale
Romeldale
Rough Fell
Shorthorn
Southdown
Swaledale
Teeswater
Welsh Mule
10 letters:
Clun Forest
Corriedale
Dorset Down

Dorset Horn
Exmoor Horn
Hill Radnor
Shropshire
11 letters:
Île de France
Manx Loghtan
Norfolk Horn
Rambouillet
Romney Marsh
Wensleydale
12 letters:
British Texel
13 letters:
East Friesland
Hampshire Down

Mountain sheep
Rouge de l'Ouest
Welsh Halfbred
Welsh Mountain
Wiltshire Horn
14 letters:
British Vendéen
Devon Closewool
North Ronaldsay
15 letters:
Border Leicester
English Halfbred
Hexham Leicester
Lincoln Longwool
Oxfordshire Down

Shellfish

3 letters:
Mya
Top
4 letters:
Arca
Boat
Clam
Clio
Crab
Lamp
Paua
Pawa
Pipi
Tusk
Unio
5 letters:
Bulla
Capiz
Chank
Cohog
Conch
Cowry
Doris
Drill
Gaper
Helix
Koura
Murex
Olive
Ormer
Pinna
Polyp
Prawn
Razor
Sepia
Solen
Spoot

Squid
Turbo
Venus
Whelk
Yabby
Zimbi
6 letters:
Buckie
Chiton
Cockle
Cowrie
Cuttle
Limpet
Marron
Mussel
Ostrea
Oyster
Pecten
Pereia
Pholas
Poulpe
Purple
Quahog
Sea-ear
Sea-pen
Stromb
Tellen
Tellin
Teredo
Triton
Wakiki
Winkle
Yabbie
7 letters:
Abalone
Balanus
Bivalve

Crawbob
Craybob
Craydab
Isopoda
Lobster
Mud crab
Octopod
Octopus
Piddock
Quahaug
Scallop
Scollop
Sea-hare
Sea-slug
Toheroa
Torpedo
Trochus
Vitrina
8 letters:
Ammonite
Argonaut
Ark-shell
Chelonia
Clawchie
Copepoda
Crawfish
Crayfish
Deerhorn
Escallop
Haliotis
Nautilus
Ostracod
Pteropod
Sand crab
Saxicava
Sea-lemon
Shipworm

Strombus
Trivalve
Univalve
Xenophya
9 letters:
Balamnite
Belemnite
Blue manna
Clabby-doo
Clappy-doo
Cone-shell
Crustacea
Dentalium
Gastropod
King prawn
Langouste
Monocoque
Neopilina
Scalarium

Thermidor
Tusk-shell
Wing-shell
10 letters:
Acorn-shell
Amphineura
Cuttlefish
Gasteropod
Periwinkle
Razorshell
Scaphopoda
Stomatopod
Swan-mussel
Turritella
Wentletrap
11 letters:
Banana prawn
Blue swimmer
Foraminifer

Globigerina
Langoustine
Paper-sailor
School prawn
Soldier crab
Tectibranch
Trochophore
12 letters:
Malacostraca
Pelican's-foot
13 letters:
Lamellibranch
Moreton Bay bug
Norway lobster
Opisthobranch
Paper nautilus
14 letters:
Dublin Bay prawn
Pearly nautilus

Shirts

3 letters:
Tee
4 letters:
Bush
Hair
Polo
Sark
5 letters:
Dress
Kurta
6 letters:
Banyan
Blouse
Boiled

Camise
Guimpe
Khurta
Skivvy
Sports
T-shirt
7 letters:
Chemise
Dashiki
Grandad
Kerbaya
8 letters:
Lava-lava
Swanndri®

9 letters:
Garibaldi
Jacky Howe
10 letters:
Overblouse
11 letters:
Middy blouse
13 letters:
Cover-shoulder

Shoes and boots

3 letters:
Dap
Tie
4 letters:
Boot
Clog
Flat
Geta
Muil
Mule
Pump
Sock
Soft
Spat
Vamp

Vibs
Zori
5 letters:
Court
Gatty
Plate
Sabot
Scuff
Spike
Stoga
Stogy
Suede
Track
Wader
Wedge

Welly
6 letters:
Arctic
Ballet
Bootee
Brogan
Brogue
Buskin
Chopin
Flatty
Gaiter
Galosh
Golosh
Jandal®
Lace-up

Loafer
Mukluk
Oxford
Panton
Patten
Racket
Rivlin
Saddle
Safety
Sandal
Sannie
Slip-on
Vamper
Vibram®
Wedgie
7 letters:
Blucher
Bottine
Casuals
Chopine
Cothurn
Creeper
Flattie
Galoche
Ghillie
Gumboot
Gumshoe
Gym shoe
High-low
Open-toe
Oxonian
Peeptoe
Racquet
Rubbers
Rullion
Sabaton
Slipper

Sneaker
Top boot
Trainer
8 letters:
Athletic
Balmoral
Crowboot
Deck shoe
Flip-flop
Golf shoe
Half boot
High heel
Jackboot
Larrigan
Mocassin
Moccasin
Moonboot
Overshoe
Pantofle
Platform
Plimsole
Plimsoll
Poulaine
Rock boot
Sandshoe
Snowshoe
Solleret
Stiletto
Velskoen
9 letters:
Ankle boot
Biker boot
Cothurnus
Court shoe
Doc Marten®
Field boot
Mary-Janes®

Pantoffle
Pantoufle
Rope-soled
Scarpetto
Slingback
Thigh boot
Track shoe
Veldskoen
Wedge heel
10 letters:
Bovver boot
Chukka boot
Cowboy boot
Espadrille
Kitten heel
Kurdaitcha
Tennis shoe
Veld-schoen
11 letters:
Hessian boot
Hobnail boot
Hush-puppies®
Running shoe
12 letters:
Co-respondent
Football boot
Kletterschue
Surgical boot
Training shoe
Winkle-picker
14 letters:
Brothel creeper
Wellington boot
15 letters:
Brothel creepers

Shrews and other insectivores

4 letters:
Mole
5 letters:
Shrew
6 letters:
Desman
Tenrec
7 letters:
Moon rat

9 letters:
Shrew mole
Solenodon
Tree shrew
10 letters:
Shrewmouse
Water shrew
12 letters:
Star-nose mole

13 letters:
Elephant shrew
Star-nosed mole

Shrubs

3 letters:
Box
Kat
Qat
Rue
Tea
Wax

4 letters:
Coca
Cola
Hebe
Nabk
Olea
Rhus
Rose
Ruta
Titi
Tutu

5 letters:
Aalii
Brere
Briar
Brier
Broom
Brush
Buaze
Buazi
Caper
Gorse
Hakea
Heath
Henna
Lilac
Maqui
Monte
Pyxie
Salal
Savin
Senna
Thyme
Toyon
Wahoo
Yacca
Yacka
Yapon
Yupon
Zamia

6 letters:
Acacia
Alhagi
Aucuba
Azalea
Bauera
Correa
Cotton

Crowea
Daphne
Fatsia
Feijoa
Frutex
Fynbos
Garrya
Jojoba
Laurel
Lignum
Manoao
Maquis
Matico
Mimosa
Myrica
Myrtle
Pituri
Privet
Protea
Savine
Sumach
Tawine
Tutsan
Yaupon

7 letters:
Arboret
Arbutus
Banksia
Boronia
Bramble
Bullace
Cascara
Cytisus
Dogwood
Emu bush
Epacris
Fuchsia
Geebong
Geebung
Heather
Hop-tree
Jasmine
Jibbong
Juniper
Lantana
Mesquit
Oleacea
Olearia
Rhatany
Romneya
Shallon
Skimmia
Tarwine
Tauhinu
Tea-tree

Waratah

8 letters:
Acanthus
Barberry
Bilberry
Black boy
Bluebush
Buddleia
Camellia
Clematis
Coprosma
Gardenia
Hardhack
Hawthorn
Hibiscus
Inkberry
Jetbread
Laburnum
Lavender
Magnolia
Ninebark
Ocotillo
Oleander
Rock rose
Rosemary
Saltbush
Shadbush
Spekboom
Sweetsop
Tamarisk

9 letters:
Andromeda
Blueberry
Buckthorn
Clianthus
Coyotillo
Cranberry
Daisy bush
Firethorn
Forsythia
Grevillea
Hydrangea
Jaborandi
Jessamine
Kerrawang
Liquorice
Melaleuca
Mistletoe
Patchouli
Poison ivy
Poison oak
Raspberry
Spicebush
Waxflower
Yacca bush

10 letters:
Blackthorn
Cottonbush
Cottonwood
Crossandra
Eriostemon
Frangipani
Gooseberry
Horizontal
Joshua tree
Laurustine

Mock orange
Parkleaves
Poinsettia
Potentilla
Pyracantha
Redcurrant
Strawberry
Supplejack
11 letters:
Beautybrush
Blanket bush

Bottlebrush
Honeysuckle
Pittosporum
Steeplebush
12 letters:
Blackcurrant
Rhododendron
Southernwood
13 letters:
Christmas bush
Crown-of-thorns

Silicas and silicates

4 letters:
Opal
5 letters:
Chert
Silex
6 letters:
Albite
Humite
Iolite
Pinite
7 letters:
Kyanite
Olivine
Tripoli

Zeolite
8 letters:
Analcite
Datolite
Diopside
Dioptase
Saponite
9 letters:
Chabazite
Hiddenite
Penninite
Rhodonite
Scapolite
Tridymite

10 letters:
Andalusite
Float-stone
Kieselguhr
Staurolite
Ultrabasic
11 letters:
Vermiculite
12 letters:
Cristobalite
Monticellite
15 letters:
Montmorillonite

Silks

4 letters:
Corn
Flox
Pulu
Tram
5 letters:
Atlas
Crape
Crepe
Flosh
Floss
Gazar
Ninon
Satin
Seric
Surah
Tabby
Tasar
Tulle
6 letters:
Dupion
Faille
Kincob
Pongee

Samite
Sendal
Shalli
Sleave
Tussah
Tusseh
Tusser
Velvet
7 letters:
Alamode
Brocade
Chiffon
Foulard
Marabou
Organza
Ottoman
Sarsnet
Schappe
Tabaret
Taffeta
Tiffany
Tussore
8 letters:
Barathea

Chenille
Duchesse
Florence
Lustrine
Lustring
Makimono
Marabout
Paduasoy
Prunella
Prunelle
Prunello
Sarsenet
Shantung
Sien-tsan
9 letters:
Charmeuse®
Filoselle
Georgette
Matelasse
Parachute
Sericeous
Serigraph
10 letters:
Florentine

Lutestring
Peau de soie

11 letters:
Thistledown

Skin, afflictions of

4 letters:
Boba
Buba
Rash
Yaws
5 letters:
Favus
Hives
Mange
Pinta
Tinea
6 letters:
Cowpox
Dartre
Herpes
Livedo
Morula
Sapego
Scurvy
Tetter
7 letters:
Ecthyma

Prurigo
Rosacea
Scabies
Serpigo
Verruca
Verruga
8 letters:
Chloasma
Cyanosis
Dyschroa
Exanthem
Impetigo
Miliaria
Pyoderma
Ringworm
Rose-rash
Vaccinia
Vitiligo
Xanthoma
9 letters:
Chloracne
Exanthema

Pemphigus
Psoriasis
10 letters:
Dermatitis
Dermatosis
Erysipelas
Framboesia
Ichthyosis
Pityriasis
Seborrhoea
Strophulus
11 letters:
Mal del pinto
12 letters:
Scleroderma
13 letters:
Leishmaniasis
Lupus vulgaris

Skirts

4 letters:
Bell
Full
Hoop
Hula
Kilt
Mini
Ra-ra
Tace
Tutu
5 letters:
A-line
Grass
Harem
Pareo
Pareu
Tasse
6 letters:
Dirndl
Hobble
Pencil
Peplum

Piu-piu
Riding
Sarong
Taslet
Tasset
Tonlet
7 letters:
Culotte
Divided
Filibeg
Lamboys
8 letters:
Bouffant
Culottes
Fillibeg
Half-slip
Lava-lava
Philibeg
Puffball
Wrapover
9 letters:
Cheongsam

Crinoline
Gabardine
Gaberdine
Maxiskirt
Midiskirt
Miniskirt
Overskirt
Petticoat
Waist-slip
Wrapround
10 letters:
Fustanella
Fustanelle
Microskirt
Underskirt
Wraparound
11 letters:
Drop-waisted
13 letters:
Button-through

Snails, slugs and other gastropods

4 letters:
Slug
5 letters:
Conch
Cowry
Murex
Ormer
Snail
Whelk
6 letters:
Cowrie

Limpet
Sea-ear
Triton
Winkle
7 letters:
Abalone
Sea hare
Sea slug
8 letters:
Ear shell
Top-shell

10 letters:
Nudibranch
Periwinkle
Roman snail
Wentletrap
13 letters:
Ramshorn snail

Snakes

3 letters:
Asp
Boa
Rat
4 letters:
Boma
Bull
Corn
Habu
Hoop
King
Milk
Naga
Naia
Naja
Pipe
Rock
Seps
Tree
Whip
5 letters:
Adder
Blind
Brown
Cobra
Congo
Coral
Cribo
Elaps
Glass
Grass
Krait
Mamba
Mulga
Racer
Tiger

Viper
Water
6 letters:
Carpet
Clotho
Daboia
Dipsas
Dugite
Ellops
Garter
Indigo
Karait
Python
Ribbon
Smooth
Taipan
Thirst
Uraeus
Vasuki
7 letters:
Camoodi
Coluber
Diamond
Hognose
Langaha
Rattler
8 letters:
Anaconda
Cerastes
Jararaca
Jararaka
Lachesis
Mocassin
Moccasin
Pit-viper
Ringhals

Ringneck
Rinkhals
Slowworm
Spitting
Sucuruju
Surucucu
Takshaka
9 letters:
Blue-racer
Boomslang
Coachwhip
Hamadryad
Horsewhip
King cobra
Kingsnake
Puff-adder
River jack
Sand viper
10 letters:
Bandy-bandy
Blacksnake
Bush-master
Copperhead
Death-adder
Dendrophis
Fer-de-lance
Homorelaps
Massasauga
Sidewinder
11 letters:
Amphisbaena
Cottonmouth
Diamond-back
Horned viper
13 letters:
Water moccasin

Sofas

5 letters:
Couch
Divan
Futon
Squab
6 letters:
Canapé
Chaise
Day bed

Lounge
Settee
Settle
7 letters:
Bergère
Sofa bed
Vis-à-vis
8 letters:
Love seat

9 letters:
Davenport
Tête-à-tête
11 letters:
Studio couch
12 letters:
Chaise longue
Chesterfield

Sounds

4 letters:
Jura
5 letters:
Puget
Smith
6 letters:
Achill
Nootka
Tromsø
7 letters:
Mcmurdo

Milford
Pamlico
8 letters:
Plymouth
Scoresby
The Sound
9 letters:
Lancaster
10 letters:
Kilbrennan
King George

12 letters:
Sound of Sleat
14 letters:
Queen Charlotte

Spiders and other arachnids

3 letters:
Red
4 letters:
Bird
Mite
Tick
Wolf
5 letters:
Money
Water
6 letters:
Aranea
Chigoe
Diadem
Epeira
Jigger
Katipo
Lycosa
Mygale
Redbug
Violin
7 letters:
Chigger
Hunting
Jumping

Red-back
Solpuga
Spinner
8 letters:
Arachnid
Araneida
Attercop
Cardinal
Ethercap
Ettercap
Huntsman
Itch mite
Podogona
Sand flea
Trapdoor
9 letters:
Bobbejaan
Funnel-web
Harvester
Orb-weaver
Phalangid
Ricinulei
Tarantula
10 letters:
Bird spider

Black widow
Cheese mite
Harvestman
Pycnogonid
Spider mite
Wolf spider
11 letters:
House spider
Money spider
Vinegarroon
Water spider
12 letters:
Book scorpion
Jockey spider
Whip scorpion
13 letters:
Daddy-longlegs
False scorpion
Hunting spider
Jumping spider
Red-back spider
14 letters:
Cardinal spider
Trap-door spider

Sports

2 letters:
RU
4 letters:
Golf
Polo
Pool
Sumo
5 letters:
Bandy
Bowls
Darts
Fives
Rugby
Sambo
Skeet
6 letters:
Aikido
Boules
Boxing
Hockey
Hurley
Karate
Pelota
Quoits
Savate
Shinty
Soccer
Squash
Tennis
7 letters:
Angling
Archery
Camogie
Cricket
Croquet
Curling
Cycling
Fencing
Fishing
Gliding
Hurling
Jai alai
Kabbadi

Netball
Rackets
Snooker
8 letters:
Aquatics
Baseball
Coursing
Falconry
Football
Goalball
Handball
Korfball
Lacrosse
Octopush
Pétanque
Rounders
Shooting
Skittles
Softball
Speedway
Tug-of-war
9 letters:
Autocross
Badminton
Billiards
Decathlon
Ice hockey
Potholing
Skijoring
Skydiving
Stool ball
Triathlon
Water polo
Wrestling
10 letters:
Ballooning
Basketball
Candlepins
Cyclo-cross
Drag-racing
Fly-fishing
Fox-hunting
Gymnastics

Kickboxing
Lawn tennis
Paddleball
Paraskiing
Pentathlon
Real tennis
Rugby union
Volleyball
11 letters:
Hang gliding
Parachuting
Paragliding
Parasailing
Rugby league
Table tennis
Windsurfing
12 letters:
Bullfighting
Cockfighting
Orienteering
Parascending
Pigeon racing
Rock climbing
Roller hockey
Speed-skating
Steeplechase
Trampolining
Trapshooting
Wakeboarding
13 letters:
Roller skating
Rugby football
Squash rackets
Tenpin bowling
Weightlifting
14 letters:
Gaelic football
Mountaineering
Sambo wrestling
15 letters:
Australian Rules
Greyhound racing

See also:
➤ **American football teams** ➤ **Athletic events** ➤ **Ball games**
➤ **Baseball teams** ➤ **Boxing weights** ➤ **Equestrianism** ➤ **Fencing terms** ➤ **Football clubs** ➤ **Grand Prix circuits** ➤ **Gymnastic events**
➤ **Martial arts** ➤ **Motor sports** ➤ **Swimming strokes** ➤ **Water sports** ➤ **Winter sports**

Stars and constellations

STARS

3 letters:
Sol

4 letters:
Argo
Grus
Idol
Lyra
Mira
Pavo
Pole
Ursa
Vega
Vela

5 letters:
Acrux
Agena
Algol
Ceres
Deneb
Draco
Dubhe
Hyads
Indus
Lupus
Mensa
Merak
Mizar
Norma
North
Polar
Rigel
Rigil
Venus
Virgo
Wagon
Whale

6 letters:
Alioth
Alkaid
Altair
Aquila
Auriga

Boötes
Carina
Castor
Cygnus
Dorado
Esther
Fornax
Hyades
Megrez
Merope
Octans
Phecda
Plough
Pollux
Psyche
Puppis
Saturn
Sirius
Sothis
The Sun
Uranus
Vesper
Volans

7 letters:
Antares
Calaeno
Canopus
Capella
Cepheus
Columba
Dolphin
Lucifer
Phoenix
Polaris
Procyon
Proxima
Regulus
Serpens
Triones
Wagoner

8 letters:
Achernar

Arcturus
Barnard's
Canicula
Circinus
Denebola
Equuleus
Hesperus
Pegasean
Pleiades
Pointers
Praesepe
Scorpius
Waggoner

9 letters:
Aldebaran
Andromeda
Bellatrix
Betelgeux
Big Dipper
Centaurus
Delphinus
Fomalhaut
Ophiuchus
Wolf-Rayet

10 letters:
Betelgeuse
Betelgeuze
Cassiopeia
Mogen David
Orion's belt
The Dog Star

11 letters:
The Pointers
The Pole Star

12 letters:
Little Dipper
Solomon's seal
The North Star

14 letters:
Proxima centaur

CONSTELLATIONS

Latin name	**English name**
Andromeda	Andromeda
Antlia	Air Pump
Apus	Bird of Paradise
Aquarius	Water Bearer
Aquila	Eagle
Ara	Altar

Latin name	**English name**
Argo	Ship of the Argonauts
Aries	Ram
Auriga	Charioteer
Boötes	Herdsman
Caelum	Chisel
Camelopardalis	Giraffe
Cancer	Crab
Canes Venatici	Hunting Dogs
Canis Major	Great Dog
Canis Minor	Little Dog
Capricornus	Sea Goat
Carina	Keel
Cassiopeia	Cassiopeia
Centaurus	Centaur
Cepheus	Cepheus
Cetus	Whale
Chamaeleon	Chameleon
Circinus	Compasses
Columba	Dove
Coma Berenices	Bernice's Hair
Corona Australis	Southern Crown
Corona Borealis	Northern Crown
Corvus	Crow
Crater	Cup
Crux	Southern Cross
Cygnus	Swan
Cynosure	Dog's Tail
Delphinus	Dolphin
Dorado	Swordfish
Draco	Dragon
Equuleus	Little Horse
Eridanus	River Eridanus
Fornax	Furnace
Gemini	Twins
Grus	Crane
Hercules	Hercules
Horologium	Clock
Hydra	Sea Serpent
Hydrus	Water Snake
Indus	Indian
Lacerta	Lizard
Leo	Lion
Leo Minor	Little Lion
Lepus	Hare
Libra	Scales
Lupus	Wolf
Lynx	Lynx
Lyra	Harp
Mensa	Table
Microscopium	Microscope
Monoceros	Unicorn
Musca	Fly
Norma	Level
Octans	Octant
Ophiuchus	Serpent Bearer
Orion	Orion

Latin name	English name
Pavo	Peacock
Pegasus	Winged Horse
Perseus	Perseus
Phoenix	Phoenix
Pictor	Easel
Pisces	Fishes
Piscis Austrinus	Southern Fish
Puppis	Ship's Stern
Pyxis	Mariner's Compass
Reticulum	Net
Sagitta	Arrow
Sagittarius	Archer
Scorpius	Scorpion
Sculptor	Sculptor
Scutum	Shield
Serpens	Serpent
Sextans	Sextant
Taurus	Bull
Telescopium	Telescope
Triangulum	Triangle
Triangulum Australe	Southern Triangle
Tucana	Toucan
Ursa Major	Great Bear (contains the Plough *or (U.S.)* Big Dipper)
Ursa Minor	Little Bear *or (U.S.)* Little Dipper
Vela	Sails
Virgo	Virgin
Volans	Flying Fish
Vulpecula	Fox

States and Territories

AUSTRALIAN STATES AND TERRITORIES

8 letters:
Tasmania
Victoria
10 letters:
Queensland

13 letters:
New South Wales
14 letters:
South Australia

INDIAN STATES

3 letters:
Goa
5 letters:
Assam
Bihar
6 letters:
Kerala
Orissa

Punjab
Sikkim
7 letters:
Gujarat
Haryana
Manipur
Mizoram
Tripura

8 letters:
Jharkand
Nagaland
9 letters:
Karnataka
Meghalaya
Rajasthan
Tamil Nadu

10 letters:
West Bengal
11 letters:
Maharashtra
Uttaranchal

12 letters:
Chhattisgarh
Uttar Pradesh
13 letters:
Andhra Pradesh

Madhya Pradesh
15 letters:
Himachal Pradesh
Jammu and Kashmir

INDIAN UNION TERRITORIES

5 letters:
Delhi

10 letters:
Chandigarh

11 letters:
Daman and Diu
Lakshadweep
Pondicherry

US STATES

State	Abbreviation	Zip code	Nickname	Capital
Alabama	Ala.	AL	Cotton	Montgomery
Alaska	Alas.	AK	Last Frontier	Juneau
Arizona	Ariz.	AZ	Apache	Phoenix
Arkansas	Ark.	AR	Wonder	Little Rock
California	Cal.	CA	Golden	Sacramento
Colorado	Colo.	CO	Centennial	Denver
Connecticut	Conn.	CT	Nutmeg	Hartford
Delaware	Del.	DE	Diamond	Dover
District of Columbia	D.C.	DC	—	—
Florida	Fla.	FL	Sunshine	Tallahassee
Georgia	Ga.	GA	Peach	Atlanta
Hawaii	Haw.	HI	Aloha	Honolulu
Idaho	Id. or Ida.	ID	Gem	Boise
Illinois	Ill.	IL	Prairie	Springfield
Indiana	Ind.	IN	Hoosier	Indianapolis
Iowa	Ia. or Io.	IA	Hawkeye	Des Moines
Kansas	Kan. or Kans.	KS	Sunflower	Topeka
Kentucky	Ken.	KY	Blue Grass	Frankfort
Louisiana	La.	LA	Pelican	Baton Rouge
Maine	Me.	ME	Pine Tree	Augusta
Maryland	Md.	MD	Free	Annapolis
Massachusetts	Mass.	MA	Bay	Boston
Michigan	Mich.	MI	Wolverine	Lansing
Minnesota	Minn.	MN	Gopher	St Paul
Mississippi	Miss.	MS	Magnolia	Jackson
Missouri	Mo.	MO	Show-me	Jefferson City
Montana	Mont.	MT	Treasure	Helena
Nebraska	Neb.	NE	Cornhusker	Lincoln
Nevada	Nev.	NV	Sagebrush	Carson City
New Hampshire	N.H.	NH	Granite	Concord
New Jersey	N.J.	NJ	Garden	Trenton
New Mexico	N.M. or N.Mex.	NM	Sunshine	Santa Fe
New York	N.Y.	NY	Empire	Albany
North Carolina	N.C.	NC	Tar Heel	Raleigh
North Dakota	N.D. or N.Dak.	ND	Sioux	Bismarck
Ohio	O.	OH	Buckeye	Columbus

State	Abbreviation	Zip code	Nickname	Capital
Oklahoma	Okla.	OK	Sooner	Oklahoma City
Oregon	Oreg.	OR	Beaver	Salem
Pennsylvania	Pa., Penn., *or* Penna.	PA	Keystone	Harrisburg
Rhode Island	R.I.	RI	Little Rhody	Providence
South Carolina	S.C.	SC	Palmetto	Columbia
South Dakota	S.Dak.	SD	Coyote	Pierre
Tennessee	Tenn.	TN	Volunteer	Nashville
Texas	Tex.	TX	Lone Star	Austin
Utah	Ut.	UT	Beehive	Salt Lake City
Vermont	Vt.	VT	Green Mountain	Montpelier
Virginia	Va.	VA	Old Dominion	Richmond
Washington	Wash.	WA	Evergreen	Olympia
West Virginia	W.Va.	WV	Panhandle	Charleston
Wisconsin	Wis.	WI	Badger	Madison
Wyoming	Wyo.	WY	Equality	Cheyenne

US STATES: YEAR OF ACCESSION TO THE UNION

State	Year of Accession
Alabama	1819
Alaska	1959
Arizona	1912
Arkansas	1836
California	1850
Colorado	1876
Connecticut	1788
Delaware	1787
District of Columbia	1889
Florida	1845
Georgia	1788
Hawaii	1959
Idaho	1890
Illinois	1818
Indiana	1816
Iowa	1846
Kansas	1861
Kentucky	1792
Louisiana	1812
Maine	1820
Maryland	1788
Massachusetts	1788
Michigan	1837
Minnesota	1858
Mississippi	1817
Missouri	1821
Montana	1889
Nebraska	1867
Nevada	1864
New Hampshire	1788

State	Year of Accession
New Jersey	1787
New Mexico	1912
New York	1788
North Carolina	1789
North Dakota	1889
Ohio	1803
Oklahoma	1907
Oregon	1859
Pennsylvania	1787
Rhode Island	1790
South Carolina	1788
South Dakota	1889
Tennessee	1796
Texas	1845
Utah	1896
Vermont	1791
Virginia	1788
Washington	1889
West Virginia	1863
Wisconsin	1848
Wyoming	1890

Stones

2 letters:
St
3 letters:
Gem
Hog
Pit
Rag
Tin
4 letters:
Bath
Blue
Celt
Door
Flag
Hone
Horn
Iron
Jasp
Kerb
Lias
Lime
Lode
Onyx
Opal
Plum
Ragg
Sard
Skew
Slab
Soap
Tile

5 letters:
Agate
Amber
Balas
Beryl
Black
Chalk
Chert
Coade
Culch
Drupe
Flint
Gooly
Grape
Jewel
Kenne
Lapis
Logan
Menah
Metal
Mocha
Niobe
Paste
Prase
Pumie
Quern
Quoin
Quoit
Rubin
Rufus
Rybat

Scone
Scree
Slate
Sneck
Stela
Stele
Topaz
Wacke
Wyman
6 letters:
Amazon
Ashlar
Ashler
Baetyl
Bezoar
Brinny
Cobble
Coping
Cultch
Dolmen
Flusch
Fossil
Gibber
Gooley
Goolie
Gravel
Humite
Jargon
Jasper
Kidney
Kingle

Ligure
Lithic
Menhir
Metate
Muller
Nutlet
Oamaru
Paving
Pebble
Pot-lid
Pumice
Pyrene
Rip-rap
Sarsen
Scarab
Summer
Tanist
7 letters:
Asteria
Avebury
Blarney
Bologna
Boulder
Breccia
Callais
Chuckie
Curling
Girasol
Granite
Hyacine
Hyalite
Jargoon
Lia-fail
Lithoid
Moabite
Niobean
Olivine
Parpane
Parpend
Parpent
Peridot
Perpend
Perpent
Petrous
Pudding

Purbeck
Putamen
Rocking
Rosetta
Sardine
Sarsden
Scaglia
Schanse
Schanze
Smaragd
Tektite
Telamon
Tripoli
Urolith
8 letters:
Aerolite
Aerolith
Amethyst
Asteroid
Baguette
Cabochon
Calculus
Cinnamon
Cromlech
Ebenezer
Elf-arrow
Endocarp
Essonite
Ganister
Girasole
Lapidate
Megalith
Menamber
Monolith
Nephrite
Omphalos
Onychite
Parpoint
Petrosal
Phengite
Portland
Rollrich
Sapphire
Sardonyx
Scalpins

Schantze
Tonalite
Voussoir
9 letters:
Alabaster
Asparagus
Cairngorm
Carnelian
Cholelith
Chondrite
Cornelian
Crossette
Dichroite
Firestone
Gannister
Greensand
Hessonite
Hoarstone
Lithiasis
Paleolith
Pipestone
Rubicelle
Scagliola
Trilithon
Turquoise
Ventifact
10 letters:
Adamantine
Alectorian
Aragonites
Chalcedony
Draconites
Enhydritic
Foundation
Gastrolith
Grey-wether
Kimberlite
Lherzolite
Lithophyte
Rhinestone
11 letters:
Peristalith
12 letters:
Carton-pierre
Philosopher's

See also:
➤ **Minerals** ➤ **Ores** ➤ **Rocks**

Straits

4 letters:
Bass
Cook
Mena
Palk

5 letters:
Cabot
Davis
Dover
Kerch

Korea
Sumba
6 letters:
Bangka
Barrow

Bering
Hainan
Hecate
Hudson
Lombok
Madura
Taiwan
Tartar
Torres
7 letters:
Denmark
Dolphin
Euripus
Evripos
Florida
Formosa
Foveaux
Le Maire
Malacca
Molucca

Øresund
8 letters:
Bosporus
Makassar
Minch, The
Sound, The
9 letters:
Bosphorus
Great Belt
La Pérouse
Small Belt
Solent, The
10 letters:
Gut of Canso
Juan de Fuca
Limfjorden
Little Belt
North Minch
11 letters:
Bab-el-Mandeb

Dardanelles
Kattegat, The
Little Minch
Mona Passage
12 letters:
Skagerrak, The
13 letters:
Strait of Canso
Strait of Sunda
14 letters:
Northumberland
Strait of Hormuz
Straits of Johor
15 letters:
Strait of Georgia
Strait of Malacca
Strait of Messina
Strait of Otranto
Straits of Harris
Windward Passage

Subatomic particles

1 letter:
J
W
Z
3 letters:
Chi
Eta
Psi
Tau
4 letters:
Kaon
Muon
Pion
5 letters:
Axion

Boson
Gluon
Meson
Omega
Quark
Sigma
Tauon
6 letters:
Baryon
Hadron
Lambda
Lepton
Parton
Photon
Proton

7 letters:
Fermion
Neutron
Tachyon
Upsilon
8 letters:
Electron
Monopole
Neutrino
9 letters:
Resonance
10 letters:
Higgs boson

Sugars

3 letters:
Goo
Gur
4 letters:
Beet
Cane
Goor
Loaf
Lump
Milk
Palm
Wood
5 letters:
Brown

Candy
Grape
Icing
Maple
Sorgo
White
6 letters:
Aldose
Barley
Caster
Fucose
Hexose
Inulin
Invert

Ribose
Sorgho
Triose
Xylose
7 letters:
Caramel
Cellose
Glucose
Jaggary
Jaggery
Lactose
Maltose
Mannose
Panocha

Pentose
Penuche
Refined
Sorbose
Sorghum
Trehala
8 letters:
Demerara
Dextrose
Fructose
Furanose
Honeydew
Jagghery

Powdered
Rhamnose
9 letters:
Amygdalin
Arabinose
Cassonade
Galactose
Laevulose
Muscovado
Raffinose
Trehalose
10 letters:
Aldohexose

Cellobiose
Glucosoric
Granulated
Saccharine
Saccharoid
11 letters:
Deoxyribose
12 letters:
Crystallized
Disaccharide
14 letters:
Monosaccharide

Supernatural

PEOPLE WITH SUPERNATURAL POWERS

3 letters:
Hag
Hex
4 letters:
Mage
Seer
5 letters:
Magus
Siren
Witch
6 letters:
Dowser
Medium
Shaman
Wizard
7 letters:
Diviner

Warlock
8 letters:
Conjurer
Exorcist
Magician
Sorcerer
Spaewife
9 letters:
Archimage
Enchanter
Rainmaker
Sorceress
Superhero
10 letters:
Channeller
Water witch
White witch

11 letters:
Clairvoyant
Enchantress
Necromancer
Thaumaturge
Witch doctor
Witch master
12 letters:
Clairaudient
Water diviner
13 letters:
Clairsentient
Fortune-teller

SUPERNATURAL CREATURES

3 letters:
Elf
Fay
God
Imp
4 letters:
Ogre
Peri
5 letters:
Angel
Demon
Devil
Dwarf
Fairy
Genie
Ghost

Ghoul
Giant
Gnome
Golem
Jinni
Lamia
Pixie
Sylph
Troll
Zombi
6 letters:
Djinni
Djinny
Dybbuk
Goblin
Jinnee

Kelpie
Selkie
Silkie
Sprite
Wraith
Zombie
7 letters:
Banshee
Brownie
Goddess
Gremlin
Incubus
Kachina
Monster
Phantom
Sandman

Spectre
Vampire
8 letters:
Familiar
Succubus
Werewolf
9 letters:
Hobgoblin

10 letters:
Leprechaun
Little folk
11 letters:
Lycanthrope
Poltergeist
12 letters:
Little people

13 letters:
Guardian angel
14 letters:
Fairy godmother

SUPERNATURAL TERMS

3 letters:
ESP
Hex
Obi
4 letters:
Aura
Fate
Jinx
Juju
Mojo
Rune
Wand
5 letters:
Charm
Curse
Obeah
Ouija®
Sigil
Spell
6 letters:
Amulet
Apport
Fetish
Grigri
Hoodoo
Kismet

Séance
Voodoo
7 letters:
Evil eye
Philtre
Portent
8 letters:
Exorcism
Greegree
Grimoire
Gris-gris
Talisman
9 letters:
Ectoplasm
Magic wand
Pentagram
Telepathy
10 letters:
Black magic
Divination
Indian sign
Levitation
Magic spell
Necromancy
Possession
Sixth sense

Telegnosis
White magic
Xenoglossy
11 letters:
Abracadabra
Incantation
Magic circle
Premonition
Second sight
Telekinesis
The Black Art
Xenoglossia
12 letters:
Clairvoyance
Invultuation
Telaesthesia
Witching hour
13 letters:
Clairaudience
Psychokinesis
Reincarnation
14 letters:
Clairsentience
Cryptaesthesia
Parapsychology

Surgical operations

5 letters:
Graft
Taxis
6 letters:
Bypass
7 letters:
Section
8 letters:
Ablation
Avulsion
Cesarean
Colotomy
Face-lift
Liposuck
Lobotomy

Tenotomy
Vagotomy
9 letters:
Anaplasty
Autograft
Caesarean
Colectomy
Colostomy
Colpotomy
Costotomy
Curettage
Cystotomy
Ileostomy
Iridotomy
Leucotomy

Lithotomy
Lobectomy
Necrotomy
Neoplasty
Neurotomy
Osteotomy
Plication
Resection
Rhizotomy
Skin graft
Tummy tuck
Vasectomy
Zooplasty
10 letters:
Adenectomy

Amputation
Autoplasty
Biosurgery
Craniotomy
Cystectomy
Enterotomy
Episiotomy
Gastrotomy
Iridectomy
Keratotomy
Laparotomy
Lithotrity
Lumpectomy
Mastectomy
Myomectomy
Nephrotomy
Neurectomy
Ovariotomy
Phlebotomy
Pleurotomy
Rachiotomy
Sclerotomy
Strabotomy
Thymectomy
Transplant
Varicotomy
11 letters:
Anastomosis
Angioplasty
Arthrectomy
Cryosurgery
Débridement
Embolectomy
Embryectomy

Enterectomy
Enterostomy
Gastrectomy
Gastrostomy
Glossectomy
Hysterotomy
Laminectomy
Laryngotomy
Liposuction
Nephrectomy
Osteoclasis
Osteoplasty
Ovariectomy
Phlebectomy
Pneumectomy
Pylorectomy
Rhinoplasty
Splenectomy
Tenorrhaphy
Thoracotomy
Tracheotomy
Vaginectomy
Venesection
12 letters:
Arthroplasty
Circumcision
Dermabrasion
Fenestration
Heteroplasty
Hysterectomy
Keratoplasty
Microsurgery
Neurosurgery
Oophorectomy

Paracentesis
Pharyngotomy
Replantation
Tonsillotomy
Tracheostomy
13 letters:
Adenoidectomy
Dermatoplasty
Mastoidectomy
Pneumonectomy
Prostatectomy
Psychosurgery
Salpingectomy
Stomatoplasty
Sympathectomy
Thoracoplasty
Thyroidectomy
Tonsillectomy
Tubal ligation
14 letters:
Appendicectomy
Blepharoplasty
Cardiocentesis
Clitoridectomy
Coronary bypass
Electrosurgery
Keyhole surgery
Plastic surgery
Staphyloplasty
Xenotransplant
15 letters:
Cholecystectomy
Cosmetic surgery
Staphylorrhaphy

Sweaters

4 letters:
Aran
Polo
5 letters:
V-neck
6 letters:
Indian
Jersey
Jumper
Siwash
Skivvy

7 letters:
V-necked
8 letters:
Cardigan
Cowichan
Crew-neck
Fairisle
Guernsey
Polo neck
Pullover
Rollneck

Slipover
9 letters:
Icelandic
Sloppy joe
10 letters:
Cowl-necked
Crew-necked
Sweatshirt
Turtleneck

Swellings

3 letters:
Wen
4 letters:
Bump

Cyst
Gout
Kibe
Lump

Stye
5 letters:
Mouse
Tuber

Whelk
6 letters:
Bunion
Epulis
Goiter
Goitre
Lampas
Oedema
Struma
Tumour
Warble
7 letters:
Blister
Chancre

Entasis
Lampers
8 letters:
Anasarca
Aneurysm
Capellet
Farcy-bud
Hematoma
Lampasse
Odontoma
Ox-warble
Pulvinus
Scirrhus
Teratoma

Tubercle
Windgall
Xanthoma
9 letters:
Adenomata
Apophysis
Chilblain
Haematoma
Hydrocele
Parotitis
10 letters:
Scleriasis
13 letters:
Elephantiasis

Swimming strokes

5 letters:
Crawl
7 letters:
Trudgen
8 letters:
Buttefly

9 letters:
Back crawl
Freestyle
10 letters:
Backstroke
Front crawl

Sidestroke
11 letters:
Doggy-paddle
12 letters:
Breaststroke

Swiss Cantons

3 letters:
Uri
Zug
4 letters:
Bern
Jura
Vaud
5 letters:
Berne
6 letters:
Aargau
Genève
Glarus
Luzern

Schwyz
Ticino
Valais
Wallis
Zürich
7 letters:
Thurgau
8 letters:
Freiburg
Fribourg
Obwalden
9 letters:
Neuchâtel
Nidwalden

Solothurn
10 letters:
Basel-Stadt
Graubünden
11 letters:
Sankt Gallen
12 letters:
Schaffhausen
15 letters:
Basel-Landschaft

Swords and other weapons with blades

4 letters:
Bill
Chiv
Dirk
Épée
Foil
Kris
Pike
5 letters:
Bilbo

Broad
Estoc
Jerid
Kendo
Knife
Kukri
Saber
Sabre
Skean
Spear

Sword
6 letters:
Anlace
Curtax
Dagger
Espada
Glaive
Gleave
Hanger
Jereed

Katana
Khanda
Kirpan
Parang
Rapier
Toledo
Tulwar
7 letters:
Anelace
Assagai
Assegai
Ataghan
Balmung
Bayonet
Curtana
Cutlass
Gladius
Halberd
Hatchet
Jerreed
Machete
Morglay
Poleaxe
Poniard
Semitar
Shabble
Spirtle

Spurtle
Whinger
Yatagan
8 letters:
Cemitare
Claymore
Curtal-ax
Falchion
Faulchin
Partisan
Schlager
Scimitar
Semitaur
Sgian-dhu
Skene-dhu
Spadroon
Spontoon
Stiletto
Stone axe
Tomahawk
Whiniard
Whinyard
White-arm
Yataghan
9 letters:
Arondight
Backsword

Balisarda
Battle-axe
Damascene
Excalibur
Faulchion
Jackknife
Schiavone
10 letters:
Angurvadel
Bowie knife
Broadsword
Smallsword
Swordstick
11 letters:
Sheath knife
Snickersnee
Trench knife
12 letters:
Spurtleblade
Sword bayonet
13 letters:
Andrew Ferrara

Tables and desks

3 letters:
Bar
4 letters:
Desk
6 letters:
Buffet
Bureau
Carrel
Lowboy
Teapoy
7 letters:
Counter
8 letters:
Lapboard
Tea table

9 letters:
Card table
Davenport
Drum table
Side table
Wool table
Workbench
Worktable
10 letters:
Escritoire
Secretaire
Tea trolley
Traymobile
11 letters:
Coffee table

Dining table
Reading desk
Roll-top desk
Writing desk
12 letters:
Bedside table
Breakfast bar
Console table
Folding table
Gate-leg table
Kitchen table
Nest of tables
Pedestal desk
Snooker table
Trestle table

Writing table
13 letters:
Billiard table
Dressing table
Drop-leaf table

Pembroke table
Piecrust table
14 letters:
Breakfast table
Refectory table

15 letters:
Gate-legged table
Occasional table

Teeth

5 letters:
Molar
6 letters:
Canine

7 letters:
Incisor
8 letters:
Premolar

9 letters:
Foretooth
11 letters:
Wisdom tooth

Territories of New Zealand

4 letters:
Niue
7 letters:
Tokelau

11 letters:
Cook Islands
14 letters:
Chatham Islands

Ross Dependency

Theatre terms

3 letters:
Act
Cue
Ham
4 letters:
Exit
Flat
Gods
Prop
Role
5 letters:
Flies
Fluff
House
Lines
Scene
Stage
Wings
6 letters:
Chorus
Circle
Corpse
Prompt
Script
Speech
Stalls
7 letters:
Curtain

Gallery
Overact
Resting
Scenery
Unities
Upstage
8 letters:
Crush bar
Entr'acte
Entrance
Juvenile
Offstage
Prompter
Scene bay
Thespian
9 letters:
Backstage
Downstage
Greenroom
Monologue
Noises off
Orchestra
Scene dock
Soliloquy
Soubrette
Stage door
Stagehand
Stage left

10 letters:
First night
Leading man
Opera house
Stage right
Understudy
11 letters:
Catastrophe
Curtain call
Greasepaint
Leading lady
Off-Broadway
Stage fright
Stage-struck
12 letters:
Front of house
Orchestra pit
Stage manager
Stage whisper
13 letters:
Coup de théâtre
Curtain-raiser
Curtain speech
14 letters:
Off-off-Broadway
Proscenium arch
Stage direction

Ties and cravats

3 letters:	Bow tie	Kerchief
Boa	Cravat	White tie
Tie	Madras	**9 letters:**
5 letters:	Rebozo	Comforter
Ascot	**7 letters:**	Neckcloth
Dicky	Foulard	School tie
Fichu	Muffler	**10 letters:**
Scarf	Necktie	Windsor tie
Stock	**8 letters:**	**11 letters:**
Stole	Black tie	Falling band
6 letters:	Carcanet	Neckerchief
Bertha	Dicky bow	

Time

GREGORIAN CALENDAR

January	May	September
February	June	October
March	July	November
April	August	December

JEWISH CALENDAR

Tishri	Shebat	Tammuz
Cheshvan	Adar	Av
Heshvan	Nisan	Ab
Kislev	Iyar	Elul
Tevet	Iyyar	
Shevat	Sivan	

MUSLIM CALENDAR

Muharram	Jumada I	Rhamadhan
Moharram	Jumada II	Ramazan
Safar	Rajab	Shawwal
Saphar	Shaban	Dhu'l-Qa'dah
Rabia I	Shaaban	Dhu'l-Hijjah
Rabia II	Ramadan	

FRENCH REVOLUTIONARY CALENDAR

Vendémiaire	Ventôse	Thermidor
Brumaire	Germinal	Fervidor
Frimaire	Floréal	Fructidor
Nivôse	Prairial	
Pluviôse	Messidor	

Tobacco

TYPES OF TOBACCO

4 letters:
Shag
5 letters:
Snout
Snuff
6 letters:
Burley
Filler
Rappee
7 letters:
Caporal

Perique
Sumatra
Turkish
8 letters:
Canaster
Makhorka
Maryland
Virginia
9 letters:
Broadleaf
Fire-cured

Flue-cured
11 letters:
Cigar binder
Cigar filler
12 letters:
Cigar wrapper
Dark air-cured
14 letters:
Chewing tobacco
Cuban cigar leaf

TYPES OF CIGAR AND CIGARETTE

5 letters:
Breva
Claro
Stogy
6 letters:
Concha
Corona
Havana
Maduro
Manila

Roll-up
Stogey
7 letters:
Cheroot
8 letters:
Perfecto
Puritano
9 letters:
Cigarillo
Imperiale

Panatella
10 letters:
Tailor-made
11 letters:
Roll-your-own

PIPES

4 letters:
Clay
5 letters:
Briar
Peace

6 letters:
Hookah
7 letters:
Corncob
8 letters:
Calabash

10 letters:
Meerschaum
12 letters:
Churchwarden
Hubble-bubble

Tools

3 letters:
Awl
Axe
Bit
Gab
Gad
Hob
Hoe
Saw
Sax
4 letters:
Bosh
Comb
File

Fork
Froe
Frow
Hack
Hone
Maul
Pick
Rake
Spud
5 letters:
Auger
Borer
Broad
Burin

Clink
Croze
Drift
Drill
Drove
Facer
Float
Gavel
Kevel
Plane
Punch
Shave
Slick
Snake

Spade
Swage
6 letters:
Beetle
Bodkin
Broach
Chaser
Chisel
Comber
Cradle
Dibble
Fillet
Flange
Former
Fraise
Fuller
Gimlet
Gouger
Graver
Gympie
Hammer
Jumper
Mallet
Padsaw
Pestle
Pliers
Rabble
Ripple
Rocker
Router
Sander
Scutch
Scythe
Shears
Sickle
Spider
Stylus
Trepan

Trowel
Wimble
Wrench
7 letters:
Bolster
Dresser
Flatter
Ice pick
Jointer
Mattock
Nibbler
Nippers
Rabbler
Rounder
Scauper
Scorper
Scriber
Slasher
Spanner
Spudder
8 letters:
Allen key
Billhook
Bitstock
Clippers
Driftpin
Edge tool
Screw tap
Scutcher
Stiletto
9 letters:
Alligator
Drawknife
Drawshave
Eyeleteer
10 letters:
Bushhammer
Claw hammer

Cold chisel
Drill press
Hack hammer
Icebreaker
Jackhammer
Piledriver
Power drill
Tack hammer
Tilt hammer
Triphammer
11 letters:
Brace and bit
Centre punch
Countersink
Drove chisel
Hammer drill
Mitre square
Ploughstaff
Pruning hook
Screwdriver
Spitsticker
12 letters:
Diamond point
Firmer chisel
Floatcut file
Monkey wrench
Pitching tool
Sledgehammer
13 letters:
Rawhide hammer
Soldering iron
14 letters:
Ball-peen hammer
Knapping hammer
Percussion tool
15 letters:
Half-round chisel
Pneumatic hammer

Torture

INSTRUMENTS OF TORTURE

4 letters:
Boot
Rack
5 letters:
Brake
Wheel

7 letters:
Scourge
10 letters:
Iron maiden
Pilliwinks
Thumbscrew

13 letters:
Cat-o'-nine-tails
14 letters:
Procrustean bed

TYPES OF TORTURE

5 letters:
Water
8 letters:
Gauntlet

9 letters:
Bastinado
Strappado
Water cure

12 letters:
Chinese water

Towns

3 letters:
Ems
Gao
Ife
Lod
Niš
Spa
Zug
4 letters:
Agen
Albi
Asti
Biel
Bury
Bute
Cheb
Cork
Deal
Edam
Eton
Genk
Győr
Hamm
Hove
Hyde
Kent
Lens
León
Lodi
Mayo
Melk
Mons
Mull
Niue
Oahu
Sale
Sfax
Skye
Thun
Toul
Trim
Tyre
Wick
5 letters:
Aarau
Aduwa
Ahwaz

Aksum
Alloa
Alost
Aosta
Arlon
Arras
Aruba
Ascot
Aswan
Aulis
Aydin
Balkh
Banff
Bohol
Capua
Cavan
Clare
Cluny
Conwy
Copán
Corby
Cowes
Crewe
Daman
Delft
Dinan
Doorn
Dubna
Egham
Elche
Elgin
Emmen
Ennis
Epsom
Esher
Faial
Flint
Gotha
Gouda
Hilla
Hotan
Ikeja
Ipsus
Irbid
Issus
Izmit
Jerez

Jinja
Kauai
Kells
Kerry
Korçë
Krems
Lahti
Laois
Leigh
Lewes
Leyte
Lorca
Louth
Luton
Luxor
Lydia
Maraş
Massa
Meath
Namur
Negev
Nikko
Niort
Noyon
Öland
Omagh
Ostia
Otago
Pavia
Pelée
Pemba
Płock
Ponce
Pydna
Qeshm
Rugby
Sedan
Sibiu
Sitka
Skien
Sligo
Stans
Ta`izz
Tomsk
Tours
Trier
Truro

Ujiji
Upolu
Vaduz
Vichy
Wigan
Youth
Ypres
Zarqa
6 letters:
Abydos
Actium
Aegina
Agadir
Almada
Al Marj
Amalfi
Anadyr
Antrim
Anyang
Armagh
Arnold
Ashdod
Assisi
Atbara
Aveiro
Ayodha
Bangor
Bastia
Batley
Battle
Bauchi
Bayeux
Bethel
Bingen
Biskra
Bodmin
Bolton
Bouaké
Brecon
Butung
Buxton
Can Tho
Carlow
Celaya
Cognac
Crosby
Cuenca
Dachau
Dawson
Denton
Deurne
Dinant
Dodona
Dudley
Dunoon
Eccles
Edessa

Edirne
Epping
Évreux
Flores
Forfar
Galway
Gibeon
Glarus
Guyana
Hameln
Harlow
Havant
Hawick
Huambo
Huesca
Hwange
Ilesha
Ilkley
Irvine
Kalisz
Kendal
Kirkby
Kiruna
Kokura
Kumasi
Labuan
Lashio
Latina
Lemnos
Lesbos
Lombok
Ludlow
Lugano
Lützen
Macapá
Maldon
Medway
Megara
Menton
Merano
Mérida
Miseno
Morley
Nablus
Nakuru
Nelson
Newark
Oakham
Offaly
Oldham
Örebro
Osijek
Ottawa
Owerri
Pernik
Phuket
Pleven

Poitou
Pudsey
Ragusa
Rashid
Rijeka
Sarnen
Schwyz
Sennar
Sestos
Seveso
Shache
Shiloh
Sintra
Slough
Sokoto
Soweto
Tarbes
Tivoli
Tralee
Tyumen
Verdun
Vienne
Warley
Welkom
Widnes
Woking
Zabrze
Zwolle
7 letters:
Airdrie
Alençon
Ålesund
Al Hufuf
Almadén
Altdorf
Amboise
Antibes
Appleby
Armenia
Arundel
Ashford
Augusta
Auxerre
Baalbek
Bacolod
Bamberg
Banbury
Bedford
Belfort
Bien Hoa
Blaydon
Bonaire
Burnley
Cabimas
Cambrai
Cannock
Carlton

Carrara
Caserta
Cassino
Chatham
Cholula
Chorley
Clacton
Clonmel
Colditz
Concord
Consett
Corinth
Cortona
Crawley
Crotone
Cwmbran
Cythera
Devizes
Dhahran
Donegal
Donetsk
Dongola
Douglas
Dundalk
Eleusis
Entebbe
Evesham
Exmouth
Falkirk
Falster
Fareham
Farnham
Fashoda
Felling
Fiesole
Görlitz
Gosport
Halifax
Harlech
Hasselt
Herisau
Heywood
Hoylake
Ipswich
Iqaluit
Karbala
Keswick
Khojent
Kildare
Kutaisi
La Línea
La Palma
Legnica
Leitrim
Lerwick
Leuctra
Lifford

Lisieux
Locarno
Lourdes
Louvain
Malvern
Margate
Matlock
Megiddo
Meissen
Melilla
Minorca
Morpeth
Moulins
Newbury
Newport
Newtown
Numidia
Okinawa
Olsztyn
Orvieto
Otranto
Paisley
Papeete
Peebles
Penrith
Pereira
Plovdiv
Punakha
Pushkin
Reading
Red Deer
Reigate
Renfrew
Runcorn
Sagunto
Saint-Lô
Segovia
Setúbal
Seville
Shakhty
Sheppey
Shkodër
Skipton
Sovetsk
Staines
Stanley
Swindon
Tampere
Tanagra
Taunton
Telford
Thapsus
Tobolsk
Torquay
Tripoli
Tutuila
Urmston

Üsküdar
Valence
Vellore
Walsall
Warwick
Watford
Wexford
Wicklow
Windsor
Wisbech
Woomera
Worksop
Wrexham
Zaandam
Zealand
8 letters:
Abeokuta
Aberdare
Abingdon
Amravati
Aquileia
Armidale
Aubusson
Aycliffe
Ballarat
Banstead
Barbados
Barnsley
Basildon
Bastogne
Beauvais
Bedworth
Benfleet
Beverley
Biarritz
Billiton
Boa Vista
Bornholm
Budapest
Buraydah
Caerleon
Calabria
Campania
Chamonix
Chartres
Chepstow
Chertsey
Cheshunt
Chigwell
Courtrai
Damietta
Dartford
Daventry
Demerara
Dewsbury
Dumfries
Ebbw Vale

El Faiyûm
Erlangen
Fribourg
Galloway
Golconda
Grantham
Guernica
Hamilton
Hastings
Hatfield
Hertford
Hinckley
Holyhead
Ilkeston
Jemappes
Junagadh
Keighley
Kerkrade
Kilkenny
Kirkwall
Le Cateau
Limerick
Llandaff
Llanelli
Longford
Lüneburg
Lyonnais
Mafikeng
Mainland
Maitland
Manassas
Maubeuge
Mézières
Mindanao
Monaghan
Monmouth
Montreux
Mufulira
Murmansk
Nanterre
Nazareth
Nijmegen
Nishapur
Normandy
Nuneaton
Omdurman
Paignton
Pembroke
Penzance
Peterlee
Piacenza
Piedmont
Portland
Redditch
Richmond
Rijswijk
Rochdale

Rothesay
Sabadell
Sarajevo
Seremban
Solihull
Spalding
Stafford
Subotica
Tamworth
Ternopol
Timbuktu
Touraine
Tübingen
Uxbridge
Viti Levu
Wallasey
Wallsend
Waterloo
Zlatoust
Zululand
9 letters:
Abbeville
Agrigento
Alcántara
Aldershot
Ambleside
Apeldoorn
Appenzell
Auschwitz
Aylesbury
Bebington
Beersheba
Bethlehem
Bethsaida
Blackpool
Bracknell
Brentwood
Brighouse
Capernaum
Castlebar
Chaeronea
Chantilly
Charleroi
Chernobyl
Chiengmai
Chinatown
Clydebank
Coleraine
Colwyn Bay
Deauville
Dodge City
Dolgellau
Doncaster
Dumbarton
Dunstable
Eastleigh
Elizabeth

Esslingen
Five Towns
Gällivare
Galwegian
Gelligaer
Godesberg
Gold Coast
Gütersloh
Halesowen
Harrogate
Inveraray
Jamestown
Kettering
Killarney
King's Lynn
Kitchener
Kitzbühel
Lambaréné
Lancaster
Le Creusot
Llandudno
Lockerbie
Long Eaton
Los Alamos
Lower Hutt
Lymington
Maidstone
Mansfield
Middleton
Mullingar
Neuchâtel
Newmarket
New Romney
Northwich
Ogbomosho
Paderborn
Palm Beach
Périgueux
Perpignan
Pharsalus
Pontypool
Portadown
Port Royal
Prestwich
Prestwick
Princeton
Roscommon
Rotherham
Saint Gall
Saint-Ouen
Salamanca
Santa Cruz
Sherborne
Solothurn
Sosnowiec
Southport
Stevenage

Stockport
Stralsund
Stranraer
Stretford
Surakarta
Tipperary
Tombstone
Tonbridge
Tourcoing
Tullamore
Vancouver
Viareggio
Wadi Halfa
Wad Medani
Waterford
Westmeath
Woodstock
Worcester
Wuppertal
10 letters:
Accrington
Altrincham
Amersfoort
Anderlecht
Austerlitz
Barnstaple
Bellinzona
Bennington
Bridgwater
Bromsgrove
Buckingham
Caerphilly
Canterbury
Carmarthen
Castleford
Chadderton
Cheltenham
Ciudad Real
Coatbridge
Colchester
Coldstream
Darjeeling
Darlington
Dorchester
Eisenstadt
Ffestiniog
Frauenfeld
Galashiels
Gettysburg
Gillingham
Glenrothes
Hammerfest
High Street
Huntingdon
Interlaken
Kalgoorlie
Kapfenberg

Kenilworth
Kilmarnock
Kragujevac
Letchworth
Leverkusen
Linlithgow
Livingston
Llangollen
Longbenton
Los Angeles
Maidenhead
Middelburg
Monte Carlo
Montego Bay
Motherwell
Neumünster
New Castile
New Ireland
Paramaribo
Pontefract
Pontypridd
Portlaoise
Regensburg
Ruda Śląska
Sacramento
Saint Croix
Saint-Denis
San Antonio
Scunthorpe
Shrewsbury
Simferopol
Tewkesbury
Trowbridge
Twickenham
Vijayawada
Warrington
Washington
Whitehorse
Winchester
Winterthur
Xochimilco
11 letters:
Aberystwyth
Aix-les-Bains
Alessandria
Armentières
Basingstoke
Cirencester
Clackmannan
Cumbernauld
Dawson Creek
Downpatrick
Enniskillen
Farnborough
Fort William
Glastonbury
Grande-Terre

Halberstadt
High Wycombe
Kanchipuram
Kigoma-Ujiji
Leatherhead
Marlborough
Mississauga
Missolonghi
Montbéliard
Montpellier
Nakhichevan
Northampton
Novosibirsk
Nyíregyháza
Prestonpans
Rambouillet
Saint-Brieuc
Saint David's
Saint Helens
Saint Helier
Saint Pierre
San Fernando
Sharpeville
Sierra Leone
Stourbridge
Wanne-Eickel
12 letters:
Alice Springs
Anuradhapura
Ascoli Piceno
Beaconsfield
Bielsko-Biała
Bougainville
Cerro de Pasco
Chesterfield
Chilpancingo
Christchurch
East Kilbride
Huddersfield
Kristianstad
Loughborough
Luang Prabang
Macclesfield
Marie Galante
Matabeleland
Milton Keynes
Newtownabbey
Peterborough
Saint Austell
Saint-Étienne
Saint-Quentin
San Ildefonso
Schaffhausen
Secunderabad
Seringapatam
Skelmersdale
Valenciennes

Villahermosa
Villeurbanne
Wattenscheid
West Bromwich
13 letters:
Berchtesgaden
Blantyre-Limbe
Bury St Edmunds
Carrickfergus
Évian-les-Bains
Fontainebleau
Hertfordshire
Hradec Králové
Kidderminster
Leamington Spa

Llano Estacado
Lons-le-Saunier
Melton Mowbray
Merthyr Tydfil
Middlesbrough
New Providence
Ryukyu Islands
Southend-on-Sea
14 letters:
Annapolis Royal
Ashby-de-la-Zouch
Bishop Auckland
Château-Thierry
Hemel Hempstead
Henley-on-Thames

Mariánské Lázně
Saint Augustine
Tunbridge Wells
Wellingborough
15 letters:
Ashton-under-Lyne
Barrow-in-Furness
Burton-upon-Trent
Camborne-Redruth
Neuilly-sur-Seine
Stratford-on-Avon
Sunbury-on-Thames
Sutton Coldfield
Weston-super-Mare

Trees

2 letters:
Bo
Ti
3 letters:
Ash
Asp
Bay
Bel
Ben
Box
Elm
Fig
Fir
Gum
Ita
Jak
Koa
Mot
Nim
Oak
Sal
Tea
Til
Ule
Wax
Yew
4 letters:
Acer
Akee
Aloe
Amla
Arar
Atap
Bael
Bhel
Bito
Boab
Bosk

Cade
Coco
Cola
Cork
Dali
Deal
Dhak
Dika
Dita
Eugh
Gean
Hule
Ilex
Jack
Kaki
Kiri
Kola
Lime
Lind
Lote
Mako
Ming
Mott
Mowa
Nipa
Ombu
Palm
Pear
Pine
Plum
Poon
Rata
Rhus
Rimu
Shea
Silk
Sloe
Sorb

Tawa
Teak
Teil
Titi
Toon
Tung
Tutu
Upas
Yang
5 letters:
Abele
Abies
Ackee
Afara
Alamo
Alder
Alnus
Anona
Apple
Areca
Argan
Aspen
Balsa
Beech
Belah
Belar
Birch
Bodhi
Boree
Bunya
Butea
Cacao
Carap
Carob
Cedar
Ceiba
China
Cocoa

Cocus
Coral
Ebony
Elder
Fagus
Fever
Flame
Guava
Hakea
Hazel
Hevea
Holly
Iroko
Jambu
Jarul
Judas
Karri
Kauri
Khaya
Kiaat
Kokum
Larch
Lemon
Lilac
Lotus
Mahoe
Mahua
Mahwa
Mamey
Mango
Maple
Marri
Matai
Melia
Motte
Mugga
Mulga
Mvule
Myall
Ngaio
Nyssa
Olive
Opepe
Osier
Palas
Palay
Panax
Papaw
Peach
Pecan
Pinon
Pipal
Pipul
Plane
Quina
Ramin
Roble

Rowan
Sabal
Saman
Sassy
Scrog
Silva
Smoke
Sumac
Taxus
Thorn
Thuja
Thuya
Tilia
Tsuga
Tuart
Tulip
Vitex
Wahoo
Wilga
Witch
Xylem
Yacca
Yucca
Yulan
Zaman
Zamia
6 letters:
Abroma
Acacia
Alerce
Almond
Angico
Annona
Antiar
Arbute
Arola
Balsam
Banana
Banyan
Baobab
Bilian
Billar
Bombax
Bonsai
Bo-tree
Bottle
Brazil
Buriti
Cadaga
Cadagi
Carapa
Carica
Cashew
Cassia
Cembra
Cerris
Chaste

Chenar
Cherry
Chinar
Citron
Citrus
Coffee
Cordon
Cornel
Cornus
Deodar
Diana's
Dragon
Durian
Durion
Emblic
Eumong
Eumung
Feijoa
Fustet
Fustic
Gallus
Garjan
Gidgee
Gidjee
Gingko
Ginkgo
Glinap
Gnetum
Gopher
Guango
Gurjun
Gympie
Illipe
Illipi
Jarool
Jarrah
Joshua
Jujube
Kamala
Kamela
Kanuka
Karaka
Karite
Kowhai
Laurel
Lebbek
Linden
Locust
Longan
Loquat
Lucuma
Macoya
Mallee
Manuka
Mastic
Mimosa
Mopane

Mopani
Myrtle
Nutmeg
Obeche
Orange
Padauk
Padouk
Pagoda
Papaya
Pawpaw
Peepul
Pepper
Platan
Pomelo
Poplar
Popple
Protea
Puriri
Quince
Raffia
Red-bud
Ricker
Roucou
Rubber
Sabicu
Sallow
Samaan
Sapele
Sapium
Sapota
Saxaul
She-oak
Sinder
Souari
Spruce
Stemma
Styrax
Sumach
Sunder
Sundra
Sundri
Tamanu
Tewart
Titoki
Tooart
Totara
Tupelo
Waboom
Walnut
Wandoo
Wattle
Wicken
Willow
Witgat
Yarran
Zamang
7 letters:

Ailanto
Amboina
Apricot
Arbutus
Avodire
Bebeeru
Bilimbi
Bilsted
Bubinga
Buck-eye
Bursera
Cabbage
Cajeput
Cajuput
Calamus
Camphor
Camwood
Canella
Carbean
Carbeen
Catalpa
Champac
Champak
Chayote
Coconut
Coquito
Cork oak
Corylus
Corypha
Cumquat
Cypress
Dagwood
Dogwood
Dryades
Durmast
Geebung
Genipap
Gluinap
Grey gum
Hemlock
Hickory
Holm-oak
Iron gum
Jipyapa
Juniper
Karbeen
Kumquat
Lacquer
Lagetto
Lentisk
Logwood
Lumbang
Madrono
Mahaleb
Manjack
Marasca
Margosa

Mazzard
Mesquit
Moringa
Morrell
Pereira
Pimento
Platane
Pollard
Populus
Quassia
Quicken
Quillai
Quinain
Radiata
Rampike
Redwood
Rock elm
Saksaul
Sandbox
Saouari
Sapling
Sausage
Sequoia
Seringa
Service
Shittah
Snow gum
Sourgum
Soursop
Spindle
Sundari
Tea-tree
Varnish
Wallaba
Wirilda
Witchen
Wych-elm
Xylopia
Zelkova
8 letters:
Aguacate
Algaroba
Aquillia
Bangalay
Bangalow
Banyalla
Basswood
Beefwood
Benjamin
Berrigan
Black boy
Black oak
Blimbing
Bountree
Bourtree
Breadnut
Brigalow

Bulwaddy
Calabash
Chestnut
Cinchona
Cinnamon
Cocoplum
Coolabah
Coolibah
Corkwood
Date palm
Dendroid
Dracaena
Espalier
Eucalypt
Flittern
Fraxinus
Garcinia
Ghost gum
Gnetales
Guaiacum
Hagberry
Hawthorn
Hoop pine
Hornbeam
Huon pine
Igdrasil
Ironbark
Ironwood
Jelutong
Kingwood
Laburnum
Lacebark
Lecythis
Loblolly
Magnolia
Mahogany
Makomako
Mangrove
Manna-ash
Mesquite
Mulberry
Ocotillo
Oiticica
Oleaceae
Oleaster
Palmetto
Pichurim
Pinaster
Pyinkado
Quandang
Quandong
Quantong
Quillaia
Quillaja
Quondong
Raintree
Rambutan

Rangiora
Rewa-rewa
Rivergum
Rosewood
Sago-palm
Sandarac
Santalum
Sapindus
Sapucaia
Scots fir
Sea grape
Silky oak
Simaruba
Soapbark
Sourwood
Stinging
Sweet gum
Sweetsop
Sycamine
Sycamore
Sycomore
Tamarack
Tamarind
Tamarisk
Taxodium
Umbrella
White ash
Whitegum
Witch elm
Ygdrasil

9 letters:
Agila-wood
Ailantous
Albespine
Angophora
Azedarach
Bauple nut
Bilimbing
Bimble box
Bitternut
Black bean
Blackbutt
Black pine
Blackwood
Bloodwood
Bolletrie
Boobialla
Bullwaddy
Bully-tree
Bulwaddee
Burrawang
Burrawary
Butternut
Caliatour
Caliature
Candlenut
Carambola

Casuarina
Cherimoya
Chile pine
Chincapin
Chinkapin
Coachwood
Cordyline
Courbaril
Cupressus
Currajong
Evergreen
Firewheel
Flame-leaf
Grasstree
Greenwood
Ground ash
Ground oak
Hackberry
Ivory palm
Jacaranda
Kahikatea
Kahikatoa
Krummholz
Kurrajong
Lancewood
Lemonwood
Macadamia
Melaleuca
Mockernut
Monkeypot
Naseberry
Native oak
Nux vomica
Paloverde
Paperbark
Paulownia
Persimmon
Piccabean
Pistachio
Pitch-pine
Poinciana
Ponderosa
Pontianac
Quebracho
Rauwolfia
Rose-apple
Sapodilla
Sassafras
Satinwood
Scots pine
Star-anise
Stinkwood
Tacamahac
Terebinth
Toothache
Torchwood
Wagenboom

Whitebeam
Whitewood
Yellow box
Yggdrasil
Zebrawood
10 letters:
Arbor Vitae
Bitterbark
Bitterbush
Blackbully
Bulletwood
Bullwaddie
Bunya-bunya
Calamondin
Calliature
Candle-wood
Cannonball
Celery pine
Chamaerops
Chaulmugra
Cheesewood
Chinaberry
Chinquapin
Cottonwood
Cowrie-pine
Douglas fir
Eucalyptus
Fiddlewood
Flamboyant
Flindersia
Flooded gum
Frangipani
Grapefruit
Green-heart
Hackmatack
Ilang-ilang
Jaboticaba
Jippi-jappa
Kentia palm
Letter-wood
Lilli pilli
Lilly pilly

Macrocarpa
Manchineel
Mangabeira
Mangosteen
Marblewood
Mudgerabah
Palisander
Paper birch
Pohutukawa
Quercitron
Ribbonwood
Sandalwood
Sappanwood
Silverbell
Sneezewood
Spotted gum
Strawberry
Tallowwood
Turpentine
Witch-hazel
Witgatboom
Woollybutt
Yellowwood
Ylang-ylang
11 letters:
Appleringie
Black wattle
Blanket-leaf
Cabbage-palm
Chaulmoogra
Chokecherry
Cryptomeria
Dipterocarp
Eriodendron
Flamboyante
Fothergilla
Leatherwood
Lignum vitae
Liquidambar
Maceranduba
Mountain ash
Pomegranate

Purpleheart
Pussy willow
Radiata pine
River red gum
Scribbly gum
Shittimwood
Silver birch
Sitka spruce
Stringy-bark
12 letters:
Bangalow palm
Golden wattle
Gympie nettle
Hercules' club
Insignis pine
Liriodendron
Mammee-sapota
Masseranduba
Monkey puzzle
Monterey pine
Washingtonia
13 letters:
Camphor laurel
Celery-top pine
Horse chestnut
Moreton Bay ash
Moreton Bay fig
Paper-mulberry
Peppermint gum
Queensland nut
Weeping willow
14 letters:
Antarctic beech
Bunya-bunya pine
Cedar of Lebanon
Illawarra flame
Stinking wattle
15 letters:
Bastard mahogany
Cabbage tree palm

Trousers and shorts

5 letters:
Cords
Jeans
Levis®
Loons
Slops
Trews
6 letters:
Breeks
Capris

Chinos
Denims
Flares
Slacks
Trouse
7 letters:
Combats
Joggers
Kachera
Pyjamas

Shalwar
8 letters:
Bloomers
Breeches
Britches
Culottes
Flannels
Hipsters
Hot pants
Jodhpurs

Knickers
Leggings
Overalls
Ski pants
9 letters:
Buckskins
Churidars
Corduroys
Dungarees
Loon pants
Plus fours
Trunk hose
Wranglers®
10 letters:
Capri pants

Cargo pants
Drainpipes
Hip-huggers
Lederhosen
Oxford bags
Pantaloons
Salopettes
Stovepipes
11 letters:
Bell-bottoms
12 letters:
Galligaskins
Gallygaskins
Palazzo pants
Pedal pushers

Smallclothes
13 letters:
Bermuda shorts
Cycling shorts
Spatterdashes
Toreador pants
14 letters:
Knickerbockers
Riding breeches
15 letters:
Jogging trousers

Tumours

3 letters:
Wen
Yaw
4 letters:
Crab
Mole
Wart
5 letters:
Grape
Gumma
Myoma
Talpa
Wilm's
6 letters:
Anbury
Cancer
Epulis
Glioma
Lipoma
Myxoma
Struma
7 letters:
Adenoma
Angioma
Dermoid

Fibroid
Fibroma
Myeloma
Neuroma
Osteoma
Polypus
Sarcoma
Thymoma
8 letters:
Crab-yaws
Ganglion
Hepatoma
Lymphoma
Melanoma
Seminoma
Steatoma
Teratoma
Windgall
Xanthoma
9 letters:
Carcinoid
Carcinoma
Chondroma
Condyloma
Encanthis

Exostosis
Granuloma
Haematoma
Papilloma
10 letters:
Meningioma
11 letters:
Astrocytoma
Encephaloma
Gioblastoma
Haemangioma
12 letters:
Angiosarcoma
Endothelioma
Mesothelioma
Osteosarcoma
13 letters:
Neuroblastoma
Osteoclastoma
14 letters:
Carcinosarcoma
Retinoblastoma
15 letters:
Burkitt lymphoma
Medullablastoma

Typefaces

3 letters:
Gem
4 letters:
Pica
Quad
Ruby
5 letters:
Agate
Canon

Elite
Pearl
Roman
Ronde
Serif
6 letters:
Aldine
Caslon
Cicero

Gothic
Minion
Primer
7 letters:
Braille
Brevier
Elzevir
Emerald
Fraktur

Old-face
Paragon
Plantin
Quadrat
8 letters:
Bold face
Egyptian
Garamond

Old style
Sanserif
Semibold
9 letters:
Bourgeois
Brilliant
Clarendon
Columbian

Non-pareil
10 letters:
Longprimer
11 letters:
Baskerville
Black-letter
Great primer

Underwear

3 letters:
Bra
4 letters:
Body
Vest
5 letters:
Pants
Shift
Teddy
6 letters:
Basque
Boxers
Briefs
Bustle
Corset
Garter
Girdle
Shorts
Trunks
T-shirt
7 letters:
Drawers
G-string
Pannier

Panties
Singlet
Step-ins
Y-fronts
8 letters:
Balmoral
Bloomers
Broekies
Camisole
Corselet
Half-slip
Knickers
Lingerie
Thermals
9 letters:
Brassiere
Crinoline
Jockstrap
Long johns
Petticoat
Suspender
Undervest
Union suit
Waist-slip

10 letters:
Chemisette
Garter belt
String vest
Underpants
Undershirt
Underskirt
11 letters:
Boxer shorts
Panty girdle
Undershorts
12 letters:
Body stocking
Camiknickers
Combinations
Underdrawers
13 letters:
Liberty bodice
Suspender belt
14 letters:
French knickers
15 letters:
Athletic support

Units

1 letter:
K
2 letters:
SI
3 letters:
Amp
Bar
Bit
Erg
Gal
GeV
Lux
Mho
Mil
Nit
Ohm
Rem
Rep
Tog
4 letters:
Baud
Byte
Dyne
Foot
Gram
Gray
Hour
Inch
Mile
Octa
Okta
Phot
Pint
Slug
Sone
Torr
Volt
Watt
Yard
5 letters:
Crith
Cusec
Daraf
Darcy
Debye
Farad
Fermi
Gauss
Henry
Hertz

Joule
Litre
Lumen
Metre
Neper
Nepit
Ounce
Pixel
Pound
Quart
Remen
Sabin
Stilb
Stoke
Stone
Tesla
Therm
Weber
Yrneh
6 letters:
Dalton
Degree
Denier
Dobson
Gallon
Jansky
Kelvin
Kilerg
Lexeme
Micron
Morgen
Newton
Pascal
Probit
Radian
Second
Sememe
Stokes
7 letters:
Candela
Congius
Coulomb
Dioptre
Energid
Fresnel
Gigabit
Gilbert
Lambert
Man-hour
Maxwell

Megaton
Micella
Micelle
Minute
Oersted
Phoneme
Poundal
Rontgen
Semeion
Siemens
Sievert
Syntagm
Tagmeme
8 letters:
Abampere
Angstrom
Chaldron
Glosseme
Kilowatt
Magneton
Megabyte
Megawatt
Morpheme
Roentgen
Syntagma
Terabyte
Therblig
9 letters:
Becquerel
Kilderkin
Kilometre
Megahertz
Microinch
Steradian
10 letters:
Centimetre
Centipoise
Dessiatine
Microcurie
Millilitre
Millimetre
Nanosecond
Picosecond
Ploughgate
Rutherford
11 letters:
Centimorgan
Pennyweight

V

Vegetables

3 letters:
Cos
Oca
Pea
Udo
Yam
4 letters:
Beet
Cole
Corn
Guar
Kail
Kale
Leek
Neep
Okra
Okro
Puha
Sium
Spud
Taro
5 letters:
Ackee
Beans
Chard
Chive
Choko
Chufa
Cress
Ingan
Mooli
Navew
Onion
Orach
Pease
Puwha
Savoy
Swede
Syboe
6 letters:
Adjigo
Allium
Batata
Bhindi
Calalu

Carrot
Celery
Daikon
Endive
Fennel
Frisee
Greens
Jicama
Kumara
Kumera
Lablab
Mangel
Marrow
Orache
Pepper
Potato
Pratie
Quinoa
Radish
Rapini
Sorrel
Sprout
Squash
Tomato
Turnip
Warran
7 letters:
Bok choy
Cabbage
Calaloo
Cardoon
Chayote
Chicory
Cocoyam
Collard
Gherkin
Lettuce
Mangold
Pak-choi
Parsnip
Pimento
Pumpkin
Rauriki
Romaine
Salsify

Shallot
Skirret
Spinach
Spinage
Sprouts
8 letters:
Baby corn
Beetroot
Brassica
Broccoli
Capsicum
Celeriac
Cucumber
Eggplant
Escarole
Eschalot
Hastings
Kohlrabi
Pimiento
Rutabaga
Samphire
Scallion
Zucchini
9 letters:
Artichoke
Asparagus
Aubergine
Broad bean
Calabrese
Corn salad
Courgette
Finocchio
Mangetout
Radicchio
Rocambole
Succotash
Sweet corn
Tonka-bean
10 letters:
Alexanders
Bean sprout
Beef tomato
Bell pepper
Cos lettuce
Salad onion

Scorzonera
Silver beet
11 letters:
Cauliflower
Chinese leaf
Horseradish
Lady's finger
Oyster plant
Spinach-beet
Spring onion

See also:
➤ **Potatoes**

Sweet potato
12 letters:
Cherry tomato
Corn on the cob
Lamb's lettuce
Mangel-wurzel
Marrow squash
Savoy cabbage
Spanish onion
Spring greens

13 letters:
Pe-tsai cabbage
14 letters:
Brussels sprout
Chinese cabbage
Globe artichoke
Iceberg lettuce
15 letters:
Vegetable marrow

Vehicles

3 letters:
ATV
Bus
Cab
Car
Hog
JCB®
LEM
Ute
Van
4 letters:
Bike
Boat
Cart
Dray
Jeep®
Kago
Kart
Luge
Pram
Quad
Scow
Shay
Ship
Sled
Tank
Taxi
Tram
Trap
5 letters:
Artic
Brake
Buggy
Coach
Coupé
Crate
Cycle
Float
Hatch
Lorry

Moped
Ratha
Soyuz
Sulky
Tip-up
Tonga
Towie
Train
Truck
Turbo
Vespa
Wagon
6 letters:
Barrow
Camion
Camper
Chaise
Dennet
Fiacre
Gharri
Gharry
Go-cart
Go-kart
Hansom
Hearse
Jet ski
Jingle
Jinker
Jitney
Koneke
Launch
Limber
Litter
Pick-up
Rocket
Samlor
Skibob
Skidoo®
Sledge
Sleigh

Sno-Cat®
Spider
Surrey
Tandem
Tanker
Telega
Tourer
Tricar
Troika
Tuk tuk
Vahana
Waggon
7 letters:
Amtrack
Bicycle
Caravan
Chariot
Dog-cart
Gritter
Growler
Jeepney
Kibitka
Komatik
Minibus
Minicab
Minivan
Norimon
Omnibus
Pedicab
Phaeton
Postbus
Railcar
Ricksha
Scooter
Sidecar
Tempera
Tipcart
Tracked
Tractor
Trailer

Tramcar
Travois
Trishaw
Trolley
Tumbrel
Tumbril
Utility
Volante
Wildcat
8 letters:
Aircraft
Brancard
Carriage
Carry-all
Curricle
Dustcart
Motorbus
Motorcar
Panda car
Rickshaw
Runabout
Scout car
Stanhope
Steam-car
Tarantas
Toboggan
Tow truck
Tricycle
Unicycle
9 letters:
Ambulance
Autocycle
Bulldozer
Cabriolet
Camper van
Charabanc
Dormobile®
Dump truck
Dune buggy
Estate car
Gladstone
Half-track
Hansom cab

Hatchback
Jaunty car
Jinriksha
Landaulet
Land Rover
Limousine
Low-loader
Milk float
Motorbike
Police car
Racing car
Road train
Sand-yacht
Spaceship
Sports car
Streetcar
Tarantass
Trail bike
Tumble-car
Wagonette
10 letters:
Black Maria
Fire engine
Hovercraft
Jinricksha
Jinrikisha
Juggernaut
Locomotive
Motorcycle
Panel truck
Post chaise
Roadroller
Shandrydan
Snowmobile
Snow plough
Spacecraft
Space probe
Stagecoach
Tank engine
Touring car
Trolleybus
Trolley car
Tumble-cart

Two-wheeler
Velocipede
Waggonette
11 letters:
Articulated
Caterpillar®
Delivery van
Dumper-truck
Jaunting car
Jinrickshaw
Landaulette
Light engine
Steamroller
Tipper lorry
Tipper truck
Wheelbarrow
12 letters:
Autorickshaw
Breakdown van
Double-decker
Garbage truck
Motorbicycle
Motor caravan
Motor scooter
Motor vehicle
Pantechnicon
Perambulator
Single-decker
Space capsule
Space shuttle
Station wagon
Three-wheeler
Troop carrier
Utility truck
13 letters:
Fork-lift truck
Paddock-basher
Penny-farthing
People carrier
14 letters:
Conestoga wagon
Off-road vehicle
Traction engine

See also:
➤ **Aircraft** ➤ **Bicycles** ➤ **Boats and ships** ➤ **Cars** ➤ **Carriages and carts** ➤ **Locomotives**

Veins

4 letters:
Spur
6 letters:
Portal
Radius
7 letters:
Basilic
Femoral
Jugular
Saphena
8 letters:
Terminal
Vena cava
9 letters:
Arteriole
Pulmonary
Sectorial
10 letters:
Subclavian
11 letters:
Subscapular

Volcanoes

3 letters:
Apo
Aso
Puy
4 letters:
Etna
Fuji
Maui
Pelé
Taal
5 letters:
Askja
Elgon
Hekla
Kauai
Kenya
Mayon
Misti
Pelée
Teide
Teyde
Thira
6 letters:
Ararat
Asosan
Egmont
Erebus
Ischia
Katmai
Kazbek
Llaima
Semeru
Tolima
7 letters:
Aragats
El Misti
Hornito
Huascán
Iliamna
Iwo Jima
Kilauea
Ruapehu
Semeroe
Tambora
8 letters:
Antisana
Cameroon
Cotopaxi
Krakatau
Krakatoa
Mauna Kea
Mauna Loa
St Helens
Taraniki
Vesuvius
9 letters:
Aniakchak
Corcovado
Haleakala
Helgafell
Huascarán
Paricutín
Pozzolana
Puzzolana
Soufrière
Stromboli
Suribachi
Tangariro
10 letters:
Chimborazo
Lassen Peak
Montserrat
Nyiragongo
Pozzuolana
Santa Maria
Tungurahua
11 letters:
Erciyas Dagi
Kilimanjaro
Mount Erebus
Mount Katmai
Nyamuragira
Olympus Mons
12 letters:
Citlaltépetl
Ixtaccihuatl
Iztaccihuatl
National Park
Popocatépetl
13 letters:
Mount Demavend
Mount St Helens
14 letters:
Nevado de Colima
Nevado de Toluca
Soufrière Hills
Tristan da Cunha

Waterfalls

5 letters:
Angel
Pilao
Tysse
6 letters:
Iguaçú
Kabiwa
Mardel
Ormeli
Ribbon
Tugela

7 letters:
Mtarazi
Niagara
Roraima
8 letters:
Cuquenan
Itatinga
Kaieteur
Takakkaw
Victoria
Yosemite

9 letters:
Churchill
10 letters:
Cleve-Garth
Sutherland
11 letters:
Yellowstone
13 letters:
Vestre Mardola

Water sports

6 letters:
Diving
Rowing
7 letters:
Sailing
Surfing
8 letters:
Canoeing
Swimming

Yachting
9 letters:
Canoe polo
Water polo
10 letters:
Skin diving
11 letters:
Aquabobbing
Parasailing

Water-skiing
Windsurfing
12 letters:
Powerboating
15 letters:
Powerboat racing

Weapons

2 letters:
V1
3 letters:
Dag
Gad
Gun
4 letters:
Bill
Bolo
Bomb
Club
Cosh
Dart
Gade
Gaid
Kris

Mace®
Nuke
Spat
Sten
5 letters:
Arrow
Baton
Estoc
Flail
Maxim
Orgue
Pilum
Rifle
Sabre
Saker
Sting

Sword
Taser®
Vouge
6 letters:
Airgun
Binary
Cestus
Cohorn
Cudgel
Dagger
Gingal
Glaive
Jingal
Mauser®
Mortar
Musket

Napalm
Onager
Pistol
Sparke
Sparth
Taiaha
Tomboc
Voulge

7 letters:
Arblast
Assegai
Ataghan
Bayonet
Bazooka
Bondook
Caliver
Caltrap
Caltrop
Carbine
Coehorn
Cutlass
Dragoon
Enfield
Fougade
Gingall
Gisarme
Grenade
Halberd
Halbert
Harpoon
Javelin
Longbow
Machete
Matchet
Quarrel

Sandbag
Shotgun
Torpedo
Trident

8 letters:
Arbalest
Armalite®
Arquebus
Ballista
Blowpipe
Bludgeon
Calthrop
Catapult
Crossbow
Culverin
Death ray
Elf-arrow
Fougasse
Howitzer
Mangonel
Nunchaku
Partisan
Petronel
Revolver
Skean-dhu
Skene-dhu
Spontoon
Stiletto
Stinkpot
Whirl-bat
Whorl-bat

9 letters:
Arquebuse
Backsword
Battleaxe

Derringer
Doodlebug
Excalibur
Fléchette
Flintlock
Forty-five
Grapeshot
Greek fire
Harquebus
Poison gas
Sarbacane
Trebuchet
Trebucket
Truncheon

10 letters:
Broadsword
Mustard gas

11 letters:
Germ warfare
Morgenstern
Snickersnee

12 letters:
Flame-thrower
Quarterstaff
Rifle grenade

13 letters:
Knuckle-duster
Life-preserver
Manrikigusari

14 letters:
Nunchaku sticks

15 letters:
Chemical warfare

Weather

WEATHER DESCRIPTIONS

3 letters:
Dry
Hot
Icy
Raw
Wet

4 letters:
Cold
Dull
Fine
Foul
Hazy
Mild

5 letters:
Balmy

Bland
Clear
Close
Dirty
Foggy
Fresh
Humid
Misty
Muggy
Nippy
Parky
Rainy
Snowy
Sunny
Windy

6 letters:
Arctic
Baking
Breezy
Clammy
Cloudy
Dreich
Filthy
Sticky
Stormy
Sultry
Wintry

7 letters:
Clement
Drizzly

Showery
8 letters:
Blustery
Freezing
Overcast

Thundery
Tropical
9 letters:
Inclement
Perishing

Scorching
10 letters:
Blistering

WEATHER PHENOMENA

3 letters:
Fog
Ice
4 letters:
Gale
Gust
Haar
Hail
Mist
Rain
Snow
Thaw
Wind
5 letters:
Cloud
Sleet
Smirr
Storm
6 letters:
Breeze

Freeze
Shower
Squall
Zephyr
7 letters:
Cyclone
Drizzle
Tempest
Thunder
Tornado
Tsunami
Typhoon
8 letters:
Acid rain
Cold snap
Heatwave
Pressure
Sunshine
9 letters:
Dust devil

Dust storm
Hurricane
Lightning
Peasouper
Sandstorm
Tidal wave
Whirlwind
10 letters:
Waterspout
Willy-willy
13 letters:
Ball lightning
Precipitation
14 letters:
Sheet lightning

METEOROLOGICAL TERMS

4 letters:
Scud
5 letters:
Front
Ridge
Virga
6 letters:
Isobar
Trough
7 letters:
Cyclone

Lee wave
Thermal
9 letters:
Cold front
Isallobar
Warm front
10 letters:
Depression
Heat-island
11 letters:
Anticyclone

13 letters:
Occluded front
Synoptic chart

GATHERERS OF WEATHER DATA

9 letters:
Dropsonde
Met. Office
10 letters:
Radiosonde

Weatherman
11 letters:
Weather ship
12 letters:
Meteorograph

Pilot balloon
Weatherwoman
14 letters:
Weather station

WEATHER MEASURING INSTRUMENTS

Instrument	Phenomenon measured
Anemometer	Wind velocity
Anemoscope	Wind direction
Atmometer	Rate of water evaporation into atmosphere
Barograph	Atmospheric pressure
Barometer	Atmospheric pressure
Baroscope	Atmospheric pressure
Hygrometer	Humidity
Maximum-minimum thermometer	Temperature variation
Nephoscope	Cloud velocity, altitude, and direction of movement
Psychrometer	Humidity
Rain gauge	Rainfall and snowfall
Rawinsonde	Atmospheric wind velocity
Stevenson's screen	Temperature
Sunshine recorder	Hours of sunshine
Thermometer	Temperature
Weathercock	Wind direction
Weather vane	Wind direction
Wet-and-dry-bulb thermometer	Humidity
Wind gauge	Wind velocity
Wind tee	Wind direction

See also:
➤ **Atmosphere, layers of** ➤ **Clouds** ➤ **Winds**

Weeds

3 letters:
Ers
4 letters:
Alga
Dock
Nard
Ragi
Sudd
Tare
Tine
Ulva
Yarr
5 letters:
Couch
Daisy
Dulse
Lemna
Reate
Runch
Tansy
Vetch
6 letters:
Blinks

Clover
Cockle
Dallop
Darnel
Dollop
Elodea
Fat hen
Fucoid
Indian
Joe-pye
Knawel
Nettle
Nostoc
Oxygen
Sorrel
Spurge
Twitch
Widow's
Winnow
7 letters:
Allseed
Burdock
Femitar

Fenitar
Helodea
Mayweed
Ragwort
Ruderal
Senecio
Spurrey
Thistle
8 letters:
Arenaria
Bedstraw
Bell-bind
Charlock
Fumitory
Knapweed
Matfelon
Pilewort
Piri-piri
Plantain
Purslane
Sargasso
9 letters:
Adderwort

Anacharis
Chickweed
Chlorella
Coltsfoot
Groundsel
Knot-grass
Mare's-tail

Pearlwort
Sun-spurge
Tormentil
Wartcress
10 letters:
Carpetweed
Corncockle

Nipplewort
Rest-harrow
Sagittaria
11 letters:
Potamogeton
Swine's-cress
Ulotrichale

Weights and measures

IMPERIAL SYSTEM

Linear	**Square**	**Weight**
Mile	Square mile	Ton
Furlong	Acre	Hundredweight
Rod	Square rod	Stone
Yard	Square yard	Pound
Foot	Square foot	Ounce
Inch	Square inch	—
Mil	—	—

Land	**Volume**	**Liquid volume**
Square mile	Cubic yard	Gallon
Acre	Cubic foot	Quart
Square rod	Cubic inch	Pint
Square yard	—	Fluid ounce

METRIC SYSTEM

Linear	**Square**	**Weight**
Kilometre	Square kilometre	Tonne
Metre	Square metre	Kilogram
Centimetre	Square centimetre	Gram
Millimetre	Square millimetre	—

Land	**Volume**	**Liquid volume**
Square kilometre	Cubic metre	Litre
Hectare	Cubic decimetre	Millilitre
Are	Cubic centimetre	—
—	Cubic millimetre	—

Whales and dolphins

4 letters:	**8 letters:**	**10 letters:**
Orca	Bay whale	Black whale
6 letters:	Cachalot	Minke whale
Beluga	Greyback	Pilot whale
Dorado	Porpoise	Right whale
7 letters:	Sei whale	Sperm whale
Bowhead	**9 letters:**	White whale
Grampus	Blackfish	**11 letters:**
Narwhal	Blue whale	Baleen whale
Rorqual	Grey whale	Killer whale

12 letters:
Toothed whale
13 letters:
Humpback whale

Sulphur-bottom
14 letters:
Greenland whale
Whalebone whale

Windows

3 letters:
Bay
Bow
4 letters:
Rose
Sash
5 letters:
Gable
Jesse
Judas
Ogive
Oriel
Ox-eye
Storm
6 letters:
Dormer
French
Garret
Lancet
Monial

Oculus
Rosace
Wicket
7 letters:
Compass
Guichet
Lattice
Lucarne
Lunette
Luthern
Mullion
Picture
Transom
Trellis
Ventana
Weather
Windock
Winnock
8 letters:
Casement

Fanlight
Fenestra
Porthole
9 letters:
Companion
Deadlight
Dream-hole
Loop-light
Mezzanine
10 letters:
Fenestella
11 letters:
Lychnoscope
Oeil-de-boeuf
12 letters:
Quarterlight
14 letters:
Catherine-wheel

Winds

4 letters:
Berg
Bise
Bora
Bura
Föhn
Gale
Gust
Puna
5 letters:
Blore
Buran
Eurus
Foehn
Gibli
Noser
Notus
Trade
Zonda
6 letters:
Aquilo
Auster
Baguio
Boreas
Ghibli

Haboob
Kamsin
Levant
Samiel
Sciroc
Simoom
Simoon
Solano
Squall
Wester
Zephyr
7 letters:
Aeolian
Aquilon
Bluster
Chinook
Cyclone
Draught
Etesian
Gregale
Kamseen
Khamsin
Meltemi
Mistral
Monsoon

Nor'east
Norther
Pampero
Shimaal
Sirocco
Snifter
Snorter
Souther
Sumatra
Tornado
Twister
Typhoon
8 letters:
Argestes
Easterly
Favonian
Favonius
Levanter
Libeccio
Scirocco
Williwaw
Zephyrus
9 letters:
Anti-trade
Dust devil

Euraquilo
Harmattan
Hurricane
Hurricano
Libecchio
Nor'wester
Volturnus

10 letters:
Cape doctor
Euroclydon
Rip-snorter
Tourbillon
Tramontana
Tramontane

Whirlblast
Willy-willy
11 letters:
White squall
13 letters:
Northwesterly

Wines

WINE-PRODUCING AREAS

Area	Country	Area	Country
Ahr	Germany	Mendocino	U.S.A.
Alsace	France	Mittelrhein	Germany
Alto Adige *or*	Italy	Moldavia	—
Südtirol		Mornington	Australia
Anjou	France	Peninsula	
Argentina	—	Mosel-Saar-Ruwer	Germany
Austria	—	Nahe	Germany
Baden	Germany	Napa Valley	U.S.A.
Barossa Valley	Australia	Navarra	Spain
Bordeaux	France	New York State	U.S.A.
Bulgaria	—	Oregon	U.S.A.
Burgundy	France	Padthaway	Australia
California	U.S.A.	Penedès	Spain
Chablis	France	Piedmont	Italy
Champagne	France	Portugal	—
Chianti	Italy	Provence	France
Chile	—	Rheingau	Germany
Clare Valley	Australia	Rheinhessen	Germany
Coonawarra	Australia	Rheinpfalz	Germany
Côte d'Or	France	Rhône	France
Finger Lakes	U.S.A.	Ribera del Duro	Spain
Franken	Germany	Rioja	Spain
Friuli	Italy	Romania	—
Gisborne	New Zealand	Sicily	Italy
Goulburn Valley	Australia	Sonoma	U.S.A.
Greece	—	South Africa	—
Hawkes Bay	New Zealand	Switzerland	—
Hessiches	Germany	Touraine	France
Bergstrasse		Tuscany	Italy
Hungary	—	Umbria	Italy
Hunter Valley	Australia	Valdepeñas	Spain
Languedoc	France	Veneto	Italy
Loire	France	Washington State	U.S.A.
Margaret River	Australia	Württemberg	Germany
Marlborough	New Zealand	Yarra Valley	Australia
Martinborough	New Zealand		
McLaren Vale	Australia		

WINE TERMS

2 letters:
AC
NV
3 letters:
AOC
DOC
Dry
LBV
QbA
QmP
Sec
TBA
4 letters:
Aszú
Brix
Brut
DOCG
Fino
Flor
Rosé
Sekt
VDQS
5 letters:
Baumé
Cream
Cuvée
Dolce
Plonk
Secco
Sweet
Tinto
6 letters:
Medium
Solera
Sur lie
Tannin
7 letters:
Amabile
Auslese

Crianza
Demi-sec
Eiswein
Malmsey
Oechsle
Oloroso
Organic
Passito
Recioto
Récolte
Reserva
Riserva
Terroir
Trocken
Vin gris
Vintage
Weingut
8 letters:
Ausbruch
Botrytis
Grand cru
Kabinett
Moelleux
Mousseux
Noble rot
Prädikat
Ruby Port
Spätlese
Spumante
Varietal
Vigneron
Vignoble
9 letters:
Abboccato
Cru classé
Grosslage
Medium-dry
Pale cream
Pétillant

Puttonyos
Table wine
Tafelwein
Tawny Port
Vin de pays
10 letters:
Botrytized
Einzellage
Garrafeira
Manzanilla
Non-vintage
Premier cru
Second wine
Sin crianza
Vin de table
11 letters:
Amontillado
Dessert wine
Gran reserva
Halbtrocken
Late harvest
Medium-sweet
Weissherbst
12 letters:
Cru bourgeois
Vino da tavola
13 letters:
Beerenauslese
Estate bottled
Fortified wine
Qualitätswein
Sparkling wine
14 letters:
Vendage tardive
Vieilles vignes
Vin doux naturel
15 letters:
Pourriture noble
Sigle Quinta Port

See also:
➤ **Drinks**

Winter sports

4 letters:
Luge
6 letters:
Skiing
Slalom
Super-G
7 letters:
Curling
Skating

8 letters:
Biathlon
9 letters:
Bobsleigh
Ice hockey
Skijoring
10 letters:
Ice dancing
Ice skating

Skibobbing
Ski jumping
11 letters:
Tobogganing
12 letters:
Alpine skiing
Nordic skiing
Snowboarding
Speed skating

13 letters:
Figure skating

14 letters:
Downhill racing

Wonders of the ancient world

Colossus of Rhodes
Hanging Gardens of Babylon
Mausoleum of Halicarnassus
Pharos of Alexandria
Phidias' statue of Zeus at
  Olympia
Pyramids of Egypt
Temple of Artemis at Ephesus

Wood, types of

3 letters:
Ash
Box
Elm
Fir
Koa
Oak
Red
Yew
4 letters:
Beef
Cade
Eugh
Iron
Lana
Lime
Pear
Pine
Poon
Rata
Teak
Toon
Yang
5 letters:
Agila
Algum
Almug
Apple
Balsa
Beech
Birch
Cedar
Ebony
Hazel
Heben
Iroko
Jarul
Kauri
Kiaat
Kokra
Larch
Maple
Myall

Olive
Opepe
Plane
Ramin
Rowan
Sapan
Sassy
Stink
Sumac
Thorn
Tulip
Zante
6 letters:
Alerce
Bamboo
Bog oak
Brasil
Brazil
Canary
Carapa
Cherry
Citron
Fustet
Fustic
Fustoc
Gaboon
Gopher
Jarool
Jarrah
Lignum
Locust
Obeche
Orache
Orange
Padauk
Padouk
Poplar
Red fir
Red gum
Red oak
Sabele
Sabicu
Sandal

Sapele
Sappan
Sissoo
Sponge
Spruce
Sumach
Tupelo
Waboom
Walnut
Willow
7 letters:
Amboina
Amboyna
Assagai
Assegai
Barwood
Boxwood
Camwood
Cypress
Durmast
Gumtree
Gumwood
Hemlock
Hickory
Meranti
Nutwood
Palmyra
Pimento
Quassia
Sanders
Sapwood
Shawnee
Shittim
Wallaba
8 letters:
Agalloch
Alburnum
Basswood
Beefwood
Chestnut
Corkwood
Crabwood
Guaiacum

Guaiocum
Hardwood
Harewood
Hornbeam
Ironwood
Jelutong
Kingwood
Laburnum
Mahogany
Pulpwood
Pyengadu
Pyinkado
Red cedar
Rosewood
Sandarac
Sapucaia
Sasswood
Shagbark
Softwood
Southern
Sycamore
Tamarack
Tamarind
9 letters:
Briarwood
Butternut
Caliature

Campeachy
Coachwood
Eaglewood
Hackberry
Jacaranda
Lancewood
Partridge
Persimmon
Pitch pine
Quebracho
Satinwood
Scots pine
Shellbark
Stinkwood
Torchwood
Tulipwood
White pine
Whitewood
Zebrawood
10 letters:
Afrormosia
Bulletwood
Calamander
Candlewood
Coromandel
Durmast oak
Fiddlewood

Greenheart
Hackmatack
Marblewood
Nettle-tree
Orangewood
Palisander
Paraná pine
Ribbonwood
Sandalwood
Sappanwood
Sneezewood
Spotted gum
Summerwood
White cedar
Yellowwood
11 letters:
Black walnut
Lignum-vitae
Sanderswood
Slippery elm
13 letters:
Partridge-wood
15 letters:
African mahogany
Western red cedar

Works of literature and music

3 letters:
Job
Kim
She
4 letters:
Aida
Emma
Lulu
Maud
5 letters:
Brand
Comus
Faust
Fetes
Kipps
La Mer
Manon
Medea
Norma
Scoop
Tosca
6 letters:
Alcina
Amelia
Becket
Ben Hur

Carmen
En Saga
Ghosts
Hassan
Helena
Iberia
Jenufa
Lolita
Martha
Mignon
Nuages
Oberon
Otello
Rienzi
Rob Roy
Rokeby
Salome
Semele
Sylvia
Trilby
Utopia
Walden
7 letters:
Adonais
Aladdin
Amadeus

Babbitt
Beowulf
Camilla
Candida
Don Juan
Dracula
Electra
Erewhon
Euphues
Fidelio
Giselle
Ivanhoe
Lord Jim
Lycidas
Macbeth
Manfred
Marmion
Ma Vlast
Mazeppa
Messiah
Nabucco
Othello
Rebecca
Ring, The
Shirley
Sirenes

Ulysses
Volpone
Werther
Wozzeck
8 letters:
Adam Bede
Adam Zero
Alcestis
Anabasis
Antigone
Arabella
Bells, The
Born Free
Carnaval
Carnival
Catriona
Cenci, The
Coppelia
Cranford
Endymion
Everyman
Falstaff
Gloriana
Hay Fever
Hiawatha
Hudibras
Hyperion
Idiot, The
Idomeneo
Iliad, The
In the Wet
Iolanthe
Jane Eyre
King Lear
La Boheme
L'Allegro
Lavengro
Les Noces
Lucky Jim
Moby Dick
Parsifal
Patience
Peer Gynt
Pericles
Rasselas
Sea Drift
Swan Lake
Tom Jones
Turandot
Villette
Waves, The
9 letters:
Aeneid, The
Agamemnon
Beau Geste
Billy Budd
Brigg Fair

Capriccio
Cavalcade
Checkmate
Choephori
Coningsby
Cox and Box
Critic, The
Cymbeline
Dandy Dick
Don Carlos
Dr Zhivago
Dubliners
East Lynne
Egoist, The
Eumenides
Euryanthe
Hard Times
Hobbit, The
I, Claudius
I Puritani
Kidnapped
Kubla Khan
Les Biches
Lohengrin
Mein Kampf
Men at Arms
Mikado, The
No Highway
On Liberty
Papillons
Prince, The
Pygmalion
Rigoletto
Rivals, The
Ruddigore
Saint Joan
Siegfried
Tom Sawyer
Venusberg
Vice Versa
Warden, The
10 letters:
All for Love
Animal Farm
Appalachia
Bleak House
Borough, The
Cannery Row
Casablanca
Cinderella
Citadel, The
Coriolanus
Das Kapital
Die Walkure
Don Quixote
Dunciad, The
Dynasts, The

Howards End
Il Seraglio
Inferno, The
In Memoriam
Intermezzo
I Pagliacci
Jamaica Inn
John Gilpin
Kenilworth
Kingdom, The
La Gioconda
La Traviata
Les Troyens
Lorna Doone
Lysistrata
My Fair Lady
My Son, My Son
Nelson Mass
Odyssey, The
Oedipus Rex
Only Way, The
On the Beach
Our Village
Pantagruel
Persuasion
Petroushka
Planets, The
Prelude, The
Prince Igor
Relapse, The
Rural Rides
Seagull, The
Seasons, The
Semiramide
Tannhauser
Tempest, The
Tono-Bungay
Trojans, The
Uncle Remus
Uncle Vanya
Vanity Fair
Vile Bodies
War Requiem
Water Music
Westward Ho
11 letters:
American, The
Apostles, The
As You Like It
Big Sleep, The
Black Beauty
Blue Bird, The
Boule de Suif
Cakes and Ale
Child Harold
Creation, The
Cruel Sea, The

Doll's House, A
Don Giovanni
Don Pasquale
Firebird, The
Georgics, The
Greenmantle
Harp Quartet
Hedda Gabler
High Windows
HMS Pinafore
Hymn of Jesus
I Like It Here
Il Penseroso
Il Trovatore
Jack and Jill
Journey's End
Judith Paris
Little Eyolf
Little Women
Loved One, The
Love for Love
Luisa Miller
Mary Poppins
Middlemarch
Minute Waltz
Mrs Dalloway
Mr Standfast
Newcomes, The
Now We Are Six
Noye's Fludde
Ode to Autumn
Oliver Twist
Peter Grimes
Peter Simple
Pippa Passes
Princess Ida
Princess, The
Puss in Boots
Redgauntlet
Rosmersholm
Salut d'Amour
Sea Symphony
Silas Marner
Sorcerer, The
South Riding
Stalky and Co
Stenka Razin
Tale of a Tub, A
Talisman, The
Tam o'Shanter
Trial by Jury
What Katy Did
Wild Duck, The
William Tell
Women in Love
Wrong Box, The

12 letters:
Alchemist, The
Anna Karenina
Antiquary, The
Apple Cart, The
Archduke Trio
Areopagitica
Ash Wednesday
Barnaby Rudge
Blithe Spirit
Brighton Rock
Buddenbrooks
Caretaker, The
Charley's Aunt
Cosi fan Tutte
Danse Macabre
Decameron, The
Dogs of War, The
Dombey and Son
Epithalamion
Eugene Onegin
Excursion, The
Four Quartets
Frankenstein
Golden Ass, The
Grand Duke, The
Guy Mannering
Handley Cross
Julius Caesar
Karelia Suite
Khovanschina
Kinderscenen
Kreisleriana
La Sonnambula
Le Pere Goriot
Les Huguenots
Les Sylphides
Linz Symphony
Little Dorrit
Locksley Hall
Lost Chord, The
Madame Bovary
Major Barbara
Manon Lescaut
Moll Flanders
Moonstone, The
Old Mortality
Owen Wingrave
Paradise Lost
Piers Plowman
Porgy and Bess
Precious Bane
Private Lives
Prothalamion
Rheingold, Das
Rip Van Winkle

Rogue Herries
Romany Rye, The
Sardanapalus
Spring Sonata
Trout Quintet
Twelfth Night
Valkyries, The
Whisky Galore
13 letters:
Albert Herring
Almayer's Folly
Andrea Chenier
Angel Pavement
Arms and the Man
Art of Fugue, The
Bab Ballads, The
Black Arrow, The
Black Mischief
Blue Danube, The
Boris Godounov
Brave New World
Cancer Ward, The
Carmina Burana
Chanson de Nuit
Clock Symphony
Crown Imperial
Death in Venice
Der Freischutz
Dido and Aeneas
Doctor Faustus
Doctor Zhivago
Fame is the Spur
Finnegan's Wake
Ghost Train, The
Gondoliers, The
Harold in Italy
Hatter's Castle
Jungle Book, The
Just So Stories
La Cenerentola
L'Elisir d'Amore
Mabinogion, The
Magic Flute, The
Magistrate, The
Mansfield Park
Metamorphosen
Nutcracker, The
Odessa File, The
Orb and Sceptre
Path to Rome, The
Peg Woffington
Private Angelo
Religio Medici
Schindler's Ark
Sketches by Boz
Songs of Travel

Sons and Lovers
Stamboul Train
Tarka the Otter
Timon of Athens
Under Milk Wood
Utopia Limited
Virginians, The
White Devil, The
Winnie-the-Pooh
Winslow Boy, The
Zuleika Dobson
14 letters:
Ambassadors, The
Andrea del Sarto
Battle Symphony
Bee's Wedding, The
Book of Snobs, The
Brief Encounter
Chanson de Matin
Choral Symphony
Cider with Rosie
Claudius the God
Coral Island, The
Country Wife, The
Crotchet Castle
Darkness at Noon
Decline and Fall
Deep Blue Sea, The
Die Zauberflote
Ein Heldenleben
Emperor Quartet
Entertainer, The
Eroica Symphony
Forsyte Saga, The
Four Just Men, The
Gay Lord Quex, The
Golden Bough, The
Goodbye Mr Chips
Goodby to Berlin
Great Gatsby, The
Handful of Dust, A
Horse's Mouth, The
Jude the Obscure
Kreutzer Sonata
Le Morte d'Arthur
London Symphony
Loom of Youth, The
Lord of the Flies
Lord of the Rings
Lost Horizon, The
Lyrical Ballads
Madam Butterfly
Man and Superman
Masterman Ready
National Velvet
Nightmare Abbey
Nine Tailors, The

Of Human Bondage
Our Man in Havana
Passage to India
Pickwick Papers
Plain Dealer, The
Prague Symphony
Quentin Durward
Rhapsody in Blue
Rights of Man, The
Robinson Crusoe
Roderick Random
Romeo and Juliet
Separate Tables
Shropshire Lad, A
Siegfried Idyll
Sinister Street
Sins of my Old Age
Slavonic Dances
Spring Symphony
Stones of Venice
Time Machine, The
Town Like Alice, A
Tragic Symphony
Treasure Island
Tristram Shandy
Uncle Tom's Cabin
Venus and Adonis
Vicar of Bray, The
Voices of Spring
Water Babies, The
Widowers Houses
Winter's Tale, The
Woodlanders, The
15 letters:
African Queen, The
Allan Quatermain
Ariadne auf Naxos
Bartholomew Fair
Beggar's Opera, The
Child of our Time, A
Christmas Carol, A
Clarissa Harlowe
Dangerous Corner
Daphnis and Chloe
Divine Comedy, The
Emperor Concerto
Emperor Waltz, The
Essays of Elia, The
Faerie Queene, The
Fanny by Gaslight
Farewell to Arms, A
Frenchman's Creek
From the New World
Golden Legend, The
Gone with the Wind
Gotterdammerung
Haffner Symphony

Hansel and Gretel
Heartbreak House
Huckleberry Finn
Iceman Cometh, The
Invisible Man, The
Italian Symphony
Jupiter Symphony
Le Nozze di Figaro
Letters of Junius
Life for the Tsar, A
Look Back in Anger
Moonlight Sonata
Northanger Abbey
Old Wives Tale, The
Our Mutual Friend
Pearl Fishers, The
Peregrine Pickle
Peter and the Wolf
Puck of Pook's Hill
Put out More Flags

Raindrop Prelude
Rite of Spring, The
Rupert of Hentzau
Samson Agonistes
Samson and Dalila
Scholar Gipsy, The
Serenade to Music
Simon Boccanegra
Soldier's Tale, The
Tanglewood Tales
Three Men in a Boat
Titus Andronicus
To the Lighthouse
Waiting for Godot
Waldstein Sonata
Weir of Hermiston
Woman in White, The
Yarrow Revisited
You Never Can Tell

Worms

3 letters:
Bob
Dew
Fan
Lob
4 letters:
Tube
5 letters:
Acorn
Arrow
Fluke
Leech
Lytta
Piper
6 letters:
Caddis
Guinea
Nereid
Paddle
Palmer
Palolo
Ribbon
Scolex
Taenia
Teredo
Tongue
7 letters:
Ascarid
Bladder
Bristle
Catworm
Cestode
Cestoid
Filaria

Gordius
Hair-eel
Ragworm
Sabella
Serpula
Stomach
Tag-tail
Tenioid
Triclad
Tubifex
Vinegar
8 letters:
Bootlace
Capeworm
Caseworm
Clamworm
Filander
Gilt-tail
Hairworm
Hookworm
Inchworm
Nematoda
Nematode
Nemertea
Paste-eel
Seamouse
Strongyl
Toxocara
Trichina
Wheat-eel
Whipworm
9 letters:
Bilharzia
Brandling

Diplozoon
Heartworm
Horsehair
Lumbricus
Peripatus
Planarian
Strawworm
Strongyle
Tiger tail
Trematode
Wheatworm
10 letters:
Anguillula
Liver-fluke
Polychaete
Threadworm
11 letters:
Oligochaete
Schistosome
Scoleciform
Trichinella
Trichinosed
Turbellaria
12 letters:
Enteropneust
Hemichordata
Night-crawler
Sipunculacea
13 letters:
Platyhelminth
Sipunculoidea

Writers

3 letters:
Eco, *Umberto*
Lee, *Sophia*
Paz, *Octavio*
Poe, *Edgar Allan*
RLS
4 letters:
Amis, *Martin (Louis)*
Asch, *Sholem*
Aymé, *Marcel*
Bede, *the Venerable*
Bolt, *Robert (Oxton)*
Cary, *(Arthur) Joyce Lunel*
Cole, *Babette*
Dahl, *Roald*
Fine, *Ann*
Gide, *André (Paul Guillaume)*
Hope (Hawkins), *Sir Anthony*
Hugo, *Victor (Marie)*
Hunt, *E(verette) Howard*
King, *Stephen (Edwin)*
Lamb, *Charles*
Loos, *Anita*
Loti, *Pierre*
Lyly, *John*
Mann, *Thomas*
More, *Henry*
Nash, *(Frederic) Ogden*
Opie, *Iona*
Ovid
Pope, *Alexander*
Saki *(Hector Hugh Munro)*
Sand, *George*
Shaw, *George Bernard*
Snow, *C(harles) P(ercy)*
Ward, *Mary Augusta*
West, *Nathanael*
Zola, *Émile*
5 letters:
Acton, *Sir Harold Mario*
Aesop
Albee, *Edward (Franklin)*
Auden, *W(ystan) H(ugh)*
Ayres, *Noreen*
Banks, *Lynne Reid*
Bates, *H(erbert) E(rnest)*
Blake, *William*
Blume, *Judy*
Burke, *Edmund*
Caine, *Sir (Thomas Henry) Hall*
Camus, *Albert*
Corvo, *Baron*
Crane, *Stephen*
Defoe, *Daniel*
Digby, *Anne*

Doyle, *Arthur Conan*
Dumas, *Alexandre*
Eliot, *T(homas) S(tearns)*
Ellis, *(Henry) Havelock*
Genet, *Jean*
Gogol, *Nikolai Vasilievich*
Gorky, *Maxim*
Gosse, *Sir Edmund (William)*
Greer, *Germaine*
Grimm, *Wilhelm Carl*
Hardy, *Thomas*
Henry, *O (William Sydney Porter)*
Henty, *G(eorge) A(lfred)*
Hesse, *Hermann*
Heyer, *Georgette*
Homer
Ibsen, *Henrik*
Innes, *(Ralph) Hammond*
James, *Henry*
Jones, *Diana Wynne*
Joyce, *James (Augustine Aloysius)*
Kafka, *Franz*
Kempe, *Margery*
Lewis, *C(live) S(taples)*
Lodge, *David (John)*
Lorca, *Federico García*
Mason, *Alfred Edward Woodley*
Milne, *A(lan) A(lexander)*
Munro, *H(ector) H(ugh)*
Musil, *Robert*
Nashe, *Thomas*
Ouida
Paine, *Tom*
Pater, *Walter Horatio*
Paton, *Alan (Stewart)*
Pepys, *Samuel*
Pliny
Pound, *Ezra (Loomis)*
Powys, *John Cowper*
Reade, *Charles*
Renan, *(Joseph) Ernest*
Rilke, *Rainer Maria*
Sagan, *Françoise*
Scott, *Sir Walter*
Seuss, *Dr (Theodor Seuss Geisel)*
Shute, *Nevil*
Smith, *Dick King*
Spark, *Dame Muriel (Sarah)*
Stark, *Dame Freya Madeline*
Stein, *Gertrude*
Swift, *Jonathan*
Synge, *(Edmund) J(ohn) M(illington)*
Twain, *Mark (Samuel L Clemens)*
Verne, *Jules*

Waugh, *Evelyn (Arthur St John)*
Wells, *H(erbert) G(eorge)*
Wilde, *Oscar (Fingal O'Flahertie Wills)*
Woolf, *(Adeline) Virginia*
Yates, *Dornford*
Yonge, *Charlotte Mary*
6 letters:
Alcott, *Louisa May*
Ambler, *Eric*
Arnold, *Matthew*
Artaud, *Antonin Marie Joseph*
Ascham, *Roger*
Asimov, *Isaac*
Austen, *Jane*
Balzac, *Honoré de*
Baring, *Maurice*
Barrie, *J(ames) M(atthew)*
Belloc, *(Joseph) Hilaire (Pierre)*
Bellow, *Saul*
Blyton, *Enid (Mary)*
Borges, *Jorge Luis*
Borrow, *George Henry*
Braine, *John (Gerard)*
Brecht, *Bertolt (Eugen Friedrich)*
Bronte, *Emily Jane (Ellis Bell)*
Buchan, *John*
Bunyan, *John*
Butler, *Samuel*
Capote, *Truman*
Cicero, *Marcus Tullius*
Colfer, *Eoin*
Conrad, *Joseph*
Cowper, *William*
Cronin, *A(rchibald) J(oseph)*
Daudet, *Alphonse*
Dryden, *John*
Durrel, *Laurence George*
Engels, *Friedrich*
Fowles, *John (Robert)*
France, *Anatole*
Gibbon, *Edward*
Godwin, *William*
Goethe, *Johann Wolfgang von*
Graves, *Robert (Ranke)*
Greene, *(Henry) Graham*
Harris, *Joel Chandler*
Heller, *Joseph*
Hobbes, *Thomas*
Hughes, *Thomas*
Hutton, *R(ichard) H(olt)*
Huxley, *Aldous (Leonard)*
Inkpen, *Mike*
Irving, *Washington*
Jarvis, *Robin*
Jerome, *Jerome K(lapka)*
Jonson, *Ben(jamin)*

Le Fanu, *(Joseph) Sheridan*
London, *Jack*
Lucian
Lytton, *Bulwer*
Mailer, *Norman (Kingsley)*
Malory, *Thomas*
Mannin, *Ethel*
Miller, *Henry (Valentine)*
Milton, *John*
Morgan, *Edwin (George)*
Murphy, *Jill*
Nerval, *Gérard de*
Nesbit, *E(dith)*
Onions, *Charles Talbut*
Orwell, *George*
Parker, *Dorothy*
Proust, *Marcel*
Racine, *Jean (Baptiste)*
Runyon, *Damon*
Ruskin, *John*
Sachar, *Louis*
Sapper *(H C McNeile)*
Sayers, *Dorothy L(eigh)*
Sewell, *Anna*
Smiles, *Samuel*
Steele, *Richard*
Sterne, *Laurence*
Storey, *David (Malcolm)*
Thomas, *Dylan (Marlais)*
Updike, *John (Hoyer)*
Virgil
Walton, *Izaac*
Wilder, *Laura Ingalls*
Wilson, *Jacqueline*
7 letters:
Addison, *Joseph*
Aldrich, *Thomas Bailey*
Aretino, *Pietro*
Beckett, *Samuel (Barclay)*
Bennett, *(Enoch) Arnold*
Bentley, *Edmund Clerihew*
Boileau, *Nicholas (Despréaux)*
Boswell, *James*
Burgess, *Anthony*
Carlyle, *Thomas*
Carroll, *Lewis (Charles Lutwidge Dodgson)*
Chaucer, *Geoffrey*
Chekhov, *Anton Pavlovich*
Cobbett, *William*
Colette, *(Sidonie-Gabrielle)*
Collins, *Wilkie (William)*
Coppard, *A(lfred) E(dgar)*
Corelli, *Marie*
Cranmer, *Thomas*
Cushman, *Karen*
Deeping, *(George) Warwick*

Dickens, *Charles (John Huffam)*
Drabble, *Margaret*
Dreiser, *Theodore Herman Albert*
Durrell, *Gerald (Malcolm)*
Emerson, *Ralph Waldo*
Erasmus, *Desiderius*
Fénelon, *François de Salignac de la Mothe*
Forster, *Margaret*
Gissing, *George (Robert)*
Golding, *Sir William (Gerald)*
Grahame, *Kenneth*
Haggard, *Sir H(enry) Rider*
Hazlitt, *William*
Herbert, *George*
Hichens, *Robert Smythe*
Johnson, *Samuel*
Kipling, *(Joseph) Rudyard*
Lardner, *Ring(gold Wilmer)*
Marryat, *(Captain) Frederick*
Maugham, *W(illiam) Somerset*
Mauriac, *François*
Mérimée, *Prosper*
Mitford, *Jessica Lucy*
Moravia, *Alberto*
Murdoch, *Dame (Jean) Iris*
Nabokov, *Vladimir (Vladimirovich)*
Naipaul, *Sir V(idiadhar) S(urajprasad)*
Peacock, *Thomas Love*
Pullman, *Philip*
Pushkin, *Aleksander Sergeyevich*
Ransome, *Arthur Mitchell*
Riddell, *Chris*
Rostand, *Edmond*
Rowling, *J(oanne) K(athleen)*
Saroyan, *William*
Sassoon, *Siegfried (Louvain)*
Shelley, *Mary (Wollstonecraft)*
Simenon, *Georges (Joseph Christian)*
Sitwell, *Sir (Francis) Osbert*
Stephen, *Leslie*
Stewart, *Paul*
Surtees, *Robert Smith*
Terence
Thoreau, *Henry David*
Tolkien, *J(ohn) R(onald) R(euel)*
Tolstoy, *Count Leo (Nikolayevich)*
Travers, *Ben(jamin)*
Wallace, *(Richard Horatio) Edgar*
Walpole, *Sir Hugh Seymour*
Wharton, *Edith (Newbold)*
Whitman, *Walt(er)*
8 letters:
Andersen, *Hans Christian*
Beaumont, *Sir John*

Browning, *Robert*
Caldwell, *Erskine*
Chandler, *Raymond*
Childers, *(Robert) Erskine*
Christie, *Dame Agatha (Mary Clarissa)*
Constant, *Benjamin*
Coolidge, *Susan*
De la Mare, *Walter (John)*
Disraeli, *Benjamin*
Faulkner, *William*
Fielding, *Henry*
Flaubert, *Gustave*
Forester, *C(ecil) S(cott)*
Goncourt, *Jules*
Ishiguro, *Kazuo*
Kingsley, *Mary St Leger*
Lawrence, *T(homas) E(dward)*
Mannheim, *Baron Carl Gustav Emil*
Melville, *Herman*
Meredith, *George*
Morpurgo, *Michael*
Perrault, *Charles*
Plutarch
Rabelais, *François*
Rattigan, *Sir Terence (Mervyn)*
Remarque, *Erich Maria*
Rousseau, *Jean-Jacques*
Salinger, *J(erome) D(avid)*
Schiller, *(Johann Christoph) Friedrich von*
Smollett, *Tobias George*
Stendhal *(Marie-Henri Beyle)*
Taffrail *(Henry Taprell Dorling)*
Traherne, *Thomas*
Trollope, *Joanna*
Turgenev, *Ivan Sergeyevich*
Voltaire *(François Marie Arouet)*
Williams, *Tennessee*
9 letters:
Aeschylus
Ainsworth, *William Harrison*
Blackmore, *R(ichard) D(oddridge)*
Boccaccio, *Giovanni*
Brent-Dyer, *Elinor M(ary)*
Burroughs, *Edgar Rice*
Dos Passos, *John Roderigo*
Du Maurier, *Dame Daphne*
Edgeworth, *Maria*
Goldsmith, *Oliver*
Hawthorne, *Nathaniel*
Hemingway, *Ernest (Millar)*
Isherwood, *Christopher (William Bradshaw)*
Jefferson, *Thomas*
Lermontov, *Mikhail Yurievich*

Linklater, *Eric*
Mackenzie, *Sir (Edward Montague) Compton*
Madariaga, *Salvador de*
Mansfield, *Katherine*
McCullers, *Carson*
Oppenheim, *Edward Phillips*
Pasternak, *Boris Leonidovich*
Pratchett, *Terry*
Priestley, *J(ohn) B(oynton)*
Santayana, *George*
Sholokhov, *Mikhail Aleksandrovich*
Steinbeck, *John (Ernest)*
Stevenson, *Robert Louis (Balfour)*
Thackeray, *William Makepeace*
Wodehouse, *Sir P(elham) G(renville)*
10 letters:
Ballantyne, *R(obert) M(ichael)*
Chesterton, *G(ilbert) K(eith)*
Dostoevsky, *Fyodor Mikhailovich*
Fitzgerald, *F(rancis) Scott (Key)*
Galsworthy, *John*

Richardson, *H(enry) H(andel)*
11 letters:
De Cervantes (Saavedra), *Miguel*
De Montaigne, *Michel Eyquem*
Machiavelli, *Niccolò*
Maeterlinck, *Count Maurice*
Shakespeare, *William*
Streatfield, *Noel*
12 letters:
Aristophanes
Chesterfield, *Lord*
De Mandeville, *Sir Jehan (or John)*
De Maupassant, *(Henri René Albert) Guy*
Solzhenitsyn, *Alexander Isayevich*
13 letters:
Sackville-West, *Vita (Victoria Mary)*
14 letters:
Wollstonecraft, *Mary*
15 letters:
De Chateaubriand, *Vicomte (François René)*

See also:
➤ **Diarists** ➤ **Dramatists** ➤ **Novelists** ➤ **Poets** ➤ **Shakespeare**

Yellow, shades of

4 letters:
Buff
Ecru
Gold
5 letters:
Amber
Beige
Lemon
Maize
Ochre
Straw
Topaz
6 letters:
Almond
Bisque

Bistre
Citron
Golden
7 letters:
Gamboge
Jasmine
Mustard
Nankeen
Oatmeal
Old gold
Saffron
Tea rose
8 letters:
Cinnamon
Daffodil

Eau de nil
Eggshell
Magnolia
Primrose
9 letters:
Butternut
Champagne
12 letters:
Canary yellow
13 letters:
Tortoiseshell

Z

Zodiac

SIGNS OF THE ZODIAC

Name	Symbol
Aquarius	the Water Carrier
Aries	the Ram
Cancer	the Crab
Capricorn	the Goat
Gemini	the Twins
Leo	the Lion
Libra	the Scales
Pisces	the Fishes
Sagittarius	the Archer
Scorpio	the Scorpion
Taurus	the Bull
Virgo	the Virgin

CHINESE ANIMAL YEARS

Chinese	English	Years				
Shu	Rat	1960	1972	1984	1996	2008
Niu	Ox	1961	1973	1985	1997	2009
Hu	Tiger	1962	1974	1986	1998	2010
Tu	Hare	1963	1975	1987	1999	2011
Long	Dragon	1964	1976	1988	2000	2012
She	Serpent	1965	1977	1989	2001	2013
Ma	Horse	1966	1978	1990	2002	2014
Yang	Sheep	1967	1979	1991	2003	2015
Hou	Monkey	1968	1980	1992	2004	2016
Ji	Cock	1969	1981	1993	2005	2017
Gou	Dog	1970	1982	1994	2006	2018
Zhu	Boar	1971	1983	1995	2007	2019

Zoology

BRANCHES OF ZOOLOGY

3 letters:
Shu
7 letters:
Zootomy
8 letters:
Cetology
Ethology

Zoometry
9 letters:
Mammalogy
Ophiology
Zoography
10 letters:
Entomology

Malacology
11 letters:
Arachnology
Herpetology
Ichthyology
Myrmecology
Ornithology

Primatology
12 letters:
Protozoology

Zoogeography
13 letters:
Palaeozoology

14 letters:
Archaeozoology

ZOOLOGY TERMS

3 letters:
Fin
4 letters:
Gill
Prey
Pupa
5 letters:
Biped
Imago
Larva
Spawn
Spine
6 letters:
Caudal
Cocoon
Coelom
Colony
Dorsal
Raptor
Rodent
Sucker
Thorax
7 letters:
Abdomen
Antenna

Bivalve
Decapod
Primate
Reptile
Segment
Ventral
8 letters:
Anterior
Arachnid
Chordate
Dipteran
Edentate
Omnivore
Pectoral
Placenta
Predator
Ruminant
Skeleton
9 letters:
Amphibian
Appendage
Arthropod
Carnivore
Chrysalis
Gastropod

Herbivore
Marsupial
Migration
Passerine
Posterior
Protozoan
Quadruped
10 letters:
Crustacean
Echinoderm
Gasteropod
Parenchyma
Vertebrate
11 letters:
Aestivation
Hibernation
Insectivore
12 letters:
Coelenterate
Invertebrate
Lepidopteran
13 letters:
Metamorphosis

ZOOLOGISTS

5 letters:
Elton, *Charles Sutherland*
6 letters:
Cuvier, *Georges*
Darwin, *Charles (Robert)*
Kinsey, *Alfred Charles*
Lorenz, *Konrad Zacharias*
Morgan, *Thomas Hunt*
7 letters:
Dawkins, *Richard*
Driesch, *Hans Adolf Eduard*
Durrell, *Gerald (Malcolm)*

Lamarck, *Jean Baptiste Pierre
  Antoine De Monet*
Medawar, *Peter Brian*
Wallace, *Alfred Russel*
8 letters:
Kammerer, *Paul*
9 letters:
Lankester, *Edwin Ray*
Tinbergen, *Nikolaas*
Von Frisch, *Karl*
Zuckerman, *Solly*